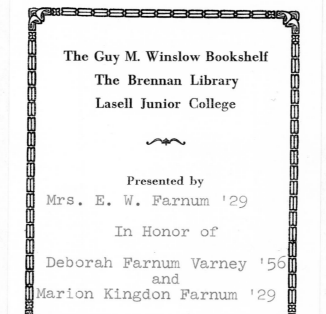

THE ILLUMINATED BOOK
its history and production

THE
ILLUMINATED BOOK

its history and production

by

DAVID DIRINGER

Revised Edition

FREDERICK A. PRAEGER, *Publishers*

NEW YORK · WASHINGTON

BOOKS THAT MATTER

Published in the United States of America in 1967
by Frederick A. Praeger, Inc., Publishers
111 Fourth Avenue, New York, N.Y. 10003

This is a new edition, revised and augmented with the assistance
of Dr. Reinhold Regensburger, of the book originally published in 1958
by Faber and Faber Limited, London, and by Philosophical Library, New York

Library of Congress Catalog Card Number: 66-12525

Printed in Great Britain

ACKNOWLEDGEMENTS

EVERY conscientious effort has been made to give due acknowledgement and full credit for borrowed material, but if through any unwitting oversight some trespass has been committed by quoting from secondary sources, forgiveness is sought in advance, apology is freely offered, and correction promised in any subsequent editions.

Thanks are gratefully given to the following persons, institutions and publishers for quotations from books, and for some of the illustrations used in this volume: Alnwick Castle, Northumberland: Duke of Northumberland Library. Baltimore, Md.: Trustees of the Walters Art Gallery. Bamberg, Germany: State Library. Barcelona: Archivio de la Corona de Aragon. Basel: University Library. Berlin: Sarre-Humann Collection, State Library, State Museums. Bologna: Civic Museum. Brescia: Queriniana Library. Burgos, Spain: Public Library. Cairo: Egyptian Department of Antiquities, Egyptian Library, Egyptian Museum. Calci, near Pisa: Carthusian Monastery. Calcutta: Ajit Ghose Collection. Cambridge, England: Corpus Christi College Library, Fitzwilliam Museum, St John's College Library, Trinity College Library, University Library. Cambridge, Mass.: Fogg Art Museum (Harvard University). Capua, Italy: Cathedral Library. Castelfiorentino, Italy: Collegiata dei SS. Lorenzo e Ippolito. Chantilly, France: Condé Museum. Chatsworth House, Derbyshire: Duke of Devonshire Library. Cincinnati, Ohio: Art Museum and Dr. Philip R. Adams, Hebrew Union College Library. Coïmbra: University Library. Copenhagen: Royal Library. Darmstadt, Germany: State Library. Dublin: National Library and Dr. R. J. Hayes, Royal Irish Academy, Sir Chester Beatty Library, Trinity College Library and Prof. H. W. Parke. Durham: Cathedral Library. Edinburgh: Royal Scottish Museum, University Library. Engelberg, Switzerland: Abbey Library. Erlangen, Germany: University Library. Escorial Library, prov. of Madrid. Florence: F.lli Alinari, Laurentian Library, National Library, National Museum, Opera del Duomo, Riccardiana Library, S. Croce Church, S. Frediano in Cestello Seminary, S. Marco Museum, Superintendent of Antiquities and Archaeological Museum, Superintendent of Medieval and Modern Art and Uffizi Gallery. Frankfort on Main: City Library. Glasgow: University Library. Hague (The): Royal Library. Heidelberg: University Library. Hereford: Cathedral Library. Impruneta, near Florence: S. Maria Basilica. Jerusalem: Schocken Library. Kremsmuenster, Upper Austria: Chapter Library. Leningrad: State Library. Léon, Spain: Cathedral Archives. Letchworth, Herts.: Sassoon Library. Leyden: Royal Museum van Oudheden, University Library. Lichfield: Cathedral Library. Lisbon: National Archives, National Library. London:

ACKNOWLEDGEMENTS

British Academy, British Museum, Dyson Perrins Library, Embassy of the U.S.S.R., India Office Library–Commonwealth Relations Office, Lambeth Palace Library, Soane Museum, Society of Antiquaries, University of London: Courtauld Institute and its Photographic Department, Warburg Institute and its Photographic Department, Journal of the Warburg and Courtauld Institutes, Victoria and Albert Museum (Crown Copyright). Los Angeles, Cal.: Guggenheim Library. Madrid: Duke of Alba Library, National Library, its Photographic Laboratory and Sr. T. Magallón. Manchester: The John Rylands Library. Milan: Ambrosiana Library, S. Ambrogio Basilica, Trivulziana (or Trivulzio) Library and Prof. C. Santoro. Modena: Estense Library. Montalcino, Italy: Communal Library. Montecassino: Badia Archives. Montepulciano, Italy: Communal Museum and Library. Moscow: Historical Museum, Museum of Fine Arts. Munich: State Library. Naples: National Library. New York: Pierpont Morgan Library, Public Library. Oslo: University Library. Oxford: Bodleian Library, Lincoln College, University College Library. Padua: Cathedral Treasury. Paris: Arsenal Library, Gillet Collection, Louvre Museum, National Library, Sainte-Geneviève Library, Vever Collection. Perugia: Capitulary Library. Pisa: Civic Museum. Porto, Portugal: Municipal Library. Princeton, N.J.: University Library and Mr. Alexander P. Clark. Rome: Corsiniana Library, Enciclopedia Italiana and Dr. P. Calisse, Italian National Photographic Institute, National Library, S. Paolo fuori le Mura. St. Gall: Chapter Library. Saint-Omer, France: Municipal Library. Schaffhausen: Ministerial Library. Siena: Osservanza Convent, Piccolomini Library, State Archives. Stockholm: Royal Library. Tehran: Gullistan Museum. Trèves, Germany: Civic Library. Turin: Civic Museum, Egyptian Museum, National Library, Royal Library. Upsala (Uppsala): University Library. Utrecht: University Library. Valenciennes, France: Municipal Library. Vatican City: Vatican Apostolic Library, Vatican Museums and Galleries. Venice: Marciana Library. Vienna: Austrian National Library, Treasury (Schatzkammer). Volterra: Communal Library Guarnacci. Washington, D.C.: Freer Gallery of Art. Winchester: Cathedral Library. Zagreb: Academy of Fine Arts. Zara: S. Francis Church. Zurich: Central Library.

CONTENTS

7

CONTENTS

CONTENTS

CONTENTS

CONTENTS

CONTENTS

ILLUSTRATIONS

COLOUR PLATES

ILLUSTRATIONS

CHAPTER I
between pages 32 and 33

CHAPTER II
between pages 80 and 81

ILLUSTRATIONS

CHAPTER III

between pages 144 *and* 145

CHAPTER IV

between pages 192 *and* 193

CHAPTER V

between pages 256 *and* 257

ILLUSTRATIONS

CHAPTER VI

between pages 304 *and* 305

CHAPTER VII

between pages 384 *and* 385

PREFACE

The exceedingly favourable reviews and unexpectedly wide circulation of my book on *The Alphabet* has filled me with a desire to present to the cultured layman—against the background of such almost watertight compartments as Far Eastern, Amerindian, Indian, Semitic, Classical and Arabic studies, epigraphy, palaeography, history, history of art, and archaeology—a series of companion volumes dealing with various aspects of book production in its millennial development. These volumes have one major aim—to bring to the intelligent reader sifted results of the most reliable research in the various fields, presented in readable form devoid of technicalities. I venture to hope that the man or woman seriously interested to know something of the making of books will welcome these volumes as a comprehensive, readable, and up-to-date synthesis of our present knowledge.

I can hardly emphasize sufficiently that these volumes are not designed primarily as analytic works of scholarship. If they were, their shortcomings would render them more or less valueless. Nor are they intended as source-books for scholars. For such material, scholars will turn to some of the works mentioned in the bibliographies (at the end of each chapter or section) or to articles of learned journals. To all of these works and articles my debt is great and gladly acknowledged. However, since the series is world-wide in scope, I trust that it may be of some value also to the scholar, particularly for information I have tried to furnish outside his field of specialization. Indeed, I well remember how immensely helpful a work of this kind would have been to me when—thirty years ago—I first engaged upon the study of book-production.

In the present book, while trying to note the chief points in the fascinating history of the medieval book, I could not hope to deal adequately with the vast subject of manuscript-illumination in all its complicated aspects. This subject would, indeed, require not one book of handy size, which is all my publishers can allow in the present series, but a great number. Nor is it my intention to deal with the subject from the artistic standpoint, or from that of the historian of art. Art and its history are now beyond the sphere of my scientific interest (which, however, was not the case when I sat at the feet of the great master Prof. Piero Toesca, of the University of Rome, to whom I am greatly indebted for my love of the history of art and for what I know of that fascinating field). I thus cannot enter into the interesting discussion of the artistic relations between book-painting styles of the various countries, nor can I venture any comparison of the art of book-illumination with other forms of pictorial art, especially wall-painting. I am mainly concerned with the history of book production, and here I have limited myself on the whole to one aspect of illumination, namely, the meaning of the pictures (though I do my best not to neglect other aspects where I feel these to be essential). In other words, I approach an example of book-illumination essentially as a manuscript written in a sort of pictorial script, for it is with scripts that I am most accustomed to deal.

Indeed, in a certain way I am going back to one of the original purposes of illumination, that of instruction: in that early period, the great majority of the faithful were illiterate. It was the duty and responsibility of the Church to find a means of instructing them in the mysteries of their faith. Pope Gregory the Great (590–604) is said to have stated that 'painting can do for the illiterate what writing does for those who can read'. Thus, for many centuries book-illumination served mainly as a pictorial synthesis of the text. I am aware, however, that from the modern point of view the other purpose of illumination—to beautify the book—may appear more interesting.

As to method, I have devoted much more space to problems which are still unsolved, or have been a matter of controversy, and to matters less known to the general reader, or which are dealt with in works or journals not easily accessible to the general reader, than to subjects, whatever their importance, which are more widely known or are treated in more accessible publications. Some sections may, in consequence, seem disproportionate in comparison with others, since unanimity cannot be achieved on matters of treatment; questions which seem most important to one person, may appear unimportant to others. Nevertheless, admirers of for instance Carolingian or Spanish or German book-illumination may be assured that I do not underestimate the importance of these branches. Moreover, owing to space limitation, the text must be as concise as possible, but the illustrations, in generous number, will enable the reader to supplement the descriptions.

Need I emphasize that throughout I have endeavoured to keep in mind the idea of affording the patient reader information regarding the origins and development of this most fascinating aspect of man's intellectual and artistic activity, as we trace its history across many lands and through many centuries. It is also my earnest hope that this book may stimulate an interest in the subject, and lead to study of some of the numerous books and articles listed in the bibliographies.

I should like to add that, however high the aim of the author and however much he may have wished to produce a comprehensive book, practical considerations make it imperative that certain sections be reduced to a minimum and others be omitted. To make good the shortcoming, the author's intention is to publish two further editions. While the present edition has been written mainly for the English reader—hence, the emphasis on the Hiberno-Saxon (Chapter IV) and the English illumination (Chapter V)—a European edition would include sections dealing with Scandinavian, Slavonic, Baltic, Hungarian, Portuguese, and other illumination; an Oriental edition would lay more emphasis on Moslem, Indian, Chinese and Japanese book-painting; and pre-Columbian book-illustration may find its place in a still further edition. On the other hand, if the present work is translated into other languages—Italian, French, German, Spanish, and so on—it would be the author's wish to enlarge the chapter, or to add a chapter, on the development of

PREFACE

illuminated book-production in the country concerned. At the same time, with regard to certain countries, in the present work only superficial reference may be made.

I can hardly express adequately my most sincere gratitude to the Trustees of Bollingen Foundation Inc., New York, for the generous grant which has facilitated my researches in various libraries and has enabled me to reduce the costs of this volume. I also wish to express appreciation to those who have given encouragement and counsel in the matter of bringing the work to publication, and my particular thanks go to Mr. Richard de la Mare, M.A., Chairman of Faber and Faber Ltd. and Mr. David Bland, a Director of the same firm. Furthermore, as one might expect in the case of a book dealing with so vast a subject, there are many people to whom an author is indebted. It seemed advisable to have all sections carefully checked by experts in the respective fields. Many such persons are mentioned in the list of acknowledgements, but it may perhaps be convenient to mention here some, such as Prof. A. J. Arberry, Dr. S. Bosticco, Dr. H. Buchtal, Prof. G. Caputo, Mlle. Thérése d'Alvergny, Dr. Sirarpie Der Nersessian, Miss P. M. Giles, the late Sir Frederic Kenyon, J. Leveen, M.A., Prof. F. Magi, Dr. F. Masai, Miss Dorothy Miner, Mr. Cyrill Moss, Prof. R. A. B. Mynors, Dr. O. Paecht, Miss D. W. Pearson, Professors F. Pérez Castro, U. Procacci, D. Talbot Rice, E. Robertson, F. Rossi, Dr. Cecil Roth, Professors M. Salmi, P. Toesca, K. Weitzmann, Mrs. R. Wischnitzer, and Prof. F. Wormald.

I am glad to acknowledge also my indebtedness to Mrs. Hilda Freeman, to Miss Jocelyn Hill, and to Messrs. Louis A. Freeman, William C. Ivory and Dr. R. Regensburger, who carefully read part of or the whole book in manuscript and made many valuable criticisms and suggestions. A special expression of thanks is also due to Miss Albinia de la Mare, Mrs. Martha Fader, and Mr. Daniel Fader for help and advice in correcting the proofs.

It is impossible for the author to express adequately his most sincere gratitude to all the librarians, historians of art, and private collectors who have collaborated in the production of the book; I feel in a special degree, however, my debt to the following:

Dr. Frederick B. Adams, Jr.; the late Cardinal Anselmo Albareda, O.S.B.; Sir Leigh Ashton; Prof. A. F. L. Beeston; Dr. L. Bieler; Monsieur É. Drioton; Dr. R. Ettinghausen; Mrs. E. Frankfort; Dr. Guerriera Guerrieri; Mlle. F. Henry; Dr. R. W. Hunt; the late Rabbi Dr. B. Italiener and Mrs. Italiener; Sir Thomas Kendrick; Prof. E. A. Lowe; Dr. Berta Maracchi; Dr. Irma Merolle; Dr. Antonietta Morandini; F. C. Morgan, M.A., F.S.A., F.L.A.; Dr. C. Nordenfalk; Rabbi S. D. Sassoon; Mr. S. C. Sutton; Prof. G. Zarnecki.

D.D.

University of Cambridge
Easter term, 1955

PREFACE TO THE SECOND EDITION

The preparation of the present edition gives me an opportunity to bring the contents up to date in certain material respects, to correct a number of inaccuracies, and to add the more important bibliographical notations of the advancing research in various branches of book-illumination. I am indebted to various readers and reviewers for help in these matters.

I must also record my gratitude to my publishers—in particular to Mr. Richard de la Mare, the Chairman, and Mr. David Bland, a Director of the firm—for having enriched the edition with as many as ten new colour plates. The only other major change is the interchange of the former Chapter III and Chapter IV. The reasons for this change are readily explained: Islamic illumination, and partly also the Hebrew and Mozarabic (now Chap. III) are more related to the Byzantine illumination (Chap. II); and English illumination (Chap. V) may be regarded as a continuation of Hiberno-Saxon and Carolingian illumination (now Chap. IV).

To the scholars mentioned in the Preface to the first edition, as having so very kindly helped in the production of the work, might I add the name of Mr. Christopher Spottiswoode, B.A., to whom I am grateful for the help he has given in the correction of the proofs of the present edition.

D.D.

UNIVERSITY OF CAMBRIDGE
2nd January 1967

INTRODUCTION

ILLUMINATION

Medieval Illuminators (or 'Miniators')

The Medieval mind delighted in the ornate and colourful; to this the books of the period bear ample witness. Besides the mere copyists of manuscripts, there were in the Middle Ages artists—monks and others—called in Latin *illuminatores*, or 'illuminators', whose profession was to embellish or ornament manuscripts by painting and drawing. Illumination, of course, added much charm. No wonder that this art—expressing itself in coloured illustrations, known as 'miniatures', decorated lettering, and ornamentation in gold (or, rarely, in silver) and brilliant colours—was much practised in the Middle Ages.

While the coloured illustrations and the designs were based largely on the art of the painter, the embellishment of the initials and of the lettering in general was based mainly on the art of the penman, the scribe, or the calligrapher. However, illumination of manuscripts as a form of art cannot be said to be an exclusive and direct development of the art of writing. Indeed if we disregard illustrations of the text, which cannot be considered true illumination (see p. 23), until the early Middle Ages the written pages were simple and unadorned. In the earliest Middle Ages, even when parchment was dyed purple and the writing was in gold and silver, it was still unadorned. In the course of time, however, there appeared enlarged initial letters and calligraphic ornaments. Still later we see whole title-pages, and especially the *Canon-tables* (see p. 102) of the Gospels, richly ornamented.

As mentioned in *The Hand-produced Book*, it was for the illuminators to do their part when the copyists had finished, and we frequently find in manuscripts blanks left for the illuminators which were never filled in.

What is Book-illumination?

Book-illumination, or illumination of manuscripts, or simply, book-painting, is the art of embellishing vellum-manuscript books by painted pictures and/or ornamented letters and geometric designs, in gold and colours, particularly on the borders of the pages. It is a medieval art *par excellence*, and even the term 'illuminated manuscript' seems to be a medieval one meaning a manuscript which is 'lighted up' with coloured decoration.

The English terms 'to illuminate' and 'illuminators' (from the Latin and Italian verb *illuminare*, 'to throw light upon', 'light up', 'brighten') have replaced the old forms—used as far back as the thirteenth century—'to enlumine', also *enlumyne* or *enlomyne*, and *enlumineurs*, derived from Old French *enluminer* and Late Latin *inlūmināre*.

The word 'miniatures' is commonly used for the individual pictures of the illuminated codices, but it would not be exact to consider 'miniature painting' as a synonym for 'illumination'. Miniatures may be executed without the use of gold or silver while illuminations may not. Although there are illuminated miniatures—*i.e.*, pictures finished with touches of gold to represent the lights—many miniatures are not 'illuminations'.

According to some scholars, the words *miniature*—from the Latin *minium*, or red paint (red ochre or red lead), and *miniare*, 'to colour with *minium*'—and *vermilion*, are of the same root; among the Romans, incidentally, bright red was the chief colour of 'illuminated' letters, the pigments used being either sulphide of mercury (or 'vermilion') or, particularly, a lead oxide (now called 'red lead'). 'Miniare' was originally applied to a picture in an 'illuminated' manuscript, but later to the highly specialized art of painting manuscripts. It is only of late years that the word 'miniature' has been used in the restricted sense as applied to a small portrait. This usage of the term is due to its accidental confusion by the French writers with the French word *mignon* and the Latin *minus*.

The term 'miniator' used as a synonym for 'illuminator' is not exact. The Romans used this word for penmen, who applied the *minium* (to mark the initial letters, or titles of sections of the MS., or rubrics), but it was never used for painters of MS. illustrations or portraits.

The art of illuminating begins—as the American leading authority, C. R. Morey, writes—with the end of antiquity, rising, so to speak, from the very ruins of antique culture, and dies with the development of printing, which may be considered the definitive symptom of the modern age. The greatest Italian poet, Dante Alighieri (1265–1321), in the eleventh canto of the *Purgatorio* (verses 80–81), speaks of the perfection of illumination as

> *quell'arte*
> *Ch' alluminar chiamata è in Parisi*

('the art which in Paris is called illuminating').

Jean, Sire de Joinville (*c.* 1224–1317), in his *Histoire de Saint Louis*, likens the deeds of Louis IX to a scribe *qui a fait son livre l'enlumine d'or et d'azur*. Chaucer (*c.* 1340–1400) writes *Kalendeeres enlumyned ben they* (*A.B.C., 73*).

Illumination reached its highest degree of perfection in the fourteenth and fifteenth centuries. It survived the introduction of printing by over a century and was especially applied to devotional books intended for use by semi-literate people.

As a class—writes Canon F. Harrison—they are usually spoken of as 'illuminated manuscripts' because, owing to their lovely colours of gold (in the form of gold-leaf) and silver, and all the colours of the rainbow, their ornamentation and their small pictures illuminate or 'light up' the grey of the parchment and the black of the ink. And F. Madan wrote: Even the red rubrics, the plain alternate blue and red letters common in headlines in the fourteenth century, relieve the eye; but when the capital letters are floriated, when the margins are filled with leaf-and-branch work, and when every few pages exhibit a delicately painted miniature, some scene from the artist's own experience—a market-place, it may be . . . or some banquet at the court of Burgundy in the fifteenth century, . . . or, again, a religious scene rivalling in effect and minuteness of detail the greater pictures of Italian artists— then, indeed, we feel that the accessories have invested the written page with a beauty and attractiveness beyond the powers of a scribe alone.

'Book-illustration' and 'Book-illumination'

Illumination in the full sense of the word—as just mentioned—originated in the early Middle Ages, perhaps in the sixth century A.D. If, however, we take the aims of illumination to be beautifying books and gratifying those who take pleasure in beautiful books, the art would appear to have evolved from the ancient methods of illustrating books, one of the most conservative fields in all the fine arts. Indeed, the desire that books should be made attractive is of great antiquity; we can trace its progress as far back as the twentieth century B.C., when the Egyptians were decorating their funeral rolls in the most gorgeous colours.

The methods of making books attractive are, of course, numerous and varied. Illumination is but one, though a particularly important one. While it may not always be easy to preserve a clear distinction between 'illumination' and 'illustration', one would be safe in assuming that the latter is but a part of the former, which would include the use of gold and/or silver, rich colouring, decorative lettering, and any forms of ornamentation which have no connection whatever with the contents of the text. Mere pictures or ornamental letters elegantly drawn in attractive colours do not constitute illumination (though, as said, they do form an essential part in its composition)—the page of an illuminated book has to be 'lighted up' (see p. 21) with bright colours and burnished gold or silver foil. *Perfect illumination* —writes John W. Bradley—*must contain both colours and metals.*

On the other hand, manuscript paintings and outline-drawings are so intimately connected that the early history of book-illustration can hardly be excluded from a history of book-illumination. The main purpose of 'illumination'—as distinct from 'illustration'—is, however, 'the desire to beautify the object of devotion rather than to clarify its contents' (C. R. Morey).

Illustrated book-production of pre-Columbian America—as well as, generally speaking, of the ancient Far East—having no connection with the history of the illuminated book, will not be dealt with in the present volume. It has been treated, though very briefly, in *The Hand-produced Book*, pp. 425–38 (and pp. 383–425).

To sum up, while the art of 'illustration' was practised early in Egypt, the other aspects of illumination, including pure decoration and ornamentation of the initials and of the script in general, would seem to have begun only in the Middle Ages.

INTRODUCTION

Elements which Influenced Book-illumination

The traditions of Egyptian art—and particularly of Hellenistic art, which was centred mainly in Alexandria and some cities of Asia Minor—had a great influence on the origin and development of illumination in Eastern Christianity, where, naturally, local elements played an important part in its formation (see p. 76 ff.).

Medieval art, it is to be remembered, was mainly Christian. Its main purpose, indeed, was to decorate the churches, great and small, which were then being built in great numbers in towns, castles and monasteries. If art may be said to be the materialized expression of man's delight in beauty, medieval art was mainly the expression of religious aspirations in terms of beauty. Indeed, it is a characteristic tendency of the medieval mind to express its faith in emotional form, to sing a hymn rather than to recite a creed. This is true of sculpture, and even more of painting in all its main aspects—frescoes, panel-paintings, mosaics, and illumination of manuscripts.

Iconography, or representation of sacred images, was a main feature of the medieval art of painting, and, at least until the thirteenth century, the individual form of expression used by the artist played very little part in comparison with conventional forms, which were nearly always symbolic. Though generally very primitive from the artistic point of view, the conventional style, by making the products appear more solemn and their contents more sure, emphasized their symbolic and religious meanings. This style is particularly evident in Byzantine, Eastern Christian, and perceptible in all the illumination produced before the period of the thirteenth-fourteenth centuries. Hiberno-Saxon elements, Carolingian art, the renaissance of Classical traditions, Persian, and other influences, contributed to the transformation of the 'primitive' style into the superb art of Renaissance illumination, which, however, may be considered a branch of pure art rather than of book-production.

In conclusion, between the artistic man in ancient Egypt and his brother in the modern West there exists—in this field—one long chain of more or less successful achievements in the direction of mutual understanding. We shall travel through ages and across a great part of the globe, and we shall see how various peoples in the far past or in times nearer to us, in the East—the Near East, the Middle East, and the Far East—and in the West, have played important parts in the development of this branch of human craving for beauty. Indeed, the illuminated book reflects the channels through which the art of painting of ancient Egypt, of the Graeco-Roman world, of the ancient peoples of Asia, and of the medieval peoples of Europe developed into the modern art of the Renaissance. But it also reflects the channels through which ancient thought and learning, literary cravings and scientific achievements, the ancient Egyptian longing to placate the gods of the Underworld, and particularly the medieval monk's desire to please God, the medieval romantic troubadour's aim to please a lady, and the Renaissance artist's endeavour to please the bibliophiles, combined to create masterpieces which are a delight even to us of the atomic age.

Book-painting compared with Panel-painting

On the surface book-painting and panel-painting appear to be closely connected. It might therefore seem reasonable to suppose that the great masters in the one field should have been great masters in the other field as well. As a matter of fact, relatively few artists practised both arts, and great masters who excelled in both book-painting and panel-painting were very few. We shall understand the reason for this if we realize that the miniature has an essential character of its own, that it is not a panel-painting on a reduced scale.

Up to a point the development of the two arts ran parallel—the most perfect kinship is apparent during the Gothic period (see pp. 263 f., 378 ff., and *passim*). Gothic art—minute, refined, delicate—was specially suited to the limitations under which the illuminator worked, and it produced the most perfect realization of the aims and ideal proper to his art. But as soon as the aesthetic equilibrium of Gothic illumination broke down, book-painting, to use Dr. Paecht's words, no longer belonged to the leading arts, notwithstanding the production of masterpieces such as the *Most Rich Hours* or the *Sforza Hours*.

Writing of Flanders, which in the fifteenth century was the leading centre in book-illumination, Paecht has pointed out that with the formation in the fifteenth century of the naturalistic art in painting, book-painting soon found itself in an inferior position. The new artistic creed—he writes—demanded that pictorial conception should be based exclusively on the subjective experience of the human eye and the picture plane be treated as imaginary space. To the self-contained picture—continues Paecht—the addition of spatial depth brought a higher degree of compositional unity. For the picture as an element of book-decoration, however, the conquest of the third dimension was a dubious gain. With the transformation of a section or the whole of a book-page into imaginary space a heavy strain was put on the artistic organization of the illuminated book. Paecht concludes thus: There was now the script, inviting the reader's eye to a movement over and along the flat expanse of the page. Then the picture suggesting to the spectator a recession of depth behind the surface of the page and finally a border decoration whose function seemed to be that of reconciling the conflicting claims of reader and spectator.

The essential difference between book-painting and panel-painting is immediately evident. Panel-paintings are displayed, and can be visited simultaneously by a considerable number of people. Books, on the other hand, lend themselves but poorly to public exhibition: they would deteriorate rapidly under the appreciative but uninformed turning of the pages by the crowd. In general, illuminations are contained in volumes belonging to private or public collections, and are available to a few qualified readers, who study and consult them individually. Indeed, the mission of the book is a personal one: it addresses the reader privately and as his mood dictates; this is the great charm, the great power of the book; it has ever been so, since the most ancient times. When—in exceptional cases only— illuminated books are exhibited to the general public, they are in glass cases and only one or two pages are shown. Book-paintings are evidently far more delicate and fragile than panel-paintings, so the non-qualified visitor must *imagine* the endless majestically superb or graciously whimsical diversity of the illuminated pages which are not exhibited, and the soft touch of the velvety smooth vellum of the whole codex.

Finally, panel-paintings should preferably be studied from a certain distance, while miniatures have to be examined at a very close range. Similarly, in medieval times panel-painting was for the congregations of people, while book-painting was for the few rich devout who loved books and could afford them.

At the same time, it should be borne in mind that illuminated books sometimes contain pictures which are independent paintings rather than miniatures. The easy interchange between the separate paintings and the book-paintings is particularly evident in the last stage of the flourishing Flemish school of illumination, *i.e.* in the early sixteenth century. Indeed, there was then an increasing tendency to introduce into the pages of books what are essentially independent paintings—without connection with the text of the book. Some 'miniatures', which belong to illuminated books, were originally intended not as book illustrations but as independent pictures to be mounted in a frame (see, for instance, p. 456 f.). In the strict sense of the term, these pictures—which have often been cut out and preserved as individual paintings—are not 'miniatures' and should not be dealt with in the present volume. An excellent example of such work is a very fine Annunciation (measuring $6\frac{7}{8}$ by $5\frac{1}{2}$ in.), preserved in the Robert Lehman Collection, New York City (*No. 72*). Other examples will be referred to on p. 456 f.

Chapter I

ANCIENT METHODS OF

BOOK ILLUSTRATION

EGYPT

(Fig. I-1-6)

The earliest illustrated book extant is a papyrus roll, known as the *Ramesseum Papyrus*, belonging to the early twentieth century B.C., and containing a ceremonial dramatic play written for Pharaoh Sesostris I of the Twelfth Dynasty, on the occasion of his accession to the throne. The illustration, consisting of about thirty figures, quite simply drawn, appears along the bottom of the roll: Fig. I-1*a*.

This highly interesting roll, now measuring about 7 ft. $\frac{2}{3}$ in. by $10\frac{1}{5}$–$10\frac{1}{2}$ in., was found (together with some other papyri) in a box, in 1895–6, by the English Egyptologist J. E. Quibell, excavating on behalf of the Egyptian Research Account in the backrooms of the Ramesseum, in West Thebes. In 1902, the find was transferred to Dr. (later, Sir) Alan Gardiner, who entrusted the editing of the papyrus to Prof. Kurt Sethe. Sethe began work on it in 1913, but because of the First World War it did not appear until 1928. The text is written in cursive hieroglyphs, that is, in the earliest hieratic bookhand. All the scenes of the illustrations centre round Sesostris I represented as Horus.

Book of the Dead (Fig. I-1*b*–4*b*)

Some illustrated copies of the *Book of the Dead* have been discussed in *The Hand-produced Book, passim*. Here again mention may be made of the fine *Hunefer Papyrus* (preserved in the British Museum, *Pap. 9901*). In Professor K. Weitzmann's opinion we have here an early example of the cyclic method of illustration. Indeed, the papyrus contains a funeral procession consisting of mourners, wailing women and the reader who recites the funeral service. Besides this scene, there is a somewhat more elaborate composition with Anubis holding the outer coffin in front of the celebrating family of Hunefer, filling nearly the full height of the roll. The *Psycho-stasia* consists of the following three scenes: (1) Anubis leads Hunefer into the Judgment Hall; (2) Anubis tests the tongue of the balance, while Thoth, the scribe of the gods, notes the result; and (3) Hunefer is brought by Horus before Osiris enthroned. Finally, in the seventeenth chapter of the *Book of the Dead* (as it appears in the Hunefer Papyrus) a long frieze runs all along the top of the papyrus 'being interrupted only in the middle by Hunefer and his wife Nasha who occupy nearly the full height of an intersection' (Weitzmann).

One of the most splendid copies of the *Book of the Dead* is preserved in the Erzherzog Rainer Collection (*Egypt., 10110*) of the National Library, Vienna. It shows Osiris in the judgment scene outlined in black, while the pattern of his garment is indicated by bright red dots. The golden neck-ornament and the crown are inlaid in gold, and the various outlines are in black ink, which also defines the borders. Here we already have the technique which very many centuries later was used by Christian and Moslem book illuminators.

Fig. I-1c reproduces sheet 3 of the 76 feet long *Ani Papyrus* (preserved in the British Museum, *Pap. 10470*), which the late Sir Frederic Kenyon considered 'probably the finest extant Egyptian book'.

The text of the papyrus is enclosed within a double border composed of two lines of colour, the inner one of brick-red, the outer of dull yellow. The text, arranged in vertical columns, is adorned at intervals with brightly coloured and well-drawn pictures and vignettes, illustrating the passage of the deceased personage named Ani (hence the name of the papyrus)—a royal scribe and overseer of granaries at Thebes—and of his wife to the abode of bliss; there is also the representation of many strange gods.

In the centre of Fig. I-1c we see Anubis weighing the heart of Ani in the great Scales against the Feather (*i.e.* the symbol of the law). To the right, the ibis-headed god Thoth notes the result. Behind him, we see the monster Amemit, the devourer of the souls condemned in the Great Judgment. Thoth reports the result of the heart-weighing to the great Gods.

Fig. I-1b and 2a represent two other funerary papyri (one preserved in the Turin Egyptian Museum, the other in the Egyptian Museum at Cairo).

Not all the copies of the *Book of the Dead* are so richly illustrated. The *Greenfield Papyrus* (*The Hand-produced Book*, p. 129) contains remarkable drawings, but these consist mainly either of a frieze running along the top of the roll, or of vignettes inserted in the text—see Fig. I-3b.

Similar methods of illustration may be seen in the copies of the *Book of the Dead* in the British Museum, in the Louvre, in the University Library of Princeton, N.J., in the Egyptian collection of the Turin Museum, and in other main collections. Some copies, such as the late-hieroglyphic papyrus of Trinity College Library at Dublin, a Cairo papyrus belonging to the period of Amenophis III, the *Nesikhonsu Papyrus* of the Cairo Museum, of the Ptolemaic period, or the *Rhind Papyri* of the Edinburgh Museum, belonging to the Roman period, are illustrated with vignettes. See Fig. I-2b and 3a, c, d.

Alexandria. In Hellenistic times, book illustration flourished particularly in Egypt, the great centre of artistic and literary production, the country of papyrus and a world-market for the book-trade. Alexandrian models—writes S. Runciman

Guests and musicians in an Egyptian wall-painting (Thebes, reign of Amenophis III, *c.* 1411–1375 B.C.). The study of Egyptian wall-painting is of great importance for the study of Egyptian book-painting.

—went out and were copied all over the Graeco-Roman world. Although no early illustrated classical Greek or Roman book extant can be attributed to Alexandria, and not many specimens can be assigned to a period earlier than the fourth century A.D., there is no doubt that several of the preserved later codices are more or less exact copies of Greek or Latin originals, some of which were certainly produced at Alexandria.

Greek Book Illustration influenced by the Egyptian (Fig. I-4–6). A fragment of a Greek illustrated papyrus roll, generally attributed to the second century A.D.—and now preserved in the National Library at Paris (*Suppl. Gr. 1294*)—shows that the Greek artist was strongly influenced by the style of copies of the Egyptian *Book of the Dead*.

The fragment, containing an unknown Greek romance, has three writing columns, each containing a scene. Of the third picture, only a portion of a figure is preserved, whereas in the first picture—damaged at the bottom—there are two figures, and in the central column there are three figures (the right being damaged), one of them sitting on a throne. The method of illustration is in Egyptian style, but the figures are in thick, black brushstrokes. The colours of the garments (tunics with clavi, etc.) are pink and blue-grey, the faces are painted in brown.

A *Chronicle of the World*, written in Alexandria by a Christian monk, on a papyrus roll, was formerly preserved in the Golenishcheff Collection, and is now in the Museum of Fine Arts at Moscow; it is tentatively assigned by O. M. Dalton to Upper Egypt and dated to *c.* A.D. 400; Dr. Kurz suggests a seventh-century date. It seems, however, to follow old Egyptian illustrative methods: see Fig. I-4.

Mention may also be made of *Pap. No. 13296* of the State Museum at Berlin, containing illustrations of the late fourth or early fifth century A.D., which also seem to follow earlier Egyptian models.

Finally, according to Weitzmann, some Greek illustrated magical rolls, such as the papyri of Leyden and Oslo, are probably translations and copies from Egyptian texts such as, for instance, *Pap. 1005* of the British Museum, written in hieratic and belonging to the period of the Twenty-sixth Dynasty. The *Leyden Papyrus* (preserved in the Royal Museum van Oudheden, *Pap. I. 384*), about 12 feet long, comes from Thebes. It contains a demotic text, but on the *verso* there are Greek magical *formulae* attributed to the first half of the fourth century A.D. Three of them are illustrated in Egyptian style. The fourth-century A.D. *Oslo Papyrus* (preserved in Oslo University Library, *Pap. No. 1*), about $8\frac{1}{3}$ feet long, is the most richly illustrated Greek papyrus. It contains twelve columns of Greek text, of which seven are illustrated by figures of the demons invoked. The method of illustration is also Egyptian. See Figs. I-5 and I-6.

It may, therefore, be argued that even if we have not sufficient evidence to show that the Greek art of book illustration *descended* from the Egyptian, there can be no doubt that the latter had a strong influence on the origin and development of the Greek ornamentation and illustration of books. In Weitzmann's opinion, the so-called *papyrus style* probably originated in pre-Hellenistic Egypt and was only adapted and further developed by the Greeks; furthermore, 'Alexandria was probably the actual centre which provided the facilities for the development of roll illustration as a new branch of Greek art'.

There is no evidence, however, that 'illumination' of books was practised in ancient Greece or Rome on a large scale. Indeed, the earliest preserved MSS. are free from ornamentation, and the earliest codices extant show a minimum of colour.

GRAECO-ROMAN BOOK ILLUSTRATION
(Fig. I-4–14)

Prof. Kurt Weitzmann, a leading authority in this field, has pointed out that in early Greek history a representational art gradually developed. In the beginning, the relation between this art and works of literature was quite vague, but the closest union was achieved when both picture and literature were physically united in the illustrated papyrus roll, and the text and the picture intermingled. This development covered the entire range of Greek history from the archaic to the Hellenistic period, but, as the original remains of classical book illustration 'are pitifully few', most of its history must be reconstructed on the basis of contemporary copies in other media—such as figured vases, metalwork, stelae, friezes, sarcophagi, and so on—or else from medieval copies of classical MSS. See Fig. I-7.

In the classical development of representational art, three stages can usually be distinguished, which Weitzmann has classified as follows: (1) The 'simultaneous method', used from archaic times until the fifth century B.C., by which several actions, taking place at the same time, are represented in a single scene; (2) the 'monoscenic method', from the fifth century B.C. to the Hellenistic period, which is based on the principle of the unity of time and place; and (3) the 'cyclic method', which in its fully developed form appears in the Hellenistic period, and in which the contents of a literary source could be rendered by a series of consecutive compositions with separate and centred actions—the modern strip cartoon in embryo. Etruscan artists—who produced such masterpieces as those shown in Fig. I-7—used coherent picture cycles as models as far back as the third century B.C.: see Fig. I-7a.

Only after the invention of the illustrated papyrus roll—argues Weitzmann—could the full text and the full picture cycle be brought together in a complete unity. The Ambrosian *Iliad* (see p. 33 f.) is the most direct evidence for the existence of illustrated Homer rolls. Weitzmann suggests that a great number of other epic poems were also extensively illustrated, as well as dramas, such as those of Euripides, and prose texts, both literary and scientific. There is much to say in favour of his view (which is opposed to the commonly held theory) that the representation of scenes from the Greek epics and the Attic dramas on ancient vases, cups, sarcophagi, tablets, etc. (Fig. I-7 and 8a), did not precede illustrated editions of the literary works, but were derived from papyrus rolls, which probably contained the 'iconographic storehouse' of all the representations.

Furthermore, it is suggested that in Hellenistic times the vast cycles of illustrations —that of Homer may have comprised as many as six hundred individual scenes— were consolidated, and that selections were made of favourite subjects, which became more and more stereotyped. There were epitomized picture-cycles illustrating biographies of gods or heroes, such as Achilles, and there were cycles illustrating other leading motives, such as the Power of Love.

However, there can be little doubt that in Hellenistic times, under the traditional influence of Egyptian painting, there grew up in Alexandria, and probably also in other cities, important schools of book illustration. Very little of the original work of these schools survives, but the style may be studied from the later copies of Greek and Latin works. Both the scientific works, dealing, for example, with geography, botany, and medicine, and the literary works, such as romances, epics, and lyric poetry, were illustrated. The style was mainly pictorial, not ornamental; the objects depicted were aptly chosen to illustrate the texts.

Although it may be assumed that a great number of classical painted manuscripts have perished, it is generally believed that such books must have been relatively rare, and must have appealed chiefly to a very restricted class which had the means—books with paintings were of course much more expensive than non-illustrated copies—and enjoyed beauty and small, detailed refinements. It has been pointed out that the scarcity of Roman painted manuscripts seems strange in view of the wealth of material which the masterpieces of Greek and Roman literature provided for sculptures, paintings on vases, frescoes, and so on. Amongst the various answers which have been suggested by leading scholars, the following deserves emphasis: the genius of Roman art was an art of display, expressed chiefly by statuary, architecture, fresco paintings, triumphal arches, splendid tombs, beautiful streets, so that comparatively little effort may have been expended on the detailed work of enrichment of books.

DEVELOPMENT OF GRAECO-ROMAN BOOK ILLUSTRATION

The earliest illustrated books were executed on papyrus rolls (see *The Hand-produced Book*, Chapter IV), and the illustrations represented continuous scenes without division into 'miniatures', and without the rich ornament of the medieval book-illumination; the Vatican *Joshua Roll* (see p. 42 ff.) retained the method of continuous illustration.

Once a picture, or a cycle of pictures, illustrating a literary or religious or scientific text, was created, it usually became the pictorial archetype of later illustrators of the same text: Weitzmann. Thus, the cycles illustrating the Bible, or Homer, or else scientific or other important texts, can be reduced to relatively few archetypes. Furthermore, single pictures often 'migrated' from one text to another, which dealt with the same or kindred subjects.

With the adoption of the codex book-form (see *The Hand-produced Book, passim*), there appeared the separate page-illustrations (equivalent to the 'plates' of the modern book), which excellently suited the Greek taste for defined composition;

sometimes there were also painted margins round the text. This Hellenistic style of book illustration can best be studied in the codices produced in the Byzantine period, and it will, therefore, be described in the section on Byzantine book-illumination.

By the close of the third century A.D.—writes S. Runciman—Graeco-Roman art could go no further. The old Greek naturalism, tastefully and gracefully arranged, had been embellished in the Hellenistic age, and still more under the Romans, with an elaboration of detail. The fourth century brought a reaction from the East.

The Egyptian and Graeco-Roman papyrus rolls, as already mentioned, had no ornament, but simply illustrations depicting events described in the text. In the Byzantine period, however, ornament assumed a growing importance. Already before the sixth century (A.D.), after the vellum codex had superseded the papyrus-roll books, the method of combining pictures with ornament, or of using ornament as something quite distinct, replaced the plain Egyptian and Graeco-Roman styles. Nevertheless, even in later times the non-ornamented style of illustration was employed in the copying of illustrated papyrus-roll books.

The *Joshua Rotulus* and the *Octateuchs* (see p. 44) may also show an influence of Jewish art (see p. 44).

EARLIEST PRESERVED GREEK ILLUSTRATED MSS. (Fig. I-8*b*–11*a*)

These are not only 'pitifully few' but also utterly insignificant from the artistic standpoint. This is easily explained by the fact that all of them are accidental findings from the rubbish piles of Egypt (see *The Hand-produced Book*, Chapters IV and VI). 'They cannot, therefore, be taken as a norm to judge the artistic standard of book illumination in the Hellenistic and Roman period.'

The earliest MSS. extant contain only some rude diagrams. By far the earliest is a papyrus roll (Fig. I-8*b*), measuring two metres (about 2 ft. 8 in.) in length, preserved in the Louvre (*Pap. Letronne 1*). It is perhaps a fragment of a schoolbook and contains, amongst other matter, propositions from the astronomical *tékhnē* of Eudoxus. Eudoxus of Cnidus (*c.* 407–355 B.C.), astronomer and geometer, founded a school at Cyzicus, and later at Athens. Several of Euclid's propositions, the 'method of exhaustions', the determination of volume of pyramids and cones, and the beginnings of scientific astronomy, are attributed to him. The present copy is usually assigned to 165 B.C.

The *Ayer Papyrus* (preserved in the Field Columbian Museum, Chicago, *Pap. No. 1*), apparently found at Hawara (Fayyûm), belongs to the first or second century A.D. and contains part of a treatise on mensuration. A fragmentary papyrus roll of the State Museums, Berlin (*Pap. No. 11529*) belongs to the second century A.D., and contains a series of geometrical and stereometrical propositions.

The second-century (A.D.) papyrus fragment of the National Library, Paris (*Suppl. Gr. 1294*), already referred to, is perhaps the earliest specimen extant of representational art.

I–1. *a, Ramesseum Ceremonial Papyrus:* ceremonial play in dramatic form, written and illustrated on the occasion of the accession to the throne of Sesostris I (*c.* 1971–1930 B.C.). *b, Kha' Papyrus* (Turin Egyptian Museum): adoration of Osiris by the dead man and his wife. *c, Ani Papyrus,* sheet 3 : Anubis weighs the dead man's heart; Thoth records the result, which is anxiously awaited by Ani and his wife; above, various gods attend the judgment.

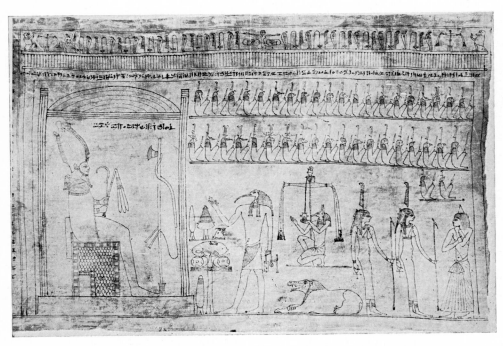

I–2. *a, Funerary Papyrus* of the 22nd Dynasty (Egyptian Museum at Cairo): adoration of Amūn (represented as a ram) by the dead woman. *b,* Portion of the *Garrett Papyrus,* illustrating a heart-weighing scene. This papyrus belongs to the *Saite Recension* of the *Book of the Dead.*

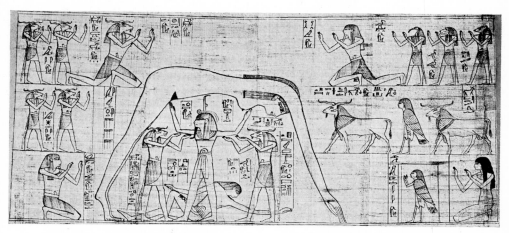

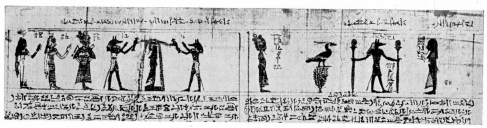

I-3. *a, Book of the Dead,* chapt. 83-85 dealing with the transformation of the dead man into a phoenix, a heron, and a human-faced bird (period of Amenophis III, 1413-1377 B.C.; Egyptian Museum at Cairo). *b, Greenfield Papyrus:* cosmogonic scene of the lifting of the goddess Nut (sky) by the god Shu (air); various gods and sacred animals in state of adoration. *c,* Copy of the *Book of the Dead* of the Saitic period (Trinity College Library, Dublin): vignettes representing monstrous genii of the nether world. *d, Rhind Papyrus:* vignettes representing various gods and purification scenes of the dead man.

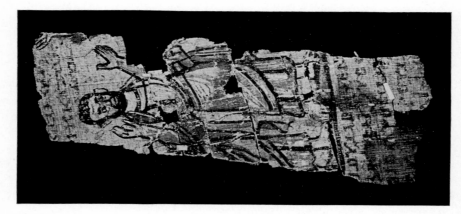

1–4. *Alexandrian World Chronicle. a*, Fragment 1 r (Prophets Obadiah and Jonah). *b*, Fragment 1 *v* (Prophet Nahum). *c*, Portion of the best-preserved fragment, 8 *r*, representing the victory of Christianity (personified by the Alexandrian Bishop Theophilos, with nimbus and Bible) and the destruction of the temple of the Serapeum.

I-5. *Oslo Papyrus*: The most richly illustrated Greek papyrus; the illustrations represent the demons invoked.

I–6. *Leyden Papyrus. Verso* of the Papyrus; it contains Greek magical formulae.

I–7. Greek sagas and myths in Etruscan and Greek art. *a,* Etruscan sixth-century B.C. fresco-painting ('Tomba dei Tori', near Tarquinia, Tuscany): Achilles in ambush behind a well trying to slay the young Trojan prince Troilus. *b,* Earliest extant illustration of the wedding of Perithous and Hippodameia: Perithous and his para-nymph Theseus defend Hippodameia against the Centaurs (Attic Crater, *c.* 460 B.C.; Archaeological Museum, Florence). *c,* Part of an Etruscan alabaster-urn of the third century B.C. representing the slaying of Mirtilus (Archaeological Museum, Florence).

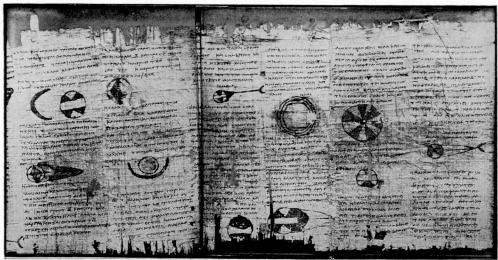

I-8. *a, François Vase* (Archaeological Museum, Florence) made by the potter Ergotimos, and painted by the artist Klitias (*c.* 560–550 B.C.); it was discovered in 1844 by A. François at Fonte Rotella near Chiusi (Tuscany). *b, Papyrus Louvre Letronne 1* : Eudoxus.

I-9. *a*, Amor and Psyche represented on a papyrus fragment of A.D. the second century, found at Behnesa (Oxyrhynchus), and now in the Archaeological Museum, Florence (*Inv. 8682*). *b*, Christ in the Boat on the Sea of Galilee drawn on a papyrus fragment, apparently found at the same site; it is attributed to A.D. the fifth or sixth century (Archaeological Museum, Florence, *Inv. 8683*).

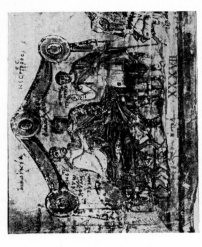

I–10. a and b, Ambrosian Iliad. a, Pict. xxi, representing two battle-scenes combined in a common frame. b, Part of Pict. xxvii (fol. 13 v), representing Nestor's tent with Eurypylos, Patroklos and Achilles. c, Sams 23. l: British Museum, Pap. 10016—Egyptian satirical fables. This procession of animals is a caricature of the great ones of the earth and their courtiers and servants of the lower classes; the lion (i.e, the king) and a unicorn gazelle (a lady of his harem) play a game of draughts; a fox plays a double pipe while animals of the gazelle class strut in front of him; there is a cat driving geese, etc.

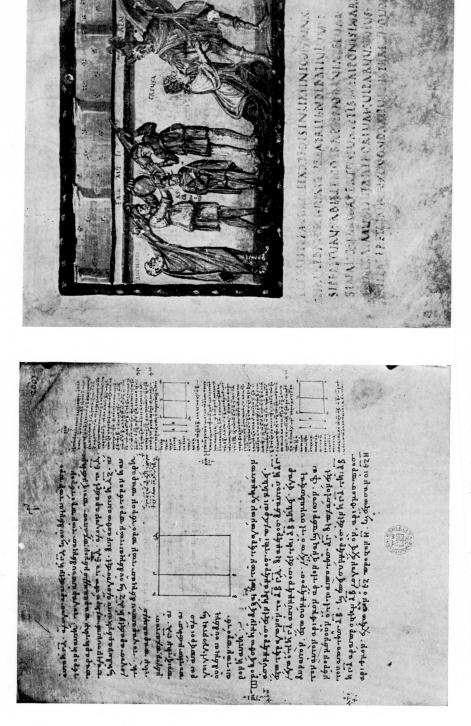

I–II. *a, Euclid's Elements. b, Codex Vaticanus Vergilius*, fol. 22 r: *Aeneid* ii, 671 ff. and 681 ff.

I–12. *a* and *b*, *Codex Vaticanus Vergilius*, fol. 17 *r* (*Aeneid* i, 657 f.) and 7 *v* (*Georg*. iv, 125 f.). *c*, *Codex Romanus Vergilius*, fol. 100 *v*, representing Dido's *Convivium*. See also *The Hand-produced Book*, Fig. VI–13.

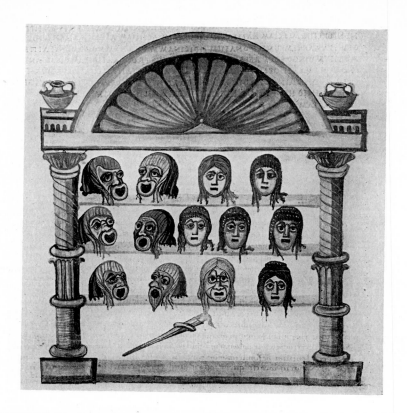

I-13. *a, Vatican Terence*, fol. 77 *r:* masks representing *dramatis personae. b, Bodleian Terence,* fol. 125 : *v: Adelphi,* 958 ff.

I-14. *a*, Horace, *Carmina* (*Vat. Lat. 1592*, fol. *20 r*): *Epistola ad Augustum* and the 'portrait' of Augustus. This 'portrait' is probably the best of the three in this codex (the others being of Horace, fol. *1 r*, and of Maecenas, fol. *6 v*), but while the others contain some classical elements, the 'portrait' of Augustus, in the attire of a medieval emperor, is in the contemporary style of the manuscript (thirteenth century). *b*, Prudentius, *Psychomachia* (British Museum, *Add. MS. 24199*, portion of fol. *11 v*) :v. 172.

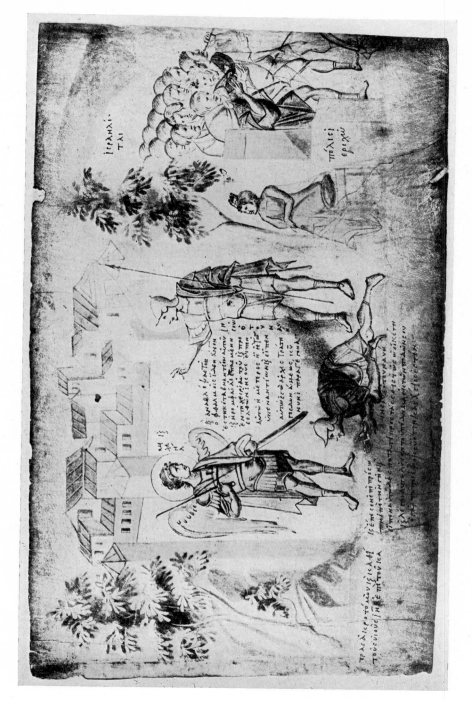

I-15. *Joshua Roll: Joshua, v, 13 ff.*

I–16. a, Joshua Roll, fol. VIII: Joshua, ii, 1 ff. b, Octateuch (Vat. Gr. 746, fol. 55 v): Noah's Ark (Genesis, viii, 14 ff.).

I-17. *a*, Octateuch (*Vat. Gr. 747*, fol. 35 *r*): Abraham and Sarah before Pharaoh (*Gen., xii, 15* and *18*). *b, Smyrna Octateuch*: birth and circumcision of Isaac (*Gen., xxi, 5*). *c, Dioscorides Neapolitanus*.

علا ماده هو يجنان في الطريق بين يديه رجلس الغلام يبول في اصل حايط يخرج حية صغيره كابا

I–18. *a, Vienna Dioscorides,* fol. 5 *v. b, Arabic Dioscorides (Cod. Arab. Vindob. A. F. 10),* fol. 2 *v.*

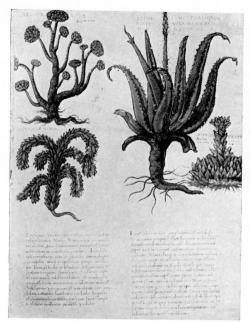

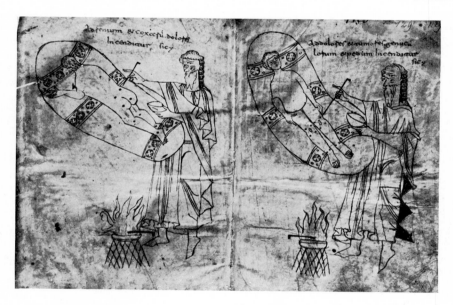

I-19. *a, Dioscorides Codex Vindobonus 2277, fol. 2 r. b, Codex Medicus Vindobonus Lat. 93, fol. 27 v. c, Codex Medicus, Herbal, Bestiary, etc. (Laurentian Library, MS. Plut. 73. 41), folios 128 v–129 r.*

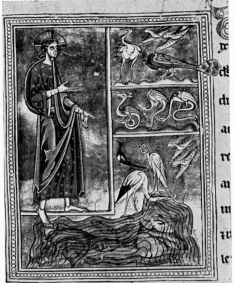

I–20. *Bestiaries and Herbals. a, MS. Bodley, 130, fol. 18 v. b, MS. Ashm. 1511, fol. 6 r. c, Liber Bestiarum Hugonis de B. Victore* (C.U.L., *MS. li. 4. 26*), *fol. 32 r. d, MS. Plut. 73. 16, fol. 132 v.*

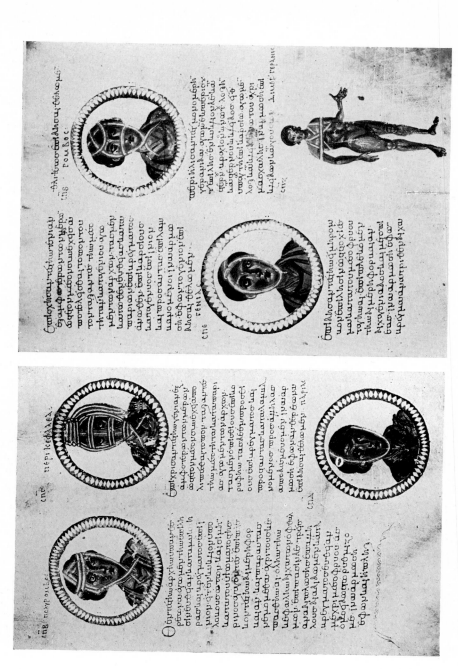

I-21. Soranus of Ephesus, *On Bandaging* (MS. *Plut.* 74. 7), folios 232 *v*–233 *r*.

I-22. Oppian of Apamea, *Cynegetica*, fol. 8 *v*. Three pictures without borders: (1) The horse Bucephalus in a cage behind an iron grating. (2) Pursuit of Darius by Alexander the Great. (In Weitzmann's opinion, these two pictures depend on the *Alexander Romance*: see p. 35). (3) Bellerophon on Pegasus kills the Chimera; landscape setting.

I-23. *Cosmas Indicopleustes. a, Vat. Gr. 699, fol. 38 r. b, MS. Plut. 9. 28, fol. 113 r: Joshua, iii, 14 f.*

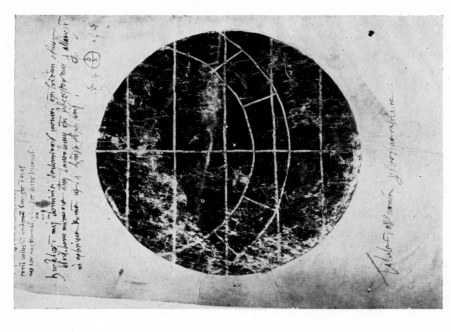

I-24. *a*, Ptolemy, *Tables* (*Vat. Gr. 1291*), fol. 4 *v. b*, *Cosmography, c. 1220* (Walters Art Gallery, *MS. 1073*), fol. 1 *r.*

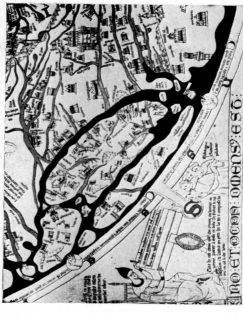

I-25. *Hereford Mappa Mundi. a,* The Map. *b,* The top of the surround, representing the Day of Judgment. *c,* Lower left-hand corner of the map, representing (within the circle) the British Isles and a great part of Europe, and (in the surround) Caesar crowned giving instructions for the survey of the world.

trifinii interdum quadrifinii aliquando pentago
ni recipiunt rationē
& hoc si exigerit loci
commoditas. hii uero
pontes hac ratione de
seruiunt quorum al

uea proxi me eos finer ultro citroq. non transmit
tunt perquos & itinera publica currunt. quibus limis
lege colonica seruit. NAM sunt & alii pontes in ui
cinalibus & priuatis uiis quorum aluea uaruntur que
tamen intrifinii ratio
nem ex conuenientia
limitum atq. signorū
cursus frequenter
accipi possunt.
AQUARUM ductus per medias possessiones diri
guntur quae a possessoribus
ipsis uice temporum repurgan
tur propter. quod & leuia tributa
persoluunt quarum putea ali
quotiens in cursorio aterminib. demonstrantur que
si in extremis finibus occurrerint ex conuenientia
centuriarum intrifinio uel quadrifinio obseruari de
bebunt. Idem uaratio fluminum riuorum cursus ca
nabulae uel nouercae quod tegulis construitur sepe

I–26. *Agrimensores* (*Vat. Pal. Lat. 1564*), fol. 119 *r*.

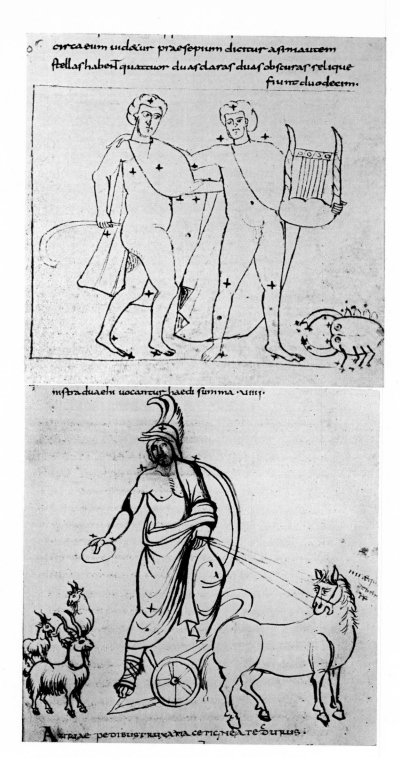

I-27. *Aratos—Codex Germanicus* (Basel, *A. N. iv. 18*). *a*, Part of fol. 20 *v*. *b*, Part of fol. 22 *r*.

I–28. *a* and *b*, Boëthius, *De Institutione arithmetica libri II* (Bamberg, *H. J. iv. 12*), fol. 2 *v* and 28 *r*.
Fol. 2 *v*: Boëthius presents his work to his learned father-in-law Symmachus; fol. 28 *r*:
beautifully illuminated graphic table. *c* and *d*, *Chronographer*: personification of the city of
Alexandria (*c*) and Calendar—picture of March with the personification of Mars (*d*).

I–29. *The Menōrāh* (the seven-branched candlestick) and the *Arōn ha-qōdesh* (cabinet containing the Scrolls of the Law) depicted on Jewish monuments. *a*, Gilded glass, showing the *Arōn ha-qōdesh* guarded on each side by a crouching lion; underneath, two *Menōrāh's* and cult objects. *b*, Wall-painting in a Jewish catacomb on Via Nomentana, Rome, showing the *Arōn ha-qōdesh* flanked on each side by a *Menōrāh*, and various cult objects.

1–30. Frescoes : Dura Europos Synagogue. (above) Exodus and passage of the Israelites through the Red Sea. (below) Infant Moses found in the bulrushes on the River Nile, and brought to Pharaoh's daughter.

An extremely interesting fragmentary literary papyrus of *c.* A.D. 250 was published in 1954 by E. Lobel and C. H. Roberts (*Oxyrhynchus Papyri*, Part XXII, No. 2331 and Pl. XI). The lower margin is completely filled by painted drawings, which apparently are referred to in the text (so D. L. Page, in *Classical Review*, 1957, pp. 189 ff., and P. Mass, in *Greece and Rome*, 1958, pp. 171 ff.) by the term γρύλλῳ, meaning a kind of caricature, as opposed to serious drawing.

There are various papyrus fragments belonging to the second to sixth centuries A.D., which may be considered remnants of Greek illustrated papyrus rolls: a fragment preserved in the Archaeological Museums, Florence; National Library, Vienna, *Pap. Gr. 30507*; State Museums, Berlin, *Pap. No. 9927*; State Library, Munich, *Gr. Mon. 128*; a fragment of the Johnson Collection, Oxford; a Christian fragment of the Archaeological Museum, Florence. There are, moreover, several illustrated magical rolls—partly already referred to—of the third to fifth centuries (preserved in the British Museum, *Pap. Gr. CXXI, CXXII, CXXIII*; the *Mimant Papyrus* in the Louvre, *Pap. No. 2391*; Leyden Museum, *Pap. I. 1384*; State Museums, Berlin, *Pap. No. 5026*; University Library, Oslo, *Pap. No. 1*, and some others).

See also p. 29 and Figs. I-5, 6, 8*b*, 9.

Ambrosian Iliad (Fig. I-10*a* and *b*)

A fragmentary copy of the *Iliad* on vellum, of uncertain origin, but since 1609 in the Ambrosian Library, Milan (*Cod. F. 205, inf.*), is the earliest extant example of a Greek 'illuminated' MS. The manuscript is precious not only for its uniqueness, but also as an indication of the style of much work which has vanished for ever. There is no doubt that in this work we have a specimen of Greek artistic book-production not in its beginnings, but rather in its final stage of development.

The book was preserved purely for the sake of its pictures—all the plain leaves have long ago disappeared; it contains fifty-eight pictures (on fifty-two separate leaves of vellum), which are perfectly classical in treatment. It may be assumed that this codex was originally a complete *Iliad*, profusely illustrated: the editor of the *editio princeps*, A. M. Ceriani, suggested that the present copy contained 386 leaves with about 240 miniatures.

The miniatures cover the full page of the *verso*, but are of various heights; they are assigned by some scholars to South Italy. According to Dalton, however, the MS. is based upon the Alexandrian style, and in Prof. Toesca's opinion the miniatures have descended from Graeco-Eastern models.

Amongst the various colours, white, red, green, blue, purplish-blue, and purple predominate; bright yellow is used instead of gold. Of interest are the nimbi of the gods—in purple for Zeus, in green for Aphrodite, and in blue for the other gods. Some outlines are in pale ink; except for two pictures, with landscape backgrounds, all the backgrounds are plain. All the pictures are enclosed in plain banded frames of red and blue.

This codex is assigned variously to the third, fourth, or fifth century A.D., but the pictures may go back to earlier models. S. J. Gąsiorowski attributes this MS. to the fourth century A.D., and considers it an excellent copy of an original produced not much earlier. The text, which is written on the *recto* of the preserved leaves, is Greek, the script being uncial writing of the fourth or the fifth century A.D. The preservation of this fragmentary copy is due to the 'artistic', though barbarous, attitude of a thirteenth-century collector, who went so far as to cover the *verso* pages with a paper backing. The leaves have been cut down as far as possible without encroaching on the pictures.

At any rate, here we have some of the most beautiful illustrations of all those which have survived from the classical period, although even the best miniatures here are artistically and technically inferior to the best pictures of the *Vatican Virgil*. The work is most unequal: some compositions are full of dignity, abounding with life and vigour, for example a few battle scenes; and many single figures are extremely charming, such as the river-god Scamander, the winged Night, the god Apollo, and a few others; but other compositions are weak, childish, and without proportion—Troy, for instance, is represented as a tiny walled space containing half a dozen soldiers, and the slain in the battle scenes are only half the size of the living. On the whole, however, there is a fine juxtaposition of mass. Unfortunately, most of the pictures are so stained and worn that it is difficult to judge of their original appearance, and the grand and gracious manner of the classical art is retained in an enfeebled form.

This precious manuscript with many others was in a vessel captured by the Turks. They eagerly broke open the caskets in which the treasures were packed. 'Moidores, perhaps, guineas we hope, manuscripts by Jingo!' the sanguine but disappointed sailors are said to have exclaimed; and they threw the MSS. overboard. This fragmentary treasure survived by sheer miracle.

Interesting is another illuminated *Iliad* MS., preserved in the Marcian Library, Venice (*A. 354*), which belongs to a much later period. It is perhaps of the late tenth or the eleventh century, and from Mount Athos. It has 327 leaves, measuring 39·3 cm. ($15\frac{7}{10}$ in.) by 28 cm. ($11\frac{1}{5}$ in.), and contains miniatures and marginal illustrations.

Miscellanea (Fig. I-10c–11a)

There are hardly any other illuminated Greek codices extant of secular literary subjects, containing illustrations which go back to Graeco-Roman models, though a fourteenth-century codex of the bucolic idylls of Theocritos—a native of Syracuse (Sicily) who flourished at Alexandria in the third century B.C.—is preserved in the National Library, Paris (*Gr. 2832*), and this contains miniatures which are based ultimately on Hellenistic models.

In some instances it is not easy to determine the archetype of the preserved copies, especially if they bear no title. This is the case, for example, with three English copies—the earliest of them being *Cotton. Vitell. A.XV* of the British Museum—of

Earliest preserved illustrated (fragmentary) copy of *Iliad* (Ambrosiana Library, Milan, *Cod. F. 205,* inf.):
Aphrodite shows Zeus her hand which Diomedes has wounded; Hera and Athene laugh at her.

a text which M. R. James calls *Marvels of the East*. According to James, it is based upon the so-called *Letter of Fermes*, attributed to the fourth or fifth century A.D., and going back to a much earlier Greek source. The latter, in the opinion of some scholars, was the *Alexander Romance* of Pseudo-Callisthenes (third cent. A.D.), which is known from the following copies: a fourteenth-century Greek MS. of S. Giorgio dei Greci, Venice; part of the *Cod. Gr. 479* of the Marciana Library, Venice; a fifteenth-century Serbian MS.; some Armenian codices; and numerous Latin copies. This work was very popular in the Middle Ages, and various French and English versions (containing a number of accretions or changes) are extant. The most popular French version, *Li romans du boin roi Alexandre* by Lambert li Tors, continued by Alexander de Bernay (or de Paris), is preserved in various MSS., of which *MS. Bodley 264* in Oxford (see also p. 380) is the most rich in pictorial and decorative illumination, this work (by Jehans de Grise) being completed on 18.4.1344. The codex contains also a fragmentary *Alexander Romance* in English alliterative verse, written in the fifteenth century in the West Midland dialect.

The late Egyptian or Graeco-Roman *Pap. 10016* in the British Museum represents animal fables. See Fig. I-10c. See also under *Graeco-Roman Scientific Texts*, p. 44 ff.

Finally, mention may be made of the commentaries on secular and religious works. These commentaries—which are often illustrated—arose out of the critical notes, annotations and explanations of words, which scholars, or even intelligent readers, wrote between the columns of the text in literary or scientific MSS. The earliest preserved MSS. containing such annotations belong to the first century A.D.

The earliest codices extant containing text and commentary, or marginal *scholia*, are Christian; these are the *Codex Zacynthius* (preserved by the British and Foreign Bible Society), a New Testament MS. attributed to the sixth century A.D.; the *Book of Job*, preserved at Patmos (*Cod. 171*), of the seventh or early eighth century, and others. Of the scientific scholia, of great importance are Euclid's *Elements* preserved in the Bodleian Library, Oxford (*Cod. d'Orville, 301*), belonging to the year A.D. 888. See Fig. I-11a.

Euclid (Eucleides), who flourished in Alexandria about 300 B.C., in his *Elements* (*Stoicheia*) has preserved all the best discoveries of his predecessors in the field of geometry. His work, which amongst other things includes five books on plane geometry and three on solid geometry, was for many centuries the textbook on geometry in all schools; indeed many of his demonstrations, in point of brevity, clearness, and accuracy have never been improved upon.

ROMAN ART OF BOOK ILLUSTRATION

(Fig. I-11b-15)

Although no true examples of classical book illustration are extant, the art of painting books is referred to by Roman authors. Pliny attests in his *Nat. hist.* (xxxv,

2, 11) that Varro wrote the lives of seven hundred illustrious Romans (*Imagines illustrium aliquo modo hominum*), enriching the work—which was published in 39 B.C.—with their portraits. This great biographical work of Varro is said to have contained a number of miniature portraits by Iaia of Cyzicus (or Kyzikos)— Pliny, XXXV, 40, 147.

Thus, this lady artist who lived in the days of Augustus Caesar, is the first miniaturist on record. She is said to have produced excellent portraits 'in little', especially those of ladies, on both vellum and ivory. All her work, as far as is known, has perished, but some scholars have suggested that her own portrait representing her engaged in painting a statuette is to be seen on a Pompeian fresco-painting now preserved in the Museum of Antiquities at Naples.

According to Cornelius Nepos, Pomponius Atticus (Chap. 18), friend of Cicero, was the author of a work on the actions of great Romans, which was illustrated with their portraits (see also *The Hand-produced Book*, Chapter VI). See also pp. 38 f. and 56 f.

An interesting definite reference to an 'illuminated' vellum manuscript of the late first century A.D. is Martial, xiv. 186, which mentions a Virgil with a frontispiece containing a portrait of the poet as one of various kinds of gifts:

> *Vergilius in membranis*
> *Quam brevis immensum cepit membrana Maronem!*
> *Ipsius et vultus prima tabella gerit.*

See also p. 39.

EARLIEST LATIN ILLUMINATED CODICES EXTANT

No illuminated Latin MS. has come down to us which can be assigned to a period earlier than the fourth century A.D.

It must be borne in mind that from the late second century A.D. onwards the Roman Empire gradually declined, especially in Italy herself. The emperors—as a leading British art-historian, N. Pevsner, has pointed out—were proclaimed by some provincial army of barbarian troops, often barbarians themselves, rude soldiers of peasant stock, ignorant of, and unsympathetic to, the achievements of Roman civilisation. There was constant internecine warfare, and constant attacks of barbarians from outside had to be repulsed. Cities declined and were in the end deserted. Soldiers of the Roman army sacked Roman towns. Goths, Alamans, Franks, Persians sacked whole provinces. Trade, seaborne and landborne, came to an end. The educated bourgeoisie, decimated by wars, executions, murder, and a lower and lower birthrate, no longer had a share in public affairs. Men from Syria, Asia Minor, Egypt, from Spain, Gaul and Germany, held all the important positions. Soon Rome was no longer the capital of the Empire; Constantinople took her place. Then—concludes Pevsner—the Empire fell into two: that of the East to prove mighty, that of the West to become the prey of Teutonic invaders, the Visigoths, the Vandals, the Ostrogoths, the Lombards, and then for a while to be part of the Eastern—the Byzantine—Empire.

Under such conditions, no wonder that not many 'illuminated' books could be produced, no wonder that none of the previous productions could be preserved.

Virgil (Fig. I-11b–12)

Of the two early illustrated Latin codices, both copies of Virgil, and both preserved in the Vatican Library, the *Cod. Vat. Lat. 3225* (also known as the *Vatican Virgil*) and the *Cod. Vat. Lat. 3867* (known as the *Roman Virgil* or *Codex Romanus*, or *Codex R.*), the former belongs roughly to the same period as, and may even be earlier than, the earliest preserved copy of the *Iliad* (see p. 35 f.)—with which it has much in common—thus being perhaps our earliest illustrated codex. The miniatures of both these precious Virgils are undoubtedly of Roman origin.

The *Vatican Virgil* contains 76 leaves, measuring 29·5 cm. (nearly 12 in.) in width by between 31·8 and 32 cm. ($12\frac{7}{10}$ and $12\frac{4}{5}$ in.) in height, and includes 50 pictures. These are not all of equal merit, but the best are painted in so mature a manner and with such excellent technique, as to induce us to accept the suggestion that we have here the only surviving work of a well-developed school of book-painting.

The text is badly damaged; it contains, with some *lacunae*, books three and four of the *Georgics* (ten leaves)—which are illustrated by nine miniatures, these pastoral pictures being the best of the whole series—and the first nine books of the *Aeneid* (sixty-five leaves) illustrated by forty-one miniatures; all in rectangular frames bordered by bands in three colours, red, black, and white (the red being decorated with gilt lozenges). An extraneous leaf, from the Medici codex, was added after 1671. The miniatures of the *Aeneid*—with some exceptions (miniatures 26–32, 40–44, 46)—are, as mentioned, not as fine as those of the *Georgics*. We may assume that the codex contains about one-fifth or one-sixth of the original manuscript.

Of the miniatures, six cover full pages including two frontispieces, the remainder being inserted in the text, mainly in its upper part. The illustrations 'preserve the fresh naturalism of the antique to a remarkable degree, with impressionistic rendering of the figures, and depth of landscape background' (C. R. Morey). See Figs. I–11b, 12a and b.

The following—all deep, rich, and harmonious—are the main colours used in this codex: dark and light blue, dark and light yellow, brown, green, red, pink, light purple, orange, grey, white, black, and gold. Brick-red is always used for the flesh-tints; the high lights of draperies and accessories are touched with gold. Apparently there was no preliminary outline-drawing. The colours are thick and some have flaked off.

While the text, written in rustic capitals of the fourth or fifth century A.D. (rustic capitals cannot be dated with great accuracy), is ascribed to one hand, the miniatures appear to have been executed by three or perhaps four artists, probably belonging to the same period, perhaps even to the same school, but having different degrees of merit. The pictures do not afford great help in the chronological problem, but all of them are in the classical style of the first four centuries A.D. This pure classical style—good proportion, pose and grace in the figures, the natural aspect of the animals, sense of space, and especially the fine execution of the earlier miniatures—showing great skill and taste, is decisive in assigning the codex to a period prior to the barbarian conquest. The diaperies—soft as they are—are quite different from those, for instance, which we find in Byzantine pictures. In S. J. Gąsiorowski's opinion, this codex should be dated to the first half of the fourth century A.D., and its original model to the late second or early third century A.D.

The codex was known to Raphael, who was inspired by more than one of its designs, but nothing is known of its history until the fifteenth century, when it was at Naples in the possession of Giovanni Pontano, the famous Italian poet and humanist (1422/26–1503). It has been preserved in the Vatican since 1600.

The *Roman Virgil* from the eighth to the fifteenth century belonged to the Abbey of S. Denis, near Paris, and since 1475 has been preserved in the Vatican Library. It contains 309 leaves—measuring 33·2 by 32·3 cm. (nearly $13\frac{1}{10}$ by $13\frac{1}{2}$ in.), thus being almost square—and is illustrated by nineteen miniatures: seven from the *Bucolics*, two from the *Georgics*, and ten from the *Aeneid*; the last twelve cover full pages. The full-size pictures are thus fewer than those of the *Vatican Virgil* which, however, on the average are smaller. Gold, black, white, yellow, brown, purple, blue, green, yellowish-green, and red are the main colours used.

The illustrations follow the same scheme as those of the *Vatican Virgil*; they are naturalistic, but are much less elegant and probably in a late classical style, already decayed—when it had become 'a dead tradition' rather than 'a living force'—perhaps of the late fifth or early sixth century A.D.

The Text is in rustic capitals of an early type, which induced some scholars—for instance the editors of the Palaeographical Society's *Facsimiles* (Series 1, Introduction, p. vii and pl. 113–114)—to attribute it to the first half of the fourth century or even to the late third century A.D. Other authorities, on the basis of the corruptness of the text and the crudeness of the painting, have suggested the sixth century or an even later period. It may be assumed, however, that the codex cannot be earlier than the fourth century A.D. and not later than the sixth.

Some scholars assign this codex to a provincial artist; others consider it 'a schoolboy's Virgil', 'a sort of artistic joke for the amusement of a Roman schoolboy'. At any rate, this coarsely executed codex is probably the work of a second-rate artist. Indeed, the figure style—writes the American expert C. R. Morey—has lost its vitality and become childish. Yet even in this crude work the antique tradition is maintained, however feebly, for the costumes are those of the later empire, the nimbus, given to distinguished personages, is a thoroughly Hellenistic notion, the furniture is of ancient pattern, and—concludes C. R. Morey—the round infantile faces with their enormous eyes, show in their very simplicity of type the basic idealism of the ancient world. See Fig. I-12c.

While this codex is, as already mentioned, artistically much inferior to the other MS., it is in certain respects more original, whereas the *Vatican Virgil* appears to be an exact copy of a classical original. An interesting feature of *Vat. Lat. 3867* is that it contains a portrait of Virgil—one of the very few extant remains of classical portrait-illustrations: see *The Hand-produced Book*, Fig. VI-13.

There are (or were) numerous medieval illuminated codices of Virgil, of which the following are most important: a tenth-century codex produced in Campania, and now in the National Library at Naples (*MS. ex-Vindob. 58, Lat. 6*), containing four interesting scenes in pen-drawing, beautiful initials at the beginning of each book, and so on; a twelfth-century Virgil MS. of the Vatican Library (*Cod. Lat. 1575*), containing some drawings; a MS., containing the *Aeneid*, which was illuminated in 1198 by the monk John Alighieri, and which until 1782 was preserved in the library of the Carmelites at Ferrara; the Ambrosian codex which belonged to Petrarca, with a frontispiece painted by Simone Martini (*c.* 1284–1344): the miniatures of this codex are excellent specimens of the art of illumination of the fourteenth century (see also p. 311); *Cod. Vat. Lat. 1579* of the Vatican Library, containing Virgil's *Carmina*: this MS., written in 1465, contains three miniatures which are in pure Renaissance style.

Beautiful Renaissance illuminated codices of Virgil are found in many important libraries: the Vatican Library possesses various magnificent copies, including *Urb. Lat. 353* (Urbino, 1475–82; this contains the emblem and arms of Federico di Montefeltro, duke of Urbino); *Urb. Lat. 350* (belongs to the same period; decoration of a school of Central Italy); *Urb. Lat. 642* (decoration of a school of Northern Italy of mid-quattrocento; arms of the Montefeltro family); *Pal. Lat. 1632*, with rich decoration of a German school of 1474; this contains many large historiated initials and two full-page sumptuous miniatures with the emblems and arms of the Elector Palatine. Fig. VI-34a is from a beautiful copy of the Riccardian Library at Florence.

MEDIEVAL COPIES OF CLASSICAL BOOKS

With some exceptions, the Graeco-Roman art of book illustration can best be studied in some secular MSS. of the Byzantine period, and even of the late Middle Ages. Indeed, the comparative study of these MSS.—allowing due consideration for changes in costume, conscious deviations or misunderstandings, and other alterations in composition or in details—show that they go back to prototypes written and illustrated in the Hellenistic period. The conservative attitude of the Byzantine and late medieval illustrator of scientific books, as observed for instance in the illustration of herbals (see p. 45 ff.), has been clearly demonstrated by Prof. Charles Singer. Indeed, quite often 'a later miniature separated from its archetype by fewer intermediate copies is iconographically nearer to it, than an earlier MS. separated from it by more repeated copying' (Weitzmann).

We start this section with the well-known medieval codices containing the comedies written by Terence—Publius Terentius Afer, 185–159 B.C., an African by birth originally brought to Rome as a slave, who wrote six comedies.

Terence (Fig. I-13)

There are about a dozen Terence MSS. extant, of which four have special importance. These are preserved in the Bodleian Library, Oxford (*Auct. F.2. 13*, of the twelfth century); in the Vatican Library (*Cod. Vat. Lat. 3868*)—written and illuminated by the German monk Adelricus of Corvey under Abbot Adelardus (822–26); in the National Library at Paris (*Lat. 7899*, a Carolingian copy); and a tenth-century copy in the Ambrosian Library, Milan (*H.75. inf.*). *Vat. Lat. 3868* is perhaps the most important of the four. According to G. Jachmann, the illuminator worked upon a Terence of the fourth century, although he may have added a few touches of his own, particularly the characteristic modern movement of the figures. Other copies, such as *Vat. Lat. 3305*, also deserve consideration. According to some eminent scholars, most of the MSS. were copied in France from a ninth-century manuscript containing miniatures derived from originals attributed to the Graeco-Roman period. For the *Térence des ducs* see p. 402.

The Terence miniatures are of paramount importance for our knowledge of the Roman theatre of the second or third century A.D., to which period the prototypes of these illustrations would seem to have belonged.

Masks of the *dramatis personae* are shown before each play in an *aediculum*, or a sort of open shrine—see Fig. I-13a. Some scholars have suggested that this feature was probably of Syrian origin. Another feature of the introductory pages is a portrait-bust of the author next to the page representing the *aediculum* with the masks.

Miscellaneous Literary Texts (Fig. I-14)

The only surviving work of Lucan, or Marcus Annaeus Lucanus (*c.* A.D. 38–65), is the famous epic *Pharsalia*, dealing with the struggle between Caesar and Pompey. A beautifully written and illuminated codex of the tenth century contains this work; it is preserved in St. Gall (*No. 863*).

There was an early Latin translation of the immortal fables of Aesop. An illuminated copy produced in the eleventh century in the monastery of S. Martial, near Limoges, is now preserved in a miscellaneous codex at Leyden (*Cod. Voss. Lat. Oct. 15*). This interesting codex—containing 212 folios, mainly measuring 21 by 15 cm. ($8\frac{1}{4}$ by $5\frac{9}{10}$ in.)—belonged to Presbyter Adhemar de Chabannes (Limoges, *c.* 1000). It also contains a complete set of illustrations of Prudentius (see further), and forty pen-drawings illustrating Deutero-Hyginus, *De Astronomia*. There are 78 fables of Aesop, the majority of them illustrated. While the composition of the illustrations and many of their features are ancient, the drawing, the motifs, and often the stylization, follow Carolingian tradition.

The *Satires* of Persius, or A. Persius Flaccus (A.D. 34–62), are preserved in an eleventh-century codex in the Public Library, Leyden (*Lat. 82*); it contains an elegant miniature which represents the author himself. According to Gąsiorowski, it is an interesting example of the representation of a pagan author in the style of an Evangelist without the *halo*.

Ovid's works are contained in a richly illustrated twelfth- or thirteenth-century codex in the Vatican Library (*Vat. Lat. 1596*). Horace's *Carmina* also find a place in the Vatican Library (*Vat. Lat. 1592*). Written and illuminated in the thirteenth century, its miniatures have preserved some Graeco-Roman characteristics. Seneca's tragedies are included in an elegant fourteenth-century MS. containing 78 miniatures (this is in the Library of the Congreg. Orat., Naples, *No.* XLIV); excellent Vatican codices are *Urbin. Lat. 356*, of the early fifteenth century, and *Vat. Lat. 7319* of the mid-fifteenth century. Macrobius (Ambrosius Aurelius Theodosius), a Roman grammarian and writer of the late fourth and fifth century A.D., of whose works only very few have been preserved (including the *Saturnalia* and the *Dream of Scipio*), is represented by *Cod. Vat. Lat. 1546* of the eleventh or twelfth century. See Fig. I-14*a* (Horace, *Carmina*).

Prudentius (Fig. I-14*b*). Aurelius Prudentius Clemens (348–*c.* 410), one of the most independent of the medieval Latin poets, is regarded by some scholars as the foremost poet of the early Latin Church; indeed, he is the only Christian Latin poet in whom Erasmus recognised real literary power (this judgment, however, is not uncontested). He was a contemporary of Jerome, Augustine and Ambrose. Prudentius was born in Spain and held important governorships and military posts. His works include graceful lyrics (written in various metres, with the iambic predominating), didactic poetry in hexameters (such as *contra Symmachum*), the twelve hymns of the *Kathemerinon*, poems on religious subjects (such as *Perì Stephanon*, on Christian martyrs), and particularly the religious allegory *Psychomachia*, on the conflict between the Vices and the Virtues. *Psychomachia* had much influence in the Middle Ages. It was even copied in sculpture on stone, bronze, and ivory, in mosaics, on enamels, and so on.

An interesting sixth-century copy of Prudentius (preserved in the National Library, Paris) may be considered one of the latest works written in rustic capitals. There are many medieval editions of *Psychomachia* containing outline drawings interspersed in the text. They were produced between the ninth and eleventh century in France, Germany and England. The earliest preserved illustrated MS. is apparently a ninth-century codex, which is in the National Library, Paris: *Lat. 8085*; another copy of the same collection is *Lat. 8318*; this is a tenth-century copy, but, in K. Weitzmann's opinion, it preserves most faithfully the system of illustration of the now lost archetype. The latter, on a papyrus roll, may have belonged to the fifth century. The *Codex Paris Lat. 8085* is written in two columns, each of which contains, at the proper place, one or two miniatures. Sometimes there are even three miniatures in a single column. The figures—writes Weitzmann—stand on a wavy groundline, which perhaps is already a later addition, since other copies, in conformity with the papyrus style, do not have it, but other than this there is no background or frame. (This latter feature is also characteristic of the miniatures in Terence.)

Extremely interesting is the copy preserved in a portion of the miscellaneous early eleventh-century MS.—already referred to—of the University Library at Leyden (*Cod. Voss. Lat. Oct. 15*). On ten pages it contains a complete set of illustrations to *Psychomachia*. By superimposing four or even five rows, and filling each with as many scenes as the space permitted, the whole cycle of more than seventy scenes was condensed on ten pages : Weitzmann.

Some authorities consider the English manuscripts—belonging to the Winchester School (see p. 198)—superior to those done on the Continent at the same time. Indeed, the latter—as O. Elfrida Saunders has pointed out—appear to be for the most part drawn with a weak, continuous outline, and show little energy, whereas the English ones have a quality of freshness and vigour which is essentially suited to these narrative subjects. The best English manuscript comes from the Abbey of Malmesbury (Wiltshire); it was produced about the middle of the eleventh century, and is preserved in Corpus Christi College, Cambridge (*Cod. 23*). Another important manuscript of the early eleventh century comes from Bury St. Edmunds, and is now in the British Museum (*Cleopatra, C. viii*). To the same period belongs British Museum *Add. MS. 24199*—see also p. 198. A later copy, produced in St. Albans between 1119 and 1146, and now preserved in the British Museum (*Titus, D. xvi*), for chronological reasons can hardly be attributed to the Winchester School. Unlike the other manuscripts, its drawings are lightly tinted.

Fig. I-14*b* reproduces a portion of fol. 11*v* from British Museum *Add. MS. 24199*. This is a miscellaneous MS. containing, in addition to *Psychomachia* (fol. 2–38), short pieces by bishops Hildebert and Marbodus. The illustrations of *Psychomachia* consist of line drawings in the style of the middle eleventh century, executed in green, red, violet, blue, and light brown. Whilst the under-drawing is assigned to one hand, at least three hands are distinguished in the drawings.

A ninth-century copy of Venantius Honorius Clementianus Fortunatus, *Carmina*, is preserved in the British Museum (*Add. MS. 24193*); it also contains prose works and letters by the same author.

BIBLICAL MSS. BASED ON CLASSICAL MODELS
(Fig. I-15–17)

Joshua Roll (Fig. I-15 and 16*a*)

The *Joshua Roll* (preserved in the Vatican Library, *Palat. Gr. 431*), which has been variously dated to the sixth-seventh century and the ninth-tenth century (A.D.), is probably a reproduction of an Alexandrian Hellenistic original of the fourth to the sixth century A.D. (probably the fifth century). In the thirteenth century the MS. was still in Greek hands, as is shown by some accounts on the back, written in Greek in a thirteenth-century hand. In 1571 it appeared in a list of the manuscripts owned by the rich Augsburg merchant Ulrich Fugger, whence it passed into the Palatine Library of Heidelberg, and with this into the Vatican Library.

Until 1902 it formed one long roll of vellum, thirty-five feet by about one foot; originally it must have been much longer, for it is clearly imperfect at the beginning and end. It is now in fifteen separate sheets of various sizes placed between the leaves of a large album.

While the back was left blank (in the thirteenth century it was used for the transcription of various *excerpta* and for various annotations), the obverse is covered with coloured drawings of the deeds of Joshua illustrating Chapters ii to x of the *Book of Joshua*. There are abridged extracts from the Greek text of the *Book of Joshua*, explaining the several scenes, written in short columns below them. They are written in minuscules of the tenth century, though some of the figures have titles written against them in capitals.

The drawings of the present copy, in continuous style—which may have been intended to supply models for mural paintings—are outlined in brown ink, and some parts have been lightly tinted and gracefully graduated. There can be no doubt—notwithstanding some suggestions to the contrary—that this incomplete colouring is the original one. The drawing is Hellenistic and presents very few orientalizing features; perspective is attempted, and figures are represented in a variety of attitudes. Also the personifications, Joshua's costume, and other details, are in Hellenistic style.

All scholars agree that the Roll is a masterpiece: the drawings are broad in treatment, anatomically correct, and full of movement; the figures have unity with their surroundings. In the scenes in which crowds appear, such as that of the carrying of the Ark of Covenant, depth as well as linear extension is suggested.

The *Joshua Roll* is one of the most disputed works that have been preserved, and all sorts of theories have been suggested as to its origin. We have already referred to its various late Hellenistic elements; and were it not for the script, one could easily consider it a third- or fourth-century production. Indeed, a theory has been put forward that a tenth-century scribe, having found the pictured roll, proceeded to fill in the text. More likely, though not conclusive, is the theory that the pictures are a faithful copy of a much earlier original (it has even been suggested that some gaps in the text may be explained by the scribe being unable to read his original). It may, at any rate, be assumed that the compositions of the *Joshua Roll*, at least in the main outlines, were taken from earlier designs (Venturi, for instance, has pointed out that many of the subjects are found in the mosaics of S. Maria Maggiore, Rome—see p. 69), but it cannot be admitted that the skilful artist of the Roll was a mere servile copyist.

Some scholars have suggested that the original book, which served as a model for the *Joshua Roll*, may have been Jewish, not Christian. In C. Roth's opinion, the soldiers' costume bears the unmistakable stamp of military dress of the 2nd century, and was conceivably made for Jewish rather than for Christian use.

The date tenth century, suggested by Prof. Kurt Weitzmann, is based upon his interpretation of Byzantine art of that period: he sees in the *Joshua Roll*, as in some other works, the effect produced on art by the revival of interest in classical culture and art, which took place under the inspiration of Constantine VII Porphyrogenitus (913–59). The *Joshua Roll* is considered by Weitzmann to be the key monument of the Macedonian renaissance; it was made for Constantine, and in its combination of classical, biblical, and imperial aspects it constitutes a fitting epitome of the reign and personality of this strange Emperor.

The German scholar Th. Birt, who suggested that classical illustrated books were picture rolls containing friezes in continuous method without any accompanying text—this being written in separate rolls—based his theory mainly on the *Joshua Roll*, the Egyptian satirical papyri, and the Trajan Column at Rome. In Weitzmann's opinion, (1) the existence of a picture roll without text cannot be proved by the Egyptian satirical papyri; (2) intrinsic probabilities speak against a roll as model for the gigantic relief monument (*i.e.* for the Trajan Column); and (3) the Joshua Rotulus is far removed from the archetype, showing more changes, errors and reinterpretations than the corresponding pictures in the Octateuchs.

Octateuch (Fig. I-16b–17a–b)

However, closely akin to the style of the *Joshua Roll* but far inferior in execution are the illustrations of the preserved copies of the *Octateuch* (*i.e.*, codices containing the first eight books of the Bible), dating from the eleventh and twelfth centuries A.D. Five are well known; they are, or were, preserved in Istanbul (*Codex Seraglio No. 8*), in the Vatican Library (*Codd. Gr. 746* and *Gr. 747*), in the Vatopedi monastery on Mount Athos (*Cod. 602*), and in Smyrna (*Cod. A.I.*). As a matter of fact, the last codex is no longer preserved: it perished during the destruction of Smyrna, in 1923.

According to Weitzmann, these copies of the *Octateuch* go back to the same archetype as the *Joshua Rotulus*. He also divides them into two branches, one represented by *Vat. Gr. 747*, and the other by the remaining MSS., the first being a purer copy of the archetype than the more numerous group.

GRAECO-ROMAN SCIENTIFIC TEXTS
(Fig. I-17c–28a–b)

Vienna Dioscorides or Diosc. Vindob. (Fig. I-17c–19a)

One of the most remarkable examples of a sixth-century copy of a classical work is the *Vienna Dioscorides*, also known as *Constantinopolitanus* (preserved in the

National Library at Vienna, *Cod. Med. Graec. 1*). It is a splendid copy of the medical treatise compiled in the first century A.D. by the great Greek botanist Dioscorides of Anazarba (in Cilicia), which for many centuries, 'has been the chief source whence... herbalists of all nations have drawn their inspiration' (R. T. Gunther). This Vienna codex was illuminated *c.* A.D. 512 for a lady bearing a Roman name, Juliana Anicia, the daughter of Galla Placidia and Anicius Olybrius (Emperor of the West in 472), and wife of the Consul Aerobindus. The manuscript contains 431 leaves, measuring 38 by 33 cm. (about $15\frac{1}{5}$ by $13\frac{1}{5}$ in.). It is the oldest preserved MS. in which a gold background is employed; its miniatures may be divided into the following two classes:

(1) The six full-page illustrations, which precede the text, are copies of traditional pictures. These form a symbolic link between the decaying Graeco-Roman art and the later Byzantine school. The miniatures are badly rubbed, and the first— a peacock with outspread tail—is mutilated. The second and third are of famous physicians (in groups of seven), including Chiron the Centaur; the fourth illustrates the fable of the mandrake uprooted at the cost of a dog's life.

Of particular interest is the fifth miniature, depicting Dioscorides writing at a desk (he is writing the description of the mandrake while its picture is being painted by a female figure personifying the Discovery): we have here an early surviving specimen of the author's portrait, copied in East Christian representations of the Evangelists, as in the case of the *Rossano Gospels* (see p. 87 f.). Another miniature (the dedication-page) represents the princess herself, seated and holding a diptych or book. In the same miniature are three other figures personifying Magnanimity, Wisdom, and Gratitude for the Arts, while a fourth figure holds a book. Round the central composition and separated by a geometrical arrangement of cabled bands are small genii in grisaille on blue grounds, engaged in building operations: Dalton.

Fig. I-18*a* represents the fifth miniature.

Miniatures 2–5 are enclosed in banded frames ornamented with wreaths, quatrefoils, lozenges, and scroll-work. These ornamental borders constitute the only Oriental influence. Otherwise the MS. is in perfect classical style. The composition of the dedication-page is exactly that of contemporary consular diptychs (see *The Hand-produced Book* and the forthcoming volume on *Binding*), but the framing rather recalls mosaic ornament of an earlier period.

(2) The second class consists of numerous and exquisite coloured drawings, inserted in the text, and representing medicinal plants or animals; they are admirably coloured. Some are probably original drawings and paintings, others are based upon ancient models. Pliny mentions Crateuas and other Greek medical writers who endeavoured to illustrate their works with coloured paintings of herbs. Crateuas was a rhizotomist and author, physician to Mithradates or Mithridates VI Eupator (120–63 B.C.), who himself described the plants of his kingdom (Pliny, xxv. 62). Some of the drawings of the *Vienna MS.*—writes Gunther—may have been made from originals based upon Crateuas' sketches; Crateuas was considered the 'father of plant illustration' and his work, reported to have comprised

the most life-like pictures of plants drawn from nature, was of first-rate importance in the history of botany.

There are many other MSS. of this work. Also in Vienna was the *Cod. Neapolitanus*, formerly *Vindob. Gr. 1: Suppl. Graec. 28*, of the late sixth century A.D., containing 170 pages illustrated with medical plants, in colour, accompanied by descriptive text; there are no human figures or animals. In Vienna there are preserved *Vindob. 2277*, of the sixteenth century, a MS. on paper (*Vindob. 22478*), two copies printed from woodcuts (*Vindob. 12437* and *12448*), and an early Arabic translation (*Cod. Arab. Vindob. A.F.10*). In Paris there is the *Cod. 2179* in the National Library, of the tenth century, as well as an Arabic translation (*Ancien Fonds Schefer*, National Library); in New York, there is the tenth-century MS. of the Pierpont Morgan Library (*M. 652*); on Mount Athos, the eleventh- or twelfth-century *Cod. Ω 75* of the Lavra monastery; in Rome there is the *Cod. Chigianus*, of the early fifteenth century. A good Latin copy is preserved in the State Library, Munich (*Cod. Lat. 337*): it is a South Italian MS., written in the tenth century. A few other Arabic copies may also be mentioned; for instance, the beautiful codex illuminated in 619 A.H. (=A.D. 1222) by 'Abdallah ibn al-Fadl, now in Martin Library, Stockholm: Fig. I-17c, 18b, and 19a. See also Fig. III-4.

The *Vienna Dioscorides* may be regarded as the common ancestor of all the illuminated herbals of the Middle Ages and the Renaissance. In this respect, too, the MS. connects classical with medieval art. Pliny (*Naturalis Historia*, xxv. 4) tells us that it was the custom for Greek medical writers to illustrate their works with paintings of herbs.

The medieval illuminated *Herbals* are often found in conjunction with illuminated *Bestiares*: see also p. 49 and p. 269 Fig. I-20.

An interesting *miscellanea* codex is preserved in the Laurentian Library, Florence (*MS. Plut. 73. 16*). It contains Hippocrates, *De diversis herbis*; Sextus Papirius Placitus, *Ex animalibus et ex diversis avibus*, and *Ex libris Dioscuridis ex herbis*, etc., as well as Pseudo-Apuleius (see next Section). The manuscript is richly illuminated; the illuminations, by various artists, of the first half of the thirteenth century, are based on a Byzantine copy of the sixth century, but contain numerous features of late classical style. The codex is assigned to South Italy or Sicily. There are full-page miniatures, schematic representations of cities, drawings of plants and animals, illustrations of pharmacopeia, scenes with sick people; there is the symbolical representation of the *precatio terrae* and *precatio omnium herbarum*, and so on. Fol. 2v represents Hippocrates between Plato and Dioscorides, and two other physicians; Hippocrates is also represented on fol. 17v, Dioscorides on fol. 178r, 'Plato *medicus*' on fol. 150v; Aesculapius is represented on fol. 20r. Fol. 132v is reproduced in Fig. I-20d.

Even more interesting is another *miscellanea* codex in the Laurentian Library, *MS. Plut. 73.41*: Fig. I-19c. Executed in the early ninth century, in 1474 it belonged to the famous Verona physician Gabriele Zerbi. It contains Antonius Musa, *De herba betonica*, Pseudo-Apuleius (see next Section), *Herbarium*, Sextus Placitus Papiriensis, *De bestiis*, Pseudo-Dioscorides, *De herbis* etc. There are numerous pen-drawings of human figures, animals, birds, decorated initials, and (on fol. *122r–129v*) sixteen scenes representing surgical operations.

Medical and Natural Sciences

The earliest preserved illustrated copy of a Greek work on surgery is a commentary of Apollonius Citiensis—who lived in the first century B.C.—to Hippocrates' work *Perì Árthrōn*, 'Concerning the Joints'; the MS. deals with dislocation of bones. The codex, preserved in the Laurentian Library, Florence (*Cod. Plut. 74.7*), is attributed to the tenth or eleventh century A.D.; it contains other medical works besides Apollonius, such as *Perì Epidésmōn* ('Bandaging') by Soranus of Ephesus, who lived in Alexandria and Rome in the early second century A.D. The illustrations undoubtedly go back to Graeco-Roman models. There are numerous miniatures in gold and colours, the greater part being full-page.

See Fig. I-21.

Apollonius' work is also preserved in other copies, such as *Gr. 2247* and *2248* in the National Library, Paris; *Cod. 3652* in the University Library at Bologna.

An interesting group is formed by copies of Latin medical works. The earliest preserved copy is the Pseudo-Apuleius, *De herbarum virtutibus* (*Cod. Leid. Voss. Lat. Quarto, 9*). The original text was falsely attributed to Apuleius, a Platonist and rhetorician, born *c.* A.D. 125 at Madaura (Africa), but it probably was a fifth-century A.D. compilation from Dioscorides and other sources. The Leyden MS., which contains 97 leaves (measuring 19 by 16 cm.—about $6\frac{3}{10}$ by $7\frac{1}{2}$ in.) in uncial script is attributed to the seventh century A.D. There are 71 miniatures.

Later copies of Pseudo-Apuleius are preserved in the Laurenziana, Florence (73.16), in the *MS. 93* of the National Library, Vienna (see also, under *Cod. Medicus Vindob.: Lat. 93*, p. 48), and in about ten more codices.

A ninth-century copy, containing numerous coloured drawings of plants and animals, was produced in Northern Italy, and is now in Lucca (State Library, *Cod. 296*). Similar copies are in the Vatican Library (*Vat. Lat. 187*). in Montecassino (*Cod. 97*), and in Vienna (National Library, *Vindob. 2425*). A tenth-century copy (perhaps written in Fulda) is preserved in Cassel (State Library, *Cod. Phys., Fol. 10*).

Two good copies are in England: an eleventh-century MS. in the British Museum (*Cotton. Vitellius, C. iii*), and an early twelfth-century MS. in Oxford (*Cod. Bodley, 130*). See Fig. I-20a.

There is a famous Latin treatise on gynaecology and obstetrics, attributed to a physician named Muscio or Mustio, who lived in North Africa in the sixth century A.D. An extant Greek text, dealing with the same subject, bears the name of Moschion; some scholars consider it the work of Theodorus Moschion, a Greek physician of Smyrna, of the first century B.C.; according to others, it is a Byzantine Greek translation of the Latin treatise of Mustio. Furthermore, some scholars have produced sufficient evidence to show that Mustio's treatise is a translation and elaboration of a treatise by Soranus of Ephesus, and that the illustrations in the copies of Mustio's work are based on Greek archetypes.

Indeed, according to the most recent authority on the subject (Diepgen, *Geschichte der Medizin*, I, Berlin, 1949, p. 198), Mustio was really only an elaborator of Soranus, whereas the name Moschion is not even mentioned.

However, the treatise by Mustio was often copied in the Middle Ages, especially in the twelfth to fifteenth centuries, and was also used for the woodcuts by Eucharius Roesslin of Worms, in *Rosengarten*, 1513. The earliest preserved copy is *Cod. 3701–3715* of the Royal Library, Brussels, containing fourteen miniatures, and attributed to the ninth century. Another excellent copy is the twelfth-century codex of the Royal Library, Copenhagen (Thottske Saml., *No. 190*).

Other illuminated copies of medical works are the following: *Codex medicus*, in Montecassino (*Cod. xcvi*, of the ninth century), and at Paris National Library (*Lat. 6862*, of the tenth century); an Italian MS. with Old English and High German glosses (preserved in the British Museum, *Harl. 4986* and *5294*, of the eleventh or twelfth century); *Cod. A. ii. 15* of the Casanatense Library, Rome; the Vienna *Cod. Lat. 93*; portion of a twelfth-century English MS. in the Cathedral Library at Durham (*Cod. Hunter No. 100*); to the same period belong three other English MSS. (British Museum, *Sloane 1975* and *Harley 1585*, and Bodleian Library, Oxford, *Cod. Ashmole 1462*).

Fig. I-19b represents *Cod. Medicus Vindob. Lat. 93*.

Another group of medico-botanical MSS. are copies based on the work *De simplici medicina*, also known as *Circa instans*, which was written by Mattaeus Plataearius (who died in the year 1161), and is the most important pharmacopoeia of the Middle Ages. The illustrations of the plants, excellently executed and painted, are undoubtedly based on classical archetypes. The most important MS. of this group is the copy of Plataearius in the State Library at Berlin (*Cod. Hamilton 407*), containing 210 miniatures, and executed *c.* 1315.

Other 'natural' subjects are dealt with in the following books:

(1) The *Theriaca* of Nicander (second century A.D.)—a treatise on remedies against poisonous bites—containing numerous pictures of snakes, scorpions, and healing plants, as well as mythological scenes. A tenth- or eleventh-century copy is extant (preserved at the National Library, Paris, *Suppl. Gr. 247*). It contains 46 leaves, measuring 14·8 by 11·8 cm. (about $5\frac{4}{5}$ by $4\frac{1}{8}$ in.); the text is written in elegant minuscules. There are 54 miniatures, which form an incomplete cycle. A few drawings are similar to those of the *Vienna Dioscorides*. The illuminations are picturesque, with garden and landscape scenes in an Alexandrian style evidently based on a very Hellenistic model: Dalton. Some scholars date the prototype of this MS. to the third or fourth century A.D., others to the second century A.D., that is, to the time of the author himself.

(2) Even more important is the *Physiologus*, or 'Greek Bestiary', a work on symbolic beasts which, in M. Wellmann's opinion, was written at Alexandria; it is attributed to the third or fourth century A.D. The oldest extant copy is a ninth-

century Carolingian codex of the Civic Library, Berne (*Cod. 318*). Another important copy is a tenth-century MS. in the Royal Library, Brussels (*Cod. 10074*); this is a Western version of the work 'with a scheme of illustration apparently free from oriental influences' (Dalton).

The illustrated *Bestiarium*, a favoured book in England in the twelfth and the thirteenth centuries, contains many moralizing animal stories some of which go back to the Latin *Physiologus*, itself a translation from the Greek original; some stories may be traced to other Greek or Latin sources. Among the best English copies of the *Bestiary* are *MS. Ashm. 1511* and *Cod. Bodl. 764* of the Bodleian Library, Oxford, of the late twelfth century, the twelfth-century *MS. Ii.4.26* and the thirteenth-century *Cod. K.k. IV. 25* of the Cambridge University Library: see also p. 269.

Fig. I-20 reproduces the following *Herbals* and *Bestiaries*: (*a*) *MS. Bodley, 130* (Bodleian Library, Oxford), (*b*) *MS. Ashm. 1511* (Bodleian Library, Oxford), (*c*) *MS. Ii. 4.26* (University Library, Cambridge), and (*d*) *MS. Plut. 73.16* (Laurentian Library, Florence): see p. 46.

The Eastern version of the *Physiologus* was preserved in a copy in the library of the Evangelical school at Smyrna (*Cod. B. viii*), of *c.* A.D. 1100; it was destroyed in 1923; the style of its pictures recalled that of the marginal Psalters. The presiding influence in both cases was monastic: Dalton.

A possible relation of the *Physiologus* with the animal art of Buddhist India, through the medium of Graeco-Asiatic art, has been suggested by Strzygowski.

(3) A copy of the treatise in hexameters on the chase, known as the *Cynegetica*, by Oppian of Apamea (called 'Pseudo-Oppian'; the poem was written *c.* A.D. 200), is preserved in three copies, of which the tenth- or early eleventh-century MS. (in the Marciana Library, Venice, *Cod. Gr. 479:881*), already referred to, is in pseudo-classical style, and based on an early Hellenistic model probably belonging to the second or third century A.D.; some of the compositions may have been included in fresco paintings. In Runciman's opinion, however, this MS. represents the neo-classical Byzantine style of the tenth century. It has numerous historical and mythological subjects, in addition to the lively little hunting and fishing scenes, represented in narrow zones across the text and decorative medallions. Nearly all the pages are illuminated.

See Fig. I-22.

Another copy of the same work, though of the fifteenth century, is in the National Library at Paris (*Gr. 2736*); it contains 59 leaves, and on almost every one there are one, two, three, or even four miniatures. Their model was either the Venetian codex or a similar MS.

In general, it may be emphasized that the *Cynegetica* and similar works had a strong influence in the Middle Ages in keeping alive classical traditions.

Geography—Surveying—Astronomy—Engineering

(Fig. I-23–27)

Ancient Cartography (Fig. I-25). Apart from Babylonian cuneiform maps and plans, and Egyptian papyri with local plans, the earliest geographic map of which there is any record was engraved on a copper plate by Anaximander of Miletus (*c.* 575 B.C.). He and Hecataeus plotted out the entire world so far as known to the Milesians of the period. Apparently, by the fifth century there existed text-books for geography and also maps for general reference. In a later period—*c.* 150 B.C.—a huge globe, ten feet in diameter, is said to have been set up at Pergamum by Crates of Malles. Of other cartographers of ancient times, may be mentioned Dicaearchus, Posidonius, Hipparchus, Strabo, Marinus of Tyre, and, the greatest of all, Ptolemy. Of all the maps produced by these geographers, nothing survives save the medieval copies of maps, which are appended to some of the extant manuscripts of Ptolemy's *Geography*.

Geography (Fig. I-24). Early geography is represented by a copy of Ptolemy's *Tables* (preserved in the Vatican Library, *Gr. 1291*), written *c.* A.D. 814, containing pictures—many of them in the form of Hellenistic personifications—of the sun, the moon, the months and hours, signs of the zodiac, on blue or gold grounds. The beautiful MS. (measuring 28 by 20 cm.—nearly 11 by $7\frac{9}{10}$ in.) contains 95 leaves; it is written in uncial script, and was probably executed in Constantinople for the Emperor or another important personage. F. Boll has suggested that the original was painted *c.* A.D. 250. One of the earliest preserved copies of Ptolemy's work on *Geography*—the standard textbook on the subject till the fifteenth century—is *Cod. Vatopedi 754* (on Mount Athos), of the late twelfth or early thirteenth century. 54 leaves are preserved, containing 66 pages of text and 42 maps. Even more important is a twelfth-century copy preserved in the Vatican Library (*Urb. Gr. 82*): it is regarded as the most authoritative of all the extant works of Ptolemy. It contains 111 pages; the map of the world is in Book VII, the twenty-six partial maps of Europe, Asia, and Africa in Book VIII (see further).

Ptolemy, or Claudius Ptolomaeus (first half of the second century A.D.)—see also *The Hand-produced Book*, p. 245 and *passim*—astronomer, geometer, geographer, wrote a number of works. Here we are concerned with his *Geography*; there are fifty-two copies containing the whole work or a portion of it. These MSS. may be divided into two versions.

Of the fifty-two Byzantine MSS. of *Geography*, eleven, *i.e.*, those containing *version A*, include twenty-six large maps, which form a portion of the eighth Book; whereas five (*i.e., version B*) contain sixty-four maps interspersed in the text. Some manuscripts also contain a Universal map of the then known world, consisting either of one sheet or of four sheets. Some copies nowadays without maps contain evidence that they once included them. It is uncertain whether the maps of either *version A* or of *version B* go back to Ptolemy or to his period. Moreover, a few specimens containing the one-sheet Universal map, are signed by a certain

Agathodaemon, an Alexandrian map-designer, of whom very little is known: it is even uncertain when he lived.

(Marcus Vipsanius) Agrippa (c. 63–12 B.C.), friend, counsellor, consul and minister of the Emperor Augustus, was a great patron of arts, literature, and science. He was also a geographer and author of various books. His *Descriptio orbis* was a commentary on a revised map of the world, which reproduced his survey of the Roman Empire on a reduced scale. Some authorities regard Books II–VII of Ptolemy's *Geography* as an index to Agrippa's general map.

Fig. I-24*a* reproduces fol. 4*v* of Ptolemy's *Tables* (*Vat. Gr. 1291*); Fig. 24*b* reproduces fol. 1*r* of an extremely interesting North-French codex on *Cosmography*, of *c.* 1220 (Walters Art Gallery, Baltimore, *MS. W. 73*): see also p. 377.

Tabula Peutingeriana (*Peutinger Table*). This world-map is so called because it was acquired by Konrad Peutinger (1465–1547), antiquary, scholar and author (*Inscriptiones Romanae*, 1520, and other works), and keeper of the archives in his native city, Augsburg. The *Peutinger Table* is a long narrow roll of parchment in twelve sections (the first being lost), measuring 6·8 m. in length (or nearly 22 ft. 4 in.). It was intended to serve as a portable road map. Land is painted in buff colour, the sea in green, roads are in red, and the rivers in blue.

The map extends from Britain to the Ganges mouth (though most of Britain, all Spain, and West Mauretania are missing), and is very elongated from East to West. The main roads (all shown rectilinear), the cities (about five hundred), the distances from city to city, the chief mountains and rivers are indicated. It is generally agreed that the *Table* is a twelfth- or thirteenth-century copy of a much earlier map.

The prototype is variously dated—K. Miller and others suggest the fourth century A.D.; O. Cuntz, Philippi, and others, the second century A.D. Some authorities attribute the prototype to Castorius, a Roman grammarian of *c.* A.D. 340. According to other scholars it may even go back to Agrippa (see above), though there must have existed some connecting links, all lost.

The *Peutinger Table* belonged to Prince Eugene of Savoy (1663–1736), and since 1731 it has been deposited in the Imperial Library (now National Library) in Vienna.

Bibliography: K. Miller, *Itineraria Romana etc.*, Stuttgart, 1916; R. V. Tooley, *Maps and Map-Makers*, London, 1949; L. Bagrow, *Die Geschichte der Kartographie*, Berlin, 1951; *Grosser Historischer Weltatlas*, Vol. I, Munich, 1953; K. Miller, *Die Peutingersche Tafel*, Stuttgart, 1962.

Hereford Mappa Mundi (Fig. I-25). Less famous, but certainly not less important is the late thirteenth-century World Map, preserved in Hereford Cathedral. It is the largest 'map' which has survived intact. In fact, it is rather an illustrated and annotated representation of the 'round world'. Its careful examination—wrote Prof. Roberto Almagià—may lead to a general re-evaluation of the medieval cartographic tradition and its relation to that of the classical world. The archetype may go back to the fourth, or perhaps even to the first century A.D. The name of the author of the Hereford Map, Richard of Haldingham and Lafford (who can be identified with a certain Richard de Bello, prebendary of Lafford, 1276–83, and of Norton, 1305–13) appears in a corner of the Map.

The whole (reproduced in Fig. I-25*a*) is drawn on a sheet of vellum measuring 64 by 54 inches (1·62 by 1·37 m.), attached to a framework of oak. The earth is represented as a circle (of 52 inches in diameter) surrounded by the Ocean. East (India) is on the top, West (Spain and Mauretania) at the bottom, South (Africa) on the right, and North (Norway, Germany, Scotland) on the left. In the centre is Jerusalem, regarded as the centre of the world. At the top, in the extreme East of the earth, is the Garden of Eden (the Paradise), a circular walled island. The British Isles (on the edge of the Map in the lower, left-hand side) are on a larger scale than the rest of Europe; in fact, with the exception of Matthew Paris (see p. 272 ff.) maps, this is the earliest attempt at a detailed map of Great Britain.

Outside the circular map is a decorative surround. At its top (see Fig. I-25*b*), surmounting the whole world, is the Day of Judgment: Christ in Glory with attendant angels, the Virgin Mary interceding for the faithful; in the lower left-hand corner, is Julius Caesar, crowned with a papal tiara, entrusting the work of measurement of the world to Nikodoxus (for the West), to Theodoxus (for the North and East), and to Policlitus (for the South): Fig. I-25*c*.

The Map is executed with a wealth of colour—black for outlines and inscriptions (all in Norman French), red for capital letters and important names (*e.g.*, names of provinces) and gold leaf for the largest letters; blue (which has become brown) for rivers, lakes, and seas. The figures and buildings are drawn with a pen, but wash is used for rivers, lakes, seas, some clothing, etc. Many buildings are picked out in red, one man has a fine red cloak, the Red Sea and the Persian Gulf are blood red. There is a free use of gold (there is a gold sword, and gold is used for decoration). Towns and villages are indicated by a great variety of symbols, some of them going back to the Roman model. The Map is adorned with a great number of all kinds of animals, fishes, snakes, monsters, grotesques, abnormal people, and so on. This sort of encyclopaedia of natural history and of fabulous races is partly derived from the *Physiologus* and the Bestiaries (see p. 46 and 48 f.).

Recent bibliography: G. R. Crone, *The Hereford World Map*, London, 1948; *The World Map etc.* (Reproductions), with *Memoir* by G. R. Crone, London, 1954; A. L. Moir, *The World Map in Hereford Cathedral*, and M. Letts, *The Pictures in the Hereford Mappa Mundi*, Hereford, 1955.

Cosmas Indicopleustes (Fig. I-23). Very important—and coming within the general category of *Byzantine Illumination*—is a kind of Christian *Cosmography and Topography* written in *c.* A.D. 547 by Cosmas Indicopleustes, an Alexandrian merchant and traveller, who afterwards became a monk in the monastery of S. Catherine on Mt. Sinai. Cosmas' work is a sort of mixed bag of science (such as geography and natural history), pseudo-science (such as Chaldaean cosmogony in Persian version), and Christian religion.

This book was frequently copied; the best known, and probably the oldest copy in existence, was probably executed in Egypt. It is generally assigned to the ninth century A.D., but some critics have assigned it to the seventh or even the sixth century A.D. Since 1545 at least it has been preserved in the Vatican Library (*Vat. Gr. 699*). The art-historian Kondakoff considered it the most important of Byzantine illuminated manuscripts. It has been noted that its composition is planned on large, grandiose, statuary lines, with a simplicity, force and vigour, unusual in similar contemporary works. Some scholars have suggested that the artist was a painter rather than an illuminator used to the minute details of the art of illumination.

As the text abounds in references to the diagrams and other illustrations, it is highly probable that the miniatures extant are more or less exact reproductions of the original, which partly reflected paintings of the early Christian centuries. The miniatures, like those of most of the early Byzantine manuscripts, however, are much disfigured through the flaking-off of colours, the more so as the artist kept to the ancient method, inherited from the papyri, of painting the pictures directly on the parchment without first putting on a layer of white. But it is evident, from what remains, that in finish and technique a great advance was made on the sixth-century codices.

Most of the subjects are Biblical, and the treatment is generally non-realistic, an effect which is heightened by the entire lack of background, giving the figures a disconnected appearance. Individual figures, however, are rich in solemn charm, such as the Madonna who stands with Christ, S. John the Baptist, Zacharias, and Elizabeth in one of the full-page miniatures. In others, again, animation is portrayed with some success, as in the picture of the Babylonians amazed at the backward motion of the sun. The codex must have been executed in some great artistic centre of the East.

See Fig. I-23*a*.

There are two other interesting eleventh-century copies, one in the Laurentian Library, Florence (*Plut. 9.28*), containing fifty-nine miniatures; and the other in the monastery of S. Catherine on Mt. Sinai (*Cod. 1186*), containing, amongst others, a picture representing the movement of the heavens round the earth. Other pictures include a planisphere and signs of the zodiac.

Fig. I-23*b* reproduces fol. 113*r* of *MS. Plut. 9.28*.

From the standpoint of the history of art, this work represents the Byzantine blending of the Hellenistic style (in the personifications, and in the illustrations of the secular subjects, such as geography and natural science) and the Oriental style (in the religious illustrations). The original work was composed either in Alexandria or on Mt. Sinai, and shows the influence of Hellenistic Egypt in the formation of the East Christian styles of painting.

Surveying (Fig. I-26). In Rome, the surveyors, *agrimensores*, formed a very important profession; they were either civil servants, who, for instance, carried out the surveying of the new colonies, their subdivision into plots, and so on; or professional persons who ascertained the boundaries of private properties, and did other cadastral work: instruction in this branch was highly developed. A ninth-century illuminated codex, *Agrimensores*, probably copied in the monastery of Fulda, and now preserved in the Vatican Library (*Palat. Lat. 1564*), seems to be a copy of a fourth-century Roman original.

Even more famous is the Wolfenbuettel copy of the works of the Roman surveyors known as the *Codex Arcerianus*.

Astronomy (Fig. I-27). Aratos of Soli in Cilicia, a Greek poet of the third century B.C., wrote a celebrated astronomical poem *Phainómĕna* in 732 hexameters, describing the constellations and the circles of the sphere. Although unscientific and inaccurate, it became very popular and was translated into Latin by Cicero, Germanicus, and Avienus. (Some scholars suggested that Aratus is quoted by S. Paul in the *Acts of the Apostles*, 17, 28.) The work was illustrated in ancient times.

The only Greek copy which has come down to us is as late as the fifteenth century (it is preserved in the Vatican Library, *Vat. Gr. 1087*). There are, however, various Latin copies of which the ninth-century Leyden codex (*Voss. Lat. Quarto, 79*) is the most important. It contains 95 leaves (measuring 22·5 by 20 cm.—about $8\frac{9}{10}$ by $7\frac{9}{10}$ in.); there are numerous miniatures, some of very high artistic value; originally there were some 45 miniatures, but about five are missing. The tenth- or eleventh-century Boulogne codex (Municipal Library, *No. 188*) containing 33 leaves may supplement the missing miniatures.

Another copy is preserved at Berne (Civic Library, *No. 88*), and others are in Madrid (National Library, *A.16*; of the twelfth century), Salzburg (two copies), Munich (State Library, *No. 210*), Vienna (National Library, *No. 387*)—the last two belonging to the early ninth century; and at Saint-Gall (*Nos. 902*, of the ninth century, and *250*, of the tenth). These MSS. are probably ultimately derived from an *edition de luxe* of the fourth century A.D., which may have been based upon earlier works going as far back as the first century A.D.

Gąsiorowski distinguishes the following three classes of medieval MSS. known as *Aratea*—it is the general name applied to the astronomical MSS. and early printed books—such as *Germanicus*, ed. princeps, Bologna, 1474; *Hyginus*, Venice, 1482; *Astronomici veteres*, Venice, 1499; and others. They contain illustrations which, though influenced by Carolingian and later styles, ultimately go back to late Roman originals. These were included in an *edition de luxe* of Aratus, different from that already referred to.

(1) To the first group of the *Aratea* known as *Codices Germanici* belong: a MS. of the ninth century preserved in the University Library at Basel (*A.N. iv. 18*); the codex (already referred to) in the National Library, Madrid (*A.16*, of the twelfth century); and two codices of the fourteenth or fifteenth century, preserved in Vienna (*Cod. Vindob. Lat. 2352*, or *Wenzel Codex*) and Munich (*Cod. Monac. Lat. 826*: this has been influenced by Arabic astronomical MSS.).

Fig. I-27 reproduces two pages (fol. *20v* and fol. *22r*) from the *Aratos* in Basel.

(2) The second group, containing the *Aratea* of Cicero and the *De Astronomia* of Pseudo-Hyginus or Deutero-Hyginus, is best represented by (*a*) an elegant codex

of the British Museum (*Harl. 647*; it is partly written in rustic capitals, and belongs to the ninth or tenth century; *Harl. 2506* is a copy of it); (*b*) the Anglo-Saxon *Aratus* (preserved in the British Museum, *Cotton. Tib. B.5*), the illustrations of which seem to have been copied from a Vercelli codex described by Cyriacus of Ancona, and now lost; and (*c*) the *Guelferbitanus*, which is preserved in the Wolfenbuettel Library (*18. 16. Aug. 4°*).

(3) To the third group—containing the *Catasterismós*, or description in prose of the sky—belong, amongst others, *Cod. Berol. Phil. 1832, Meerman 130* (of the ninth or tenth century); *Cod. Vindob. Lat. 12600* (of the twelfth century); *Monac. Lat. 210* (of the ninth or tenth century); *Monac. Lat. 560*, of the twelfth century; *Cod. Colon. Eccles. Metropol. lxxxiii*, of the eighth century; *Cod. St. Gall. 250*, of the ninth century; *Cod. Cassin. No. 3*, of the eleventh century; and *Cod. Dresd. Dc. 183. Quarto*, of the ninth or tenth century.

Engineering. Heron of Alexandria, perhaps an Egyptian by birth, who lived in the late second century B.C., wrote Greek books on arithmetic, geometry, civil engineering, engines of war and simple machines. Some of his works have come down to us in Greek copies (preserved in the National Library at Paris, *Gr. 2442* and *Suppl. Gr. 607*, and others), and some in the following Arabic translations, which are accompanied by drawings: British Museum, *Add. MS. 23394*; *Cod. Leidensis, cmlxxxiii, 51*; ex-Royal Library at Cairo, *No. v*; and a codex in S. Sophia at Istanbul. Other copies of Heron's works are *Cod. 516 cl. xciii. 7* of the Marciana Library, Venice (twelfth or thirteenth century); and *Cod. B. v. 20* of the University Library at Turin, written in 1541. The drawings of these MSS. seem to go back to archetypes of Heron's times.

Miscellanea

Boëthius (Fig. I-28*a-b*). The Roman philosopher and statesman Boëthius (Anicius Manlius Torquatus Severinus), who lived from *c.* A.D. 470 to A.D. 524, and is generally considered one of the last of the great ancient Romans, produced the famous work *De Consolatione Philosophiae*. He also translated into Latin the logical treatises of Aristotle, and wrote a series of manuals on arithmetic, astronomy, geometry, and music, which were very popular. A sumptuous copy of his *De Institutione arithmetica libri II*, containing 139 leaves (measuring 23·2 by 17·5 cm.—about $9\frac{1}{8}$ by $6\frac{9}{10}$ in.) written at Tours, in the ninth century, for Emperor Charles the Bald, is preserved in the State Library at Bamberg (*H.J. iv. 12*). The codex is beautifully illuminated in Carolingian style, but the illustrations seem to be based on late Roman models. (*See* also p. 206 f.).

Warfare. An eleventh-century Byzantine codex, preserved in the Vatican Library (*Gr. 1605*), dealing with war, contains miniatures some of which seem to be based on Hellenistic models. The text of this work is assigned to Heron of Byzantium (tenth century A.D.), but is based on earlier works written by Heron of Alexandria, Apollodorus of Damascus, and others. Another codex (*Poliorceti-*

corum liber, Cod. Leidensis, Gr. F.3), of the sixteenth century, contains 53 miniatures representing war-machines and besieged fortresses; it is based on the former MS.

Chronographer (Fig. I-28c-d). There are other late copies of lost codices, belonging to a much earlier period. Particularly worthy of note is the famous *Chronographer*, or 'Calendar of the Sons of Constantine'. It is the first extant Roman Christian 'calendar', and coordinates the dying ancient and the new Christian categories of the secular conception of history. The original is reputed to have been produced at Rome, in Hellenistic style, by Furius Dionysius Filocalus, in A.D. 354, for a patron named Valentine. The date is fixed by the *Natales Caesarum* and other chronological notes. The work was frequently copied and a copy made in the ninth century—now lost—was used for the production of further copies such as the seventeenth-century copy (now in the Barberini Collection of the Vatican: *Cod. Vat. Lat. 9135*), made for the French antiquary Nicolas-Claude Fabri de Peiresc (1580–1637).

The figures of the months, generally nude or half-draped youths symbolizing the occupations proper to those months, are of particular interest as they are forerunners of the Calendar-pictures prefixed to medieval Psalters and Books of Hours. The ornamental borders of the frames are decorated with debased classical patterns, such as the Greek scroll, cable, egg-and-dog-tooth, and so on. If the ornamental borders of the frames surrounding the pictures in the preserved copy, writes Dalton, reproduce exactly the original borders, they show that the Graeco-Roman illuminators ornamented as well as illustrated their books—a feature not found in any ancient codex extant. Indeed, here we would have the only evidence—if we consider it evidence—that classical illuminators ornamented, as well as illustrated, their books. It is not until the sixth century that we meet with other instances of the use of decorative borders and conventional ornament. Hence, it has been rightly suggested that the ornamental frame-borders may be an addition of the ninth-century copyist. The more so since an excellent fifteenth-century copy of the manuscript—now at Vienna—contains rectangular pictures without any decorative framing. Another copy is preserved at Brussels.

The *Chronographer* also contains personifications of some of the main cities of the Empire (Rome, Alexandria, Constantinople, and Trier), of the months and the planets, of the signs of the zodiac, and representations of two consuls who seem to be Constantius II and his Caesar, Constantius Gallus (suggestion by Mr. Harold Mattingly); it also contains a *Chronica Mundi* ('World Chronicle') up to A.D. 334.

'Portraits' and 'Birth-places' of Ancient Authors (Fig. I-14a, 18a, 28a, etc.)

Mention must here be made of the 'portraits' in medieval MSS. of ancient Greek and Roman authors. These portraits are mostly fictitious, but many are copies from Graeco-Roman models; see, for instance, the portraits of Theocritos in *Cod. Gr. 2832* in the National Library, Paris (already referred to). The portraits of Horace and of Maecenas in *Cod. Vat. Lat. 1592*, present mixed features of ancient Roman (see p. 40 f.) and thirteenth-century times. For the 'portrait' of Virgil see pp. 36 and 39.

Sometimes the 'birth-places' of the ancient authors and other personages, likewise copied from classical originals, are also painted in medieval codices.

In most instances, however, neither the 'portraits' nor the 'birth-places' are based on ancient models: see, for example, Ptolemy's 'portrait' in *Cod. Gr. 388* of the Marciana Library, Venice; or Aristotle's 'portrait' in *Cod. Phil. Gr. 64* of the National Library, Vienna; or the 'portrait' of Augustus in Horace's *Carmina* (see p. 41 f. and Fig. I-14a).

For the further development of Graeco-Roman book illustration and illumination in the Byzantine period, see p. 70 ff. and *passim*.

Conclusion

An analysis of the copies which we have discussed, or only mentioned, provides sufficient evidence to show that many Graeco-Roman works, both of a literary and scientific character, were illustrated in Graeco-Roman times. In the fourth or the fifth century A.D., and probably also much earlier, there existed some cycles of illustrations, such as those for the *Iliad* and the *Aeneid*.

The most important centres of Graeco-Roman book illustration were Alexandria, in the Hellenistic and Graeco-Roman periods, and Rome in the Imperial period. There were, undoubtedly, other centres, such as Constantinople, Pergamum, Antioch, Athens, Ephesus—in the East, as well as some provincial cities in the West (especially in Gaul, such as Lyons, and in Spain); but we know scarcely anything about them, as there is not sufficient evidence for assigning any illustrated book to a definite centre.

According to F. Madan, the main characteristics of the Graeco-Roman illustrations were simplicity and directness in aim, with no straining after effect, few accessories, and plenty of colour but very little shading. The background is often an olive green, and the border is noticeable, consisting of a plain band or bands of colour carried as a rectangle round the picture, sometimes with gold lozenges.

Persistence of Roman Style

The Roman style of book-illustration seems to have lingered on for some centuries in some remote parts of the Roman Empire. See also p. 70 ff. In Spain it can be traced to a surprisingly late date in the Middle Ages (see p. 162). In C. R. Morey's opinion, for instance, two manuscripts of Beatus, *Commentary on the Apocalypse*, preserved in the Pierpont Morgan Library, New York, belong to this category (*M. 644* is of the tenth century, and is thus the earliest dated copy of this text with illustrations; the other manuscript, *M. 429*, is of the thirteenth century); see also p. 166 f.

BIBLIOGRAPHY

O. Jahn, *Griechische Bilderchroniken*, Bonn, 1873.

Heraclius, *De coloribus et artibus Romanorum*, ed. Vienna, 1873.

W. de Gray Birch and H. Jenner, *Early Drawings and Illuminations etc.*, London, 1879.

C. Robert, *Bild und Lied*, Berlin, 1881.

G. Vitelli and C. Paoli, *Collezione fiorentina di facs. paleogr. greci e latini*, Florence, 1884–88.

J. Strzygowski, *Kalenderbilder des Chronographen etc.*, Berlin, 1888; *Der Bilderkreis d. griech. Physiologus*, Leipsic, 1899; *Orient oder Rom*, Leipsic, 1901; (and A. Bauer) *Eine alexandrinische Weltchronik*, Vienna, 1906.

J. H. Middleton, *Illuminated Manuscripts in Classical and Medieval Times*, Cambridge, 1892.

Pierre de Nolhac, 'Notices et Extraits,' xxxv/ii, 1897, pp. 683–791.

G. Thiele, *De Antiquorum Libris Pictis Cap. Quatt.*, Marburg, 1897; *Antike Himmelsbilder etc.*, Berlin, 1898; *Der illustr. latein. Aesop etc.*, Leyden, 1905.

E. Strong, *Roman Art. Some of its Principles and their Applic. to Early Christian Painting*, London and New York, 1900.

D. Ainaloff, *The Hellenistic Basis of the Byzantine Art* (in Russian), St. Petersburg, 1900.

A. Mancini, 'Index codicum lat. publ. Bibl. Lucensis,' *Studi Ital. di Filol. Class.*, 1900.

A. Riegl, *Die spaetroemische Kunst-Industrie*, Vienna, 1901.

P. Giacosa, *Magistri Salernitani nondum editi. Cat. rag. d. Espos. di storia d. medicina etc. 1898*, 2 vols., Turin, 1901.

A. Gayet, *L'Art copte*, Paris, 1902; *Trois étapes d'art en Egypte*, Paris, 1910.

Biblioteca Vaticana, *Picturae ornamenta complura scripturae specimina cod. Vat. 3867 qui cod. Vergilii Romanus audit phototypice expressa etc.*, Rome, 1902; *Il rotulo di Giosuè etc.*, Milan, 1905; *Fragmenta et picturae Vergiliana cod. Vat. lat. 3225*, 3rd ed., Vatican City, 1945.

N. Terzaghi, 'Index codicum lat. class. qui Senis etc. adservantur,' *Studi Ital. di Filol. Class*, 1903.

A. M. Ceriani and A. Ratti, *Homeri Iliadis pictae fragmenta Ambrosiana etc.*, Milan, 1905.

A. Bauer and J. Strzygowski, *see* J. Strzygowski, *Eine alexandrinische Weltchronik*.

A. von Premerstein, K. Wessely, and J. Mantuani, *Dioscurides etc.*, Leyden, 1906.

A. Muñoz, *I codici greci delle biblioteche minori di Roma*, Florence, 1906.

K. Sudhoff, *Kindslagen in Miniaturen etc.*, Leipsic, 1907; *Beitraege zur Geschichte der Chirurgie im Mittelalter*, Leipsic, 1914.

Th. Birt, *Die Buchrolle in der Kunst*, Leipsic, 1907.

A. Ausfeld, *Der griechische Alexanderroman*, Leipsic, 1907.

L. Frati, 'Indice d. codici lat. conservati n. R. Bibl. Univ. di Bologna,' *Studi Ital. di Filol. Class.*, 1908–9.

A. Erman, 'Zeichnungen aegyptischer Kuenstler griechischer Zeit,' *Amtl. Berichte d. Berliner Museen*, 1908–9.

C. Stornaiolo, *Le miniature della Cosmografia cristiana etc.*, Milan, 1908.

R. Engelmann, *Antike Bilder aus roemischen Handschriften*, Leyden, 1909.

D. C. Hesseling, *Miniatures de l'Octoteuche de Smyrne*, Leyden, 1909.

B. Nogara, *I mosaici antichi etc.*, Milan, 1910.

F. Mueller, *Die antiken Odyssee-Illustrationen*, Berlin, 1913.

E. H. Zimmermann, *Vorkarolingische Miniaturen*, 5 vols., Berlin, 1916.

W. Schubert, *Das Buch bei den Griechen und Roemern*, 2nd ed., Berlin and Leipsic, 1921.

G. Loumeyer, *L'Outillage et le matériel du peintre de l'Antiqu. gr. et rom.*, Brussels and Paris, 1922.

E. Pfuhl, *Malerei und Zeichnung der Griechen*, Munich, 1923; *Meisterwerke griechischer Zeichnung und Malerei*, I vol., Munich, 1924.

A. W. Byvanck, 'Die geillustreerde Handschr. v. Oppianus Cynegetica,' *Mededeelingen v. h. Nederl. Hist. Inst. te Rome*, 1925.

H. Gerstinger, *Die griechische Buchmalerei*, Vienna, 1926.

C. Singer, 'The Herbal in Antiquity', *Journ. of Hellen. Studies*, 1927; *From Magic to Science*, London, 1928; — and others, *A History of Technology*, Oxford, 1954.

E. Howald and H. E. Sigerist, *Pseudoapulei Herbarius*, Leipsic, 1927.

S. J. Gąsiorowski, *Malarstwo minjaturowe grecko-rzymskie*, Cracow, 1928.

M. R. James, *The Bestiary*, Oxford, 1928; *Marvels of the East*, Oxford, 1929; *The Romance of Alexander. A Collotype Facsimile of MS. Bodley 264*, Oxford, 1933.

K. Sethe, 'Der dramatische Ramesseumpapyrus etc.', *Dramatische Texte zu altaegyptischen Mysterienspielen. Untersuchungen zur Geschichte und Altertumskunde Aegyptens*, vol. X, Leipsic, 1929.

M. H. Swindler, *Ancient Painting*, New Haven, 1929.

H. Woodruff, 'The Illustrated Manuscripts of Prudentius,' *Art Studies, The Art Bullet.*, 1929.

K. Bulas, *Les Illustrations antiques de L'Iliade*, Lwów, 1929.

M. Wellmann, 'Der Physiologus etc.,' *Philologus*, Suppl., XXII/1, 1930.

T. de Marinis and F. Rossi, 'Notice sur les miniat. du "Virgilius" de la Bibl. Riccardi à Florence' (*MS. 492*), *Bull. de la Soc. Franç. de Repr. de Manuscr. à peint.*, 1930.

L. W. Jones and C. R. Morey, *The Miniatures of the Manuscripts of Terence etc.*, 2 vols., Princeton, 1931.

H. Degering and A. Boeckler, *Die Quedlinburger Italafragmente*, Berlin, 1932.

J. Fischer, *Claudii Ptolemaei Geogr. cod. Urb. gr. 82 etc.*, 2 vols., Leyden and Leipsic, 1932.

E. A. Lowe, 'Virgil in South Italy etc.,' *Studi Medievali*, 1932.

M. Pieper, 'Die aegyptische Buchmalerei etc.,' *Jahrb. des Instit.*, 1933.

Lambert le Tort, *Romance of Alexander*, Oxford, 1933.

M. Pieper, 'Die aegyptische Buchmalerei verglichen mit der griechischen und fruehmittelalterlichen', *Jahrbuch des deutschen archaeologischen Instituts*, XLVIII, 1923.

National Museum, Copenhagen, *Greek and Latin Illuminated MSS.* etc., Copenhagen, 1934.

P. Buberl, 'Das Problem der Wiener Genesis,' *Jahrb. d. Kunsthist. Samml. in Wien*, 1936.

E. Berti Toesca, 'Un erbolario del '300,' *Bibliofilia*, 1937.

J. C. Webster, *The Labors of the Month in Antique and Medieval Art*, Princeton, 1938.

M. C. Ferrari, 'La geogr. d. Tolomeo fatta miniare d. card. Bessarione,' *Bibliofilia*, 1938.

W. Lameere, 'Apamée de Syrie et les Cynégétiques etc.,' *Bulletin de l'Inst. Hist. Belge de Rome*, 1938.

J. Adhémar, *Influences antiques dans l'art du moyen âge français*, London, 1939.

P. Courcelle, 'La tradition antique d. les miniat. mediév. d'un Virgile de Naples,' *Mélanges d'archéol. et d'hist.*, 1939.

E. Bethe, *Buch und Bild im Altertum*, Leipsic, 1945.

K. Weitzmann, *Illustrations in Roll and Codex*, Princeton, 1947; *Greek Mythology in Byzantine Art,* Princeton, 1951; *Ancient Book Illumination*, Oxford, 1959.

S. Matalon, 'Codici arcaici alla mostra di Zurigo,' *Bolletino d'arte d. Min. d. Pubbl. Istruz.*, 1949.

H. Stern, 'Le Calendrier de 354,' Paris, 1953 (*Inst. franç. d'archéol. de Beyrouth*).

THE PROBLEM OF EARLY HEBREW
BOOK ILLUSTRATION

Did illuminated, or, at least, illustrated Hebrew books exist in the late Graeco-Roman period? It certainly seems that (1) no such books have survived, (2) we have no literary allusions to them (either in the vast Talmudic literature or in any other literature), and (3) a too-rigid interpretation of the Second Commandment by medieval Judaism produced the still generally held conception that not only were conforming Jews always hostile to art and particularly to representational art, but that such Hebrew art never existed.

The answer to point (1) is easy and will be obvious from the varied information given in *The Hand-produced Book* with regard to the destruction of Hebrew and other books. The *argumentum ex silentio* of point (2) may be valid if we refer to the 'official' ritual copies of the *Torah* as used for the public reading of the Law in the Jewish synagogues, but no conclusive evidence can be drawn with regard to the private domestic books, including copies of the Pentateuch written in codex-form. Indeed, one of the earliest copies extant is the illustrated *Leningrad Codex* (see p. 147 f.).

Point (3) will be discussed below. Here we should like to point out that the ancient Hebrews were not hostile to representational art even in the Temple, as may be seen from the Biblical references to *cherubim* (1 *Kings*, vi. 23, etc.), *seraphim*

(*Isaiah*, vi. 2, etc.), and so on. Human and animal representations are often found on early Hebrew seals from the late-ninth or the eight century B.C. onwards, some of them showing excellent or even magnificent craftsmanship. It may be assumed that the original pagan symbolic meaning of these representations had lost their religious significance.

On the Jewish coins (second century B.C.–second century A.D.), generally speaking—with very rare exceptions—only such emblems were used as would not offend orthodox religious feeling: cornucopias, flowers, bunches of grapes, anchors, etc. The *menorah*, the seven-branched candlestick, which later became the most characteristic symbol of Judaism, appeared for the first time on the coins of Antigonus Mattathia (40–37 B.C.). The silver coins struck during the First Jewish War (A.D. 66–70) contain the chalice on the obverse and the pomegranates on the reverse, whereas the contemporary bronze coins contain, for the first time, a *lulab* (palm-branch) and an *ethrog* (citrus fruit), both used at the celebration of the feast of Tabernacles, and baskets full of fruit beneath a palm tree, the latter being a symbol of Judaea. The Jewish coinage reached its highest standard of workmanship at the very time when the last serious rising against the Romans was brutally crushed (A.D. 132–35). These illustrations, showing the intensity of national and religious feeling, not only survived in the Synagogal art of the first Christian centuries, but also influenced Jewish art during the Middle Ages and have continued to be used down to our own day.

Jewish Attitude to Representational Art

In his Schweich Lectures of the British Academy, 1939, on the *Hebrew Bible in Art*, J. Leveen, the late Keeper of Oriental Printed Books and MSS. in the British Museum, has brilliantly discussed problems concerning the early history of Hebrew illuminated MSS. He thus summarized the respective attitudes of the three great Semitic religions to representational art (*i.e.*, the representation of human beings or animals). Islam is the most rigidly uncompromising in its hostility; its ban on this art was adamant and was never relaxed, although in certain individual cases it was deliberately defied or ignored. The Christian Church, both Eastern and Western, notwithstanding the recurring opposition of some Church Fathers and the iconoclastic period, finally permitted representational art, and even encouraged and patronized it. Rabbinical Judaism may be described as steering a middle course between the Moslem and the Christian attitudes. Sculpture was banned, although in certain cases the law was applied with a great deal of latitude, but synagogal wall-painting and mosaics were permitted, although reluctantly, from the third century A.D. onwards.

Eminent scholars—such as the British authority on Jewish history, Cecil Roth—have remarked how recent archaeological discoveries have revolutionized all the conceptions formerly held (which were based on late Hebrew literary sources) regarding the attitude of Judaism towards representational art. The present data at our disposal—ancient Hebrew signet-seals, floor-mosaics, wall-paintings at Dura

Europos (see p. 63 f.), in catacombs, and so on—show that the rigid interpretation of the Ten Commandments and the warnings against making any 'graven image' (which caused Jewish hostility to figured sculpture), did not prevent the Jews from having representational art, except at certain periods and in certain lands, as for instance in Moslem countries. See Fig. I-29-30.

Some literary sources confirm this view: 'In the days of Rabbi Yōḥanan they began to paint pictures on walls, and he did not prevent them; in the days of Rabbi Abūn they began to make designs on mosaics, and he did not prevent them' (*Palestinian Talmud, Abodah Zarah*, 48 d). 'A figured stone ye shall not put on the ground to worship thereto, but a colonnade with pictures and likenesses ye may have in your synagogues, but not to worship thereto' (*Targūm Jonathan* on *Leviticus*, xxvi).

The Talmudic laws were concerned only with the ritual copies of the Hebrew Bible, *i.e.* the *Scrolls of the Law*, which must be free of all illustration or decoration. No rigid uniformity or austerity, however, was imposed upon private Bibles, secular codices and other books. Although, even in later times, the Rabbis did not favour book illustration, or even book decoration, when Rabbi Meir of Rothenburg (*d.* 1293) mildly criticized the animal-and-bird decoration (see p. 156 f.) of the *Maḥăzōrīm, i.e.* the prayer-books for the festivals, he did not base his criticisms on religious considerations; indeed, he writes: 'by looking upon these figures, people would not devote their heart to their Father in heaven'; he asserts that representational illustration is not an infraction of the Rabbinical law. Moreover, the considerable number of prayer-books from the thirteenth and fourteenth centuries that were decorated in this manner—see, for instance, Fig. IV-25 and 28 —has been advanced as proof that there was no marked opposition to be reckoned with. Perhaps the best evidence of the rather tolerant attitude prevalent is found in the illustrated prayer-book (Breslau University Library) executed by a disciple of the Rothenburg Sage: R. Wischnitzer. Thus, the ample latitude that was allowed made possible the production of Hebrew illuminated MSS.

Frescoes at Dura Europos (Fig. I-30)

The discovery, in 1932–33, 1933–34, and 1934–35, of the wall-paintings of the synagogue of Dura Europos (on the Middle Euphrates), assigned to *c.* A.D. 245, deserves special mention. These frescoes preserve for us the earliest surviving examples of Bible illustration. See Fig. I-30.

On the whole, the Dura wall-paintings are arranged in four horizontal rows, or registers, running around the synagogue hall. The three upper rows, of which about thirty panels are preserved, illustrate various episodes of the Bible. There appear, amongst others, the patriarchs Abraham, Isaac, and Jacob; the twelve sons of Jacob and the two sons of Joseph; then Moses, Aaron, and Miriam; the prophets Samuel, Elijah, and Ezekiel; King Saul, King David, and King Solomon; Queen Esther with Mordecai; King Ahasuerus and Haman. The bottom row—a frieze or dado—contains animals (lions and lionesses, cheetahs), masks inscribed in circles, and geometric patterns.

The editors of the *editio princeps* on the wall-paintings have pointed out that the conception of the scenes here represented is superior to their execution. And J. Leveen writes: their spiritual intensity so often transcends the technical limitations of the artist. Still, it has rightly been pointed out that these wall-paintings are not without artistic merit. Indeed, some of the frescoes, like the Esther frieze, convey admirably a sense of vitality and dramatic force, but the noble 'portrait' panel of Moses reading the Law, which breathes such spiritual exaltation and serene dignity, easily dominates them all.

Space does not allow us to deal in detail with the various questions and problems raised by these paintings, on which an extensive literature has already been published (see R. Wischnitzer, *The Messianic Theme in the Paintings of the Dura Synagogue*, pp. 117–24). Amongst the various theories, reference may be made to that of Rachel Wischnitzer: The messianic concept which pervades the rabbinical literature of Palestine and Mesopotamia has been found to be the organizing, formative factor in the iconography of the synagogue decoration.

Dura Frescoes in relation to Book-illumination

Some scholars have suggested that these wall-paintings and some Christian book-illuminations go back to a common source. The preponderance of Old Testament over New Testament illustrations in early Christian books and in the catacombs has been attributed to the existence of Jewish prototypes.

If it could be established—writes Jacob Leveen—that the Jews came first with pictorial representations from the Hebrew Bible, then this partiality for O.T. subjects would point to the probability that the early Christians, amongst whom were so many converted Jews, borrowed from the current Jewish picture cycles. On the other hand there are some weighty objections against the thesis that the Jews borrowed their picture-sets from the early Christians.

Moreover, other scholars—such as Cecil Roth—have suggested that 'the prolific but unarticulated' representational frescoes of the Dura synagogue took over as it were the subject-matter of an antecedent manuscript tradition in book- or scroll-form—an hypothesis which would explain some of its characteristics. If this is so, concludes Dr. Roth, we have additional reason to suspect that the Old Testament subject-matter of the early catacomb frescoes and the earliest illustrated Latin Bibles were, as had long been suspected, in the full tide of an earlier Jewish tradition.

Mrs. Wischnitzer, in examining the problem of the immediate models of the Dura frescoes, that is, whether there existed at the time Jewish books with Bible illustration, writes as follows: It is conceivable that picture cycles for the Pentateuch, the Books of Samuel and Kings, and other books may have been in circulation. Less plausible is the assumption that illustrated liturgical books, such as the Passover Haggadah, existed in the third century. This hypothesis involves the problem of whether the text of the Passover Haggadah was already extensive enough to form a separate book. Those who look for allusions to festivals in the synagogue decoration presuppose the existence of liturgical picture cycles, which in fact only gradually evolved, with the completion of various types of prayer-books in the Middle Ages. The only festival unmistakably pointed to by its cult symbols, the citrus fruit and the palm branch, is the Feast of Tabernacles.

The Dura frescoes, though unique, are not our only source for the study of Jewish art of the early Christian centuries. From the mosaic decoration of synagogues, and the paintings of catacombs, discovered in Palestine, Rome, and North Africa, it can be inferred that between the fourth and sixth centuries A.D., Jewish representational art, with a Biblical content, was fairly well spread over a large area.

There is no doubt that both early Christian and Jewish art were greatly influenced by Hellenistic art blended with some Oriental elements, especially in the style and form of narration. C. R. Morey, however, has suggested that the early Christian art and the illumination of the Latin Bibles were based on Alexandrian Jewish prototypes. This theory was already envisaged in 1901 by Joseph Strzygowski; and O. Wulff, in 1918, and H. Gerstinger, in 1926, have adduced further proof; the discovery of the synagogue of Dura Europos—and, more recently, of the synagogue at Ostia—seems to have provided the connecting link. The objections of P. Buberl and E. Bethe have been disproved by other scholars.

Cecil Roth, however, correctly points out that it is only during the last few years that it has become certain that, contrary to what was once believed, representational art was tolerated in the Synagogue in the Talmudic period. The mosaics of Beth Alpha, it is suggested, provided an example of such art on the Synagogue floor, and other examples better executed though less perfectly preserved show that this phenomenon was by no means isolated in Palestine. It is obvious, writes Roth, that representations of the same sort in the pages of a book were less objectionable from the religious point of view than either of the other forms of expression (mosaic floors or wall-paintings).

It has, therefore, been argued that at least in the early centuries of the Christian Era, Jews practised book-illumination, which included also representational illustrations of the Biblical story. Dr. Roth, indeed, goes as far as to suggest the existence in early times of Hebrew Biblical manuscripts, which were in the fullest sense illuminated and which included, in some cases at least, conventional representations of the human figure. The conventional subject-matter is said to have comprised a representation of the interior of the Sanctuary, or of the Synagogue, centering upon the Tabernacle, or the Torah-shrine.

Furthermore, Roth suggests that the subject-matter of these Hebrew illuminated Bibles may have been taken over from the Jews by the Christians and thus figures in early Christian book-art. In Roth's opinion, there is additional reason to believe that the Old Testament representations, so important in early Christian art and book-illumination, were similarly taken over from Hebrew originals.

Is it therefore established that there was a direct relationship between the ancient wall-paintings and the miniatures of the Hebrew MSS.? Although many of the subjects painted, for instance, in the Dura frescoes, appear centuries later in illustrations of preserved Hebrew MSS., the connection between them is still an

open problem. We have to agree with Jacob Leveen that so many of the intermediate links in the chain of the Jewish tradition of Old Testament illustration are
missing that the task of relating the miniatures in the Hebrew manuscripts to their
prototypes is one of great difficulty. See, however, p. 70 f. 148.

Chrysography

The first recorded reference whatsoever to gold illumination in MSS. comes
from a Jewish source: it appears in § 176 of the *Letter of pseudo-Aristeas* (see *The
Hand-produced Book*, p. 176), and the statement that Hebrew scrolls were written in
letters of gold is repeated both by the Jewish philosopher Philo (*c.* 10 B.C.–*c.* A.D.
60) and the Jewish historian Josephus (A.D. 38–*c.* 100). The Talmud contains
three references to writing in gold letters; the earliest may be assigned to the period
between A.D. 10 and 220, although the Rabbis had banned the use of gold
illumination in ritual Scrolls of the Law and in other ritual objects. The Talmudic
prohibition of the use of scrolls written in gold for Synagogal purposes (*Sabbath*
103*b*, *Sopherim*, I, viii) may indicate that more latitude was permitted with codices,
i.e. manuscripts which did not serve ritual purposes.

Book Illustration

It is uncertain, however, whether Hebrew book illustration was practised as
early as Hebrew gold-writing, and whether the obscure verse *I Maccabees*, iii. 48
refers to book illustration. (The text reads, 'And they [*i.e.*, the followers of the
Maccabees] laid open the Book of the Law, concerning those things about which
the Gentiles were accustomed to inquire, seeking the likenesses of their idols.')

The existence of ancient Jewish illustrated books in Graeco-Roman times
cannot, however, be doubted. For instance, the *Sacra Parallela* (see p. 104), containing a series of pictures illustrating the sixth book of *Bellum Judaicum* and the
ninth book of *Antiquitates Judaicae*, are sufficient proof that the two works written by
Josephus were originally illustrated. The Talmud independently refers to a family
of calligraphers and book-illustrators who lived in Jerusalem before its destruction
in A.D. 70, and thereafter removed to Galilee.

Moreover, Dr. Roth, as a result of a detailed examination of the illustration of
the earliest extant Hebrew illuminated Pentateuch—the *Leningrad Pentateuch* or
Leningrad Codex, dated A.D. 929/30: see p. 147 f. and Fig. IV-17*b*—has reached the
conclusion that this illustration is so stylized, the details in it have become so
warped, that we are certainly justified in assuming that it stands at the end of a
prolonged development; *i.e.* that the tenth-century manuscript, as we have it,
demonstrates a long antecedence in the same medium, going back well beyond the
tenth century—that is, presumably, to Roman (if only late Roman) times. Thus,
there would have been no gap between, on the one hand, the representations of the
ritual objects on the gold glasses, mosaics and frescoes of the classical period (see
p. 64), and, on the other, those in the earliest preserved manuscripts. It follows,

concludes Roth, that Hebrew illuminated Bible manuscripts existed in the classical period—what has so long been imagined, but never hitherto proved.

BIBLIOGRAPHY

V. Strzygowski, *Orient oder Rom*, Leipsic, 1901.

Th. Ehrenstein, *Das Alte Testament im Bilde*, Berlin, 1923.

E. L. Sukenik, *The Ancient Synagogue of Beth Alpha*, Jerusalem and Oxford, 1932; *Ancient Synagogues in Palestine and Greece*, London, 1934; *The Synagogue of Dura-Europos and its Frescoes* (in Hebrew), Jerusalem, 1947.

C. Hopkins, 'Jewish Prototypes of Early Christian Art,' *Illustrated London News*, 29 July 1933;— and Count du Mesnil du Buisson, 'La Synagogue de Doura Europos,' *C.R.D.S. Acad. d. Inscr. et B.-L.*, April–June, 1933.

Count du Mesnil du Buisson, 'Les Fouilles de Doura-Europos sur L'Euphrate,' *L'Illustration*, No. 4717, 1933, pp. 454–7; *Les Peintures de la synagogue de Doura-Europos, 245–256 après J.-C.* With *Introduction* by G. Millet, Rome, 1939.

G. Millet, 'Les Peintures de la synagogue de Doura,' *C.R.D.S. Acad. d. Inscr. et B.-L.*, April–June, 1933.

M. I. Rostovtzeff, 'Early Christian and Judaean Art in Mesopotamia,' *Proc. of the British Academy*, 1933, pp. 319–21; *Dura-Europos and its Art*, Oxford, 1938.

J.-B. Frey, 'La Question des images chez les juifs à la lumière des récentes découvertes,' *Biblica*, 1934, pp. 265–300.

J. Sloane, 'The Torah Shrine in the Ashburnham Pentateuch,' *Jew. Quart. Review*, 1934, pp. 1–12.

R. Wischnitzer-Bernstein, *Gestalten und Symbole der juedischen Kunst*, Berlin, 1935; 'The Conception of the Resurrection in the Ezekiel Panel of the Dura Synagogue,' *Journal of Biblical Literature*, 1941, pp. 43–55; 'The Samuel Cycle in the Wall Decoration of the Synagogue at Dura-Europos,' *Proc. of the Amer. Academy for Jew. Research*, 1941, pp. 85–103; 'Studies in Jewish Art,' *Jew. Quart. Review*, 1945, pp. 47–59; *The Messianic Theme in the Paintings of the Dura Synagogue*, Chicago, 1948.

G. Wodtke, 'Malereien der Synagoge in Dura und ihre Parallelen in der Christlichen Kunst,' *Zeitschr. fuer die neutest. Wissensch.*, 1935, pp. 51–62.

E. R. Goodenough, *By Light Light*, New Haven, 1935; 'Early Christian and Jewish Art,' *Jew. Quart. Review*, 1943, pp. 403–17; 'The Crown of Victory in Judaism,' *Art Bulletin*, 1946, pp. 139–59; *Jewish Symbols in the Graeco-Roman Period*, 12 vols., New York, 1953 onwards.

The Excavations at Dura-Europos etc., New Haven, 1936 (particularly: C. H. Kraeling, *The Wall Decorations*; and *Aramaic and Greek Dipinti and Graffiti*; C. C. Torrey, *The Aramaic Dipinto from the Exodus Panel*; A. Pagliaro, *The Pehlevi Dipinto*).

H. Rosenau, 'Some Aspects of the Pictorial Influence of the Jewish Temple,' *Pal. Explor. Fund Quart. Statem.*, 1936, pp. 157–62.

BIBLIOGRAPHY

C. Watzinger, 'Die Ausgrabungen von Dura-Europos,' *Die Welt als Geschichte*, 1936, pp. 397–410.

M. Aubert, 'Le Peintre de la synagogue de Doura,' *Gazette des Beaux-Arts*, No. 898, 1938, pp. 1–24.

R. de Vaux, 'Un détail de la synagogue de Doura,' *Revue Biblique*, 1938, pp. 383–87; 'Les Peintures de la synagogue de Doura-Europos,' *ibid.*, 1940, pp. 137–43.

E. G. Kraeling, 'The Meaning of the Ezekiel Panel in the Synagogue at Dura,' *Bull. of the Amer. Schools of Orient. Res.*, 1940, pp. 12–18.

G. Kittel, 'Die aeltesten juedischen Bilder: Eine Aufgabe fuer die wissenschaft-liche Gemeinschaftsarbeit,' *Forschungen zur Judenfrage*, IV, Hamburg, 1940, pp. 237–49.

M. Narkiss, *The Ḥanukah Lamp* (in Hebrew), Jerusalem, 1940.

A. Grabar, 'Le Thème religieux des fresques de la synagogue de Doura etc.' *Revue de l'Hist. des Religions*, 1941 (cxxiii, pp. 143–92; cxxiv, pp. 5–35).

E. Hill, 'Roman Elements in the Settings of the Synagogue Frescoes at Dura,' *Marsyas*, 1941, pp. 1–15.

C. R. Morey, *Early Christian Art*, Princeton, N.J., 1941.

L. Finkelstein, 'Pre-Maccabean Documents in the Passover Haggadah,' *Harvard Theological Review*, 1942, pp. 292–332; 1943, pp. 1–38.

M. H. Ben-Shammai, 'The Legends of the Destruction of the Temple in the Paintings of the Dura Synagogue' (in Hebrew), *Bull. of the Jew. Pal. Expl. Soc.*, 1942, pp. 93–7.

W. Stechow, 'Jacob Blessing the Sons of Joseph,' *Gaz. des Beaux-Arts*, 1943, pp. 193–208.

J. Leveen, *The Hebrew Bible in Art*, London-Oxford, 1944.

N. Schneid, *The Paintings of the Synagogue at Dura Europos* (in Hebrew), Tel Aviv, 1946.

F. Landsberger, 'Old-Time Torah-Curtains,' *Hebrew Union College Annual*, 1946, pp. 353–87; 'The Origin of the Winged Angel in Jewish Art,' *ibid.*, 1947, pp. 227–54.

I. Sonne, 'The Paintings of the Dura Synagogue,' *Hebrew Union College Annual*, 1947, pp. 255–362.

K. Brandi, *Geschichte der Geschichtswissenschaft*, Bonn, 1947 (2nd ed., 1952).

C. Wendel, *Der Thoraschrein im Altertum*, Halle, 1950.

C. Roth, 'Jewish Antecedents of Christian Art,' *The Journ. of the Warburg and Courtauld Inst.*, 1953, pp. 24–44.

J. Gutmann, *Jewish Quarterly Review*, XLIV, 1953, p. 55 ff.

T. Burckhardt (ed.), *Ilias Ambrosiana*, Olten-Lausanne-Freiburg im Breisgau, 1953.

K. Weitzmann, *Ancient book illumination*, London-Oxford, 1959.

E. Wellesz, *The Vienna Genesis*, London, 1960.

Chapter II

EARLY WEST-CHRISTIAN
BYZANTINE & ALLIED ILLUMINATION

EARLY WEST-CHRISTIAN ART OF PAINTING
(Fig. II-1-4)

Scholars have rightly emphasized that book illumination (unlike book illustration) did not create new forms, but 'rather it took over pictures and ornaments from other forms of art.' At the same time, we have to accept A. Haseloff's statement that the decisive changes in the history of the book are also turning points in the art of illumination.

In some Egyptian papyrus rolls (see Chapter I) illustration runs in a continuous series of pictures from end to end, as in modern cartoon strips. A similar method may have been employed in Graeco-Roman papyrus-rolls, and the same style was adopted in the early codices copied from rolls. But in later times the single pictures were either inserted in the text (with or without frames), placed as border illustrations of the text, or they became full-page miniatures. True book-illumination probably originated in the Eastern Roman Empire, but the products of Western Christianity must also be considered.

Very few illuminated early Christian manuscripts have been preserved, but, judging from the Biblical paintings in the fourth-century basilicas of Rome and Milan, we may assume that a number of illustrated Western Christian religious books existed in that period.

It has, however, been said that the Christian paintings—such as those of the catacombs of Rome—of the first four centuries A.D. were not so much Christian as Graeco-Roman art depicting Christian subjects. The early Christians adopted the then prevailing style of the pagan Graeco-Roman art, probably with some Jewish influence, and, being as yet unable to create a new technique, they worked out new subjects on old lines.

Early Christian Paintings and Mosaics (Fig. II-1-2). As to this early Christian art, mention may be made of the wall-paintings of the Roman catacombs of the third or fourth century A.D., the mosaics of the Roman church of S. Pudenziana, and the so-called mausoleum of S. Constanza. This, indeed, was a profane art, and reflected the late Roman-Hellenistic style. The splendid mosaics of the triumphal arch of S. Maria Maggiore in Rome—probably belonging to the late fourth or early fifth century, and apparently based on illustrated Biblical manuscripts which have not come down to us—may be considered amongst the latest works of this style. This free adaptation of late classical art to early Christian art-productions is also conspicuous in the earliest extant Christian illuminated manuscript: see further on.

The same may be said of the even more superb mosaics of the so-called mausoleum of Galla Placidia, in Ravenna, of the first half of the fifth century, and of the slightly less important mosaics of the Battistero degli Ortodossi of Ravenna Cathedral (of the mid-fifth century), while the mosaics of the Ravenna basilica of S. Apollinare Nuovo, built by Theodoric the Great in the first half of the sixth century, and those of the Ravenna church of S. Vitale, belonging to the same period, reflect the change of style which occurred in the late fifth and early sixth centuries. A similar style of art may be seen in the mosaics of Parenzo Cathedral, and of a few other ancient churches of southern and northern Italy (Naples, Capua, Milan, and so on). As to the Byzantine mosaics of early churches of Rome, see p. 80.

In the darkness of tribal barbarism which dominated western Europe after the fall of the Roman Empire, the Church was the main tie with the glorious past.

Itala Fragment (Fig. II-3a)

The earliest extant illuminated MS. of Western Christianity is the Quedlinburg fragment of the *Itala*, or Old Latin version of the Bible (see *The Hand-produced Book, passim*)—probably written and illuminated in Northern Italy—now preserved in the State Library at Berlin (*Cod. Theol. Lat. fol. 485*); it is assigned to the late fourth century A.D.

Nothing is known of its history until the seventeenth century when it came to light in Quedlinburg (Saxony, Germany), where it was used by a bookbinder for lining up the covers of municipal and ecclesiastical records. It has been suggested that one of the Saxon emperors may have brought the codex from Italy and presented it to the monastery of Quedlinburg. The five leaves extant were rediscovered in 1865 (two), 1869 (two), and 1887 (one).

The last leaf contains text only, but the other four are of particular interest for our purpose. They have one side filled with text (portions from *Samuel* and *Kings*) and the other with pictures which in style and technique closely approach those of the *Vatican Virgil* (see p. 37 f.), though the *Itala* fragment seems to present greater originality. There is the same antique conception of the human figures, the same use of gold for heightening effects in draperies and accessories, but—unlike the *Virgil*—the pictures had preliminary outline drawing; curiously enough, thanks to the peeling of the colours, even the instructions to the artist, written in cursive script across the field of the pictures, are now visible.

Four scenes in square compartments (formed by broad red bands) usually fill one page. The paintings are in thick body-colour, but much of it has now disappeared. Only traces of the bright colouring and forcible modelling of the pictures are still preserved. The style is clear and simple in character, and the pictorial conception, calm and naturalistic, is without a trace of the Byzantine style, but there are already traces of the method—which we find later in Byzantine art—of treating the face with sharp highlights upon the forehead.

For the slightly later *Cotton Genesis* and *Vienna Genesis*, and for other early Christian illuminated codices which reflect the Hellenistic-Oriental style, see p. 84 ff.

S. Augustine Gospels

From the fifth century A.D. onwards, the West Roman style of book illustration deteriorated, but the very few remaining manuscripts bearing witness to the survival of late Antique and early Christian art in the West hardly allow us to trace this development in detail. See also p. 68. An interesting initial with the primitive drawing of the Christian symbol and of a decorative device is represented in Fig. II-3*b* (S. Jerome, *Tractatus in librum Psalmorum*, preserved in the Nat. Libr., at Paris, *Lat. 2235*).

A *Gospel* in Corpus Christi College, Cambridge (*Cod. 286*) which was illuminated in Italy in the sixth century A.D., and was perhaps one of the codices sent by Pope Gregory the Great (590–604) to Augustine in Canterbury, is a remarkable example of an early Western Christian illuminated codex of the period. Fig. II-3*c* reproduces the frontispiece from the *S. Augustine Gospels*.

The Corpus Christi codex contains two interesting miniatures, which reflect the complex artistic traditions—including the classical Graeco-Roman elements as well as some Oriental influences—displayed in the Roman church wall-paintings of that period, as, for instance, those of the presbytery of S. Maria Antiqua. This codex may, therefore, be assigned to Rome or, perhaps, to Southern Italy.

On the whole, there are very few illuminated Gospels (complete or fragmentary) belonging to this early era of Christianity. One is in Latin (at Munich), two are in Greek (the *Rossano codex*—see p. 87 f.; and the *Sinope fragment*—see p. 89), and two are in Syriac (the *Rabbūlā Gospels*—see p. 117 f., and the Syrian *MS. 33* in the National Library at Paris—see p. 118).

Ashburnham Pentateuch (Fig. II-3*d*)

The *Ashburnham Pentateuch* in the National Library, Paris (*Nouv. Acq. Lat. 2334*) is in a category of its own. It contains various miniatures of great stylistic and iconographic interest. Also the representations of public and private buildings, religious ceremonies, domestic scenes, costume and furniture, are of paramount importance. The codex consists of 142 folios; the text, in uncials, is written in two columns of twenty-eight lines; there are also initials of much larger size. The MS. belonged to the church of S. Gatien, at Tours; later it was owned by Lord Ashburnham, on whose death it passed to the National Library at Paris.

The place of origin of this codex is still uncertain. Springer, Schultze, and Krauss assign it to northern Italy or southern France. Gebhardt does not exclude North African influences; Rand, Webber, and Porter connect it with Tours; Strzygowski, Dalton, Wulf, and Woerman consider it a Western product based on a Semitic model from Egypt; finally, S. Berger, Leprieur, Beissel, Haseloff, García Villada, and Dominguez Bordona assign it to the Visigoths of Spain (in that case, it would be the only historiated manuscript of Visigothic origin). None of these attributions can be accepted without qualification. Whatever the place of origin of the MS., the miniatures seem to be based on Oriental models.

Of the nineteen pages with miniatures, sixteen contain pictures exclusively. The first, or frontispiece, represents a portal with round-headed arch, and with curtains and peacocks drawn in the spandrels. (The peacock is a symbol of eternal life: see H. Lother, *Der Pfau in der altchristlichen Kunst*, Leipsic, 1929.) The remaining miniatures illustrate the Old Testament from the Creation to Moses. The Story of the Deluge occupies an entire page; other pictures are divided into two or three horizontal bands. The smaller miniatures are arranged in rectangular or square spaces extending over the whole width of the page, or are distributed irregularly in the text and inserted by the side of the script. The paintings are in water-colour, painted in successive layers upon a monochrome ground (red, green, or blue), and framed in a red fillet having in each corner a small leaf of approximately the same colour as the ground.

A point of unique interest has recently been referred to by a British scholar. In this somewhat intriguing Spanish seventh-century codex (the *Ashburnham Pentateuch*)—writes Dr. Cecil Roth—there figures in one of the pages at the outset a sort of chest, partly concealed by curtains—in just the same way as the Palestinian Torah-shrine of the early centuries is shewn in the contemporary records. The curtains are gathered round pillars, which also were apparently a characteristic of the Palestinian Synagogue interior; and the chest is placed in a rounded apse, with a conch-shaped decoration above. Within it are lying the books of the Pentateuch, or rather their titles in the original Hebrew, transcribed into Latin characters. The resemblance in particular to the Beth Alpha mosaic representation of the Synagogue interior is obvious, and has already engaged the attention of scholars. Dr. Roth thus suggests that the *Ashburnham Pentateuch* (or rather its prototype—for 'the preceding manuscripts in the series have been lost') is, as it were, nothing other than a Christian version of a Jewish historiated Bible, each feature of which it piously copies.

Miscellanea (Fig. II-4*a*–*b*)

As to the so-called *Psalter of S. Augustine* (British Museum, *Vesp. A.1.*), which notwithstanding the tradition that it is another of the codices sent by Pope Gregory (see p. 70), its miniatures seem to have been copied by an eighth-century English artist from a Roman original: *see* p. 188 and Fig. II-4*a*.

The *Codex Brixianus* (preserved in the Queriniana Library, Brescia, North Italy) of the first half of the sixth century—see *The Hand-produced Book*, p. 280—contains the Eusebian Canons (fols. 1*r*–34*v*) in classical arches drawn in silver, whereas the Corinthian capitals of the columns (and sometimes the base), the ornamentation of the upper part and the titles are in gold. Each page contains in its lower part the concordances written in silver under arches also drawn in silver: Fig. II-4*b*.

A fifth-century (A.D.) Boëthius *diptych* (see *The Hand-produced Book*, p. 29), also in Brescia (in the Civic Christian Museum), contains two seventh-century miniatures very badly preserved. One represents the Resurrection of Lazarus, the other the Saints Augustine, Jerome, and Gregory.

A relatively late MS., containing the *First Book of the Maccabees*, is preserved in the University Library at Leyden (MS. *Perizoni 17*). It was written and illuminated in the monastery of St. Gall. The miniatures cover twenty-eight full pages, and go back to an earlier model. An illuminated codex in the monastery of S. Paul im Lavanttal (in Carinthia) was also probably copied (in the early seventh century) from a much earlier original.

All these manuscripts bear witness to a survival of late Antique and early Christian art in the West. See also p. 290.

Illumination of manuscripts in the Frank and Lombard kingdoms will be dealt with on pp. 199 ff. and 292 f.

Illuminated Bibles and Gospels rarely occur in early Western Christianity (see, however, p. 68 ff. and *passim*). Indeed, hardly any have come down to us. The earliest extant illuminated full Latin Bibles belong to the Carolingian period (see p. 206 f.); they are the *Grandval Bible* of the British Museum (*Add. MS. 10546*), the *Vivian Bible* of the National Library, Paris (*Cod. Lat. 1*)—both produced at the school of Tours (see p. 206 f.)—and the *Bible of S. Paolo fuori le Mura*, Rome, a product of the Corbie school. According to W. Koehler, however, the archetype of these Bibles must have belonged to the fifth century A.D.

Byzantine Influences

Apart from the classical Graeco-Roman elements in early illumination, there was another, and more important, element which affected particularly the Christian illuminated devotional works. This was the florid Byzantine art of adorning MSS. of the Gospels with brilliantly painted ornamental designs, gilt or silver lettering, and finely executed miniatures embellished with highly gilded backgrounds.

The influence of the Byzantine style in miniature-painting may also be seen in the universal type of the Evangelists, often recurring in medieval European codices; the pose of the figure, the chair, the foot-stool, the writing desk, the bookstand, are all of the Byzantine style. See also p. 92 and *passim*.

BYZANTINE ILLUMINATION

(Fig. II-4d–28b)

From the standpoint of the history of civilization, this section is one of the most important of the present book. Until recent times, Byzantine art—'that Orientalized Graeco-Roman' art (Runciman's term), which, not altogether correctly, is called East Christian—has been misinterpreted. It was generally regarded by scholars either as a decadent continuation of Roman classical art, or as something static, *i.e.* without evolution or change.

Indeed, it has been the custom to identify Byzantinism with formalism in art: with stately decoration rather than life, with the presentation of ideas rather than of action. It has been known as the conserving force which kept intact for centuries the traditional composition of sacred themes. Its last descendants were seen in the icons of the Greek Church, which still interpret the eternal truths to the twelfth century in the artistic language of the tenth and the preceding centuries.

These theories are superseded, and it is now generally held that between the fourth century A.D.—in which Byzantine art originated—and the fourteenth century—when it last flourished—it was a living art with periods of florescence and decay, and, as Sir Steven Runciman has pointed out, it is the truest mirror of the synthesis that made up Byzantine civilization. There all elements, Greek, Roman, Aramaic, and Iranian, can be seen in varying proportions, but always blended perfectly into a whole, into something unique and original for all its derivations. The art, Sir Steven concludes, was essentially the art of Imperial Constantinople, lasting in its fundamental characteristics as long as Emperors reigned on the Bosphorus.

Byzantine Art

A new period in the study of Byzantine art began in 1925. New discoveries—such as those of dated wall-paintings on Cyprus or of dated panels at the Sinai monastery or the uncovering of Byzantine mosaics in Constantinople and of Byzantine panel-paintings in Moscow—new research and publications, have provided additional material for study. But—we have to agree with Father Mathew —it is still too early to hope to be definite on any point connected with the development or with the influence of Byzantine painting. The discoveries of the last thirty years have made nearly all earlier generalizations untenable, but the chance evidence they are continuing to provide is both heterogeneous and self-conflicting.

The static, traditional, symbolic quality—to which reference has been made— only represents one of the aspects of early Byzantine art, although it happens to be the one which has survived to the present day (in the Russian and other icons), and which, in the Italo-Byzantine mosaics, has become familiar to the casual tourist. In the Byzantine illuminations we find not one but three or four or more styles or ideals, and endless combinations and permutations of these, struggling for mastery.

Mathew rightly emphasizes that it seems increasingly clear that the conservative character of Byzantine civilization has been much overestimated. Until the fifteenth century it remained characterized by zest for experiment and for a sophisticated modernity in thought, in science, in literature and in painting. Even new barbarian sources would at times be utilized precisely because exotic and bizarre: Mathew.

In the East—writes the American authority in this field, C. R. Morey—a different fate awaited the classic tradition. In the first place, the illumination of books in the eastern portion of the Empire started with the stronger tradition behind it of Greek art, as distinguished from Latin. It thus eventually retained the essential dignity of Hellenic work, but it met at the outset a powerful counter-current from Persia. As life dies out of the scenes and motifs, concludes Morey, a new splendour of colour comes to take its place, showing the effect of a growing tone-instinct unknown to antiquity and traceable to Persian influence.

In A.D. 330 Byzantium became the seat of the Roman Empire and became not only its political centre, but also one of the main intellectual and artistic centres of the whole ancient world. The pagan world and its Graeco-Roman art were then in complete decadence; a new cultural world was being created, which took over the main elements derived from the past and transformed them in the light of new inspirations mainly originating in the Near and the Middle East. The details of the origin and early development of the new culture and art, particularly in their bearing on the history of book-illumination, are now hardly ascertainable; the preserved manuscripts of this period are very few in number, and their birth-place and date are still uncertain.

However, the distinctive style, which resulted from the conflicting influences and eclectic culture of the Byzantine Empire in its formative period, is found fully developed in sixth-century mosaics.

Painting, including book-illumination, was the most important of the formative arts of the Byzantine Empire. From the sixth century A.D., Byzantine painting was a Christian art, or rather an 'East-Christian' art, *par excellence*, and interestingly enough, an organic unity.

On the whole, Christian art was then mainly Byzantine; it began to develop distinctive characteristics, such as the peculiar angularity of outline, the meagreness and elongation of form, the richness of costume indicating oriental influences, and so on. It was during the glorious reign of Justinian (527–65) that this art reached its first Golden Age.

Centres and Chronological Subdivisions of Byzantine Art

There were various centres of 'Byzantine' culture, where 'Byzantine' illuminated manuscripts were produced—we have already referred to Italy, particularly to South Italy. Many also were doubtless produced in the cities and monasteries of Western Asia, until the Turkish invasion swept away their civilization. But it is convenient and appropriate to group these MSS. all together under the name

74

'Byzantine', for a certain well-marked and easily recognizable manner is common to all; and this manner, whencesoever it primarily drew its chief inspiration, certainly flourished conspicuously in and about Byzantium itself, under the patronage of the Imperial Court.

Byzantine art on the whole may be divided into the following periods: (1) fourth and fifth centuries: formative period; it may not be exact to apply the term 'Byzantine' to this transitional period and some scholars prefer the general name of *Early Christian*; here we have an art still in a fluid state: old, traditional and pagan elements, employed in combination with new Christian influences; elements of pagan symbolism adapted to Christian use; (2) sixth century: first Golden Age of that peculiar and well-defined manner which is known as the Byzantine style; (3) late seventh century to late ninth century: decadence of Byzantine art; (4) tenth to twelfth century: second Golden Age of Byzantine culture and art, probably the most brilliant period of Byzantine civilization; and (5) fourteenth and fifteenth centuries: short period of renaissance, followed again by decadence.

This subdivision is not dogmatic. It is based on the general connotation of the term 'Byzantine' to designate all that concerned the Byzantine Empire between *c.* A.D. 330 and the mid-fifteenth century. Not all scholars agree with this connotation. For Pierce and Tyler (in *Art Byzantin*, 1932 and 1934), for instance, the term 'Byzantine' applies only to the works of the earlier centuries, whereas an authority on Byzantine painting, Gervase Mathew, O.P., agrees with the modern Greek and Roman scholars that true Byzantine art started only in the late eighth century. He points out that the traditional dates of the beginning of Byzantine history (11 May A.D. 330, when Constantine established the administrative centre of the Roman Empire at Byzantium) and its end (29 May 1453, when the Turks conquered the city) are arbitrary, 'outside the unrealities of a pure political history'. Much that can be considered as characteristically Byzantine art, in civilization and in technique of administration, writes Father Mathew, is first apparent in the late third century, is only fully developed in the late eighth century and survived under Turkish rule until the late seventeenth century. In his opinion, it is perhaps simplest to follow the practice of the Athens school and to apply the term Byzantine from the late eighth century. While many scholars will agree with Father Mathew as regards his general remarks, for practical reasons we cannot here accept this simpler and narrower sense of Byzantine painting, implying 'painting practised within the frontiers of the Byzantine Empire under the Macedonian, Comnenian and Palaiologan dynasties from the middle of the ninth to the middle of the fifteenth century'.

On the other hand, with regard to the restriction of the term 'Byzantine' as to place, we do agree with the wider connotation given by Mathew and other scholars, rejecting both (1) the restriction of the term to the products of Constantinople and of the regions strictly connected with the capital, and (2) the widest meaning of the term, *i.e.*, including not only Italy and Syria, but also Armenia. Unlike, for instance, Italian art, it is only possible, emphasizes Mathew, to classify Byzantine painting in terms of such centres of production, not of individual painters. This, he writes, is due to the fact that the artist had none of the special status of the writer. Whether he was monk or layman, as a painter he was a journeyman. For the same reason it is difficult to classify Byzantine painting in terms of the medium employed. It is increasingly clear how close was the relation between wall-painting, panel-painting and manuscript-painting; perhaps because all three might be commissioned from the same workshop whether lay or monastic. Again, concludes Mathew, it is unsatisfactory to attempt to formulate too strict a division between Constantinopolitan and provincial styles.

MAIN SOURCES OF BYZANTINE ART, ESPECIALLY ILLUMINATION

In the past, there was error regarding the origin of Byzantine art. Most scholars considered Roman classical art as its main or even its only source. Nowadays it is known that Byzantine art originated from the following main sources:

(1) *Hellenistic art*, with its main centre at Alexandria. This was calm and naturalistic in style, concerned with the portrayal by illusionist and picturesque methods of living forms and of the idealized human form, plastically conceived and displayed against an extensive background. The subjects were illustrated by continuous scenes, in historical sequence, without division into single pictures (later known as 'miniatures'), and there was no ornamentation unrelated to the subject. There were numerous personifications of cities, mountains, rivers, and so on, as well as personfications of qualities, such as Strength, Repentance, etc. Classical influence is sometimes also evident and strongly marked in the treatment of individual figures and groups, and occasionally in the composition of a whole picture, as in the celebrated representation of David as Orpheus. In the drawing of landscape, with panorama-like backgrounds, true perspective was attempted and architecture was shown in picturesque detail. On the whole, Greek design is essentially proportional, i.e., stable, depending for its harmony on the different but proportionate size of its units: C. R. Morey.

Generally speaking, in illustration little, but delicate, colour was employed. 'Greek colour is essentially local colour, i.e., colour used to pick out and emphasize form' (C. R. Morey). The illustrations covered the full page and formed a complete picture, but they lacked the deep emotion, the passion and the drama of life of Semitic art. By the third century A.D. 'Hellenistic painting had degenerated into graceful prettiness' (Runciman).

(2) *'Oriental', Semitic, or Syrian art*, its main centre being Antioch. This showed, to a certain extent, a search for truth. It was more realistic and dramatic, disregarding historical sequence. A dramatic energy combined with a mystical, austere spirit permeated the pictures. This lively and primitive manner, full of brisk movement and vividly depicted action—so noticeable, for instance, in the *Vienna Genesis* (see p. 85 f.)—is shown in a high degree in many of the best manuscripts of the tenth and eleventh centuries.

BYZANTINE ILLUMINATION

There was rarely a suggestion of perspective; instead, we find a 'vertical projection': the two parts of a scene are placed one above the other and landscape is reduced to a few schematic features. On the whole, it may be said that the 'Oriental' artist was inferior to the Hellenistic in accomplishment, and in the power of composition and logical arrangement. But he saw his subject swiftly in a comprehensive view, and conceived it simply in bold outline and mass. He did not labour a deliberate process, but gave a schematic rendering straight from perception. In Runciman's words, the Aramaean brought a new force—directness of vision and intensity of feeling.

An inferiority of skill in drawing and composition, and a want of variety in depicted attitudes and gesture, were compensated for by a love of apocryphal events, by a logical simplicity of composition, by a highly developed art of brilliant colouring—especially in the characteristic brightly coloured costumes—by a magnificent even exaggerated ornamentation, as well as by a profusion of purely decorative motifs, such as arcades surmounted by monsters, beasts, birds, vases, trees, plants, flowers, and even more so by interlaced borders and crosses.

The illustrations were mainly marginal (see p. 97 ff.); these seem to have been popular in Syria and Palestine. In Weitzmann's opinion, however, marginal illustration was not invented for Syrian book-illumination; indeed, this method of illustration did not and could not develop before the invention of the codex, though the miniature cycles, which are represented in these margins, go back to earlier archetypes, which were not marginal.

(3) *Monumental and Liturgical Elements*. Many Byzantine illuminations were largely influenced by the art of mosaic; indeed, they are but mosaics in little, and reproduce the usual accessories of such mosaics as are still to be seen in churches of the Byzantine style. To the influence of mosaics may probably be traced the stiffness of the forms; the majestic pose of the figures; perhaps, too, the depth and richness of the colouring. At the same time, there is a close parallel between Byzantine art of this kind and those formal liturgies and grave ceremonies which succeed by their very stateliness and remoteness from actuality in raising the mind to a plane of rapture and awe. See also section (5).

Indeed, this art at its best possessed a power of rendering spiritual values and of translating supernatural or natural majesty into terms of colour and line, which no other artistic system has ever approached. The main purpose of this art was theological, liturgical and dogmatic; profoundly anti-realistic, it preferred the static, solemn presentation of mysteries to the representation of events. It achieved its purpose by a deliberate subordination of naturalism to ideas, by the representation of arrested action, not violent movement; it aimed at dignity, not energy. Its personages are symbols of something greater than themselves; their formal outlines, their carefully folded draperies, enhance, like the vestments of priests, the hieratic effect. The static style sometimes appears actually in conjunction with the lively, dramatic manner as described under (2). In the representation of a martyrdom, for instance, the executioners are often animated figures going about their gruesome work with the utmost vigour, while the saint—a symbol of divine patience rather than the portrait of a living man—seems wrapped in another atmosphere than that of his persecutors.

(4) *New artistic influences*, which may be discerned in Byzantine art of the fourth period, *i.e.*, from the tenth century A.D. onwards. These were derived from Oriental sources, principally Persian. Eminent scholars, such as Runciman, have already pointed out that 'Mithraism, the Iranian-born religion in worship of the all-glorious Sun', or the Mazdaism from which it derived, had its own art, not prettily naturalistic like the Hellenistic, nor emotionally realistic like the Aramaean, but a symbolical art of pattern. It employed, indeed, a magnificent series of landscape, trees, hills and houses, arranged in flowing design, richly coloured and gracefully drawn, but pattern not composition is the basic intent.

This art, thus, did not aim at representation, but was rather based upon formal design, sometimes employing natural shapes as symbols, and in general using them as conventional parts in a system of geometrical ornaments. Persian art, writes C. R. Morey, may be naturalistic in detail, but it is always ornamental in composition; its effect on the illumination of the Eastern Empire was to introduce an absolute colour harmony, by which we mean one to which the forms are subordinated, and a rhythmic design, whereby the eye instead of resting on a stable unity is forced to move about the pattern by the alternation or recurrence of units that do not differ much in size or emphasis. See also further on.

These main elements make up Byzantine art.

(5) *Christianity completed the movement.* The Christian public, points out Runciman, demanded art with a direct emotional appeal rather than technical excellence. The Hellenistic artists, having exhausted every technical secret of their art, had a new problem to face, how to adapt their technique to the new world. The Oriental artist provided the ingredients for the solution of this problem. Thus, during the fourth century A.D. a new art arose, of which Constantinople became the main centre.

Origin of the Persian Trend. The origin of this artistic trend is uncertain: in the opinion of the great art-historian Strzygowski, it originated in the 'Altai-Iran corner', *i.e.*, the region between the Caspian and the Altai, where about the middle of the second century B.C. two 'racial influences' met, the nomadic Saka (Scythian tribe, speaking an Iranian dialect), and the nomadic East-Turki tribes, the nomadic life being naturally favourable to an art of geometrical ornament. The arrival of the Arabs, with the spread of Islam, secured a complete triumph for this Iranian-Turkish style.

Thus, according to Strzygowski, this 'Altai-Iran corner' should be regarded as the creative centre of the Islamic art, and not the southern Iranian territory of Persia, where the Sasanian dynasty arose. Furthermore, certain motifs suggested by the text of *Avesta* (see *The Hand-produced Book*) united with forms of decorative ornament, constituted a 'Mazdean symbolic art', which directly influenced the early Christian art.

In Herbert's opinion, it seems likely that this style may have been borrowed from the Arabs, whose civilization was more or less in touch with that of Byzantium from the seventh century onwards. But it must be admitted, he argues, that a scheme of decoration, out of which that now in question might conceivably have been evolved, appears at a still earlier date in Byzantine architecture, e.g., in the altar-screen and capitals at the church of S. Vitale, Ravenna.

Another eminent art-historian, Dalton, has suggested, instead, the following theory: (1) Some of the features characteristic of Persian art may have been already present in the art of ancient Mesopotamia, the tradition of which seems certainly to have survived in Syrian, i.e., North Mesopotamian, representation. (2) A definite Iranian influence may have penetrated northern Asia Minor long before the Christian era.

Such facts may in large measure explain certain influences underlying Syrian art between the fourth and sixth centuries A.D., without the need for supposing a fresh Iranian importation, suggested by Strzygowski. This is also hinted at by S. Runciman, in whose opinion the Iranian art of pattern and design was already influencing the Aramaean artists, and in some way compensated for their neglect of the Greek sense of composition. On the other hand, there is the probability that this new art-style may have been encountered by the numerous Christian communities in Persia, Armenia, and northern Iran.

The Persian artistic trend was essentially artificial; the colours were rarely naturalistic; there was a love of bright, daring, and invariably effective colours; elaborate borders were introduced wherever possible; the ornamental square 'head-pieces' (see p. 94 f.) became common, the colour and design of which have 'been aptly compared to that of fine Persian prayer-carpets' (O. M. Dalton): see, for instance, Fig. II-7, 20, 29, 39. The decorative art of Islam (see p. 133 ff.) carried out to their logical conclusion these ornamental principles, and attained a great mastery of geometrical and conventional design.

Thus there originated the first broad and quaint forms of that vast variety of ornament usually described as 'arabesque', consisting of flowers, foliage, and so on. Some of this conventional leaf-work seems to have developed from the earlier vine motifs, out of which exquisitely beautiful borders were subsequently designed. The influence of this Persian-Arabic art may be seen in the actual introduction of the Kufic script as an ornamental motif (see, for instance, the MS. Gr. 660 in the National Library at Paris), and may be traced, although fully assimilated, in more elaborate ornaments (as, for instance, in the MS. Suppl. Gr. 75 in the National Library at Paris). See, e.g., K. Erdmann, 'Arabische Schriftzeichen in d. Abendl. Kunst d. Mittelalt.' Abhandlung. d. Akad. d. Wiss. u.d. Lit., Wiesbaden, 1953.

G. Mathew emphasizes this influence of Islamic art upon Byzantine painting. It is becoming increasingly clear—he writes—how very closely Byzantine and Islamic art forms were interwoven. From their beginnings they had been united in common sources and from the ninth to the twelfth century Islamic art possessed some of the prestige of fashion at Constantinople. It was perhaps considered novel and bizarre and yet was closely enough allied to Byzantine art to be intelligible. The Islamic-Byzantine relationship, in Mathew's opinion, is best illustrated by the sporadic use just referred to of Kufic script in Byzantine decoration.

HISTORICAL IMPORTANCE OF BYZANTINE ART

While in the West the barbarian invasions more or less destroyed the Graeco-Roman culture, Byzantine art formed a sort of bridge uniting the ancient art of Egypt and Greece with the medieval art of Western Europe, and the art of the East with that of the West. Having received various elements from Hellenistic Alexandria, from Syrian Antioch, from Ephesus, and numerous other important art centres, Constantinople created a syncretistic art, which was handed on to Italy and to the West generally.

Indeed, Byzantine influences may be seen, for instance, in frescoes and mosaics (already referred to) of Roman churches of early medieval times (fifth to eighth centuries A.D.); some specimens are in pure Byzantine style, some even containing Greek inscriptions, others are 'Byzantinizing'; some obviously were done by Byzantine artists, others perhaps by local schools of art. We refer here to the Roman frescoes of S. Maria Antiqua, of the churches of S. Saba, S. Maria in Via Lata, S. Maria in Cosmedin, S. Clemente, S. Martino ai Monti, and S. Prassede, and others, mainly belonging to the eighth century A.D. Of the mosaics belonging to an earlier period, it will suffice to mention those of the apses of SS. Cosma e Damiano (of the time of Felix IV, 526–30), of S. Lorenzo fuori le Mura (of the period of Pope Pelagius, 578–90), and of S. Agnese fuori le Mura (625–38). See also p. 68 f. and *passim*.

Thus, already in the sixth to the eighth centuries, but more particularly in the tenth to the thirteenth centuries, Italy and other countries borrowed artists from Constantinople, and these carried Byzantine style and technique to distant places, so that Byzantine art lost its purely local significance as well as its definite geographical position and became general throughout the greater part of Europe.

It was, for instance, partly out of Byzantine richness that there came those intricate ornaments—known as 'tessellated' and recalling the mosaic pattern—of interlaced fretwork, or twining branches of gold or white, delineated over a background of variegated colours; this style became almost general in Western Europe. The relationship—if there was one—between this and the ornamental style of the Irish school of illumination is uncertain: see the section on the Hiberno-Saxon style.

As to the importance of Byzantine book-illumination, it will suffice to note the opinion of Sir Steven Runciman: it is in the manuscripts that the continuity of Hellenistic influence is seen and through the manuscripts that it made itself felt, for mosaic and fresco artists largely relied for their inspiration on thin, small and easily portable miniatures.

It goes without saying that Byzantine art is not without blemish. Indeed, as an

II-1. Early West-Christian Art. *a*, One of the earliest representations of Jesus Christ (youthful and beardless). Gilded glass, showing raising of Lazarus from the dead. *b*, Earliest representation of the Holy Eucharist (Priscilla Catacombs, second century A.D.). *c*, Earliest representation of the story of the virtuous Susanna (Peter and Marcellino Catacombs, Rome, third century A.D.). *d*, Christ in Glory: Mosaics in the apse of the church of S. Pudenziana.

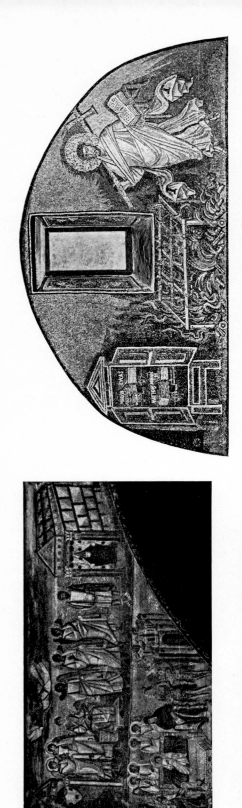

II–2. Mosaic-art in early Italian churches. *a*, Part of the mosaics of the Triumphal Arch in the church of S. Maria Maggiore, Rome. *b*, S. Lawrence and a book-shrine in the fifth-century mosaics *mausoleum* of Galla Placidia, Ravenna. *c*, The Three Magi: mosaics in S. Apollinare Nuovo, Ravenna. *d*, The Sacrifice of Isaac: sixth-century mosaics in the church of S. Vitale, Ravenna.

II–3. *a*, *Quedlinburg Itala Fragment*. *b*, Sixth-century A.D. fragment with primitive Christian drawing and initial: S. Jerome, *Tractatus in librum Psalmorum* (National Library at Paris, *Lat. 2235*, fol. 12 r). *c*, *S. Augustine Gospels* (fol. 129 b): S. Luke and his symbol and scenes from the life of Christ. *d*, *Ashburnham Pentateuch*: Noah's Ark after the Deluge.

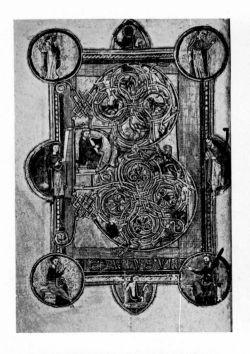

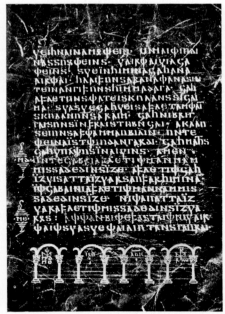

II–4. *a, S. Augustine Psalter:* initial B representing King David. *b, Codex Brixianus: Canon Table. c,* Page from *Codex Argentus:* this beautiful Gothic manuscript, preserved at Uppsala (Sweden), contains 187 pages written in silver and gold on purple parchment. *d, Cotton Genesis:* Creation of Eve.

II–5. a, *Vienna Genesis*, Pict. 14: Rebecca at the well; Rebecca tells her parents of her adventure (*Gen.*, xxiv, 23–31.). b, *Rossano Gospels*, fol. 121 *r*: S. Mark.

II–6. *a, Rossano Gospels,* fol. 8 *r*: Christ before Pilate (upper zone) and Judas returning the thirty pieces and hanging himself (lower zone). *b, Codex Sinopensis*: Christ healing the two blind men; on the tribunes, David (on the left) and Isaiah.

II–7. Headpieces and Initials. *a*, Beginning of *S. John's Gospel* (Bodleian Library, *MS. Misc. Graec. 307*: *Auct. T. inf. II. 7*). *b*, Headpiece and initial of *S. Luke's Gospel* (Walters Art Gallery, *MS. 10. 528*): on the right, interesting representation of a pelican (in the curious shape of a peacock) ripping open her breast to feed her brood or to resuscitate them to life (see *Physiologus*)—symbol of Christ. *c*, Headpiece to *S. Matthew* (*Vat. Gr. 361*, fol. 15 r). *d*, Headpiece and initial to *S. Matthew* (*Urb. Gr. 2*, fol. 21 r).

II–8. The *Great Bible* (*Vat. Reg. Gr. 1*). *a*, Fol. 450 *v* : 2 *Macc.,* vi. 18–vii. 42 : King Antiochus, the scribe Eleazar, and the story of the Mother and her seven Sons. *b*, Fol. 461 *v* : *Job,* ii. 11 : Job, his wife and his three friends.

II–9. *a, Cod. Plut. 5. 9*
(*Prophets*), fol. 128 *v* :
messianic prophecy ; the
prophet Jeremiah pointing
at Christ. *b, Cod. Plut. 5. 38*
(*Old Testament*), fol. 6 *r* :
four zones, representing (1)
the creation of the animals ;
(2) the creation of Eve,
Eve and Serpent, Eve and
Adam ; (3) Eve hands the
apple to Adam ; Eve,
Adam, and the fig-tree ;
(4) God calls Adam and
Eve to account ; the
expulsion from Paradise ;
Adam and Eve as
labourers.

II-10. Frontispiece (representing S. Mark on golden background) and first page of *S. Mark* (National Library at Paris, *Gr. 70*, folios 113 *v* and 114 *r*).

II-11. 'Aristocratic' Psalters. a, Vat. Pal. Gr. 381, fol. 381 v. b, Morey's comparison of heads from the Paris Psalter (c), the Joshua Roll (a), and S. Maria Antica (b). c, Isaiah's Prayer in Paris Psalter (fol. 435 r).

II–12. *Paris Psalter* (fol. 1 *v*) : David with the harp, inspired by Melody.

II-13. *Khludoff Psalter,* fol. 147 *v*: David playing the harp.

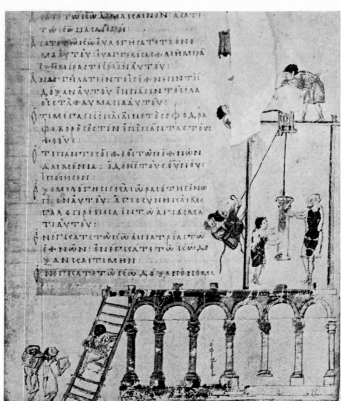

II–14. 'Monastic'
Psalters. *a, Paris Cod.
Gr. 20,* fol. 4 *r* :
Construction of the
Temple (see *Psalm* xcv,
1). *b, Barberini Psalter,*
fol. 40 *v* : David playing
the harp (*Psalm* xxvii).

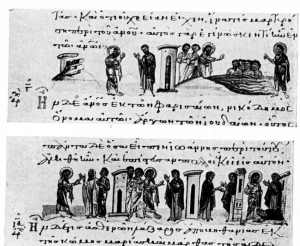

II–15. Gospel-books. *a, Vat. Gr. 1156,* fol. *252 v. b, Plut. 6. 23,* fol. *172 r* (upper part)—*S. John ii, 23–iii, 2*—and fol. *192 r* (lower part)—*S. John,* x, 40–xi, 3. *c, Vat. Urb. Gr. 2,* Nativity. *d, idem,* fol. *19 v*: Christ, between Charity and Justice, blessing the Emperors Alexios (1081–1118) and Joannes Comnenos (1118–1143).

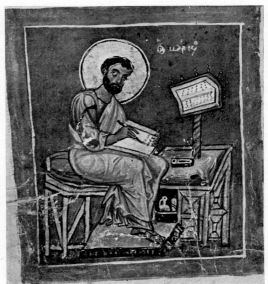

II–16. S. Mark: *a,* Walters Art Gallery, *MS. 530 a;* early eleventh century. *b, Rylands Gr. MS. 15,* fol. 219 *v;* eleventh or twelfth century. *c,* Walters Art Gallery, *MS. 527,* fol. 1 *v;* early twelfth century. *d, ibidem, MS. 530 e;* twelfth century.

II–17. *a*, Marciana Library, *MS. Gr. 1. 8 (1397)*, fol. 182 *v* : S. Luke writing his Gospel; above, Annunciation. *b*, National Library at Naples, formerly *Vienna Gr. 9 (Vindob. Suppl. Gr. 102)*; written by Constantine Bischianites, in 1192; fol. 77 *r* : S. Luke. *c*, Walters Art Gallery, *MS. 530 d*; twelfth century: S. Matthew. *d, ibidem, MS. 530 g*; fourteenth century: S. John.

II–18. S. John with S. Prochorus; S. James. *a,* Pierpont Morgan Library, *M. 748,* fol. 151 *v*: S. John with S. Prochorus. *b, Plut. 6. 23,* fol. 167 *v*: S. John, inspired by God (represented by a hand), dictates to his disciple S. Prochorus, who is writing. *c,* Similar composition in a *Gospel-book* at Naples, formerly *Vienna Gr. 3 (Vindob. Suppl. Gr. 6),* fol. 316 *v. d,* Bodleian Library, *MS. Can. Gr. 110,* fol. 106 *v*: S. James.

II–19. *a*, Walters Art Gallery, *MS. 524*: S. James preaching. *b*, Bodleian Library, *MS. Auct. I. inf. 1. 10*, fol. 310 *r*: S. Jude (the text is *Third Epistle of S. John*, verses 14–15). *c*, Walters Art Gallery, *MS. 530 c*: S. Paul, S. Peter, and the four Evangelists. *d, ibidem, MS. 530 b* (detached leaf from a Psalter): Moses on Mt. Sinai.

II–20. Later Gospels. *a, Vat. Gr. 1158,* fol. *4 v* : Canon Table. *b,* Pierpont Morgan Library, *M. 692,* fol. *214 r* : Symeon Stylites (most famous Syrian saint of the early Church, *c.* 390–459). *c,* Walters Art Gallery, *MS. 531* (fourteenth century); fol. *1 v* : Raising of Lazarus. *d,* The same collection, *MS. 530 g, v* (fourteenth century): Christ appearing to the disciples.

II-21. *a–c*, S. Mark and S. Luke in thirteenth- and fourteenth-centuries Gospels, all three being preserved in the Walters Art Gallery: *a*, MS. *523* (S. Mark); *b*, MS. *525* (S. Mark); *c*, MS. *530 f* (S. Luke). *d*, S. John of Damascus, *Sacra parallela* (Paris, *Gr. 923*), fol. 80 *r*.

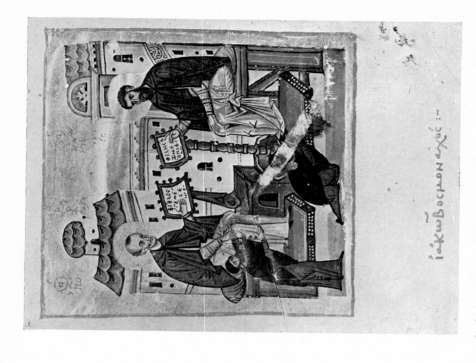

II–22. *Homilies.* *a,* National Library at Paris, *Gr. 510,* copy of the *Homilies* by S. Gregory of Nazianzus; by far the most rich in illuminations; here, fol. 165 *v*: scenes from Christ's life. *b,* The same collection, *Gr. 1208*; copy of *Homilies* by Jacobus Monachus of Kokkinobaphos; fol. 1 *v.*

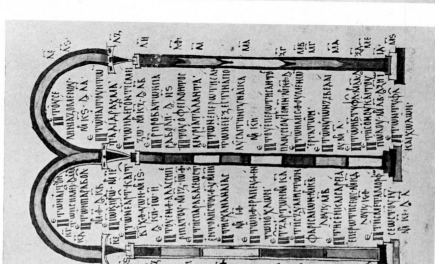

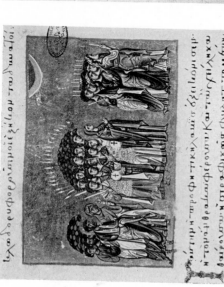

II-23. a, *Vat. Gr. 1162* (*Homilies by Jacobus Monachus*), fol. 64 r. b, *Vat. Gr. 1613* (*Menologium of Basil II*): Adoration of the Magi. c, *Vat. Gr. 354* (*Klimax, Spiritual Ladder*), fol. 15 r. d, *Melissenda Psalter*, Fol. 206 r.

II-24. *Coislin 79*. This copy, made in the second half of the eleventh century, perhaps for Emperor Michael VI, was presented to his successor Nicephoros III Botaneiates, Emperor 1078–1081, and later belonged to the Imperial Library in Constantinople. Fol. 2 *v*, here reproduced, represents Nicephoros between S. Chrysostom and S. Michael. The other three miniatures of folios 1–2 represent (1) Nicephoros and monk Saba; (2) Nicephoros and Empress Mary; (3) Nicephoros and high dignitaries.

II-25. *Menologia. a, Vat. Gr. 1613 (Menologium of Basil II)*, fol. 320 *r. b,* State
Historical Museum, Moscow, *Sin. Gr. No. 183 (Menologium),* fol. 239 *r:*
Annunciation. *c,* Walters Art Gallery, *MS. 521 (Imperial Menologium* for
January), fol. 202 *v.*

II–26. *a,* National Library at Paris, *Gr. 2144* (Hippocrates: paper-manuscript copied for Grand-Duke Alexios Apocaucos, d. 1345), fol. 10 *v. b, MS. Lincoln College Gr. 35 (Typikon),* fol. 8 *r. c,* National Library at Paris, *Gr. 1242; de luxe* copy of Emperor John VI Cantacuzen's (1347–1354) theological works, produced 1371–1375 in the monastery of S. Anastasia on Mt. Athos; here, fol. 92 *v*: Transfiguration of Christ between Moses and Elia, with Saints Peter, James, and John, at the bottom. *d, Vat. Gr. 1208;* fol. 4 *v.*

II–27. *a,* Walters Art Gallery, *MS.
534 (Horologion),* fol. 85 *v:* David
prostrates himself before Nathan.
b, Vat. Lat. 5974 (*Grottaferrata
Gospels*), fol. 10 *v:* headpiece
(containing the 'portrait' of S.
Matthew), initial, and beginning of
S. Matthew's Gospel.

c, Bodleian Library, *MS. Gr. Th.f. 1*
fol. 3 *v:* Transfiguration of Christ.
d, Walters Art Gallery, *MS. 526
(Athos Gospel),* fol. 201 *v.*
e, Walters Art Gallery, *MS. 535
(Cyprus Lectionary),* fol. 4 *r.*

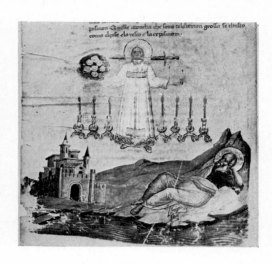

II–28. *a, Vat. Gr. 2138 (Capua Evangelistarium)*, fol. 16 *r. b*, Walters Art Gallery, *MS. 335* (*Commentary on the Apocalypse*), fol. 1 *r. c–d*, Earliest Glagolithic codices: *c,* Portion of page from *Codex Marianus* (formerly in the S. Mary monastery on Mt. Athos, and now in Moscow); *d, Codex Zographensis* (formerly in the Zographu monastery on Mt. Athos, and now in Leningrad, *Cod. Glag. 1*), fol. 43 *v.*

II–29. Early Russian Illumination. *a, Izborniki* ('Collected Treatises') *of Sviatoslav* (former Moscow Synodal Library, *MS. 30*), of the years 1073 and 1076, portion of fol. 251 *r. b, Miroslav Gospels,* of the twelfth century, fol. 70 *r. c, Pandects of Monk Antioch* of the eleventh century; beginning of the MS. *d,* Initial *Π* (= P) from *MS. 235* (a *Psalter*) of former Synodal Library, of 1296.

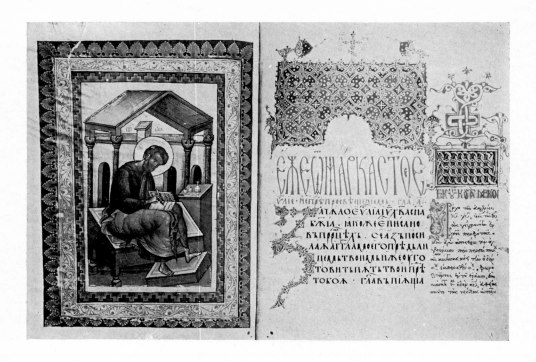

II-30. *Greek-Slavonic Gospels* (Bodleian Library, *MS. Can. Gr. 122*); above, fol. 89 *v*–90 *r* (S. Mark and the first page of his Gospel); below, fol. 144 *v*–145 *r* (S. Luke and the first page of his Gospel).

II–31. *Rabbūlā Gospels,* fol. 13 *r*: magnificent full-page composition in two zones. Upper zone, Crucifixion; Lower zone, Resurrection of Christ (on the left, the Maries at the Tomb; on the right, Christ appears to them.).

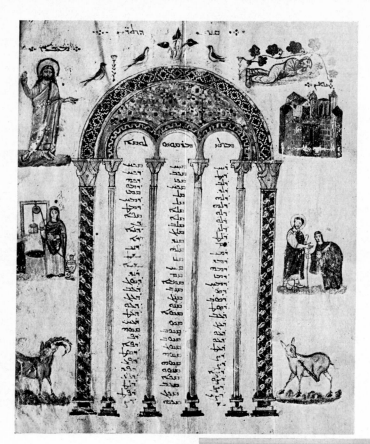

II–32. Syriac Illumination.
a, Rabbūlā Gospels, fol. *6 r*:
Eusebian Canon Table under
a beautifully decorated arch
with internal columns; above
the arch, birds; to the right and
left, Biblical scenes, figures
and animals. *b,* Pierpont
Morgan Library, *M. 774*:
S. Luke.

II–33. Armenian Illumination.
a, Queen Mlqé Gospels, fol. 3 *v* :
Canon Table. *b, Adrianople
Gospels,* A.D. 1007 (Venice,
No. 887), fol. 6 *v* : SS. Matthew
and Mark.

II–34. Armenian Illumination. *a–b, Queen Mlqé Gospels,* folios 4 *r* (Ascension) and 5 *v* (S. Luke). *c, Adrianople Gospels,* fol. 8 *r* (Donor: John Protospatharios). *d, Venice Gospels, N. 1635;* fol. 5 *v* (Canon Table).

II-35. Armenian Illumination. *Trebizond Gospels,* folios 7 *v* (Canon Table), 1 *r* (Annunciation), and 3 *v* (the Four Evangelists).

II-36. Armenian Illumination. *a, Gospels of the Translators*: SS. Mark and Luke. *b, Kirakos Gospels,* fol. 270 *v*: SS. John and Prochorus. *c, Freer Gospels* (Freer Gallery, *32. 18*), pages 8–9: Mary with Child, Joseph, and an angel, in Bethlehem (*S. Matthew,* ii. 11); the Three Magi (the same passage).

II–37. Armenian
Illumination. *a,* Pierpont
Morgan Library,
M. 740 : Canon Table.
b, Walters Art Gallery,
MS. 539 (Gospels,
written in 1262 at
Hromkla, and
illuminated by T'oros
Roslin), fol. 163 *r* :
Transfiguration.

II–38. Armenian Illumination. *a*, Walters Art Gallery, *MS. 538*, fol. 4 *v*: Epistle of Eusebius. *b*, Armenian Patriarcate at Jerusalem, *No. 2660*, fol. 1 *v*: also Epistle of Eusebius. *c*, *MS. 538*, fol. 12 *v*: Dedicatory page. *d*, *Keran Gospels* (Armenian Patriarcate at Jerusalem, *No. 2563*), fol. 362 *v*: Crucifixion.

II–39. Armenian Illumination. *a*, Armenian Patriarcate at Jerusalem, *No. 2568*, fol. 295 *v*: Washing of the Feet. *b*, The same collection, *No, 2566*, fol. 93 *r*: first page of *S. Mark*. *c*, The same collection, *No. 1973*: Nativity. *d*, Venice, *No. 151 (134)*, fol. 268 *r*: first page of *S. John*.

II-40. Coptic Illumination. *a*, Naples, *MS. I. B. 18*, fol. 4 *v*: pen-drawing depicting Job and his three daughters. *b*, Pierpont Morgan Library, *M. 612*, fol. 1 *v*: the Nursing Madonna. *c*, Paris, *Copte 13–48*: Transfiguration of Christ between Moses and Elia with Saints Peter, James, and John, at the bottom (*S. Matthew*, xvii. 1–13).

eminent scholar points out, the miniatures, though classical in style, are not only dull and flat in colouring, but the whole form of the figures of the saints or other personages represented is constrained and unprepossessing. One monotonous, mesmerizing rhythm fills whole manuscripts—no secondary motifs weaken their fanatical single-mindedness. There is no articulation in the long rows of saints or martyrs to arrest our eyes, and the solemn, silent figures, austere and gaunt, with their motionless faces and stiff garments, are all that men tired of rational human intellect could provide. The invisible, the mysterious, the immaterial, the magical, the irrational were their need. The means employed for achieving mystical expression are sometimes so complex and sophisticated that only men of high sensibility could discern and appreciate them.

CHRYSOGRAPHY

Court life at Byzantium was characterized by pomp and ostentatious splendour of all kinds, and this taste for the luxurious found expression in the production of sumptuous manuscripts.

It may be said that medieval illumination began with gold writing, or *chryso-graphy*, of Byzantine MSS., though it is known that gold was used as a writing fluid at a much earlier period (see, for instance, Chapter I). Manuscripts produced for presentation to imperial persons were often written in gold or silver inks, in beautiful uncials, on leaves of vellum stained with a rose-coloured purple dye. The *codex purpureus* ('purple codex'), the *codex aureus* ('golden codex'), the *codex argenteus* ('silver codex'), were early imitated in the West, and books of this kind were written for Charlemagne and other Western monarchs. The finest purple colour, the 'Tyrian' purple, derived from *murex*, was employed for this purpose, especially in the Byzantine MSS. Indeed, it was by his materials that the Byzantine artist achieved the requisite sumptuousness. Even in his panel-painting he would use a background of gold: Runciman.

In Dr. Regensburger's opinion, expressed orally, the rich employment of gold may have a mystic meaning, gold representing the synthesis, the unity of all colours, as heaven is the unity of created things. The golden background may attempt to express the conception that the scene does not occur on earth, but in heaven.

The production of Christian luxurious manuscripts seems to have begun in the third century. Bishop Theonas, writing to Lucian, Diocletian's chamberlain (late third century A.D.), mentions *in purpureis membranis et litteris aureis totos codices*; and early in the fourth century, Julius Capitolinus puts into the possession of the young emperor Maximinus *libros Homericos omnes purpureos . . . aureis literis scriptos* (books of Homer written in gold on purple vellum).

Blue or violet vellum with gold and silver writing was generally used for diplomas, for official documents of the Byzantine emperors, and for their official letters to the Arab courts in Baghdād and Cordova. This combination of blue and yellow (or gold) was later borrowed for Moslem book-illumination. Its origin has been sought in more eastern regions, but eminent scholars have pointed out that blue and yellow were the favourite colours in ancient Mesopotamia as well as in Egypt (lapis-lazuli in gold setting).

One of the main purposes of luxurious book-production in the Byzantine Empire was to preserve copies of the Holy Scripture, of which some extremely valuable specimens are extant. Manuscripts in silver lettering are even rarer than manuscripts in gold. This may be due to the fact that it was costly to stain the vellum purple in order to display the white metal, whereas manuscripts in gold lettering could be executed on white as well as on purple grounds.

Incidentally, this magnificence was condemned by the Fathers: S. Jerome, in his preface to the *Book of Job* and in his *Letterae familiares*, xviii (to Eustochium) mentions with disapproval writing with gold or silver on purple vellum ('burdens rather than books'); S. Chrysostom also condemns such luxurious writing. For Hebrew chrysography see p. 65.

Most of the large libraries possess manuscripts written in gold, but they belong mainly to the Carolingian period. In Western Christianity very early examples, however, are: *Codex Palatinus* attributed to the fifth century A.D.— apparently the earliest preserved purple Gospels of the *Vetus Latina* (see *The Hand-produced Book*, Fig. VII-2); *Codex Sarzanensis*, also a Gospel-book of the early sixth century (see *The Hand-produced Book*, Fig. VII-3); *Codex Brixianus*, a Gospel-book of the first half of the sixth century (see *The Hand-produced Book*, Fig. II-13), all three containing Gospels of the *Vetus Latina* (*The Hand-produced Book*, p. 283 ff.). See also p. 72 and Fig. II-4*b*.

Of Eastern MSS. written in gold, the Greek *Codex Sinopensis* (see p. 89), of the first half of the sixth century, and *Codex Rossanensis*, in part (see p. 87 f.), are the most important. A later *Gospel-book* (of the ninth century), preserved in the Marciana Library, Venice (*MS. Gr. I, 8: 1397*), contains the *Epistle* of Eusebius and the *Gospel of S. Matthew* written in gold. The most famous codices written in silver are the Gothic *Codex Argenteus* of Upsala (Fig. II-4*c*), the Greek *Vienna Genesis* (see p. 85 f.), and *Codex Rossanensis*, in part (see p. 87 f.).

Noteworthy also are the seventh-century Greek Psalter preserved at Zurich, and the following three Latin uncial codices belonging to the sixth century: the *Psalter of S. Germain* (who died in 576), at Paris; the *Metz Gospels*, also at Paris; and the *Naples Gospels*, at Vienna. Writing in silver appears to have ceased contemporaneously with the disuse of stained vellum.

Gold Grounds

From chrysography, the introduction of entirely gold grounds, with the characters traced in black ink, seems to have been the main result of the natural progress of Byzantine luxury. These gold backgrounds were probably laid before the painting-in of the figures was completed. Firstly, a red or crimson priming was applied; the designs were then sketched with a fine brush or pen, often in a shade of brown which suggests the use of diluted ink; and after the painting of the gold background, the figures were finished by the application of successive coats of colour, the first being so thin that the outline drawing beneath shows through.

The colours employed by the Byzantine and other East Christian illuminators are more liable to flake off than those used in medieval Western Europe (where a rougher vellum was employed, the surface being sometimes intentionally roughened); also, the gold employed was inferior, in both adhesive power and brilliance, to that of the West-European codices of the thirteenth century.

Ultramarine

As to the blue colour, it was not the Egyptian blue employed by Roman painters, but—as Dalton has pointed out—an ultramarine prepared from lapis lazuli by a crude washing process, and apparently, in the generality of MSS., not improved.

A remarkable exception, however, the *Melisenda Psalter* (see p. 107 f.) provides the earliest example of a really fine ultramarine yet known. On the whole, the Byzantine ultramarine did not share in the changes made in the West (except Ireland).

DEVELOPMENT OF BYZANTINE ILLUMINATION

What has been said about Byzantine art in general concerns especially the art of illumination. Indeed, the Greeks gave Christian art its vertebrate system, but they failed to give it a heart, while the Semitic spirit gave the new arts fire and mystery: Dalton. It has already been mentioned that the East Christian art originated probably in the late fourth and the fifth centuries A.D. as a mixed art containing Hellenistic and Oriental elements. We have seen that each of these main elements was too strong to give way to the other, and that the church was moved to demand a compromise. 'This uneasy alliance endured down to the last years of the Byzantine Empire.' For a time, however, 'The two styles existed side by side, each checking the faults of the other' (Runciman).

Formative Period (Fourth-Fifth Centuries A.D.)

It is uncertain (see also p. 74 ff.) whether this compromise was achieved in any particular place; there is no evidence to suggest in which of the main artistic and cultural centres of the Byzantine Empire it was realized, or whether tentative movements were made simultaneously in various centres, such as Alexandria, Antioch, Ephesus, and Constantinople. In addition, the date of the consummation is uncertain, but it has been suggested that by the reign of Justinian (A.D. 527-65)—'perhaps the greatest individual patron in the whole story of art' (D. Talbot Rice)—the new, definitely Christian art was already in existence. The climax of the new style, argues Talbot Rice, was reached in Justinian's great cathedral of Sancta Sophia, which was to become not only the principal church of Christianity, but also the very centre of the cultured universe. It has survived to this day, though it was converted to the service of Islam soon after the Turkish conquest of Constantinople (1453). It is still not only the greatest monument of Byzantine art, but perhaps also the greatest monument of Christian art. Justinian, when he entered it, on its completion, exclaimed in awe, 'Glory be to God, who has found me worthy to finish so great a work, and to excel thee, O Solomon.' Solomon's temple has not survived. But no other faith—concludes Talbot Rice— no other benefactor, has ever been responsible for a structure that can in beauty, in spatial conception, or in its religious atmosphere, surpass the Church of the Holy Wisdom at Constantinople.

It must, however, be emphasized that the syncretistic Syro-Hellenistic art was not employed on uniform lines: the proportion of the main elements, belonging respectively to the two chief components, varied geographically, chronologically, and according to literary *genre*. In the productions of the Alexandrian school, which influenced the Constantinople school, the Hellenistic elements predominated; in those of the Antioch school, the Syrian elements were the stronger. Further to the East—especially in the great monasteries of Eastern Christianity, which were important centres of culture, learning and art, and constituted the great missionary force of early Christianity—the Oriental elements always predominated.

EARLIEST MANUSCRIPTS

Very few early Byzantine manuscripts have come down to us. In *The Hand-produced Book* (p. 240 and *passim*) various causes of book-destruction have been mentioned. Here a few more may be added in the case of Byzantium: its Senate House and its great church of Sancta Sophia, with all their treasures and their libraries, were twice burnt down before the end of the sixth century; numerous illuminated codices were destroyed by the Iconoclasts in the wholesale destruction of sacred images and pictures, which lasted for over 125 years (717–843): see p. 91 f.; Constantinople was twice sacked (in 1204, during the Latin occupation of the city, and in 1453, the year of its capture by the Turks), and great havoc was made of its libraries.

Cotton Genesis (British Museum, *Otho. B. vi*)—Fig. II-4*d*

One of the most lamentable sights in the Manuscript Department of the British Museum is that of the charred remains of many manuscripts of the greatest value which were burnt in the fire among Sir R. Cotton's books in 1731: Kenyon. Perhaps the most valuable of all the volumes then destroyed was the so-called *Cotton Genesis*—containing in its original state the Septuagint version of *Genesis*; the text was written in fifth-century uncials. The volume was brought from Philippi, in Macedonia, by two Greek bishops, who presented it to King Henry the Eighth, informing him that according to tradition it had belonged to Origen. Queen Elizabeth gave the book to Sir John Fortescue (her preceptor in Greek), who placed it in Sir Robert Cotton's Library.

This codex, commonly assigned to the fifth century A.D., was adorned with 250 curious paintings in water-colours 'in a manner evidently derived directly from the ancient Greek style of painting' (Kenyon). The miniatures, of the same width as the text, were placed either above or below it, in some instances two on a page, with or without a few lines of text between them. Only twenty-one fragmentary pictures escaped the fire at Ashburnham House: 150 pieces, now inlaid on paper leaves, are preserved in the British Museum, and some are in the Baptist College, at Bristol. The miniatures are enclosed in plain banded borders of red, black, and white or pale yellow.

The backgrounds were richly coloured, generally blue, and finely executed in a classical style, similar to those of the best pictures in the *Ambrosian Iliad* or the *Vatican Virgil*: see p. 33 f. and 37 ff. The colours were harmonious, the figures, beautiful and in rich draperies, were well drawn and modelled, and the landscapes —as seen, for instance, in the preserved fragment of Lot receiving the Angels (fol. 26b)—were treated naturalistically, in the Alexandrian manner. On the whole, it may be assumed that the prototype of this manuscript was a product of the Alexandrian Hellenistic style, but the present copy may perhaps be assigned to Constantinople. We see here, emphasizes Prof. D. Talbot Rice, the first instance of the use of thin gold lines to pick out the high-lights on the costumes, a custom which becomes very common in later Byzantine painting. It gives an effect akin to that obtained by the gold partitions of a cloisonné enamel.

Some of the designs of the *Cotton Genesis* miniatures recur in later representations of scenes from *Genesis*; for instance, in the S. Marco mosaics, at Venice.

In 1618 Cotton lent the MS. to Peiresc (see p. 56), for whom many of the pictures were copied; unfortunately only two of the copies are preserved (National Library at Paris, *fr. 9350*, fols. 31–2).

Weitzmann has suggested that the miniatures of the *Grandval Bible* (British Museum, *Add. MS. 10546*), and also of a twelfth-century copy (preserved in the Rudolfinum Museum, Klagenfurt) of an illustrated Middle-High-German Biblical version in rhyme written in the eleventh century, are based on early Christian models related—through Latin intermediaries—to that of the *Cotton Genesis*.

Vienna Genesis (Fig. II-5a)

Several specimens of interesting paintings appear in the *Vienna Genesis* (*Vindobon. Theol. Gr. 31*); this codex is in an excellent state of preservation, and has long been one of the most famous of Early Christian MSS. It is executed upon dull purple-stained vellum, and consists of twenty-six leaves (*i.e.*, fifty-two pages), the first twenty-four of which contain fragments of *Genesis* and are adorned with forty-eight fine pictures (one on each page) in water-colours.

Some pictures are divided into two compartments, one above the other, without dividing line except for a strip of colour, representing the ground of the upper picture. Some pictures have a red rectangular frame. Some contain backgrounds, which either are required for the comprehension of the subject, or—in a few instances—serve to heighten the pictorial effect (in which case the background is of greyish-blue colour).

The text, in silver uncials, was added later; it is written above the miniatures: the scribe seems to have aimed merely at supplying a continuous narrative to explain the illustrations. The suggestion has, therefore, been made that the codex was originally a sumptuous Bible picture-book, and that we have here the sole representative of a once large class of book-production.

The codex has been in the National Library (formerly the Imperial Library) at Vienna since the seventeenth century, but very little is known of its previous history; according to some scholars it had previously been in Italy.

The miniatures lack the charm of the *Cotton Genesis*; the drawing is crude (often grotesque), the figures are stiff and with absurd proportions, the features are coarsely marked, the colouring inharmonious, but the scenes are represented with such extraordinary freshness and vivacity that 'they display a positive genius for the direct telling of a story. Never was artist more "literary" than the illustrator of this book. The telling of Bible history, not the production of beauty, was his aim . . .' (J. A. Herbert).

The *Vienna Genesis* is the earliest manuscript which uses persistently the 'continuous' treatment (already employed in classical times: it appears, for instance, in the Laocoon scene of the *Vatican Virgil*); this style became very popular in the Middle Ages. With this method, the picture contains a representation divided into successive scenes representing successive moments in a story.

The style, if naturalistic, is archaic: there are Hellenistic personifications—such as that, in two miniatures, of a half-draped nymph, of distinctly classical type, at a spring (see the picture of Rebecca at the Well, Fig. II-5a)—and other classical survivals. On the other hand, Oriental influence is obvious from the vivid realism of the figures and the lively method of narration and Byzantine influence may be recognized in many details of costume and ceremonial; nevertheless the style of these pictures has very little in common with the style of the fully-developed Byzantine miniatures.

The manuscript has been assigned to every region of the early Christian world except Greece, and to the fourth, the fifth, and the sixth centuries. However, North Syrian and East Anatolian, as well as Ravennate, influences are marked. According to some scholars, the work of several hands is clearly discernible, some Hellenistic, some Oriental in style; but Wulff's suggestion that this codex should be assigned to a Constantinople Palatine school (which produced such sumptuous volumes for use as Imperial gifts) is most tempting, especially in view of the representation of the herald, which is unquestionably in Byzantine style. The early sixth century A.D. is the most likely date.

Some authorities suggest that the *Vienna Genesis*, the *Rossano Gospels*, and the *Codex Sinopensis* not only belong to the same class of luxurious codices, but have such striking resemblances that all three of them should be assigned to the same period and the same locality. While, indeed, the period—early sixth century—is more or less agreed to, there is no agreement as to the provenance.

Vienna Genesis, fol. XV, 31. Upper row, left-hand scene: *Gen.* XXXIX, 9–13—Potiphar's wife tempting Joseph; to the right: Joseph looking back; women of Potiphar's household. Lower row: women of Potiphar's household in various occupations, and two trees.

Codex Rossanensis (Fig. II-5b and 6a)

Related to the *Vienna Genesis*, but indicating the growing influence of the
Oriental style, is the *Rossano Gospel-book*—preserved in Rossano Cathedral,
Calabria (Italy)—of which only about half survives, containing 188 sheets.

Rossano has a curious history; it long maintained its Byzantine character; the
Greek language and rite were used there till the fifteenth century; on Palm Sunday
the Gospel was read in Greek down to the middle of the eighteenth century.

The codex has been assigned to the fifth or sixth centuries A.D. According to
Dalton it cannot be later than A.D. 500. Like the Vienna codex, it is written—
except the opening lines of each Gospel, which are in gold—in silver uncials on a
background of pure purple vellum. The text contains nearly the whole of the
first two Gospels.

Fifteen miniatures are preserved; the portrait of S. Mark, a full-page miniature,
is prefixed to his Gospel; all the other miniatures are at the beginning of the MS.
The miniature of S. Mark was in certain respects the prototype of the Evangelist-
portraits which were so popular in medieval illumination, but in certain details the
Rossano miniature is unusual. S. Mark sits on a sort of basket-work arm-chair (his
implements on a table beside him) and writes his Gospel on a roll spread over his
knees; a nun-like woman, perhaps a personification of Divine Wisdom, stands
over him and dictates to him; in Western illumination her place is taken by the
emblem of the Evangelist. The unusual architectural setting consists of a semi-
circular shell-pediment (coloured blue, pink, and gold, in strips radiating fan-wise
from the centre), flanked by sharp-pointed gables terminating in gold discs, and
rests on an entablature supported by two pillars, Fig. II-5b.

There are, as very early examples of purely decorative pages, a decorative
frontispiece to the Tables of Canons, and an ornamental border framing the first
page of the *Epistle* from Eusebius to Carpianus; the text is surrounded by a
rectangular frame of gold, bounded by black lines, with pink rosettes, flowering
plants in natural colours, black doves with white wings, and ducks of varied
plumage.

Twelve miniatures represent scenes from the life and parables of Christ. Two of
these miniatures fill the whole page, one consisting of two compartments—representing Christ before Pilate and Judas returning the thirty pieces and hanging
himself—and the other representing the scene 'Christ or Barabbas'. Fig. II-6a.

The other miniatures occupy the upper half of the page, the lower half being
occupied by an unusual symbolic device: four contain half-length figures of O. T.
worthies (Moses; David and Solomon, distinguished by their crowns; Isaiah,
Hosea, Sirach, and others) and figures of Christ; all wear a nimbus and stand in
tribunes inscribed with appropriate texts; each points forward with his right hand,
to the fulfilment of his 'prophecies'. They all appear as heralds of the Messiah,
proclaim His presence, and point out the mystical significance of His acts.
Theologically very important, too, are 'Christ or Barabbas', the pictures representing the wise and foolish virgins, the good Samaritan and the distribution of

bread and wine symbolizing the mystical institution of the Mass. The conception of the characters is marked by a great dignity, particularly in that Christ is no more shown as the beardless young man of Western Christian art, but as a mature man with dark hair and beard, a figure of grave, serene, and most impressive majesty.

Also of great theological interest—a point to which J. A. Herbert has drawn attention—is that at this early date the iconography of some of the principal scenes in the life of Christ, as they appear in medieval liturgical manuscripts, had already been settled; so had, for instance, the arrangement of the personages and the way of telling the story.

The illustrations are probably based on wall-paintings which decorated Oriental churches, and in the details they are quite different from those of the Western MSS. They are on a more monumental scale than those of the Vienna manuscript, and the 'illusionist' Hellenistic representation, which may still be seen in some of the miniatures of that manuscript, is almost wholly abandoned in the *Rossano Gospels*: indeed, the superbly bright geometrical composition of the frontispiece to the Canon-table is absolutely alien to the naturalistic style.

The landscape is schematized, and no background is employed, except in the Gethsemane scene; 'vertical projection' is employed, as a result of which there is little perspective.

The resemblance to the Vienna codex lies mainly in some details of costume and architecture, in types of face, and so on. These superficial resemblances seem to point to the two codices being of much the same date of provenance, although the standpoints of the painters of these books are quite different. Moreover, while the decorative patterns of the *Rossanensis* are superior to those of the *Vienna Genesis*, its miniatures are quiet in manner and, as already mentioned, the conception of characters is marked by great dignity.

The *Rossano codex* by its style and iconography illustrates for us in a striking manner the spirit of illumination in the first Byzantine Golden Age, when Oriental influences had been fully assimilated by the new Byzantine art, which resulted from the compromise between the Hellenistic and the Syrian elements. Certain characteristics of its iconography recur in Byzantine art down to the period of Giotto (1276–1337).

The *Rossano MS.* has been assigned variously both to Egypt (theory preferred by D. Talbot Rice) and Syria-Palestine (preferred by O. M. Dalton). Some scholars have suggested that it was a gift to an Emperor or by a Patriarch of Constantinople. It is not known when and how the codex reached Rossano Cathedral, where it was discovered in 1879 by A. Harnack and O. von Gebhardt.

According to Weitzmann, it may be assumed that in the *Rossano MS.*, as well as in other codices (such as the *Rabbūlā Gospels*), we have a 'selective cycle' of miniatures, derived from a more fully illustrated Gospel-book with column pictures; whereas in Nordenfalk's opinion, the New Testament scenes of the Syrian Canon-tables were invented for their present purpose, and from the very beginning constituted a rather short cycle of their own.

Sinope MS. or Codex Sinopensis (Fig. II-6b)

This fragmentary codex, consisting of forty-three leaves of purple vellum—another leaf is (or was) preserved in the Mariupol Gymnasium, near the Sea of Azov—and obtained at Sinope in 1900 (and now in the National Library at Paris, *Suppl. Gr. 1286*), is akin in date and style, in iconography of the pictures, and in text, to *Codex Rossanensis*.

The text, in Greek, belonging to the same recension as the *Rossanensis*, contains about a third of S. Matthew's Gospel, and is written in gold uncials, a unique feature in the extant Greek Gospel-books.

The miniatures are on a much smaller scale than in the *Rossanensis*; they occupy the bottom margin of the page, following the text which they illustrate. The figures (as in the *Rossanensis*) are painted directly on the purple vellum. The subjects represented are the death of S. John the Baptist, the two miracles of feeding the multitude, Christ (represented with dark hair and beard) healing the two blind men, and cursing the barren fig-tree. There are two prophets, nimbused, to each miniature (David appears four times, wearing a crown with a double row of pearls; Moses three times; Isaiah, Habakkuk, and Daniel, once); each stands on a tribune, one on each side of the picture, and looks down upon it, extending two fingers. Whilst in the *Rossanensis* the execution is much more artistic, the five Sinope miniatures, much cruder, less finished and dignified, show nevertheless greater vivacity, individuality, and expressiveness. The *Sinopensis* may be assigned to Asia Minor.

Other fragments executed in the same style, and also obtained at Sinope, are now in the Leningrad Library. These formed part of a dismembered codex now known as *Codex N*, which was apparently executed either at Constantinople or in Asia Minor.

Rabbūlā Codex (Fig. II-31 and 32a)

The Oriental style is to the fore in the Syriac Gospels of the Laurentian Library at Florence (*Cod. Plut. I, 56*)—known as the *Rabbūlā Gospels*—which will be dealt with on p. 117 f.

Etchmiadzin Gospels: see also p. 121

This codex, preserved in the monastery of Etchmiadzin, Armenia (*Cod. No. 229*), is another important MS. in which the Syrian style is predominant. It is dated to A.D. 989, but it contains illuminations at the beginning and at the end which, according to Strzygowski and Dalton, appear to be as early as the sixth century. More recently, Weitzmann has tried to show that these illustrations are to be assigned to the same date as the book. However, their style and iconography are essentially Eastern. The ornamental work is analogous to that of the *Rabbūlā*

Gospels, especially the arcades decorated with birds (peacocks, ducks, etc.), and plants (with foliage); the rare marginal illustrations occupy the inner margin between two parallel columns of texts.

Also many of the compositions are the same as in the *Rabbūlā Gospels*. The most interesting feature, perhaps, is a sanctuary with a sort of dome somewhat resembling a Chinese pagoda, surmounted by cross and orb, and supported by Corninthian columns. It also appears—though in a slightly different form—in the *Rabbūlā Codex*, and is repeated, curiously enough, in the 'Fountain-of-Life'-miniatures of the ninth-century Carolingian Gospels, thus being one of the proofs of the indebtedness of Carolingian to Eastern art.

Miscellanea

Of some early illuminated Greek Gospels, richly decorated in Syrian style, only a few loose leaves have come down to us, such as *fols. 10* and *11* of the British Museum *Add. MS. 5111*, and *fols. 1–6* of *MS. No. 847* in the Vienna National Library. Both fragments belong to the sixth or early seventh century.

Add. 5111, fols. 10–11, consisting of two imperfect leaves of vellum gilded on both sides, contains parts of the *Epistle to Carpianus*, framed in a depressed arch, and of the *Eusebian Canons*, the Canon-tables being in round-arched arcades. They are on gold grounds, and are profusely decorated with geometrical patterns, floral scroll-work, medallion-heads of saints, birds, fishes, flowers, and so on. The colours, in which blue and carmine predominate, are wonderfully fresh, the flowers being exquisitely naturalistic.

Vienna No. 847, fols. 1–6, contains the *Eusebian Canons*: the Canon-tables, in arcades usually round-arched, are richly ornamented with a zigzag-pattern, strap-work, cable-pattern, birds pecking at fruit, etc. There is also a frontispiece, and a title-page (in a double-banded, decorated frame) for the Four Gospels. This fragment is bound at the beginning of a Latin MS. (*Rufinus*), assigned to the same period and having an almost identical frontispiece; both frontispieces are of rigidly symmetrical design, consisting of a cross enclosed by two concentric circles, and standing on a sort of Y-shaped device which spreads out at the foot into two wavy lines. In the Greek frontispiece, the device supports two peacocks facing one another, and in the Latin page, two birds of uncertain species.

Decadence of Byzantine Art

The last years of the Justinian dynasty and the period of the Heraclean (610–717), the Isaurian (717–820), and the Amorian (820–67) dynasties were marked by wars with the Persians, the Goths, the Arabs, the Bulgars, and the Slavs of Russia, and wars are hardly conducive to the development of art. In addition to the misfortunes of these wars and to the Arab conquest of a great portion of the Byzantine Empire, there were iconoclastic, *i.e.* image-breaking, disturbances. Between 717 and 843—writes D. Talbot Rice—no representation of the Divine, even of the saintly form, was permitted in religious art. Numerous earlier monuments, more especially mosaics, which depicted Christ, the Virgin, or important saints were actually destroyed, while any new church decoration was strictly confined to non-representational subjects, such as the cross, or some form of decorative floral or geometrical motif.

It has not yet been established whether the Byzantine iconoclasm and the Islamic hostility towards representation were directly or indirectly connected. Indeed, according to some scholars, such as R. Wischnitzer, the mere threat of an Arab avalanche affected this cultural policy of the Byzantine Empire.

Other authorities connect the movement with the Imperial hostility towards the growing power of the monasteries: an attempt at a general dissolution of the monasteries being screened under a popular cry of artistic impropriety. Still other scholars, particularly Talbot Rice, distinguish two main aspects of the movement, the question of image worship, which had undoubtedly become a danger owing to the tremendous reverence accorded to the painted representation of the divine or saintly form, and that of the legitimacy of religious art, which had been brought to the fore by the teaching of Islam. However, 'perhaps the most important characteristic of the movement, from the point of view of art, is its eastern character' (D. Talbot Rice).

In Sir Steven's opinion, artistically the iconoclastic movement represents the struggle between the Aramaean art, with its stark, intense figures, which became the sole property of the monks of Byzantium, the Iranian art, with its rich foliate and geometrical ornament, and the Hellenistic style, intervening and emerging victorious, but having learnt much from its rivals. In fact, however, the classical, or rather neo-classical, style emerged victorious only at a later period (see p. 93 ff.). In the Iconoclastic period the Imperial authorities encouraged an art of patterns, geometric figures, and still more those flowering designs of birds and leaves in which the Iranian and Armenian delighted.

Considering the wars and the Iconoclastic controversy, we need hardly be surprised at the decadence of Byzantine art from the late seventh to the late ninth century. The very few Greek illuminated MSS. which can be assigned to this period show fantastic animal decoration (such as beasts, monsters, and birds) often combined with rich foliage, interlaced borders and crosses, or other geometrical ornament, which proves that the Iranian-Armenian influence was constantly growing.

Two unusual MSS. may here be mentioned; both are Greek Gospel-books and come from the Skiti of S. Andrew of the Russians, on Mt. Athos, and both are now in the Library of Princeton University. *Garrett MS. 6*, of the twelfth century, contains five full-page miniatures which, on the basis of style, colouring, and ornament, are attributed to the ninth century, and are connected with the East Christian art of the Syrian region. The miniatures, of unusual style, represent

Christ, the Virgin, S. Mark, S. Luke, and S. John, all standing frontally under arches or pediments. *Garrett MS. 1*, of the ninth century, contains ornamented head- and tail-pieces. The text of each page, written in small uncials without separation between words, is disposed in the shape of a cross. This arrangement occurs on occasional pages of other MSS., but is rather unusual for an entire book. It also appears, however, in *M. 692* of Pierpont Morgan Library, New York.

Influence upon the West

There is an Italian saying, *non c'è male che non riesca un bene*—'out of evil cometh good', or 'It's an ill wind that blows nobody any good'; this is illustrated by some of the results of Iconoclasm. Indeed, one of its striking results was the flight of numerous Byzantine artists to the West, especially into South Italy, where Basilian communities flourished—at least from the tenth century onwards.

Iconoclasm was never accepted generally in Eastern monastic circles, and the connection of Eastern monasticism with South Italy had already begun in the late fourth century. Moreover, in Italy there is an evident continuity of tradition between the Early Christian illuminators and those of the later—more definitely formed—Byzantine school. Many later manuscripts were in fact written and illuminated in Italy, especially in South Italy, where Greek influence persisted long after the decay of the Western Empire had become far advanced.

Cassiodorus. In the sixth century Cassiodorus established the monastery of Vivarium on the bay of Squillace (in the modern province of Catanzaro, Calabria). Flavius Magnus Aurelius Cassiodorus, Roman historian, statesman, minister, man of letters, and monk, who lived beyond the age of ninety (*c.* 480–*c.* 575), is probably the best personal link between the Roman age and the Middle Ages. A descendant of a distinguished family, he rose to high position, being sole consul in 514, secretary to Theodoric, and chief minister. He wrote important historical works.

In 540 he retired from public life, and founded the monastery of Vivarium on his ancestral estate, which became an important seat of classical and sacred learning. He himself composed an encyclopaedic work dealing with classical and religious subjects. In Sir John Sandy's opinion, Cassiodorus was apparently the first to make the cultivation of learning part of the systematic organisation of the common life of the convent, and thus to contribute in no small measure to the preservation of the ancient Classics. He also gave detailed instructions to his copyists with regard to accuracy in copying. Moreover, he was the author of a revision of the Vulgate (see *The Hand-produced Book*, p. 284), which was adopted in the whole of South Italy, and his monastery of Vivarium—where he brought numerous codices from Constantinople and the East—became an important centre for copying manuscripts.

In the same century, *Codex Rossanensis* and other important books were brought to South Italy. During the Iconoclastic period the influence of the Eastern illuminated book deepened in South Italy, and extended far beyond this region.

This influence is apparent in the history of the surviving books of Italy and West Europe. As research makes us more familiar with Carolingian art—writes D. Talbot Rice—we shall come to realize more and more how considerable was the role that the Eastern fugitive artists played in its development.

Various manuscripts produced in Italy in pure Byzantine style will be discussed further on (p. 112 f.). Here, in passing, we might note an earlier production: a striking eighth-century *Gospels* is preserved in the Cathedral Museum at Perugia (*Codex No. 2*): Fig. VI-1e–f, with illustrations representing Christ, S. Luke and his symbol.

SECOND GOLDEN AGE

The period of the Macedonian and the Comneni dynasties (867–1056 and 1057–1183, respectively)—particularly the tenth and eleventh centuries—was one of very successful foreign policy (defeat of Arabs in Syria, 995; of Bulgarians, 1014; reconquest of South Italy, 915; conversion of Russia, 989), and of great economic prosperity. The long drawn-out struggle between image-destroyers and image-worshippers—writes Mathew—had closed, and the bitter Monophysite controversies were forgotten. Constantinople had come to possess an inevitable and unquestioned predominance in all Greek-speaking lands. It was the new Rome on the Bosphorus. It was the heir of Antioch and of Alexandria. All that was still dynamic in Greek culture moved in the sheltered reaches of the Court. From the ninth to the fifteenth century the Byzantines conceived of themselves as Romans and of the Greek classics as their special heritage: Mathew. Moreover, the Hellenistic revival blended with Islamic influences. Court ceremonial, colour, wealth were at their highest.

Arts, such as architecture, sculpture and painting, and craftsmanship, such as superb textiles, mosaics, enamels, delicate metal-work, reached a very high level, indeed their highest point of perfection. A vast quantity of illuminated MSS., both religious and secular, was produced in this period, and many of them have come down to us.

Neo-Classical Style

It is evident that under Basil I, the Macedonian, and his successors, after the long puritanical period of the Iconoclasts, beauty came into fashion again, and artists were called upon to satisfy the aesthetic taste, as well as the religious instincts, of their clients.

The style of the Second Golden Age has been called neo-classical or pseudo-antique: there was a frequent reversion to older models; masterpieces of classical art, of which many have since perished, were pressed into service as models. Some miniatures, especially of the tenth century, are so imbued with the classical spirit that, rightly or wrongly, they have been held to be copies of lost originals dating back to the earliest periods of Christian art. At the same time the new style was enriched by some Eastern patterns such as the design of peacocks and of twining

93

foliage. The two strains, Hellenistic and Aramaean—writes S. Runciman—can still be seen, but they had come close together. Indeed, they are now reconciled, and neo-classicism is no longer an inanimate relic or a soulless copy of ancient originals.

Though Hellenism was beaten, it did not die. Its conceptions—to quote again Sir Steven—were too deeply inherent in the blood of the Greek. At intervals throughout the lifetime of the Byzantine Empire, it would emerge to turn Byzantine art back towards the old naturalism. At Thessalonica especially, Hellenistic ideas persisted longer than in certain other parts of the Empire, and it is natural that, with the Macedonian dynasty, a revival of the classical style should occur.

The neo-classical wave did not last long. The eleventh- and twelfth-century manuscripts are direct imitations of older models, rather than original productions influenced by classical art. According to Mathew there is probably no break in the history of Byzantine painting. He notes three main tendencies in fashion during the ninth–twelfth centuries: the fashion for the reproduction of the Antique, the influence of Islamic art motifs, and the desire for fresh expressions of dramatic tension. Even within a pre-determined iconographic convention such tension could be conveyed by new rhythms in the grouping of the figures or by experiment in contrasted colours. In this connection Mathew refers to the British Museum *Add. MS. 11870* (see p. 105), fol. 197*b*: In the beheading scene the headsman unsheaths his sword as the wind blows back his cloak and as the saint's red-clad body sways abruptly towards the dark blue crag. On Patmos S. John stands bent and listening even as he dictates.

The art was refined and realistic, but there was little attempt at invention in the composition, and the iconographical types were constantly and monotonously repeated. However, there was still room for the creative talent of the artist, especially with regard to the costumes of the personages represented, the proportion of their features, limbs, and so on. At the same time, new classes of MSS. came into existence, such as *Menologies* (see p. 103 ff.). Illuminated MSS. of other classes, such as Psalters, became more numerous.

Headpieces (Fig. II-7, 10, and 30). The purely decorative motifs—the headpieces—became a characteristic conventional ornament of the Byzantine style. In the richest and most beautiful examples this ornament reminds all who see it for the first time of some Oriental pattern-work, and especially of Persian carpets or enamels. It is generally used at the beginning of a book or chapter, sometimes forming a framework or pendant to a miniature, but more often it is alone, the miniature—if any—being on a separate page within a plain banded frame (as in most of the Gospel-books, see p. 99 ff.). The form is square or oblong, sometimes with short depending borders.

The decoration consists of a repetitive pattern of geometrical elements—circles, lozenges, and quatrefoils—together with strictly conventionalized flower and leaf ornaments. Sometimes the design is so close as to seem a mere floriated network. Sometimes it has a richer border, and a more open pattern within. The ground is gold; the pattern is in the deep blue of Persian enamel, with myrtle-green and a little red. In later work, pink, light blue, mauve, and other secondary shades are introduced, but as a general rule the better the specimen the nearer it keeps to the original blue-and-green effect. The whole is relieved with minute touches of white, which become coarse and heavy as the style deteriorates. A really good specimen of this ornament looks like a fine Persian praying-rug on a small scale. See also p. 79.

The origin and early development of this headpiece is still uncertain (see p. 78 ff.), but its successive stages of decadence may easily be seen from the long series of Gospel-books which have been preserved.

Initials (Fig. II-7, 10, 29–30). Headings and beginnings of single books are written in very large golden capitals, so that six or seven letters frequently occupy the whole page. These letters are painted over a richly decorated background covered with floreated ornament and the whole is framed in an elaborate border, all glowing with the most brilliant colours, and lighted by burnished gold of the highest decorative beauty.

On the whole, the initial-ornament—especially in some of the earlier manuscripts—is rich. An excellent specimen is the British Museum *Arundel MS. 547*: an early tenth-century *Evangelistarium* or Gospel-lectionary, written in 'Slavonic' uncials. Its initials are of the type usually called Lombardic, and the ornamentation abounds in variety and humour: fishes, birds, human limbs, human trunks without limbs, pitchers—these and other objects are combined in all sorts of fantastic ways. Herbert refers to initials of a similar character in Eastern manuscripts of the tenth and eleventh centuries, from the monastery on Mount Sinai.

Bibles (Fig. I-16–17; II-8–10).

A good specimen of neo-classical art is the illuminated *Septuagint* (the only one preserved), known as the *Great Bible*, of which the first volume (preserved in the Vatican Library, *Cod. Vat. Reg. Gr. 1*), containing books from *Genesis* to *Psalms*, is extant. It was produced for Leo the Patrician, a high official at the court of Constantinople, in the first half of the tenth century. Leo presented it (and the second volume, now missing) as a votive offering in honour of the Virgin. It was probably executed by one of the best court-illuminators of the time. It contains eighteen full-page miniatures, which are related both to the miniatures of the *Paris Psalter* (see p. 96 f.) and to those of the Paris copy of *Gregory Nazianzen* (see p. 103 f.), its artistic merit being a sort of midway mark between the two: finer than the *Gregory*, it is coarser than the *Psalter*. Some of its miniatures correspond closely to those of the *Psalter* (Moses on Mount Sinai and Samuel anointing David), others to those of the *Gregory*. Modern critics have suggested that many of the miniatures are copies of a much earlier original, and were done by an artist who well understood the ancient art of painting and illuminating. Fig. II-8.

Other important codices representing this art are *Plut. 5. 9 (Prophets)* and *Plut. 5. 38 (Old Testament)* in the Laurenziana Library at Florence; the *Octateuchs,* already referred to, in the Vatican Library (*Gr. 746* and *747*); *Cod. Chig. Gr. R. viii. 45* (*Prophets*), also in the Vatican Library; *Cod. Gr. Z. 538: Gr. 540* (Olympiodorus on *Job*) in the Marciana Library, Venice, which is a superb, richly illuminated manuscript, dated 905 : the last miniature (*fol. 246v*), in two compartments, represents Job, his wife, their seven sons and three daughters; an Armenian *Gospel* of the year 862 or 902, preserved in S. Lazzaro degli Armeni, Venice (see p. 120 f.); *Cod. 5* (*Gospels*) of the Palatine Library, Parma; and *MS. Gr. 70* (*Gospels*) in the National Library at Paris : Fig. II-10. See also Fig. II-9.

PSALTERS (Fig. II-11–14)

The earliest illuminated Psalters extant are ninth- and tenth-century MSS., such as the *Khludoff Psalter*, formerly in the monastery of S. Nicholas at Moscow, and now in the Historical Museum of that city. Comparative study of various MSS., frescoes and mosaics, by leading scholars, such as Morey (see Fig. II-11*b*), show that the preserved Psalters follow closely earlier copies, and that Psalters must already have existed in the fourth or the fifth century A.D., based on Hellenistic models. The fact that older copies are not now available is thus due not to any absence of Psalter illumination in earlier times, but to their destruction.

The Psalters are generally divided into two classes: the 'aristocratic' or 'aulic' and the 'monastic'.

'Aristocratic' or 'Aulic' Psalters (Fig. II-11–12)

The predominantly Hellenistic class is the 'aristocratic', or 'aulic', so called because the copies of this class were produced mainly for members of the Imperial court and the Constantinople 'aristocracy'.

Interesting MSS. belonging to this group are preserved in the National Library, Paris (*Cod. Gr. 139*, of the tenth century); in the Mount Athos monasteries of Vatopedi (*Nos. 609* and *760*) and Pantokrator (*No. 49*); in the Marciana Library, Venice (the *Psalter of Basil II, Cod. Gr. Z. 17: 421*); in the Ambrosian Library, Milan (*No. 54*); in the British Museum (*Add. MS. 36928*), and in the Vatican Library (*Palat. Gr. 381* and *Gr. 752*) : Fig. II, 11*a*.

The illustrations of this group are based upon the Constantinopolitan-Alexandrian redaction, and may go back to Alexandrian-Hellenistic prototypes of the fourth and later centuries A.D. (Dr. Cecil Roth suggests that the *Paris Psalter* is based on a Jewish prototype belonging perhaps to the second century A.D.), especially in the style employed in landscapes, architecture and personifications, such as that of Mount Sinai in the *Pantokrator Psalter*. Although there are some slight traces of Oriental influence, the illustrations abound in evidence of a classical renaissance. They form veritable pictures, conceived as wholes, and executed in the style of the neo-classical revival which followed the period of Iconoclasm. It will suffice, in this connection, to mention the beautiful miniature of the *Paris Psalter*, representing the shepherd David : Fig. II-12.

The *Paris Psalter* is the best and the earliest of this group, belonging to the tenth century. In the sixteenth century it was acquired by a French ambassador in Constantinople where it must have belonged to the Imperial Library. The text is in Greek tenth-century minuscules.

The manuscript contains fourteen full-page miniatures, also assigned to the tenth century. The leaves bearing the miniatures (on the *verso* pages, the *recto* being blank) are independent of the quires of the text—it has been suggested that they may have been inserted later. The miniatures may be divided into two classes: six show classical influence and rise to a high artistic level; eight—probably the work of an inferior hand—are akin to the Biblical scenes in the *Gregory Nazianzen*, showing little or no trace of classical influence (except in a few isolated figures); they contain crowded compositions, ill-proportioned figures, and decayed colouring.

The most famous of all—and superior in freedom, grace, and proportion—is that of David with the harp, inspired by Melody who sits at his right hand, with her hand on his shoulder, the reclining figure in the foreground symbolising Bethlehem; even the individual animals have been charmed to stillness by the music. It is generally believed that the miniature owes its original idea to some Graeco-Roman picture of Orpheus taming the beasts, but there is no doubt that we have in this miniature the work of a brilliant artist who had absorbed the spirit of his model, rather than an exact copy made by a patient craftsman (Herbert). This composition became very popular, and in some MSS. we have exact copies of it. Amongst the various reproductions is the British Museum *Add. MS. 36928* (fol. 44*b*). Fig. II-12.

The other fine miniatures of the *Paris Psalter* are: David slaying the Lion, with a personification of Strength coming to his assistance; Isaiah receiving inspiration, standing between the Dawn (a boy holding a torch) and the Night (a noble woman with a drooping and half-extinguished torch); Nathan rebuking David, with the figure of Penitence; the prayer of Hezekiah; David between Wisdom and Prophecy; Crossing of the Red Sea. Fig. II-11*c*.

Most remarkable is fol. 3*r* of the *Psalter of Basil II*: it is a full-page miniature on gold background; in the centre, we see the Emperor Basil II in Imperial robes, holding in his right hand the lance handed to him by Archangel Michael. He is crowned by Archangel Gabriel. Above, Christ in half figure, holding in His left hand a book, and in His right a crown, which is suspended over the Emperor's head. On each side of the Emperor there are three saints in half figure; whereas beneath there are eight subjects kneeling, prostrating, or in similar Eastern servile attitudes.

'Monastic' Psalters (Fig. II-13–14)

The 'monastic' group employs the Oriental method of marginal illustration; there are no full-page miniatures.

The marginal illustrations would seem to go back to prototypes of the sixth century, and to have been inspired by the composite art demanded by the Church; in this art, Syriac monasticism, 'under the direction of North Mesopotamian theology, played so large a part' (Dalton). Nevertheless, the illustrations are rich in picturesque Hellenistic detail.

The convention of the marginally illustrated Psalter became increasingly popular in the tenth century and increasingly fashionable in the eleventh. No convention in Byzantine art gave freer play for studies from contemporary life and from nature, or illustrated more perfectly the fusion of secular and religious painting (Mathew).

The 'monastic' Psalter may have originated in Syria-Palestine or in Cappadocia.

To this group belong the following codices: the *Khludoff Psalter*, already referred to; a fragmentary codex of the National Library at Paris (*Cod. Gr. 20*), of the tenth century; the *Theodore Psalter* of the British Museum, of A.D. 1066 (*Add. MS. 19352*), as well as the *Psalter* British Museum *Add. MS. 40731,* of the eleventh century; the *Cod. Vat. Gr. 1927*; the *Barberini Psalter* (preserved in the Vatican Library, *Barb. Gr. 372*), from the Imperial Scriptorium of the Comneni, of the twelfth century; the *Hamilton Psalter* (now preserved in Berlin); the *Pantokrator Psalter* (preserved in the monastery of Pantokrator, on Mount Athos, *Cod. No. 61*), which by some scholars is attributed to the ninth century, by others to A.D. 1084; and some other specimens. Psalters of this group continued to be produced in later centuries in Serbia and Russia.

See Fig. II-13-14.

The *Theodore Psalter*—containing a Greek Psalter, a metrical life of David (in dialogue form), and some hymns and canticles (including the psalm traditionally composed by David when he had killed Goliath)—is of particular interest. Completed in 1066 by the priest and monk Theodore of Caesarea (probably in Cappadocia) for Michael, Abbot of the *Studion* monastery in Constantinople, it contains 208 leaves, almost every one with the margins filled with delicately executed paintings.

Its main interest lies in the wealth and variety of its illustrations, vividly portrayed, some naïvely literal (*Ps. xi. 2, xii. 3, lxxviii. 25,* and so on), others elaborately symbolical (*Ps. xlii. 6, cxiii. 7,* etc.). Pictures from the life of David are dispersed throughout the volume, but really charming are ff. 189b and 190. Of particular 'monastic' character are the scenes from the New Testament, many being drawn from the lives of saints and the history of the Eastern Church. Many of the subjects (such as the Crucifixion) are repeated in different parts of the book, but with striking variations in treatment, rather unusual in Byzantine style at a time when iconography had already become settled.

On the whole the figures are well drawn, but are deeply felt and have not been given the distraction of a background (Runciman). Indeed, the figures are painted direct on the plain vellum page, having the appearance of standing or walking upon nothing. The pigments have flaked away in many places, so that we can now see that while the gold leaf was laid on a red priming, the colours were employed without any preliminary preparation of the vellum surface. But before the colours were laid on, the outlines of the figures were drawn very lightly, with the pen, in watered ink. Watercourses are represented by broad wavy lines of blue. Generally speaking the colouring is subdued, leaden blue being frequently used, but the pages are brightened up with gold highlights in the draperies and with frequent use of red.

A late eleventh-century Psalter is preserved in the Walters Art Gallery, Baltimore (*MS. suppl. 14*). It contains 145 marginal illustrations distinguished for the vivacity and vividness of the representations, which range from extremely literal renderings of the text, to symbolic interpretations and liturgical allusions (M. Ch. Ross). Originally it probably contained about two hundred illustrations, as far as can be judged from a nearly complete copy, made in 1397, and preserved in Kiev.

The fourteenth- or fifteenth-century *Serbian Psalter* at Munich, with the popular style of its border-illustration showing early Oriental motifs, points, in Strzygowski's view, to direct relations between Serbia and Eastern monasteries without Byzantine intermediaries—although, according to Millet and Wulff, it seems to have derived from a Byzantine model based on a Syrian prototype and to have been produced at the Serbian monastery of Chilandari on Mount Athos.

Other Old Testament Books. Here mention may be made of the illuminated copies of the *Book of Job*—such as the richly illuminated copy in the Marciana Library, Venice (*Cod. Gr. Z. 538: 540*), of A.D. 905—and especially of the *Prophets*, of which several illuminated codices are preserved in the Vatican Library (*Cod. Chig. Gr. R. viii. 54*, already referred to), in the Laurentian Library, Florence, and in other collections.

GOSPEL-BOOKS (Fig. II-10, 15-21)

The Gospels are the most common of all illuminated codices and the most typical of the Byzantine period which we are discussing.

These sumptuous *Evangeliaria*, or *Textus*, as they were called in the West, soon came to be something more than merely magnificent books. They developed into one of the most important pieces of furniture belonging to the High Altar in all important cathedral churches of the Middle Ages.

Comparative study of a few copies, especially those belonging to the tenth or eleventh centuries—such as those in the Laurentian Library (*Plut. 6. 23*), the British Museum (*Add. MS. 28815*), the National Library at Paris (*Nos. 74, 115, 139*), and so on—shows that the production of Gospel-books was parallel to that of the books of the Old Testament: the earliest productions were probably in the form of rolls illustrated in the Hellenistic style; they were followed by codices produced in the mixed Hellenistic-Oriental style.

British Museum *Add. MS. 28815*, containing the four *Gospels*, the *Acts of the Apostles*, and some of the *Pauline Epistles*, was probably written in Constantinople in the late tenth century. It contains, amongst others, two fine portraits of S. Luke (fols. *76b* and *162b*), chosen by Mathew to illustrate the conscious imitation of the antique. This is apparent not only in the details of costume and of architectural setting and in the almost sculptured monumental rendering of the figures but most significantly of all in the conception of an Evangelist as a Philosopher. Here behind S. Luke as author of his Gospel and S. Luke as author of the Acts there lie two variants of the Philosopher convention on third century sarcophagi (Mathew).

The Gospels show two main redactions: (1) that of Alexandria-Constantinople —represented, for instance, by the Laurentian codex *Plut. 6.23*, the British Museum *Add. MS. 28815*, by *Cod. Gr. 540* of the Marciana Library, Venice, or even *Cod. F. 7* of the Vallicelliana, Rome, which is as late as 1330—in which classical ornamentation with Hellenistic features predominates; and (2) that of Antioch, with the predominance of Oriental influence—as, for instance, *Cod. No. 74* of the National Library, Paris, and a few codices of the Vatican Library (*Gr. 361, 1156, 1158* and *1208*), of the Ambrosiana (*Cod. D. 67 sup.*), and of the Marciana (*Cl. i. xx* and *xxii*): Fig. II-15.

The Gospels may be divided into two classes, (1) the *Tetraevangelia* ('four Gospels'), or complete version of the four canonical Gospels, in which the illumination follows the historical sequence of the Gospels; and (2) the *Evangelistaria*, or liturgical Gospels, in which the historical sequence is disregarded; the text, which is aided by illustrations, consists of the 'pericopes' or lections in the order of the Church calendar. See p. 106 (*Lectionaries of the Gospels*).

Portraits of Evangelists (Fig. II-16–18, 30). With certain exceptions (see below), the decoration of the Gospel-books consists of portraits of the Evangelists and headpieces prefixed to the Gospels (see p. 94 f.), sometimes with arcades for the Eusebian Canons and ornamental initials. The four Evangelists are represented on full-page miniatures placed at the beginning of the codex. Each Evangelist, sometimes enthroned like an Emperor under an arched canopy supported on Corinthian columns of marble or porphyry, sits holding in his hand the manuscript of his Gospel, or, in some cases, writing it. A fifth full-page miniature represents 'Christ in Majesty' usually enthroned within an oval or vesica-shaped aureola.

The portraits of the Evangelists thus form the chief decoration of a very large number of Greek Gospel-books belonging to the period of the tenth to the fourteenth centuries. The series is, however, of much earlier date—the portrait of S. Mark appears in the *Rossano Gospels* (see p. 87 f.), and the *Lindisfarne Gospels* (see p. 182 f.) contain the four portraits, which are probably of Italo-Byzantine origin. As to Byzantine book-illumination of the period between the seventh and the ninth century, nothing is known.

In the Evangelists' portraits in the Greek Gospel-books, the Evangelists are usually at work on their respective Gospels; the first three seated and engaged in the actual writing, usually with a book on a stand to copy from. For S. John there are two different compositions: in one he stands dictating to S. Prochorus and is looking to heaven for inspiration (symbolized by a hand issuing from part of a disc); in the other he sits alone writing: here also there is the symbol of inspiration. Fig. II-16–18, and 30.

In some particular instance the Evangelist is shown standing, holding the Gospel in his hands. This is the case—Fig. II-10—of the beautiful *Gospel-book* preserved in the National Library at Paris, *Gr. 70*, dated 964. Opposite the portrait there is an elaborate head-piece and initial.

In a tenth-century *Gospel-book* preserved in the Walters Art Gallery, Baltimore (*MS. 524*), the composition of the miniatures of the Evangelists is quite unusual: each Evangelist is writing in the presence of a companion—S. Luke with S. Paul, seated; S. Mark with S. Peter; S. John with S. Prochorus; the fourth miniature of the MS. represents S. James addressing a multitude. Fig. II-19*a*.

An eleventh-century *Gospel-book*, which comes from the Orthodox Church of Keiroussis on the Black Sea, and is preserved in the Pierpont Morgan Library, New York (*M. 748*), is assigned to a provincial *scriptorium* (for instance, to South Italy), but the architectural backgrounds, the modelling of the draperies, the fairly light colouring, etc., suggest that we have here a copy from a fifth- or sixth-century Gospel-book. There are two full-page miniatures (representing Evangelists with a standing companion figure), marginal illustrations, illuminated Canon Tables, and head-pieces. Fig. II-18*a*.

A single leaf from a *New Testament*, of the eleventh century, preserved in the Walters Art Gallery (*MS. 530c*), represents the four Evangelists with S. Paul and S. Peter, standing in two zones, against a blue background. Fig. II-19*c*.

With some exceptions (as in British Museum *Add. MS. 22736*, dated 1179, in which both he and S. Luke have almost girlish faces), S. John is represented as an old man, with long white beard and bald head, the forehead very large and dome-shaped. The cast of countenance is usually grave, thoughtful, ascetic, especially in the earlier manuscripts, with bulging, wrinkled forehead and prominent chin.

S. Matthew is always an old man, with white hair and beard. S. Mark is much younger, dark haired, sometimes of a strikingly Semitic type, for instance, in the British Museum *Add. MSS. 4949* and *22740*, both of the twelfth century. An interesting portrait is that of an eleventh-century MS. from the Escorial Library, near Madrid (now in the British Museum, *Burney MS. 19*). Finally, S. Luke is a young man in his prime, a non-Semitic type, fair with good features of the conventional Greek mould; he has a slight, pointed beard, and is sometimes tonsured (British Museum *Burney MS. 19*, *Add. MS. 4949*, *Burney MS. 20*, dated 1285). See also Fig. II-16–19, and 21.

Symbols of Evangelists (Fig. II-3*c*). Curiously enough, the symbols of the four Evangelists appear to be almost unknown in Byzantine art before the fourteenth century. (British Museum *Add. MS. 11838*—a Greek Gospel-book of 1326—is apparently the earliest Byzantine Gospel-book containing the four emblems.) The 'four living creatures' of *Ezekiel*, i. 5, and the 'four beasts' of the *Apocalypse*, ix. 6, were regarded as the symbols of the four Evangelists from very early times, and they occur in the Baptistry of S. Giovanni in Fonte, at Naples, of *c.* A.D. 400. In Western MSS. they appear almost invariably from the seventh century onwards, and the fact that Byzantine art, with its highly developed symbolic imagery, did not use them, induces Herbert to suggest that these symbols were an invention of Latin Christianity. See also Fig. IV-*5a–b, c–d*, 12, 14*c*, 15*a*, 17, 19*b*, 22*c*, 24*b–c*, 29*b*, 33*b*, VI-*e–f*, etc.

Accessories (Fig. II-16–18, 21, 30). Accessories depicted in miniatures of Evangelists are of great importance to the student of the history of book-production, though of course the fanciful variations of the artist have to be taken into account: the book which, in the miniature, serves as model, may be—according to the fancy of the artist—a roll or a codex; and so, too, but independently, the Gospel which is shown in the process of being written. The model in the British Museum *Burney MS. 20* (dated 1285), referring to S. Matthew's Gospel, is a roll written in Arabic; it seems to indicate the then current tradition that Arabic was the original language of this Gospel.

Of great interest in our study is the complete outfit of writing implements (inkstand, knife, scissors, compasses, sponge, and so on) as they often appear on the table by the Evangelist's side. The stand for the model-book, the patterns of the chair, of the table, and of the other furniture and accessories, such as the hanging lamp suspended over S. Luke's table in the tenth-century British Museum *Add. MS. 28815*, are also of interest to the student. Fig. II-18*d* represents the Apostle S. James in an interesting MS. of the Bodleian Library (*MS. Can. Gr. 110, fol. 106v*).

Eusebian Canons (Fig. II-20*a*). The Eusebian Canons—*i.e.* the 'Canons' of Bishop Eusebius—are a set of ten tables giving lists of parallel passages in the four Gospels. These Tables are usually framed by columns supporting a semi-circular arch, richly decorated with architectural and floral ornaments in gold and colours. Frequently birds, especially doves and peacocks (see Fig. II-32 ff.), are introduced into the spandrels over the arches. They are often arranged in pairs drinking out of a central vase or chalice—a motif which occurs very often among the reliefs on the sarcophagi and marble screens of Byzantine churches both in Italy and in the East. These birds appear to be purely ornamental, in spite of the many attempts made to discover symbolic meanings in them. Other birds, such as cocks, quails and partridges, are also commonly used in these decorative illuminations. See particularly the Syrian and Armenian *Gospels* (Fig. II-32–35, and 37).

Additional Miniatures (Fig. II-15*c, d*). Reference may here be made to two exceptional manuscripts which contain additional miniatures—the British Museum *Harley MS. 1810*, of the twelfth century, and the Vatican MS. *Urbin. Gr. 2*, executed in 1128–9. The former contains as many as sixteen miniatures of the life of Christ, each occupying about three-quarters of the page. The composition and the design are nearly identical with those of the *Melissenda Psalter* (see p. 107 f.), but the

Harleian MS.—in best Byzantine style—is much superior in colouring, dignified gestures, gentleness of faces, and so forth; the miniatures of the Incredulity of Thomas and the Annunciation are the best. The *Vat. Urbin. Gr. 2*, apparently executed for John Comnenus (1118–43), has the following additional illuminations: Christ blessing the Emperors Alexios and Joannes Comnenos, the Nativity, Baptism, Birth of S. John the Baptist, and Harrowing of Hell.

A leaf from a fine eleventh-century *Psalter*, preserved in the Walters Art Gallery, Baltimore (*MS. 530b*), represents Moses removing his sandals, Moses receiving the Law on Mt. Sinai, and Moses giving the Law to the Israelites. Fig. II-19d.

Additional miniatures occur in other illuminated manuscripts, for instance, in the Pierpont Morgan *MS. M. 692*, belonging to *c.* 1160, Fig. II-20b. See also p. 106.

Later Byzantine Gospels (Fig. II-15c–d, 17d, 20, 21). The later Byzantine *Gospels* exhibit great differences of style and colouring. The illustrations are generally in the text (and not placed all together at the beginning of the MS.), sometimes filling a whole page—as, for instance, in the *Vat. Urbin Gr. 2*, already referred to, and sometimes constituting simply a marginal painting (*e.g.*, already in the MS. National Library at Paris, *Gr. 115*, of the tenth century: in this *Tetraevangelion* the illustrations are reduced).

Gold grounds occur frequently, and gold is also employed for the highlights on costumes, with free imitation of jewels. The colours are bright and daring: marine blue, a brilliant green, yellow, red, opaque whites. There are full-page portraits of the Evangelists, sometimes shown standing, but generally shown seated. Opposite these portraits there is often an elaborate headpiece in bright colours, giving an impression of enamel.

Homilies and Menologia (Fig. II-21d–24b, 25)

Certain scholars have remarked that the Byzantine illuminated codices—notwithstanding their great number and the variety of the material they offer—are peculiarly qualified to illustrate the conservatism of East Christian tradition. It has been said that there was little attempt at invention. This is not correct. After the Iconoclastic period, new classes of manuscripts came into existence; but their illumination presented the same dualism of style as the classes already discussed. At any rate, the ninth to the twelfth centuries produced many manuscripts of great beauty and interest.

The Paris copy of the homilies of S. Gregory of Nazianzus (preserved in the National Library at Paris, *Gr. 510*) is a large volume. It is illustrated by about 200 miniatures, of which forty-six are full-page, including the magnificent portraits of the Emperor Basil I (867–86), his empress, Eudocia, and her two sons Leo and Alexander, the eldest son, Constantine, who died in 879, being omitted—which date this MS. between A.D. 880 and 886. This codex is a typical production of the

Constantinople school of Macedonian revival, in which the neo-classical style prevails. Other styles, however, are also shown, as represented for example by the animated compositions in the 'continuous' method (for instance, in the story of Jonah), and by the stately, bejewelled, highly decorative pages which recall the most gorgeous of the Byzantine mosaics: this is most noticeable in the portraits of Basil and Eudocia, and particularly in the impressive figure of S. Helena, who stands, vested as an empress, with three other saints in a splendid full-page miniature of an angel proclaiming the Redemption. The prevailing classical influence may be seen, for instance, in the famous Vision of Ezekiel, with its freer pose of classically conceived figures. Fig. II-22a.

The Jerusalem copy of *Gregory*, dating from the eleventh century, is full of scenes in the fields and of mythological pictures. Another interesting copy is the MS. of the Ambrosian Library, Milan (*Cod. E. 49. 50 inf.*; it belongs perhaps to the ninth century), containing illustrations to all forty-five homilies of Gregory. An eleventh-century copy is preserved in the Panteleimon monastery on Mount Athos: Weitzmann thinks that its miniatures are related to an eleventh-century copy of the commentary written by Pseudo-Nonnus (who lived in the sixth century A.D.), preserved in the Patriarchal Library at Jerusalem. S. Gregory's homilies provided 'pericopes' for the Church feasts.

The best copy of S. John Chrysostom is in the National Library at Paris, *Coislin: 79*. In addition to the religious miniatures, beautiful though rigidly formal portraits—those of Nicephorus Botaneiates, Emperor in the years 1078–81—are contained in this volume of *Homilies* of S. John Chrysostom: Fig. II-24.

A tenth-century copy of S. John Chrysostom, *Homilies on S. Matthew*, from the monastery of Kosinitza in Macedonia, is preserved in the Library of Princeton University (*Garrett MS. 14*). Its scribe was the notary Nikephoros; the date 955. It contains portrait medallions and ornaments in ink.

Akin to the Gregory of the Ambrosian Library is the ninth-century codex of the *Sacra Parallela* of S. John of Damascus (preserved in the National Library at Paris, *Gr. 923*), which is a *florilegium* with passages arranged alphabetically according to their catchwords: Fig. II-21d.

An eleventh-century copy of ecclesiastical hymns for Sunday services, collected by S. John of Damascus, is preserved in the University Library at Messina (*MS. Gr. 51*): there are eight miniatures on gold grounds. These miniatures are assigned to Sicily.

In the *Homilies* of Jacobus Monachus of Kokkinobaphos (preserved in the Vatican Library, *Cod. Vat. Gr. 1162*; National Library at Paris, *Gr. 1208*, both of the early twelfth century), which contain fine frontispieces, the neo-classical style is replaced by something rigidly religious, dogmatic and liturgical, exhibiting, however, some features of the Hellenistic style. On the whole, we have here perfect examples of the Byzantine monastic style (particularly in the Vatican MS.), with its exquisitely finished, if formal, groups of saints and angels. Fig. II-22b and 25a.

Simeon Metaphrastes, *Lives of the Saints* (B.M., *Add. MS. 11870*), fol. *197v*:
S. John with S. Prochorus.

A similar style is employed in the *Menologium* (or Menology) of Basil II (preserved in the Vatican Library, *Cod. Vat. Gr. 1613*). This is a superb work of art
(though partly retouched and fragmentary—only the portion from September to
February is extant), containing 430 miniatures, *i.e.*, a miniature on each page, on
gold background, signed in all by eight different painters, including two (Michael
and Simeon) 'of Blachernae', who probably belonged to the Imperial scriptorium
of Constantinople. Simeon of Blachernae, Pantaleon and Michael the Little seem
to be the best artists, the finest miniatures being the Nativity and the Adoration of
the Magi, by Simeon, and the Miracle of S. Michael and the hermit Archippus,
by Pantaleon. In Dalton's opinion, this manuscript, being an abridged edition of a
menologium, should rather be called a *synaxarium*. Copies of the *menologium* are
preserved in Moscow (*Sin. Gr. No. 183*) and in Baltimore (Walters Art Gallery,
Cod. No. 521): see further on. Fig. II-23*b* and 25. See also Baronius (*ad a. 886*,
No. 14).

The important and richly decorated theological works of the eleventh and
twelfth centuries, known as *menologia*, are kinds of general liturgical calendars in
which the exploits of the saints are recorded in the order of the Church calendar:
they are based on the compilation by Simeon Metaphrastes (a great lay official who
had been Logothetes and Magister) of the *Lives of the Saints*, written during the
reign of the Emperor Basil II. There are several such MSS. extant, but they are not
identical; an extremely fine example, for the twenty-five feasts of September, is in
the British Museum (*Add. MS. 11870*, late eleventh or early twelfth century): see
Plate facing p. 106.

At the head of each legend is a miniature, richly framed in ornament. The
backgrounds are in reddish gold; the figures, painted in body-colour, are long and
slender, the faces dignified, the draperies carefully shaded and arranged in fine folds.
Some of the miniatures occur frequently in Byzantine Gospel-books (fol. 197*b*: S.
John dictating the Gospel to his disciple S. Prochorus; fol. 60: the Archangel
Michael turning aside a torrent); six headpieces—in series of four or five small
medallions—contain scenes from the lives and passions of saints, and sixteen have
single miniatures, representing either martyrdoms, or miracles, or saints standing
upright, sometimes holding a small cross. The treatment is mainly conventional,
there is no perspective, and the colouring is far from natural.

Mention may also be made of *Cod. Gr. 586* of the Marciana Library, Venice; it
is an exquisite eleventh-century MS. of the *Lives of the Saints*.

Imperial Menologium: MS. 521 (already referred to) in the Walters Art Gallery,
Baltimore, which comes from the Greek Patriarchal Library at Cairo, is the only
surviving copy of the *Lives of the Saints* for January, of the 'Imperial Menologium'.
The twenty-four miniatures are in the best style of the Imperial atelier at Constantinople. Each miniature precedes a 'biography'. In Dr. Der Nersessian's opinion,
this menology was produced for the Emperor Michael IV the Paphlagonian
(1034–41). Fig. II-25*c*.

Lectionaries of the Gospels

Important lectionaries were also produced, such as that of the Public Library at Leningrad (*Cod. Gr. 21*), which is dated by C. R. Morey to the eighth century, and by K. Weitzmann to the tenth; another is the *Phocas Lectionary*, in the monastery of Lavra on Mount Athos.

An interesting tenth-century *Lectionary of the Gospels*, which comes from the Convent of S. Clement, Ochrida (Yugoslavia), is preserved in the Walters Art Gallery, Baltimore (*MS. 520*). It is written in large uncials by a certain Theodoros. It contains decorated headpieces and initials.

A very fine *Lectionary*, produced in Constantinople in the eleventh century, and now preserved in New York (Pierpont Morgan Library, *M. 639*), contains five large miniatures and twenty-one delicate marginal miniatures.

In another fine *Lectionary*, also produced in Constantinople (about 1160), and now preserved in the Pierpont Morgan Library (*M. 692*), all pages are arranged in the form of a cross (Fig. II-20a). Similar method is adopted in a ninth-century *Gospels* from the Skiti of S. Andrew of the Russians on Mt. Athos, now in Princeton University Library, *Garrett MS. 1*. In several MSS. such arrangement occurs only on occasional pages.

Miscellanea (Fig. II-23c)

Of other extant East Christian theological works, one of the finest and most interesting is the *Klimax*, or *Scala Paradisi* ('Spiritual Ladder'), written in the sixth century by Abbot John Klimax of the monastery of S. Catherine, on Mount Sinai; in the preserved copies (Vatican Library, *Cod. Vat. Gr. 354*, eleventh century; a twelfth-century copy in the Monastery of S. Catherine; and a few other copies, with independent but inferior illustrations), are set forth, by means of allegorical miniatures and drawings, the toilsome ascent of the spiritual ladder; the pictures are executed in a manner somewhat resembling that of the *Metaphrastes* (see p. 105). There are here many illustrations of religious and monastic life, with allegorical subjects relating to progress up the 'ladder'.

An eleventh-century copy of the *Scala Paradisi*, preserved in the Marciana Library, Venice (*MS. Gr. II, 32: 1013*) contains fifteenth-century additions with illuminations and pen-drawings without colour. They are attributed to the region of the Adriatic Sea.

Religious poetry is represented by the well-known *Akathistos*, or Akathistic Hymn to the Virgin—so called from the fact that it was sung standing—attributed to Photius (A.D. 629); it contains twenty-four episodes from the life of the Virgin, and is preserved in several late illuminated copies. Some scholars (such as L. Bréhier and V. Cottas) have studied this Hymn in connection with the drama *Christos Paschon* and with the text and illustrations of the *Homilies* of the monk Jacobus—already referred to—and have tried to reconstruct the Byzantine religious theatre and to discern its influence on European art and the origins of the European theatre.

Mathew refers to a curious British Museum manuscript (*Add. MSS. 5111–5112*), containing a considerable portion of a twelfth-century MS., of the Eusebian Canons, and fragments from the fourteenth and fifteenth centuries. He suggests that the book was constructed in a monastic scriptorium, perhaps in the seventeenth century, by dismembering earlier manuscripts, and was intended to include the Four Gospels, the Creeds, a selection of Canons, and extracts from Cyril and Athanasius. At a later period, however, further fragments and loose leaves were added to it. Amongst the various miniatures of this codex there is a mid-fourteenth-century portrait of an Evangelist containing perhaps fifteen shades of colour. In the slender doorway of the high blue-walled house a red curtain is being blown back by the wind to balance the turning leaves of the Gospel; the Evangelist is counter-balanced by the small figure erect on the locked casket: Mathew.

Exultet. A group of peculiar illuminated parchment rolls, known as *Exultet*, was produced in the eleventh to thirteenth centuries in Italy—for instance, at Beneventum, which had close relations with Eastern Christianity. These manuscripts, though in Byzantine style, will be dealt with in Chapter VI, relating to Italy.

Portraits of Authors and Patrons (Fig. II-26a). Numerous manuscripts contain beautiful portraits of authors and/or patrons, some drawn from actual life—for instance, the portrait of Admiral Apocaucos on the title-page of a Hippocrates MS., National Library at Paris, *Gr. 2144*. See also p. 56 f. and Fig. II-26a.

Melissenda Psalter (Fig. II-23d)

This unique manuscript (preserved in the British Museum, *Egerton MS 1139*), covered with a beautiful and unique binding (which will be discussed in the book on *Binding*), is strictly speaking not Byzantine, but it is preferable to deal with it in this Chapter, not only for want of a more suitable place, but also because of its miniatures. The book is relatively well preserved, and there is none of the flaking off which we find in the Byzantine MSS. It is the only preserved example of—if we may name it thus—the Crusaders' art of illumination.

The MS., it is commonly agreed, was made for Queen Melissenda or Melissande, eldest daughter of Baldwin II du Bourg, King of Jerusalem from 1118 to 1131. Eminent scholars suggest that the MS., ordered by Melissenda, was intended to be presented to some lady in a religious house, perhaps her sister Iveta, an Abbess at Bethany. Melissenda was the wife of Fulk (or Foulques) of Anjou, who succeeded Baldwin II when the latter retired to the monastery of the Holy Sepulchre. Melissenda took an active part in the government, and after Fulk's death in 1143, held the regency for some years for their son Baldwin III (1129–62). She died in Jerusalem only one year before her son.

The MS. is in Latin minuscules and is beautifully written. It contains (1) interesting Calendar-ornaments, Western (perhaps French) in character, consisting of the zodiac-signs, on gold grounds, in small medallions; (2) miniatures which are Byzantine in style and iconography, but not in colouring; and (3) elaborate decorative gilded initials, Western in character (though not without Islamic influence), at the beginning and principal divisions of the Psalter.

The miniatures, all on gold grounds, may be distinguished in two groups: (1) twenty-four full-page pictures at the beginning, representing scenes from the life of Christ, and (2) nine half-page miniatures of saints, towards the end of the manuscript. The former, an unusually complete series, are of great importance for study of iconographical details. All seem the work of a single painter with a Greek name, Basilios, whose signature is recorded on the scene of Christ's enthronement. The form of his signature, *Basilius me fecit*, proves that he was working for some Western patron. Mathew assumes that this artist Basil may be identical with the Byzantine *Basilius Pictor*, who worked on mosaics at Bethlehem which were completed in 1169. An ascription to the second half of the twelfth century is also supported by the similarity of technique with early thirteenth century paintings in the Lectionary of Joseph of Malatea. Thus, in Father Matthew's opinion, the MS. may be assigned to a date between 1131 and 1187.

However, while the composition is in pure Byzantine style, the colouring (vivid but unharmonized: deep ultramarine marred by the juxtaposition of ill-matched shades of crimson, green, and a harsh crimson) and the design of the figures (ill-modelled, with impossibly long necks, sullen and peevish faces, etc.) betray other influences. There is no perspective at all, and the scenes seem as if cut against the gold background. The proportions of the figures are often absurd; the types monotonous; there is no facial expression. Nevertheless, some scenes possess much beauty and symmetry (particularly the miniatures representing the Ascension and the Harrowing of Hell) or include personifications (the miniature depicting Baptism).

The half-page miniatures, by the same painter who executed the zodiac-medallions, are copies from a traditional Byzantine menology, but the effect has been much improved by greater freedom and naturalism, brighter colouring, and more skilful treatment of the faces, imparting to them an animation, in some cases even a touch of coquetry, quite alien to the spirit of Byzantine hagiographical art: Herbert.

SECULAR SUBJECTS

The style of the early Byzantine secular books, of which not many have been preserved, was based mainly on Alexandrian Hellenistic models; it has been referred to in Chapter I. In later times the neo-classical style was employed particularly for secular books. It may be seen, for instance, in two important historical works of the fourteenth century: a copy—preserved in the National Library, Madrid—of Johannes Skylitzes (eleventh century), Byzantine history from 811 to the middle of the eleventh century, containing over 600 miniatures painted by different hands; and a Bulgarian translation of Constantine Manasses: see p. 115. Manasses, *Sýnopsis historikḗ*, written in the second half of the twelfth century, is a historical compilation, based on Dionysius of Halicarnassus, John of Antioch, Pseudo-Simeon, and Zonaras. This *Chronicle* is known from various copies, particularly from Slavonic versions, preserved in Moscow (*Codex S*; just before 1345), in the Vatican Library (see p. 115), in the Serbian monastery Chilandari on Mt. Athos (*c.* 1510), in Tulča, Dobrudja (sixteenth or seventeenth century), in Leningrad (sixteenth century), and in several later copies.

A *de luxe* copy of the medical works by Hippocratus has been referred to on p. 107.

The *Liber de arte venandi cum avibus*, which was written by Emperor Frederick II (1194–1250) and enlarged by his natural son, King Manfred (*c.* 1231–66), was beautifully illuminated in Byzantine style by an anonymous artist, and is now preserved in the Vatican Library (*Pal. Lat. 1071*). See Chapter VI, dealing with Italy.

Various secular illuminated manuscripts in Byzantine style are discussed in Chapter I. Here we may refer to some other codices, such as the thirteenth-century codex of Orpheus, *Argonautica et Hymni*, preserved in the Riccardiana Library, Florence (*53–e–1a*).

END OF BYZANTINE ILLUMINATION

The later Byzantine codices, though as a rule fully illustrated, are generally speaking not as beautiful as those of the tenth, eleventh, and twelfth centuries, and show no new artistic movement of importance. The ground is almost invariably gold—but occasionally blue, as already in the British Museum *Add. MS. 4949*, of the twelfth century. The backgrounds are either plain or filled with buildings. Landscape is restricted to one subject, S. John dictating to S. Prochorus (see p. 100 f.).

The Latin occupation of Constantinople (in 1204), in effect the sack of the richest city in the world—one of the greatest sackings in history—and the temporary establishment there of Latin rule, naturally resulted in a decadence of Byzantine art, including book-illumination.

Signs of decay had begun to show themselves, especially in the sense for harmonious colouring, before the end of the twelfth century. The instinct for decorative fitness and for the solemn effects proper to religious art, which had been its distinguishing characteristic for at least three centuries, gradually died away, and very little remained apart from the outward mannerisms which had always been a characteristic—though not a very happy feature—of the Byzantine style. As to the broad lines of composition, there is a conservatism verging on monotony, though the details vary in a way calculated at once to delight and to perplex the student of these MSS.—and that not only from one codex to another, but also from page to page within the same volume. At the same time, however, Byzantine art of illumination provided a starting-point for the new Italian school, which continued its tradition with great success through the thirteenth and fourteenth centuries (see Chapter V).

Fourteenth and Fifteenth Centuries (Fig. II-26–27). In the fourteenth century there was a short renaissance, in which Italian artistic influence may be discerned. Then book-painting fell gradually into decadence, until at last, lifeless in conception and coarse and weak in execution, it no longer deserved the name of artistic book-production.

This Byzantine production is amply represented in Eastern monastic libraries, in the Vatican Library, the British Museum, the National Libraries in Florence, Venice, Vienna, Paris, and other great European, as well as American, collections of manuscripts. The following manuscripts are outstanding: *Cod. F. 7 (Gospels)* of 1330, of the Vallicelliana Library, Rome (already referred to); *Vat. Lat. 375 (Lives of the Holy Fathers)*; *Vat. Gr. 361 (Gospels)*; *Vat. Gr. 1156 (Gospels)*; *Vat. Gr. 1158* and *1208 (Gospels)*; the already mentioned codices *Cl. i. xx (Gospels*; of the year 1302) and *xxii (Gospels)* of the Marciana Library, Venice, and *Cod. Cl. i. 8 (Gospels)* of the same collection; *Cod. D. 67 sup.* of the Ambrosian Library, Milan, already referred to *(Gospels)*; a *Life of Alexander*, preserved in S. Giorgio dei Greci, Venice. See Fig. II-26d.

In Mathew's opinion, the zest for pure experiment mars much late fourteenth- and early fifteenth-century Byzantine painting. A late fourteenth-century *Typikon* (part Rule, part Cartulary) of the rich convent of the All Holy of the Protovestiary, at Constantinople, belongs to Lincoln College, Oxford *(Gr. MS. 35)*, and is now preserved in the Bodleian Library, Oxford. Consisting of 163 folios, it contains the rules and customs of the convent, a survey of the buildings, edifying exhortations, an account of the family of a co-foundress, a calendar, and portraits of twenty-one Palaeologan benefactors and benefactresses, including ten full-page portraits. Apparently it was commissioned about 1360 by Euphrosyne Comnena Ducaena Palaeologina, grandniece of the Emperor Michael VIII. Palaeologus, in order to commemorate her mother, who had died as a nun in the convent under the name Theodulia. It is suggested that the MS. was not accomplished at once, but grew slowly, the miniatures being executed by at least three hands. The fol. 12—which Mathew considers possibly a late addition made not long after 1400— is rather unusual: it represents the Abbess and her community; the Abbess leans upon her staff of office, her counsellors and the senior nuns are grouped around her, whereas the novices or out-sisters stand below. Fols. 161–162v contain entries of donations in 1397, 1398, and 1402: Fig. II-26b.

Some MSS. contain superb miniatures showing a perfect artistic taste and study of life. Remarkable in this respect is the codex of John Cantacuzen (Johannes VI Kantakuzenos, 1347–1354), National Library at Paris, *Gr. 1242*—Fig. II-26c; here also is rich and varied ornamentation, due in part to strong Oriental, mainly Arabic or Persian influences. The Transfiguration reproduced in Fig. II-26c is a great composition. We find it also in the Bodleian *MS. Gr. Th. fol. 1*, fol. 3*v* (Fig. II-27*c*).

Several *Menologia* in the form of small pictorial handbooks, on parchment or paper, are extant; they served as Church calendars. A charming little Service-book, a *Horologion*, of the late fourteenth century is preserved in Walters Art Gallery, Baltimore (*MS. 534*). It measures 4 by 2¾ in., and contains 260 leaves with sixteen miniatures, executed 'not in the formal style of the court ateliers' (Miner): Fig. II-27*a*. It is bound in old wooden boards and green silk.

An interesting Byzantine MS. is preserved in the British Museum (*Add. MSS. 5111–5112*). 'It contains a considerable portion of a twelfth century manuscript which, from an obit, was possibly Western Greek. But it includes fragments of a far older manuscript of the Eusebian Canons and fragments from the fourteenth and fifteenth centuries. Its most probable history is that it began as a commonplace book of Sacred Parallels constructed in a monastic scriptorium perhaps in the seventeenth century, by dismembering earlier manuscripts ... and that further fragments and loose leaves were added to it before it came into the possession of the British Museum.'

Mount Athos (Fig. II-26*c* and 27*d*) [*see now* F. Doelger, *Aus den Schatzkammern des Heiligen Berges*, Munich, 1948; K. Weitzmann, *Aus den Bibliotheken des Athos*, 2 vols., Hamburg, 1963, and so on.] Following the conquest of the Empire and of Constantinople, and its terrible sack by the Turks (in 1453), many Greek artists retired to the convents of Mount Athos, and this 'Holy Mountain' became one of the main centres of Byzantine art. To this day the libraries of these monasteries contain wonderful treasures of finely illuminated and bound MSS. On the whole, however, there was no attempt at invention in technique or style.

Work produced in the previous centuries in the Mt. Athos monasteries has already been referred to. Here mention may be made of an interesting *Gospel-book* from the Skiti of S. Andrew of the Russians on Mt. Athos, now preserved in the Walters Art Gallery, *MS. 526*. Written in the eleventh century by the scribe Theodoulos, the codex contains four contemporary headpieces (painted in brown and green), but in the fifteenth century five full-page miniatures were added on pages that were left blank. See Fig. II-27*d*.

Apart from Mt. Athos and from Italy—see further on—Greek-Byzantine illuminated book-production was carried out in various places. Here it will suffice to refer to a *Lectionary of the Gospels*, which belonged to the Temple of the Resurrection, Jerusalem, and is now in the Walters Art Gallery, *MS. 535*. It is on paper, and was written in 1594 by Lukas of Cyprus, Bishop of Buzeos, who was the scribe of other important works. The present codex—Fig. II-27*e*—contains illuminated headpieces, 58 small miniatures and four full-page ones, in a 'late, somewhat hardened style', but 'particularly interesting in that the illumination is unfinished and shows us the various stages from outline sketch to finished miniature' (D. Miner).

Finally, we may refer to illuminated book-production in other Greek centres.

An interesting sixteenth-century MS. in the British Museum (*Add. MS. 40724*), containing 375 illuminations, is a copy of a Greek poetical paraphrase of *Genesis* and *Exodus* by Georgios Chumnos of Candia (Crete). Two other copies are in Vienna and Venice (they are not illuminated).

Influence on Italian Painting (Fig. II-27*b* and 28*a*; see also p. 290, 301, and *passim*)

The growing influence of Byzantine art of the Second Golden Age upon Italian painting, especially in the period which preceded the great Giotto, may be seen not only in the works of Cimabue (a famous Florentine painter, 1240–1302), of Duccio di Buoninsegna (founder of the Sienese school, ? 1260–1340), and of the two great Roman painters of the late thirteenth and early fourteenth centuries, Pietro Cavallini and Jacopo Torriti, but also in some beautiful illuminated codices, such as a *Pisa Bible* of 1169 (see p. 302), and especially in the Gospels of 1259 in the treasury of Padua Cathedral (see p. 305 f.). In the celebrated Grotta-ferrata monastery (near Rome), excellent Byzantine book-illumination was produced by Greek monks: see, for instance, Fig. II-27*b* (Vatican Library, *Vat. Lat. 5974, fol. 10v*).

Particularly important is the influence exercised by Byzantine illumination on the early Italian masters in depicting landscape backgrounds. In certain respects, the Byzantine painters—as represented, for instance, by the paintings in the *Menologium of Basil II* (see p. 105)—have been considered a link between the classical frescoes—as seen, for example, in Pompeian wall-paintings—and the Tuscan paintings, down to Benozzo Gozzoli and Filippo Lippi. Although the treatment was far from naturalistic, it soon (during the tenth century) became traditional in Byzantine painting and lingered on till the fifteenth century.

The most striking feature in Byzantine landscape is the curiously conventional treatment of hills, which are represented as *tells*—as seen in hundreds all over the Near East—*i.e.*, truncated cones with smooth, level table-tops, and with steep, symmetrical and absolutely smooth and arid slopes, often interrupted at regular intervals by ledges of the same evenness as the summits. Lower down are boulders and crags of similar form, like the stumps of neatly sawn-off tree-trunks.

Byzantine influences reached Italy in various ways; here it will suffice to mention the beautiful mosaic decorations executed in Sicily and at Venice by Byzantine artists and craftsmen, or the close relations which existed between the merchants of the maritime city-states, such as Amalfi, Pisa, Genoa, Bari, and Venice, on one hand, and the Byzantine Empire and its neighbouring countries on the other. Numerous South Italian illuminated MSS. extant—particularly those of the Benedictine monasteries—show strong Byzantine influences; mention may be made of Montecassino *Cod. 73* (*S. Gregory*; early eleventh century), *109* (*Homilies* illustrated by the monk Grimualdus), and *98* and *99* (*Homilies* illuminated by the monk Leo, 1072); *Vat. Lat. 1202* (*Vita S. Benedicti*); *Vat. Lat. 3741* (*Gospels*); *Vat. Ottob. 296* (*Gospels*); and *Urbin. Lat. 585* (*Psalter*; thirteenth century); *Cod. vi. B. 2* (*Homilies*; early eleventh century) and *Cod. viii. C. 4* (a *Martyrology*) in the National

Library at Naples; and *MS 31* (*Lectionary*) in Traù Cathedral. See also p. 290 ff.

An *Evangelistarium* of Capua, dated 991, written by a Sicilian monk (preserved in the Vatican Library, *Vat. Gr. 2138*), and a Gospel-book, of 1023, probably written in South Italy (preserved in the Ambrosian Library, Milan, *B. 56. Sup.*) contain interesting humorous initials of the Lombardic type, similar to those mentioned on p. 296. In Herbert's opinion, they are of Eastern-Byzantine origin. Fig. II-28*a*.

As to the later period, reference may be made to an interesting copy of the Greek Gospels written in Rome in 1478 for Cardinal Francesco Gonzaga, and now preserved in the British Museum (*Harley MS. 5790*). The scribe was a Cretan priest named John; the illuminations were executed by an Italian artist, as may be seen from the style of the miniatures of the Evangelists and of the charming head-pieces, prefixed to the Gospels (following the Byzantine method—see p. 94). The single figures and some small marginal groups were copied from Byzantine models, related to such MSS. as the *Theodore Psalter* (see p. 98 f.).

Fig. II-28*b* reproduces an interesting miniature from a copy of the *Commentary on the Apocalypse* by the Dominican Fredericus de Venetiis, illuminated by a Greek artist working in Venice. According to the colophon, it was completed on 10.10.1415 (Walters Art Gallery, *MS. 335*, fol. 1*v*).

Finally, we may refer to a copy of *Prophecies* by Emperor Leo, written between 1566 and 1574, formerly preserved in the Jesuit Collegio Massimo in Palermo, and now in the National Library of that City (*MS. I. E. 8*). The copy contains the fifteen oracles, each one illustrated by a miniature and coloured pen-drawings of figures; although based on earlier Byzantine models, they present other Western and Eastern features, and were probably executed in Sicily.

BYZANTINE ILLUMINATION IN THE BALKANS AND IN RUSSIA

From the cultural standpoint, these lands were Byzantine colonies. The whole culture of Bulgaria, Serbia, Russia and Roumania is, indeed, based on Byzantine foundations. When Duke Vladimir the Great became a Christian in 988, he married the Byzantine princess Anne and made the East Christian Church the State religion of Russia. He ordered the wholesale baptism of his people in the waters of the Dnieper, invited from Constantinople numerous priests and artists to supply the newly created need of the Christian churches, and sent intelligent people from Russia to Constantinople to learn their culture and art.

RUSSIA

Throughout the eleventh, twelfth, and thirteenth centuries, the inspiration of Russian art in the main Russian cities was Byzantine-Greek or Constantinopolitan. From the eleventh century a school of illumination developed in Russia, but its works at first are scarcely to be distinguished from those of Constantinople.

After the fall of Constantinople, in 1453, the Russian rulers regarded themselves as the direct successors of the Byzantine line. Indeed, Zoë—the niece of the last Byzantine emperor, Constantine Palaeologus—married Ivan III the Great, Grand-Duke of Moscow, and when Constantinople fell, the Grand-Duke considered himself heir of Byzantium and Head of Eastern Christianity. He assumed the title of Monarch of All the Russias. The 'double-eagle' of the Eastern Roman Empire —it was argued by some scholars that this originally symbolized the division of the Roman Empire into an eastern and western portion, but this is questionable— became the coat of arms of the Muscovite Grand-Dukes, and later of the Russian Tsars. The Russian court assumed the pompous form of the Byzantine court. This strange inheritance which the dying Byzantine Empire bequeathed to an unsuspecting world, continued to live with great vigour until the Russian Revolution in 1917.

In 1589, the Bishop of Moscow was declared the fifth Patriarch (of the Orthodox Church) to take the place of Rome, and as all the other Patriarchates were then minority groups isolated in the Moslem ocean, Moscow became the main centre of Eastern Christianity. In later times the Serbian and Roumanian churches became self-governing, and now the Greek Church has again become the most important centre of Orthodox Eastern Christianity.

During her virtual isolation from Western Europe from the fourteenth to the seventeenth centuries, Russia, while seeking her development along distinctive lines, preserved the main traditional Byzantine features in her art and culture.

Bulgaria and Serbia

The culture and art of Bulgaria and Serbia were even more closely related to Byzantium than were those of Russia. Byzantine influence penetrated to Bulgaria by way of Salonica, which was the most important city of the Byzantine world after Constantinople. As to Serbia, when the founder of her independence from Byzantine rule, Stephen Nemanja, abdicated, he retired to the Serbian monastery of Chilandari on Mount Athos, and in this and other monasteries on Mount Athos, Serbian as well as other Slavonic monks lived in absolute equality with the Greek monks.

Roumania

Although most of her art and culture came only indirectly from Byzantium, Roumania may nevertheless be considered to be culturally within the Byzantine orbit.

ILLUMINATED MANUSCRIPTS (Fig. II-28–30)

There are extant a number of manuscripts of the twelfth to fifteenth centuries written in Glagolitic or Cyrillic characters (see *The Alphabet*, pp. 475–88), though couched in the Bulgarian, Serbian, Russian or Roumanian languages. They are illuminated with miniatures in Byzantine style. The Bulgarian codices, such as the

Manasses MS., already referred to, and the *Curzon Gospel*—an illuminated manuscript written in Old Bulgarian, and now in the British Museum—are examples.

Fig. II-28 reproduces specimens from the earliest and most important Glagolitic codices: *c*, from *Codex Marianus*, of the tenth century, formerly in the S. Mary monastery on Mt. Athos, and now in Moscow; *d*, *Codex Zographensis*, also of the tenth century, formerly in the Zographu monastery, on Mt. Athos, and now in the Public Library at Leningrad (*Cod. Glag.* 1). Fig. II-29 reproduces various early Cyrillic miniatures and initials.

Vat. Slav. 2, containing the Bulgarian prose translation of the *Chronicle* of Constantine Manasses, is the most important of the Slavonic manuscripts belonging to the Vatican Library. It is also the only fully illustrated of all the known copies of the *Chronicle*. Moreover, it is one of the three secular Byzantine manuscripts which are richly illustrated. The superb codex was executed *c.* 1345, during the reign of John Alexander (1331–71), and was probably commissioned by him.

An interesting illuminated MS. preserved in the British Museum (*Add. MS.* 39627) may be referred to. It was produced in 1355–56 by the monk Simon for Tsar John Alexander of Bulgaria. The text is in Bulgarian, but it is based on a Greek original.

An interesting *Hymn-book*, written in 1404 for Hervos, Duke of Spalato, is preserved in the University Library at Bologna (*MS. 3575 B.*). The text is written in Serbo-Croatian Church Slavonic and in Cyrillic characters. The codex, of 359 leaves, contains a number of miniatures, decorated Eusebian Canons, and initials. Some of the miniatures are influenced by the Italian Gothic style—the Apostles (two on a page), Christ (fol. 3r), S. John the Baptist, Ascension (fol. 162v), Stoning of S. Stephen (fol. 171v), the figures of David, Moses, S. James, S. Peter, S. John, S. Jude, S. Paul, and a few other pictures; other miniatures are in local Slavonic style—Annunciation (fol. 13v), the miniatures preceding the Four Gospels (representing the Evangelists and their symbols), and Christ with the Apostles on fol. 38r.

Illuminated Letters: an interesting *Psalter* of the beginning of the fourteenth century was on the book-market several years ago. It was probably produced in South Russia, or rather Ukraine. The codex, measuring 210 × 160 mm., contains 282 leaves with one large miniature and 105 initials, large and small, illuminated in gold and colour.

Fig. II-30 represents the Evangelist Mark (fol. 89v) and Luke (fol. 144v) and the initial pages of their Gospels in a beautiful Slavonic-Greek Gospel-book of the Bodleian Library (*MS. Can. Gr. 122*).

SYRIAC ILLUMINATION (Fig. II-31–32)

The importance of the role played by the Syrian strain in the development of Byzantine and other East Christian book-illumination has already been indicated, the main features of this strain being crude rather than good composition, true perspective, ideal or superficial beauty; but also realism, dramatic energy, inner meaning, the significance of an idea; the desired effect being achieved by the most forceful means, such as, for example, the enlargement of an individual figure to emphasize its importance.

Syrian Art

It is outside the scope of the present book to discuss the problem of the dependence of this art upon the ancient Semitic civilization of Mesopotamia or the Hittite-Aramaic of Syria. The origins of Aramaic or Syrian culture and art were probably of a fairly complex nature; and though their principal ingredients were either original or drawn from the East, Hellenistic and Roman influences were not excluded.

In the wall-paintings of a Christian chapel at Dura Europos, on the Middle Euphrates, dated before A.D. *c.* 250, which show Christ walking on the water and other episodes of the Gospels, we have one of the earliest figures of Christ known in art. (For the importance of the frescoes of the Dura synagogue, see the section on early Hebrew book-illustration and decoration in Chapter I.)

There can be no doubt that from this time onwards Christian paintings must have been quite common in Syria, but as very few, if any, examples are extant, it is not easy to determine the development of their style. In the fourth century A.D. religious art of Syrian or Syro-Egyptian origin had been growing more popular throughout the world. Its votaries—writes Runciman—were fundamentally esoteric and fundamentally dissatisfied with the world. The complacency of Hellenistic naturalism was meaningless to them. Nature to them was often ugly and they were prepared to face its ugliness. They were insensitive to delicacy of drawing and balance of composition; they required an art that would speak to them directly without compromise, that would rouse them to an intensity of emotion rather than lull them in aesthetic content.

Scholars agree that the triumph of Christianity meant the furthering of this Semitic conception of art. Indeed, as Runciman points out, Christ could not be depicted as Apollo had been. He was the God that suffered, the Great Judge, the Redeemer. Religion demanded an impressionism unknown in the Graeco-Roman world.

Syria may have developed a decorative art of her own, an art which Mesopotamian tradition may also have enriched. Indeed, geometrical surface-covering designs, conventional beast-ornament, a love of polychromy, and so on, were already present in the ancient Assyrian art.

However, even from the late paintings at Kuseir Amra (711–15), and from the ninth-century Samarra paintings, we can assume that Syrian art was strongly influenced by Hellenistic art on the one hand, and by Sasanian or Persian art on the other; there were also some Byzantine affinities, and, for later times, even Far Eastern influences can be traced.

Illumination: Dependence on Byzantine Art and Local Influences

The rich and abundant ecclesiastical art of the Syrian Churches depended, partly at least, on Byzantine art. At the same time, however, there were strong local influences derived from the indigenous art of northern Syria, Mesopotamia, and Persia. Unfortunately, owing to the numerous forces of destruction that overran western Asia from time to time—religious persecution, wars of devastation, massacres, incendiarism, looting, orthodox fanaticism or iconoclast bigotry, pestilence, and so on, all implying the destruction of works of art and conditions making for the growing ignorance of native populations, with a consequent neglect of art—only a few illuminated MSS. have come down to us, and hardly any belonging to the early period. Furthermore, even those still extant have received little attention from students of the history of art.

Rabbūlā Gospels (Fig. II-31 and 32a)

The earliest extant and without doubt the most celebrated Syriac *codex* is the *Rabbūlā Gospel-book*, which is illuminated in Byzantine style. It is preserved in the Laurentian Library at Florence (*Cod. Plut. 1. 56*). It was written and illuminated by the monk Rabbūlā in A.D. 586, at the monastery of S. John at Zagba, in Mesopotamia; the name and date—features all too rare in early codices and unique in the earliest ones—are given in an inscription.

The connection of this codex with early Byzantine art is unmistakable. In the rich colour of its twenty-six illuminated pages, in the representation of the many scenes and subjects—which also probably derived from wall-paintings or mosaic decorations of Palestinian or Syrian churches—it is related to the *Rossano Gospels*. It shows, in addition, various characteristic features of the distinctively Syrian style, such as the method of marginal illustration, the profusion of decorative motifs, especially arcades, and so on. Finally, the Hellenistic style is recalled by some marginal scenes, more specifically by the seven full-page illustrations (including four at the end of the codex: the Crucifixion, the Ascension, Pentecost, and Christ enthroned in a sanctuary), which are of surpassing interest for the history of Christian art; this style is also brought to mind by the colouring, and by the background of mountains and bushes.

There is, indeed, a theory that the *Rabbūlā Codex* was copied from a Greek original—a suggestion which, however, is not probable, although the blundered inscription *Loginos* in Greek uncials over the head of Longinus (piercing Christ's right side with a lance), seems to lend support to it. However, this splendid codex particularly reflects the great activity of the Syrian artists in the formation of the iconographic system, an activity which continued during the whole of the Middle Ages. Fig. II-31.

It has been suggested that at least some of the illustrations of the *Rabbūlā Gospels* are later interpolations, but in the opinion of Ainaloff their prototypes may have been lost mosaic designs belonging to early memorial churches of the Holy Land.

As O. M. Dalton says, if their date is that of the book they are of exceptional importance, and the Crucifixion, for instance, containing iconographic themes which appear much later in painting, would be the earliest example in illumination. Syro-Palestinian art must have had a paramount influence not only upon the formation and diffusion of iconographic or picture-cycles of Biblical stories, but also perhaps in fixing the type of Christ—bearded, long-haired, mature, with suave looks and definite ethnical features of Oriental type—which (almost completely) replaced the young and idealistic type previously created by Hellenistic art, which was in vogue in the early centuries of Western Christian art: see, for instance, Fig. II-1a.

There is a sketchiness and lack of finish about all the illuminations in the volume—their special importance being iconographical rather than artistic—but the work is always wonderfully effective and expressive, and at times (for instance, in the composition of the Pentecost scene, which we find repeated down to the end of the fifteenth century) succeeds in conveying the idea of spiritual beauty and grandeur.

The arcades of the Eusebian Canons are decorated with zigzag, check, meander, and other patterns; peacocks and other birds appear on many of the pages, usually standing on the arches. On the margins outside the arcading is a series of small paintings of scenes from the Gospel-story, including the Annunciation (in the divided form familiar to students of medieval Italian art), the 'Double Communion', and the entry into Jerusalem. Fig. II-32a.

Another important early Syrian MS. is *Codex Syr. 33*, in the National Library at Paris, also attributed to the sixth century A.D.

Part Played in the Formation of Byzantine Illumination

Monks, trained chiefly in the theological schools of Edessa, Nisibis, and other Syrian centres (see *The Hand-produced Book*, p. 295 and *passim*) flocked to religious houses which were soon founded in Palestine and the neighbouring countries. From the fifth century onwards, Syrian monks took a predominant part in the formation of Christian iconography—see p. 76 f.—and contributed to Byzantine art its main non-Hellenistic qualities. Syrian religious art was always predominant in Palestine, Syria, North Mesopotamia, and Persia, and it strongly influenced Cappadocia, Pontus, Armenia, and other Asiatic countries, as well as Christian Egypt and particularly Sinai.

Furthermore, the Eastern monasteries since early times had frequent and close intercourse with the monasteries of the West, especially of South Italy; in consequence, influences of Syrian art were felt strongly in the West. The possible influence of Syrian book-illumination has been suggested by Mlle. G. L. Micheli: specimens of interest are a *Book of Daniel* (preserved in the British Museum, *Syr. 14445*), dated to the eighth century, and a *Book of Kings* (preserved in the National Library at Paris, *Syr. 27*), dated A.D. 705.

Nestorian and Jacobite Illumination (Fig. II-32b)

Of the various Syriac Churches, those of the Jacobites and, particularly, of the Nestorians, need special mention; see also *The Hand-produced Book*, p. 296 ff. Several illuminated service-books and illustrated copies of the Gospels have been preserved. Sir Thomas Arnold has shown that the miniatures in the service-books are ultimately connected in technique and style with those of the Byzantine schools. But the artists who belonged to the schismatic Oriental Churches carried on their work for centuries with little direct connection with the sources from which they derived the tradition of their art.

In these circumstances, it is understandable that the illumination of the Nestorian and Jacobite books was strongly influenced by the indigenous art that formed part of the Persian national inheritance. This was to be expected since the consciousness of the national (Persian) affiliation was highly developed, not only amongst the large and flourishing community of Persian Christians belonging to the Nestorian Church, but also amongst the smaller community of the Jacobites.

British Museum *Add. MS. 7170* and *Vat. Syr. 559* are the most important Jacobite illuminated manuscripts. They are strictly related and are almost the only surviving examples of the very active *scriptorium* of the monastery of Mar Mattaï. Father Jerphanion, the editor of *Syr. 559*, has shown that 'numerous features borrowed from the Islamic arts, and principally from the illuminations which, by common agreement, have been attributed to the so-called "Baghdād" school, but which it would be more correct to call Seljuk, came to be inserted on a common iconographic basis of Syro-Palestinian or Byzantine origin in which Western derivations are not lacking'. The Vatican MS., executed in 1220, contains 50 miniatures, a few having been lost. An interesting feature of the MS. is a pen-sketch showing how the design was altered according to the corrections suggested by the scribe.

Fig. II-32b reproduces the portrait of S. Luke, standing, holding a book with the opening words of his Gospel (a detached leaf from a Syriac *Gospels*, Pierpont Morgan Library, *M. 774*). Of particular charm is the ornamentation of a Jacobite *Lectionary of the Gospels*, of the year 1220 (*Cod. Syr. Harris*, 78; now, Castle Museum, Colchester, *MS. 228. 32*). It is a copy of the Harqleian version (see *The Hand-produced Book*, p. 302), which was in great favour with the Jacobites, who introduced it in all their churches.

Christian Arabic Illumination (Fig. III-8a). Moslem Arabic illumination will be dealt with in the next Chapter, where it will also be indicated how strong was Syrian influence. Here it will suffice to mention that Christian Arabic illumination, on the whole, was Syrian. A fragmentary *Gospel-book* in Arabic, containing the text describing the infancy of the Saviour, is preserved in the Laurentian Library, Florence (*MS. Orient. 387*). It was written in 1299 at Mardin (in Mesopotamia), by Isaac son of Abulfaraj. Nearly all pages contain pen-drawings illustrating the text.

ARMENIAN ILLUMINATION

Although relatively early paintings have been discovered in Armenian churches (at T'alish, Tekor, Mren, and T'alin), little was found to be contemporary with the construction of these seventh-century churches; and although these paintings show that Armenian Christianity had a full New Testament picture-cycle, this art was not native to the region, but was introduced, on the one hand, through Byzantine influences, and, on the other, through Syrian and Iranian influences.

Illuminated Codices (Fig. II-33–39)

According to the treatise attributed to Vrt'anes K'ert'ogh, who flourished in the early seventh century A.D., painting was introduced into Armenia 'from the country of the Greeks' shortly before his own time. Magnificent Gospel-books were then already available in Armenia 'painted and bound not only with gold and silver, but with ivory and purple parchment'. However, the earliest dated Armenian MSS. which have come down to us belong to the ninth and tenth centuries A.D., and almost all the illuminated codices of this period are Gospels.

The decoration of these Gospels is confined to the initial quire on which is written the Epistle of Eusebius to Carpianus, explaining the concordance between the Four Gospels, as well as the concordance (or Canon) tables. In the words of Miss S. Der Nersessian, ornate arcades frame the Canon tables, the entire composition recalling a church portal. Floral, animal, and geometric motifs fill the lunettes of these arcades, and flowers and birds are also drawn around them. The illuminated quire also contains a full-page miniature—representing, for instance, a round church, in addition to portraits of Christ, the Virgin, the four Evangelists (the portraits of the latter being sometimes at the end of the respective Gospels), and some Gospel scenes.

On the whole, Armenian book-illumination was developed along lines parallel to the Byzantine, but with absolute predominance of Oriental influences. Many Armenian illuminated codices are extant, produced mainly between the tenth and the seventeenth centuries, and mainly at Melitene and Van—at this latter place generally between the fifteenth and the seventeenth centuries. In addition, there have been preserved a certain number of illuminated Gospels, which were owned by members of the Royal family of Cilicia, by catholicoses (or heads of the Armenian Church), and by other high dignitaries of the State and Church.

Classification. Miss Der Nersessian has recognised the following groups:

(1) The earliest extant and best illuminated codices, being those produced under the influence of the Byzantine MSS. of the ninth and tenth centuries. The most important MS. of this group is the magnificent *Gospel-book of Queen Mlqé*, the wife of Gagik Ardzruni; she presented this MS. to the monastery of Varag, near Van. This codex, which is generally attributed to A.D. 902—though N. Adontz would

prefer the date A.D. 862—is now preserved in the Mekhitharist Library, S. Lazzaro degli Armeni, near Venice (*MS. 1144*). Though the inspiration is derived from Byzantine art, the form is translated and adapted to Armenian artistic taste and feeling.

The *Mlqé Gospel* shows rich headpieces, which seem to combine Syrian and Iranian decorative motifs, though some motifs may ultimately go back to Alexandrian models. The miniature of the Ascension and the portraits of the Evangelists are exquisite: Fig. II-33*a* and 34*a*–*b*.

Other illuminated codices belonging to this group are: the Gospel-book of Etchmiadzin Library, *No. 229* (executed in 989 at Noravank', province of Siunik'), which has been discussed on p. 89 f., and *No. 369/311* (of the year 1066); the eleventh-century codices preserved in the library of the Armenian Patriarchate at Jerusalem (*No. 2556*) and in Venice, S. Lazzaro, *Nos. 887* (*Adrianople Gospels*) and *1400*; the latter MS. (*Trebizond Gospels*) is perhaps the work of a Greek artist: Fig. II-33*b*, 34*c*, 35.

(2) More numerous—though, to some degree, of inferior quality—are the illuminated codices produced by artists who were not affected by Byzantine influences, but followed the Syrian or the Iranian styles. Miss Der Nersessian assigns the following MSS. to this group: the *Gospels of the Translators*, now preserved in Walters Art Gallery, Baltimore; codex *No. 81* of the Erivan State Library (*Gospels*, of the year 986); the *Jerusalem Gospels No. 2555*; a few Gospels of the Etchmiadzin Library (*Nos. 363/3793*, of the year 1053, *993/4804*, of 1018, and *6201*, of 1038), and some other manuscripts.

Fig. II-36*a* reproduces the interesting miniature representing S. Mark and S. Luke in the *Gospels of the Translators*: this traditional name of the *codex* is due to the old belief that the text goes back to the original translation of the Gospels into Armenian. The MS. is written in capital letters; its scribe was Sargis, who produced the *codex* in 966 for his fellow-priest Thoros.

(3) Other preserved MSS. show a similar style, but are of a later date, and display a strongly marked local style seemingly developed from the original Syro-Byzantine models; so that from the twelfth century onwards Armenian book-illumination is somewhat distinct. In Prof. Runciman's opinion, the Armenian artists worked according to the Iranian synthesis of patterns and naturalism. Iran, working through Armenian artists, was teaching how to use animals as a decorative pattern rather than as a picture without sacrificing accuracy in the drawing.

Cilician Schools of Illumination. In the twelfth and thirteenth centuries, famous Armenian schools of book-illumination flourished in Cilicia, and particularly at Sis, Skevra, Mlidj, Hromkla, Drazark, Grner and Akner. The designs are drawn with delicate precision, and 'preference is given to interlace designs and to geometric motives such as the multi-coloured discs, chevrons and the rainbow' (Der Nersessian).

Fig. II-36*b* reproduces fol. 270*v* (SS. John and Prochoros) of a *Gospel-book* written in 1248 at Hromkla by Kirakos. This interesting MS. is preserved in the Armenian Catholicosote (*Cod. No. 1*) at Antilias (Lebanon).

Some of the codices, such as the *Venice Gospels, No. 1635,* have a great variety of colours and ornamental motifs, which have derived from different sources but are combined in a manner that 'makes them richer than anything produced by Byzantine book-illumination, and produces the effect of cloisonné enamel' (Der Nersessian). There is the rich gold background, and the colours used are various shades of red, blue, green, yellow, lilac, pink, etc. There are delicate zoomorphic initials and floral arabesques, consisting of bands of intricate interlace with birds and animals—real or fantastic—fighting or with intertwined necks. Above all, there is such a variety that hardly two pages are identical in colouring and ornamentation. Fig. II-34*d.*

While the greater part of these artistic features is due to Byzantine or Syro-Iranian influences, there are some characteristics which Miss Der Nersessian considers independent developments of the Armenian illumination of Cilicia. Amongst these features are the medallion framing the portrait of a prophet, represented in bust and holding a scroll with a passage from his prophecies (*Jerusalem Gospels No. 251*): see further on; fantastic figures, such as goat-headed men holding flowers, or nude women with long flowing hair (Pierpont Morgan Library, New York, *M. 740*); or nude men riding lions (*Gospels,* Etchmiadzin Library, *No. 1035*). There are new iconographic episodes from the New Testament —for instance, in *Gospels* preserved in the Freer Gallery at Washington; in the Walters Art Gallery at Baltimore (*No. 539*); in the Library of the Armenian Patriarchate at Jerusalem (*No. 1956*). There are new interpretations. We should also note the dramatic intensity of certain compositions and the expressiveness of some gestures and motions.

See Fig. II-36*c,* 37, 38*b* and *d,* 39*a.* Fig. II-37*b* and 38*b* are specimens from codices written in 1262 at Hromkla and illuminated by T'oros Roslin, the greatest Armenian illuminator of the thirteenth century; 37*b* is from a MS. preserved in Baltimore (Walters Art Gallery, *MS. 539*); 38*b* is from a MS. now in the Armenian Patriarchate at Jerusalem (*No. 2660*).

Numerous Gospels belong to the Cilician group, the following being the most important: the *Tuebingen Codex* (written in Drazark in 1113); the MSS. preserved in Walters Art Gallery (*No. 538,* written in 1193 in the monastery of Poghoskan, near Katen), in S. Lazzaro (*No. 1635,* written in 1193 at Skevra), in Lviv (written in 1198 partly at Skevra and partly at Mlidj), and in Trebizond. Outstanding are the *Gospels* written in the middle of the thirteenth century for Leo, son of Het'um I (now in Jerusalem, *No. 2660*), the Gospels written for the same Leo and his wife Keran (now in Jerusalem, *No. 2563*), and for the catholicos Constantine I, a great patron of art (now in Jerusalem, *No. 251*). Mention may also be made of the collection of prayers written by Grigor of Narek and copied in 1173 for Nerses of Lambron, now in the Etchmiadzin Library (*No. 1561/1568*).

Fig. II-38*a* and *c* reproduce folios 4*v* and 12*v* from Walters Art Gallery *MS. 538.* Fig. II-38*d* reproduces a full-page Crucifixion from the *Queen Keran Gospels,* already referred to, which were written in 1272 by the scribe Avetis for Queen Keran (and her husband Leo), and presented by her to the Cilician monastery of Akner (it is preserved in the Armenian Patriarchate, Jerusalem, No. 2563). Roughly to the same period belongs No. 2568 of the same collection; it is a *Gospel-book*, written for Prince Vasak (Fig. II-39a). Another interesting *Gospel-book*, preserved in the same collection (No. 2566), was written in 1301 by Grigor and painted by him and his son Sargis. A beautiful headpiece, the beginning of S. Mark's Gospel (fol. 93r), is reproduced in Fig. II-39b.

In the fourteenth century, Armenian book-illumination abandoned the delicate and varied ornament and the extensive narrative cycle, and returned to the simpler style. In contrast with T'oros Roslin, the foremost Armenian illuminator of the earlier Cilician school, Sargis Pidzak, the outstanding book-illuminator of the fourteenth century (who has left us more than fifteen illuminated codices) does not use the elegant blending of naturalism and stylization, and is much less varied in design and in colour, though—as Miss Der Nersessian has pointed out—his ornamental pages produce a pleasing impression, 'for the drawing is sure and the composition harmonious and clear'. His style was much more influenced by Eastern art, and was, therefore, more deeply felt in Greater Armenia than the artistic productions of T'oros and his contemporaries.

No. 1973 in the Armenian Patriarchate, Jerusalem, is an excellent specimen of the work produced by Sargis Pidzak. It is a *Gospel-book*, which was written in 1346 in Sis (Cilicia) for Queen Marium, wife of Constantine II, Cilician king 1342–44. Fig. II-39c reproduces the full-page miniature representing the Nativity.

Greater Armenia. In Greater Armenia, the Seljuk conquest caused a decadence of all arts, including book-illumination, but this was resumed in the thirteenth century, mainly in the monasteries of Haghbat and Horomos (near Ani). Eastern motifs, such as geometric designs, multicoloured discs, the rainbow, stylized plants, birds and griffins, predominated except in the representation of figures, which were still under Byzantine influence.

Interesting specimens of this art are the codex No. 207 of the Erivan State Library (a *Gospel* illuminated at Haghbat in the late twelfth or early thirteenth century); the *Gospels of T'argmantchats*, of 1202, now preserved in the Etchmiadzin Library (No. 2743/1058); the *Gospels of Gedashen*, written at Haghbat in 1211, and also preserved in the Etchmiadzin Library (No. 6288); and the numerous Gospels of Ignatios who painted mainly at Horomos—for instance, the *Gospel-book* of 1236 now preserved in New Djulfa (No. 36), which contains seventeen full-page miniatures. Important centres of this art were Erzerum (*Gospels*, of the year 1230, preserved in S. Lazzaro degli Armeni at Venice, No. 325), Erzindjan (*Bible*, of 1269, now at Jerusalem, No. 1925), and a few others.

A good specimen of Ignatios' art is reproduced in Fig. II-39d; it shows fol. 268r (first page of S. John) of the *Gospels*, written by Ignatios in 1214 at the monastery of Havut'ar; it is now preserved in S. Lazzaro degli Armeni, Venice, No. 151 (134).

In the fourteenth century, the illumination of Greater Armenia, though continuing local artistic tradition, shows closer connections with the art of Cilicia. The best artist of this period in Greater Armenia is T'oros of Taron, who worked at the monastery of Gladsor (Siunik'), and produced many illuminated codices, such as the *Gospels* now preserved in S. Lazzaro degli Armeni, Venice, *Nos. 1907* and 1917.

Decadence. From the fifteenth century onwards the Armenian art of book-illumination decayed, though excellent work was still done as late as the seventeenth century, and numerous illustrated manuscripts were also produced in the Armenian colonies of northern Persia, Constantinople and Crimea.

Influence upon Byzantine Illumination. Armenian influence upon Byzantine book-illumination has already been mentioned. This influence is particularly strong in those Byzantine MSS. which have no representational but only ornamental decoration; this is Eastern in character, and in Miss Der Nersessian's opinion it was introduced by Armenian craftsmen.

COPTIC ILLUMINATION

The position of Coptic art was peculiar. While Alexandria was the main centre of Hellenistic art and culture, upon which, at least in the fourth and fifth centuries A.D., the Copts were largely dependent, much of the distinct Coptic art of the hinterland goes back to prototypes based on ancient Egyptian models.

In addition, from the fourth or fifth century onwards, Coptic art gradually assimilated Syro-Palestinian influences embodying—as D. Talbot Rice points out—the realism and forceful expression, the frontal pose, and the vertical projection of the Semitic strain. Thus arose a commingling of the Syrian and the Hellenistic (Alexandrian) influences.

In monasteries of Upper Egypt, writes C. R. Morey, the naturalism which was taught by the Hellenistic schools of Alexandria to the nascent Christian art of Egypt was gradually lost as Oriental habits regained their sway, and figures and ornament were gradually devitalized without a compensating gain in decorative effect. The figures grew more and more primitive.

At the same time, parts of the old mythology were taken up into the new system, and familiar old forms assimilated to those of Christianity. Conceptions of Osiris, Isis, and Horus were linked with those of Christ and the Virgin; the types of the mounted saint and of the *orans* became associated with Egypt; the pagan Egyptian *ankh* was often used for the cross; the beast symbolism of the old belief was in part adopted by the new.

Illuminated Manuscripts (Fig. II-40*a–c*). The earliest extant illustrated Coptic manuscript is a fifth-century fragment of eight leaves, from the Old Testament. It contains *Job*, xl. 8—*Proverbs*, iii. 19, and it is written in Coptic Sahidic dialect (see below). This important fragment was part of the Coptic-Sahidic collection of the Borgia Museum in Velletri (south of Rome), and in the early nineteenth century it was acquired by the Bourbon Library at Naples, which later became the Naples National Library. The MS. is now classed *I. B. 18*. On fol. 4*v* (Fig. II-40*a*), at the end of the Book of *Job*, it contains an interesting pen-drawing of Job and his three daughters. This drawing may be considered the earliest specimen of Coptic linear-narrative style as distinguished from Hellenistic art of composition.

The Pierpont Morgan Library, at New York, has a unique collection of illuminated Coptic manuscripts. Fig. II-40*b* reproduces folio 1 *verso* of a *Coptic Synaxary* (*M. 612*). The manuscript comes from Upper Egypt and is written in Sahidic (see *The Alphabet*, p. 470, and *The Hand-produced Book*, p. 310 ff.). It contains seventeen leaves (measuring $13\frac{1}{4}$ by $10\frac{3}{8}$ ins.), including one full-page miniature as frontispiece; there is initial and marginal decoration. The manuscript was found in 1910; then it was complete, but later the last six leaves were separated, and now are preserved in the New Museum, at Berlin (*P. 11965*). The colophon states that the scribe was the priest Apa Isaac of Ptepouhar, in the Fayyûm, and the work was written in A.D. 893, for Papostolos, monk of S. Michael of the Desert. The frontispiece, which represents the Nursing Madonna—an early occurrence in Christian pictorial art—bears the signature of the artist, Isaac.

Even under Islam, the Copts continued to illuminate Gospel MSS. in their mixed style, as may be seen from the Coptic manuscript in the National Library at Paris, *MSS. Coptes-Arabes 13–48*. Fig. II-40*c*.

Coptic influence upon Islamic illumination was very great—see p. 135.

BIBLIOGRAPHY

O. von Gebhardt and A. Harnack, *Evangeliorum Codex graecus purpureus Rossanen-sis*, Leipsic, 1880.

O. von Gebhardt, *The Miniatures of the Ashburnham Pentateuch*, London, 1883.

A. Springer, *Die Genesisbilder in der Kunst d. fruehen Mittelalters* etc. ('Abhandl. d. koen. saechs. Gesellsch. d. Wissensch.'), Leipsic, 1884.

W. Stassoff, *L'Ornement slave et oriental d'après les manuscrits anc. et modern*, St. Petersburg, 1884; 2nd ed., 1887.

J. Strzygowski, *Ikonographie der Taufe Christi*, Munich, 1885; *Das Etschmiadzin Evangeliar* etc., Vienna, 1891; *Orient oder Rom*, Leipsic, 1901; *Kleinarmenische Miniaturmalerei* etc., Tuebingen, 1907; *Origin of Christian Art* (Engl. transl.), Oxford, 1913; *Altai-Iran und Voelkerwanderung*, Leipsic, 1917.

N. P. Kondakoff, *Histoire de l'art byzantin cons. princ. dans les miniatures*, 2 vols., Paris, 1886–91; *The Iconography of Jesus Christ* (in Russian), St. Petersburg, 1905; *The Iconography of the Virgin* (in Russian), St. Petersburg, 1911.

J. J. Tikkanen, in *Archivio Storico dell'arte*, I (1889), and *Acta Societ. Scient. Fennicae*, XVII (1891).

BYZANTINE AND ALLIED ILLUMINATION

I. Carini, 'Codici greci del SS. Salvatore di Messina,' *Archivio Storico Siciliano*, 1890.

H. Brockhaus, *Die Kunst in den Athos-Kloestern*, Leipsic, 1891.

E. Martini, *Catalogo di manoscritti greci esistenti nelle biblioteche italiane*, 2 vols., Milan, 1893–1902.

E. Rostagno and N. Festa, 'Indice dei codici greci laurenziani non compresi nel catalogo del Bandini,' *Studi Italiani di Filol. Class.*, 1893.

E. Narducci, *Catalogus codicum manuscr. praeter graecos et orientales in Bibliotheca Angelica*, I, Rome, 1893.

W. von Hartel and F. Wickhoff, *Die Wiener Genesis*, Vienna, 1895.

J. Ficker, *Archaologiesche Studien zum christlichen Altertum und Mittelalter*; also *Studien ueber christliche Denkmaeler*, Leipsic, 1895 onwards.

C. Castellani, *Catalogus codicum graec. qui in Bibl. D. Marci Venet.*, Venice, 1895.

A. Haseloff, *Codex purpureus Rossanensis*, Berlin, 1898.

V. Schultze, *Die Quedlinburger Itala-Miniaturen*, Munich, 1898.

H. S. Cronin, 'Codex purpureus Petropolitanus,' Cambridge, 1899 (*Texts and Studies*, V-4).

C. Errard, *L'Art byzantin*, Paris, 1900.

D. Ainaloff, *The Hellenistic Bases of the Byzantine Art* (in Russian), St. Petersburg, 1900.

A. Gayet, *L'Art copte*, Paris, 1902.

J. E. Weis-Liebersdorf, *Christus- und Apostelbilder*, Freiburg, 1902.

C. Keller, *Ueber Maler und Malerei in Abessinien*, Zurich, 1903–4.

C. Bayet, *L'art byzantin*, 2nd ed., Paris, 1904.

A. Kruecke, *Der Nimbus etc.*, Strasbourg, 1905.

G. Milet, *L'Art byzantin*, in A. Michel, *Histoire de l'art*, 1905 (see GENERAL BIBLIOGRAPHY); *L'Ancien Art serbe*, Paris, 1909; *Récherches sur l'iconographie de L'Evangile*, Paris, 1916.

A. Muñoz, *I codici greci miniati delle minori biblioteche di Roma*, Florence, 1905; *L'Art byzantin à l'Exposition de Grottaferrata*, Rome, 1906; *I codici greci delle biblioteche minori di Roma*, Florence, 1906; *Il codice purpureo di Rossano e il frammento sinopense*, Rome, 1907; *Studi bizantini*, Naples, 1924.

Biblioteca Vaticana, *Il menologio di Basilio II*, 2 vols., Turin, 1907.

A. Mancini, *Codices graeci monast. Messan. S. Salvatoris*, Messina, 1907.

C. Stornaiolo, *Le miniature della Cosmografia Cristiana*, Milan, 1908; *Miniature delle Omilie di Giacomo Monaco*, Rome, 1910.

S. Abdullah and F. Macler, *Études sur la miniature arménienne*, Paris, 1909.

L. Bréhier, 'L'Art du Moyen Age est-il d'origine orientale?' *Revue des Deux Mondes*, 1909; *L'Art byzantin*, Paris, 1924; *L'Art chrétien etc.*, 2nd ed., Paris, 1928; see also further on.

J. Reil, *Die altchristlichen Bildzyklen des Lebens Jesu*, Leipsic, 1910.

O. M. Dalton, *Byzantine Art and Archaeology*, Oxford, 1911; *East Christian Art*, Oxford, 1925.

BIBLIOGRAPHY

A. Lambros, *Empereurs byzantins. Catalogue (Athènes-Roma. Exposition intern. de Rome, 1911)*, Athens, 1911.

M. Laurent, *L'Art chrétien primitif*, Paris, 1911.

F. Macler, *Miniatures arméniennes*, Paris, 1913; *L'Evangile arménien*, Paris, 1920; 'Documents d'art arménien,' *De arte illustrandi*, Paris, 1924; *L'Enluminure arménienne profane*, Paris, 1928.

O. Wulff, 'Altchristliche und byzantinische Kunst,' in *Handbuch der Kunstwissenschaft*, 2 vols., Berlin, 1914–18.

E. Blochet, *Les peintures des manuscrits orient. de la Bibl. Nat.*, Paris, 1914–20.

J. Wilpert, *Die roemischen Mosaiken und Malereien der kirchlichen Bauten*, Freiburg, 1917.

P. Buberl, *Die Miniaturhandschriften der Nationalbibliothek in Athen*, Vienna, 1917; *Die byzantinischen Handschriften*, Leipsic, 1937.

J. Garber, *Wirkungen der fruehchristlichen Gemaeldecyclen*, Berlin and Vienna, 1918.

B. Filof, *L'Ancien Art bulgare*, Bern, 1919, and Paris, 1922; Germ. ed., Berlin and Leipsic, 1933.

L. Réau, *L'Art russe*, Paris, 1921; *L'Art primitif. L'Art médiéval*, Paris, 1934.

N. Jorga and G. Bals, *L'Art roumain*, Paris, 1922.

A. Colasanti, *L'arte bizantina in Italia*, 2nd ed., Milan, 1923.

J. Ebersolt, *Les Arts somptuaires de Byzance*, Paris, 1923; *La miniature byzantine*, Paris, 1926; *Orient et Occident etc.*, 2 vols., Paris, 1928–9; see also further on.

P. Pargoire, *L'Eglise byzantine de 527 à 847*, Paris, 1923.

H. Breasted, *Oriental Forerunners of Byzantine Painting*, Yale, 1924.

P. Muratov, *L'Ancienne Peinture russe*, Rome, 1925; *La pittura bizantina*, Rome, 1929; French ed., Paris, 1932.

C. Diehl, *Manuel d'Art byzantin*, 2nd ed., 2 vols., Paris, 1925–6; *L'Art chrétien primitif et l'art byzantin*, Paris, 1928; *La Peinture byzantine*, Paris, 1933.

J. Ebersolt, *La Miniature byzantine*, Paris and Brussels, 1926; — and L. Bréhier, *Histoire de l'Art byzantin*, 3 vols., Paris, 1933.

A. Grabar, *La Peinture religieuse en Bulgarie*, Paris, 1928; *Recherches sur les influences orient. de l'art balkan.*, Paris, 1928; *Les Miniatures du Grégoire de Nazianze de l'Ambrosienne*, Paris, 1943.

N. L. Okunev, *Monumenta artis Serbicae*, Zagreb and Prague, 1928 onwards.

J. C. S. Runciman, *The Emperor Romanus Lecapenus and his Reign: a Study of tenth-century Byzantium*, Cambridge, 1929; *Byzantine Civilization*, London, 1933; *The Iranian Influence on the Mediaeval Culture of Europe etc.*, Teheran, 1944; *The Medieval Manichee: a Study of the Christian Dualist heresy*, Cambridge, 1947; *A History of the Crusades*, 3 vols., Cambridge, 1951–54.

J. Baltrusaitis, *Études sur l'Art médiéval en Géorgie et en Arménie*, Paris, 1929.

A. Gruenwald, *Byzantinische Studien (Zur Entstehungsgeschichte d. Pariser Psalters, MS. Grec. 139)*, Prague, 1929.

(Recueil) Uspenskij, *L'Art byzantin chez les Slaves*, 2 vols., Paris, 1930–32.

Archaeological Society and National Museum, Belgrade, *La Peinture serbe du M.A.*, Belgrade, 1930.

H. Gerstinger, *Die Vienna Genesis*, Vienna, 1931.

V. Cottas, *L'Influence du drame 'Christos Paschon' sur l'art chrétien d'orient*, Paris, 1931.

W. H. P. Hatch, *Greek and Syrian Miniatures in Jerusalem*, Cambridge, Mass., 1931.

H. Degering and A. Boeckler, *Die Quedlinburger Italafragmente*, Berlin, 1932.

F. Volbach, G. Salles and G. Duthuit, *Art Byzantin*, Paris, 1933.

K. Weitzmann, *Die armenische Buchmalerei etc.*, Bamberg, 1933; *Die byzantinische Buchmalerei etc.*, Berlin, 1935; *Aus den Bibliotheken des Athos*, Hamburg, 1963. (See also BIBLIOGRAPHY to Chapter I.)

National Museum, Copenhagen, *Greek and Latin Illuminated MSS. etc.*, Copenhagen, 1934.

D. T. Rice, *Byzantine Art*, Oxford, 1935; 2nd ed., London, 1954; *Russian Art*, London, 1935; *The Byzantine Elements in Late Saxon Art*, London, 1947; *Russian Icons*, London, 1947; *Byzantine Painting and its Development in the West*, London, 1948; *The Art of Byzantium*, London, 1959; *Art of the Byzantine Era*, London, 1963.

G. Der Nersessian, *Manuscrits arméniens illustrés*, 2 vols., Paris, 1937; *Armenia and the Byzantine Empire*, Cambridge, Mass., 1947.

K. W. Clark, *A Descriptive Catalogue of Greek New Testament Manuscripts in America*, Chicago, 1937.

S. Bittini, *La pittura bizantina*, Florence, 1937–8.

C. Nordenfalk, *Die spaetantiken Kanontafeln*, Goeteborg, 1938.

E. Panofsky, *Studies in Iconology*, New York, 1939.

A. N. Svirine, *La Miniature dans l'ancienne Arménie* (in Russian, with titles in French), Moscow and Leningrad, 1939.

W. H. P. Hatch, *The Principal Uncial Manuscripts of the New Testament*, Chicago, 1939.

Simaika Pasha, *List of Arabic and Coptic MSS. in the Coptic Museum*, Cairo, 1939.

W. Koehler, *Byzantine Art in the West*, 'Dumbarton Oaks Papers,' Harvard University Press, 1941.

C. R. Morey, *Early Christian Art*, Princeton, N.J., 1942.

A. M. Friend, Jr., *The Princeton University Library Chronicle*, III, 1942.

P. Lemerle, *Le Style byzantin*, Paris, 1943.

L. G. E. Bunt, *Russian Art*, London and New York, 1946.

H. Boissin, *Le Manassès Moyen-Bulgare*, Paris, 1946.

F. Deichmann, *Fruehchristliche Kirchen*, Basel, 1948.

G. Mathew, *Byzantine Painting*, London, 1950.

E. H. Swift, *Roman Sources of Christian Art*, 1951.

H. Thorossian, *Histoire de la littér. arménienne*, Paris, 1951.

M. Bowra, J. Carcopino, and others, *Golden Ages of the Great Cities*, London, 1952.

O. Paecht (ed.), *Byzantine Illumination*, Oxford, 1952.

I. E. Grabar, V. N. Lazarev, and V. S. Kemenova (ed.), *History of Russian Art* (in Russian), vol. I, Moscow, 1953.

H. Buchthal, *Miniature Painting in the Latin Kingdom of Jerusalem*, Oxford, 1957.

BIBLIOGRAPHY

A. U. Pope (ed.), *A Survey of Persian Art from Prehistoric Times to the Present*, 6 vols. (New York, 1938), London, 1958.

C. Roth, *Jewish Antecedents of Christian Art*: see Chapter III.

J. C. Sloane, 'The Torah Shrine in the Ashburnham Pentateuch,' *The Jewish Quarterly Review*, n.s. XXV.

E. Wellesz, *The Vienna Genesis*, London, 1960.

T. Burckhardt (ed.), *The Rabbula Gospels*, Olten and Lausanne, 1960.

L. A. Dournovo, *Armenian Miniatures*, London, 1961.

J. M. Hussey, *The Byzantine World*, 2nd ed., London, 1961.

E. Will, 'L'art sassanide et ses prédéc.,' *Syria*, Vol. XXXIX, 1962.

F. Dvornik, *The Slavs in European History and Civilisation*, Cambridge (Mass.), 1963.

Chapter III

ISLAMIC, HEBREW, AND

MOZARABIC ILLUMINATION

ISLAMIC ILLUMINATION

Very little is known about the early Islamic book in general, because—after the various destructions mentioned in *The Hand-produced Book* (p. 334 f.)—few specimens have survived which belong to a period earlier than the thirteenth century A.D. Islam had no art of its own in the first centuries of its existence, and the Moslems were receivers rather than givers. Prof. D. Talbot Rice's statement that in the life and thought of the Moslems 'there was nothing in the nature of a creative or even of a preservative artistic instinct' is probably exaggerated, but there is much truth in his assertion that Byzantine, Syrian or Persian methods, motifs and forms were taken over wholesale by the Moslems, 'in order to effect the establishment of the individual culture which this new religious state demanded'.

Thus, with the establishment of the first Islamic ruling dynasty Omayyad, its capital city being Damascus, there was introduced a culture which was essentially Syro-Byzantine. The culture of the splendid Abbasid empire (see *The Hand-produced Book*, p. 333)—which was established in 749, and had its capital in the Baghdād of the *Arabian Nights*—was derived mainly from Persian sources. Moreover, the Moslems, as they advanced eastwards, 'found in Iran an ornamental art admirably suited to them. They adopted it and revitalized it' (Runciman). A similar state of affairs characterized Egypt with the establishment of the Fāṭimid dynasty (*The Hand-produced Book*, p. 333). However, all this being true, it would still be inadequate to suggest that Islam had no creative art.

The artistic culture of Islam was derived from all the countries which came under Moslem domination, and certainly from many that lay around this new religious empire: that is, not only from Byzantium, Syria and Persia, but also from South Arabia, Abyssinia, Egypt, China, India, the countries of the North-Eastern Iranians, and so on. In effect, this vast community determined what should survive, and what, however eagerly prized and however strongly imposed, should wither and disappear. What remained was welded and tempered in a great and splendid form. Incessant contact with Chinese, Mongolian, Indian, and other civilizations of Eastern, South-Eastern and Central Asia, and with Eastern and Western Christianity, had modified many of the elements inherited from the ancient traditions of Egypt, the Graeco-Roman world, Byzantium, Syria or Persia, and—with the foundation of native qualities—learning, art, craftsmanship and life itself were enriched and vivified. As a result, a civilization was created which had no parallel and for a time no rival.

Beginnings

The Islamic art of ornamenting books, which was later developed to a high degree, grew out of modest beginnings, like the early medieval Christian art.

In later times the various branches of the art of book-making were so highly specialized that, according to an Arabic manuscript in the National Library at Vienna (*MS. H.O. 131, Ch. 5, fol. 57*), there were as many as nine completely separate crafts, each devoted to a single branch: painters, leaf-cutters, gilders, draughtsmen, binders, preparers of the gold-sprinkled paper, designers of the lined borders, restorers of old manuscripts, and the masters who put together the wonderful albums. But in early times the scribe, the draughtsman, the painter and the decorator were probably one and the same person.

This, indeed, can be seen in very early manuscripts; in two of the earliest dated 'it is actually stated that both the writing and the illustration were done by the same person' (Grohmann). These manuscripts are an Arabic translation of the third treatise by Dioscorides (see p. 44 ff.), dated A.D. 1222, and an *al-Hariri MS.* (formerly in the Ch. Schefer collection, now National Library at Paris, *Arabe 5877*), dated 1237, which was written and illuminated by Yaḥyā bin Maḥmūd bin Yaḥyā bin Abi'l-Ḥasan of Wāsiṭ.

The earliest Arabic illuminated codices, which until half a century ago were available for study, do not date earlier than the thirteenth century A.D. Because of this, and also because of the anti-representational attitude of orthodox Islamic circles, it was concluded that Moslem book illumination was a late creation. In addition, as all the earliest specimens then known came from Western Asia, it was thought that this art was originally confined to Syria and Mesopotamia. Finally, according to some scholars, the Manichaean miniatures were the basis of almost all Islamic book illustration. This opinion, however, is nowadays rejected, although it is agreed that Manichaean art exercised a strong influence on Moslem illumination.

In the problem of the beginnings of Islamic illumination, Egypt has come to our rescue, as in the case of the preservation of Graeco-Roman literature (see *The Hand-produced Book, passim*). 'In the land of Egypt nothing decays', runs the proverb; this, indeed, is due to the wonderful Egyptian climate, and the consequent dryness of the soil. In fact, some decades ago, in the Fayyūm district, there was a sensational discovery of several fragments of Arabic illustrated books belonging to the early centuries A.H. (*i.e.*, of the Moslem era). These important fragments, as well as other documents, from al-Ushmūnayn, are now preserved in the famous Erzherzog

Rainer collection of papyri (abbreviated into *PER*) in the National Library at Vienna. They have been studied and edited by Prof. A. Grohmann, the leading Czech expert on Arabic papyri.

Among the finds from the Fayyūm and al-Ushmūnayn are ninth- and tenth-century fragments of miniatures, pen-drawings, sketches, book ornaments, impressions from engraved blocks, inlaid filigree works, and book-bindings which, belonging to the earliest centuries of the Moslem area, are of great importance in the history of the art of book-making in early Islam. In 1918 and 1919, Prof. Grohmann made a thorough examination of this material. More recently, similar researches were made in the Berlin State Museums, in the Heidelberg University Library, and in the then Royal Egyptian Library in Cairo.

Thus it is now possible to distinguish two main periods in Moslem book-production: (1) the early period from the seventh century till 1258, the year in which Baghdād was captured by the Mongols; (2) from the thirteenth to the eighteenth century.

EGYPTIAN-ARABIC ILLUMINATION

The oldest specimen of illustrated fragments (*PER., Inv. Chart. Arab. 25612*; paper MS.; 16 by 14·5 cm. or $6\frac{3}{10}$ by $5\frac{3}{4}$ in.) may be dated to the third century A.H. (ninth-tenth century A.D.). Only the end-vignette of the original manuscript is preserved. It represents a tree—in strong, bright colours with vermilion fruits—between two low hills sloping down in three stages. The coarse, wavy lines which fill these stages, as well as the branches and trunk of the tree, are painted dull green and edged a dull yellow. In Grohmann's opinion, while the technique recalls Hellenistic models, the primitive composition savours of the Egyptian.

Another Fayyūm fragment (*Inv. Chart. Arab. 25613, a–e*; five scraps which when united give a leaf of 16 by 14·1 cm. or $6\frac{3}{10}$ by $5\frac{3}{5}$ in.; paper MS.; probably early tenth century A.D.) is the only survival of early Arabic erotic literature. The text, written with dark brown ink, gives a portion of the forty-sixth chapter of the book. The miniature—added after the text was written—represents a *symplegma* of a long-haired woman and a bearded, kneeling man, both with breast and face front-covering, and feet in profile, a feature characteristic of old Egyptian representation as well as of Coptic and Ethiopic paintings. The same artistic affinity may be suggested by the strong emphasis on the eyebrows and the large eyes in the physiognomy of the woman; this feature is also given prominence in Egyptian-Hellenistic portraits. It has been suggested that this fragment may have belonged to a book based on a model having some connection with an old Egyptian erotic papyrus preserved in the Turin Museum.

Similar pen-and-ink technique in drawing is seen in *PER. Inv. Chart. Arab. 25615* (from al-Ushmūnayn; very yellow paper; 9·8 by 13·1 cm. or $3\frac{9}{10}$ by $5\frac{1}{8}$ in.; late ninth or early tenth century A.D.). Artistically it is on a much higher level than the fragments already referred to. While the colour used for writing was originally dark brown, those for painting were black, vermilion and chrome changing to greenish-yellow. The drawing shows the characteristic features of ornamentation of the Ḥaram of Ibn Tūlūn's mosque; it is divided into compartments enclosed by sharp black lines, outlined with vermilion. There is represented a standing bearded male figure, and there are also spiral flourishes, a network of lozenges, a small trefoil and other ornaments.

Another paper fragment (*No. 954* of the same collection), roughly belonging to the same period, represents a horseman, in a style similar to that of the Coptic pictures of the mounted saints. It is the only early illustrated fragment which gives us the signature of the artist: Abū Tamīm Ḥaydara.

The best book-drawing of the early Moslem period is said to be *PER. Inv. Chart. Arab. 13682* (dingy white paper, 5·7 by 8·1 cm., or $2\frac{1}{4}$ by $3\frac{1}{5}$ in., tenth century, probably from al-Ushmūnayn). It represents a dog squatting on its haunches and a slender clay jug; the colours used were black, dark yellow, ruby, white, grey and bright yellow ochre. Grohmann thinks that the style of this drawing is connected with the work of Eastern Asiatic schools of painting brought to Western Asia by the Turks.

All the fragments mentioned are text illustrations, without any background, like those of the old Egyptian papyrus illustrations, and are either drawn in outline or coloured. There is, however, one fragment (*PER. Inv. Chart. Arab. 25751*; very yellow paper; 12·5 by 11·8 cm., or $4\frac{9}{10}$ by $4\frac{3}{5}$ in.; tenth century A.D.), which by its composition and frame has been considered a typical decorative page. This fragment comes from the central part of the first page of a splendid manuscript. We see in it a hexagon with a dark green and yellowish-green background, enclosed by dark green borders, having black lines outside and bright red lines within. Inside the hexagon there are two parrots facing each other, while a third bird is in a triangular corner. To the right, on an upper plane and against a crimson background, there is a distinguished, richly clothed, male figure, seated on a low, dark green couch; and below there is a still more richly dressed man, who probably represents a Caliph, the representation being 'undoubtedly not only one of the earliest, but certainly also one of the most interesting' of the 'Commander of the Faithful' (Grohmann). This fragment, artistically probably the most valuable of the early Moslem period, seems to be stylistically connected with the miniatures and wall-paintings of the Buddhist and Perso-Manichaean schools of Central Asia, though it cannot be established whether this manuscript was imported or actually produced in Egypt.

EARLY ILLUMINATED COPIES OF THE KORAN

The importance of the Koran in the history of books has already been indicated in *The Hand-produced Book*. Here it may be observed that, first, owing to the already mentioned hostility of Moslem orthodox circles to representational art—*i.e.*, that of representing living forms, especially human figures—the sacred book of Islām possibly holds among the followers of that faith an even higher and more exclusive place than that of the Bible among the Christians; the reason being that the Christians, in their devotional books and in their churches, made large use of representational art, for instance in the form of icons of the Virgin or statues of Christ and of the saints, so that the Bible, unlike the Koran, did not really become the almost exclusive focal point of devotional interest. Secondly, because of the hostility to representational art, especially in decorating the Moslem sacred book, Islamic art had to find other methods of adornment and illumination. Even the early copyists of the Koran laid great emphasis on fine calligraphy; indeed, in the opinion of some scholars, at quite an early date the Koran was written in golden letters, though, as amongst Jews and Christians—with reference to their sacred books—the more orthodox Moslems insisted on the traditional simplicity in the form of the Koran, and disapproved of such gorgeous productions.

The Christian influence on the development of the external form of the Koran has already been recognised. So, for instance, the Christian folio missals may have had some influence upon the origin of the large format of the Koran kept for reading in the mosque. More important was the Christian influence upon the decoration of Islamic books in general.

Early Decorations

A preserved sheet of vellum from a copy of the Koran belonging to the late seventh or early eighth century A.D. (*PER. Inv. Perg. Arab. 2:* 27 by 22 cm. or $10\frac{3}{5}$ by $8\frac{5}{8}$ in.) has the simple method of dividing verses by six dots. In MSS. of the second century A.H. (eighth-ninth century A.D.), however, appear the elaborate 'ashīra marks, *i.e.*, marking the divisions between groups of ten verses.

Similarly, it is only from the early second century A.H. onwards that the beginnings of the Sūras (*i.e.*, chapters of the Koran) are marked by suitable formulas, as can be seen, for instance, from a sheet of vellum (*PER. Inv. Perg. Arab. 186:* 38·5 by 27 cm. or $15\frac{3}{8}$ by $10\frac{3}{5}$ in.) where the formula—that is, a kind of title—is written in crimson ink, but without ornamentation. In a very early copy of the Koran, the valuable codex *Maṣāḥif No. 139* (Egyptian Library, at Cairo; *c.* A.D. *725*), the formulas have been added by a later hand; the writer had also left an empty space at the end of each Sūra which was later filled in by a decoration (similar to those which appear in Eastern Christian manuscripts) consisting of trellis-work, knots, square or circular patterns, rows of arches, and including a decorative scroll running across the whole page and crowned by the colonnade of a mosque partly hung with lamps, having triangular pinnacles. In some sections the latter are replaced by winged palm-leaves, which also are the terminal ornamentation of the narrow ends of the decorative scroll.

The terminal Sūra decorations were later (already, however, in the same eighth century A.D.) combined with the formulas of the succeeding Sūras, and thus were produced the rich and more and more elaborate Sūra divisions. An excellent early specimen of these as well as of other 'ashīra marks is *Maṣāḥif No. 1* (written before A.D. *765*, and now preserved in the Egyptian Library at Cairo).

In later copies the pages of elaborately decorated codices have generally a rectangular field of decoration, and are marked off on the narrow side by a kind of peak of arabesque tendrils which rise up out of a vase formed of winged palm-leaves. The title vignette, too, is enclosed in a rectangular frame, and finishes off with a peak-like tendril ornament, while the title itself is left white in the central area. The peak-like tendril ornament is sometimes transformed into a circular medallion—later serving as a marginal decoration—as may be seen in the splendid, large Koranic codices of the Mamlūk period. The first and the last page in them—points out Grohmann—is usually ornamented in such a way that two of the usual kind of preliminary leaf-ornaments with scrolls of writing form the top and bottom of the ornamental framed page.

In the main collections of Europe, America, North Africa, and West Asia, complete or fragmentary copies of the Koran are preserved containing various decorations in gold. The Freer Gallery of Art, Washington, D.C., has a good collection of such fragments. A leaf from an eighth-century Koran (*No. 32.62*) contains a rectangular ornament with foliated medallion projecting into the margin; there is gold and a slight colour. Single leaves from two eighth- or ninth-century Korans (*Nos. 30.60* and *30.66*) contain texts in *kūfī* script in dark brown ink; diacritics are in red, or in red and yellow. Punctuation marks are in gold; one specimen has also a terminal ornament in gold. On one of the two leaves, the Sūra heading is in ornamental kufī in white reserve on a gold patterned ground. A leaf from a ninth-century Koran (*No. 37.11*) is decorated on both sides with designs executed in gold and blue, which mark the end of a chapter or section, or the beginning of another. A decorated fragment of a late eighth-century Koran, preserved in The John Rylands Library, Manchester (*Arabic MS. 703*), consists of fifty leaves with various decorations: Fig. III-1.

Naturally, the decorative style of copies of the Koran influenced that of the more valuable secular books; it is shown, for instance, by two splendid copies of al-Būṣīrī's *Burda* preserved in the National Library at Vienna; they are *A.F. 4*, dated 746 A.H. = A.D. 1345 (it was written by Aybak bin 'Abd Allāh as-Sayfī), and *N.F. 381*, written in 741 A.H.; the latter is ornamented with a round medallion: Fig. III-2.

Coptic and Persian Influences

In some specimens, already referred to, the Sūra formulas are in red or chrome yellow, and the *'ashīra* marks are enclosed in a red-green circular ornament, or else consist of two small dark green circles with a larger circle in chrome yellow between them. The main colours of the terminal decorations in early Korans are also yellow ochre, dark green and crimson, and the same combination of colours appears in the Coptic manuscripts; moreover, many geometrical patterns of Koranic decoration have probably been borrowed from Coptic art.

Some decorative elements in the early Koranic copies, however, seem to have been borrowed from Pahlavi books; the Arabs also adopted the Pahlavi method of punctuation. Indeed, according to Prof. Grohmann, the Arabic employment of a plain circle as a full stop must have been taken over from such texts as the Pahlavi literary texts on papyri (*PER. Inv. Pap. No. 446*, and *Papyri Berol. No. 4442*).

Finally, Grohmann considers decorated Persian, Coptic and other textiles as a connecting link between Persian and Coptic art and Arabic illumination. Some textiles contain rich ornaments consisting of festoons with spirals, arabesques, a network of lozenges, and so on, in beautiful colours such as sepia-brown, clay-brown, enamel-like crimson, carmine, ultramarine, grass-green, bright-green, white, and gold.

CHRYSOGRAPHY

We have already dealt with the custom amongst the Christians and the early Hebrews of writing in gold ink, and further on we shall treat of medieval Hebrew chrysography. Here we must say a few words of this custom amongst the Moslems. It has been pointed out by specialists in this field that the preference for the combination of blue and gold dominated practically the whole of Moslem book-decoration. Indeed, one can open hundreds of Islamic illuminated manuscripts and always find gold on a blue ground as the prevailing combination of colours.

A portion—consisting of 52 leaves—of a splendid copy of the Koran written in gold is still preserved in the Egyptian Library (in Cairo). There are also some fragments extant of a gorgeous copy written on dark blue parchment in gold ink, which al-Ma'mūn (813–37) presented to the chief mosque of Meshhed. But what has come down to us is only a small fraction of the number of copies once kept at the splendid courts or in the libraries and mosques of Baghdād, Cordova and Cairo. It is known, for instance, that the famous Fāṭimid library possessed several copies of the Koran written in gold, which were placed in the so-called old mosque in the year A.D. 1012–13, along with 1,298 other precious copies.

Because of the influence of Koranic copies written in gold, chrysography was later applied to other books, and especially to collections of prayers. Occasionally, other works, such as the poems of the Caliph al-Mu'tamid (870–92), were also written in golden ink. It has already been mentioned in *The Hand-produced Book*, p. 343, that the sect of al-Ḥallāj (annihilated in A.D. 921–2), who were influenced by Manichaeism, were famous for their books produced on Chinese paper, some of them written in gold. See also p. 140 f.

Sketches and Decoration-patterns in Secular Manuscripts

(Fig. III-3).

Apart from the illustrated fragments referred to on p. 132 ff., various specimens of sketches, studies for designs of arabesques and geometrical figures, and so on, have come to light. They are either on papyrus (*PER. Inv. Arab. Pap. 10006, 10047, 10052, 10053*, and others) or on paper (*PER. Inv. Chart. Arab. 12514, 25620, 25641, 25656*, and others).

The oldest of them (*No. 10053*, measuring 5·8 by 6·6 cm. or $2\frac{3}{10}$ by $2\frac{3}{5}$ in.) is attributed to the ninth or tenth century A.D. It contains a black-ink drawing representing two intersecting quadrilaterals with a bird in the centre. Another one (*No. 10052*), shows—among its various studies for arabesques, done with a reed pen—the head of an animal rising out of a half palm-leaf. Grohmann argues that it heralds the free use of the bodies of animals in decoration, which later became unexpectedly popular in marginal decorations and in initials on Coptic and Armenian manuscripts. The interesting fragment *No. 12514*, measuring 9·1 by 8·8 cm. (or $3\frac{3}{5}$ by $3\frac{1}{2}$ in.), contains studies in tendrils with flowers, arabesques and birds.

Even in early days, in fine manuscripts of secular literary texts, the beginning of the book contained a more or less decorative framework, although no such specimen has come down to us. There are, however, fragmentary papyrus-manuscripts extant—belonging to the eighth to tenth centuries A.D., and coming mainly from the Fayyūm (*PER. Inv. Arab. Pap. Nos. 600a* and *b, 9998*, and others)—in which the end of a section is occasionally marked by a simple ornamental border such as a rectangle with a zigzag band, or a rectangle with two intersecting zigzag bands, or else a row of ornamental dots, and so forth. The end of the whole book is sometimes marked by a more elaborate combination of geometrical figures, or else by a vignette consisting of a bird-ornament, or of an ivy-leaf with a face drawn in it and terminating in a trefoil, or by a combination of leaves or knots with geometrical figures.

Furthermore, even in secular manuscripts, at least in the more valuable copies, writing in gold must have been employed for titles and chapter headings at a quite early date (see also p. 136). Probably decorated inscribed borders were also used in early Arabic codices; at any rate such a specimen—although belonging to the eleventh or twelfth century A.D.—is preserved in two small fragments (*PER., Inv. Chart. Arab. 1924* and *25647*, together measuring 9·7 by 7·6 cm. or $3\frac{4}{5}$ by 3 in.), which formed part of a copy of *Ḥadīth*, or 'Tradition'; the fragments are of yellow paper, which originally was probably white.

Colours

The main colours of the early Egyptian-Arabic illuminated manuscripts (red, yellow and green) were also used in the Coptic manuscripts (indeed, these colours were also included in the palettes of ancient Egyptian and Egyptian-Hellenistic painters). In the early Egyptian-Arabic MSS., the main colours appear in different shades, such as pale red, bright red, brilliant vermilion, crimson and bright crimson, ruby, dingy yellow, chrome yellow, bright ochre, dark dull green, yellowish green, and dark green. There is also a dingy white, and a deep black for outlines.

Only in *Nos. 13682* and *25751* of the illustrated manuscripts already referred to, has the problem of light and shade been tackled, and only in the latter of the two has gold-leaf been used to represent gold ornaments; the technique employed was very simple, the trinkets were imitated by laying on thin gold.

In early specimens the colours have suffered severe chemical changes, partly in consequence of the process of disintegration to which they have been exposed for almost a thousand years, so that it is not possible in every instance to be sure of the original shades of colour.

MOSLEM REPRESENTATIONAL ART

The hostility of orthodox Moslems towards representations of the human figure, and even of any living being whatsoever, is well known. Many eminent scholars have stated that Islām had no representational art at all. That theory has been proved wrong. It is even probable that Islām had a religious representational art, but the task of the Moslem painter was like that of a modern illustrator of books, and—unlike Christian religious art—it was never intended to stimulate devotion. We may go further, and, in view of recent evidence, accept Prof. Sir H. A. R. Gibb's opinion that Sir Thomas Arnold's statement that no illustrated MS. of the Koran is known ever to have existed, may now require modification.

In particular, mention must be made of the so-called Baghdād or Mesopotamian school of Islamic painting of the twelfth or thirteenth century (as a matter of fact there seems to be no special reason to connect these painters either with Baghdād or even with Mesopotamia). Very little has come down to us which can be ascribed to this school. It is known, however, that this particular group of paintings comprised illustrations of treatises on astronomy and medicine, as well as collections of fables, including the cycle of animal stories of Buddhist Indian origin, known in its Arabic form as *Kalīlah and Dimnah*: Fig. III-4–5, particularly 4*e* and 5*c*.

We must also mention the famous illustrated work *Al-Maqāmāt* of al-Harīrī. This description of the adventures and rascalities of a needy wandering scholar is full of puns and witticisms of a learned type, and thus 'from its subject matter it affords suitable material for a painter with a sense of humour' (Arnold): Fig. III-5*a* and *b*.

What was the origin of this representational art? According to E. Blochet, the 'Mesopotamian school of painting' was entirely dependent upon Byzantine art. This theory has not been accepted by others, but it is generally admitted that this school was influenced by Byzantine art, partly directly and partly indirectly, by the way of Byzantine artistic elements previously incorporated in Syrian or Moslem art.

Sir Thomas Arnold has suggested that Moslem representational art, including that of the 'Mesopotamian' school, is due mainly to the influence of the Nestorian and Jacobite church service books. There is no historical evidence that the painters who were employed as illustrators of Moslem books were Christians, but we find in the illustrations of these books a striking resemblance to corresponding features in illustrations found in service books of the Oriental churches, though naturally the subject matter dealt with is quite different. A group of figures found in a *Lectionary* of the Jacobite Church (British Museum, *Add. MS.* 7170, fol. 145; probable date: thirteenth century) 'would quite readily fit into any illustration of the Maqāmāt of al-Harīrī' (Arnold).

Various circumstances point, indeed, to the conclusion that religious art in Islamic painting, which can be traced at least from the eleventh century onwards, derived its origin from representations of similar subjects in Christian painting. Some Moslem codices contain pictures which seem to have derived from Christian originals, and in a few instances there is borrowing in the representation of separate incidents of sacred history. This is indicated, for example, in a copy of al-Bīrūnī's *al-Āthār al-Bāqiya*, a work on the various systems of chronology in the world, dated A.D. 1307–8; the copy is now preserved in the Edinburgh University Library (*Arabic, No. 161*). Similar evidence is given in another MS., of the same collection (*Arabic, No. 20*), which is a copy of Rashīd ud-Dīn's *Universal History*, dated A.D. 1310–11; also in a British Museum copy of the *Maqāmāt* (*Add. M.S. 7293*); others are seen in the British Museum MSS. *Or. 4533* and *Add. 18576*. See Fig. III-8b and 13a.

The painters of such miniatures may have been Christians or converts from Christianity to Islām, or the descendants of converts, or disciples of Christians or of converts; 'what is certain is, that they worked under the influence of an artistic tradition that was Christian in its source and origin' (Arnold).

For Arabic-Christian illumination see p. 119 and Fig. III-8a.

SECOND PERIOD OF MOSLEM ILLUMINATION

The year 1258, in which Baghdād fell to the Mongols, marked in certain respects an era in the history of Asia similar to that signified by the year 1453 (the fall of Byzantium) in the history of Europe. The sack and destruction of that splendid city marked the culmination of a series of appalling acts of havoc and devastation, as the Mongolian barbarians swept over the centres of Moslem civilisation—Herāt, Bukhārā, Samarqand, Balkh, Khwārizm—from the borders of China through Transoxiana and Persia into Mesopotamia. Wherever they passed they left red ruin behind them, for one of the cardinal points of their military policy would seem to have been utter destruction. With the massacre of the Caliph and his family, 'for the first time in its history the Moslem world was left without a caliph whose name could be cited in the Friday prayers' (Hitti).

Chinese Influences

(Fig. III-7.)

When Mongol domination in Persia eventually simmered down to more or less stable rule and the Moslem world was brought under the same sway as Central Asia and China, a flood of artistic and cultural influences reached down to Persia and other Islamic countries from the East; these were felt for centuries, and their survival in Moslem art may be traced up to modern times. Hūlāgū brought with him Chinese painters and illustrated books. Later, with the establishment of a more settled government in Persia under the dynasty of the Īlkhāns, one ruler after another brought Chinese artists to reconstruct and embellish the conquered cities.

For a brief period Chinese influences predominated, and even Persian artists had to adapt themselves to the new conditions and to the taste of their new rulers. Curiously enough, long before the Mongol invasion, an admiration for Chinese painting was a commonplace of Persian literature; the Sāmānid dynasty of Bukhārā (c. A.D. 872–999) entered into relations with the Chinese court, which could hardly have been without some effect, at least in the north-eastern corner of the Islamic world. But any influences which may have come this way were neither considerable nor permanent. Indeed, even the flood of Chinese influence brought in under Mongol domination did not produce fundamental changes in Persian-Arabic arts.

Sir Thomas Arnold mentions the following conventions of Chinese origin which remained permanent, though superficial, characteristics of Persian paintings: the *Tai'* or 'cloud form', with its strange, sinuous undulating shape; the fantastic dragons with their irregularly shaped wings, and strange appendages that project from their bodies; and the magnificent bird that trails a long tail across the sky. The Mongol period—writes Sir Thomas Arnold—is further distinguished by a change in the form of the halo, which now ceases to be round and takes the appearance of a tapering mass of flame, such as Central-Asian and Chinese art gave to the representations of the Buddha.

PERSIAN-ARABIC ILLUMINATION

Persian miniature painting—emphasizes B. W. Robinson—developed from a fusion of late Classical elements derived from Byzantium, with a surviving native tradition of painting under the Sasanian dynasty, subsequently enriched and largely transformed by an admixture of Chinese ideas and methods, introduced during the fourteenth century as a result of the Mongol conquests in the previous century.

A strong artistic sense has always been a characteristic of the Iranian peoples, and there is evidence to show that the artistic tradition was kept alive as much by the Persian Christians as by the Persian Zoroastrians and those Persians who adopted the faith of the Arab conquerors.

The importance laid upon painting in Manichaean manuscripts suggests that the art of book-illumination was already widely practised in Mesopotamia and Persia at the end of the Sasanian era (late sixth and early seventh century A.D.). In this period, Zoroastrianism, the state religion of the Persian Empire, had many followers also in the larger towns of central and southern Mesopotamia, and even amongst the more settled Arab tribes, such as the Ghassanids and Lakhmids; indeed, in the capital of the latter, Hira (near Kufa), the inhabitants were partly Christians and partly Mazdaeans. There were Mazdaeans even as far as Dura Europos (see pp. 62 ff. and 116 f.).

Fig. III-6a reproduces a specimen of Manichaean book-painting.

It would follow, therefore, that the art and practice of Persian painting, includ-

One of ten parts of the illustrated Chinese book-scroll *Admonitions of the Instructress to the Ladies in the Palace*, written by Chang Hua, A.D. 232–300, and printed by Ku Kai-chih, c. 344–406. It is perhaps a sixth-century copy (Chiang Yee's opinion). Lady Feng protecting Emperor Yuan-ti (reigned 48–33 B.C.) from a bear.

ing book-illumination, must have been spread far beyond the territories of the Sasanids. However, the examples that have survived from the Sasanian period (A.D. 226–636) and from the early period of Moslem book-making (seventh to thirteenth centuries) are few indeed, but there can be no doubt that they represent only a small fraction of the original works of art.

It is by casual literary evidence that we learn of the existence of illustrated Sasanian books. Al-Mas'ūdī, an Arabian historian from Baghdād (who died in 957), describes a huge volume, which he saw in 303 A.H. (A.D. 915–16) in the possession of a noble Persian family in the city of Iṣṭakhr; it contained a history of the Persian kings and was illustrated with twenty-seven pictures of the Sasanian monarchs (including two women), dressed in royal robes and with crowns on their heads; each feature was carefully delineated, even to the hairs of the beards. Al-Iṣṭakhrī, a Persian-Arabic geographer of the mid-tenth century tells us that he saw in the castle of Shīrāz some volumes of annals of the ancient Persian kings, illustrated with pictures of each of them. In Baghdād itself, the Caliph al Ma'mūn (who reigned 813–33) was shown—by a Mazdaean priest—a portrait of the Sasanian king Anūshīrvān, in whose reign the Prophet had been born.

Earliest Preserved Illuminated Persian-Arabic MSS.

It is uncertain whether or not the destruction of the Persian illuminated books was mainly or partly due to orthodox Moslem hostility towards representational art. Curiously enough, some of the earliest extant illuminated Persian-Arabic manuscripts—they are mainly preserved in the National Library at Paris—contain examples of this art, although all of them are of a secular character.

Andarz Nāme. Recently an illuminated manuscript, also of secular character, was discovered, which was regarded as the earliest Persian-Arabic illuminated MS. in existence. A brief note on this interesting work has been published by R. N. Frye in *Serta Cantabrigiensia*, presented by the Wiesbaden publisher Franz Steiner to the XXIII. International Congress of Orientalists in Cambridge, 1954.

The MS. is a very early (?) copy—or perhaps the original itself (?)—of *Andarz Nāme*, an eleventh-century collection of sage counsels and admonitions, written by a ruler of the southern shore of the Caspian Sea for his son. It is, thus, one of the oldest New Persian prose works. The MS. contains 109 miniatures, which 'both in subject and style . . . are unique in Islamic miniature painting' (Frye): Fig. III-6c.

The manuscript was written in the court at Gurgān (capital of the Ziyarid princes of Ṭabaristān) by Shīrdā b. Shīrdīl al-Iṣfahbadī aṭ-Ṭabarī (a scribe hitherto unknown); it was finished in July 1090, that is, only seven or eight years after the original was begun. The MS. contains 187 folios and is preserved partly in the Cincinnati Museum of Fine Arts and partly in another American institution. Frye regards the discovery of this MS. as a most sensational find in the realm of Near Eastern Studies in recent times.

In Frye's opinion, the nearest relations to its miniatures seem to be the figures painted on the eleventh-century walls and pottery from Nishapur, and on the wall-

ISLAMIC, HEBREW, AND MOZARABIC

paintings discovered in the French excavations at Lashkarī Bazar in Afghanistan. 'The technique of painting the faces of men with bulging eyes, open mouths, and moles on their cheeks, is especially noteworthy. The proximity of this style of painting to pre-Islamic Sasanian art rather than to later Islamic miniature painting seems apparent' (Frye).

N.B. The first edition of the present book was in page-proof when I was informed by Prof. A. J. Arberry that this MS. has now been proved a forgery (I have preferred to maintain the description of the MS.).

Twelfth and Thirteenth Centuries. There is a Persian version of the work *Kalila and Dimna*, already referred to, copied and illustrated in Ghazna about the middle of the twelfth century. Belonging approximately to the same date are two manuscripts of an Arabic version of the same work; three MSS. of the *Maqāmāt* are dated a little later (A.D. 1222, 1237, and late thirteenth century). An interesting thirteenth-century copy of the *Shāh-nāma* is preserved in M. Charles Gillet's Collection, Paris. A beautiful three-volume copy of the large novel *Kitāb-i Samak 'Iyār* by Ṣadaqah bin 'Albī-alqāsim Shīrāzī is preserved in the Bodleian Library, Oxford (MSS. Ouseley 379–381). Fig. III-9 reproduces folios 94*v* and 302*r* of the third volume. Farāmurz bin Khudhādhādh bin 'Abdallāh Alkātibn Alajarānī, at the request of his friends, began to collect this story on 20 June 1189, but the present manuscript probably belongs to the thirteenth century.

Fig. III-4e, 5a–c, and 9.

Post-Mongol-Conquest Persian Illumination

With the Mongol conquest (1220–50), the Persian artistic tradition freed itself from the limitations imposed upon it by the Moslem anti-representational attitude, and flared up, especially as painting received the generous patronage of sultans and powerful nobles of Mongol, Turkish, or Persian stock. It is almost miraculous that in the art of painting of this period there re-emerged characteristics of the art of the Sasanians, the national Persian dynasty, whose empire had been swept away by the Arab conquerors of the middle seventh century. In some mysterious manner, it has been remarked, the same motifs and traditional methods as flourished under a Zoroastrian regime succeeded in remaining alive for a period of six centuries, and presented themselves again under an alien rule in the midst of an Islamic culture fundamentally unsympathetic to one of the most characteristic features of this art—the representation of the human form. Here we find—argues Sir Thomas Arnold—a remarkable example of that intense national feeling which has, with irrepressible vitality, refused to be crushed under successive epochs of foreign domination.

This Sasanian artistic tradition, which had been partly preserved in the Nestorian and Jacobite religious art, and which probably lingered on in Persian illuminated books, firstly reappeared in the decorated pottery of Rayy (the ancient Ragha, Lat. Rhages; about 6 mil. south of Tehran); the earliest extant examples of Rhages ware belong to the twelfth-thirteenth century (A.D.).

142

Of the fourteenth-century manuscripts, the following may be referred to: an early fourteenth-century copy of the *Shāh-nāma* preserved in M. H. Vever's Collection, Paris, and a slightly later copy preserved in Fogg Art Museum, Harvard University, Cambridge, Mass.; a copy dated 1315 of al-Jazarī's treatise on *automata* (*Kitāb fi maʿarifat al-ḥiyal al-handasiya*), the original text having been composed in 1206: Fig. III-10a. See also Fig. III-5d–f, and 6b.

Before we pass to the brilliant Tīmūrid period, mention must be made of a beautiful manuscript, dated A.D. 1388, by the anonymous author of *The Marvels of Creation* (Paris, National Library, *Suppl. Pers. 332*); it was copied for the library of Sultān Aḥmad ibn Uways (1382–1410).

GOLDEN AGE OF PERSIAN ILLUMINATION
(Fig. III-10b–c, and 11–13)

The last twenty years of the fourteenth century brought further havoc and destruction to the Moslem countries. This time it was Tīmūr Beg (or Tīmūr-lenk: the name was corrupted into Tamerlane; he lived from 1335 to 1405). After a series of bloody and cruel campaigns in which he left ruined and depopulated cities behind him, he made himself master of Central and Western Asia. Samarqand, then still a splendid city, was his capital (it is now in the Soviet Republic of Uzbekistan).

The most pleasant surprise of the Tīmūrid period, marked by a regime of blood and iron, is an extraordinary artistic productivity on a scale and of a quality without parallel in Persian history since Sasanid days. 'Like the Italian princes of the quattrocento, who were their contemporaries, the Tīmūrid princes found time in the midst of their interminable wars, for the cultivation of the fine arts' (Arnold). Shāh Rukh (1404–47)—one of the younger sons of Tīmūr (or Tamerlane)—and his sons Ulugh Beg and Mīrzā Bāysunghur, restored and beautified their capital, Herāt; the last mentioned, in particular, was a great bibliophile, and he collected around him a group of the most distinguished calligraphers from all parts of Persia.

In B. W. Robinson's opinion, Hafiz i Abru composed his *History* under Shāh Rukh's patronage. A fine large volume, containing this history may well have been executed at Herat, about 1420–30, for Shāh Rukh himself. The volume is now lost, but a detached page from it is preserved in the Victoria and Albert Museum, London (*E. 5499–1958*).

Under the patronage of Mīrzā Bāysunghur book-painting of the Herat school was still perfected: a beautiful copy of the *Gulistān* ('Rose Garden'), the famous work of the poet and moralist Shaikh Saʿadī of Shīrāz (traditionally, 1184–1292), is preserved in the Chester Beatty Library, Dublin (*MS. 119*).

B. W. Robinson also refers to illuminated MSS. produced in the contemporary school of Shīrāz: two copies of the *Khamsa* ('Five Treasures') of Niẓāmī, 1444–45 (John Rylands Library, Manchester, *Pers. MS. 36*) and about 1450–60 (Royal Asiatic Society, London, *MS. 246*). A detached page from another copy of the same work, of about 1490, was probably also produced in the Shīrāz school (Victoria and Albert Museum, London, *E. 1589–1953*). The style of this school in the second half of the fifteenth century was the Turkumān style (under the patronage of the Turkumān rulers of western Persia).

An excellent copy of Niẓāmī's *Khamsa*, apparently executed in 1463 at the school of Iṣfahān, is in the Chester Beatty Library, at Dublin (*MS. 137*).

Under the patronage of Sulṭān Ḥusayn Mīrzā Bāyqarā (1458–1505), the last of the Tīmūrid Sulṭāns, eminent artists created a style and a fashion in painting that dominated the Persian schools for a whole century. Grace and elegance and a larger freedom of movement took the place of the stiffness in the elongated figures of the earlier style. While this earlier style was still current there was a growing brilliancy and a range of colours ; now it reached the highest point of perfection. Furthermore, not only are the names of the main artists recorded, but we have some biographical data as well.

Bihzād. At least one great Persian painter must be mentioned—Kamāl ad-Dīn Bihzād, who worked under the generous patronage of Mīr 'Alī Shīr or Nawā'i (the minister of Sulṭān Ḥusayn—see above) and, later, of Shāh Ismā'īl, the founder of the Ṣafawid Dynasty (1510–22). Towards the close of his reign, Shāh Ismā'īl appointed Bihzād director of the Royal Library, with control over 'all copyists, painters, gilders, margin-drawers, gold-mixers, gold-beaters, and washers of lapis lazuli'. Bihzād built up a famous school of court-painters, which under the reign of Shāh Ṭahmāsp (1524–76) illustrated a number of works of the classical Persian poets, and produced masterpieces such as the Baron Edmond de Rothschild copy of the *Shāh-nāma* or the *Khamsah* by Niẓāmī (British Museum, *Or. 2265*). [Fig. III-11*b* reproduces a miniature by Bihzād from a copy (by Sulṭān 'Alī, A.H. 893 = A.D. 1488) of Sa'adi, *Būstān*, containing six miniatures by Bihzād, four being signed (Egyptian Library at Cairo).]

The copy of the *Shāh-nāma* contains 285 miniatures (some of which are attributed to Bihzād himself), and in execution, design, and colouring this truly regal volume marks the highest attainment of the period of Persian painting. A copy of the *Khamsah*, which was formerly preserved in the Imperial Library at Delhi, and is now in the British Museum (*Or. 6810*), contains sixteen beautiful miniatures, some attributed to Qāsim 'Alī, a pupil of Bihzād, and one to an artist known by his pseudonym Mīrak, who was considered 'unsurpassed and unrivalled in craftsmanship and painting'. Sulṭān Muḥammad, too, was one of the most able of Bihzād's pupils. See also Fig. III-11*c*, reproducing a miniature from a copy (by 'Alī al-Husainī al Harawī, A.H. 928 = A.D.1522) of Jāmī, *Khamsah*, containing ten full-page miniatures (two each) by Sulṭān Muḥammad Shāhī, Haydar 'Alī (son of Bihzād's sister), Qāsim 'Alī Chiha-gushāy, Muzaffar 'Alī (son of Bihzād's brother), and Maqṣūd (Bihzād's pupil). Seven pages are decorated with gold figures; margins have rich designs of birds, animals and human beings; page-headings are in different colours; gold borders. There are five *sarlauhs*. The MS. is preserved in the Gullistan Museum at Tehran.

Page from a *Shāh Nāmah* of the first half of the fourteenth century (B.M., *1948 12–11 022*):
Isfandiyar unhorses Gurgsar by lassoing him.

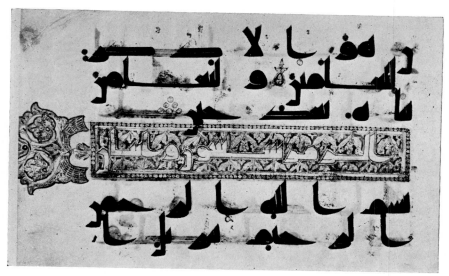

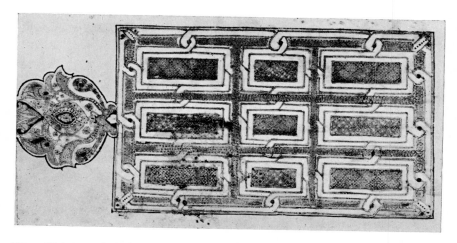

III–1. Eighth- and ninth-century Koran ornamentation in Egypt. *a, Mixt. 814,* fol. 14 *r.*
b, Freer Gallery, *No. 30. 60* : *Sūra*-heading in ornamental *kūfi* in white reserve on gold-
patterned ground; punctuation-ornaments in gold. *c,* The same collection, *No. 32.*
62 r : rectangular ornament with foliated medallion projecting into the margin: gold
and slight colour.

III–2. Early secular
ornamentation : *a–b*, Vienna,
A. F. 4, fol. *2 r*, and *N. F. 381*,
fol. *7 r*.

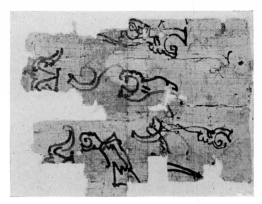

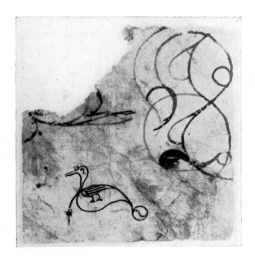

III–3. Sketches and decoration-patterns: Vienna, *Inv. Ar. Pap. 10. 053 (a), 10. 052 (b), Inv. Ar. Chart. 12. 514 r and v (c and d), Inv. Ar. Pap. 600 a (e), 600 b (f), and 9998 (g).*

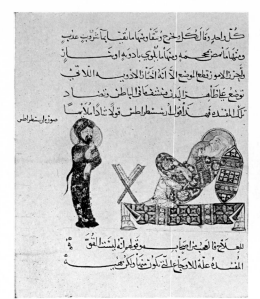

III–4. Baghdād School: 'Abdallah ibn al-Fadl. Arabic translation of Dioscorides, *Materia Medica*; illustrations in opaque colour and gold, A.D. 1224: *a*, the Greek physician Erasistratos lying on a low bench with an assistant standing in front of him; *b*, a prince, a physician and his assistant under a fruit tree; *c*, two physicians cutting a plant; *d*, mushrooms (Freer Gallery, *Nos. 47. 5; 32. 22; 38. 1; 43. 2 A*). *e*, *Kalilah and Dimnah*, first half of the thirteenth century (Paris, *MS. Arabe 3465*).

III–5. *a, Maqāmāt,* A.D. 1237, Paris, *MS. Arabe 5847,* fol. 69 *v*: literary discussion in a garden at Baghdād. *b,* Another illustration from the same MS. *c, Kalīlah and Dimnah,* Bodleian Library, *MS. Poc. 400,* fol. 46 *r*.

d–f, Early copies of the *Shāh-nāma. d,* Thirteenth century; Charles Gillet Collection, Paris: two rows of knights fighting. *e,* Early fourteenth century; M. H. Vever Collection, Paris: Iraj's coffin brought to Farīdun. *f,* Fourteenth century; Sachs Collection, Fogg Art Museum, Harvard University: Rustam fighting a dragon.

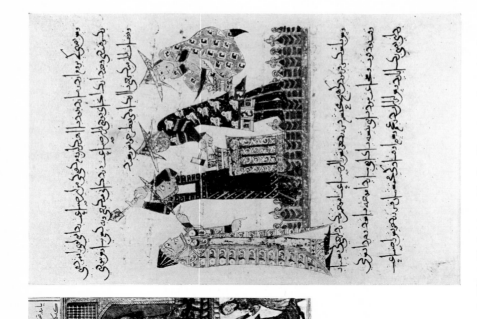

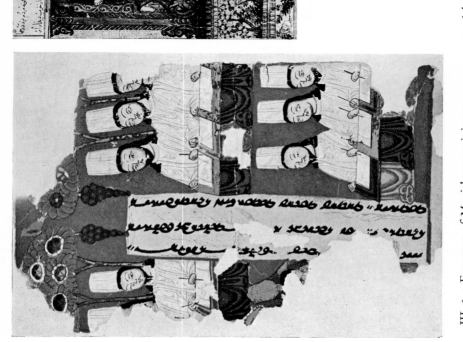

III-6. *a*, Fragment of Manichaean miniature, on paper, A.D. eighth or ninth century; discovered 1904 in Idiqut-Shahri (near Turfán, Eastern Turkestan). The men are Manichee Elders. *b*, *Vever Shāh-nāma*: Farīdūn mourning for Iraj. *c*, Earliest extant Persian illustrated MS., Cincinnati, *MS. 1954. 112. 17*, fol. 119 r: Gushtasp and the Byzantine blacksmiths (this MS. appears to be a forgery: see *N.B.* on p. 215).

III-7. Chinese painting on paper *makimono*; late T'ang period or early Sung (A.D. ninth or tenth century): two inscriptions in ink, two seals, and illustration to a Buddhist *sūtra* representing the Buddha addressing Yamarāja at Kusinagara (Freer Gallery, No. 26. 1).

III–8. *a*, Arabic-Christian MS., written by Isaac son of Abulpharagius in the city of Mardin (Mesopotamia), A.D. 1299; there are 48 folios; nearly all of them contain pen-drawings (in Oriental style, with Byzantine influences) illustrating various episodes from Christ's infancy (Laurentian Library at Florence, *MS. Orient. 387*), fol. 36 *v. b*, Al-Bīrunī, *Āl-Athār al-Bāqiya,* copy by Ibn al-Qutbī, dated A. H. 707 (A.D. 1307), Edinburgh University Library (*Arabic. MS. No. 161*), fol. 532 *v*: Annunciation.

III–9. Bodleian Library, *MS. Ouseley,* 381, fol. 94 *v* and 302 *r.* (Third volume of a large novel *Kitāb-i-Samak ʿIyār* by Ṣadaqah bin ʿAlbī-alqāsim Shīrāzī). This copy is of the thirteenth or fourteenth century.

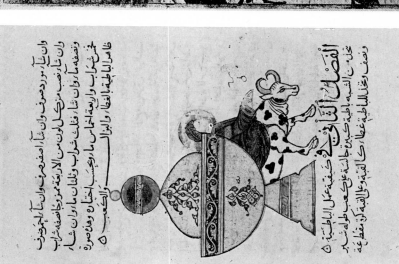

III-10. *a*, Al-Jazari, *On automata* (*Kitāb fī maʿārifat al-hiyal al-handasiya*, A.D. 1315; Āmida, N. Mesopotamia; text in black ink; illumination in colour and slight gold (Freer Gallery, *No. 30. 72*) : table device for holding several wines. *b*, Timuridae School, *Anthology of Sultān Iskander* : Game of Polo (Gulbenkian Collection). *c*, Incomplete paper-MS., *c.* 1430, *Shāh-nāma*, Fitzwilliam Museum, *MS. 22–1948* (detached miniatures from this MS. are in the British Museum), fol. 11 *v*: King Jamshed.

III–11. *a*, Herat School, late fifteenth century: Tree of the *Houri* (*Sūra*, lvi), Sarre Collection, Berlin. *b*, Saʿadi, *Būstān*, A.D. 1488: King Dum with his tribesmen and horses grazing. *c*, Jāmī, *Khamsah*, A.D. 1522 (Gullistan Museum, Tehran): lower scene, the ladies of Egypt are astonished at Joseph's beauty.

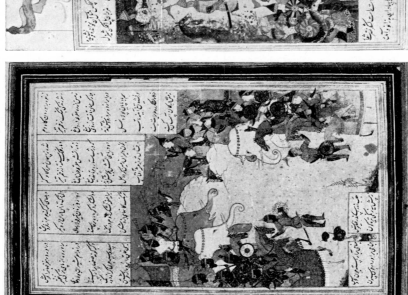

III-12. *a, Khamsah-i-Nizāmi*, copy of 1505–10 (India Office Library, *No. 387, E. 976*), fol. 364 *v*: Alexander the Great on a hunting expedition. *b*, The same work, copied by Muḥammad Muḥsin Tabrīzī, 1542 (Fitzwilliam Museum, *MS. 373*), fol. 60 *v*. *c*, *Zafarnāmah*, copy dated A. H. 939 (= A.D. 1533), India Office Library: Tamarlane reviewing his army before his campaign against Tuqtamish Khān.

III-13. *a*, Sixteenth-century MS.; Ajit Ghose Collection, Calcutta: Mary with the infant Jesus, at an oasis in the desert. *b*, Qazwīnī, *Wonders of Creation* (On Cosmology), copy of 1566 (C.U.L., *MS. Nn. 3. 74*). *c* and *d*, *Shāh-nāma*: *c*, copy of 1569/70, with strong Chinese and Indian influences (National Library at Naples, *MS. III. G. 68*); *d*, copy of 1582; thirty full-page miniatures, illustrating the deeds of the ancient Persian kings (Laurentian Library, *MS. Orient. 5*), fol. 59 *v*.

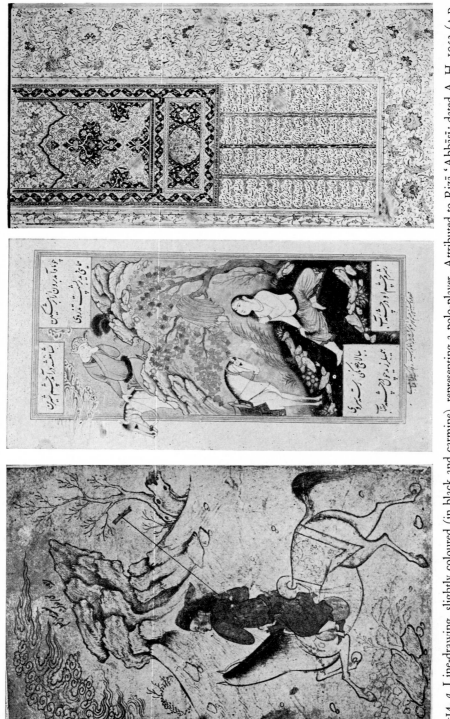

III-14. *a*, Line-drawing, slightly coloured (in black and carmine), representing a polo-player. Attributed to Riẓā 'Abbāsī; dated A. H. 1052 (A.D. 1642); Sarre-Humann Collection, Berlin. *b*, Riẓā Abbāsī's masterpiece: Niẓāmī, *Khusraw and Shīrīn* (Victoria and Albert Museum, London, *J*. 1389). *c*, Luxurious sixteenth-century MS., ornamented in gold (*Rylands Persian MS*. 35).

III–15. Hindu Illumination. *a*, Rāz Bahādur and Rupmati, *c.* 1590 (National Library at Paris, *Prints, OD. 44*). *b*, General Kandurān, seventeenth century (the same collection, *OD. 43*, fol. 25).

III–16. Turkish illumination.
a, Paris, *Suppl. Turc. 190,* of
1436, fol. 34 *r*: Ascent of
Mohammed. *b, Rylands Turkish
MS. 3* (sixteenth century), fol.
34 *r*.

III–17. Earliest illuminated Hebrew MSS. *a, Codex Leningradensis* (*Bible L*, Leningrad State Library, *Cod. B. 19*, dated *c.* 1008), fol. 489 *v* : colophon and Massoretic ornamentation. *b, Leningrad Pentateuch* : Interior of the Temple with Sacred Vessels. *c, Hagiographa B. M. Or. 9880*, tenth century : decoration in gold (rosettes, chain-like ornamentation, etc.).

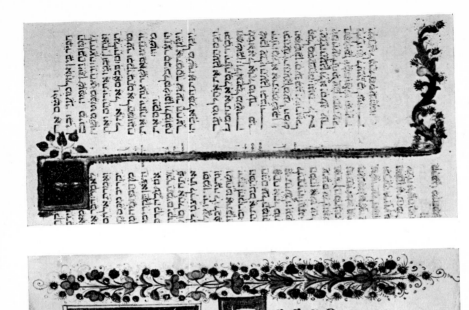

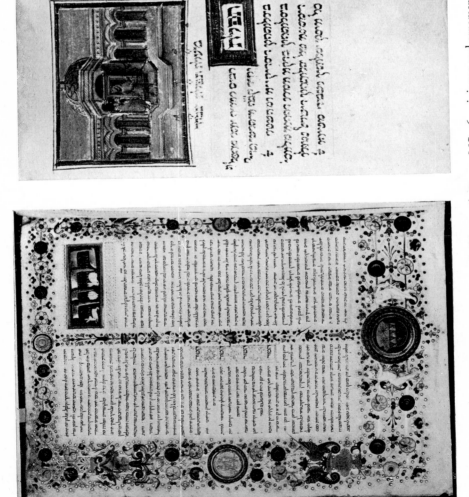

III-18. *a*, Copy of *Arbāʿ Ṭurim* (*Harl. MS. 5716*), fol. 79 *r. b*, *Garrett MS. 26*: miniature and ornamentation in late fifteenth-century Renaissance style. *c*, U.L.C. *Add. MS. 468*, fol. 68 *r*: initial *w* (the first letter of the Hebrew *Book of Leviticus*) and beginning of *Leviticus*.

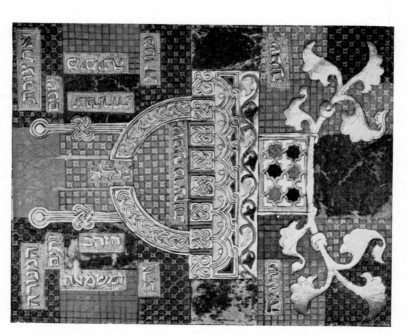

III-19. *a, Farḥi Bible*, p. 150: the Golden *Menōrah. b, Lisbon Bible*: first page.

III–20. *Kennicott 1.—a*, Upper portion of fol. 3 *r. b*, fol. 6 *r.*

זה לויתן

III–21. *a–b, B.M. Add. MS. 11639—a*, Fol. 114 *r*: Aaron puts oil into the *Menōrah*; *b*, 'the Leviathan'.

 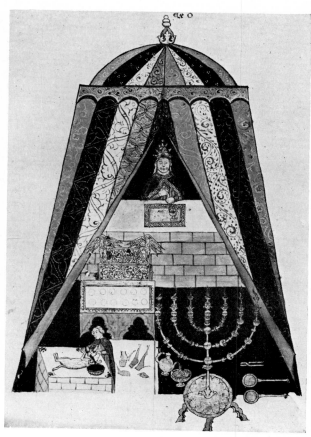

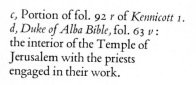
c, Portion of fol. 92 r of Kennicott 1.
d, Duke of Alba Bible, fol. 63 v:
the interior of the Temple of
Jerusalem with the priests
engaged in their work.

III–22. *a, B. M. Add. MS. 15282,* fol. *179 v* : frontispiece to the *Book of Numbers. b,* Felix Guggenheim Collection, Los Angeles—MS. containing *haphṭaroth* : ornamented letters.

III-23. *Schocken Bible*: frontispiece containing the illuminated initial word of the Hebrew Bible surrounded by forty-six small medallions, illustrating various episodes recorded in the Pentateuch.

III–24. *a*, Trinity College Library, Cambridge, *F. 12. 71*, fol. 205 *v*: first word of the *Book of Lamentations* with various ornamentation. *b*, Darmstadt, *Cod. or. 13*, fol. 202 *v*: Sacrifice of Isaac. *c*, Munich, *Cod. Hebr. 4*: the word *melekh* ('king') ornamented with animals, birds, etc. *d*, Sassoon *Haggādāh* (*Cod. 514*), p. 13: instructions concerning *maṣah* ('leavened bread').

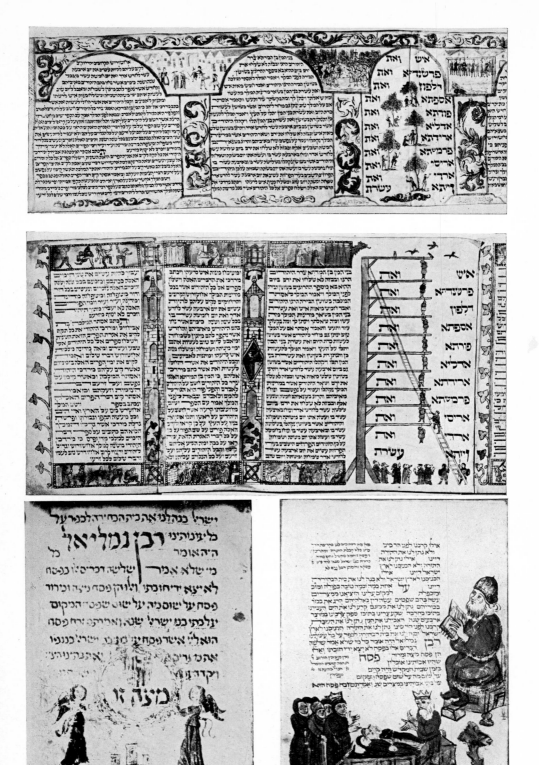

III–25. *a–b, Book of Esther,* ix. 7 till the end, in two fine copies belonging to the Felix Guggen-heim Collection, Los Angeles. *c, Nîmes Prayer-book,* fol. 112 *v*: two angels with heraldic garland. *d,* Sixteenth-century Italian *Maḥăzōr* fol. 172 *v*: right, Jew reading the *haggādāh*; bottom, Pharaoh at the funeral of the firstborn.

III–26. *a, Hamilton 288,* fol. 19 *r*:
letters in form of animals
(*Kennicott 1,* fol. 447 *r* contains
the colophon in letters pictured
in human or animal form and
grotesques). *b,* Paris, *Fonds hébr.
21* (*Bible*; also, at the beginning of
the MS., *Calendar,* starting with
1295; and in the last pages
epitome of *Cosmology*), p. 263 *v*:
text in geometrical
ornamentation; in the centre,
violet-coloured lion: decorated
border.

III–27. a, B. M. *Haggādāh Add. MS. 14762,* fol. 4 r: left, man seated with raised left hand; bottom, hare-hunt, b, Frankfort o. M. City Library, *MS. 725/17,* fol. 7 v: curious decoration including a square consisting of twenty-five fields in which well-drawn faces or grotesques are alternated with other designs (*cf. MS. 2* in the Jewish Theological Seminary of America).

III–28. *a–b, Prayer-books,* Guggenheim Collection—*a,* afternoon-service for Passover. *b, Psalms,* xcvii.10–xcix.2. *c–d, Haggādōth—c, Rylands Hebr. MS. 6,* fol. 29 *v*: ornamented letters, hare-hunt, grotesques, birds, snakes, and other decoration. *d, Rylands Hebr. MS. 7,* fol. 5 *r*: richly decorated beginning of the *haggādāh* service.

III–29. *Haggādōth. a,* Munich State Library, *Cod. 200,* fol. *15a*: illuminated letters; bottom, arrival of prophet Elia; other ornamentation. *b,* Frankfort, *MS. 725/17,* fol. 21 *r*: family at the *seder* (ceremonial meal on the first two nights of Passover).

III-30. *First Cincinnati
Haggādāh*: fol. 1 *v* (above)—
ritual of disposal of
ḥameṣ (remains of leavened
bread) on eve of Passover; fol.
2 *r*: (below)—two men with
maṣah (unleavened bread).

III-31. *a*, Madrid, *AL. 69 (Mozarabic Breviary)*, fol. 165 *r*: initial. *b*, Madrid, *Hh. 68*, (*Lives of Saints*, copied by Armentarius), fol. 139 *r*: initial. *c*, *Bible of S. Isidore de Léon*, of 960: I *Kings*, xviii. 39 ff. (Elijah and the priests of Ba'al) and xix, 4 ff. (Elijah under the juniper tree). *d*, *Madrid Beatus*: World map.

III–32. *a, Rylands Beatus,* fol. 181 *v*: Mystic explanation of *Apocalypse* xviii.
b, Escorial Beatus: beginning of the MS.

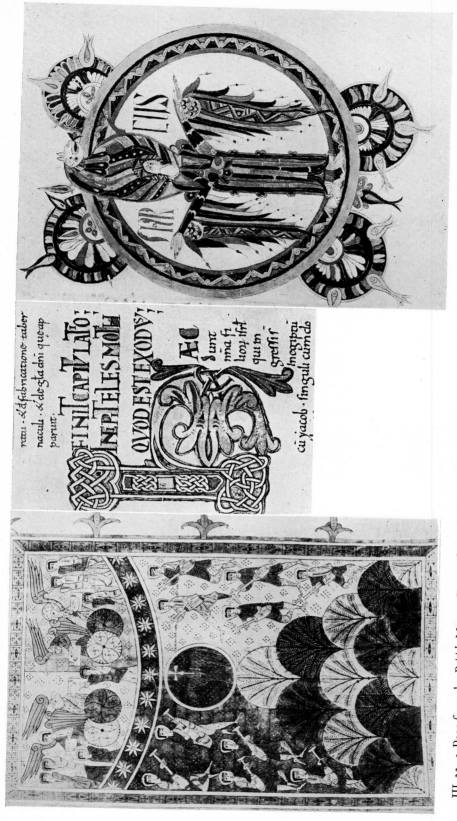

III-33. *a*, Page from the *British Museum Beatus*: the symbols and Gospels of the four Evangelists; worship of the Antichrist (?). *b*, Initial from the *Farfa Bible*, fol. 23 *r*: beginning of *Exodus* (see also Fig. III-21). *c*, *Léon Bible*, fol. 209 *r*: allegory of S. Mark.

III-34. *a*, Thirteenth-century codex of Léon Cathedral (*Libro de las estampas de Léon*), fol. 21*v*. *b*, *Pierpont Morgan Beatus*, fol. 231 *r*: S. John going to Ephesus—the Evangelist prostrated before the Son of Man; the Evangelist addressing himself to the Church of Asia. *c*, Twelfth-century *Burgos Bible* (Public Library at Burgos), fol. 13 *v*: upper zone, Fall of Man (*Gen.* iii. 6–15): lower zone, right: Christ and the four Evangelist-symbols; various Biblical episodes.

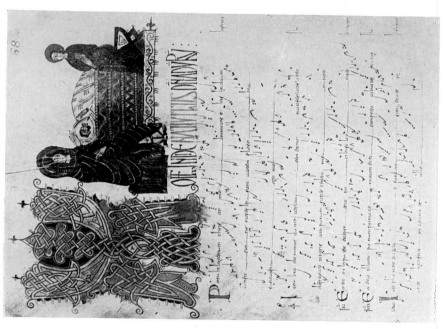

III-35. *a*, Eleventh-century *Mozarabic Antiphonary* (Léon Cathedral), fol. 68 *r*: Nativity. *b*, *Liber Feudorum Maior*, of the twelfth or thirteenth century (Arch. de la Corona de Aragon, Barcelona, *Cod. 1*), fol. 1 *r*: frontispiece.

III-36. a, *Mozarabic Old Testament*, twelfth century (Municipal Library, Porto, *MS. 32*), fol. 1 r: S. Jerome, *Prologus* to the five Books of Moses. b, *Book of the Birds*, written in 1183 at the monastery of Lorvão (Armario dos Tratados, National Archives, Lisbon). c, *Lorvão Apocalypse*, late twelfth century (the same collection): Beginning of explanation of *Apocalypse*, xvi. 10–11. d, *Bible* (University Library, Coïmbra, *MS. 31432*), vol. 1: Jacob's sons (beginning of *Exodus*).

Decline of Persian Illumination

Riẓā 'Abbāsī, who worked during the reign of Shāh 'Abbās (1587–1629) and his successors, was not a court-painter, but he may be accounted the last of the great Persian book-illuminators. His main work is a copy of Niẓāmi's *Khusraw and Shīrīn* (preserved in the Victoria and Albert Museum). Thenceforth, although now and again a good artist appeared, Persian illumination declined: Fig. III-14*a* and *b*.

Excellent Persian-Arabic illuminated manuscripts of the sixteenth century are preserved in all the main collections of Europe, America, Asia, and North Africa: Fig. III-12–14.

From the seventeenth century onwards the fashion of imitating European models set in, and the decay of Persian painting rapidly followed.

INDIAN ILLUMINATION

(Fig. III-15)

It seems that Moslem India had no book-illumination before the Mogul conquest. Under the new rule, however, this art reached a very high level. The Mogul emperors—who descended from the art-loving Tīmūrid princes of Persia —were great patrons of art. Fakhr ad-Dīn Muḥammad Bābur (or Bābar or Bāber), 1483–1530, who conquered Hindūstān in 1526, had remarkable talents in military and civil affairs, as well as in administration, science and the arts. He was a great collector of finely illuminated manuscripts, which had been adorned by some of the best painters of Persia. He wrote, in the Tatar language, a history of his life and conquests—an illuminated Persian version of this book, preserved in the collection of the ex-Mahārājā of Alwar, is a sample of the art of his period.

Under the rule of Bābur's son, Humāyūn (1508–56), painting received considerable impetus. Humāyūn spent some years of exile in Persia, and on returning to his throne he brought with him Persian painters who influenced the Hindu school of book-illumination. The most important example of this art is provided by the splendidly illuminated *Romance* by Emīr Ḥamza (twenty-five pages are preserved in the India Museum, South Kensington, London; the rest is in Vienna); the pages are 22 by 28¼ in. (56 by 72 cm.); and fifty painters—under the superintendence of two great Persian painters, first Mīr Sayyid 'Alī, and later 'Abd aṣ-Ṣamad—are said to have worked on this masterpiece.

Akbar

Jalāl ed-Dīn Muḥammad, Humāyūn's son, known as Akbar ('the Greatest'), the Napoleon of India (1542–1605), although illiterate, was a monarch of great enlightenment and power. Despotic and cruel, he was the wisest of the Moguls; in religious matters he was exceedingly tolerant; indeed, he was far more liberal in the matter of religion than the contemporary sovereigns of Europe. Himself a Moslem, he called for Portuguese Jesuit missionaries from Goa; they brought to his court the influences of Western art, and introduced Western woodcut illustrations. Akbar's reign also marked the beginning of an important period in the literary history of India. His interest in the religion and mythology of the Hindus prompted him to have translated into Persian the two great Sanskrit epics (the *Mahābhārata* and the *Rāmāyana*: see *The Hand-produced Book*, p. 357 f.).

Akbar had a great predilection for the arts of painting and book-illumination. The work of all the painters is said to have been submitted to him every week, and he then conferred rewards according to the excellence of the work done. These painters, however, appeared to have been mainly occupied in illustrating the works of literature which Akbar delighted to have read to him.

He had, it would seem, more than a hundred painters working for him—the majority Hindu; the names of many are known; some introduced methods and techniques of the native traditional style of painting as practised in Rajputana, Bundelkhand and Punjab; the style was derived from the Rajputana mural art, and was concerned mainly with illustrating the stories of Hindu legend and religious epic. The subjects chosen were sometimes portraits of men of the time, and sometimes scenes chronicling contemporary events. The native colouring was mainly flat, while the main features of Mogul-Persian painting were gradations of tone and effects of light and shade.

Akbar collected a great library, and when, in 1641, in Shāh Jahān's reign, the Imperial Library of Agra was visited by a Spanish priest, it contained 24,000 volumes. One of the finest illuminated books extant, now preserved in Jaipur, is Akbar's copy of the Persian version of *Mahābhārata*, containing 169 miniatures. The execution of this volume is said to have cost £40,000.

Decadence of Indian Illumination

Akbar's successors, Jahāngir, who reigned 1605 to 1628, and Shāh Jahān, 1628 to 1659, continued the cultivation of the fine arts, and maintained a group of excellent court-painters; but during the long reign of Aurangzīb, also known as Aurangzeb or Aurungzebe (1659–1707), who was a brilliant but despotic emperor and also a bigoted Moslem, the arts were discouraged for religious reasons, and the art of book-illumination decayed. For some decades painting continued to be cultivated, but both drawing and colour were poor. During the reign of Muḥammad Shāh (1719–48) there was even a brief renaissance, but the break-up of the Mogul empire struck the death-knell of Indian book-illumination.

Eighteenth-century Garhwal (N. India) painting; *c.* 1780;
Kasturbhai Lalbhai Collection, Ahmadabad. Lovers in a moon-lit retreat.

(Fig. IV-16)

In Turkey, as in India, book-illumination was based upon Persian models. The precious illuminated manuscripts brought to Constantinople by Badī ʿaz-Zamān Mīrzā—a son of Sulṭān Ḥusayn, referred to on p. 144—apparently served with other fine works of contemporary Persian artists as models for the Ottoman artists, until, towards the end of the seventeenth century, fashion changed and they began to imitate the new manner of the Ṣafawid painters.

Court Book-illuminators

The names of a few great Turkish book-illuminators are recorded: Ṣanʿullah, born at Brussa, was a poet and painter; he is said to have worked under Murād II (1422–51), and Muḥammad II (1430–81). The latter also patronised the Italian painter, Gentile Bellini, who trained the Turkish painter Shiblīzāda Aḥmad. Walī Jān, born in Tabrīz, was another court-painter, though of the second half of the sixteenth century; he painted two miniatures in the splendid album—see further on—of Sulṭān Murād III, compiled in 1572.

Under Ottoman rule there was no such liberal patronage as in Persia or India, but Suleymān the Magnificent (1496–1566) had a few excellent painters, such as ʿOsmān, who illustrated a history of his patron's reign, or Ḥaydar, who was under Western influence, and Sharīf Shafīʿ, the reputed inventor of the albums called *Subḥat al-Akhbār*. This was a collection of something resembling illustrated genealogical tables—mainly in the form of rolls—of the Ottoman imperial family; the earlier Sulṭāns are represented by 'portraits', which are generally fictitious, especially as many of the albums begin with Adam.

Ottoman book-illumination, however, shows little originality, and the hostility towards representational art—apart from the works of the famous secret cabinet of the Imperial Seraglio—prevented the emergence of an eminent school.

HEBREW ILLUMINATION

Jewish attitude to representational art and the possible existence in ancient times of illuminated or illustrated manuscripts have been discussed on pp. 60 ff.

PRESERVED HEBREW ILLUMINATION MSS.

The earliest preserved Hebrew illuminated MSS. belong to the tenth and eleventh centuries (A.D.), and they were executed in the East (Palestine, Egypt and Syria); the earliest dated is the fragmentary *Pentateuch* of A.D. 929/30, in Leningrad (*Cod. II. Firk.* 17). It was written, possibly in Egypt, by one Solomon ha-Levi ben

Buya'a. It includes a page representing in the centre the Vessels of the Sanctuary and the Candelabrum; on the left, the censer and sacrificial implements; on the right, the Altar, the Laver, and other cult objects; above the Candelabrum there is an *aedicula* with two rectangular doors and a triangular apex, surrounded by liturgical and ritual appurtenances. This feature is in Dr. Cecil Roth's opinion not only identical with the *Torah*-shrine (*i.e.*, the shrine in which the Law Scrolls are kept) of the later representations, but it presents a striking similarity to the representations on the gold glasses, the frescoes, and particularly to those in the sixth-century (A.D.) mosaic of Beth Alpha (North Israel). It is now generally believed that the reason why earlier Hebrew illuminated manuscripts have not come down to us is not that such codices were not produced, but that they have been lost or destroyed. Fig. III-17.

Classification

J. Leveen classifies the Hebrew codices into representational and non-representational art, the latter category being by far the larger; indeed, the splendid codices produced in Spain or Portugal show little or no representational art. In the sphere of pure ornament one aspect of the Jewish artistic genius is seen at its best. The finest examples in this class can challenge comparison with the corresponding products of Christian and Islamic art.

On the whole, these manuscripts may be classified (1) according to whether they are Eastern or Western; and (2) according to contents. There are religious works as well as secular codices. To the former belong: (*a*) Bibles or single Biblical books, particularly the *Book of Esther* (these are in Hebrew); (*b*) the Aramaic version (*Targum*); (*c*) the Hebrew traditional textual *apparatus* of the Bible, known as the *Māsōrah* (compiled by the Masorites, in the sixth to the ninth centuries of the Christian era); it was the object of special ornamentation, often assuming fantastic shapes; (*d*) prayer-books for daily prayers (*Siddūrim*), and for festivals (*Maḥăzōrim*); (*e*) the ritual of the two first nights of the Passover (*Haggādāh*, pl. *Haggādōth*), which occupies a special place in the realm of illumination (see p. 157 ff.).

Secular Works. Here we may refer to such codices as David Qimḥī's (1160–1235) grammatical treatise (*Sēpher hamikhlōl*); and the code of Jacob ben Asher (*Arbā' Ṭurim*), copied in 1473–5, probably in Italy, and now in the British Museum (*Harl. MS.* 5716–17). A beautiful copy of the same work—in pure Renaissance style—executed at Mantua (N. Italy) in 1435, is preserved in the Vatican Library (*Rosiano 555*). Of particular interest is a profusely illuminated copy of the Hebrew translation of Avicenna's *Canon Medicinae*. This most famous of medieval medical works, by Abû-l-Hasan ibn-Sînâ, better known as Avicenna (980–1037), was translated into Hebrew by Joseph Lorki, Nathan ha-Meati, and Zeraḥyah Ḥen. The present copy, written on paper and vellum, executed in Spain in 1468, is preserved in the Elkan N. Adler Collection of the Jewish Theological Seminary of America, New York. Fig. III-18*a*.

The most celebrated copy of Avicenna's *Canon* is the finely illuminated Hebrew codex preserved in the University Library at Bologna, *Codex 2197* (see also p. 346); it was one of the Italian masterpieces which Napoleon ordered to be carried away to Paris, where it remained till 1815. Amongst other medical works, reference may be made to the illuminated copy of Maimonides, *Peraqīm*, or 'Medical Chapters', preserved in the Bodleian Library, Oxford (*Codex 2113*). See also p. 170.

An excellent example of an illuminated *Legal Code*, produced in Italy, is preserved in the British Museum, *Or. 5024*, containing the *Responsa* of 'Isaia of Trani the Younger'; it was executed in 1374. Amongst its charming illustrations, there is one at the beginning of the section dealing with the sale-transaction of a ship; it is painted in pleasing colours and it represents a ship and the buyer handing the money to the seller.

Of semi-religious and semi-secular character are a De' Rossi codex (Palatina Library at Parma, *No. 878*), containing commentaries by Rashī and Abraham ibn Ezra; there are other copies of Rashī's commentary, and similar works. A mid-fifteenth-century copy of Moses Naḥmanides (1195–c. 1270), *Commentary on the Pentateuch*, written in Italy in Spanish hand, is preserved in the Jewish Theological Seminary of America, New York. It is decorated in beautiful Spanish style.

A fifteenth-century copy of a portion of Moses Maimonides, *Mishneh Tōrah* (Code of Jewish Law), formerly in the Library of the city of Frankfort, is now part of a private collection in Brooklyn, N.Y. The whole work, which consisted of four volumes, was once the property of Isaac Abravanel (1437–1508), minister of state in Portugal, and chancellor in Spain, before the expulsion of the Jews. The work, richly illuminated, was executed in Spain, probably for Abravanel himself. At the beginning of each section, there is a miniature referring to the subject dealt with in the section. Another illuminated copy of the same work, also written in Spain, but somewhat earlier, is preserved in the Elkan N. Adler Collection in the Jewish Theological Seminary of America, New York. The opening of each book is beautifully illuminated

Another interesting fifteenth-century copy of *Mishneh Tōrah* is preserved in the British Museum (*Harley MS. 5698–9*): it was produced in Spain, but it also shows Italian influence by the arabesque design richly worked over with foliage, blossoms, fruit, birds, etc.

A very fine specimen of Maimonides' *A Guide to the Perplexed* is preserved in the Royal Library at Copenhagen; it is dated 1348, and was produced in Barcelona.

Illuminated works dealing with religious philosophy may also be referred to, such as *Malmad ha-Talmidīm* by Jacob ben Abbamari (who lived in the thirteenth century), *Mishlê Shuʿalim (Parabolae Vulpium)* by Berakhya Naqdān, identified with Benedictus le Poncteur of Oxford, thirteenth century; the *Fables (Mashal ha-qadmonî)* by Isaac Sahula, and others.

Of great charm and interest is an early fourteenth-century manuscript *Hanhagot mikol ha-shanah* ('Customs of the whole year'), a sort of manual for practical Jewish ritual. It is a compilation of Jewish customs, rites and ceremonies. The

MS.—now preserved in the Princeton University Library (*Garrett MS. 26*)—contains two full-page miniatures, twenty-six smaller ones and ornamented borders. Although the subject matter is Jewish—being the representation of the religious life of pious Jews from the cradle to the grave—the style of the pictures is pure Renaissance, not specifically Jewish; it is partly related to the style of Ferrara. The illumination is now assigned to the last two decades of the fifteenth century. A forged letter on an originally blank leaf of the book, attributes the text to Moses Maimonides and the paintings to Giotto; but this forgery has been exposed by Dr. Panofsky. Fig. III-18*b*.

Noteworthy is a Portuguese manual, written in Hebrew character by a Jew (Abraham ben Judah ibn Ḥayyīm), on the art of book-illumination; it is preserved in the De' Rossi collection of the Palatina Library, Parma (*Cod. 945*, of the year 1265).

Eastern Manuscripts

In the earliest preserved Hebrew illuminated codices, which were produced in the East, the influence of Islām precluded representational art, while—as has been rightly remarked—'the process of ornamentalization and geometrization of real objects of the visible world is found to be completed'. There was no objection to the representation of the Tabernacle or the Temple, the seven-branched candlestick (*Menōrah*), or the Sacred Vessels. Leveen mentions a good example of a later representation: *Cod. 7* in the National Library at Paris, written and illuminated in 1299 by Solomon ben Raphael in Perpignan. Similar representation, which appears 'immerged in ornamental design' is to be found in the *Leningrad Pentateuch*, already referred to.

As Mrs. Wischnitzer points out, the skill of the artist is exhibited in penmanship. She argues that dedications to patrons in huge gold lettering on diapered backgrounds became an outstanding feature of the magnificent parchment codices, and the masoretic notes of the Bible (see p. 148) written in Rabbinic script were arranged in marginal and full-page ornamental pieces.

Mr. Leveen discusses the Leningrad codices and other Hebrew illuminated MSS. (British Museum, *Or. 2540, 9879* and *9880*) which show the marked influence of the Islamic style of ornamentation. It was the Qaraite sect rather than Rabbinic Judaism which absorbed so much of Arabic culture. Two Eastern Hebrew vellum codices of the British Museum (*Or. 2363* and *1467*) plainly show the source of inspiration for the beautiful Spanish Hebrew Bibles of the fourteenth and fifteenth centuries. *Or. 2363* is the more complete: the decoration—executed in red, green and yellow—is limited to the beginning of each pericope, to the end of each book of the Pentateuch, and to the two Songs of Moses (*Exod. xv* and *Deut. xxxii*). Fig. III-17*c*.

Experts have thus suggested that the Qaraites, who at the period were very numerous in Palestine and Egypt, were the first to follow the lead of Moslem illumination. Whilst representational miniatures remained (at least, for a certain period) strictly excluded, rich non-representational ornamentation (including illuminated illustration of the Temple and its Sacred Vessels, the Tables of the Ten Commandments, the *Menōrah*, and so on) occurs in several codices. Early examples are the Leningrad codices, already referred to, and the British Museum manuscripts, also mentioned above. Another interesting specimen is the British Museum *MS. Or. 2540* (undoubtedly Qaraite), which exhibits ornamentations in gold to mark the 'open' and 'closed' sections of the text.

Later examples come mainly from Spain and Portugal (which naturally enough were under Moslem influence: see next Section). Here we may refer to British Museum *Add. MS. 12250*, of the thirteenth century (with the text neatly shaped in the form of *Menōrah* etc.) and particularly to the magnificent *Sassoon Codex 368*, or *Farḥi Bible* (see p. 160), of the second half of the fourteenth century. A still later specimen comes from Portugal—it was produced in Lisbon in 1483—and is the beautiful *Hebrew Bible* British Museum *Or. 2626–8*. Several pages at the beginning and at the end are placed within finely executed arabesque borders and whole sentences are written in gold. Finally, reference may be made to illuminated Hebrew MSS. of Yemenite origin, such as the British Museum *MS. Or. 2348*, of 1496, and those of North-African provenance, such as British Museum *MS. 15283*, formerly in the Duke of Sussex Collection. See Fig. III-19a.

Western MSS.

While Eastern Hebrew book-illumination exhibits Moslem influence, the Western MSS. show clear signs of Christian influence. From the thirteenth century onwards (when Christian illumination became partially secularized), the Jews not only borrowed their general scheme of decoration from Christian art, but also drew largely upon its iconography—in some cases adapting the illustrations to suit their own requirements. At the same time Hebrew illuminated MSS. included numerous specifically Jewish subjects, such as the Tents of Jacob, Aaron lighting the *Menōrah* (or the seven-branched Temple candlestick), the Death of Moses, the Temple restored, and so on. See also p. 152 ff. and *passim*.

Interesting specimens—containing elaborate illustrations of the *Menōrah* and of the Sacred Vessels—are preserved in the British Museum (for instance, *King's MS. 1*, of 1383). British Museum *Add. MS. 21160*, produced in Germany *c.* 1300, contains charming grotesques (see also further on). The beautiful British Museum *Add. MS. 15282*, executed in Franco-German style, will be discussed further on. Another MS. of Franco-German origin is preserved in Cambridge University Library (*MS. Ee. 5.9*); it is dated 1347. Particularly interesting is its frontispiece to the *Book of Job*, representing Job seated on a dunghill, tormented by Satan, whilst his wife stands before him giving evil counsel. Various other MSS. of Franco-German origin will be referred to under *Hebrew Bibles*. Concerning Italy—which Prof. David Kaufmann, the first historian of Hebrew illumination, described as 'the blessed country of illustration of Hebrew manuscripts'—it will suffice to refer to British Museum *Add. MS. 15423*, formerly in the Duke of Sussex Collection.

Hebrew Bibles

Continuous Biblical picture-cycles are rare, and there is not one Bible illustrated throughout; Mrs. Wischnitzer is probably right in suggesting that there must have been a certain reluctance to do so. In the magnificent Bible codex *Kennicott 1* in the Bodleian Library, Oxford (produced in La Coruña, Spain, in 1476)—in which 'we find the calligrapher and illuminator collaborating in the production of a perfect work of art' (Leveen)—only a few figures are represented, the decoration being chiefly animal and floral: see also p. 160. Fig. III-20 and 21c. See particularly C. Roth, *The Kennicott Bible*, Oxford, 1957.

In other codices, beasts, birds, and all sorts of plants crept even more into the interlacings of the arabesques of the decoration. One of the earliest and finest of these codices is now in the British Museum (*Add. MS. 11639*). Produced in Northern France and assigned to the late thirteenth century, it consists of over 700 leaves of the finest vellum—containing the Pentateuch and other portions of the Hebrew Bible, as well as selections from the liturgy and other miscellaneous literature—and of forty-one full-page miniatures, painted upon a thicker and darker kind of parchment, which contain a sort of Biblical picture-cycle. In the opinion of the late G. Margoliouth these magnificent miniatures were executed by a Christian artist. Fig. III-21a and b.

Moreover, almost every leaf of the first 400 folios is provided with excellent and lavishly produced ornamentation, which was probably not the work of the artist who painted the full-page miniatures. This ornamentation contains initials illuminated in gold, a profusion of marginal decorations with beautifully executed figures of animals, grotesques, shields and coats of arms, and also other patterns, all displayed with 'great resourcefulness, variety and superb skill' (Leveen).

A few other Hebrew illuminated Bibles—Fig. III-18c, 19b, 22–24a—deserve special mention: (1) British Museum *Add. MS. 15282*, once belonging to the Duke of Sussex, contains the Pentateuch (accompanied by the *Targūm*), the Five *Megillōth* (see *The Hand-produced Book*, p. 175), and the *haphṭārōth* (i.e., the sabbatical readings from the Prophets); each of the five books of the Pentateuch has a frontispiece executed in gold and colours, also containing the first word of the book in large gold letters; all the other books, except *Lamentations*, have initials in large gold letters enclosed in ornamental borders; the codex is assigned to the late thirteenth or early fourteenth century, and is in Franco-German style. (2) In the same style, and probably also of the same date, is a codex of similar contents, which was sold at Sotheby's on 20 July 1936 and is now in the Schocken library, at Jerusalem; its illumination consists in the frontispiece, containing the first word of *Genesis* enclosed in a frame in the centre of the page and surrounded by forty-six small medallions illustrating various events recorded in the Pentateuch. (3) A magnificent copy of the Bible with *Māsōrah*, executed in Spain in the late thirteenth century, belongs to a private collector in Brooklyn, N.Y. (it was formerly in the City Library at Frankfort). At the beginning are twenty-six illuminated pages, some containing pictorial representations of the sacred vessels and utensils employed in the Tabernacle. (4) A copy in two volumes of the Hebrew Bible, accompanied by the *Māsōrah*, is preserved in the Spencer Collection of the New York Public Library. This copy contains many illustrative and decorative pen-and-ink drawings, and was executed, according to the colophon, by Joseph of Xanten, son of Kalonymus from Neuss (Rhine). It was completed in January 1294. (5) British Museum *Add. MS. 9405*, dated 1309, has a representation of two mourning figures at the beginning of the *Book of Lamentations*. (6) British Museum *Add. MS. 21160* 'contains designs constructed out of Masoretic notes' (Leveen), such as the Tree of Jesse. (7) Of particular interest is an illuminated Hebrew Bible of Trinity College Library at Cambridge (F. *12.71*). (8) A fourteenth-century Hebrew Bible, executed at Regensburg or Ratisbon (see also p. 155), is (or was) preserved at Cracow: it contains six pages of miniatures interspersed through the text and several decorated initials. (9) A thirteenth-century Hebrew Bible, executed in north-east France, and containing illustrations taken from a *Bestiary* (see p. 49 and 269), was described by Z. Ameisenowa in *Miesięcznik Żydowski*, 1933. (10) Another Hebrew Bible described by the same scholar, and now lost, was attributed to Spain and assigned to the fifteenth century. Originally it seems to have contained sixty illustrations; in 1905 some forty-five remained, and about 1935 the codex disappeared. (11) A copy in two volumes of the Bible, written in fine Spanish script, contains beautifully illuminated initials of the first word of each book. Vol. I (*Pentateuch* and *Early Prophets*) is preserved in the University Library at Cambridge (*Add. MS. 468*); Vol. II (*Latter Prophets* and *Hagiographa*) is in the Library of the Hebrew Union College, Cincinnati (Ohio, U.S.A.). (12–15) A superb Hebrew Bible, in two large octavo volumes, illuminated in Renaissance style, was in 1877 acquired by Baron Edmond de Rothschild. Also British Museum *Add. MS. 15251* (a Hebrew *Bible* dated 1448) and Bodleian Library, *Can. Or. 62* (a Hebrew *Pentateuch* dated 1472) are outstanding. We end this list with the beautiful *Lisbon Bible* (National Library, Lisbon, *Illum. MS. 72*) of the fourteenth century, which is partly in Mozarabic style (see p. 163).

On f. 72*b* of a beautiful British Museum Bible (*Add. MS. 19776*), written in Franco-German hand, and dated to 1395, there is an extremely interesting illumination showing a teacher (holding a whip) and a pupil; in the background, a synagogue is represented.

A Castilian version of the Hebrew Bible, containing some 334 magnificent miniatures, for the most part inserted in the text, but comprising also six full-page miniatures, is preserved in the Duke of Alba's Library, at Madrid. It was written and illuminated in 1422–30. The beautiful codex was made—the miniatures were probably executed by Christian artists—by Rabbi Moses Arragel of Maqueda and Guadalajara on the commission of Don Luis de Guzman, Grand Master of the Order of Calatrava, Toledo. One page apparently represents the interior of the ancient Temple of Jerusalem, with the priests engaged in their work; there is the *Candelabrum*, the Table of Shewbread, the implements of sacrifice, the Ark, and—according to Dr. Cecil Roth—also the two great curtains 'sweeping down from top to bottom on either side'. 'It would seem'—argues Dr. Roth—'that the ancient original ... in the Chapter Library of Toledo, on which the illustrations in this codex were based, preserved an old Hebraic tradition. ...' Fig. III-21*d.*

Of the individual Bible books, one should be singled out: the *Book of Esther,* known in Hebrew as *megillath Esther* or, simply, *megillah*—'roll', the roll *par excellence* (see *The Hand-produced Book,* p. 175). This book has always been in much favour among the Jews, and a Talmudic regulation prescribes that it should be recited annually on the Feast of Purim. See also p. 148.

A leading scholar in this field, Dr. M. Metzger, has pointed out 'that, with the exception of one which can be ascribed to the end of the fifteenth century (the *Kirschtein Megillah*), it is only in various *megilloth* dating from the seventeenth century onwards that we begin to find a fully-developed cycle of illustrations to the Book of Esther.' *See,* particularly M. Metzger, 'The John Rylands Megillah and some other Illustrated Megilloth of the XVth to XVIIth Centuries', and 'A Study of some Unknown Hand-painted Megilloth of the Seventeenth and Eighteenth Centuries', *Bullet. of the John Rylands Library, Manchester,* Vol. 45/1 (1962), pp. 148–184; and Vol. 46/1 (1963), pp. 84–126.

Here reference may be made to the sixteenth-century British Museum *MS. Or. 1047,* executed in Franco-German style, which contains on the upper and lower margins and in the spaces between the columns a large variety of extremely charming coloured drawings, representing incidents recorded in the book. Two other copies are reproduced in Fig. III-25*a–b.*

Non-representational Illuminated Bibles

There are extant numerous non-representational illuminated Bibles—produced in Spain, Portugal, Italy, and France or Germany—containing representations of inanimate objects mentioned in the Bible (such as the sacred vessels of the Sanctuary or the Golden *Menōrāh*; or ritual objects, such as the *shophar,* or ram's horn, and the *lulab,* or palm-branch), as well as arabesques, patterns of foliage and flowers, animals and grotesques. Occasionally, however, 'a picture will insinuate itself upon the margin depicting a figure or episode out of the Hebrew Bible' (Leveen).

Dr. Cecil Roth has shown that in the illuminated Hebrew Bibles, following the Spanish, South European, and Mediterranean tradition, it was conventional to include a double page (sometimes, rather more than this), representing the Vessels of the Sanctuary, as a sort of solitary representational illustration (whereas the other ritual objects were in most cases purely decorative). While, however, it would have been natural to have such pictures inserted in the *Book of Exodus,* where the text deals with the subject, they are invariably or almost invariably placed before the entire Biblical text.

The precise details that went to make up this composite picture—writes Roth— vary from one manuscript to the other, and indeed the precise ascription of the objects shown is not always certain. Invariable or almost invariable, however, are the central features—the Ten Commandments, the *Candelabrum,* the Table of the

Shewbread, the Altar, the Laver—precisely the same in fact as those we find depicted in the later cult-objects of Central European synagogues.

Roth has suggested—see also p. 65 f.—that there is a very close parallel between the representations of these ritual objects in the medieval illuminated Bibles and the representations found on various media—frescoes, mosaics, carvings, gold glasses—in widely-separated areas of the Diaspora, in the late classical period. The *Leningrad Pentateuch* (see p. 147 f.)—argues Roth—may be considered a connecting link between the late classical representations and those of the medieval Hebrew illuminated Bibles.

Beautiful lettering and ornamentation of letters, particularly initials, appear in the great majority of the illuminated, and also non-illuminated, Hebrew codices. Here we cannot go into details. It will suffice to refer, as an example, to a charming book in the Felix Guggenheim Collection (ex-Collection Kirschstein), Los Angeles: Fig. III-22*b*.

Hebrew Bibles Containing Representations of Ritual Objects. Ritual objects are shown in the following illuminated Hebrew Codices—listed by Dr. Roth: Bodleian Library, Oxford, MSS. *Kennicott I* (see p. 152 and further on) and *Kennicott II* (executed by Joshua son of Abraham ibn Gaon, at Soria, in 1306); *Sassoon MSS. 368* (*Farḥi Bible*: see further on) and *16* (*Rashbā Bible*; executed in Cervera in 1383); National Library at Paris, *Ancien fonds 3, fonds hébr. 7* (Perpignan, 1299), and *MSS. 1314–15* (apparently seventeenth century); Ambrosian Library, Milan, *Cod. C. 105 sup.* (Spanish, fourteenth century); Laurentian Library, Florence (*Plut., 3, 10*); Palatina Library, Parma, *Cod. de' Rossi 782* (Toledo, 1277); two manuscripts were in Germany—one in Frankfort, of *c.* 1300, and another, formerly *MS. 12* in the Jewish Theological Seminary at Breslau (now, Wrocław, in Poland), is Italian, of the fourteenth century; two in Leningrad—the *Leningrad Pentateuch*, see pp. 147 f., 150, and *passim*, and *Cod. Guenzbourg 119*: a copy of Solomon Crescas, fourteenth century; one formerly in Cracow (Jewish Community, Cracow; in German style of the fourteenth century); one in Copenhagen (in the Royal Library, manuscript dated 1301); one formerly in the Collection D. Henriques de Castro (*Sale Catalogue*, 1899, No. 475); and three in the Cairo Synagogue, including one dated wrongly 895, and one, Spanish, probably of the fourteenth century. See also Fig. III-17*b*, 19*a*, 21, 23, etc.

Hebrew Psalters and Prayer-books

Hebrew illuminated Psalters are very rare: there is the De' Rossi codex of the Palatina Library, Parma, *No. 510*. Some of its miniatures illustrate the contents of the accompanying psalm; for instance, *Psalm 137*:

'By the rivers of Babylon, There we sat down, yea, we wept, When we remembered Zion. Upon the willows in the midst thereof We hanged up our harps,' ...

is illustrated by a miniature depicting weeping exiles who have hung up their harps in affliction; other miniatures illustrate David playing the harp, Saul in flight, and so on. Another illuminated Psalter of the same collection is *Cod. 490*.

Of Prayer-books we may mention the British Museum *Add. MS. 22413*, which is a *Maḥāzōr* of the late thirteenth century, in the Franco-German style. A charming *Maḥāzōr*, executed in Hammelburg in 1348, is (or was) preserved in the State Library at Darmstadt (*Cod. Or. 13*). A *Siddūr* in the Hamilton Collection (*Cod. 288*) of the State Library at Berlin also belongs to the fourteenth century. A fifteenth-century *Siddūr* is preserved in the Nîmes Municipal Library (*Cod. 13709*). Fig. III-24*b*, 25*c*, and 26*a*. See also Fig. III-24*c*, from a beautiful fourteenth-century *Maḥāzōr* in Munich.

Particularly interesting are two fifteenth-century *Maḥāzōrīm* in Italian style, preserved in the British Museum, *Add. MSS. 19944-5* and *Harley MS. 5686*. The former, a Jewish Florentine masterpiece, was produced in Florence in 1441, and was partly related to the fourteenth-century *Responsa-Codex* British Museum *Or. 5024* and to the fifteenth- or sixteenth-century *Bible* British Museum *Add. MS. 15423*, both produced in Italy. *Harley MS. 5686*, executed in 1466, contains several ornamented initials and border illuminations, as well as pictorial illustrations, including a very interesting one of a bridal procession (fol. 27*v*–28*r*).

A beautifully illuminated *Maḥāzōr* of the Bodleian Library, finished in 1501, is also in Franco-German style (*Laud. Or. 321*). Another *Ashkenazi Maḥāzōr*, profusely illustrated, in two folio volumes, is preserved in the Louis M. Rabinowitz Collection, New York. It was probably written in the Rhine valley, and was finished in 1380; the scribe was David bar Pesaḥ. In the same collection there is a magnificent *Maḥāzōr* of Italian rite, also in two volumes, copied in the latter decades of the fifteenth century; it includes a *Haggādāh*, illustrated by two striking miniatures. A beautiful fourteenth- or fifteenth-century Italian *Maḥāzōr* is in the Felix Guggenheim Collection, Los Angeles. Charming, but rather unusual—unique one may say—are the pen-drawings (including a pig!) in another *Prayer-book* in the Guggenheim Collection. A sixteenth-century Italian *Maḥāzōr* is preserved in the Jewish Theological Seminary, New York. Eight leaves of an illuminated *Maḥāzōr*, executed in Germany in 1296, are preserved in the same collection. Fig. III-25*d* and 28*a–b*.

An interesting *Prayer-book*, executed in Italy in the fifteenth century, is preserved in the Elkan N. Adler Collection, also in the Library of the Jewish Theological Seminary of America. It contains numerous colourful illustrations. In the same collection there is a thirteenth-century *Siddūr Miṣrayim* (daily prayers in Egyptian rite), containing musical notes for the blowing of the *shofar* etc.

A collection of *piyyūṭim* (*i.e.*, liturgical hymns) and other liturgical texts is also in the Jewish Theological Seminary. It was written in 1300 in Austria, and contains numerous miniatures.

Haggādōth

The illuminated *Haggādōth* (see p. 148) occupy in Hebrew book-production a position analogous to the profusely illustrated copies of the *Book of Hours* in the Christian Church (see p. 402 ff. and *passim*). The fascinating power of this little book—writes Dr. A. Galliner—seems immortal. It begins in a true religious-ethical spirit with the manifestation of purest social feeling; it ends with the belief in the eternal justice of Divinity! Heinrich Heine (1797–1856), the great German poet of Jewish descent, though converted to Christianity, describes in his *Rabbi of Bacharach* the sweet melancholy of the serious, fairytale-like, mysterious character of the *Haggādāh* service, of the traditional singing, of the sounds so intimate and at the same time so stirring, that even those Jews who had long forsaken the faith of their fathers in their search for alien pleasures and honours, are moved in the depth of their hearts whenever by chance they hear the familiar old Passover melodies. It was, therefore, only natural—concludes Galliner—that out of such a lively, vivid representation of the birth of a people, a picture-story should arise telling the miraculous story once again, in pictures accompanying and illustrating the text. The *Haggādāh*-ritual is sometimes also contained in Prayer-books (see, for instance, Fig. III-25c–d, and 26a).

In the *Haggādōth* as well as in the *Book of Esther* (see p. 154)—that is, in the copies designed for private use—the artist was allowed some measure of freedom and in-formality. Copies of both have survived in large numbers, and they are distinguished, especially the *Haggādōth*, either by occasional illustrations or by picture-cycles.

Preserved manuscripts, however, do not go back beyond the thirteenth century. One of the earliest is preserved in the Elkan N. Adler Collection of the Library of the Jewish Theological Seminary of America. It was illuminated in Spain in the thirteenth century in the Byzantine style.

Haggādōth have been classified into two main groups: (1) To the first group belong manuscripts, mainly assigned to Spain, containing a kind of picture-cycle of illustrations unrelated to the text.

It is interesting, indeed, that illustrations beginning with Adam and Eve are found in *Haggādōth* rather than in *Genesis* of the Bible. The splendid *Haggādāh* of the British Museum (*Add. MS. 27210*), in the French Gothic style of the late thirteenth century, contains fourteen folios—painted only on one side—illustrating Biblical history from the Creation to the Exodus. All the miniatures are executed in bright colours upon a gold background.

Rather better known, but of somewhat later date, is another MS. of the same group, the *Haggādāh* of the Serajevo Museum (where it came in 1894) produced in Northern Spain: it is assigned to the early fourteenth century. It has thirty-four folios, mostly containing two sketches on each; there are two full-page miniatures painted in luminous colours, in blue and light red, one representing the *seder* (the ceremony of the Eve of the Passover), and the other showing Rabban Gamaliel (these last two words being in bold Hebrew characters in gold) instructing his pupils. The text also contains beautiful initials. Of the sketches, the most interesting is the representation of the Creation; each of the six weekdays is represented by a disc of the earth showing the successive improvements, while the seventh day is represented by God, depicted as a young and beardless man, seated on a bench and enjoying His rest. Other pictures show affinities with themes illustrated in the Dura wall-paintings (see p. 62 f.).

(2) Manuscripts belonging to the second group come mainly from German lands; the illustrations keep closely to the contents of the narrative, illustrating the main events of the *Haggādāh*: the sketches are often full of witticism. The best representative of this group is the *Second Haggādāh* of the Germanic Museum, at Nuremberg, dated to the late fifteenth century.

A few other interesting *Haggādōth* may be mentioned: the Spanish *Haggādāh* in the British Museum, *Or. 2737*; it contains—apart from the ornamental drawings— many full-page miniatures depicting the story of Moses as told in Exodus. Other illuminated Spanish *Haggādōth* preserved in the British Museum are *Or. 2884* and *Add. MS. 27210*, both belonging to the fourteenth century. British Museum *Add. MS. 14762* is a beautifully illustrated *Haggādāh* of the fifteenth century. It is of German origin; on fol. *4r* it contains the humorous feature of hare-hunting (see below), which we find in other German MSS. of this kind: Fig. III-27*a*. A beautiful thirteenth-century Spanish *Haggādāh* is preserved in the Sassoon Collection (*MS. 514*): Fig. III-24*d*.

We may also refer to a striking and rather unusual copy of the early fourteenth century preserved in The John Rylands Library, Manchester (*Hebrew MS. 6*). Rylands *Hebrew MS. 7* belongs to a later date. An excellent fifteenth-century copy is in the State Library at Munich (*Codex 200*). Fig. III-28*c–d* and 29*a*.

In the *First Haggādāh* of Nuremberg symbolic animal and human figures express artistically 'the relation of the festival with the ultimate aims of mankind, the messianic idea' (Galliner). The *Rothschild Haggādāh*, included in a fifteenth-century MS., contains also the daily prayers and books of the *Psalms, Job* and *Proverbs*. The (Elkan N.) *Adler Haggādāh*, preserved in the Jewish Theological Seminary, and the *Darmstadt Haggādāh* must also be mentioned; the latter masterpiece contains two large miniatures with numerous figures, architecturally framed, a hunting scene and a fountain, superb initials and other beautiful lettering and ornamentation. Whereas the text was written in the first half of the fourteenth century (by the scribe Israel ben Rabbi Meir), the illumination was executed by several artists of a later date, probably in the second decade of the fifteenth century. The colours are still gay and vivid.

British Museum *Or. 1404* contains twenty-four miniatures; *Or. 2884* contains more than thirty sketches on eighteen pages, from Creation to Exodus, and also two sketches representing Eve-of-Passover ceremonies; *Or. 2737* contains many full-page miniatures illustrating the story of Moses. The Palatina Library, Parma, possesses some beautiful *Haggādōth*, including *Cod. No. 111* and *Cod. No. 958*, which are probably fifteenth-century products, the former of Northern Italy the latter of Tuscany.

וייבלעמטה אהרן את מטותם

The 'Golden Haggadah'—Brit. Mus. 27210, fol. 11r.
Early 14th cent. MS. Script in Spanish style; illuminations in French style.
Illustrations from the Bible (based on the Book of Exodus).

Several beautiful *Haggādōth* show Italian or—to a lesser degree—French influence. In this respect the *Kaufmann Haggādāh* (Jewish Theological Seminary at Budapest, *No. 422*) deserves special mention. It belongs to the fourteenth century and contains 104 pages with miniatures (partly full-page and partly in the text) showing Italian-French influence. These illustrations either refer to the ritual of Passover or depict incidents recorded in the text: similar illustrations appear in the *Second Haggādāh of Nuremberg*, already referred to, and in the *Yahuda Haggādāh* (edited by M. Narkiss, Jerusalem, 1955).

A charming Italian *Haggādāh* is preserved in the Schiff Collection, Jewish Theological Seminary of America (*MS. 2*). It was executed in 1454 by Joel son of Simon, called Feibush Ashkenazi, from Cologne, and contains many beautifully illuminated letters, as well as human figures and animals, frequently grotesque. The first word *h'* forms the centre 'of a square consisting of thirty-six fields in which well-drawn faces alternate with other designs' (J. Bloch).

The *First Cincinnati Haggādāh* is another fifteenth-century treasure preserved in an American Jewish institution (Library of the Hebrew Union College, Cincinnati, Ohio). The text, in elegant square letters (each page having no more than nine lines), was written by Meir, son of Israel Jaffe, of Heidelberg. It is beautifully illuminated. One of the pages 'shows a hunter brandishing a large lance and pursuing two hares while running behind his dogs over the hilly landscape. It illustrates the mnemonic Hebrew word *Yaqnehaz*.' This jocose scene, found in many *Haggādōth* (already referred to), has its origin in a curious, or perhaps intentional, misunderstanding of *Yaqnehaz* as the almost homonymic German words '*er jagt den Has(en)*' = 'he chases the hare'. In fact *Yaqnehaz* consists of the initials of the Hebrew words for 'wine', 'blessing (over the cup)', 'candle', *habhdalah* (ceremony of separating Sabbath and festivals from working days), and 'time'; it thus indicated the idea of time, or seasons, lying at the base of all festival celebrations. Fig. III-30.

After the introduction of printing, the variety in *Haggādāh* illustration for the most part ceased. The illustrated *Haggādāh* of Prague, 1526, followed by that of Augsburg, 1534—points out Galliner—set the example for the whole of Northern Europe; for the South, the Italian type of Mantua, 1550 and 1560, is of at least equal importance.

Kethūbōth, or Marriage Contracts, constitute a very large class of Hebrew illuminated manuscripts, but the preserved copies are mainly of relatively recent date. Some *Kethūbōth*, however, go back to much earlier times (they come from the Cairo *Genizah*: see *The Alphabet*, p. 261), but they are not provided with illumination. An interesting *Ketūbah*, which comes from Modena (North Italy) and is dated to 1557, is preserved in the British Museum. It produces the effect of a beautifully illuminated title-page. It contains the design of an archway richly decorated, and bounded by waving pillars like those in S. Peter at Rome; there are cupids with trumpets and budding branches; at the bottom there are figures representing Abraham, Sarah, and Lot, and perhaps Isaia, with verses from the

Bible; the outer illumination contains arabesques with blossoms, fruit, birds, signs of the zodiac, and portions of the *Song of Songs, Psalms,* etc.

Hebrew Illuminators. A question has often been asked: why is a mention of the artist's name so rare in the Hebrew manuscripts? As a matter of fact, in other kinds of illuminated codices names are even more scarce. Indeed, quite a number of Hebrew illuminators are known by their names. Some of these have already been referred to. Here at least two more may be added: Israel ben Israel of Toledo is known from two illuminated Hebrew *Bibles* of the years 1272 (preserved in Paris) and 1277 (in Parma). Two illuminated *Bibles* were executed in 1306 and 1312 by Joshua and Shemtob, sons of Abraham ibn Gaon: one is preserved in the Bodleian Library (*Kennicott II*), the other was preserved in a private collection in Tripolis, and is now in Paris: Fig. III-26b.

It may be added that whilst most of the illuminators of Hebrew MSS. were Jews, a certain number were undoubtedly Christians.

Hebrew Masterpieces. 'The finest examples of illuminated Hebrew Bibles of the non-representational kind are to be found in the manuscripts of Spanish and Portuguese origin' (Leveen). The most important Hebrew Bibles belonging to this class are: (1) the *Farḥi Bible* (so called because it belonged to that family for many years), or *MS. Sassoon 386*, already referred to; this was written and illuminated by Elisha' ben Abraham ben Benveniste ben Elisha' Crescas, who worked upon it for sixteen years (1366–82). It contains thirty full-page arabesques of various patterns and intricacy. Apart from these arabesques (on pages 42–71), there is a picture of the seven walls of Jericho (p. 22), of the four Matriarchal Tents (p. 23), full-page illustrations of the *Menōraḥ* (p. 150 and p. 182), the Tabernacle and Noah's Ark (p. 154), the Table of the Shewbread, the Altar, etc. (p. 183), of the Musical Instruments of the Temple, Aaron's Rod, etc. (p. 186), and the Tables of the Ten Commandments (p. 187); there is border decoration on pages 183–9. All the book-headings are illuminated except that for *Lamentations*. This masterpiece contains 1056 pages. Fig. III-19a reproduces page 150. (2) The Hebrew Bible in three volumes acquired in 1882 by the British Museum (*Or. 2626–8*), is one of the most profusely illuminated copies in existence. It was written and illuminated at Lisbon, 1476–82. (3) The copy of the Bodleian Library already referred to (*Kennicott I*) 'is easily the finest existing example of Jewish art as applied to a manuscript' (Leveen). It contains 445 folios of the finest white vellum, including seventy-seven full-page illuminations and 173 smaller decorations scattered in the text. See also pp. 151 f. and 157, and Fig. III-19, 20, 21c.

With the last two works Jewish book-illumination reached its zenith. The invention and spread of printing on the one hand, and, on the other, the expulsion of the Jews from Spain (1492), and their increasing misfortune in Germany which was 'accompanied by a marked decline in the quality of their books' (R. Wischnitzer)—the sketchy coloured book-drawings 'reflect haste and carelessness'

—mark the end of Hebrew illumination. There was, however, a notable exception. In Italy, as Mrs. Wischnitzer has pointed out, Hebrew illumination and, especially, illustration remained on a high level during the fifteenth and sixteenth centuries. They show an unparalleled variety and wealth of imagination and finesse of execution. However, as J. Leveen has remarked, from the sixteenth century onwards, the illuminated Hebrew codices shared the fate of the Christian illuminated book, and, as in the latter case, their art rapidly declined.

SPAIN: MOZARABIC ILLUMINATION

Moslem Spain was one of the main links between the learning of the classical world and the European Renaissance. In the eighth to eleventh centuries, when Graeco-Roman tradition was entirely lost to West-European Christianity, it was nurtured and developed in al-Andalus (hence the modern name of the Spanish region, Andalusia), which was the Arabic name for Spain. This country was then one of the main world-centres of learning and culture.

Indeed, the Moslems, when they conquered the South of Spain in the eighth century, as against the Christians in Spain (Visigoths) and France (Franks), were highly civilized. Their science, their cities, their art, were far ahead of those of their Christian neighbours.

Cordova. The capital, Cordova—especially under the rule of Caliph 'Abd al-Raḥman III, who reigned from 912 to 961, and of his son and successor Al-Ḥakam II (961–76)—became the most magnificent city of Western Europe. It is said to have then had a population of half-a-million inhabitants, living in 113,000 homes, spread over the city and its twenty-one suburbs. This city was embellished by a magnificent royal palace, containing nearly five hundred rooms, a great university—the earliest of the Moslem universities—and twenty-seven free schools, seven hundred mosques (including the main mosque, a building of eleven aisles, each twelve bays long, with interlaced arches and complicated star-ribbed vaults, rich in elegant filigrees), three hundred public baths, the imperial library—said to have contained 400,000 volumes—and several public libraries, numerous book-shops, and beautiful palaces.

Men from all parts of the Moslem world as well as from Christian countries—Italy, France, England—came here to study the arts and sciences: astronomy, geography, chemistry, natural history. The great mosque of Cordova, founded in 788, but not completed until 990, was transformed into a Christian cathedral in 1236, and is now the largest of Christian temples next to S. Peter's. The flourishing leather industry of this city is associated with such terms as 'Cordovan leather' and 'cordwainer', the ancient English word for 'shoemaker'.

Other famous centres of Moslem Spain were Seville, Granada, Malaga, Almeria, and Toledo (capital of Castile).

Moslem Rule in Spain. The Hispano-Roman inhabitants of Spain—who were not yet amalgamated with the Visigoths—regarded the Moslems simply as successors of their previous masters; to them, generally speaking, it was a matter of indifference whether they were ruled by Moslems or Visigoths. At first they were interfered with but little by the Moslems, and they were far better governed by representatives of the Caliph than they had been by the Visigoths. As has been mentioned, the Moslems who came into Spain in the early days were tolerant; the Christians not only retained their religion, their bishops, their churches and their monasteries—indeed, some churches were even shared between the two faiths, as for instance, for a certain period, the Cordova basilica of S. Lawrence—but they were also allowed to retain their courts and their judges and an almost complete civil autonomy. The government was, of course, officially Moslem, and carried with it ecclesiastical functions, such as appointing bishops and calling church councils. Finally, the serfs fared better under the new regime than before.

Like other subjects, the Christians had to pay the customary dues—a poll-tax and a land-tax in kind (which, however, was higher for Christians). They often lived in separate quarters, and therefore, to a great extent, were able to preserve their old way of life. They kept their craftsmanship and their guilds.

Moreover, the princes and chiefs of the highlands of Galicia, the Asturias and Cantabria, as well as parts of Aragon, Navarre and North-Western Catalonia, succeeded in preserving their political autonomy, and many refugees from the South, both nobles and ecclesiastics, came to join them. The *Reconquista* started in the Asturias, and in the late ninth century the whole north country was freed from the Moslems.

SPANISH CULTURE

Spanish culture is the result of many civilisations—Visigoth, Jewish, Berber, Arabic, and so on—which were grafted upon the Romanized Celt-Iberian population, previously colonized by Carthage. It had also strong influences from Constantinople, Asia Minor, Syria, Egypt, and even from Persia and Arabia. Experts have shown how this mixed culture was welded and tempered so as to form a great and splendid spirit. Professor Georgiana Goddard King, the American leader in Hispanic studies, has pointed out that Spain probably derived her coenobitic ideals from Egypt, but S. Basil's Rule, as well as S. Benedict's, underlie the Rule made by Isidore of Seville (see p. 165), whose influence altered the organization of the Church in Spain. 'In Spanish use to this day fragments of the Coptic use are conserved, but more remarkable are the Greek elements persisting in the Mozarabic rite'. Prof. King has pointed out that numerous ancient Spanish churches were strongly influenced by early Syrian architectural sculpture. Thanks to all these influences Spanish culture and style are unlike anything else in the world.

Mozárabe and Mudéjar

The term 'Mozarabs', from Spanish *mozárabe*, derives from Arabic *musta'rib*, meaning something like 'Arabized'. This literary term is given to the Christians who lived in the Iberian Peninsula under Moslem rule. They adopted in a fairly large measure the customs of their conquerors. By the merging of the ancient Christian tradition of church-building and the Moslem traditions of mosque-building arose a definite architectural style, known as 'Mozarabic'. This style was created by the day-to-day proximity of Moslem to Christian civilization. Even in liturgy the Christians succeeded in retaining their own Mozarabic rite, which is still used in a chapel of Toledo Cathedral and in Salamanca. A Mozarabic style is also recognisable in book-illumination.

Mudéjars, an Arabic word meaning 'domesticated', is the term applied to the Spanish Moslems who were able to preserve their customs, laws, art, and religion after the country had been reconquered by the Christians. They spoke *Aljamia* (adj. *Aljamiado, Aljamiada*), i.e., a Spanish dialect written in Arabic letters. The last Mudéjars were not Christianized until the sixteenth century. Their rich and enchanting art, which lasted for at least seven centuries, presents essentially the same characteristics as the Mozarabic art; it was, indeed, a mixed Christian-Arabic art, though based mainly on the latter and adapted to Christian requirements.

It may be said that, in certain respects, Mudéjar art became the Spanish national style. The typical Spanish house is still built in Moslem style around a courtyard, or *patio*, planted with orange-trees and cooled by splashing fountains. But the Mudéjars' most important architectural contribution is the employment of the horseshoe arch and vault where practicable. It was used in the ancient Near East, as well as in Visigothic Spain, but it was the Spanish Moslems who adopted it and developed it generally. The Mozarabic builders introduced this type of structure into Toledo and the northern Christian kingdoms of Spain. In Western Europe the horseshoe arch became known as the Moorish arch. As Prof. King has pointed out, it is one of the things in Spain—and there are several—which have no parallel elsewhere. 'It extended . . . over nearly the whole of Spain, it penetrated into the sanctuary and the dwelling, it was part of every man's daily existence.'

Ancient Christian traditions, together with East Christian influences, modified by Visigothic influence and combined with strong influences of the Moslem culture, helped to create the Mozarabic style, which in its development felt also the influence of the Carolingian, Romanesque and Gothic styles. Finally, it must be pointed out that it would be preferable to speak of Mozarabic 'styles' rather than 'style'; indeed, various regions have their own local variants.

In the present chapter, which deals with the development of book-illumination, we are naturally concerned with the Mozarabic style of illumination. With the Mudéjar style we are concerned only indirectly, since this relates mainly to architecture and handicraft, and has only an indirect bearing on later book-illumination. The style, however, is recognizable and definable, and there is nothing similar in the art of the Christian countries of Europe. The great S. Domingo abbey of Silos (Old Castile) was one of the main centres of both the Mozarabic and Mudéjar styles.

Alfonso VI (1065–1009), who in 1085 took the city of Toledo, and made it his capital, had an Oriental education at the court of Toledo under the protection of the Moslem ruler. He called himself King of the Two Religions and indeed, he did not at first molest his Moslem subjects. His little kingdom was highly civilized; his capital was magnificent, 'the pearl in the necklace', as the Arabs called it.

In the splendid art of Toledo, which had a deep-seated Mozarabic life, it is impossible to draw a line between pre-Reconquest and post-Reconquest: the style of its architecture, sculpture, and so on, is continuous. In Christian times it continued to be a most important centre of Arabic and Hebrew learning and culture, and famous men from Italy, England, and France went there to be instructed in the Hellenistic learning, which was then available in Arabic and Hebrew translations. Adelard of Bath (twelfth century), Michael Scot (thirteenth century), Daniel of Morley, Gerard of Cremona, Plato of Tivoli, and others, particularly the French Benedictine Gerbert of Aurillac, afterwards Pope Sylvester II (999–1008), the foremost scholar of the century, were witnesses of the international character of pre-Reconquest or post-Reconquest Toledo, Ripoll, Barcelona, and other centres.

ILLUMINATION OF MSS.

Apart from the Spanish book-production in Arabic, which of course is included in the sections on the Moslem book, the style of the earliest Spanish books is mainly either Mozarabic or influenced by the Mudéjar style. These two styles, but particularly the Mozarabic, were the Spanish main original contributions in the field of illumination. In later centuries excellent production was accomplished in the Spanish *scriptoria*, or otherwise by Spanish masters, but it is not comparable, particularly in originality, with the productions of France, Italy, and Flanders.

Not all the early Spanish illuminated MSS. extant are in pure Mozarabic style. Some reflect rather Coptic, Syriac, or Byzantine, others Visigothic influences. This may be said of the *Bible of S. Isidore of León* (tenth century), in which the Incarnation at the moment of the Annunciation is represented by a baby's head emerging from the Mother's dress; the same theme is found in a Coptic fresco of the sixth century. Also the frameless miniatures of this Bible are evidence of the ancient origin of its illustrations: Fig. III-31c.

The tenth-century *Bible of Seville* shows strong Byzantine influences. The *Moralia* of Gregory the Great (*c.* 590–604), copied in 945 by Florencio of the Baralangas monastery (Burgos), and preserved in the National Library at Madrid, contains miniatures in Visigothic style, though according to some scholars they represent the Mozarabic style of Castile. A tenth-century vellum codex is preserved in the National Library at Madrid, and consists of 345 folios containing miniatures in Byzantine style; it is a collection of deliberations of ecclesiastical councils, drawn up for the Head Abbot. An illuminated Bible of the late eleventh and early twelfth century—the so-called *Avila Bible*—now preserved in the National Library at Madrid, is partly in the Italian Carolingian style, and partly in the French style.

Mozarabic Manuscripts

The earliest Mozarabic liturgical books (ninth and tenth century) have a very primitive illumination; it consists principally in ornamented and coloured initials, based mainly on Carolingian prototypes, which probably came ultimately from Italy; but the colouring (including blue, red, and black) is due to Arabic influence.

Amongst the earliest illuminated or illustrated Mozarabic MSS. special mention must be made of the following:

A ninth- or tenth-century copy—preserved in the National Library at Madrid (*Lat. N. Acq. 2169*)—of the work *Originum seu Etymologiarum Libri*, a sort of encyclopaedia, written by S. Isidore, Archbishop of Seville, 600–636, who may be considered the last representative of ancient Latin learning in Spain; he was mainly instrumental in shaping the Mozarabic liturgy. This copy, which comes from Silos and consists of 163 folios in parchment, contains geometrical and astronomical figures in blue and red. Mention may be made of a *Lectionary* in the National Library at Madrid (*Lat. N. Acq. 2171*), which also comes from Silos. A ninth- or tenth-century *Breviarium*, preserved in the Madrid National Library (*AL. 69*), is illuminated in the Mozarabic style of León. The *Fuero Juzgo*, or Book of Laws for the Courts, preserved in the National Library at Madrid, was written in 1058; it consists of 186 folios of parchment, and contains marginal ornaments in red and blue, and sketches in the Mozarabic style of Toledo. A tenth-century *Lives of Saints*, also in the Madrid National Library (*Hb. 68*), is in the Mozarabic style of Old Castile: it was copied in 902 by Armentarius. Fig. III-31*a–b*. Finally, another tenth-century MS., the *Codex Vigilanus* (executed in 976, in the Aldelba monastery, by the monk Vigila) was produced in a style related to the Mozarabic, but shows also other Spanish Romanesque influences. The codex contains a collection of Council-decrees and numerous miniatures both of Biblical and Spanish history. The interesting codex is preserved in the Escorial Library.

Bibles. A few Bibles should be mentioned: the *León Bible* (Cathedral Archives at León, *Cod. 6*), written and illuminated in 920 in the monastery of Albores, by Juan and Viviara for Abbot Mauro; the *S. Isidore de León Bible*, of 960; the great *Hispalensis*, also known as *Codex Toletanus*, written in 988, on 375 folios of parchment, and illuminated in the Mozarabic style of Andalusia, is preserved in the National Library at Madrid. Another tenth-century Bible, which was preserved in the University of Alcalá, was partly destroyed during the last Spanish Civil War, and was found in the trenches of the University City of Madrid; it is now preserved in the University Library at Madrid. An eleventh-century Bible, which came from the monastery of S. John de la Peña, and is now preserved in the National Library at Madrid, is in the Mozarabic style of Aragon. For the beautiful, illuminated *Bible of Ripoll*—known as the *Bible of Farfa* (*Vat. Lat. 5729*)—written in Catalonia in the late tenth or early eleventh century, and the famous tenth-century *Bible of Ronda*, see p. 211 f. Fig. IV-21; III-32*c*, 33*b–c* and 34*c*.

Beatus (Fig. III-31*d*, 32, 33*a* and 34*b*)

We have a most interesting group of Mozarabic MSS. in certain copies—numbering almost twenty-five—of the famous *Commentary* by S. Beatus de Liébana (monk of Liébana in the Asturias; he died in 798) on the *Apocalypse* of S. John. It was written about 776; in the late ninth and in the tenth century it was copied in Spanish monastic scriptoria with abundant illuminations, representing an extensive picture cycle (see also page 269 ff.). Although the *Beatus* illuminations go back to late classical models, the majority of the preserved copies are strongly Mozarabic in appearance. 'The scenes are converted into almost abstract patterns of a highly decorative character, the stylized figures and banded backgrounds presenting a mosaic of rich and lively colour, most skilfully handled' (D. Miner). In the early eleventh century, manuscripts of this work, bound up with Jerome's *Commentary on Daniel*, were brought to France and copies of them were made in French Benedictine monasteries. The fine copy preserved in the National Library at Paris (*Lat. 8878*) comes from the Abbey of S. Sever on the Adour, and was written in Gascony in the second or third quarter of the eleventh century. On the whole, the influence of the *Beatus* manuscripts on medieval illumination was very great.

The earliest *Beatus* copy extant, written in A.D. 926, is the Ashburnham-Yates Thompson codex, now preserved in the Pierpont Morgan Library, New York (*M. 644*): it is a very fine manuscript. It has a colophon indicating that it was illuminated in 926 A.D. (formerly it was thought that the date was 894) by a certain Maius or Magius, commissioned by Abbot Victor, for a monastery dedicated to S. Michael. (It has been suggested that this monastery may be identified with S. Miguel de Camarzana, not far from Távara.) Maius's *scriptorium* was in the monastery of S. Salvador de Távara. Another copy, illuminated by Maius in A.D. 968 in the same Távara monastery, and now preserved in the National Historical Archives, Madrid, is illuminated in the Mozarabic style of Old Castile. The copy preserved in the Cathedral of Gerona (Catalonia), is dated to 975 and is illuminated in pure Mozarabic style. Still another tenth-century codex, written in the monastery of S. Millán, and illuminated in the Leónese Mozarabic style, is preserved in the National Library at Madrid.

Eleventh- and twelfth-century copies are in London and Manchester, in the Chapter of La Seo de Urgell, and in the Madrid National Library. The last mentioned copy, which comes from S. Isidor de León, is a splendid MS.; it was completed in 1047 by one Facundus, and consists of 316 folios of vellum, containing over one hundred miniatures in the Leónese Mozarabic style, of which some are full-page and others double-page. Apparently it was written and painted for King Ferdinand I of Castile (*c.* 1000–65) and Doña Sancha. The British Museum *Add. MS. 11695* was executed at the monastery of Santo Domingo de Silos, and completed in 1109. The John Rylands *Beatus* (*Lat. MS. 8*), of the second half of the twelfth century, is one of the finest Spanish manuscripts of this period in existence. The text is apparently complete (a comparatively rare occurrence in pre-thirteenth-century copies). There are 110 large miniatures, painted on grounds of deep and vivid colour, and a world-map.

Other twelfth-century copies are preserved in various collections, such as the Corsiniana Library, Rome (*MS. 369 : 40. E. 6*), containing six miniatures (including two full-page), two schematic figures, and a pen-drawing; and the National Library at Turin (*MS. I. II. 1*), containing numerous miniatures (including several full-page or double-page) and pen-drawings in vivid colours. The Corsiniana *Beatus* shows two different styles, one partly going back to the Visigothic style. The Turin MS. is a product of the Catalonian school influenced by the Mozarabic style. A thirteenth-century copy (of *c.* 1220), written near Burgos, is preserved in the Pierpont Morgan Library, New York (*MS. 429*).

See also p. 57.

Mysticism of Mozarabic Illumination

The illustrations in these codices, which give a strange vision of the end of the world, are unlike anything else: the strong deep colours—writes Prof. King—that cover all the picture with bands, for instance, of green, yellow and violet, as the ocean shows bands of colour under approaching tempest; the monsters, seven-headed, hundred-eyed, or horned and striped, saddled and bridled to bear a queen pacing slowly against the pale lift of an amber horizon; the golden cup of trembling, uplifted in silhouette against purple heavens; the shrouded figure with fluttering birds about him that are *las animas*; the angel of a more terrible Pentecost brooding over a city's flames, *ubi Babilon id est iste mundas ardet.*

In the words of Gómez-Moreno, we have here a mysticism of terrible virility, evoking a new emotion and a new ideal, the antithesis of the Classic, which was to inform the art of the latter Middle Ages throughout all Europe, but which Spain anticipated by nearly two centuries—'precipitated by the tension of spirit, the struggle of ideas, the stimuli that the close approximation of Moors and Christians produced'. This mysticism, which, as Prof. King has remarked, replaced that fear of the year 1000 which oppressed the French and the Rhenish mind, was the Arabic mysticism of the desert and the apocalyptic terrors of Syrian dreamers, which passed into the minds of the Castilians and Leónese, impregnated as these were with ancient Christian and Visigothic, Carolingian, Oriental, and other influences.

Dr. Joan Evans has suggested that the fantastic subject matter and the Spanish background of the *Commentaries*, have derived from the supernatural intention—which sometimes disquiets the modern observer—of Romanesque sculpture, and had produced that force and exaggeration of reality to which nothing but blind faith can aspire.

This mysticism of Mozarabic art can also be seen in various other MSS., written and illuminated in the eleventh and twelfth centuries in the numerous monasteries, scattered all along the north of Spain, from Escalada and Liébana to Ripoll and Urgel.

An interesting MS. of the Capitulary Library of Tortosa (*MS. No. 20*) contains four miniatures, of which the first represents the Celestial City, the Terrestrial, the Angelical and the Diabolical; the second, which partly resembles a miniature in the *Rabbūlā Gospels* (see p. 117 f.) represents the Ascension; the third depicts the Assumption of the Virgin Mary; and the fourth, the twelve signs of the Zodiac. The MS. was written, and probably also illuminated, by Nicolaus Bergedanus, whose name appears to indicate that he was a man from Berga (Catalonia). Indeed, the style of these miniatures can be compared with some frescoes of the Bergada churches.

Miscellanea

Many other MSS. deserve mention, but we limit ourselves to the following copies: John Cassianus (*c.* 360–*c.* 433), *Incarnation of Jesus Christ*; Paul Orosius, *Contra paganos*; John Diaconus, *Life of Gregory*; and *Crónica Najerense* (all four of them belonging to the twelfth century, and now preserved in the National Library at Madrid). To the same or the next century belong a copy of S. Bernard, *Sermons*, in Aragonese style; S. Ildefonso, *De Virginitate*, in Toledan style (both preserved in the National Library at Madrid), and the *Cartulario* ('Registry') of Ovarra, written on a roll, and preserved in the National Historical Archives, Madrid.

We conclude this short list with the works written by, or for, Alfonso X, *el Sabio* ('the Wise'), the king who as Infante took part in the reconquest of Seville, in 1248. His court was not unlike his Spanish-Moslem predecessor's al-Mutamid; he was a great patron of learning and culture; Moslem, Jewish, and Christian scholars worked for him. The *Crónica general*, which he compiled (or which was compiled for him) is fundamental for Spanish history, as *Siete Partidas* (an excellent copy of the fourteenth century, illuminated in the style of Old Castile, is preserved in the National Library at Madrid) is of paramount importance for the study of Spanish law; 'there was nothing like them until the *Code Napoleon*', writes Prof. King. The *Alfonsine Tables*, as well as treatises on astronomy and the *astrolabe*, are other important works due to Alfonso X, though actually the *Tables*—according to Abraham Zacuto—are not the work of Alfonso but of Isaac ibn Sid, the ḥazan of Toledo; they are based on the Toledo *Tables* by Az-Zarqālī (in Spanish, Azarquiel); their fame lasted till the seventeenth century. The *Alfonsine Tables* and the other astronomical treatises, which were either translated from Arabic or compiled from Arabic sources, were published in 1836–67 in five large volumes (*Libros del Saber de astronomia*).

More important from the standpoint of the development of Spanish book-illumination are three illuminated works by King Alfonso X, a copy of *Lapidary*, a *Book of Chess*, and a copy of *Cantigas*. Their miniatures are 'full of charm and grace in the Gothic manner. Here horseshoe arches alternate with *arcs en tiers-point*, cusped and crocketed . . . yet nothing is ever quite French, or quite Italian' (G. G. King). Prof. King has indeed pointed out that, for instance, in the interiors of the buildings depicted in the *Book of Chess*, we find sometimes the king and a Moor, sometimes Moors together, in a public place, or in the women's quarters. 'The turban and the open crown fleur-de-lysée mark the meeting of south and north.' Also *Kalilah and Dimnah* (see p. 138) and other Arabic literary works were translated into Spanish.

Fig. III-34*a* and 35 reproduce specimens from other Spanish illuminated codices.

Of particular interest for its composite artistic style, showing French and Italian influence, as well as Catalan style of composition, of colouring and of the marginal decoration, is a beautiful *Breviary of Martin d'Aragon*, the last king of Aragon of the Catalan branch (1395–1410). This codex, formerly belonging to Baron Charles de Rothschild of Frankfurt a/M. (Rothschild, *No. 2529*), has been presented in 1949 to the Paris National Library by Baron Henri de Rothschild. It measures 351 mm. × 252 mm. and contains 451 leaves, 5 full-page and 24 half-page illuminations, as well as 68 small illuminations and many hundreds gold and coloured initials and border-decorations.

An interesting illuminated MS. of the Renaissance period—a fragmentary *Toledo Missal*—is in the British Museum. The border-frames—writes Herbert—are a modification of the familiar Italian branch-work type, with *putti*, birds, and human figures interspersed somewhat stiffly; they are chiefly distinguished from those found in undoubtedly Italian manuscripts by the greater thickness of the curving stems. The initials are mostly gold, filled with conventional foliage, and have the marked peculiarity of being made to appear as if cut out of the solid.

Another excellent work of the Renaissance period is the *Breviary* of Philip II (1527–1598), illuminated in the Escorial by the monks of St. Jerome Order Julián de la Fuente el Saz and Andrés de León; this sixteenth-century master-piece is preserved in the Escorial.

A charming MS. was for sale at Deighton, Bell & Co., Cambridge (Engl.)—see *Catalogue 95* (Autumn 1965), No. 755. It is a *Patent of Nobility*, a royal patent for ennobling Laso de la Vega. The codex, executed in 1575 at Granada, measures $12\frac{1}{4} \times 8\frac{1}{4}$ ins. and contains 67 leaves. The text is written in long lines (34 to a page), in a rounded Roman hand, and is ruled in red throughout. There are 32 initials in gold with silver decorations on crimson ground. Among the several miniatures, there is a three-quarter page miniature of a king (Philip II?) enthroned; an armorial bearing emblazoned in gold and colours (on f. 1); the miniature of a knight on a charger in battle (f. 2, verso); some leaves are decorated with elaborate borders of angels, flowers, etc.

Toledo School of Translators

In the last centuries of the first mill. A.D. and in the first centuries of the second mill., Arabic became the vehicle for research work in science, including medicine. Moslem Spain, particularly, became a torch of culture and civilization, and after the Christian conquest, the kingdom of Castile with its splendid capital Toledo, became a meeting-point of Islamic and European cultures. Under the aegis of Archbishop Raymond of Toledo (1125–1151) a famous school of translators arose in Toledo. Here we refer particularly to Gherardo de Cremona (+1187), who translated into Latin the famous *Canon Medicine*, by Avicenna (see p. 148), and the book on *Surgery* by Khalaf ibn Abbâs uz-Zahrâwî, known as Abû-l-Qâsim (tenth-century court physician at Cordova). Copies of these translations are preserved in the Vatican Library, *Urbino MS. 241* (Avicenna's *Canon*); Venice, Biblioteca Marciana, *Lat. 320*; and National Library, Vienna, *N.S. 2641* (the last two, being Abû-l-Qâsim's *Surgery*).

PORTUGUESE ILLUMINATION

Limitation of space does not allow us to deal in detail with Portuguese illumination. On the whole it may be said that in certain respects it was parallel with Spanish illumination. However, very fine works are preserved in various collections at Lisbon (National Archives, National Library, Library of the Academy of Sciences, Ajuda Library, and the Museum of Ancient Art), in the University Library at Coïmbra, in the Municipal Library at Porto, in the Public Libraries at Mafra, Braga, and Evora, as well as in the National Libraries at Madrid, Vienna, and Paris, in the British Museum, and in the Pierpont Morgan Library, New York. Precious codices are also preserved in the ancient monasteries of Lorvão, near Coïmbra (a splendid *Missal* with Calendar-pictures), of Alcobaça (a twelfth-century *Gospel-book* with illuminated Canon Tables), and others. Fig. III-36 reproduces four outstanding specimens of Portuguese illuminated book-production of the twelfth and the thirteenth centuries.

BILLIOGRAPHY

J. Zedner, *Catalogue of the Hebrew Books in the British Museum*, London, 1867.

J. Bourgoin, *Les Arts arabes*, Paris, 1873; *Les Eléments de l'art arabe*, Paris, 1879.

H. Mueller and J. von Schlosser, *Die Haggadah von Sarajevo*, Vienna, 1898.

Van de Put, *Hispano-moresque Ware*, London, 1904.

Z. García Villada, 'Un nuevo ms. d. coment. sobre el Apocalypsis de San Beato de Liébana,' *Rason y Fé*, 1905.

A. Ronflard, L. Bouvat, and Y. Rioche, 'L'Art musulman. Essai de bibliographie,' *Archives Marocaines*, Paris, 1905.

M. Gómez-Moreno, *Arte Mudéjar Toledano*, Madrid, 1906; *Iglesias Mozárabes*, Madrid, 1919.

BIBLIOGRAPHY

G. J. de Osma, *Apuntes sobre cerámica morisca*, Madrid, 1906–11; *Catálogo de azabaches compostelanos*, Madrid, 1916; *The Valencian Styles of Hispano-Moresque Pottery* etc., New York, 1938.

H. Saladin, *Manuel d'art Musulman*, Paris, 1907.

A. Musil, *Kusejr Amra*, 2 vols., Vienna, 1907.

C. Huart, *Les Calligraphes et les Miniaturistes de l'Orient musulman*, Paris, 1908.

R. Tyler, *Spain, a Study of her Life and Arts*, London, 1909.

F. Sarre, *Seldschukische Kleinkunst*, Leipsic, 1909; *Die Kunst des alten Persien*, Berlin, 1922; — and E. Herzfeld, *Archaeologische Reise im Euphrat- und Tigrisgebiet*, 4 vols., Berlin, 1911–20 (for Herzfeld see also next item).

E. Herzfeld, 'Die Genesis der islamischen Kunst,' *Der Islam*, I, Strasburg 1910.

E. Kuehnel, *Die Buchkunst auf der mohammedanischen Ausstellung zu Muenchen—1910*, Munich, 1910; *Miniaturmalerei im islamischen Orient*, 2nd ed., Berlin, 1923; *Maurische Kunst*, Berlin, 1924; *Jāhangīr. . . . Indian Book Painting* etc. (with H. Goetz), London, 1926; *Islamische Stoffe aus aegyptischen Graebern*, Berlin, 1927; *History of Miniature Painting and Drawing*, London, 1939; *Kunst und Kultur d. arabischen Welt*, Heidelberg, 1943; *Moghul-Malerei*, Berlin, 1955; *Persische Miniaturmalerei*, Berlin, 1959.

V. A. Smith, *A History of Fine Arts in India and Ceylon*, Oxford, 1911.

H. Viollet, 'Un Palais musulman du IXe siècle,' *Mémoires de L'Acad. d. Inscriptions*, 1911.

F. R. Martin, *The Miniature Painting and Painters of Persia, India, and Turkey, etc.*, 2 vols., London, 1912; *Miniaturen und Buchkunst*, Munich, 1922 (*Die Ausstellung von Meisterwerken mohammedanischer Kunst in Muenchen, 1910*).

J. Ribera and M. Asin, *Manuscritos arabes y aljamiados en la Biblioteca de la Junta*, Madrid, 1912.

G. Marteaux and H. Vever, *Miniatures persanes*, Paris, 1913.

M. A. Dieulafoy, *Art in Spain and Portugal*, London and New York, 1913.

A. L. Mayer, *Geschichte der spanischen Malerei*, Leipsic, 1913.

H. Dozy, *Spanish Islam* (transl. by F. G. Stokes), London, 1913.

P. W. Schulz, *Die persisch-islamische Miniaturmalerei*, 2 vols., Leipsic, 1914.

E. Blochet, *Les Peintures des manuscrits orient. de la Bibl. Nat.*, Paris, 1914–20; *Les Enluminures des manuscrits orientaux . . . de la Bibliothèque Nationale*, Paris, 1926; *Musulman Painting*, London, 1929.

E. Diez, *Die Kunst der islamischen Voelker*, Berlin, 1916; — and H. Glueck, *Die Kunst des Islam*, Berlin, 1925.

S. Flury, *Islamische Schriftbaender*, Bâle and Paris, 1920.

M. Pézard, *La Céramique archaïque de L'Islam*, 2 vols., Paris, 1920.

P. Ricard, *Pour comprendre l'art musulman*, Paris, 1921.

A. Cresswell, *A Provisional Bibliography of Painting in Muhammadan Art*, London, 1921.

A. del Castillo López, *Riqueza monumental y artística de Galicia*, Coruña, 1921.

A. Mez, *Die Renaissance des Islâms*, Heidelberg, 1922.

W. Neuss, *Die katalanische Bibelillustration etc.*, Bonn and Leipsic, 1922; *Die*

Apokalypse des Hl. Johannes in der altspanischen und altchristlichen Bibel-illustration, 2 vols., Muenster in Westphalia, 1931.

S. Kheiri (introd.), *Indische Miniaturen der islamischen Zeit*, Berlin, s.d.

E. Mâle, 'Les influences arabes de l'art romane,' *Revue des Deux Mondes*, 1923.

A. von Le Coq, *Die manichaeischen Miniaturen*, Berlin, 1923; *Bilderatlas zu Kunst und Kulturgeschichte Mittel-Asiens*, Berlin, 1925.

F. Brown, *Indian Painting under the Mughals*, London, 1923.

Ausgrabungen von Samarra, 4 vols. (E. Herzfeld, vols. I and III; F. Sarre, vol. II; C. J. Lamm, vol. IV), Berlin, 1923–8.

T. W. Arnold, *Survivals of Sasanian and Manichaean Art etc.*, Oxford, 1924; *Painting in Islam*, Oxford, 1928; *Bihzād and his Paintings in Zafar-Nāmah*, London, 1930; *The Old and New Testaments in Muslim Religious Art* (The British Academy, Schweich Lectures 1928), London, 1932; *The Library of A. Chester Beatty: a Catalogue of the Indian Miniatures*, 3 vols., London, 1939; — and A. Grohmann, *The Islamic Book*, Paris, 1929.

E. Kuehnel and H. Goetz, *Indische Buchmalereien aus dem Jahângir-Album der Staatsbibliothek zu Berlin*, Berlin, 1924.

G. G. King, *Pre-Romanesque Churches of Spain*, Bryn Mawr, Pa., 1924; *Mudéjar*, Bryn Mawr, Pa., 1927.

H. Glueck, *Die indischen Miniaturen des Hamza-Romanes im oesterr. Mus. f. Kunst u. Ind. in. Wien u. in anderen Sammlungen*, Zurich-Vienna-Leipsic, 1925.

H. Terrasse and J. Hainault, *Les Arts décoratifs au Maroc*, Paris, 1925; see also further on.

G. Marçais, *Manuel d'Art musulman*, Paris, 1926; *L'Art de Islam*, Paris, 1946.

Nizami MS. illuminated by Bihzad, Mirak and Qasim Ali. Written 1495 for Sultan Ali Mirza Bartes, ruler of Samarqand. British Museum (*Or. 6810*), Vienna, 1926.

The Miniatures in Hilāli's Mystical Poem, Vienna, 1926

Miniatures from the Period of Timur, Vienna, 1926.

B. Italiener, *Die Darmastaedter Pessach-Haggadah*, Leipsic, 1927.

A. Marx, in the *Jewish Quarterly Review*, 1928–9.

L. Binyon, *The Poems of Nizami*, London, 1928.

A. Sakistan, *La miniature persane du XIIe au XVIIe siècle*, Paris, 1929.

C. Glaser, S. Kramrisch, E. Kuehnel and others, *Die aussereuropaeische Kunst*: ostasiatische Kunst, indische Kunst, islamische Kunst, etc. in *Handbuch d. Kunst-geschichte*, 6, Leipsic, 1929.

J. Shtchoukine, *La Peinture indienne à l'époque des Grands Moghols*, Paris, 1929; *La peinture iranienne sous les derniers Abbassides et les Il-Khans*, Bruges, 1936; *Les peintures des manuscrits timurides*, Paris, 1954; *Les Peintures des manuscrits safavis de 1502 à 1587*, Paris, 1959.

A. K. Coomaraswamy, *Les Miniatures orientales de la collection Goloubew au Museum of Fine Arts de Boston*, Paris and Brussels, 1929.

J. Domínguez Bordona, *Exposición de códices miniados españoles. Catálogo*, Madrid, 1929; *La miniatura spagnuola*, 2 vols., Florence, 1930.

BIBLIOGRAPHY

G. Swarzenski and R. Schilling, *Die illuminierten Handschriften ... in Frankfurter Besitz*, Frankfort, 1929.

A. Grohmann and T. W. Arnold, *Denkmaeler islamischer Buchkunst*, Florence and Munich, 1929.

E. Cohn-Wiener, *Die juedische Kunst*, Berlin, 1929.

B. Gray, *Persian Painting*, London, 1930; *Persian Painting from Miniatures of the XIII–XVI Centuries*, London, 1947; *Indian Miniatures from the Collection of H.H. the Maharaja of Bikaner*, The Arts Council, London, 1949; *Persian Painting*, London, Paris, Cleveland (Ohio), and Lausanne, 1961; *Persian Miniatures from Ancient Manuscripts*, Fontana UNESCO Art Books, 1962.

R. Grousset, *Les Civilisations de l'Orient. L'Inde*, Paris, 1930.

A. Baghat Bey and F. Massoul, *La Céramique Musulmane de l'Egypte*, Cairo, 1930.

G. Gabrieli, *Manoscritti e carte orientali nelle biblioteche ... d'Italia*, Florence, 1930; — and F. Gabrieli, 'I manoscritti persiani del poema di Firdusi in Italia,' *Accademie e Biblioteche d'Italia*, 1935.

H. A. Sanders, *Beatus of Liebana. In Apocalypsin*, Rome, 1930.

J. Daridan and S. Stelling-Michaud, *La Peinture séfévide d'Ispahan*, Paris, 1930.

J. V. S. Wilkinson, *The Shahnama of Firdausi from a Fifteenth Century Manuscript in the Possession of the Royal Asiatic Society*, Oxford, 1931; *The Chester Beatty Library. A Catalogue of the Turkish Manuscripts and Miniatures* by V. Minorsky, Dublin, 1958.

E. Lambert, 'L'Art mudéjar,' *Gazette des Beaux-Arts*, 1932; *Art musulman et Art chrétien dans la peninsule ibérique*, Paris–Toulouse, 1956.

H. Terrasse, *L'Art hispano-mauresque des origines au XIIIᵉ siècle*, Paris, 1932; see also above.

R. Dos Santos, 'Les principaux manuscrits à peintures conservés en Portugal,' *Bullet. de la Soc. Franç. de reproduct. de manuscr. à peinture*, 1932.

M. H. Zaky, *Les Tulunides*, Paris, 1933.

L. Binyon and others, *Persian Miniature Painting*, Oxford, 1933.

R. Wischnitzer-Bernstein, *Gestalten und Symbole der juedischen Kunst*, Berlin-Schoeneberg, 1935. (See also Chapter I.)

M. S. Dimand, 'Studies in Islamic Ornament,' *Ars Islamica*, Michigan, 1937.

M. Fooner, 'Joel ben Simeon, Illuminator of Hebrew MSS. in the XVth Cent., *Jew. Quart. Rev.*, 1937.

N. A. Reath and E. B. Sachs, *Persian Textiles*, Yale, 1937.

A. J. Arberry, *The Library of the India Office etc.*, London, 1938; *Specimens of Arabic and Persian Palaeography*, London, 1939.

A. V. Pope, *A Survey of Persian Art*, Oxford, 1939.

Z. Ameisenowa, 'The Tree of Life,' *The Journal of the Warburg Institute*, 1939.

M. Schapiro, 'From Mozarabic to Romanesque in Silos,' *Art Bulletin*, 1939.

E. Camps, *El arte hispano-visigodo*, and A. Ferrandis, *Las artes industriales visigodos*, in R. Menéndez-Pidal, *Historia de España*, Vol. III, Madrid, 1940.

F. Landsberger, 'The Cincinnati Haggadah and its Decorator,' *Hebrew Union*

College Annual, 1940; *History of Jewish Art*, Cincinnati, 1946; 'The Washington Haggadah and its Illuminator,' *Hebrew Union College Annual*, 1948; 'The Second Cincinnati Haggadah, *ibid.*

E. Panofsky, 'Giotto and Maimonides in Avignon,' *The Journal of the Walters Art Gallery*, 1941; and *note, ibid.*, 1942.

J. Leveen, *The Hebrew Bible in Art* (The British Academy Schweich Lectures, 1939), London, 1944.

Metropolitan Museum of Art, *Persian Miniatures* (ed. by M. S. Dimand), New York, 1944.

Staatliche Museen, Berlin, *Indische Miniaturen* etc., Berlin, 1949.

G. Dunham Guest, *Shiraz Painting in the Sixteenth Century* (Smithsonian Inst.-Freer Gallery of Art), Washington, D.C., 1949.

M. Gómes-Moreno, *El arte Árabe Español hasta los Almohades, Arte Mozárabe*, in *Ars Hispaniae: Historia Universal del arte hispan.*, vol. III, Madrid, 1951.

Early Medieval Illumination (introduction by H. Swarzenski), London, etc., 1951.

K. Holter, *Persische Miniaturen*, Vienna, 1951.

G. Wickens (ed.), *Avicenna: Scientist and Philosopher: a Millenary Symposium*, London, 1952.

B. W. Robinson, *Persian Paintings*, London, 1952 (2nd ed., 1965); *Persian Miniatures*, Oxford, 1957.

Bodleian Library, *Mughal Miniatures of the Earlier Periods*, Oxford, 1953.

S. J. Sierra, 'Hebrew Codices with Miniatures belonging to the University Library of Bologna,' *The Jewish Quarterly Review*, 1953.

S. Radojcic, *Haggadah of Sarayevo*, Belgrade, 1953.

R. N. Frye, 'The Andarz Nāme of Kāyūs b. Iskandar b. Kāpūs b. Vušmgīr,' *Serta Cantabrigiensia*, Wiesbaden, 1954.

H. Rosenau, 'Notes on the Illuminations of the Spanish Haggadah in the John Rylands Library,' *Bulletin of the John Rylands Library*, Vol. 36 (1954); 'Contributions to the Study of Jewish Iconography, *ibid.*, Vol. 38 (1956).

D. Barrett, *Persian Painting of the Fourteenth Century*, London, 1955.

B. Gray and A. Godard, *Iran. Persian Miniatures—Imperial Library* (UNESCO World Art Series), Paris, 1956.

M. Dimand, *Persische Miniaturen*, Wiesbaden and Milan, 1956.

R. H. Pinder-Wilson, *Persian Painting of the Fifteenth Century*, London, 1958.

E. Preetorius (Preetorius Collection Munich), *Persische Miniaturen*, Munich, 1958.

A. U. Pope, 1958: see under Byzantine and Allied Illumination (Chap. II).

W. G. Archer, *Indian Miniatures*, Toronto, 1960.

S. E. Lee, *Rajput Painting* (vast literature), New York and Tokyo, 1960.

R. Ettinghausen (Pref.), *Turkey. Ancient Miniatures* (UNESCO World Art Series), Paris, 1961.

Beatus de Liébana, Commentaire sur l'Apocalypse, . . . Édit. en facsimilé . . . , Leiden, 2 vols., 1962.

BIBLIOGRAPHY

T. Burckhardt (ed.), *Die Apokalypse von Gerona (S. Beati a Liébana in Apocalypsin Codex Gerundensis)*, Olten-Lausanne-Freiburg im Breisgau, 1963.

G. M. Meredith-Owens, *Turkish Miniatures* London, 1963; *Persian Illustrated Manuscripts*, London, 1965.

See also Chapter I (last section).

Chapter IV

HIBERNO-SAXON, CAROLINGIAN,
AND OTTONIAN ILLUMINATION

HIBERNO-SAXON STYLE

In the seventh and eighth centuries the early art of book-illustration in the centres of Roman culture was apparently extinguished, or nearly so—in Italy a reaction seems to have set in only in the ninth and tenth centuries with the development of a new art—but an additional centre of illumination of manuscripts arose, strangely enough, in the Anglo-Celtic countries, and flourished particularly in the eighth and early ninth centuries.

ORIGINS OF HIBERNO-SAXON STYLE

The traditional view is that this art developed in partial independence of the Graeco-Roman art, its origin being due mainly to local Celtic and Saxon influences. Intertwined ribbons and spiral patterns were already to be seen in local stone monuments of previous centuries, and in later metal-work. For instance, according to O. Elfrida Saunders, of the spirals: the trumpet-pattern seems to be native to Ireland, and was used in simple form even before Christian times. It consists of spirals unfolding into broadening bands of trumpet shape which connect with other spirals, either convergent or divergent, in an endless variety of ways. The same art-historian also points out that spirals, zigzags, and dots were used in Ireland in very early times, and may well have arisen spontaneously there, as well as elsewhere, as motives for decoration.

Some scholars also suggest, however, the penetration of Egyptian-Arabic influences, brought to Ireland by Egyptian monks in the sixth century A.D. This theory is improbable generally, and certainly highly improbable for the sixth century. Other scholars argue that Irish book-production was originated under strong influences from Italy and Gaul.

Until recent times it was usually assumed that the Hiberno-Saxon art of illumination (and, indeed, Hiberno-Saxon book-production in general; see *The Hand-produced Book, passim*) was of Irish origin, and that the *Lindisfarne Gospels* and other illuminated Northumbrian MSS. were either derived from the Irish art, or contained both Irish and Mediterranean elements.

176

Nowadays, however, the experts disagree among themselves. A. W. Clapham suggested in 1934 that the decoration of the *Book of Durrow*—which eminent scholars now consider to be the earliest known book in the Hiberno-Saxon style— is of Northumbrian origin; in Sir Thomas Kendrick's opinion, expressed in 1938, this codex (regarded by him as the earliest known example of the new Christian art) is Irish, and 'the requisite English art of that period in Northumbria is purely hypothetical'.

Writing in 1944, though his book was not published until 1947, F. Masai, the leading Belgian authority on the subject, stated that the *Book of Durrow*, and all the other illuminated MSS. of the so-called Irish style (including the *Book of Kells*, the 'Irish' codex of Durham *A. ii. 7*, and the *Echternach Gospels*) were of Northumbrian and not Irish origin: see also *The Hand-produced Book*, pp. 445 and *passim*. W. Oakeshott, in 1949, agreeing that the *Book of Durrow*, the Durham codex *A. ii. 7*, the *Echternach Gospels* and similar MSS. are Northumbrian, considers the *Book of Kells* Irish, though produced under the influence of the Northumbrian *Lindisfarne Gospels*; he holds that Northumbria was the meeting place of a number of cultural influences from Ireland, from England, and through England, from Italy.

A leading authority on the Hiberno-Saxon style, Mlle. Françoise Henry, in her book on *Irish Art*, published in 1940, not only considers Irish the *Book of Kells*, the *Echternach Gospels*, and so forth, but maintains that the *Book of Durrow* has survived to bear witness to the ability of Irish painters of the seventh century. Moreover, in her opinion, the monks of Lindisfarne, in the time of S. Colman and his immediate successors, had evidently been trained in the art of manuscript decoration evolved in Ireland. On the whole, in the *scriptoria* of Lindisfarne and Northumbria, Irish influence remained strong until a very late date.

In *The Hand-produced Book* it has been pointed out that the problem of the artistic relationship of the Irish and English manuscripts is still open. The argument that the earliest illuminated North English manuscripts extant may be older than the Irish—if we agree that the *Book of Durrow* is Northumbrian—is of no great significance, as preserved illuminated manuscripts of this period are very scarce indeed; there is the possibility that there were illuminated Irish manuscripts in the seventh century, but they have not come down to us. Generally speaking, it is commonly agreed that in Britain two fundamentally different tendencies, the Irish and the English, must be distinguished. The development in England was determined by the Roman mission and by the close relations kept up between the Italo-Saxon churches and monasteries and Rome itself.

In her excellent article on the origins of Irish book illumination (*Gazette des Beaux-Arts*, Paris, 1950), Mlle. Henry maintains that these origins go back to the beginning of the seventh century, or even to the sixth century if we accept the early date of the *Cathach* (see *The Hand-produced Book*, p. 458 ff.). This early art was based partly on the Irish pre-Christian art, and partly on the early Christian art. The former is shown by the ornamentation of stone monuments in Ireland, such as those of Turoe, Castlestrange, and Killycluggin, or of objects of stone and bronze from Broigther, Lough Crew, and so on; the latter style may be seen, for instance, in that of the earliest Coptic binding in the Pierpont Morgan Library (it will be discussed in the forthcoming book on *Binding*). This style may have been imported into Ireland from the fifth century onwards. Fig. IV-1*a*.

Specimens of early Irish ornamented manuscripts—containing decorated initials and elementary decorations—which came from the monastery of Bobbio, an Irish foundation, and are preserved in the Ambrosian Library, Milan (*S. 45. sup., D. 23. sup., C. 26. sup., I. 61. sup., O. 212. sup.*), are partly attributed to the early seventh century. The *Codex Usserianus Primus* (*The Hand-produced Book*, p. 460 ff.), attributed by Prof. Lowe to the early seventh century and also assigned to the Bobbio *scriptorium*, may belong to the same group. Fig. IV-1*b–c*, and 2*a*.

The Irish manuscripts of the *Cathach* (already referred to), assigned to the late sixth century, and the *Antiphonary of Bangor* (*The Hand-produced Book*, p. 466 f.), of the seventh century, the Durham *Codex A. ii. 10* (by some scholars assigned to the seventh century and held by Mlle. Henry to be an Irish production) and the other manuscripts just referred to, are by the latter considered specimens of sixth- or seventh-century Irish book-illumination.

To conclude, with regard to the problem of the origins of the Hiberno-Saxon book-illumination, it may be observed that a considerable degree of caution should be exercised in coming to dogmatic conclusions or even in forming theories, because the evidence is so fragmentary, and in that respect so much inferior to what we possess of many other branches of illumination. Moreover, it is not easy to determine the origin of such masterpieces as the *Book of Kells* or the *Lindisfarne Gospels*. It is obviously not always possible to know everything behind the achievements of great artists, as the scribes and decorators of the codices undoubtedly were. Indeed, we have to oppose the current theories which minimise the part consciously played by individual artists.

Main Characteristics of Hiberno-Saxon or Anglo-Celtic Illumination

(Fig. IV-1*d*-2, 4*c*-*d*, 5*d*, 6*a*-9*a*, 10*b*)

The style of the illuminated copies of the Scriptures which have come down to us from the Hiberno-Saxon *scriptoria* is aptly described by the late Sir Frederic Kenyon: the special feature of this style is its extraordinarily intricate system of interlacing patterns, sometimes geometric and sometimes including animal forms, combined and continued with marvellous precision over a whole page throughout the pattern of a huge initial letter. Looked at from a little distance, a page of one of these manuscripts resembles a harmonious mosaic or enamelled pattern in soft and concordant colours. Examine it closely, even with a magnifying glass, and the eye wearies itself in following the intricacy of its pattern, and the hand strives in vain to reproduce its accuracy even for a few inches of its course. The use of gold—concluded Sir Frederic—gives to later illuminations a greater splendour of appearance at first sight; but no other style shows a quarter of the inexhaustible skill and patient devotion which is the glory of the Anglo-Celtic school.

A point of interest is that the early Hiberno-Saxon illumination dispensed entirely with historical illumination of the text, thus showing a complete disregard for realism; with its impassioned understanding of conventional ornament, it assumed a purely decorative character. Whereas classical book 'illumination' (see Chapter I) was entirely historical-pictorial and Byzantine illumination was mainly pictorial, the Hiberno-Saxon style was, indeed, purely ornamental. Generally speaking, it consisted in (1) delicate designs of interlaced—plaited or knotted—ribbon-work (used also in the borders), thread-like lines plaited or knotted, tangled knots, intricate zigzag and spiral patterns (including the divergent spiral or trumpet pattern), the triquetra (or three-spoked wheel pattern), dots, generally red, arranged in patterns, or outlining letters and frames, tessellated patterns (tartans, key patterns, lozenges, checks), and network patterns of fine lines; and (2) a profusion of monstrous forms—extravagantly elongated and knotted—of 'lacertines', such as hounds, birds, snakes, lizards and mythical monsters (such as dragons), plaited and twined together with a wonderful dexterity, their tongues and tails being prolonged into ribbons, and knotted or woven into a compact space-filling decoration. Also the human figure—but always in a purely conventional manner—is made use of for grotesques, corner-pieces, and terminals. Plant-forms (such as the shamrock or the vine) are used rather rarely.

The plainted designs—writes O. Elfrida Saunders—vary from the simplest borders of interlacing bands to the most intricate all-over patterns of animal forms whose legs and wings can barely be distinguished in the maze of wide and narrow bands and knots into which their bodies have been elongated. The creatures used in the lacertine patterns are generally of dog or bird form; occasionally they even have human heads, as in the *Book of Kells*. The accurate workmanship of these incredibly complicated patterns—points out O. E. Saunders—is perhaps more to be wondered at than anything else in the whole course of illumination. There are also z-patterns, T-patterns, and I-patterns. It is interesting to compare this art with Oriental art as described, for instance on p. 76 ff.

Trees and flowers are avoided, and the rare representation of the human figure—apart from its use as an ornamental motive—and of historical scenes is very poor (see, for instance, Fig. IV-8–10). The whole, however, is executed with marvellous precision and minuteness. Indeed, in its disposition of lines and masses, its dexterous manipulation of only a few forms and colours to form patterns of endless variety, it has never been surpassed. This style of decorative motifs—which belongs primarily and properly to work in three dimensions—seems to have been an adaptation from the allied, yet essentially distinct, arts of metalwork and sculpture.

The Irish artists—as emphasized by Saunders—refused to attempt naturalistic representation in order to make as free play with the figures of a picture as if they were calligraphic designs. It is often difficult to see what these plaited figures really mean. This anti-naturalistic method of representation stands in sharp contrast to the whole range of classical antique art in all its derivations. Irish MSS. show a richness of decoration unparalleled, as far as is known, up to that time. The various Gospels are preceded by whole pages with carpet-like designs, and the initials at the beginning of the text grow and spread until they, too, cover the whole page.

The colouring is milder and much more delicate than in Byzantine art. Gold is not used at all, nor silver—thus, considering the term 'illumination' as defined on p. 23, one may even regard the ornamentation of the Anglo-Celtic MSS. as non-'illuminated'—and the colours are mingled in such a way that no one colour predominates, but a soft and blended effect is produced by the many small surfaces of different colours.

Almost all the early Celtic illuminated codices are Gospel-books, which were evidently at that time considered the only books worthy of the skill and care of the illuminator. 'Two psalters exist (the Blickling Psalter, and the Salaberga Psalter in Berlin) but they are very much the exception at this early period' (Saunders).

Classification of Hiberno-Saxon Features of Illumination. O. Elfrida Saunders distinguishes the following five main features in the decoration of the complete copies of the Gospels:

(1) Pages containing the Canon-tables (*i.e.*, lists of parallel passages in the various Gospels) framed in ornamental columns and arches.

(2) Full-page pictures of the Evangelists, one before each Gospel, enclosed in a border.

(3) Initial pages to each Gospel, containing the first few words of the text, elaborately decorated.

(4) A few full-page ornamental designs, usually based on the form of a cross.

(5) One or more pages containing figure subjects, such as scenes from the Life of Christ (or, in Psalters, scenes from the Life of David).

Some codices, moreover, have ornamental pages on which the four Evangelist symbols appear together, or other decorations.

Book of Durrow (Fig. IV-2b–c)

The earliest extant codex fully illuminated in the style commonly known as Hiberno-Saxon, is the *Book of Durrow*, or *Durmachensis*, a Gospel in Latin preserved in Trinity College Library at Dublin (*A. IV. 5*). Its pages measure 9¾ by 6½ ins. (25 by 16·5 cm.). It contains a relatively pure text of the Vulgate, *i.e.*, S. Jerome's translation of the Bible into Latin, and is named after the Columban monastery of Durrow (near Tullamore, in Co. Offaly), where it is known to have been kept, and where it is said to have been written.

It contains a 'colophon' saying that the MS. was copied in twelve days by S. Columba, the founder of the monastery of Durrow (who died *c.* 597). It seems, however, that this colophon refers to the original, from which our MS. was copied.

Book of Durrow: Symbol of S. Mark.

Thus, neither the place of origin nor the date of the *Book of Durrow* is certain. Kendrick attributes it to *c.* 650; Mlle. Henry to the second half of the seventh century; Oakeshott to a date between 664 and 675; Zimmermann and Masai to the early eighth century—the date *c.* 650–75 is more likely.

While the representations it contains of the Evangelists and their symbols are grotesque and unreal, the ornamental decoration is magnificently designed and brilliantly executed. The ornament varies from page to page; almost every page is surrounded by a border of interlacing. There are wide ribbons—yellow, red and green, zigzag and twisting on a background of deep black—spirals, fantastic animals, the trumpet-pattern, the panel type of pavement, and the *millefiori* pattern.

In general the Durrow-style—writes Sir Thomas Kendrick—is characterised by a bold spreading rhythm that brings the intricate patterns up on a large scale to usurp the page and lessen the effect of the heavy panelling. And Mlle. Henry rightly emphasizes that the style of the *Book of Durrow* achieves effects by a simplicity, a directness of means, which is illustrated by the use of only four colours: the black-brown, a sort of brick red, a bright yellow, and a green.

Codex Amiatinus (Fig. IV-3 and 4a–b)

Before we discuss the Lindisfarne Gospels, the most beautiful Anglo-Saxon book in existence, we have to deal (at least, shortly) with a book strictly connected with it in its contents (see also *The Hand-produced Book*, p. 504 f. and *passim*). The *Codex Amiatinus* is so-called from its former home (from *c.* 900 onwards), the monastery of S. Salvatore on Mount Amiata (Tuscany), whose Abbot falsified the original colophon and inserted his own name.

This celebrated codex, of paramount importance for Bible study, is now preserved in the Laurentian Library at Florence (*MS. Amiatino 1*) and it is also known as *Codex Am.* or *A.* It contains 1030 leaves, measuring $50\frac{1}{2}$ by 34 cm. (nearly 20 by $13\frac{1}{2}$ ins.), and is written in Northumbrian uncial in two columns of 44 lines to the page. Scholars agree that—together with two other copies of the Vulgate—it was written and illuminated in Northumbria, at the twin monasteries of Jarrow and Monkwearmouth, in the late seventh or the early eighth century, on the orders of Abbot Ceolfrid (690–716) who intended to present this volume as a gift to the Pope, but who died on his way to Rome in A.D. 716.

Thus the *Codex Amiatinus* is an Anglo-Saxon production, having been illuminated by a native artist, though in its three main miniatures painted in colours and gold it is 'almost entirely Italian in style and shows no weakening whatsoever in the direction of a barbaric Celtic or English ornamental apparatus . . .' (Kendrick). On the other hand, its most important miniature, representing the Christ in Majesty between two angels, and containing also the symbols and figures of the Evangelists (folio 796*v*.), preceding the New Testament, 'is crude and unsophisticated' as compared with the *S. Augustine Gospels* of Corpus Christi College at Cambridge (see p. 70), 'though the original the artist had before him must have been very close in style to the pictures in the Corpus book' (Oakeshott). Fig. IV-4*b*.

The importance of the *Amiatinus* text has been emphasized in *The Hand-produced Book* (*passim*). Here reference may be made to its two illuminations of the Old Testament books, which were copied from an older model. Some scholars have suggested that this model was the famous MS. now lost, known as *Codex Grandior* or *Pandects of the Old Testament* by Cassiodorus, which had been seen by Bede, and which was brought to England by Ceolfrid. Of particular importance is the double-page illumination (fols. 2*v*–3*r*) representing schematically the interior of the Israelite Sanctuary in the Wilderness. 'With the looped curtains round the enclosure and the careful grouping of the Sanctuary vessels, it displays obvious analogies with the Jewish and Samaritan representations' (C. Roth). Fig. IV-3.

The other large Old Testament illumination (folio 5*r*) represents a bearded man writing in or copying a book; he is seated in front of a book-chest, the doors of which are open showing the volumes within. At the side of the chest is a table. The scribe holds his feet on a four-legged foot-stool, which in Dr. C. Roth's opinion has some analogies with the conventional altar. The book-chest contains nine volumes, which according to some scholars may represent the five Books of Moses and the four Gospels. The scribe wears a *halo*, and from the middle of his forehead there projects a curious object which, according to Roth, may represent a phylactery. The practice of wearing phylacteries (based on *Exod.* xiii. 9 and 16, *Deut.* vi. 8–9, xi. 18) is still continued by strict Jews at the weekday prayers, and by scribes while engaged in copying the Scroll of the Law. In 'Jewish imagery "Ezra the Scribe" would naturally be depicted in this fashion. But no Christian artist would have thought of including this detail' (Roth).

A Latin inscription above the scribe—attributed to Alcuin—implies that the figure represents Ezra renewing the Law. Fig. IV-4*a*.

Fol. 4 (on purple) contains (on *r*) the Prologue, and (on *v*) the Canon or index of the Old and New Testaments, written in yellow in a double arch decorated with interlacement and other motifs. Folios 6*r*, 7*r*, and 8*r* contain schematic and symbolic figures of the Old and New Testaments (the figure of Christ in half-bust, the Holy Ghost in the form of a dove, and so on). Fig. IV-3*b*.

Lindisfarne Gospels (Fig. IV-5*a–c*)

With the exclusion of the *Amiatinus*, the illuminated Anglo-Saxon codices of the seventh (if any can be assigned to this date) and eighth centuries present in colour the ornamental characteristics of the 'Irish' codices, gold being employed in profusion; moreover, the human figures are represented in a more natural manner, and there are other influences of Italian and Byzantine models. Thus, until recently, it was generally assumed that Anglo-Saxon art developed under the influences of both local and Roman-Byzantine art (see also p. 176 ff.). Indeed—as has been shown in Chapter X of *The Hand-produced Book*—while Irish monks and missionaries brought Christianity to the North of England, the South of England was in direct contact with Rome, and from the period of Augustine onwards both missionaries and Christian codices were sent from Rome to Canterbury and to other centres.

The best example of Anglo-Saxon illumination is the *Lindisfarne Gospels*, generally attributed to *c.* A.D. 700. It is now preserved in the British Museum (*Cotton. Nero, D. IV*). It is also known as the *Book of Lindisfarne*, or *Lindisfarnensis*, and in scientific editions it is quoted as *Codex Y*; it was also called the *Gospels of S. Cuthbert*.

All scholars agree that this book is the finest example of early English book production. It has 258 leaves (measuring $13\frac{1}{2}$ by $9\frac{5}{8}$ ins. or 34 by 24·5 cm.), containing the text of the Gospels, with some introductory matter. Several pages have magnificent illuminations, including full-page pictures of the four Evangelists, five full-page crosses, and much other ornamentation, including pictures of birds, such as cormorant, 'which have their homes on the Lindisfarne Island and the Farne Islands' (F. Harrison).

According to O. E. Saunders, the pictures of the Evangelists, not Irish in style, are only explained by the influences of the Italo-Saxon monasteries. The designs are somewhat simpler and more orderly than those of the 'Irish' codices. The initials are balanced by partial borders, and a profusion of red dots is used to outline the main initials and form a patterned background to the lesser ones. The skilful use of these dots does much to lighten the general effect of the richly decorated pages. Some of the 'smaller initials are filled in with plain washes of colours; this was a favourite practice at this time' (Saunders).

The colours employed are gold, dark red, blue, green, mauve, yellow, purple and pink.

In Mlle. Henry's opinion, the decoration of the *Lindisfarnensis* is based to a great extent on the style of the *Book of Durrow*. Spirals, interlacings, animal interlacings—the elements are the same, but, far from being kept apart, they are constantly juxtaposed and sometimes mingled. The spirals, however, are much bolder than those of the *Book of Durrow* and blossom over the page in easy-flowing, well-balanced curves.

According to Sir Thomas Kendrick, the *Book of Lindisfarne* shows in some respects that there is a tendency towards barbarian over-elaboration which is to be observed in the crowded and multitudinous array of intricate details with which the Lindisfarne illuminator filled his pages. Kendrick compares this system of ornamentation with that of Irish contemporary metal-work, such as the Tara brooch. Of many of the pages in the Gospels—he concludes—we may truly say that they are a veritable Celtic bewilderment in which pattern and background spread themselves in a rich and almost endless parade of dexterous designs, a perpetual challenge to the eye and a perpetual delight.

Book of Kells (Fig. IV-4c–d)

There is only one other book with which, in style and beauty, the *Lindisfarne Gospels* can be compared, and that is the *Book of Kells*, which is considered by some scholars to be the finest MS. ever produced. The taste and delicacy, the originality, the elaboration of the colouring and design, place the *Book of Kells* among the wonders of the world. According to the late Sir Frederic Kenyon, however, this book is more barbaric in colouring than that of the English school, its reds and yellows contrasting with the more sober lilacs and pale greens of the *Lindisfarne Gospels*; its interlacements and figure drawings are also more extravagant. Splendid as it is in its wealth of ornament, in Kenyon's opinion, it lacks the restraint and good taste of the English style.

On the other hand, the noble script, the generous margins, the ample spacing, the huge initial letters at the opening of each Gospel, the single-column text, the mere magnitude of the ornament, the ocean of colour and the forest of ornate capitals (more than two thousand one hundred of them), the large number of pages devoted to ornament, and the sustained beauty and dignity of the six hundred 'ordinary pages' of the *Book of Kells*, induce the Rev. Prof. A. A. Luce to consider it infinitely finer than the *Lindisfarne Gospels*: Fig. IV-4d.

The *Book of Kells*, also known as *Codex Cenannensis*, or *Codex Q* (at one time it was called the *Great Gospel-book of S. Columkille*) is now preserved in Trinity College Library at Dublin (*A. I. 6*). This 'supreme masterpiece of the Celtic illuminator' is a Gospel-book, written in beautiful half-uncials, on 339 leaves of thick glazed vellum measuring 13 by $9\frac{1}{2}$ ins. (33 by 24 cm.). A few leaves are missing; moreover, over one hundred years ago the margins were clipped by the binder of the book.

According to Mlle. Henry, this MS. can only have been produced in one of two places: Iona or Kells. Masai questions whether it was made in Ireland, but his doubts are not warranted. As to its date, *c.* A.D. 800 is generally agreed upon; in Mlle. Henry's opinion, since most of the decoration points to a date within the eighth century, it is probable that an important part of its illumination is due to the Irish monks working in the *scriptorium* of Iona.

The text is incorrect and careless, full of misspellings and misreadings; there is even a certain carelessness in the decoration and in its finish: witness the uneven quality of the paintings, conflicting styles, unfinished state of some ornamentation, and pages left blank here and there. Still, nothing we have seen before—writes Mlle. Henry—approaches the *Book of Kells* for elaborate decoration. A continuous chain of ornamentation runs all through the text. The capitals at the beginning of each paragraph—two, three, four to a page—are made of the brightly coloured entwinements of birds, snakes, distorted men and quadrupeds, fighting or performing all sorts of acrobatic feats. Sometimes these painted letters are linked together in a continuous decorative band. And here and there—concludes Mlle. Henry—a sentence of the text blossoms suddenly into ornaments and is treated as a full page of illuminations.

Tradition has it that the unerring lines of its ornamentation—in one space of about $\frac{1}{4}$ inch square may be counted, with a magnifying glass, 158 interlacements—must have been traced by angels.

In addition to this magnificent ornamentation there are 'portraits' of the Evangelists, cruciform pages bearing their symbols, porticos framing the Canons, and other important artistic features.

It is in the initial page of each Gospel—points out O. Elfrida Saunders—that the full freedom of the Celtic designers is displayed. These pages contain the first words of the Gospel, elaborately decorated. In S. Matthew the initial words are *Liber Generationis*, introducing the genealogy of Christ, contained in seventeen verses. This genealogy is sometimes treated as a sort of preface, and the first words of verse 18 form a second initial page. S. Matthew has the Great Sacred Monogram *Khi-Rho* (for Christi) followed by *autem generatio*; S. Mark has *Initium evangelii*; S. Luke *Quoniam quidem*; and S. John *In principio*. The rounded uncials of the Irish script—emphasizes O. E. Saunders—lend themselves well to designs of sweeping curves; the large initials are generally filled with panels of various lacertine and geometrical designs, and within the spaces they enclose, as well as all around them, luxuriates an intricate maze of patterns, among which spiral whorls take a preponderant place. The background is often filled in with black, but little of it is to be seen.

Particularly interesting is the 'Great Monogram' or *Khi-Rho* of the opening of the eighteenth verse in the Gospel of S. Matthew ('Now the birth of Jesus Christ was on this wise'): the Sacred Monogram dominates the whole page. Sir Thomas Kendrick has rightly remarked that while the page of the *Khi-Rho* of the *Book of Durrow* is relatively unpretentious, and in the *Lindisfarne Gospels* there are four lines of text below the Monogram, in the *Book of Kells* we reach such a climax that the ornamented *Khi-Rho* leaves room for no more than the words *autem generatio*. Furthermore, the ornamental style of the Irish metal-work, which, according to Kendrick, is to be recognised in the *Lindisfarne Gospels*, is to be seen in even more stupendous exuberance in the *Book of Kells*: Fig. IV-4c.

To sum up with O. E. Saunders' words, on the whole, the *Khi-Rho* page in the *Book of Kells* is the most elaborate in any of these initial pages. Its design, although freely adapted to fill the uneven spaces of the lettering, preserves a certain symmetry; circular and spiral patterns are very much in evidence, and geometrical and animal lacertine motifs are also used; but the artist does not restrict himself to these traditional themes; at least thirteen human heads are found, on close inspection, to be included in the design, and near the bottom there is a little group of cats and mice.

Other Hiberno-Saxon MSS. (Fig. IV-5d–11)

With regard to the Evangeliary of Lichfield Cathedral, which is known as the *Gospels of S. Chad*, in Mlle. Henry's opinion it is more than likely, from the appearance of the decoration, that it had been sent to Wales from Ireland. Sir Thomas Kendrick, who also assigns this work to an Irish monk, dates it to the mid-eighth century. In the eighth or ninth century this MS. was presented by a certain Gelhi to S. Telian, *i.e.*, the monastery of Llandaff, in South Wales: Fig. IV-8d.

According to other scholars it is of Northumbrian origin, and W. Oakeshott has suggested that it may have been made in Wales under strong Northumbrian influence.

The Gospel fragment of Corpus Christi College, Cambridge, *Codex 197*, and the fragment in the British Museum, *Cotton. Otto, C. V.* are part of a Northumbrian MS. to which the famous *Codex Epternacensis* seems to be strictly related. The latter MS., which comes from the monastery of Echternach, and is also known as the *Echternach Gospels*, is preserved in the National Library at Paris (*Lat. 9389*). It is attributed to the late seventh or early eighth century, and 'was probably brought from Northumbria where it had been written and decorated' (F. Henry). It is—writes Kendrick—the most grimly splendid of the barbaric manuscript styles, and it is doubtful if any English illumination excels the *Echternach Gospels* in meticulous draughtmanship and cunningly displayed richness : Fig. IV-5d.

Other known Echternach MSS. such as the *Gospel-books* preserved at Maihingen, in Bavaria, and at Trèves (Cathedral Treasury, *Cod. 61*), and the *Martyrologium Hieronymianum*, preserved at the National Library at Paris, are of relatively minor importance : Fig. IV-11a.

The monastery of Echternach, near Trèves, now in Luxembourg, was founded by S. Willibrord (*c.* 657–739)—see also *The Hand-produced Book*, p. 510 f. and *passim*—who was born in Northumbria, and educated in a monastery at Ripon. Consecrated Archbishop by Pope Sergius I, Willibrord also founded the monastery of Utrecht, and established his metropolitan cathedral in that city. In Mlle. Henry's opinion the monasteries of both Echternach and Utrecht were semi-Irish, semi-Northumbrian.

The fragmentary *Gospel-book* in Durham Cathedral Library (A. *ii.* 17)—from the point of view of its illuminations—seems to be related to the *Lindisfarne Gospels* ; so is also the *Cassiodorus in Psalmos* in the same Cathedral Library. Both seem to belong to the mid-eighth century. The *Vatican Gospels* (Vatican Library, *Barb. Lat. 570*), and especially the *Leningrad Gospels* (*Lat. F. V.I.N.8*), which formerly belonged to the Abbey of S. Germain des Près, at Paris, are also 'founded solidly upon the earlier Northumbrian art'. The central panel of the Canon Tables in the *Vatican Gospels* (fol. 1r), in Kendrick's opinion, is a fantastic design of such flippant and whimsical impertinence that it is without rival outside the *Book of Kells*. Fig. IV-6—and 10a.

An early eighth-century fragmentary *S. Mark's Gospel* (Durham Cathedral Library, A. *ii.* 10 and A. *ii.* 16) contains beautiful initials : Fig. IV-9b.

Later developments of the Hiberno-Saxon art of book-illumination, are shown by the following codices, amongst others.

Armagh Gospels or *Book of Armagh* or *Liber Ardmachanus*, preserved in Trinity College at Dublin, is also known as the *Gwynn MS.* or *Codex Dublinensis*. Formerly it was assigned to S. Patrick, but it is now known that it was written by Ferdomnach, of Armagh, from the dictation of Torbach, abbot of Armagh in 807–8. See also *The Hand-produced Book*, p. 466 and *passim*. Fig. IV-7c.

Mac Regol Gospels, also known as the *Rushworth Gospels*, was written and illuminated by Bishop Mac Regol, abbot of Birr (Co. Offaly), who died in 822. This book is preserved in the Bodleian Library at Oxford (*Auct. D. 219, no. 3946*). See also *The Hand-produced Book*, p. 464.

The *Book of Dimma*, preserved in the Trinity College Library at Dublin (*No. 59*), was probably written in the abbey of Roscrea (Tipperary)—see *The Hand-produced Book*, p. 468. For the *Book of Mulling* or *Moling*, also known as *S. Mulling's Gospels* (Trinity College Library at Dublin, *No. 60*), see *The Hand-produced Book*, p. 467 f. The *Stowe Missal* and *Gospel of S. John* bound with it, now in Dublin, in the Royal Irish Academy, Ashburnham Collection (*Stowe MS. D. 2. 3.*)—see *The Hand-produced Book*, p. 468 f.; the *Irish Psalter*, in St. John's College, Cambridge (*C. 9: No. 59*); the *Book of Mac Durnan* or *Mac Durnan Gospels* (Lambeth Palace, London)—see *The Hand-produced Book*, p. 469; the *Book of Cadmug* (Hess. Landesbibl., Fulda, *Cod. Bonif. III*); a *Commentary on the Psalms* (Ambrosian Library at Milan, *Cod. C. 301 inf.*)—are other important examples of illuminated Irish manuscripts: Fig. III-*c*–*d*, 7*a*–*b*, 8*c*, and 11*c*.

In Mlle. Henry's opinion, some other illuminated manuscripts seem to be quite certainly Irish work of the eighth and ninth centuries; amongst them are three St. Gall MSS. (*No. 51, Gospels*; *No. 904, Grammar of Priscian*; *No. 1395*, two fragments); the *Grammar of Priscian*, in the University Library of Leyden (*Lat. 67*); the *Collectio Canonum* in Cologne; four disconnected pages from Bobbio, preserved in the Turin National Library (*O. IV. 20*), and one page from Bede's *De Rerum Natura*, preserved in the Library of Reichenau. The Bobbio fragment comes from a palimpsest codex. One folio is filled with ornamentation in 'pure' Insular style; another folio represents the Ascension (Christ in half-length, Angels, Apostles); on a third folio we see Christ in Glory holding the Cross, and figures of Saints in a number of small compartments. An early ninth-century codex, preserved in Rome (National Library, *MS. 1258, Sessor. 40*), contains four charming initials of Insular style: Fig. IV-8*a* and *b*, 9*a*, and 11*b*.

Mention may also be made of an interesting *Gospel-book* preserved in the Library of the Hereford Cathedral (*P. 1. ii*). The MS., assigned to the eighth or ninth century, is written in a script, which by some scholars (for instance, Schenkl) is considered 'Irish', by others (Lindsay) 'Welsh'. There are coloured titles to each Gospel, but the title to S. Luke is missing: Fig. IV-9*c*–*d*. Finally, a few later MSS. have also been regarded as Irish: a *Psalter* of the Trinity College Library, Dublin (*MS. 50*), of c. 1090; two *Gospels* of the Brit. Mus. (*Harley MS. 1802*, of 1138, and *Harley MS. 1023*, of c. 1150); and a *Psalter* of the Brit. Mus. (*Add. MS. 36929*).

Fig. IV-11*d* reproduces fol. 16*v* from the *Book of Deer* (Cambridge University Library, *Ii. 6. 32*), belonging to the ninth century. It is the earliest MS. containing Scottish Gaelic glosses: see *The Hand-produced Book*, p. 483 f.

Canterbury School (Fig. IV-12)

Canterbury appears to have been the earliest centre of artistic book-production in Southern England. In the eighth and the early ninth century, from which period a series of splendid manuscripts have been preserved, the Canterbury *scriptorium* produced works partly based on the early Christian figurative tradition in stiffly outlined forms, and partly on the superb, though barbaric, ornamentation of the Hiberno-Saxon art. Very little is known of the origins and development of this school of illumination, but apparently the activity of the school at that period did not last long. If the *Lindisfarne Gospels* (p. 182 f.) may represent a sort of compromise between Celtic and Continental illumination, the products of the Canterbury school probably represent this trend to a greater degree.

Their decoration—argues O. E. Saunders—is predominantly Celtic, although diluted with foreign importations such as leaf-scroll patterns, rosettes and acanthus-leaf borders. But the figure subjects, in their whole setting, pose and technique, show close analogy to the manuscripts produced in the various Carolingian schools of illumination which were springing up at this time in France. Solid, round-headed figures, ample drapery, heavy and opaque colouring, and a somewhat streaky attempt at modelling, are the main features of Carolingian work, and they appear in those pictures also.

Other affinities between the styles of the Canterbury school and the Carolingian schools are the device of framing a figure-subject by columns and an arch, the striped backgrounds of various colours, and some other features. Moreover, gold is used for lettering and decoration. The *Canterbury Gospels* and the *Codex Aureus* of Stockholm have some pages stained purple.

On the whole, we have to accept Sir Thomas Kendrick's statement that the style of the so-called Canterbury School is hybrid, but it is hybrid in an intelligent and organized manner. The columns with their patterned gold lozenges on a background of interlace reveal a cunning southern enrichment of northern style; and the introduction of the new animal 'portrait' style, pictures, of Merovingian origin, of little beasts and birds in the roundels that purport to be the capitals and bases of these columns—concludes Kendrick—is yet another sign that this Canterbury art is a disciplined hotch-potch of many fashions.

Canterbury Psalter. To this school belongs the *Canterbury Psalter*—also known as *S. Augustine's Psalter*—in the British Museum (*Cott. Vespasian A. i.*) dated to c. 750. See also p. 71 f. and Fig. II-4b. The famous folio 30b of the Psalter, which is a full-page miniature and represents David seated on a cushioned throne, surrounded by musicians, dancers and scribes, 'is a gorgeous polychrome page of rich shaded colours and much gold' (Kendrick), but, as Walter Oakeshott points out, it has Hiberno-Saxon motifs in the decoration, fine trumpet spirals, fret pattern and so forth, interspersed with Frankish and classical ornaments. On the other hand, the figures are untouched by 'Irish' influence and aspire to be classical, as do the Evangelists of *Codex Aureus* (see p. 212). O. Elfrida Saunders, indeed, considers the style of this miniature very near to that of the Carolingian 'Palace school' or 'Palatine school' (see p. 204): Fig. IV-12b.

The *Stockholm Gospels* or *Codex Aureus* of Stockholm, the other main product of the early Canterbury school, also belongs to the eighth century: Fig. IV-12a.

A mid-eighth century Latin *Psalter* (with Anglo-Saxon and Latin glosses), produced in South England, perhaps at Canterbury, is preserved in the Pierpont Morgan Library, New York (*M. 776*). The text, in a fine even Insular majuscule script, is a Roman Psalter (that is, Jerome's earlier version) with some Gallican readings. There are ornamental initials to each Psalm, and ornamental first lines to four of the Psalms. Ornamentation is in rich black and it consists of lacertine and interlace motifs, with outlines of red dots and fillings of lavender, orange, and green; there are also a few touches of powder-gold.

An interesting manuscript, known as *Cuthbert Evangeliar*, is preserved in the National Library at Vienna (*Lat. 1224*). It is dated *c.* 770; by some scholars it is assigned to South England: see, however, p. 219. Fig. IV-10b.

Canterbury Gospels. This interesting MS. (British Museum, *Royal 1. E. vi*) of the Carolingian period, represents a slightly later development of the Canterbury style and of the Anglo-Saxon art. It is attributed by some scholars to the archbishopric of Wulfred (805–832). It is a sumptuous book; its ornament—writes Kendrick—is most opulent and continentally splendid in appearance, particularly because of the great purple pages in the Byzantine and Carolingian manner, and the new abundant use of gold. The Evangelist picture—which some scholars consider a later addition—has affinities with the style of the Rheims school (see p. 204 f.), where a swift and sketchy method of drawing prevailed: Fig. IV-12c.

The problem of the origins of the Canterbury style is partly chronological. Its connection with the Hiberno-Saxon style can be explained, and its relationship with Continental art may be partly explained by the facts that numerous manuscripts were brought over from the Continent (see *The Hand-produced Book, passim*) and that there was constant intercourse with Rome and Frankish Europe.

The difficulty arises if we assume that at least two of the three principal Canterbury manuscripts belong to the eighth century, and at the same time admit that the Canterbury school was influenced by Carolingian styles which belong to a later period. The possibilities are: (1) that the common elements were borrowed independently from the same primary sources; and (2) that the Canterbury miniatures were copied from, or influenced by, eighth-century Frankish manuscripts which have not survived, but which were already foreshadowing the new Carolingian style.

For the later Canterbury productions, see pp. 193, 196, 257 f., 274 f.

MERCIAN SCHOOL (Fig. IV-14c)

Under the great king Offa, who reigned for nearly forty years (755–94), Mercia rose to a height unknown before. Offa was in close connection with the Emperor Charlemagne, and concluded with him a treaty which secured protection for the English merchants and pilgrims who were making their way in growing numbers to Rome. He founded the great monastery of St. Albans, and, because of his intense hostility towards the Archbishop of Canterbury, he set up for a while a rival archbishopric at Lichfield, which became a centre of culture and art.

The best representative of the Lichfield *scriptorium* is undoubtedly the *Book of Cerne*—its name derives from the fact that for a certain period it belonged to Cerne Abbey (Dorset); the *codex* is preserved in the University Library of Cambridge (*Ll.1. 10*). It was written and illuminated in the early ninth century, and it contains a collection of the Passion and Resurrection narratives from the Four Gospels. T. D. Kendrick describes its style as far more barbaric in treatment than any work of the Canterbury school. Nevertheless, he continues, the aim of the principal decorative pages was to simulate the serene and spacious dignity of the Carolingian grand manner; the architectural structure is light and thin. Furthermore, in Kendrick's opinion, the colouring is applied in the northern mosaic style rather than in the southern painterly fashion, and a warm purplish-brown assembly of cinnamon red, pink and blue, takes the place of the rich and more varied palette of the south. Gold is used only three times in the initials. Ornament is sparingly used, the favourite animal being a little biped with a long, curly tail.

Another important work of this school, containing beautiful ornamental pages though no figure drawing, is a copy of Bede's *Ecclesiastical History* (preserved in the British Museum, *Tiberius C. ii*).

PERIOD OF DECADENCE (Fig. III-10)

In *The Hand-produced Book* it has been pointed out that, particularly in the ninth century, Anglo-Saxon civilization, just as it began to rise, was met by a new blow and sank down once more. During many decades the same atrocities which had attended the victory of the Saxon over the Celt were now, after the lapse of ages, suffered by the Saxon at the hands of the Dane. The Danish raids and invasions shattered the organisation of the English Church. Religious houses were destroyed and their inmates put to the sword; the whole monastic life, especially in the North and the East, was disrupted; the libraries were plundered, and the pursuit of learning became a matter of the greatest difficulty.

The description of the havoc brought by the Vikings reminds us of the Gothic destruction in the Roman Empire, of the Mongol plunderings in Asia, or of the 'Vandalism' in Spain and North Africa. Monasteries and other centres of culture were favourite objects of attack. 'No scholars, no clerics, no books, no holy relics were left in church or monastery through dread of them'—wrote the historian Keating (first half of the seventeenth century).

The Irish author of the *Wars of the Gael with the Gaill* (a copy of which is preserved in the Irish *Book of Leinster*, written *c.* 1150)—see *The Hand-produced Book*, p. 453 f. and *passim*—after describing the endurance of the few remaining scholars, mentions that 'their writings and their books in every church and in every monastery where they were, were burnt and thrown into water by the plunderers from beginning to end (of the Viking invasion)'. In the South, King Alfred the Great (*c.* 849–99), in the preface to his *Cura Pastoralis* (see *The Hand-produced Book*, p. 514)—see further on—wrote: 'I saw, before all were spoilt and burnt, how the churches throughout Britain were filled with treasures and books.'

The obvious results of these destructions were: (1) Great numbers of books, both illuminated and non-illuminated, must have perished. (2) Numerous monks and missionaries fled to the Continent with such books and manuscripts as they could save from the violence of the invaders. And (3) when the condition of life became such that men could no longer cultivate the arts, the production of books became increasingly rare, or even—at least in some parts of the Island—non-existent. In consequence, there followed a long period of sterility in book-production, and particularly in manuscript-illumination. Curiously enough, this period corresponded with the flourishing Carolingian period, in which illumination was being extensively practised on the Continent (see p. 198 ff.).

It would be wrong, however, to assume that artistic book-production ceased altogether. Indeed, as a leading British authority, F. G. Wormald, has recently proved, the Anglo-Saxon style to a certain degree lingered on up to the end of the Romanesque period—particularly in the field of outline drawings and decorated initials. Extant manuscripts, although rather rare, show that both the Hiberno-Saxon schools (see p. 185 ff.) and the Southern schools produced illuminated books. In the South, the synthetic style—as observed in the sections on the Canterbury and Mercian schools—still prevailed. The British Museum copy of Bede's *History* (*Tiberius C. ii*), already referred to, may be cited as a characteristic specimen of this art. The *B*—writes O. E. Saunders—is of Celtic form, but some of the panels of the decoration contain scroll work, and the conventionalized animals of the centre filling recall, if anything, the patterns on Oriental stuff.

At the same time, Saunders rightly remarks that for the lesser initials in some eighth-, ninth-, and even early tenth-century manuscripts, light and graceful designs in black ink, sometimes picked out with red dots, and formed of interlacing and knotted strands, ending in heads of birds or animals, are frequently used. They often show much taste and invention, and form a suitable decoration to the very beautiful hand-writing of the period. See, for instance, Cassiodorus, *Commentary on the Psalms*, one of the most important manuscripts produced in Northumbria in the middle of the eighth century, referred to on p. 186 (see also Fig. IV-10*a*); Aldhelm, *De Virginitate*, Lambeth Palace Library, ninth century; and *Codex Vossianus* of Bodleian Library, Oxford (*Junius 27*), early tenth century.

King Alfred's literary activity has been dealt with in *The Hand-produced Book*;

generally speaking, however, the books written by him, or rather by his court school, were not illuminated, and we know very little about the production of illuminated books in South England during his reign. It may be inferred, however, that men thought little of books and their decoration during the period of the wars between Wessex and the Danes.

However, a copy of King Alfred's reputed translation of Pope Gregory the Great's *Regulae* or *Cura Pastoralis* ('Pastoral Care'), probably written in Winchester during the last years of Alfred's reign, is preserved in the Bodleian Library at Oxford (*Hatton MS. 20*). It contains little decoration, but 'it must represent as good a style of illumination as the king could command in his own capital' (Kendrick). The poorly decorated *Durham Rituale* (Durham Cathedral Library, *A. iv. 19*), also belonging to the late ninth or early-tenth century, is assigned to a Midland or Southern style. See also *The Hand-produced Book* (p. 514 f. and *passim*, and Fig. X-21).

Tenth-Century Renaissance

Foreign elements were already introduced into England by the ninth century through the Carolingian school of Rheims (see p. 204 f.). Indeed, as Saunders argued, the Rheims style was to have a notable influence on the Anglo-Saxon school of outline drawing. The acanthus border with medallions seems to have been the basis from which the Winchester border was evolved two centuries later.

During the first half of the tenth century the Anglo-Celtic elements gradually disappeared, and in the second half of the century a new style developed—a great and truly English national style—which lasted until the decadence of the Anglo-Saxon art of illumination was brought about by the Norman Conquest. The main centre of the new style was the Winchester school, the greatest English school of illumination; it flourished particularly in the last decades of the tenth century, and in the early eleventh century.

WINCHESTER STYLE

King Alfred did much to revive culture and learning, but it took some decades before his reforms bore fruit in the field of artistic book-production. At the same time, but mainly in the South, the early tenth century brought a remarkable Christian revival, together with the re-establishment of English monasticism. The great reform of English monasticism was mainly associated with S. Dunstan (*The Hand-produced Book*, p. 515 ff.), with whom collaborated S. Aethelwold, Bishop of Winchester (963–84) and Dunstan's greatest pupil, and S. Oswald, a pupil of the monks of Fleury on the Loire, himself the founder of the great abbey of Ramsey, who succeeded Dunstan as Bishop of Worcester, and later became Archbishop of York. The years 955 to 980—with relative peace in England—were the best in this movement. Fig. IV-10c.

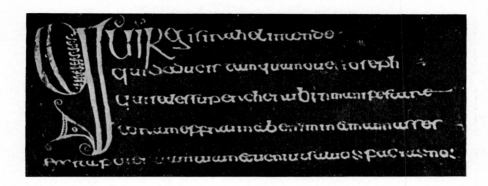

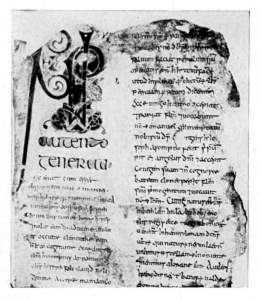

IV–1. Early Irish Initials. *a, Cathach of S. Columcille*, fol. 40 *r*, middle portion. *b*, Ambrosian Library, *MS. S. 45. sup. c*, The same collection, *MS. D. 23. sup. d*, Stowe Missal, fol. 1. *e*, *Book of Mulling*, p. 30.

IV–2. *a, Codex Usserianus Primus,* fol. 149 *v. b–c, Book of Durrow—b,* fol. 11 *v*: symbol of S. Luke. *c,* fol. 77 *v–*78 *r*: frontispiece and first page of *S. Mark.*

IV–3. *Codex Amiatinus*, fol. 2 *v* and 3 *r*.

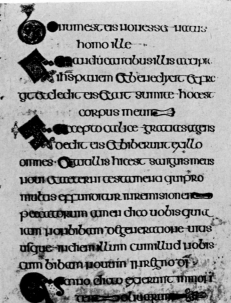

IV-4. *a–b, Codex Amiatinus,* fol. 5 *r* and 796 *v. c–d, Book of Kells, Khi-Rho* page (fol. 34 *r*) and fol. 177 *r*.

IV–5. *a–c, Lindisfarne Gospels* (*a*, S. Matthew; *b*, S. John; *c*, full-page cross). *d, Codex Epternacensis,* fol. 18 *v* : symbol of S. Matthew.

IV–6. *Vatican Gospels,*
fol. 8 *r* (initial) and
11 *v* (S. Matthew).

IV–7. *a–b, Book of Dimma,* pp. 30–31 (S. Mark and first page of his Gospel) and 104 (symbol of S. John). *c, Book of Armagh,* fol. 53 *v* : symbol of S. Mark.

IV–8. *a–b, St. Gall Gospels*: S. John and Crucifixion. *c, Mac Durnan Gospels*: S. Matthew (fol. 4 *v*). *d, Gospels of S. Chad*: S. Luke.

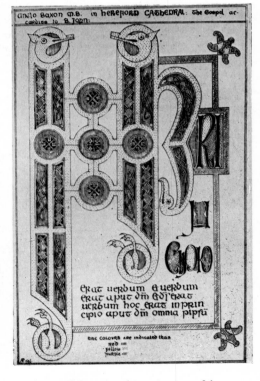

IV–9. *a*, St. Gall, *No. 1395*, p. 418 : S. Matthew (?). *b*, Initial from Durham A. *ii. 10*, fol. 2 *r*.
c–d, Hereford, *P. 1. ii*, fir st pages of *S. Matthew* and of *S. John* (reconstructed).

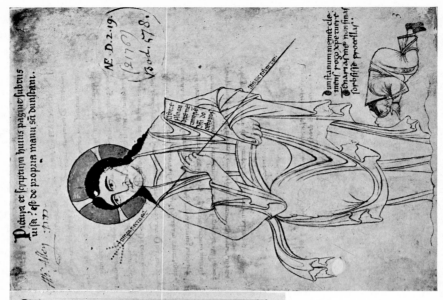

IV-10. *a, Cassiodorus in Psalmos* (Durham, *B. ii. 30*), fol. 172 *v*: David the Warrior. *b, S. Cuthbert Gospels,* fol. 110 *v*: S. Luke. *c,* Bodleian Library, *Auct. F. 4. 32 (—NE. D. 2. 19 (2176) Bod. 578)*: S. Dunstan prostrates before Christ.

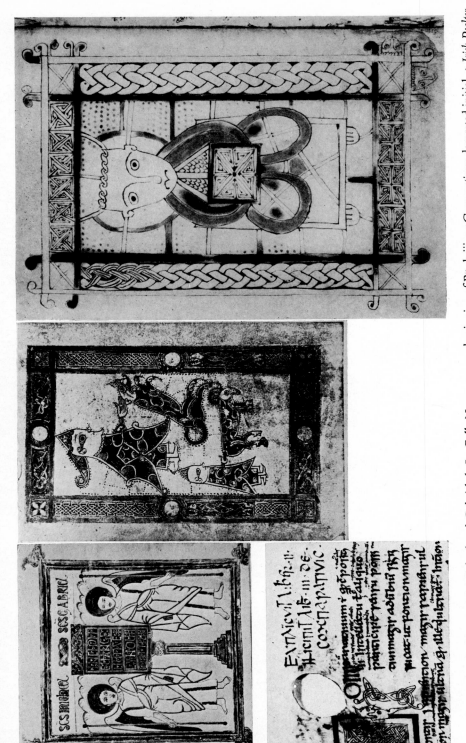

IV–11. *a*, Trèves, *No. 61*, fol. 9 *r*: SS. Michael and Gabriel. *b*, St. Gall, *No. 904*, p. 39: beginning of Book iii on *Comparatives*; decorated initial. *c*, *Irish Psalter*, fol. 4 *v*: frontispiece to the *Psalter*—two men (King David) and two beasts. *d*, *Book of Deer*, fol. 16 *v*: S. Mark.

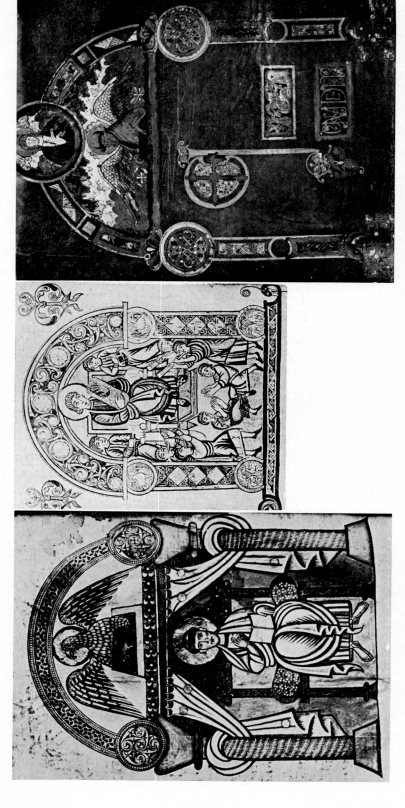

IV–12. Canterbury School. *a, Codex Aureus*, fol. 150 *v*: S. John. *b, Canterbury Psalter*, fol. 30 *v*: David playing the harp; his musicians and dancers. *c, Canterbury Gospels*, fol. 43 *r*: S. Luke and his symbol.

IV-13. *a, King Athelstan's Psalter*, fol. 35 *r*: Christ in Glory. *b–d, Benedictional of S. Aethelwold*: Ascension; the Three Maries; Entry into Jerusalem.

IV–14. a, *Arundel Psalter*, beginning of *Psalm i. b, S. Swithin Psalter*: Archangel Michael and Satan; Christ in the Limbo with Adam and Eve, and other N.T. scenes. *c, Book of Cerne*, fol. 21 v: S. Luke and his symbol. *d–e, Eadwine Psalter: Psalms* xliv and lxix.

IV-15. *a, Sacramentarium Gellonense,*
fol. 1 *v*: beginning of the
Sacramentary; the initial
reproduces the Virgin. *b, Ada*
Gospels: S. Mark.

IV–16. *a, Godescalc Evangeliarium, fol. 3 r:* Christ on the throne with the Gospels. *b, Charlemagne Gospel-book, fol. 15 r.*

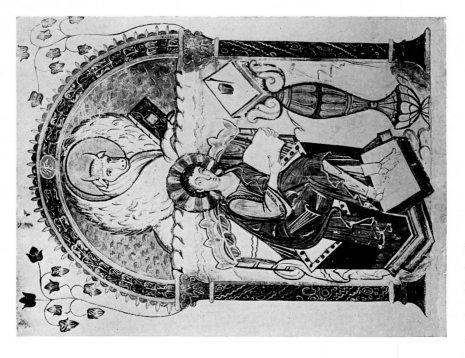

IV-17. *Lorsch Gospels*: SS. John (*a*) and Luke (*b*).

IV–18. *a, Rheims Gospels (M. 728)*, fol. *141 v* : S. John (a rather unusual
representation). *b, Utrecht Psalter,* fol. *100 r* : *Gospel* title-page.

MATTHEVS

IV-19. *a*, School of Otto von Freising (South Germany): *Gospels, c. 875*; S. Matthew. *b–c*, Tours *Scriptorium*: *b, Dufay Gospels*—S. Mark; *c*, Apicius, *De re coquinaria* (Cookery Book), fol. 2 *r. d*, Metz *Scriptorium: Drogo Sacramentarium.* Initial D, containing the representation of the Three Maries at the Tomb (decorative page for Easter Sunday).

IV–20. Corbie School: *Great Bible of S. Paolo fuori le Mura* (Rome)—incidents from the life of S. Jerome (the author of the Vulgate translation of the Bible).

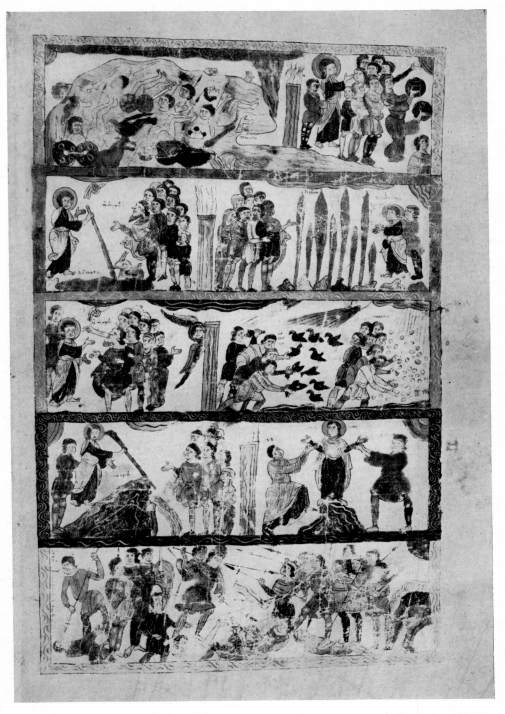

IV–21. Catalan Carolingian School: *Farfa Bible*, fol. 1 *r*—illustration of incidents described in *Exodus*, xiv–xvii (see also IV–33*b*).

IV–22. *a*, North-French Provincial School: *Gospels W. 3*. fol. 20 *r*—first page of *S. Matthew*.
b, Franco-Saxon School: *Second Bible of Charles the Bald*, fol. 285 *r* (1 *Chronicles*)—initial *A*.
c, *Erlangen Evangeliarium*: S. John. *d*, *Psalterium Aureum* (*St. Gall Cod. 22*), frontispiece: King
David and dancers.

IV–23. *a*, Early Ottonian
School: *Otto Gospels*, fol.
16 r: frontispiece to *S.
Matthew* with medallions of
Otto I. *b*, Weser School:
Gospels M. 75 (cf. pl. III–
25b), fol. *16 v*
(a whole word in
monogrammized form)
Initium (sncti)—frontispiece
to *S. Mark*.

IV–24. *a, Pruem Gospels*, fol. 45 *v*–46 *r*: Christ's entry into Jerusalem. *b, Codex Aureus Harley MS. 2788*: S. John. *c, McClean MS. 20*: S. Matthew.

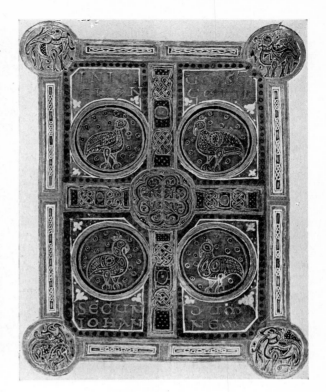

IV-25. *a*, *Helmarshausen Psalter W. 10*: Crucifixion. *b*, *Corvey Gospels W. 751*: frontispiece to *S. John. c*, Cologne School: *Abbess Hitda von Meschede Gospels*—Christ and disciples on the sea of Galilee. *d*, Echternach School: *Escorial Codex Aureus (Vetrinas 17)*: Virgin enthroned, with Henry II and Queen Agnes.

IV–26. a, *Hitda von Meschede Gospels*: Christ baptized in the River Jordan by S. John the Baptist; lower right, personification of River Jordan. b–c, Reichenau School: *Codex Egberti* (b, Rescue from Cross and Deposition; c, Adoration of the Magi).

IV-27. Reichenau School: *a, Pericopē-book* (book containing portions of *Gospels* read at public worship) of the Bamberg Cathedral Treasury, now in the State Library at Munich: New Testament scenes (right, Christ before Caiaphas and Crucifixion). *b, Bamberg Apocalypse:* SS. Peter and Paul crowning Henry II, the founder of the Abbey, and scenes from his life.

IV–28. Reichenau School:
a, Commentary to Isaia (State
Library at Bamberg)—
the Lord appears in the
midst of *Cherubim. b,
Bamberg Perícopē-book*:
Madonna and Child.

IV–29. *a*, Saxon ornamentation : *M. 827*, fol. 14 *v*—
decorated Canon Table.
b, Reichenau Gospels W. 7,
fol. *67 v* : S. Mark.

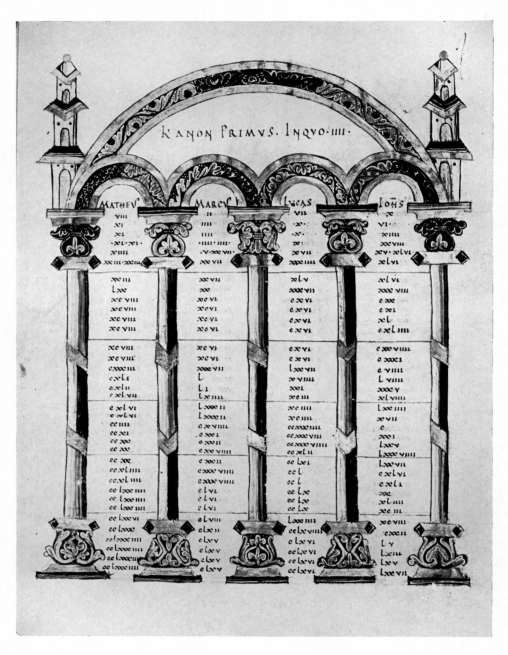

IV–30. Ratisbon School: *Henry II Gospels* (Vatican Library, *Ott. Lat. 74*), fol. 9 *r*: first Canon Table.

IV–31. *a, Engelberg Codex
47* : Venerable Bede
sharpening his pen.
b, Salzburg School :
Gospels M. 781, fol. *189 r*—
frontispiece to *S. John*.

IV-32. Austrian Schools. *a, Custos Bertolt Lectionary,* fol. 60 *v*: Crucifixion. *b,* Honorius, *Expositio*: symbolic illustration in polychrome outlines and strongly coloured background. *c,* Giselbertus of Auxerre, *Glosa in Threnos Jeremiae,* fol. 3: Scenes from War with Babylonia. *d, Melk Missal*: Crucifixion.

IV-33. Austrian Schools. *a–b, Kremsmuenster Gospels* (Kremsmuenster, Upper Austria, *Cod. 1*): S. Matthew and his symbol. *c, M. 808*: Canon Table. *d, Prayer-book of Leonhard Layming,* fol. 1 *v.*

IV–34. *a*, *Rheinau Psalter*, fol. 52 *v* : Christ's arrest; kiss of Judas. *b*, *Cologne Gospels* : S. John. *c*, *The Hague Gospels* (Royal Library, 76. F. 1) : S. Mark. *d*, S. Augustine, *On the Trinity* (Ministerial Library, Schaffhausen, Cod. 20) : first initial. *e*, *German Bible*, MS. *Laud. Misc.* 752, fol. 122 *r* : beginnings of 1 *Kings*— the priest Zadok anoints Solomon (i. 39) ; death of David (ii. 10).

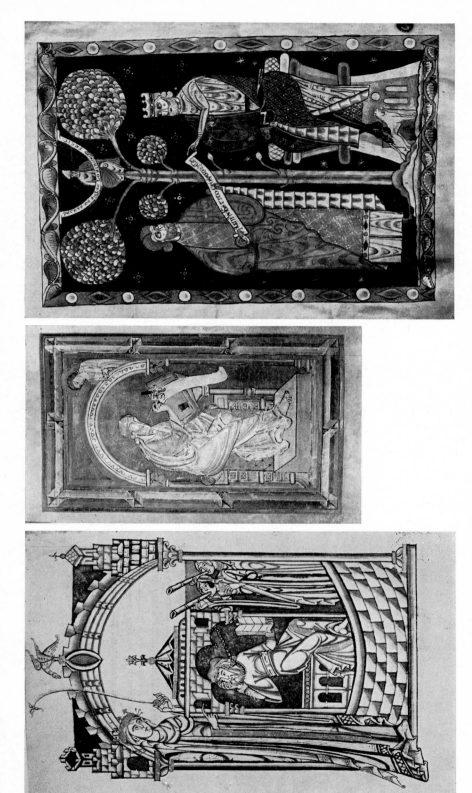

IV–35. *a*, Boëthius, *Philosophiae Consolatio* and other works, MS. *Auct. F. 6. 5*, fol. 1 *v*: 'While I ruminated these things with myself . . . I saw a woman stand above my head' (Book i, Chapt. i). *b*, McClean MS. *21*, fol. 11 *v*: S. Matthew; in gold on purple background. *c*, MS. *Plut. 82. 1*, fol. 2 *v*: Pliny.

IV–36. Some *minnesinger* in the *Manesse Codex. a,* Emperor Henry VI, himself a poet. *b,* Conradin with his friend Friedrich von Baden, in the attitude of hawking. *c,* Walter von der Vogelweide. *d,* Meister Johannes Hadloub, the last *minnesinger* of the *Manesse Codex*: two incidents from his autobiographical *minne*-lyric.

IV-37. Czech and Polish Illumination. *a, Coronation Evangeliar of Wratislav,* of the eleventh century. *b, Codex Aureus Pultoviensis,* another eleventh-century Czech MS. *c, Płock Codex No. 140* (formerly in Płock Cathedral Library; destroyed during last war); Polish, under Mosan influence, before 1160; fol. 32 *r*: Flagellation of Christ. *d, Adalbert Gasztold Hours, c.* 1528 (National Museum at Munich): S. Jerome.

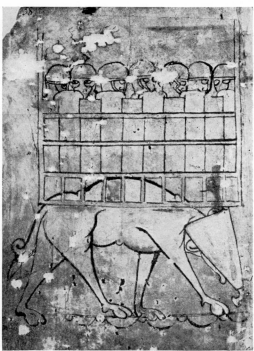

IV–38. Scandinavian and Icelandic Illumination. *a, Dalby-boken,* fol. 26 *v* : S. Matthew. *b,* Early Icelandic copy of *Physiologus,* fol. 7 *v* : Elephant. *c, Lund Gospels,* fol. 116 *v* : S. John. *d,* Royal Library, Copenhagen, *E don. var.* 55, 2° (*Necrology*), thirteenth-century Danish MS., fol. 43 *v* : Abraham holding the souls of the Faithful.

In this period, the illumination of manuscripts flourished again in England, appearing almost at once in a homogeneous and fully developed style, although only in the last decades of the tenth century did the matured Winchester school reach its full splendour.

As has already been stated, Winchester—with its two great monasteries, the Old Minster or the Priory of S. Swithin, and the New Minster, afterwards Hyde Abbey —was the main centre of this art; it soon spread to Ely. But many other monasteries —such as Canterbury, Bury St. Edmunds, Peterborough (the new name of the old Medeshamstede, given after the reform of Aethelwold) and even the far distant monasteries of York and Durham (see p. 196)—produced richly illuminated Gospel-books, Benedictionals, Pontificals, Sacramentaries and Service-books (see also p. 196 ff.). This rich outburst of artistic book-production was not equalled by anything on the Continent at that period.

Origins of Winchester Style

Both the chronological and artistic problems of these origins are still not quite certain. Sir G. F. Warner and other experts date the beginnings of the Winchester school to the period of S. Aethelwold's bishopric, *i.e.*, after 963. Indeed, the earliest known manuscript illuminated in this style is the Charter of King Edgar to New Minster, dating from 966 (British Museum, *Vespasian A. viii*). It contains one full-page dedication picture, enclosed in a leaf-work border, and shows the style already fully developed.

Aethelwold, emphasizes Saunders, himself a craftsman like his contemporary, S. Dunstan, had been in close touch with the Continent while he was Prior at Abingdon, and is known in particular to have been in communication with the monasteries of Fleury and Corbie. The sudden appearance of this new style in England, with only such slight preparation, makes it reasonable to suppose that he had stimulated his monks by examples of Carolingian art imported from northern France.

It is commonly agreed that the Winchester style is closely related to that of the school of Rheims (see p. 204 f.), and it is suggested that Aethelwold had brought Rheims manuscripts to Abingdon or Winchester. It should be added that the Carolingian minuscule writing—introduced into England roughly in this period —appeared first in Winchester manuscripts. On the other hand—again quoting O. E. Saunders—the Winchester border as seen in the Benedictionals, clearly shows its derivation from earlier manuscripts of the type of the *Canterbury Gospels* (p. 189). The acanthus foliage is enclosed between gold bars, except at the corners, where it juts over the framework of the medallions; the leaves are coloured in various soft shades, and occasionally in gold.

Beside the rich and formal initials, which will be referred to on p. 197, in several manuscripts of the tenth century there appear initials of a freer type, which are similar to, and appear to have developed from, the lesser initials of Anglo-Celtic manuscripts as described on p. 191. They use similar motifs of knot-work, leaves and biting heads, but are painted with opaque colours in a variety of tones. Examples occur in the *Codex Vossianus* (see p. 191).

Moreover, as Saunders points out, it is not easy to determine how much the Winchester monks, in forming their new style, borrowed from Frankish models (especially from those of Rheims and Metz), and how much they created. The border may certainly be claimed as an original development with its bright colours, gold bars, and freely branching foliage, although the mere element of acanthus foliage in a border was not new (it may be seen, for instance, in Metz ivories). An interesting innovation is the relation of the figure-subjects to the border, over which they frequently project. Moreover, although the actual figures are Carolingian in type, there is a freedom of treatment in the Winchester work which is characteristically English. This is shown, for instance, in the combination of outline figure drawings with coloured decoration, which frequently appears in Anglo-Saxon illumination, both at Winchester and elsewhere.

In Oakeshott's opinion, it was the great development of ceremonial in the tenth century which inspired the illumination of the Winchester school.

Thus, in general, it may be surmised that while Carolingian illumination—particularly the Rheims style—greatly influenced the development of the Winchester style, it was not its only source. At the same time, it may be assumed that while under Aethelwold's bishopric the Winchester style crystallised and flourished, it actually originated earlier, or, rather, it gradually developed from other styles. It is always to be remembered that not many codices of this period have come down to us, and that many illuminated manuscripts which could have been important links in the chains of development of various styles may have perished. Thus, whatever theory one may suggest, there will hardly be sufficient evidence to prove it.

However, there is an interesting codex—*King Athelstan's Psalter* (British Museum, *Galba A. xviii*)—which seems to foreshadow the Winchester style proper. It is attributed to Germany, whence it was sent as a present to King Athelstan, but it contains four full-page miniatures, which were apparently added in England in the period between 925 and 940. Although differing in style, all seem to have been copied from originals painted in Oriental style. Two of the miniatures represent Christ in Glory (long-haired and, curiously, beardless), one is of the Ascension, and the fourth (now preserved in the Bodleian Library, Oxford) represents the Nativity. Certain characteristics are closely related to the Winchester style—*e.g.*, the large hands, the conventional treatment of the features, and the colouring, but there is nothing here of the fluttering drapery, humped attitude, or extravagant gesture that are the most striking characteristics of the Winchester style. The border has some foliage of the acanthus type, but it has not yet developed into anything approaching the Winchester border: Fig. IV-13a.

Masterpieces of Winchester School

Benedictional of S. Aethelwold (Fig. IV-13b–d). Its most representative work—although by Tolhurst assigned to Ely—is the *Benedictional of S. Aethelwold*, Bishop of Winchester (see p. 192 f.). This codex, which W. Oakeshott considers the most important monument of later Anglo-Saxon illumination, is now preserved in the library of the Duke of Devonshire, at Chatsworth, Derbyshire. It contains several beautifully illuminated pages, such as S. John, Baptism, Entry into Jerusalem, and Ascension (which some scholars consider the only one in an English manuscript which shows Hellenistic treatment). Moreover, the initials with their luxuriant decoration (the foliage being interlaced into intricate patterns overflowing the frame) are of particular interest.

An authority in this field has rightly remarked that the *Benedictional of S. Aethelwold* stands out far above any of the other Winchester manuscripts for the elaboration and beauty of its decoration, and is a proof of the great skill to which the best English artists had already attained by 980, the date by which it was probably finished. Experts agree that this masterpiece shows influences of the Rheims school, but there is no trace of the influence of the *Utrecht Psalter* (see p. 205 f.). Godeman is given as the name of the scribe, and he probably also illuminated the codex—Godeman later became abbot of Thorney (*c.* 984–1012).

The celebrated *Winchester Psalter*, preserved in the British Museum (*Harl. MS. 2904*), has also been attributed to the period of S. Aethelwold, *i.e.*, to the late tenth century. *See* also p. 257.

Related Works. Amongst the MSS. closely related to *S. Aethelwold's Benedictional* are two eleventh-century productions of New Minster, which are preserved at Rouen: (1) the *Benedictional of Archbishop Robert* (archbishop of Canterbury, 1051; formerly bishop of London—*see* further on), with three beautiful miniatures. In comparison with the *Benedictional of S. Aethelwold*, it shows a less heavy type of figure, and in borders a freer and more rounded form of foliage; and (2) the *Missal of Robert of Jumièges*, with thirteen miniatures (much inferior, however, to those of the two Benedictionals). It was written and illuminated for Robert, bishop of London (1044–50), and sent by him to Jumièges, where he had been abbot.

Three other illuminated codices have been attributed to the same school: the *Ramsey Benedictional* (preserved in the National Library at Paris, *Lat. 987*), which, however, has no figure subjects; a *Gospel-book* in Trinity College Library at Cambridge (*B. 10. 4*); and a *Gospel-book* in the British Museum (*Royal 1. D. ix*), which was apparently donated by King Cnut to Canterbury, where it was in 1013.

Other Works (Fig. IV-14*a–b*). One of the best representatives of the Winchester style in its later period is the famous *Arundel Psalter* (preserved in the British Museum, *Arundel MS. 60*) which belongs to the late eleventh (perhaps 1060) or early twelfth century; 'its illuminations are in the finest style of English art' (Esdaile). Most interesting is the initial B of its *Beatus* page, Fig. IV-14*a*. Slightly earlier (perhaps of *c.* 1050) is another British Museum *Psalter* (*Cott. Tiberius C. vi*).

Other illuminated MSS. were produced, particularly in the eleventh century, but also later, at the two aforementioned monasteries of Winchester—the Old Minster or Priory of S. Swithin (most important is the *S. Swithin Psalter* of the first half of the twelfth century, now in the British Museum, *MS. Cotton. Nero C. iv*—Fig. IV-14*b*) and the New Minster (*Liber Vitae*, of the early eleventh century, also preserved in the British Museum, *MS. Stowe 944*; the *Grimbald Gospels*, of the same period, now in the British Museum, *Add. MS. 34890*). An interesting *Winchester Gospel-book* is preserved in the National Library at Paris (*Lat. 14782*). *See* also pp. 256 f.

Artistic MSS. in the same 'Winchester Style' were produced also in the monasteries of Durham, York (the *York Anglo-Saxon Gospels, c.* 1000, preserved in the York Minster Library), Bury St. Edmunds (the *Psalter Vat. Reg. Lat. 12*, and the eleventh-century *Bury Gospels*, British Museum, *Harl. MS. 76*), Peterborough, and especially in Christ Church, at Canterbury. To the latter is attributed a *Psalter* preserved in the British Museum (*Add. MS. 155*), which was written and illuminated between 1012 and 1023; it not only contains elaborate Winchester borders in dull colours and much gold, but—as O. E. Saunders has pointed out—also a miniature of S. Benedict giving his rule to his monks—, a rare example of a fully coloured figure-subject produced elsewhere than at Winchester. The leading authority Prof. F. Wormald (*Brit. Mus. Quart.*, IX-4, 1935, pp. 113 f.) has attributed to Christ Church, Canterbury, the Brit. Mus. *Cott. MS. Tiber. A. III*, and perhaps also Durh. Cath. *MS. B. iii. 32*, both belonging to the middle of the eleventh century; both are collections of miscellaneous matter with Anglo-Saxon glosses. The Durham Cathedral MS. contains the Latin hymnal, Proverbs, Canticles for Matins throughout the year, Aelfric's grammar, and part of S. Paulinus of Aquileia's hymn for S. Peter and S. Paul.

Richly illuminated Gospel-books intended for ceremonial use (such as the *Grimbald Gospels*, already referred to), Benedictionals, Pontificals, Sacramentaries and especially magnificent Service-books were produced at this time.

General Characteristics of Winchester Style

The Winchester style is quite different from the barbaric Anglo-Celtic style, which was based upon elaborate decoration rather than illustration. It is, in a certain way, a renaissance of the Graeco-Roman and Continental 'narrative tradition, but in a fresh, lively and delicate new form' (Oakeshott).

In the eleventh-century productions of the Winchester school, the structural bars of the border are often half-covered, and sometimes almost hidden, by the luxuriant foliage. Moreover, the medallions at the corners and sides are often almost absorbed in the rest of the decoration. One of the main exceptions is the *Arundel Psalter* already referred to.

In the twelfth century (p. 261 ff.)—see, for instance, the *Westminster Psalter*, late-twelfth century (preserved in the British Museum, *Royal 2. A. xxii*)—the free, decorative border died out (in the thirteenth century it was gradually revived, but in a totally different form); the medallions disappeared; and the miniatures were enclosed by severe borders. Thus, writes Saunders, nothing is left but shaded conventional leaf-designs enclosed between plain bars. These are more strictly picture frames than borders, and do not occur as free designs on a page containing writing.

Apart from the lesser initials referred to on p. 191, the initials used to introduce the Gospels or the principal divisions of the Psalms are generally elaborately decorated with conventional foliage, interlacing stems, and with heads of animals. They are painted in opaque colours, the colours employed being, generally speaking, violet, soft shades of blue, light green, yellow, pink shading to purple, vermilion, and gold. Outline drawing was mainly executed in brown ink and was lightly tinted with washes of colour; there are, however, exceptions in which coloured ink was employed without any touch with the brush.

In iconography, especially for scenes from the Bible, productions of the Carolingian schools (p. 202 ff.) were used as models. Also in the technique of drawing and colouring, the Winchester school was largely influenced by Carolingian styles, particularly by the schools of Rheims and Metz (p. 204 ff.).

Because of the apparent prejudice against monks receiving credit for their work as individuals, not many names of the illuminators have come down to us. Godeman, the illuminator of the *Benedictional of S. Aethelwold*, has already been referred to (p. 195). The names of two other illuminators of New Minster are known: they are Ethric and Wulfric, but very little else is known about them.

Influence of Utrecht Psalter

The later Winchester style, especially, was greatly influenced by the *Utrecht Psalter* (p. 205 f.). Already, *c.* A.D. 1000, a copy of it was produced at S. Augustine's Abbey at Canterbury, which is now preserved at the British Museum (*Harl. MS. 603*); whereas the original had no colour, in this copy inks were used for drawings. *Lat. 8846* in the National Library at Paris is another English copy of the *Utrecht Psalter*. Apparently there was another copy, now lost, which was the model of the *Eadwine Psalter*, produced in Canterbury about 1147–50 by the monk Eadwine, and now in Trinity College Library at Cambridge (*R.17.1*)—Fig. IV-14. This codex is also known as the *Canterbury Psalter*, but to avoid confusion —*see* p. 188—we prefer to use the term *Eadwine Psalter*. Some other English illuminated codices, such as the *Hildesheim Psalter* or *St. Albans Psalter*, produced at St. Albans in the twelfth century, are copied from similar models.

Various defects and mannerisms of the later Anglo-Saxon style, such as all marked exaggerations—hunched and distorted shoulders, necks stretched forwards, shrugging gestures, curved, jointless fingers, legs spindle-thin and dwindling to threadlike ankles—were borrowed from the *Utrecht Psalter* or similar works.

At the same time, the eleventh-century Anglo-Saxon drawings, 'full of life and movement', some having 'real gaiety and humour' (Oakeshott), the fluttering scarf-ends, the manner of indicating rocky ground by a series of swirls, have also been borrowed from the *Utrecht Psalter* school. The drawings 'are often heightened with colour, or executed in coloured inks', and rapid characterisation is 'achieved by a few lines or by the poise of the body' (Oakeshott).

Prudentius. Various other manuscripts that were produced in the Winchester style have already been discussed in other sections. Special mention must be made of the interesting copies of *Psychomachia*, by Prudentius, which have been discussed on p. 41 f. An eleventh-century copy from Bury St. Edmunds, preserved in the British Museum (*Add. MS. 24199*), is a good representative of the contemporary English art: the exaggerated gestures of the figures, the expressions on their faces, the movement of their garments, greatly contribute to the liveliness of the scenes. See Fig. I-14*b*.

ANGLO-SAXON CHRYSOGRAPHY

Chrysography appears to have been introduced into England in the latter half of the seventh century, when Wilfred, archbishop of York, caused to be made and presented to the monastery of Ripon a celebrated purple codex written in gold (*de auro purissimo in membranis depurpuratis coloratis*), but then it was *inauditum ante seculis nostris quoddam miraculum*. In 735 S. Boniface, writing to Eadburg, abbess of S. Mildred's, Thanet, asked her to get transcribed for him in gold the *Epistles* of S. Peter.

The preserved English MSS. written in gold are of a relatively late date, one of the earliest being the Latin *Hamilton Gospels* (or *King Henry VIII's Gospels*), formerly at Berlin, now in the Pierpont Morgan Library, New York; it is attributed to the eighth century. The *Benedictional of S. Aethelwold* (p. 194 f.) contains a page written in gold.

CAROLINGIAN ILLUMINATION

The late eighth and early ninth century A.D., with the reign of Charlemagne, mark the beginnings of a new period in the history of civilization and of European culture. While Charlemagne was reconstructing and consolidating the Western Empire, culture and art revived at his court, to which were invited men of learning, such as Alcuin of York (see *The Hand-produced Book*, p. 547), and Eginhard or Einhard (Charlemagne's historiographer, 770–840). Charlemagne—though he himself never wrote with ease—pursued a constant programme of building up a Christian civilization. Hence he gathered round his person the flower of European scholarship and culture: men—all ecclesiastics—from the British Isles, France, Italy, and Spain. Carolingian culture and art spread to the main centres of the Frankish Empire, and later to other countries, including the British Isles.

Among the most important documents of Carolingian art are the numerous manuscripts extant, which were written and illuminated under Charlemagne and his successors, and which thus belong to the late eighth and to the ninth centuries.

The productions of the Carolingian schools of illumination are rightly considered to be among the chief glories of Carolingian art.

Furthermore, the preservation of the Carolingian manuscripts is the more important as few of the wall-paintings (see, for instance, p. 204) and mosaics which decorated the churches built at that time have survived.

See now, W. Braunfels, D. Kœtzsche, G. Mœrsch, and others, *Karl der Grosse*, Aachen, 1965.

Origins of Carolingian Illumination

The origin of the Carolingian art of illumination has been investigated by various scholars, and particularly by the German authority on the subject, H. Janitschek. In his opinion, the colouring and drawing were mainly based on models reproduced in Hellenistic style, while the various elements of ornamentation and iconography were borrowed from the Anglo-Celtic (Chapter IV), Byzantine (Chapter II), Syrian (Chapter II), and Merovingian art-forms.

Merovingian Illumination (Fig. IV-15a). The *Sacramentarium*, or 'Sacramentary', played a great part in the Western Christian liturgy; it included the Evangeliary, the Epistolary, the Gradual, the Deacon- and sub-Deacon-book, the Hymnal, and the Prayerbook. At a later period, it became very fashionable, and in the thirteenth century it completely replaced the Missal. The *Sacramentarium Leonianum* (it is so called, because it was attributed to Pope Leo the Great, who died 461; but actually it was a liturgical collection of the first half of the sixth century) is the earliest extant sacramentary; it is preserved in an early seventh-century MS. (*Cod. Veron. 85*). The second-oldest is the *Sacramentarium Gelasianum*, which was attributed to Pope Gelasius (+496). Two codices (*Vat. Reg. 316* and *Paris Lat. 12048*) are excellent examples of the Gelasian Sacramentary. The so-called 'Gregorianised Gelasian Sacramentary' is preserved in the *Cod. Sangall. 348*, the *Sacramentaire d'Angoulême* (Nat. Libr., at Paris, *MS. Lat. 816*), the *Sacramentarium Fuldense*, of the tenth century, and the *Sacramentarium Rossianum*, of the eleventh century. Historically, the most important is the *Sacramentarium Gregorianum*, attributed to Pope Gregory the Great (+604)—exemplified by *Cod. Vat. Reg. 337*, of the ninth century. We may also refer to the *Sacramentarium Gallicanum* and to the sacramentaries of the liturgies of Ireland, Milan, the Mozarabic Church of Spain, and so on.

In this section on *Merovingian Illumination* it will suffice to refer to the two copies of the Gelasian Sacramentary, mentioned above, which may be regarded as representatives of Merovingian production. The *Sacramentarium Gelasianum Vat. Reg. 316* was executed about the middle of the eighth century in a scriptorium of N.-E. France. This beautiful codex once belonged to the Parisian Senator Petavius and later to Queen Christina of Sweden, with whose library it passed to the Vatican Library. The codex *Paris Lat. 12048* is generally known as *Sacramentarium of Gellone*. It dates from the second half of the eighth century (755–87?).

It has 270 leaves (300 × 180 mm.) and contains a great number of zoomorphic initials, typical of the Merovingian manuscripts of this period. In the opinion of V. Leroquais, it may be attributed to Flavigny Abbey (Diocese of Autun).

A *Gospel-book*, preserved in Autun (*MS. 4*), is another contemporary production of the Flavigny *scriptorium*. Several other *scriptoria* were active in the seventh and eighth centuries (though their artistic productions consisted mainly in initial-decoration: see further on). The preserved works come from Luxeuil, Fleury, Laon, Corbie, Amiens, Saint-Riquier, Mondsee, and a few other *scriptoria*.

With the same merciless cruelty in which the Angles and Saxons revelled in Britain, the Visigoths in Spain, and the Vandals in North Africa, all but exterminating what had remained of the Roman civilization in these countries, the princes of the Merovingians sought to exterminate whole families of rivals. The pagan outlook of the native tribes did not greatly change even after 496, when Clovis I was converted to Christianity. 'The pages of Gregory of Tours, who wrote in the second half of the sixth century, are full of assassination, rape and perjury' (Pevsner). The position was not much better even at the time of Charlemagne, who himself had grown up illiterate.

As a result, the Merovingian book-production was rather poor. On the whole, the illuminated manuscripts produced in the seventh and eighth centuries in Frankish and Lombard monasteries (*i.e.*, in Gaul and Northern Italy), completely differ from those of other countries. Only a few have figurative representations; ornamentation, mainly based on the art of the calligrapher, is restricted to initial letters with zoomorphic decoration in red, green and yellow, and to decorated pages. Examples are: a copy of S. Augustine, *Homilies*, produced in 669 in Luxeuil, and now in the Pierpont Morgan Library, New York (*M. 334*); two copies of Gregory of Tours, *History of the Franks*, preserved in the National Library at Paris—*Lat. 17655*, executed in the late seventh century in Luxeuil, and *Lat. 17654*, of the early eighth century, from a *scriptorium* in East France; a *Gallican Lectionary*, produced in Luxeuil in the seventh or eighth century (preserved in the National Library, *Lat. 9427*); a *Gospel-book*, of the early eighth century, from North France (preserved in the National Library, *Lat. 256*); a *Lives of the Prophets*, from Fleury, eighth or ninth century (preserved in the Orléans Municipal Library, *MS. 17*); *Homilies*, three volumes, mid-eighth century (preserved in the National Library, *Nouv. Acq. Lat. 1598-99* and Orléans, *MS. 154*); a *Gospel-book*—known as the *Gudohinus Evangeliar*—, executed in 751-54 in Burgundy (Fleury?), and preserved in the Autun Municipal Library (*MS. 3*); *MSS. 137* and *423* in the Laon Municipal Library (executed in Laon in the eighth century); eighth-century productions of Corbie (preserved in the National Library, *Lat. 3836, 11627, 12135, 12155*); Poitiers Municipal Library, *MS. 17*; Cambrai Municipal Library, *MS. 300*, and some others.

Of paramount significance is the celebrated codex *Leges barbarorum*, executed about 793 in the Besançon region and now preserved in the St. Gall Stiftsbibliothek, *No. 731*. Artistically the codex does not show any Carolingian influence, but it is related to continental pre-carolingian art.

CAROLINGIAN ILLUMINATION

It has been shown that compared with the simplicity of the script in Late Antique manuscripts, Merovingian and Lombard ornamentation 'is a complete revolution'. This art seems to have originated in southern Gaul and in Lombardy, and its beginnings are dated by some scholars as far back as the early seventh century. But it flourished mainly in the eighth century, particularly in the latter half of the century, after its transplantation to central and, especially, northern France, at a time when the Hiberno-Saxon art of book-illumination had reached its zenith. Indeed, 'the majority of the MSS. and especially those richest in decoration, arose in north France in the latter half of the eighth century' (Saunders).

Foreign Influences. With one or two exceptions, scholars agree that Carolingian illumination originated in the late eighth century under the influence of, or at least greatly influenced by, Hiberno-Saxon art which partly was brought to Tours by Alcuin of York. However, in the study of the human figure and in the extended use of gold, the Carolingian artists followed Byzantine and West-European (Continental) models. This resulted in the Carolingian style of illumination being of a mixed type, and combining the best elements of the 'Irish' and the Anglo-Saxon, as well as of the Hellenistic, Roman, Byzantine, Oriental, and Merovingian styles.

This opinion is held, in part, by the leading British authority on the subject, Prof. F. Wormald, who considers that the two main influences at work in Carolingian manuscript decoration were: (1) The influence of 'Insular' illuminated MSS., brought to the Continent by English and Irish missionaries in the eighth century—this can be seen most clearly in the MSS. of the Franco-Saxon school—and (2) Classical and Late Antique influences, which may be seen, for instance, in MSS. produced at Metz. However, other scholars—particularly the Belgian authority on the subject, F. Masai— disagree with this theory. In Monsieur Masai's opinion, both the Frankish and Northumbrian (commonly known as Hiberno-Saxon) arts of book-illumination are parallel and are of Italian origin; see p. 177.

However, it is in the Carolingian period that we first find books lavishly and systematically embellished.

The codices of this period are almost exclusively of a religious nature. The pure ornament outweighs the illustrations or miniatures; the latter generally relate to scenes or characters from the Gospels. Another outstanding characteristic of this art is the large and profusely embellished initial letters on most of the pages.

MAIN CLASSIFICATION OF CAROLINGIAN SCHOOLS

The manuscripts written and illuminated in Carolingian style have been classified into various groups or main schools, one of them being the so-called *Schola Palatina* (or 'Palace School') at Aachen, or Aix-la-Chapelle. It should, however, be borne in mind that this classification is far from certain, and that not all the nomenclature of these schools has been generally accepted. For instance, the earliest school which developed in the entourage of Charlemagne and which was mainly influenced by Oriental models, is generally called, following Janitschek's theory propounded in 1889, the 'Ada School', because its most famous production is the *Ada Gospels*, connected with Ada, otherwise hardly known, who is alleged to have been Charlemagne's sister. Other authorities call this school the 'Trèves School'. More recently, Jean Porcher, the *Conservateur en chef* of the *Cabinet des manuscrits* in the National Library at Paris, has suggested the term 'Rhine School', as its productions were executed in the three main centres of the Middle Rhine region, Trèves (or Trier), Mayence (or Mainz) and Aix-la-Chapelle (or Aachen), where Charlemagne and his *entourage* usually resided.

Moreover, the list of 'schools' is far from complete. Now and then the existence of some new school has been suggested. Recently Prof. Wilhelm Koehler has identified a Liége school (Flemish), which imitated the Rheims style. This group of Liége manuscripts would include the ninth- or tenth-century *Gospel-book* of the Pierpont Morgan Library (*M. 640*), the *Gospels of Notger* (bishop of Liége, 972–1008), preserved in the University of Liége, the ninth- or tenth-century *Gospels* of The John Rylands Library, Manchester (*MS. 10*), and a *Sacramentary* at Leningrad (*MS. Q.v.1—No. 41*).

The classification of the Carolingian schools into the following two groups is that which is generally adopted, the first group being the Carolingian proper.

(1) To this group belong the schools situated mainly in France and on the left bank of the Rhine, but also in German, Italian and Catalonian lands. These schools flourished until the middle of the ninth century. The main schools of this group were the abbeys or monasteries of Tours, Trier or Trèves, Rheims, Metz, the Franco-Saxon school in Northern France (Saint-Denis, Amiens, Chartres, Saint-Amand, Noyon, Arras, and other centres), Corbie; the early schools of Fulda and St. Gall; the early schools of North and Central Italy, and of Catalonia.

(2) The second group consists mainly of the schools in German lands (see p. 218 f.), which flourished in the second half of the tenth and in the eleventh century, *i.e.*, from the Ottonian period onwards, when the Holy Roman Emperors (Otto I, or the Great, who reigned from 936 to 937, and his successors) resided in Germany. In the tenth century, indeed, Carolingian book-illumination was introduced into Germany, where new schools arose, or old schools began to show characteristics of their own, especially in stylization of form. Thus developed the calligraphic mannerisms of the later German art of book-illumination. The Ottonian centres of illumination will mainly be discussed on p. 218 ff.

Masterpieces of Carolingian Illumination

The most famous products of the Carolingian and Ottonian schools of book-illumination are the following:

Rhine School (Fig. IV-15*b*, 16*a*, 17). The most precious Carolingian codices, mainly written in gold, and often on purple-stained vellum, were produced in the *Scriptorium of Trèves*; these MSS. were mainly written for, or on the orders of, Charlemagne and members of his family. Byzantine influence is here very strong. Among the most celebrated codices of this school are:

The celebrated *Ada Gospels* of the Trèves Civic Library (*Cod. No. 22*), end of the eighth century, produced for the Abbess Ada, who, according to tradition, was Charlemagne's sister. The *Charlemagne* or *Godescalc Evangeliarium* (preserved in the National Library at Paris, *Nouv. Acq. Lat. 1203*), written in the Mainz diocese between 781 and 783 by Godescalc, on Charlemagne's order, for him and his wife, Hildegarde, who died in 783. It is the most ancient, the most precious and the most famous of the Carolingian manuscripts which have been preserved. It is written in gold on purple vellum, in uncial characters (except the dedication, which is written in Caroline minuscule), and contains six full-page miniatures (the Evangelists; Christ; and the Fountain of Life, which appears for the first time in the West), a title-page (f. 4) in capital letters with decorated initials, a Calendar and Easter tables (f. 121*v*–126), where a note, written in rustic capitals, relates that in 781 Charlemagne was in Rome and the Pope baptized his son Pepin.

The *Dagulph Psalter*, a masterpiece preserved in the Vienna National Library (*Cod. No. 1861: Theol. 652*), written between 783 and 795, and presented by Charlemagne to Pope Adrian I (772–95). This magnificent codex is also known as *Psalterium aureum Caroli Magni*. Executed for Charlemagne, it was probably written in the Schola Palatina, at Aachen, by the calligrapher Dagulf. The letters are partly in gold, partly in silver, but mainly in *minium*. Its excellent ivory binding is at Paris in the Louvre (Départ. d. Objets d'Art, Iv. 9/10). Fig. IV-15*b* and 16*a*. In A. Boeckler's opinion (*Deutsche Buchmalerei vorgotischer Zeit*, n. 12), the Wuerzburg *Gospels* (*Univ. Libr., MS. theol. fol. 66*), produced at Wuerzburg about 800, belongs to an important artistic branch related to the Ada Gospels.

The *S.-Riquier Gospel-book* (executed *c.* 800 and preserved in the Abbeville Municipal Library, *MS. 4*), was apparently presented by Charlemagne to Angilbert, the Abbot of Saint-Riquier (790–814). It is written in gold uncials on purple vellum, and contains four full-page miniatures of the Evangelists, Canon Tables, initials in gold and colours, and medallions. The *S.-Médard Gospel-book* (preserved in the National Library at Paris, *Lat. 8850*), which in 827 was presented by Louis I le Débonnaire and his wife Judith to Angilbert, Abbot of Saint-Médard de Soissons, is regarded as the most luxurious codex of this group. It is entirely in gold uncials, and contains several full-page miniatures, Canon Tables, initials, or initial words, in gold and silver on purple ground, and so on.

The *S.-Martin-des-Champs Gospels*, or the *Golden Gospels* or *Charlemagne Gospels* (preserved in the Arsenal Library, Paris, *MS. 599*), of the early ninth century, is written entirely in gold minuscules, and contains the Canon Tables, large initials in gold and silver on purple ground, etc. Finally, the *Lorsch Evangeliarium* (preserved partly in the Vatican Library, *Cod. Pal. Lat. 50*, and partly at Alba Julia, Rumania: Alba Julia, the ancient Apulum, the Hungarian Gyula Fehérvár and the German Karlsburg, is situated to the south of Klausenburg or

Clŭj, Siebenbürgen or Transilvania), of the ninth century, is an elegant MS. which represents, however, the beginning of the decay of the Trèves school: Fig. IV-17.

In the Ottonian period (see further on), the Trèves (or Trier) *scriptorium* receives a new lease of life. An illuminated copy of the *Registrum Gregorii*, executed in Trèves *c.* 983, is still preserved in this city (Munic. Libr., MS. *1711/626*): the codex was donated by Archbishop Egbert (see also p. 219 f.); a detached leaf, preserved in the Condé Museum, Chantilly, represents Otto II with the personifications of four provinces (*Germania, Francia, Italia, Alemannia*) rendering homage. In Prof. Boeckler's opinion, the portrait of the Emperor is the most imposing in all Ottonian illumination. It was copied in later times—see p. 228.

A contemporary, but different, school of Trèves is represented by an *Evangeliarium* from S. Maria ad Martyres (at Trèves), now preserved at Koblenz (State Archives, *Cod. 701*). It contains a majestic miniature of Christ, copied from a great ninth-century Bible of the school of Tours (see pp. 206 f.).

Schola Palatina (Fig. IV-16b). This name was given by Janitschek on the assumption that the *scriptorium* of Aachen was more directly connected with the artists of Charlemagne's court. The products of this school show little ornamentation but much illustration. In this respect they are similar to those of Graeco-Roman book-illustration (see p. 30 ff.). Some authorities—such as Jean Porcher, have suggested a relationship between the *Schola Palatina* (as well as the Rheims school) and wall-paintings, still preserved, of Carolingian churches, particularly of the crypt in the ancient Abbey of Saint-Germain, Auxerre (Yonne).

One of the best specimens to show the derivation from models based on ancient originals in Late Antique style is the *Charlemagne Gospel-book*, which is said to have been found in the tomb of the Emperor. The superb codex, written on purple-stained vellum, is preserved in the Vienna Treasury (*Cod. No. 7621*). Two other famous products of this school are: the *Aachen Gospel-book*, preserved in the Treasury of Aachen (or Aix-la-Chapelle) Cathedral, which was written and illuminated in the early ninth century, and the roughly contemporary *Xanten Gospel-book*, preserved in the Royal Library at Brussels (*Cod. No. 18723*, formerly *462*). Fig. IV-16b.

Scriptorium of Rheims (Fig. IV-18): This was strictly connected in style with the *Schola Palatina*. The earliest known work of this school is the *Épernay* or *Ebbon Gospel-book* (preserved in Épernay Municipal Library, MS. *1*), written in gold minuscules and containing several full-page miniatures, decorated Canon Tables, initials in gold and colours, etc. It also contains (in gold rustic capitals) the dedication of Abbot Peter de Hautvillers to Ebbon, archbishop of Rheims (816–45). Other important productions of the Rheims school are: a *Psalter* of the mid-ninth century (Troyes Cathedral); contemporary *Gospel-books* in the Rheims Municipal Library (MS. 7) and in the Duesseldorf City Library (MS. 113); the *Loisel Gospels*, executed between 845 and 882, and the ninth-century *Blois Gospels*, both preserved in the National Library (*Lat. 17968* and *265*); the *Celestin Gospels* of the mid-ninth century (preserved in Arsenal Library, *MS. 1171*); and several Gospel-books of the second half of the ninth century, including the *S. Frambourg Gospels* (preserved in S. Geneviève Library, *MS. 1190*) and the *Morienval Gospels* (Noyon Cathedral), and others, such as Rheims Municipal Library, *MS. 11*, and National Library, *Lat. 17969*.

A *Gospel-book*, preserved in the Pierpont Morgan Library (*M. 728*), is written in fine minuscule script on burnished gold, and contains four full-page miniatures, four ornamented introductory pages, and ornamented Canon Tables, all in gold, silver and colours. It is according to Miss Dorothy Miner 'certainly the most monumental example of Carolingian painting' in the U.S.A. The MS. was executed in the diocese of Rheims under Archbishop Hincmar (845–82). The miniatures represent the Evangelists; they are 'based closely on late classical models, but the modelling in light and shade, which merely gives solidity to ancient painting, is here handled in a tensely dynamic manner'. The Canon Tables are ornamented with a more fluid and impressionistic version of this characteristic Rheims style, the vivacious poses and rapid technique giving great liveliness to the classical satyrs and other creatures that clamber over the pediments and columns. The ornamental introductory pages show large golden strap-work initials and archaic capitals, mostly on backgrounds of purple: Fig. IV-18a.

Two interesting copies of Latin works come from Rheims: a ninth-century MS. of Terence, *Comedies* (preserved in the National Library, *Lat. 7899*), copied from a fifth-century MS.; and a late ninth-century Prudentius, *Psychomachia* (preserved in the National Library, *Lat. 8085*), copied from a fifth- or sixth-century MS. See also pp. 40 and 41.

A fine codex, the *Collectio canonum Dionysiana* (now preserved in the Vallicelliana Library at Rome, *Cod. D. 4. 5*) is a copy of a Roman book. It contains two great full-page miniatures and a great number of initials. It is attributed to the Rheims *scriptorium*.

One of the most famous products of the Carolingian schools is the *Utrecht Psalter*, i.e., a Latin Psalter preserved in the University Library of Utrecht (*Cod. No. 32*); in this superb work, the agitated movements of the pen-drawings, according to the Italian authority Pietro Toesca, are almost beyond comparison with any other illuminated MS. of Western art. Indeed, unlike the usual elaborated miniatures of Carolingian manuscripts, the drawings of the *Utrecht Psalter* are really sketches which give the appearance of having been executed with great speed and lightness. Also, unlike other Western Psalters, it gives a full illustration of the text of each Psalm, and takes symbolism literally. Its influence on the late Anglo-Saxon school has already been mentioned (p. 197 f.): Fig. IV-18b.

The origin and date of this masterpiece have been a matter of controversy, but the opinion most generally held is that it was probably written and illustrated in the ninth century in Northern France, and it seems to be a product of the school of Rheims, although it also reflects the style of a much earlier manuscript. Indeed, there can be no doubt that it is a copy of an older manuscript: the script in which the whole codex is written would suffice to dispel any such doubt. It is in rustic capitals 'in the last stage of its existence', and—as E. M. Thompson has pointed out—it reproduces the rustic capital writing of the archetype apparently as the best method of maintaining the exact relative positions of text and drawings. There was indeed, by this time, no practical reason for continuing the use of rustic capitals; the less cumbersome, but still not altogether convenient uncial hand having been in full use for some centuries. Moreover, as Prof. Wormald has remarked, also the number of columns to the page supports the theory that the *Utrecht Psalter* is the copy of a much older manuscript.

The *Utrecht Psalter* was for a time in England (British Museum, *Cott. Claudius. C. vii*).

The Rheims school influenced some provincial *scriptoria* of North-East France. This influence may be recognized in a *Gospel-book* strictly allied with the *Loisel Gospels*, which is preserved in the Pierpont Morgan Library, New York (*M. 640*). It contains two Evangelist-portraits and four ornamented initial pages. The portraits are drawn with brown outline, with washes of light brown brushed in to intensify the modelling. Dull gold picks out the halo, footstool, lectern, etc. (D. Miner).

A *Gospel-book*, of 860–70, from N. France, in the classical style of Rheims is preserved in the Schnuetgen-Museum at Cologne.

In South Germany there was another *scriptorium* influenced by the Rheims school. A good example of this centre is a *Gospel-book* of c. 875 preserved in the Walters Art Gallery, Baltimore (*W. 4*). It contains the portraits of the four Evangelists (with a strong reflection of the late Classical prototypes), and ornamented Canon Tables: Fig. IV-19a.

Scriptorium of Tours (Fig. IV-19b–c): One of its best products is the *Vivian Bible* or *First Bible of Charles the Bald*, now preserved in the National Library at Paris (*Lat. 1*). This splendid work was written and illuminated c. 846, its archetype being attributed to the fifth century A.D. (see p. 72). There are 423 pages, measuring 49·5 by 37·5 cm. (nearly $19\frac{1}{2}$ by $14\frac{3}{4}$ in.), and containing as many as eighty large painted initials. The illumination of this codex shows much stronger influence of Hellenistic models than do other important products of this school. These are: The *Evangeliarium of Emperor Lothaire I* (795–855), which was written between 849 and 851 under the direction of Sigislaus, and is preserved in the Paris National Library (*Lat. 266*); the *Sacramentarium of Marmoutier* (preserved in Autun Municipal Library, *Cod. 19 bis*), of c. 850, which was written for Abbot Rainaud of Marmoutier; and a copy of Apicius, *De re coquinaria*, preserved in the Vatican Library (*Urb. Lat. 1146*).

The earliest illuminated codex produced in Tours is a *Gospel-book*, of c. 800, executed in the time of Alcuin (see *The Hand-produced Book*, p. 513). Other Tours productions are: the *Rorgon Bible*, of c. 835, in the National Library (*Lat. 3*): it was presented by Count Rorgon, Charlemagne's son-in-law, to the Abbey of S. Maur-de-Glanfeuil; the *S. Gauzelin Gospels*, of the second quarter of the ninth century (preserved in Nancy Cathedral); the *Laon Gospels* (preserved in Laon Municipal Library, *MS. 63*) and the *Dufay Gospels* (preserved in the National Library, Paris, *Lat. 9385*), of the mid-ninth century; the *Mans Gospels* (preserved in the National Library, Paris, *Lat. 261*) of the second half of the ninth century; two *Sacramentaries* of the late ninth century or the early tenth (preserved in the National Library, *Nouv. Acq. Lat. 1589,* and Tours Municipal Library, *MS. 684*); and perhaps also two ninth-century *Gospel-books* in the National Library (*Lat. 9386* and *11959*).

An interesting tenth-century MS. of Prudentius is preserved in the National Library (*Lat. 8318*, fol. 49–64); it is a copy from a sixth-century Oriental MS.

On the whole, it may be noted that the influence of the Hiberno-Saxon style of illumination is very strong. It may be seen particularly in the decoration of the miniatures, although a certain influence of models based on Hellenistic originals is evident.

The magnificent *Grandval Bible* (preserved in the British Museum, *Add. MS. 10546*) and the splendid *Vivian Bible* (Paris, National Library, *Lat. 1*) have been referred to on pp. 72 and 85.

The '*Alcuin Bible*' (so called from a *carmen*, now lost, which was contained at the end of the MS.), of the ninth century, preserved in Rome (Vallicelliana Library, *MS. B. 6*), is by Rand considered a product in the Franco-Saxon style of the Tours *scriptorium*. In the opinion of other scholars (Koehler, Micheli, and others) it shows characteristics of the Rheims school. It contains ornamental Eusebian Canons and a number of initials with zoomorphic motifs, either in pen-drawing or coloured in red, green, and yellow.

The Walters Art Gallery, Baltimore (*W. 3*), possesses a *Gospel-book*, executed in the late tenth century in a North French provincial atelier influenced by various Carolingian schools, particularly that of Tours. It contains one drawing, four ornamented initial pages and twelve ornamented Canon Tables. In Miss D. Miner's opinion, like most of the provincial works of the period, it depends upon a few colours: orange, yellow ochre, lavender, light green, and a dull blue: Fig. IV-22a.

One of the most original schools of illuminations was developed in the *Scriptorium of Metz* (Fig. IV-19d), its main characteristics being richly decorated initials, including little picturesque scenes. There was, however, a certain stylistic affinity with the products of the school of Rheims. Most famous of its products is the luxurious *Drogo Sacramentarium* (preserved in the National Library at Paris, *Lat. 9428*), which was written *c.* 850, for Drogo, Charlemagne's son and bishop of Metz from 826 to 855. There are 130 pages measuring 26·6 by 21·4 cm. (nearly 10½ by 8½ in.), and containing numerous beautiful historiated initials.

Another important codex of this school is the *Gospel-book of Louis le Débonnaire*. This codex, also known as the *Metz Evangeliarium*, is preserved in the National Library at Paris (*Lat. 9388*), and contains 196 pages, each measuring 32 by 24·5 cm. (about 12⅗ by 9⅝ in.). Thr *Drogo Sacramentarium* and the *Metz Evangeliarium* are closely related to each other, and apparently show Classical and Late Antique influences. Wormald has pointed out that the splendid symbol of S. Luke—on fol. *99 verso* of the *Metz Evangeliarium*—whose golden wing sweeps up to meet the swishing tail, forms a monumental letter Q which has no contact with Insular illumination.

Other Metz Gospel-books are preserved in the National Library; they are *Lat. 8849* and *9383* of the ninth century, and *Lat. 9390* and *9393* of the tenth century.

The products of the *Franco-Saxon school* show strong influence of the 'Hiberno-Saxon' style; this influence can be seen most clearly in the *Second Bible of Charles the Bald*, especially in its initials. Indeed, according to Wormald, both the shapes of the letters and the ornamental details—such as biting animals—are derived from Insular manuscripts. This superb codex, executed between 871 and 877, is now preserved in the National Library at Paris (*Cod. Lat. 2*). There are 444 pages, measuring 43 by 33·5 cm. (17 1/10 by 13⅖ in.), and containing 74 large painted initials: Fig. IV-22*b*.

Apart from the codex just mentioned, as many as eighteen preserved codices were assigned to the Franco-Saxon school by the French scholar L. Delisle. Of these, the following illuminated manuscripts may be mentioned: the *Evangeliarium of Saint Vaast d'Arras* (preserved in the Municipal Library at Arras, *MS. 233*), assigned to the second half of the ninth century; the roughly contemporary *Evangeliarium* (preserved in the National Library at Paris, *Cod. Lat. 257*), known as the *Gospel-book of Francis II* (1544–60), on whose order the codex was bound; the *S. Matthew Gospel* (preserved in Boulogne Municipal Library, *MS. 12*); ninth-century Sacramentaries: the *Cambrai Sacramentary* (preserved in Cambrai Municipal Library, *MS. 162*), the *S.-Denis Sacramentary* (preserved in the National Library, *Lat. 2290*), and the *Noyon Sacramentary* (Rheims, *MS. 213*); also several *Gospel-books*, preserved in the following collections: National Library (*Lat. 11956*); Tours (*MS. 23*); Grand Séminaire, Meaux; Lyons Municipal Library (*MS. 431*); Valenciennes (*MS. 69*), all of the ninth century; the tenth-century *Gospels* in Cambrai, *MS. 327*; in the S. Croix church, Gannat; and in the National Library (*Nouv. Acq. Lat. 305*); and an eleventh-century *Gospels* in the Arsenal Library (*MS. 592*).

The *Corbie school* (Fig. IV-20), also, shows strong Anglo-Saxon influences; it is known that English monks worked at Corbie in the late eighth century. A famous product of the Corbie school, already referred to on p. 72, is the *Great Bible of S. Paolo fuori le Mura*, at Rome. It is the richest MS. of the Carolingian period: it is uncertain whether this codex, which was executed about 880 by the Frank calligrapher Ingobertus, was dedicated to Charles II, who reigned 875–7, or Charles III ('the Fat') who reigned 881–7.

Another precious MS. of the Corbie school is the *Codex Aureus*, which the Emperor Arnulf (late ninth century) presented to the monastery of S. Emmeram (Ratisbon), and which is now preserved in the State Library at Munich (*Cod. Lat.*

14000); it was produced at Corbie *c*. 870. The codex measures 403 × 304 mm. It is written in gold letters and contains many full-page miniatures and decorated pages, initials and border decorations. It is based on an *Evangeliarum* by Alcuin of the Tours school (see p. 206 f.), which is now lost.

A luxurious volume written by Liuthard between 842 and 869, and preserved in the National Library (*Lat. 1152*), is known as the *Psalter of Charles the Bald*. The National Library also possesses the following Corbie productions: a *Sacramentary* of the second half of the ninth century (*Lat. 1141*), the contemporary *Noailles Gospels* (*Lat. 323*), the *Nonantola Sacramentary* (*Lat. 2292*), of the ninth century, and a ninth-century *Gospel-book* (*Lat. 324*).

In Prof. Wormald's opinion, the MSS. of the Corbie school show a compromise between the two extremes of the *scriptorium* of Metz (whose products, as has already been pointed out, show strong Classical and Late Antique influences), and of the Franco-Saxon school, which was strongly influenced by Insular illumination. He mentions, for instance, the Gospel-book of the school of Corbie, which is known as the *Evangeliarium of Claude Fauchet* (preserved in the National Library at Paris, *Lat. 270*), in which the shape of the initials has a Franco-Saxon source, while the border and general planning of the pages is derived from Late Antique MSS. This codex was restored and partly re-painted by Claude Fauchet (1530–1601).

Some Corbie productions are in a different style altogether. To this group belong a *Psalter* in Amiens (*MS. 18*), of the early ninth century; a copy of *Joshua* and *Ruth*, in Amiens (*MS. 7*); and two ninth-century *Sacramentaries* in the National Library (*Lat. 12050* and *12051*).

Minor Schools and Codices of uncertain Provenance. The *Theodulphus Bible* (preserved in the National Library, *Lat. 9380*), of the early ninth century, was executed in Orléans or Fleury, under the direction of Theodulphus, bishop of Orléans and Abbot of Fleury. Another illuminated copy is preserved in the Treasury of Puy Cathedral. Various works were produced in Fleury: a *Gospel-book*, of *c*. 800 (Tours, *MS. 22*); a copy of Terence, *Comedies*, ninth century (preserved in the National Library, *Lat. 7900*); a copy of Isidore of Seville, *De natura rerum*, ninth century (preserved in the National Library, *Lat. 5543*); a copy of Martianus Capella, tenth century (preserved in the National Library, *Lat. 7900 A*).

Saint-Amand productions are: an *Apocalypse*, late ninth century (preserved in the National Library, *Nouv. Acq. Lat. 1132*); a copy of Prudentius, *Psychomachia*, ninth century, Valenciennes Municipal Library (*MS. 412*).

St.-Germain-des-Prés(?): An important MS., preserved in Stuttgart (Württembergische Landesbibliothek, *Bibl. fol. 23*), has been by W. Koehler attributed to the St.-Germain-des-Prés scriptorium. It is a Psalter executed about 820–30; it measures 265 × 175 mm., and contains 168 leaves. The text is written in minuscules (in two hands); each Psalm begins with a decorated initial and a line in capital or uncial style. There are numerous illuminations representing Old and New Testament scenes: these seem to go back to a sixth-century prototype.

The following three *Gospel-books* were produced in Brittany: Alençon Municipal Library, *MS. 84*, of the ninth century; Boulogne Municipal Library, *MS. 8*, of the ninth century; and Troyes Municipal Library, of the early tenth century. A *Benedictine Psalter*, produced in the mid-ninth century in a North-Eastern *scriptorium*, perhaps in the Abbey of S. Rémy de Sens, is preserved in the Angers Municipal Library (*MS. 18*). Autun Municipal Library, *MS. 5*, a ninth-century *Gospel-book*, was perhaps executed in the Autun *scriptorium*; and Laon Municipal Library, *MS. 422*, a copy of Isidore of Seville, *De natura rerum*, also of the ninth century, may have come from the Laon *scriptorium*.

National Library, *Lat. 1979* and *4404*, both of the ninth century, have been tentatively attributed to *scriptoria* in South France. The provenance of Rheims, *MS. 10* (a *Gospel-book* of the mid-ninth century); National Library, *Lat. 9384* and *9387* (ninth-century *Gospel-books*); Cambrai, *MS. 386*, and Valenciennes, *MS. 99* (ninth-century copies of the *Apocalypse*), and of several other Carolingian MSS. is uncertain.

Cologne Scriptorium: Assuming that the *Gospel-book* preserved in Cologne Cathedral Library (*MS. fol. 56*) is of local origin, this school was strongly influenced by the Byzantine style.

Scriptorium of Fulda (Fig. III-22c). Among its earlier products mention may be made of *Gospels*, belonging to the second quarter of the ninth century, and preserved in the University Library at Wuerzburg (*Ms. Theol. fol. 66*): its style seems to be related to the style of the Ada group (see p. 203), but it shows also Graeco-Italian influences. Slightly later and in a different style is the *Erlangen Evangeliarium*, preserved in the University Library of Erlangen (*Cod. No. 141*), which was written *c.* 870; and the MS. preserved in the Vatican Library (*Reg. Lat. 124*) of *De Laudibus S. Crucis* by Hrabanus Maurus (*c.* 776–856), who was abbot of the monastery of Fulda in the first half of the ninth century. Another copy of this work, also a ninth-century production of the Fulda *scriptorium*, is preserved in the National Library at Turin (*MS. K. II. 20*). A still later copy—early tenth century—of English production is preserved in Trinity College, Cambridge (*MS. B. 16. 3*).

Later products may be exemplified by the *Codex Wittekindeus*, written in the latter half of the tenth century and preserved in the State Library at Berlin (*Theol. Lat. Fol. 1*); the *Goettingen Sacramentarium*, also in Berlin (*Theol. Lat. Fol. 231*), written *c.* 975; another *Sacramentarium* of the tenth century, preserved in the State Library, at Munich (*Lat. Mon. 10077*); a fragmentary *Lectionary*, preserved in the Court Library at Aschaffenburg (*MS. 2*); a fragmentary *Sacramentary* in the State Library at Berlin (*Theol. Lat. Fol. 192*)—both of the last thirty years of the tenth century; and the *Sacramentarium Fuldense*, written about the middle of the eleventh century, and preserved in the Vatican Library (*Vat. Lat. 3548*).

Among the most outstanding products of the *St. Gall School*, with its particular predilection for ornamentation, there are two luxurious Psalters of the ninth century, preserved in the St. Gall Chapter Library (*Codd. 22* and *23*), i.e., the *Psalterium Aureum*, written between 872 and 920, and the *Folcardus Psalter*, written between 841 and 872: Fig. IV-22d.

A copy of Wandalbert's *Martyrology* (preserved in the Vatican Library, *Reg. Lat. 438*) is an example of other religious works, whereas a copy of Prudentius (see pp. 41 f.), *Psychomachia* (preserved in the Civic Library at Berne, *MS. 264*) may represent St. Gall's secular book-production. Both manuscripts belong to the last quarter of the ninth century.

The later manuscripts of St. Gall, produced in the late tenth and in the eleventh and twelfth centuries show strong influences of the schools of Reichenau and Salzburg (see further on).

(Finally, even as late as in the sixteenth century excellent illumination was produced in St. Gall—we may refer to the *Antifonarium* of 1544 preserved in the St. Gall Chapter Library (*Cod. 541*).)

Italian Carolingian schools (see also p. 294): famous MSS. produced in Carolingian style are the following: the *Ambrosian Psalter* of the Vatican Library (*Vat. Lat. 83*), written in the late tenth century, which shows strong Anglo-Saxon influences. A similar style may be seen in the *Munich Psalter* of the early eleventh century, preserved in the State Library at Munich (*Lat. 343*). The *Gospel-book of Matilda*, Countess of Tuscany (1046–1115), preserved in the Pierpont Morgan Library, New York, shows certain influences of the schools of St. Gall and Reichenau. Of great interest are the miniatures of the *Register* of the church of Tivoli (Vatican Archives, *A.A. Arm. I–XVIII. 3658*), and those of the *Bobbio Missal*, which is preserved in the Ambrosian Library, Milan (*D. 84, inf.*).

Catalan schools. Spanish book-illumination is discussed on page 164 ff. Here we may note that in Catalonia, or the *Marca Hispanica*, conquered by the Franks, a new school was developed which produced illuminated codices in Carolingian style, although showing influences of the Visigothic style in drawing, and of the Arabic style in colouring and in the drawings of arches and palms, and so forth. The most outstanding products of this school are two famous Bibles—the tenth-century *Bible of S. Peter of Ronda*, preserved in the National Library at Paris (*Lat. 6*), and the so-called *Farfa Bible*, preserved in the Vatican Library (*Vat. Lat. 5729*), which was written in the tenth or the eleventh century at S. Maria of Ripoll (North Catalonia): Fig. IV-21.

Concerning the later Catalan illumination, at least one must here be referred to, the *Breviary of Martin d'Aragon*. This magnificent codex was written and illuminated for Martin I, the last king of Aragon of the Catalan branch (1395–1410). A great bibliophile, he himself gave exact instructions for the production of this breviary. The liturgy of the breviary is that of the Cistercian abbey of Poblet, near Barcelona; the Aragon kings are buried here. The volume, formerly in the Paris Rothschild Collection, in 1949 was given by Baron Henri de Rothschild to the National Library, Paris (now, *Rothschild 2529*).

The codex, measuring 351 × 252 mm., contains 451 leaves, including five full-page miniatures, 24 half-page, 68 small illuminations and many hundreds of borders and initials illuminated in gold and in colour. Like the contemporary Catalan art, this volume is strongly influenced by the art of Italy, with which Catalonia was then bound by political and commercial ties. Moreover, the breviary shows also strong French influences. At the same time, the style of the compositions, the 'solid gravity', the vivacity of the colours, the richness of the border decorations, and several other characteristics—in the opinion of Jean Porcher—are rather Catalan. *See*, particularly, J. Porcher, *Le Bréviaire de Martin d'Aragon*, Paris, 1950(?).

Chrysography (Fig. IV-24b)

Chrysography, or gold-writing, has already been discussed, and it has been indicated that most of the large libraries possess MSS. written in gold. In the Carolingian period a fresh impetus was given to such luxurious writing, and to this period belong a great number of preserved MSS.—see p. 203 ff. and *passim*.

Two beautiful codices written in gold are in the British Museum; they are *Gospels*, the previously mentioned *Codex Aureus* (Harl. *MS. 2788*), in uncial letters, and *Harl. MS. 2797*, written in minuscule script. The former is a very fine manuscript of *c.* A.D. 800, and contains miniatures of the Evangelists, and illuminated borders; the latter, belonging to the ninth century, comes from the monastery of S. Geneviève, at Paris. In the British Museum there are, in addition, a few beautiful leaves written in gold and contained in *Cotton MS. Tiberius A. ii* which the Emperor Otto presented to King Athelstan.

A superb Latin *Gospel-book*, written throughout in burnished gold uncial letters upon leaves dyed purple, is preserved in the Pierpont Morgan Library, New York (*M. 23*). It contains 144 leaves. Its ample format (14½ by 10½ in.), the beauty of its script, and the colours of its pages are outstanding. 'The pages range in shade from royal purple to tones of blue and of rose-lavender, the opposing pages being carefully matched in colour' (D. Miner). Authorities now attribute it to North France and date it to the early ninth century.

An illuminated Latin Psalter, written in golden Caroline minuscules, is preserved in the Bodleian Library, Oxford (*Douce MS. 59*). Finally, there are the Latin *Gospels* at Paris, written for Charlemagne by Godescalc (see p. 203); a Latin *Gospels* at Vienna; the *Psalterium Aureum* of St. Gall (see p. 210 f.); the *Codex Aureus* of Stockholm (see p. 188 f.), and many other MSS. already referred to.

Gold writing as a practice died out in the thirteenth century, although there are several later cases (*see* Index, under *Chrysography*).

Decadence of Art

Carolingian book-illumination taken as a whole cannot be considered the real start of West European illumination. It appears—to use Prof. N. Pevsner's words with regard to architecture—a premature flowering doomed to wither under the grim frosts of the later ninth and the tenth centuries. Less than thirty years after Charlemagne's death, in 843, the Empire was divided. France and Germany henceforth took separate courses. But internal struggles, earl against earl, duke against duke, shook both. And from outside, the Vikings ravaged the North-West; the Hungarians menaced the East; the Saracens the South. No progress was possible in art and architecture. What we know is almost as primitive as Merovingian work, although forms taken up under Charlemagne and his immediate successors were still used. But the spirit in which they were used was blunt and crude. Indeed, the period between about 850 and 950—concludes Pevsner—seems even more barbaric than the pre-Carolingian centuries. (See also p. 200 f.)

Strictly speaking, the West-European decadence in art was not general: there was always a region where art continued to flourish or linger on, or even only started to flourish. There was always a branch of art—such as book-illumination—in which here and there superb specimens were produced.

GERMANY: OTTONIAN ILLUMINATION

The decay of the Carolingian dynasty, accompanied and followed by generally troubled times in the former Carolingian Empire, was the main cause of the decadence of the Carolingian art of illumination.

OTTONIAN RENAISSANCE

Amidst the general anarchy which seemed likely to make Western Europe the prey of the Norsemen, the Magyars, and the Slavs, the first movement of reorganisation came from Germany, which for the first time began to take the leading place in West European political power and cultural achievement. In 962 Otto I was crowned Holy Roman Emperor. By the twelfth century the German Empire became the principal power in Europe; France, Italy, England, Spain were all more or less secondary.

The three emperors—Otto I the Great (912–73), Otto II (955–83), and Otto III (980–1002)—give the name of 'Ottonian' to the period immediately succeeding the Carolingian. They not only ruled Germany, but had much to do with the ruling of Italy. The death of Otto III (in 1002), who was succeeded by Henry II the Saint (973–1024), did not materially affect the steady advance of German culture and art. It was but natural that Germany should become predominant in art, as she was in politics. Also the illumination of books was drawn away from the great French centres and began to adopt new trends from the various leading cities of Germany such as Bamberg, which the Ottos had made their capital. It was, indeed, a Renaissance, an awakening in art as well as in literature and social life. Nor did its glory fade until eclipsed by the succeeding rivalries of France and Italy.

HIBERNO-SAXON, CAROLINGIAN AND OTTONIAN

The Carolingian centres of book production in German lands became the main Continental centres of illumination. The immigration in 963 of Greek artists and the introduction of Greek fashions greatly influenced the splendour of monastic illumination. A fresh impetus was given in 972 after the marriage of Otto II to the Byzantine princess Theophano, daughter of Romanos II (959–63).

Illustrious Women

The tenth century seems to have been an age of illustrious women in Germany. Otto I's mother, Matilda, was the patroness of cloister-schools for women. The women's cloisters of Germany and the Netherlands were then most active centres of learning and book-production. Otto's sister Matilda, Abbess of Quedlinburg, in 969 persuaded Abott Widukind of Corvey to write the *History of the Saxon Kings* (now in the State Library at Dresden). Hazecha, the Treasury-mistress of Quedlinburg, also employed the monks of Corvey to illuminate her own *Life of S. Christopher*.

Princess Hedwig, another of Otto's sisters, read Virgil with Ekkehard of St. Gall and taught the child Burchard Greek. Otto's niece, Gerberga, Abbess of Gandersheim, was the instructress of Hrosvita, 'the oldest German poetess'. Otto's wife, Adelheid of Burgundy, was a zealous patroness and protectress of the Abbey of Cluny (see p. 372); she was a patroness of illuminators, and many liturgical books were executed at her expense for use in her various foundations. She died in her seventy-first year in her Abbey of Selz in Alsace. Otto II's wife, Theophano, brought the Byzantine splendour to the German court at Bamberg, which became a great centre of literature, culture and art.

The great monument of feminine erudition and artistic skill, that lost treasure-house of medieval allegory, the *Hortus Deliciarum* (see p. 217), was of somewhat later date; amongst the few preserved early MSS., the beautiful and unique *Niedermuenster Gospel-lectionary* of the Abbess Uta (now in the State Library at Munich, *Cod. Lat. 13601*) is particularly interesting: see p. 222.

EARLIEST PRESERVED ILLUMINATED MANUSCRIPTS

Few German illuminated codices can be attributed to the first half of the tenth century. Of great historical (rather than artistic) interest is the *Gospel-book of King Athelstan* (preserved in the British Museum, *Tib. A. ii*), which the inscription *Odda rex, Mihthild mater regis* indicates to be a present by Otto I (Eadyth or Edith, Athelstan's sister, was his first wife) and his mother Matilda. Athelstan presented it to Christ Church, at Canterbury, where it was apparently used as the oath-book of the early English kings. It contains the portraits of the Evangelists, as well as arcades for the Eusebian Canons, and large ornamental initials. Of the Evangelists, Mark, Luke, and John—small huddled figures, with huge hands, and heads twisted round in the effort to gaze upwards, on dull green backgrounds—seem to be painted in a very debased style, showing some traces of the ninth-century Rheims

214

school; whereas the depiction of Matthew—'with its thick soft technique and pale colouring' (Herbert)—is painted in an early Ottonian style. Gold (edged with red) and silver are profusely used.

One of the finest manuscripts is preserved in The John Rylands Library, Manchester (*Lat. MS. 98*). It is the *Otto Gospel-book*, containing full-page decorative patterns executed in purple and gold at the beginning of the book and before each Gospel, as well as illuminated Tables of the Eusebian Canons. The MS. was produced for Otto I, whose portrait is painted on small medallions. The illumination was executed either in Cologne or St. Gall: Fig. IV-23a.

The earliest Saxon school of illumination is represented by a magnificent *Gospel-book* of the second half of the tenth century, which comes from the Abdinghof Monastery, near Paderborn. It was preserved in the State Library of Cassel (*Cod. theol. fol. 60*), but it was lost during the last war.

Froumund of Tegernsee, born about 960, was a *Magister scholae*, i.e., teacher, and wrote verses; he made a collection of letters and poems which give an excellent picture of monastic life in Germany about 1000. He also edited Boëthius (*see* p. 55); five copies of this MS. have been preserved. The earliest of these was acquired about 1936 by the State Library, Berlin. This codex—which once belonged to the Prince of Oettingen—Wallerstein at Maihingen—also contains a beautifully illuminated frontispiece, representing Philosophy appearing to Boëthius. This is the only miniature of the Froumund MSS., but it was probably painted by Froumund and shows that this monk of Tegernsee was not only a scholar and poet, but also an excellent painter.

Eleventh Century. The great mass of the preserved early German illuminated MSS. belongs to the eleventh century. With few exceptions, writes Herbert, these are characterized by poverty of invention, heaviness and hardness in drawing, and harshness and want of harmony in colouring. The same compositions are copied again and again with wearisome iteration of design and with steady deterioration in treatment. In initial-ornament, the interlaced branch-work of the *Heidelberg Sacramentary* is repeated with scarcely any variation until, with the twelfth century, the historiated initial begins to make its appearance. With it came the initial decorated with forms of animals and monsters, a revival rather than a new movement.

Amongst the exceptions there is the *Pruem Gospel-book* (The John Rylands Library, *Lat. MS. 7*). It contains a dedicatory inscription by Ruotpertus, Abbot of Pruem (1027–68). The illustrations are peculiar: the figures are left mostly in white, with draperies heightened by bands of gold, on a ground usually bluish-green, with circular patterns of white or red dots: Fig. IV-24a.

However, the wave of Byzantine influence which had passed over Germany had immensely benefited the Germans. We notice it especially in the miniatures of the Gospel-books. See also p. 230, where *S. Henry's Missal* is referred to. In another interesting *Missal*—preserved in the State Library at Bamberg—there is a miniature of Emperor Henry II presenting the book to the Virgin.

A late eleventh-century Gospel-book is preserved in the Fitzwilliam Museum,

Cambridge (*McClean MS. 20*): it has fine portraits of the Evangelists and very fine Canons: Fig. IV-24c.

Twelfth Century. Under Frederick I Barbarossa (1123–90), the first of the Hohenstaufen dynasty, who succeeded Conrad III as emperor in 1152, we may note a wave of new life, especially in Saxony. A charming example preceding this wave is a *Passionale*, of 1110–20, produced in Hirsau and preserved in the State Library, Stuttgart (*Bibl. fol. 57*). However, examples of twelfth-century work from Germanic lands are exceedingly numerous, even more so than those of the preceding century. They stretch over various provinces from West to East: Westphalia, the Palatinate, Switzerland, Bavaria, extending even into Bohemia. Indeed, an *Evangeliarium* in the University Library at Prague agrees altogether with those of Germany.

Twelfth-century illumination shows a marked effort towards true artistic design and subtle beauty of linear outline. Some of the noblest curve-drawings, with rich and massive grouping of foliage, are to be found in the very fine ornamental initials of white foliated branch-work, outlined in red upon soft blue and green fields, as well as in the dignified border-designs appearing in the later specimens of the century; and it is very interesting to observe the rapid pace at which the climax is reached in mere calligraphic ornament. Initials become smaller but exquisitely drawn. Dragons and birds are often added to the intertwining stems and leaves, and form effective head- and tail-pieces to the letters. Human figures, too, are sometimes introduced as part of the decorative scheme, and reasonable expressions take the place of the senseless stare or grotesque exaggeration of attitude and feature, which detract from the artistic value of all preceding efforts.

Examples are: a copy of Petrus Lombardus, *Psalm-Commentary*, written in 1166 by the scribe Michael, at Bremen, formerly in the Dyson Perrins Library (on sale, at Sotheby's in December, 1959); a *Gospel-book* from the Gegenbach monastery (in Baden), preserved in the State Library at Stuttgart (*Cod. Bibl. fol. 28*), and a *Pericope-book*, from the Cologne *scriptorium*, preserved in the National Library at Paris (*Lat. 17325*), both attributed to the mid-twelfth century; a copy of the *Weingarten Guelf Chronicle*, executed in the Weingarten *scriptorium* between 1179 and 1191, and preserved in the State Library at Fulda (*MS. D. 11*); a copy of Hildegard von Bingen (*see* also p. 217), *Liber scivias*, executed in a *scriptorium* of the region of the Middle Rhine between 1150 and 1175; it was preserved in the Civic Library at Wiesbaden (*Cod. 1*), but disappeared during the last war; a copy of the *Glossary* of Bishop Solomon of Constance, executed in Pruefening in 1165, now in the State Library at Munich (*Cod. Lat. 13002*); an *Evangelistarium*, executed *c.* 1197 in the district of Speyer, on commission by Custos Conrad von Danne for the Collegiate church of Neumuenster near Worms, is preserved in the State Library at Karlsruhe (*Cod. Bruchsal. 1*)—see, particularly, K. Preisendanz and O. Homburger, *Das Evangelistar des Speyerer Domes*, Leipsic, 1930; a copy of *Pauline Epistles*, produced in Halberstadt between 1175 and 1200, and preserved in the State Library at Berlin (*Theol. Lat. fol. 192*), and other works.

Symbolism and Allegory. Two main features of twelfth-century illuminated books are (*a*) symbolism and allegory, and (*b*) the huge size of Bibles. The former traits, as shown mainly in apocalyptic commentaries, were particularly popular in Spain from the ninth to the thirteenth centuries (see p. 167 f.).

Here a few other MSS. may be mentioned. A copy of Hrabanus Maurus, *De Laudibus S. Crucis* (see p. 210)—produced in the twelfth century in, or for, the Premonstratensian abbey of Arnstein (near Coblentz or Koblenz, Rhenish provincial capital), and now in the British Museum (*Harl. MS. 3045*)—besides richly illuminated initials in gold, silver, and deep and warm colours, contains several pages with curious mystical diagrams, enclosed in border-frames decorated with repeat-patterns in red outline on blue and green grounds.

An *Apocalypse*, preserved in the Astorga collection (National Library at Edinburgh) contains one hundred and ten miniatures, many of which are perfect curiosities of symbolism, depicting not only the four figures of the Evangelists, but the mysteries of the seals and vials, serpents, and beasts, on yellow, red, green, blue, and brown backgrounds. The draperies in some of the miniatures show Byzantine manner, but also recall the Western late Roman style.

The curious symbolism of the last-named two books links them with a far more beautiful and famous MS., already referred to on p. 214, which unfortunately was burnt with many other treasures during the siege of Strasbourg by the Germans in 1870. Fortunately, copies had previously been made of several of the miniatures and these have been published.

The manuscript composed, written, and illuminated by Herrad de Landsperg, Abbess of Hohenburg in Alsace, 1167–95, for the edification and delectation of her nuns, was a veritable treasury of medieval customs, furniture, and costumes, giving a medley of encyclopaedic information on religious and philosophical matters, illustrated by paintings of scriptural, symbolical, and other subjects. There was a figure of the Church riding upon a beast with four heads, the heads being the symbols of the four Evangelists; there were allegorical figures of the virtues and vices, and the sirens as the symbols of sensual temptation. The drawing and treatment were generally not of a very skilful kind, but the colouring was bright and in body-colour. Draperies were much folded and fluttering. The Abbess called her book *Hortus Deliciarum*, or 'Garden of Delights'. The title began *Incipit hortus deliciarum, in quo collectis floribus scripturarum, etc.* Hildegard von Bingen's (*see* p. 216) *Prayerbook*, preserved in the State Library, at Munich, was executed under the artistic influence of the *Hortus Deliciarum*.

A contrast to the *Hortus Deliciarum* in artistic ability is the *Gospel-book of Henry the Lion* (1129–95), Duke of Saxony and Bavaria, and cousin of Frederick Barbarossa, executed at the convent of Helmarshausen (later it belonged to the Cathedral Library at Prague; about 1860 it was bought by King George V of Hanover). The dedication page of this splendid book represents the Virgin with SS. John the Baptist and Bartholomew, and below them the patron saints of Brunswick, Blaize and Egidius, leading forth the Duke and his wife Matilda. Another page represents the Duke and Duchess receiving crowns. The figures are well-drawn, even elegant, the draperies good, and the colouring skilful. Some pages are framed within richly decorated borders. The page of the Eusebian Canons shows influences of the art of Lombardy and Venice. The columns rest on crouching animals. Allegorical figures are introduced striving with each other as in the later Gothic illuminations. A half-nude figure of Faith vanquishes the champion of Paganism. (The *codex* is now preserved in the private collection of the Duke of Brunswick.)

Most curious is the work *Mater Verborum* by the monk Conrad, of Scheyern, in Bavaria, who was not only a scribe-illuminator and goldsmith, but also a grammarian. It is a kind of dictionary in which not only actual objects are pictorially represented, but also music, philosophy, sacred subjects, virtues and vices are illustrated allegorically—the same method was followed by contemporary German and French glass-painters.

Huge Bibles. The best specimen of the German huge Bible is the late-twelfth-century *Arnstein Bible*, in two volumes, now in the British Museum (*Harl. MSS. 2798-9*). There are great initials in gold, silver, and colours, some containing large figures of Solomon and the Evangelists writing, with smaller half-length allegorical figures in medallions.

Less harmonious in colour and harder and drier in technique is another Rhenish production, the *Worms Bible* (preserved in the British Museum, *Harl. MSS. 2803-4*). 'The miniatures are crude, flat, and coarsely executed; it is in the initial-ornament that the illuminators of this and similar books show to most advantage' (Herbert). There is a large decorated initial at the beginning of each book; there are arcaded Canon-tables, portraits of the Evangelists, two miniatures of S. Jerome writing and one of David as harpist (prefixed to the Psalms).

MAIN CENTRES OF ILLUMINATION

The following three main centres of Ottonian book-illumination may be specially mentioned: (1) the great Benedictine abbey of Reichenau, situated on a small island in Lake Constance. This monastery was already in existence in Carolingian times, but in the second half of the tenth and in the early eleventh century it was the most important centre of book-illumination in the Holy Roman Empire, and with Fulda and St. Gall it was a pivot of German culture in the early Middle Ages. The Reichenau book-production was outstanding; it was so popular that Pope Gregory V (996-9) granted to the abbey special privileges in exchange for liturgical codices to be supplied to Rome.

There is no doubt that the Reichenau style ultimately goes back to Early Christian models of the late Graeco-Roman type (similar style may also be noted in the Reichenau frescoes discovered in 1880), but some scholars connect this style with the earlier Carolingian school at Trèves, and particularly with the *Ada Gospel-book* (p. 203). One of the characteristic features of the Reichenau school is a patterned background containing either geometrical designs (such as the repeat-pattern of crosses and rosettes of the *Vere dignum* page of the *Gregorian Sacramentary* at Heidelberg—see p. 220), or figures of birds or monsters, which are thought to have been borrowed from Oriental textiles. The great Archbishop of Trèves, Egbert (977–93), brought the influence of the school of Reichenau to Trèves (see further on).

(2) Ratisbon or Regensburg, on the Danube in Lower Bavaria, was for a time the Imperial residence; its school of illumination, the most important of the Bavarian schools, flourished particularly in the late tenth and in the eleventh century.

(3) Salzburg, now a provincial capital in Austria; its *scriptorium* had a certain importance in the eighth and ninth centuries: the *Cuthbert Evangeliarium*, in good Anglo-Saxon style (see p. 189 f.), was probably executed *c.* 770 by a scribe Cuthbert in Salzburg, where Abbot and Bishop Virgilius brought Insular art. The codex is now in the National Library at Vienna, *MS. 1224.* The best period of the Salzburg school of illumination was, however, the twelfth century. *See* p. 223.

Reichenau Productions. Many of the finest illuminated books of the Ottonian period—especially the earlier ones— emanated from the *Reichenau school.*

From this renowned *scriptorium*—writes Miss Dorothy Miner—sumptuous volumes were ordered by prelates in other centres and by the Ottonian emperors, which extensively influenced other German schools of painting. The Reichenau artists, continues Miss Miner, during their great period—the decades immediately preceding and following the year 1000— produced works of marvellous richness and beauty, characterized by monumentality and a peculiarly psychological intensity.

Curiously enough, whilst the Reichenau book-production goes back at least to the eighth century—when the monk Reginbert, librarian of the Reichenau monastery in the years 786–842, wrote a number of codices (many are still preserved)— apparently no illuminated Reichenau codex has been preserved which can be dated before the middle of the tenth century. On the other hand, about 30 illuminated codices are preserved, which were executed in Reichenau between 960 and 1010.

The most famous MS., which may be considered the Reichenau masterpiece, is the *Egbert Gospel-book,* or *Codex Egberti,* executed *c.* 980, by the monks Keraldus and Heribertus for Egbert Archbishop of Trèves (977–93), and preserved in Trèves (Civic Library, *Cod. No. 24*); it is in a style ultimately based on Graeco-Roman models. This style is particularly evident in the fifty-one miniatures of the Gospel-lessons. These are framed, writes Herbert, in rectangular bands with no ornament beyond a simple lozenge-pattern, and mostly occupy half-page spaces in the text; where they fill the whole page, they often contain two scenes with differently coloured backgrounds, but without formal partition. At the beginning of the codex there is a purple dedication-page showing the two scribes (painted in diminutive proportions) presenting the codex to Archbishop Egbert, who is represented rising aloft in dignity. There are also portraits of the Evangelists, in Byzantine style, on a background of geometrical patterns: Fig. IV-26b–c.

Strictly connected with the *Codex Egberti* is a *Pericopē-book*, also produced for Archbishop Egbert, which is preserved in the National Library at Paris (*Lat. 10514*). This codex is also known as the *S. Leo Evangeliar*: it has been suggested that it may have been donated by Pope Leo IX (who in the years 1026–49 was bishop of Toul) to the famous Poussay Abbey, a foundation of the Toul bishops. Stylistically and in the composition, the codex is based on a north-Italian proto-type. Some of the miniatures—the only ones of the Reichenau schools—are stylistically related to the wall-paintings of the Reichenau monastery.

Also *MS. Theol. Lat. Fol. 34,* in the State Library, at Berlin, is connected with the *Codex Egberti.*

Other famous products of the Reichenau school are the following: the magnificent *Gospel-book of Otto III* (983–1002), executed just before 1000, and preserved in the State Library at Munich (*Cod. Lat. 4453*), which will be dealt with further on; the *Gero Gospels* (Darmstadt, *Cod. No. 1948*), executed for Gero, Archbishop of Cologne, 969–76; the *Gregorian Sacramentary* (preserved in the University Library at Heidelberg, *Sal. ix. b*), by some scholars assigned to the first half of the tenth century; but its style is so similar to the *Gero Gospels* that many, including Janitschek, attribute both the codices to one hand. It contains two full-page miniatures (of Christ and the Virgin) in the clumsy style of mediocre Carolingian painting, though the beardless, long-haired, feminine-looking Christ goes back to an early Western Christian model; the initials of intertwined branch- and leaf work are a characteristic feature of the Ottonian style.

Similar background occurs in the *Egbert Psalter*, produced between 977 and 993, and preserved in the National Archaeological Museum at Cividale (North Italy); this MS. is also known as *Codex Gertrudianus* (it contains eleventh-century glosses by a Slavonic princess, Gertrude). The codex is the main representative of the 'Ruodpreht group' of MSS. It contains initials in pure Reichenau style and a number of miniatures, some (fol. 16v–17r) representing Ruodpreht (the scribe or illuminator) presenting the book to Egbert, its dedication by him to S. Peter (fol. 18v–19r), and fourteen of Egbert's predecessors (fols. 30v, 41v, 52v, 66v, etc.). Fol. 20v represents King David. In the eleventh century the codex was in Russia, where several miniatures in Russian style were added: fols. 5v, 9v–10r, 41r. The interesting *Pericopē-book* of the Paris Nat. Libr. (*Lat. 10514*), already referred to, also belongs to the Ruodpreht group of codices.

Also very interesting is the *Barberini Gospel-book*, written *c.* 1000, preserved in the Vatican Library (*Barb. Lat. 711*).

The *Pericopē-* or *Church Year-book*, now preserved in the State Library at Munich (*Cod. Lat. 4452*) was executed in Reichenau in 1007 or 1014 for Henry II and Cunigunda, and by them presented to Bamberg Cathedral. The *Hillinus Evangeliar* (Cologne Cathedral Library, *Cod. 12*) was produced in the early eleventh century for Hillinus, Archbishop of Cologne. The *Bamberg Apocalypse* (State Library, Bamberg, *A. II. 42*), was produced in Reichenau *c.* 1020: Fig. IV-27*a–b* and 28*b*. Fig. IV-28*a* reproduces a page from another excellent production of Reichenau, a *Commentary to Isaia*. We may also refer to the *Pericopē-books Clm. 23338*, at Munich, and *Cod. 84. 5. Aug.*, at Wolfenbuettel; to the richly decorated *Epistolary* of the British Museum, London (*MS. Add. 20629*); to the *Orationale* in the Beverin Library, at Hildesheim (*Cod. membr. U. I. 19*); to Bamberg *Cod. membr. Ed. V. 9*; to Bamberg, *Cod. bibl. 22*; to the *Sacramentary, Sal. IX b* at Heidelberg (see above), and to a few other *Sacramentaries* (Arsenal Library, at Paris, No. 610; *Hornbach Sacramentary*, Solothurn Cathedral; *St. Blasien Sacramentary*, at St. Paul, Carinthia; *MS. Lat. 18005*, in the Paris National Library); as well as to several *Gospel-books* and *Psalters* (*Cod. Augiensis CLXI*, at Karlsruhe, and others).

Other eleventh-century examples of the Reichenau school are a *Gospel-book* preserved in the Laurentian Library at Florence (*MS. S. Croce Plut. 5 dext. 7*) and, although by some authority attributed to the Einsiedeln *scriptorium*, a *Gospel-book* preserved in the Queriniana Library, Brescia (North Italy).

A tenth-century *Gospel-book* preserved in the Angelica Library, Rome (*MS. 1452*); another *Gospel-book*, belonging to the tenth or eleventh century, preserved in the Laurentian Library, Florence (*MS. Acq. e Doni 91*); and a tenth-century luxurious *Sacramentary* preserved in the National Library at Florence (*MS. B. R. 231: Magl. Cl. XXXVI, 13*) are also attributed to the school of Reichenau; the last has no miniatures; only decorative pages, containing geometrical designs or figures of beasts and long-tailed birds. For the *Bamberg Lectionary* (State Library at Munich, *Cimel. 57*), by some scholars attributed to Reichenau, see p. 228.

Of uncertain origin, but partly related to Reichenau productions, is the *Otto Gospel-book*—probably Otto III, 983–1002—or *Aix Gospels*, preserved in the Cathedral Treasury at Aix-la-Chapelle (or Aachen). We have already referred to the *Otto III Gospel-book*, executed *c.* 1000, and preserved in the State Library at Munich (*Cod. Lat. 4453*). It was however produced in Reichenau; it comes from Bamberg Cathedral, to which it was probably presented by Henry II, the successor of Otto III. According to the opinion of several scholars the *Otto III Gospel-book* was written for Henry II and not for Otto III. See particularly W. Weisbach, *The Pictures of the Evangelists in the so-called Gospels of Otto III and their Relation to the Antique* (The Warburg Institute), London, 1939.

In the eleventh century, the Reichenau productions show 'a hardening of the style and a relaxation of the energy inherent in the earlier works'. Nevertheless, they still preserve in their 'rich purple *incipit* pages and the gay, pastel hues of the paintings a reminiscence of the days of greatness' (Miner). An excellent specimen of this production, a *Gospel-book*, of *c.* 1030–40, is preserved in the Walters Art Gallery, Baltimore (*W. 7*). It contains five full-page miniatures, four ornamented introductory pages, and sixteen decorated Canon Tables: Fig. IV-29*b*.

Ratisbon Productions. The best-known product of the *Ratisbon school* is the *Gospel-*

book of Henry II, which was written and illuminated between 1014 and 1024, and is preserved in the Vatican Library (*Ott. Lat. 74*): Fig. IV-30.

Another codex produced in Ratisbon between 1002 and 1014 was presented by Henry II to Bamberg Cathedral, and is now preserved in the State Library at Munich (*Cod. Lat. 4456*). It is known as the *Henry II Sacramentary*.

Perhaps even more famous is the *Uta Codex* or *Niedermuenster Gospel-lectionary* (see p. 214), probably executed for Uta, Abbess of Niedermuenster, at Ratisbon (1002–25). Its splendid pages, writes Herbert, blend in a remarkable manner the Carolingian tradition of ornate magnificence with Byzantine wealth of symbolic imagery, and already foreshadow, in the slender figures and in the medallion-scenes set in the frames, the fully developed Gothic miniature of the thirteenth century. The mystical tendency, concludes Herbert, is shown very strikingly in the miniature of the Crucifixion. Its curious illustrations of symbolism (such as the allegorical figures of Life and Death beside the figure of Christ in the miniature of the Crucifixion, instead of the customary figures of Mary and John) and its richly foliaged geometrical backgrounds and borders, which make it one of the most interesting manuscripts in any collection, have induced some scholars to attribute it not to Abbess Uta, but to Tuota of Niedermuenster, a lady of the House of Counts of Falckenstein (1177–80).

One of its remarkable miniatures depicts the presentation of the MS. to the Madonna, who is seated on a Byzantine *sedile* with the infant Jesus on her knees. Both have the nimbus. Over the Madonna, written in letters of gold on purple, is the monogram *Maria*, surrounded by the word *Sancta* in ordinary ink. There are also other inscriptions, partly Latin, partly Greek. Below the Madonna, on the left, stands the Abbess, her knees slightly bent, holding up her book and clothed in the costume of her Order. She wears a blue veil and a claret-coloured robe. In the reversed semicircle before her is the monogram Uta, or Uota, or Tuota, which may give us the name Uta, Utta, Uota, Tuota, Ida, etc.

An interesting *Pericopē-book*, from Salzburg, but executed in Ratisbon in the first quarter of the eleventh century, is preserved in the State Library, at Munich (*Clm. 15713: Cim. 179*). Artistically, this codex forms one of the links between Byzantine and Western art.

A much later production of Ratisbon, the *Hohenwart Gospel-book*, of c. 1240, is also preserved in the State Library at Munich (*Cod. Lat. 7384*).

The Scheyern *scriptorium* was strictly related to that of Ratisbon. Amongst the most important productions of Scheyern, we may refer to a copy of *Liber matutinalis*, preserved in the State Library at Munich (*Cod. Lat. 17401*).

Saxony and Mixed Style. A *Gospel-book*, formerly belonging to the Dukes of Anhalt-Dessau, and now in the Pierpont Morgan Library (*M. 827*), is an excellent specimen of illuminated books containing mixed elements. Indeed, it contains features of the tenth-century Franco-Saxon style of the region around Arras (see p. 208), of the Anglo-Saxon style (see p. 180) and the 'Channel School', and the 'richly ornamented products' of the early eleventh-century style of Saxony. In Dr.

Hans Swarzenski's opinion, the codex (which is written in Franco-Saxon minuscules) may have been produced in a Franco-Saxon centre, such as Arras, and the Evangelists' portraits may have been executed by an artist trained in English style; and after 1000 (when the codex was brought to Saxony) 'much of the enrichment of blue and purple backgrounds was added'. The MS. contains four full-page miniatures, ten ornamented or purple pages, and fourteen Canon Tables: Fig. IV-29a.

Salzburg. A luxurious *Gospel-book* of the early eleventh century, probably produced at the Benedictine Abbey of S. Peter's in Salzburg, where it belonged from the twelfth century until 1933, is now preserved in the Pierpont Morgan Library, New York (*M. 781*). It contains seven full-page and sixteen smaller miniatures, and four decorated introductory pages. The style is partly related to that of Reichenau. More Byzantine in style and iconography is the illumination of a *Lectionary*, which *Custos* Bertolt (he signed the book), executed in the second half of the eleventh century in S. Peter's, Salzburg. This codex, too, belongs since 1933 to the Pierpont Morgan Library (*M. 780*). It contains nineteen miniatures and a great number of illuminated initials. A *Gospel-book*, preserved in the Admont Abbey (*MS. 805*), on the river Enns, North-Styrian Alps, is probably also Bertolt's work: Fig. IV-31b and 32a.

Mention may also be made of the mid-twelfth-century *Pericopē-book of S. Ehrentrud*, preserved in the State Library at Munich (*Cod. Lat. 15903*); an *Orationale*, preserved in the same library (*Cod. Lat. 15902*), attributed to the late twelfth century; an *Antiphonary*, produced in S. Peter's at Salzburg, between 1175 and 1200, and preserved in the National Library at Vienna; and the codex *Decretum Gratiani*, written in the late twelfth century, and preserved in the same collection (*Cod. Lat. 13004*).

A copy of Honorius of Autun, *Expositio super Canticum Canticorum* (belonging to a group of MSS. allied in text and illustrations, executed between 1150 and 1175 in South Germany or Austria), is preserved in the Walters Art Gallery (*W. 29*). There are three half-page miniatures, three historiated and five ornamented initials in a style influenced by the Salzburg School: Fig. IV-32b.

The Benedictine Abbey of Admont had also an active *scriptorium*. An early copy of Jeremiah's *Lamentations*, with glosses by Giselbertus (Universalis) of Auxerre (who died in 1134) has been attributed to the Admont Abbey. The copy, preserved in the Walters Art Gallery, Baltimore (*W. 30*), contains three miniatures, five pages of ornamented arcades, and three ornamented initials. An interesting volume, probably also executed in Admont Abbey, is preserved in the Howard L. Goodhart Collection, New York City. It is the best copy of the earliest Latin version of Pseudo-Philo, *Antiquitates Biblicae*. There are two interesting historiated initials in the Austrian romanesque style: Fig. IV-32c.

A *Missal* for the use of Melk (in Upper Austria), preserved in the Walters Art Gallery (*W. 33*), is an excellent example of the Austrian provincial style related to the Salzburg romanesque style. There are two full-page miniatures, six historiated and eleven ornamented initials. 'The figures are finely drawn in red and lavender inks against flat backgrounds of light blue and green. The use of inscribed frames and partitions is characteristic' (Miner): Fig. IV-32d. An interesting *modus scribendi* (*A 15th Century Modus Scribendi*) from the Abbey of Melk, was published in 1940 by S. Morison. Kremsmuenster, also in Upper Austria, had an excellent *scriptorium*. Fig. IV-33a and b are from the *Kremsmuenster Gospels* (Kremsmuenster, *Cod. 1*). Fig. IV-33c reproduces the final Canon Table from a thirteenth-century Austrian MS. now in New York (Pierpont Morgan Library, *M. 808*).

Other Centres. There were a few other important centres. Bamberg, already referred to, became a great centre of German art under Emperor Henry II and his wife Cunigunda (*see* also p. 220 f.). Both here and at Magdeburg very fine illuminated books were executed in the eleventh century. Trèves (see pp. 204 and 227) also became an Ottonian centre of illumination.

In the second half of the tenth century a small group of luxurious manuscripts were executed 'somewhere in the general region of the Weser River in northern Germany'; they are 'sometimes attributed more precisely to the monastery of Corvey'. As Miss Dorothy Miner points out, the distinguishing characteristic of this group is the use of rich introductory pages with purple backgrounds delicately shaded or boldly patterned with foliage, birds and animals, suggestive of Byzantine textile designs. With these are combined exceptionally complex initials or even whole words in monogrammized form, the elements of the ornament showing the influence of the earlier Corbie and Franco-Saxon styles.

A *Gospel-book* in the Pierpont Morgan Library (*M. 755*), containing sixteen decorated Canon Tables, and seventeen ornamented introductory pages to the Gospels, is the best known specimen of this group. But Miss Miner regards as its foremost example a *Lectionary*, preserved in the New York Public Library (*MS. 1*), which is the only one of the group containing illustrations as well as ornamental pages. There are six full-page miniatures (four represent the Evangelists; one contains the symbols of the Evangelists in four compartments, and one is Christ in Glory) and a number of elaborate initial pages and ornamental passages, complex monograms written in gold on purple ground, etc. A very fine though fragmentary *Gospel-book* preserved in the Walters Art Gallery, Baltimore (*W. 751*), is another example of the 'Corvey school': Fig. IV-23b and 25b. Wolfenbuettel State Library, *16. 1. Aug. fol.*, of the third quarter of the tenth century, may also have been produced at Corvey.

Hildesheim. S. Bernward, Bishop of Hildesheim near Hanover (993–1022) and tutor to Otto III was according to tradition an excellent penman and a good painter (see p. 251). He instituted a school of illumination in his cathedral city, and supplied it with jewelled service-books and with specimens of Greek illumination. Many of the books executed for S. Bernward are still preserved in Hildesheim Cathedral.

In the early eleventh century Hildesheim was a great centre of ecclesiastical art and craftsmanship. The style of illumination of its *scriptorium* was based on the Reichenau style (p. 219 ff.) with its patterned background, but 'the patterns seem founded less on textile designs than on those found in champlevé enamel' (Herbert) —see also below.

Hildesheim Style. Of the books executed in the Hildesheim style and now preserved in that Cathedral, the most important are the following MSS. executed for S. Bernward (see above) by Guntbald the Deacon (the attribution is not in all cases beyond doubt): *S. Bernward's Gospel-book*, probably written between 1011 and 1014; the slightly later *S. Bernward's Sacramentary*, with an interesting miniature (representing the Crucifixion) prefixed to the Canon of the Mass; it contains the opening words *Te igitur* embodied in the design, the *T* forming the cross, with elaborately plaited terminals; another *Gospels*, less richly ornamented, written in 1011; and a *Bible* (with an elaborate and interesting frontispiece) written about 1015.

The whole technique of these books, according to Herbert, suggests by its severity and disposition of line, its lack of perspective and modelling, its rigid, non-realistic rendering of the human form, an acquaintance with the arts of metal-work and enamelling rather than the more plastic ideals proper to the miniaturist. This predilection for conventional forms, adds Herbert, is joined, however, to an elaborate and sometimes impressive symbolism.

An other excellent example of Hildesheim twelfth-century (*c.* 1150–75) productions is a *Missal*, which comes from S. Michael in Hildesheim; it was preserved in the collection of Count Egon von Fuerstenberg-Stammheim, and is now in the Fuerstenberg Collection at Brabecke near Bestwig (Sauerland). The *Ratmann Sacramentary*, written in 1159 (now preserved in the Hildesheim Cathedral), and the *Riddagshausen Evangeliar*, of the second half of the twelfth century (preserved in the Braunschweig Museum) are also productions of the Hildesheim scriptorium.

Mainz. The city of Mainz (or Mayence), situated on the Rhine opposite the mouth of the river Main, also had an important *scriptorium* which was attached to its cathedral, dating back to 978. A fragmentary *Sacramentary* of the tenth-eleventh century is preserved in the Lucca State Library (*MS. 1275*). It contains eight miniatures, a great number of gold initials, a beautiful title page written in gold on purple background, etc.

A much later production of Mainz—a *Gospel-book* of *c.* 1260—is preserved in the Castle Library at Aschaffenburg (*No. 13*). It is a superb MS. written in gold, which in its very large format, organisation, iconography, etc., is based on the luxurious productions of the Carolingian and Ottonian schools; it shows strong Byzantine and French influences.

Extremely important for its style, showing the last influence of late Romanesque, is a *Psalter* executed in the second half of the thirteenth century, and attributed, with some doubt, to a Middle Rhine scriptorium. It is preserved in the Civic Library, at Besançon.

Helmarshausen. In the twelfth century, an important *scriptorium* was active in the Benedictine monastery of Helmarshausen near Kassel (Hesse). About 1175, Gertrude (daughter of Henry the Lion, Duke of Saxony and Bavaria), who later became Queen of Denmark, ordered from this *scriptorium* two interesting MSS., now preserved in the British Museum (*Lansdowne MS. 381*) and in the Duke of Brunswick Collection. A *Psalter* in very small format (rather unusual for this period), executed in Helmarshausen, probably for Gertrude or for her mother, is preserved in the Walters Art Gallery, Baltimore (*W. 10*). There are three full-page miniatures (including a portrait of the lady, for whom it was made), and four ornamented initial pages: Fig. IV-25a. A particularly interesting *Gospel-book*—for a time deposited on loan in the Cleveland Museum of Art (it belonged to a private collector)—was sold in London in December 1958 for £109,200. The codex, measuring 230 × 170 mm., contains 168 vellum leaves (written in an upright Roman hand), four full-page miniatures—portraits of the Evangelists, full-page illuminated initials, sixteen finely decorated pages of the Eusebian canons, and many initials in red.

In the late twelfth century, it became one of the most important art-centres of N.-W. Germany, and excellent work was produced in its *scriptorium* for bishops (like Henry of Werl) and princes (like Henry the Lion): a *Gospel-book*, executed by the monk Herimann for Henry the Lion, is preserved in the Collection of the Duke of Brunswick; another *Gospel-book* is in Trèves (Cathedral Treasury, *Cod. 142*); also the *Gospel-book*, of 1195, preserved in the Duke August Library at Wolfenbuettel (*Cod. Helmstadensis 65*), apparently comes from Helmarshausen. Helmarshausen was also a great centre of metalwork.

Here a few words may be said about Roger of Helmarshausen, a great craftsman active in 1100 and 1118. Of great significance is the fact that this Roger has been identified by scholars of repute with Theophilus, the author of the most famous work *De diuersis artibus* ('Of Various Arts'), in which—in several chapters—he discusses book-illumination, colours, gold-painting, and so on. See, now, the excellent monograph by C. R. Dodwell, *Theophilus* (also known as Theophilus *qui est Rugerus* = 'also known as Roger') *De Diuersis Artibus—The Various Arts*, T. Nelson & Sons Ltd., Edinburgh—London—and so on, 1961.

Cologne. From the late tenth century, the *scriptorium* of Cologne (see p. 210) was very active. Its early productions were strongly influenced by the Byzantine style both in iconography and composition. Examples are: the *S. Gereon Sacramentary*, of the late tenth century (preserved in the National Library at Paris, *Lat. 817*); *Hitda von Meschede Gospels*, of the first quarter of the eleventh century (State Library at Darmstadt, *Cod. 1640*); *Abdinghof Gospels*, c. 1040–68 (preserved in Kupfer-stichkabinett, Berlin, *MS. 78. A. 3*)—some scholars regard this *Evangeliar* as a continuation of the following: *S. Maria ad Gradus Gospels*, mid-eleventh century (preserved in the Priest-Seminary, Cologne, *Cod. 753b*): Fig. IV-25c and 26a. An interesting illuminated MS., connected stylistically with the *Abdinghof Gospels*, is preserved in the University Library of Freiburg im Breisgau (*Missale 360a*).

Rylands Lat. MS. 87 is another illuminated Gospel-book influenced by the Cologne school. It was executed *c.* 1000 for the Bremen Cathedral and according to B. Bruch ('Bull. of the John Rylands Library,' 1961, pp. 275 ff.) it is apparently the only codex to survive the Cathedral fire of 1041 and, with the sumptuous Charlemagne 'Golden Psalter', now in Vienna, it is one of the only two volumes to escape the plundering of the Cathedral Library by Henry the Lion in 1155.

Examples of later productions of Cologne are: a codex of *c.* 1200 preserved at S. Maria Lyskirchen, Cologne; an early twelfth-century copy of Bede's *Ecclesiastical History*, executed for S. Martin in Cologne, and preserved in the Civic Library at Leipsic (*MS. CXLV*); the mid-twelfth-century *Cod. Lat. 17325* in the National Library at Paris; and the early thirteenth-century *Evangelistarium* produced for S. Martin and now in Brussels (Royal Library, *MS. 9922*)—the last MS. is executed partly in the traditional twelfth-century style of Cologne, and partly in a new style, influenced by the productions of Nicholas of Verdun.

Finally, a luxurious *Bible*, of *c.* 1240, which comes from the Cologne-Aachen region (it belonged to the Cistercian Abbey in Heisterbach), was preserved in the State Library at Berlin (*Theol. Lat. fol. 379*): is now in Marburg, Westdeutsche Bibliothek.

Echternach. The Echternach *scriptorium* (see p. 186 f.) continued to produce luxurious work such as the *Codex aureus*, of the first quarter of the eleventh century, which until 1945 was preserved in the Ducal Library of Sachsen-Coburg-Gotha, in Coburg, and is now at Nuremberg, Germanisches National-Museum, *MS. 15642*; as well as the *Gold Gospel-book of Henry III* (1039–56), which this king, in 1045–6, presented to Speyer Cathedral (founded by his father), and which is preserved in the Escorial Library, near Madrid (*Cod. Vitrinas 17*): Fig. IV-25d.

Another important work is the *Echternach Sacramentary*, of *c.* 1030, preserved in the Royal Library, at Brussels (*MS. 5596*).

Trèves. Assigned to Trèves is the *Echternach Gospel-book*, which once belonged to the famous Echternach Abbey; the codex is now preserved in the Library at Gotha. The MS. is in its original binding; as to its illuminations, it is remarkable for its great wealth in the illustrations of the Parables.

Another Trèves MS. is the *Gospel-lectionary*, of *c.* 1100, preserved in the British Museum (*Egerton 809*). Apart from the uninteresting full-page miniatures and the stereotyped initials, it contains small miniatures and serpentine forms, which, as Herbert points out, are crude and insignificant in themselves, but welcome signs of incipient progress.

Bamberg. Related to the *Aix Codex* (see p. 221) and to *Codex Egberti* (p. 219 f.) is the *Bamberg Gospel-book* (having previously belonged to Bamberg Cathedral), dated 996–1002, and preserved in the State Library at Munich (*Cimel. 58*). The affinity is particularly noticeable in the miniatures representing scenes from the Gospels, whereas a two-paged dedication picture (Rome, Gaul, Germany and 'Sclavinia', *i.e.*, the Slavonic lands, bringing gifts to Otto III sitting in State surrounded by his court) has been considered almost a replica of one of Otto II painted for Archbishop Egbert's *Registrum Gregorii* (now at Chantilly): see p. 204. The painting of *Cimel. 58*, especially the general character of the draperies, is in the Byzantine manner; while the feet are ill-drawn, the faces are well-drawn (though with exaggerated solemnity of expression) and the features carefully modelled.

Allied in style is *Henry II's Lectionary* or *Bamberg Lectionary*, now in the same collection (*Cimel. 57*), dated 1002–14, which S. Henry presented to the great church founded by him at Bamberg. It also contains scenes from the Gospels; its dedication picture represents Christ crowning Emperor Henry II and his wife S. Cunigunda, presented by SS. Peter and Paul. A characteristic feature is the land-scape of boulders, probably derived from tenth-century Byzantine paintings. Some scholars—particularly K. Kuenstle—have attributed this important codex to the Reichenau school of illumination (see p. 219 ff.).

Switzerland

Several *scriptoria* were active in this region. The most famous of them, St. Gall, has been referred to on p. 211. The Benedictine Abbey of Rheinau (a small island on the Rhine)—its foundation is said to go back to 778—also had a famous *scriptorium*: the preserved MSS. are partly in the Landesmuseum, at Bern, and partly in other important collections. The *Rheinau Psalter*, a thirteenth-century masterpiece, is in the Central Library at Zurich (*Cod. Rhen. No. 167*); fol. *52v*, reproduced in Fig. IV-34*a*, represents Christ's arrest.

Another Benedictine Abbey, Maria Einsiedeln (Einsiedeln, a town in Canton Schwyz, is now the most celebrated pilgrim-resort in Switzerland), was founded in the early tenth century on the site of the cell of S. Meinhard, who was murdered in 861. It was dowered with land by two emperors, and later became an inde-pendent principality of the Holy Roman Empire. Its *scriptorium* flourished par-ticularly in the tenth and eleventh centuries. The present Abbey Library possesses over 100,000 volumes and over 1300 MSS. Schaffhausen, now the capital of the Swiss canton of this name, lies on the famous falls of the Rhine. It is celebrated for its important library, the medieval architecture of the town, and the twelfth-century Romanesque basilica of the All-Hallows Benedictine Abbey. This was founded about 1050; its excellent *scriptorium* flourished particularly in the twelfth century: Fig. IV-34*d*.

Engelberg, not far from Lucerne, now a popular summer and winter resort, was another centre of book-production. Its abbey was founded in 1120 by the Bene-dictines from St. Blasien, in the Black Forest, and soon obtained such power that its abbot ruled the whole valley until 1798. Abbot Frowin (1143–78) founded the *scriptorium*, which flourished for over two centuries. The illuminated MSS., how-ever, are interesting for their calligraphic accomplishment and the drawings rather than for their illuminations. Fig. IV-31*a* reproduces, from a twelfth-century Engelberg MS. (*Codex 47*), Venerable Bede sharpening his pen.

Katharinenthal Dominican Nunnery, near Diessenhofen (Canton Thurgau, Switzerland). A beautiful Gradual, dated 1312, formerly in the Sir C. W. Dyson Perrins collection—after Sir Dyson Perrins' death, Spring 1958—was sold on 9-12-1958 at Sotheby's, London, for £33,000, and acquired by the Schweizerisches Landesmuseum, Zurich. This masterpiece, containing 314 vellum-leaves (cm. 48 × 34), with 46 large and 25 small initials on gold-background, as well as 14 (originally 16) filigran letters drawn in red and blue, was undoubtedly produced in the Katharinenthal Nunnery.

Manuscripts of Uncertain Provenance. It goes without saying that it is not always easy or even possible to determine the origin of certain MSS.

Of uncertain provenance are, for instance, a twelfth-century *Missal* (bound with a fifteenth-century MS.), preserved in Modena (Estense Library, *MS. α. G. 8. 9: Lat. 464*), and a twelfth- or thirteenth-century copy of Pliny, preserved in Florence (*MS. Plut. 82. 1*). Miniature italiane; it may be of Danish provenance. We may also refer to a *Gospel-book* in the Fitzwilliam Museum, Cambridge (*McClean MS. 21*), of the twelfth century, with four very fine purple pages; to a twelfth-century *Bible* in the Bodleian Library (*MS. Laud. Misc. 752*); to a twelfth-century copy of Boëthius in the same collection (*MS. Auct. F. 6. 4*); to a contemporary copy of Pliny in the Laurentian Library, Florence (*MS. Plut. 82. 1*); to the beautiful *Gospels* (just before 1200) of the British Museum (*Cotton MS., Caligula A. VII*) and to numerous other books in the main European and American collections: Fig. IV-34c and e, and 35. See also p. 232 f.

Frutolf and Ekkehard, World Chronicle or *Historia ffrancorum*, formerly (though wrongly) known as *Chronicon Urpergense*; also known as *World Chronicle* of Ekkehard von Aura. There are several recensions, particularly known as A, B, C, D, E. An excellent MS. is preserved in Corpus Christi College, Cambridge (*MS. 373*): it is essentially rec. C.

Recension A is attributed to Frutolf (+ 1103), prior of Michelsberg near Bamberg, who in the years 1098/99–1101 wrote this *World Chronicle*. Ekkehard (+ after 1125) continued Frutolf's work (recensions B, C, D, E) till Henry V and his marriage with Matilda. According to Pertz, the Corpus Christi codex belonged to Henry V and Matilda, and after the former's death was brought to England by Matilda. This theory is not generally accepted.

While the beautifully written text—in neat Gothic hand—has been attributed to three scribes, the illuminations and drawings are, with one exception, by one artist only. The text is written above the pictures. The 'portraits' apparently are based on seals, medallions, and coins.

Byzantine Influence. The new wave of Byzantine influence—referred to on p. 214 f. —is especially noticeable in illuminated books of Henry II's time. The coarse handling and slovenliness of execution that mark some of the Carolingian productions are less evident; the technique is much more masterly; the painting more methodical, in soundly worked body-colour with a certain sense of harmony; expression is improved (becoming quite superior to the utterly expressionless faces of Carolingian illumination); and there is a better sense of proportion (though a tendency to rather excessive tallness).

The development of illumination from Carolingian style is best seen in the *S. Henry's Missal* (preserved in the State Library at Munich *Cimel. 60—Cod. Lat. 4456*); its illuminations were copied from the famous *Emmeram Golden Gospels* of Charles the Bald, written by Liuthard and Berenger, and presented to Ratisbon. Whilst the general composition of the illuminations is precisely the same, the stylistic details are quite different. Another remarkable difference is of great historical and political significance: Charles the Bald is beardless and bears nothing in his hands, merely sitting as if addressing an assembly; Henry II has a pointed beard and holds in his hands the symbols of imperial authority: in his right hand a sceptre and in his left an orb and cross. Indeed, it has been pointed out that the orb surmounted by the cross never appears in Western art until the time of Henry II (in the miniature of Otto III it appears as a mere symbol).

Decadence of German Illumination

In striking contrast to the English, French, and Flemish illumination, which during the thirteenth century reached, with the Gothic movement, the zenith in development, Germany in this period ceased to take a leading place in the history of illumination. The delicate Gothic style had hardly any influence on German illumination. German miniaturists, argues Herbert, were content for the most part with the artistic formulae, compounded of Byzantine and Romanesque traditions, which had been elaborated during the twelfth century. They placidly repeated the old, harsh, lifeless types, the hard flat technique, the crude and discordant scheme of colour, of the style which the Rhenish schools had brought to such perfection as it was capable of by the end of the twelfth century.

And yet, several German masterpieces (which will be referred to further on), though artistically inferior to the French Gothic illumination in dramatic and spiritual conception, in the expression of the faces, in the plastic form of the body, in ornamental imagination, are not inferior to any contemporary production of the French or other schools.

Thirteenth Century

Thus, the decadence referred to was far from general. Indeed, *e.g.*, the thirteenth-century Thuringian-Saxon school (studied by Dr. Haseloff) produced exquisite Psalters, such as some specimens preserved in the British Museum (*Add. MSS. 17687* and *18144*), *MS. 309* in the Library of Duke Fuerstenberg, Donaueschingen, and so on.

A superb *codex*, known as *S. Elizabeth Psalter* (S. Elizabeth von Hungary, 1207-31, was the wife of Louis IV, Landgrave of Turingia, the son of Hermann), which was executed for Hermann, Landgrave of Thuringia (d. 1217) and his wife, Sophie, is preserved in the National Archaeological Museum at Cividale, N. Italy (*Codici Sacri 7*). It contains Calendar-illustrations (pp. 2–13), fifteen full-page miniatures and seven large miniatures, a full-page initial *B* (p. 28), and a number of other ornamented initials, illuminated borders, etc. There are strong Byzantine and English influences. Another *Psalter*, known as *Landgrafen Psalter*, executed for the same personages and in the same *scriptorium*, between 1211 and 1213, is preserved in the Landes Library at Stuttgart (*H.B. II. Bibl. 24*).

An *Evangelistarium*, produced in the early thirteenth century in Lower Saxony, is preserved in the Cathedral Archives at Brandenburg. A Saxon *Gospel-book*, possibly produced in Goslar *c.* 1230–40, is preserved in the Goslar Rathouse; a slightly later *Missal* executed in the same school, is in the Domgymnasium, Halberstadt (*No. 114*).

An elegant *Gradual*—in a style influenced by Flemish art—written and illuminated in 1299 by the Cologne Minor Friar Johann von Valkenburg, is preserved in the Diocesan Museum, at Cologne.

Weingarten. The Benedictine monastery of Weingarten (in the diocese of Constance) had an important *scriptorium* which was particularly active in the early thirteenth century. Countess Judith of Flanders, a patron of art who in 1051 married Earl Tostig of Northumbria, collected various books in England; when in 1071 she married again, becoming the wife of Duke Welf IV of Bavaria, she became patroness of the Weingarten Abbey, and in 1094 bequeathed to it her library. These MSS. served for over a century as models of the Weingarten artistic production. But not many Weingarten codices have been preserved which are earlier than the thirteenth century. A frontispiece to a lost codex on the *Life of S. Gregory* is preserved in the Art Institute of Chicago (*No. 44. 704*). It may be dated *c.* 1180–1200; there are two full-page miniatures, representing S. Gregory writing and (on the reverse) S. Gregory celebrating the Mass. A *Welf-Chronicle*, containing also other matter, produced *c.* 1179–91, is preserved in Fulda, Landesbibliothek (*MS. D. 11*). It contains a full-page miniature, representing Frederic Barbarossa between his sons.

Berthold, Abbot of Weingarten from 1200 to 1232, was the mainspring in the artistic production of this *scriptorium*, and 'was active in enhancing his abbey with fine books and other artistic works' (Miner). The *Berthold Missal*, commissioned by Berthold, is the main product of the Weingarten scriptorium, and one of the chief monuments of German romanesque art. Byzantine, English and Flemish influences are 'here fused with southern German traditions into a unique creative achievement' (Miner). It was in the Holkham Hall Library, and is now preserved in the Pierpont Morgan Library (*M. 710*). It contains twenty-one full-page and seven smaller miniatures, eighteen historiated and seventy ornamented initials. The chief miniatures are 'by an artist of exceptional brilliance and power. . . . Particularly characteristic are the intense, almost menacing expressions and gestures of the people. . . . The extraordinarily rich use of gold and silver, as well as many ornamental motives, recall the productions of the goldsmith' (Miner).

A copy of the *Minor Prophets*, partly (eight prophets) preserved in the Public Library at Leningrad (*MS. Lat. F.V.1. 133*), and partly (the last four prophets) in the Spencer Collection, New York Public Library, is attributed to the 'Master of the *Berthold Missal*'. The New York MS. contains nine large and twenty small historiated and illuminated initials. 'Although not as rich in its pictorial scheme, its miniatures display the powerful and original conception, the dynamic drawing and plastic rendering that reach their apogee in the Missal' (Miner).

Another *Missal*, executed in Weingarten between 1225 and 1250 by a follower of the 'Master of the *Berthold Missal*', is preserved in the Pierpont Morgan Library, New York (*M. 711*). It is not as forceful and dramatic as the *Missal* of the Master, but it presents the same lyric and highly artistic qualities.

We may here refer to a magnificent *Psalter* executed in the early thirteenth century in a Cistercian scriptorium in, or near, the Constance diocese, perhaps at Weingarten. The codex, now preserved in the University Library at Freiburg im Breisgau (*MS. 24*), contains a calendar (fol. 1–7), allied to that of Weingarten codices, eighteen full-page miniatures, eleven magnificent initials, 180 smaller initials, and so on. *See* E. J. Beer, *Ein Zisterzienserpsalter in der Freiberger Universitätsbibliothek*, 'Kunstwerke aus d. Besitz der A.-L.-Univ. Freiburg i.B. 1457–1957,' pp. 22–28.

Bavaria. Examples of Bavarian productions are: an early thirteenth-century *Miscellanea Codex* from the Aldersbach monastery, and a copy of *Carmina Burana*, of the first thirty years of the same century, from the Benediktbeuren monastery; both are preserved in the State Library at Munich (*Cod. Lat. 2599 and 4660*); also a copy of Martianus Capella, *De nuptiis Philologiae et Mercurii*, executed in the early thirteenth century at the Aldersbach monastery, is preserved in the Munich State Library (*Cod. Lat. 2590*); a copy of Wernher von Tegernsee, *Drei Lieder von der Magd*, of the first quarter of the thirteenth century, was preserved in the State Library at Berlin (*Germ. oct. 109*)—the codex has disappeared during the Second World War—it contained eighty-five illustrations.

[The Lucca State Library possesses (*MS. 1425*) an eleventh-century illuminated *Prayer-book* and *Missal* which probably comes from South Bavaria. A slightly later manuscript, containing S. Hildefonsus, *De virginitatae Sanctae Mariae* is preserved in the Palatina Library, Parma (*MS. 1650*). It is attributed to a monastic *scriptorium* in Bavaria. There are twenty-five full-page (or nearly full-page) miniatures, numerous initials and ornamented borders.]

Miscellanea. Two excellent productions of Rhenish schools may be referred to: a copy of S. Hildegard (*see* also p. 216), *Revelationes*, with ten superb full-page miniatures and beautiful initials in colour on gold background (State Library at Lucca, *MS. 1942*); and a *Roman Missal*, executed for the church of Aachen (or Aix-la-Chapelle), containing a full-page miniature with border, and several initials (preserved in the Laurentian Library, Florence, *MS. Med. Pal. 4*).

A thirteenth-century *Psalter*, produced in Augsburg, is partly preserved in Prague (*MS. XIV. E.3*); two illuminated leaves from the same MS. are in the Germanisches Museum, Nuremberg; one in the Gewerbe Museum, also at Nuremberg; and one, containing two full-page miniatures (the Crucifixion, on the *recto*, and the Three Maries at the Tomb, on the *verso*), is in the Rosenwald Collection, National Gallery of Art, Washington.

Detached leaves from an illuminated codex, attributed to Franconia, possibly to Wuerzburg, are dated *c.* 1240: they are preserved in the British Museum (*Add. MS. 17687*).

A *Psalter* executed *c.* 1260 in a Cistercian monastery of the Bâle diocese, is preserved in the Besançon Municipal Library (*MS. 54*).

Fourteenth Century

The most important German school of illumination of the fourteenth century was—curiously enough—the Bohemian school of Prague (see further on). Its style was carried to Nuremberg after the marriage of the Burgrave John to Margaret, daughter of Emperor Wenzel. Good work was also produced by the school of Salzburg, *e.g.* the grand *Salzburg Missal* (now at Munich, *Lat. 15710*).

A *Lectionary of the Gospels*, produced *c.* 1300 in a Rhenish *scriptorium*, is preserved in the Library of the Congress, Washington (*MS. acc. 558564*). It contains a large historiated initial, representing Christ enthroned amongst the four symbols and the four Evangelists writing. A *Lectionary of the Bible* and *Church Fathers*, produced in the second half of the fourteenth century in a Rhenish convent of Brigittine nuns, is preserved in the Walters Art Gallery, Baltimore (*W. 148*). It contains six large and twenty-three smaller miniatures, executed in 'a vigorous gothic style on heavy burnished gold grounds' (Miner); there are also four pen-and-ink drawings on fly-leaves.

Excellent example of the Upper Austrian illumination is a *Missal*, donated in 1320 by Michael sacerdos de Newnburga to the Cistercian monastery of Wilhering (Upper Austria): it is preserved there (*Cod. 9*).

A *Missal* of the first third of the fourteenth century, from the Pruem monastery, painted in the 'high Gothic' style, and influenced by Flemish and Parisian book-illumination, was preserved in the State Library, at Berlin (*Cod. Theol. Lat. fol. 271*), and is now in the Univ. Libr. at Tuebingen.

A *Missal*, illuminated in the style of Johann von Valkenburg (see p. 231), formerly in possession of Conrad von Rennenberg (+1357), the dean of the Cologne Cathedral, is preserved in the Cathedral Library, at Cologne (*Cod. 149*).

Fig. IV-34*b* is from a fourteenth-century *Gospel-book* produced in the Cologne *scriptorium*.

A fourteenth-century copy of *Speculum Humanae Salvationis* (see p. 389), preserved in Yale University Library (*MS. Z. 109. 073*), contains 170 drawings (out of the original 200); it is an excellent example of the popular didactic manuscripts, richly illustrated with rough drawings, which were produced in Germany in great numbers during the fourteenth and fifteenth centuries. The Yale MS., which in 1714 was given by Governor Elihu Yale to the college afterwards named after him, seems to be the first medieval illuminated codex to enter an American library.

A fourteenth-century copy of the *Biblia Pauperum* (see pp. 236 and 389) produced in a Danube school (perhaps at Ratisbon), is preserved in the National Library, at Vienna (*C. 1198*).

Illuminated Vernacular MSS. (Fig. IV-36)

What has been said about German illumination concerns primarily books written in the Latin language. Very little can be said about illuminated MSS. of the early period written in vernacular. Naturally, this literature which arose in the ninth and tenth centuries and steadfastly grew in the eleventh and twelfth centuries, demanded its copyists, illustrators and illuminators.

These primarily came from the monastic *scriptoria* and probably were the same penmen and artists who did the copying and embellishment of religious books.

Not many illuminated vernacular MSS. of the early period have come down to us. J. A. Herbert mentions an interesting codex preserved in the Berlin State Library (*MS. Germ. fol. 282*)—a copy of Heinrich von Veldegke's *Eneidt* (a free German paraphrase of Virgil's *Aeneid*)—illustrated with seventy-one fine drawings in red and black outline on panelled grounds of crimson, blue, green, or buff. There are representations of castles and armed knights, ships, battles, feasts and other delightful pictures, however crude they may be.

A charming, fragmentary copy of the *Jung frauen-Spiegel*, executed in the late twelfth century in Burg Brohl, near Andernach, is preserved in the Rhein. Museum at Bonn.

Of particular importance are the *Minnelieder* or *Minnesinger*, the artificial and courtly lyric, which flourished from the period of Barbarossa (*c.* 1122–90) to the times of Rudolf of Hapsburg (1218–91), but continued until the fourteenth century. The main collection of these love- and chivalry songs and poems is contained in the *Manesse Manuscript* (the 'famous Manessian Codex', as Goethe called it). There are one hundred and thirty-seven full-page miniatures, including hunting scenes and similar outdoor amusements, which are useful as studies of costume, but otherwise of little interest. Ruediger Manesse (who died in 1304) and his son Johannes collected the main stock of these *lieder*, and Zurich may be considered its birthplace. But the manuscript wandered from place to place (Zurich, Heidelberg, Forsteck, St. Gall, again Zurich, again Heidelberg, perhaps Rome and/or The Hague, then Paris, since 1657, and finally Heidelberg) till 1888, when it found its home in Heidelberg.

The majestic figure of Emperor Henry VI (1165–97), son of Barbarossa, opens the series of the miniatures, as well as the text of the *lieder*. He is given the prominence similar to that given to Christ in religious book-production. He is followed by Conradin (1252–68), the last in the male line of the Hohenstaufen dynasty, who finished his young life tragically in the market-square of Naples. The *minne-singers* von Kuerenberg, Spervogel, Dietmar von Eist, Friedrich von Hausen, Heinrich von Morungen, Heinrich von Veldeke, Reinmar (the Older) von Hagenau, "Klingsor von Ungerlant", Wolfram von Eschenbach, Heinrich von Ofterdingen, Walther von der Vogelweide, Kristan von Hamle, Werner von Teufen, Count Kraft von Toggenburg, Hartmann von Aue, Ulrich von Lichtenstein, Walter von Klingen, von Suonegge, Reinmar von Zweter, Gottfried von Strassburg, Heinrich Frauenlob, Johan Hadloub—poets who lived in the period from the late twelfth century to the early fourteenth century—are here represented: Fig. IV-36a–d.

In the thirteenth and fourteenth centuries illuminated vernacular works became more and more popular. There appeared a German paraphrase of the *Aeneid* (see p. 234), various illustrated original productions, such as *Tristan*, *Carmina Burana*, *Mariendichtung*, and other poems of love, chivalry, and so on. A copy of Gottfried von Strassburg, *Tristan*, executed *c.* 1240 in Strasbourg, in the *scriptorium* of the *magister burgensium*, Master Hesse von Strassburg, is preserved in the State Library at Munich (*Germ. MS. 51*). In the first half of the thirteenth century, Rudolf von Ems, a Swiss-Austrian *minnesinger*, wrote *Barlaam und Josaphat*, *Alexander*, and other epic poems, and *Chronicle of the World*, dedicated to Conrad IV (1228–54). This *Weltchronik* (which remained unfinished), a rhymed version of the Bible, supplemented by additions from other sources, religious or secular, was very popular in the fourteenth and fifteenth centuries, and over forty MSS. have been preserved. An early copy—written about 1300 in the district of Lake of Constance —is preserved in the Civic Library, at St. Gall (*Cod. 312*). An excellent copy written on paper, executed in 1402, is preserved in the Spencer Collection (*MS. 38*) of the New York Public Library. There are 287 coloured drawings, notable for their narrative charm and vigour of execution. 'Placed unframed upon the rough white paper, some occupy a column's width, others sweep informally across the page and into the margins. Always, however, the arrangement of script and picture results in a fine and unified page design' (D. Miner). *Cod. germ. 6406* of the State Library, at Munich, is another important copy of the *Chronicle of the World* (E. Petzet, *Eine Prachthandschrift der Weltchronik des Rudolf von Ems*, "Germ.— Roman. Monatsschr.", I, 1909, pp. 465–90). See also p. 242.

Eike von Repgow (also known as Repchow or Repkow) from Anhalt wrote about 1221/4 a popular law-book in Middle Low German, the *Saxenspiegel* (or *Sachsenspiegel* or *Sassenspegel*), which was soon diffused in thousands of MSS., and translated into Latin, Dutch, Czech and Polish. Illuminated MSS. became soon a necessity.

The original illuminated MS. is lost, but several copies have been preserved including those in the libraries of Heidelberg, Dresden, Wolfenbuettel and Oldenburg. They belong to the foureenth century; the oldest, of Heidelberg, was produced about 1300–25, very probably in Meissen. In 1571 it belonged to Ulrich Fugger who, in 1584, gave it to the Bibliotheca Palatina, Heidelberg. In 1624, this library was sent to the Vatican Library (by Tilly, the Commander of the Bavarian army in the 30-years War), but in 1819 the *Saxenspiegel* returned to Heidelberg. The illustrations accompany the text and explain it. They are very simple—childish, one may say—but very clear. The colours are red, green, and yellow. Most illustrations represent various legal actions, and it is interesting to note the symbolic meanings of the gestures, arm- and hand-movements of the people, and so on.

The Dresden codex has been dealt with by Karl von Amira, in *Dresdener Bilder-handschrift des Sachsenspiegels*, vol. I. (1902) and II. (1, 1925; 2, 1926).

We cannot deal here with all the illuminated vernacular MSS.; even a 'dry' list would cover many pages. We shall limit ourselves to the thirteenth- and fourteenth-century codices preserved in the State Library at Berlin (see H. Wegener, *Beschreibende Verzeichnisse* etc., Leipsic, 1928): *MS. Germ. fol. 282*: Heinrich von Veldeke, *Eneit*, with 71 illustrations; Ratisbon-Pruefening school, early thirteenth century. *MS. Germ. quart. 978*: Thomasin von Zirklaere, *Waelscher Gast* (fragm.); Bavarian school, late thirteenth century. Early fourteenth century: *MS. Germ. fol. 746* and *fol. 923, No. 43*: Ulrich von dem Tuerlin, *Willehalm* and *Der starke Rennewart*; Wolfram von Eschenbach, *Willehalm*; Frankish style. *MS. Germ. quart. 357*: *Legend of S. Francis of Assisi*; South-West Germany. *MS. Germ. fol. 129*: *Saxon Worldchronicle*, with about 400 illustrations; Lower Germany. First half of, and mid-fourteenth century: *MS. Germ. quart. 1254*: *Martyrdom and Crowning of S. Lawrence*; South Germany. *MS. Germ. oct. 125*: *Nagler Fragment* (allied to the *Manesse MS.*—see above); South-West Germany, c. 1320–40. *MS. Germ. quart. 1412*: *Redemption*; North-West Germany or Holland, 1337. *MS. Germ. fol. 623*: Rudolf von Ems, *Worldchronicle*, and Stricker, *Charlemagne*; Middle German. *MS. Germ. fol. 1362*: *Biblia pauperum* (further on and p. 389), 34 illustrations; Middle German. Late fourteenth century: *MS. Germ. fol. 631*:*Sachsenspiel*; Middle Rhenish. *MS. Germ. oct. 489*: *Prayer-book*; Saxony. *MS. Germ. fol. 1109*: Cassiodorus, *Historia Tripartita*; Austria (probably, Vienna), 1385. *MS. Germ. fol. 1343*: *Speculum humanae salvationis* (see p. 389); Rhenish, c. 1400. *MS. Germ. fol. 122*: '*Chronika*' of Austria (until 1398); c. 1400.

Hugo von Trimberg (1260–1313), *Der Renner*, was a widely spread didactic poem. An excellent copy, produced in Bavaria in 1431, is preserved at Heidelberg (Univ. Libr., *Cod. pal. germ. 471*), another copy is in Stockholm (see p. 243).

Three interesting copies of Otto von Passau, *Die 24 Alten* (of the *Apocalypse*)—see, particularly, W. Schmidt, *Die vierundzwanzig Alten Ottos von Passau*, "Inaugural-Dissertation", Berlin, 9-2-1933 and 6-5-1936—may also be referred to: (1) MS. by Erhart Koch of Weingarten, produced probably at Constance in 1435, formerly in the Taenikon monastery (Thurgau), later at Meersburg, now in Donaueschingen (Fuerstl. Fuerstenberg. Hofbibl., *Cod. 242*); (2) copy written in 1446 by Nicolas Kursener of Pirna, for George I of Anhalt (now preserved at Dessau, Landesbibl., *Georgs-Hs. 230. fol.*); (3) fragmentary MS. preserved in Berlin, Munich, Venice, and Nuremberg (Germ. Nat.-Mus. *St. 378*), c. 1450: the miniatures seem to be related to the panel-painting of 1444 of the "Weilheimer Master".

A Low-German *Breviary*, now lost, but until 1904 in the collection of the von Druffel family, Muenster i. W., produced about 1475 for Sophie, wife of Johann von Hemert, in memory of her first husband, Reynald von Homoet, Lord of Dorenwerth and Valberg (near Arnhem), contained miniatures of the Lower-Rhenish master who in the years 1470–80 apparently worked in Utrecht and in 1480/85–1510 was active in Cologne, where he executed his masterwork, the Bartholomew-altar, hence is known as the "Master of the Bartholomew-altar".

A fifteenth-century German *Bible*, known as the *Ottheinrichsbibel*, partly painted about 1450, but completed only after 1530 by Matthias Gerung, for the Kurfuerst Ottheinrich v.d. Pfalz, is preserved in the Munich State Libr. (*Cgm. 8010*, vols. 1 and 2).

Eberhard Windecke of Mainz, chronicler of the period of Emperor Sigismund (1361–1437), wrote political and satirical poems and compiled a sort of chronicle (collection of biographical and other records, political poems, etc.) known as *Emperor Sigismund's Book*. A copy of 1440–50, written on paper, and illustrated with 173 very large coloured drawings, executed with strength and vigour, 'characteristic of German secular graphic art at its best' (Miner), is preserved in the H. P. Kraus Collection, New York City.

Another chronicler, Ulrich von Richenthal, wrote the *Chronicle of the Council of Constance* (1414–18), which he based on his own diary and impressions. This important work was apparently executed between 1433 and 1450. The original MS. is lost, but nine copies are preserved; they are not identical. The best, known as *MS. A*, belonged to Count Koenigsegg, at Aulendorf; *MS. K* is preserved in the Rosgartenmuseum (*HS. 1*) at Constance; and *MS. Pr.* in the University Library, at Prague. Here we refer particularly to the copy of the New York Public Library. The MS., executed in an Upper Rhenish *scriptorium*, is written on paper, in South German dialect, and contains 115 coloured drawings and 837 coats of arms (preserved in the Spencer Collection, New York Public Library). The outlines of the drawings, freely executed, are tinted with thin washes of colour. Dr. Karl Kuep, of the New York Public Library, has suggested that the drawings, depicting buildings of Constance, were derived from sketches made on the spot. The Bâle University *matricula*, of 1460, painted by a Bâle master in the tradition of the Richenthal *Chronicle*, but probably belonging to the school of the Master ES, is preserved in the Bâle Univ. Libr. (*Cod. AN. II. 3*).

Two illustrated Swiss chronicles may here be referred to: (1) the *Tschachtlan Illustrated Swiss Chronicle*, produced c. 1470 and preserved in the Central Library, at Zurich (*MS. A. 120*); and (2) The *Spiezer Chronik*, also known as Diebold (or Diepolt) Schilling, *Bern Chronicle*, preserved in the Civic Library, at Luzern, and at Bern, Civic Library (*MS. Hist. Helv.*, I. 46).

Finally, reference may be made to the German translation of the *Biblia pauperum*, 'The Bible of the Illiterates,' a series of MSS., block-books, and printed books, which contain rude illustrations of Biblical subjects, with a short explanatory text accompanying each picture. An early fourteenth-century copy, preserved at S. Florian, Austria, is the first one known to have the triple arrangement: scenes from the life of Christ, pre-figurations or types occurring in the Old Testament, and the text in rhyming Latin verse. First printed in movable types in 1462, it became very popular in Germany, Holland and France.

An excellent German copy, of *c.* 1420, is preserved in the Spencer Collection, New York Public Library. It was produced in South Germany. There are thirty-nine half-page pen-drawings, executed in outline in a light and fluent style, enlivened by thin washes of colouring. 'A scene from the New Testament occupies a central roundel on each page, while subsidiary roundels contain busts of the prophets. On either side appear scenes from the Old Testament which are considered prophetic symbols of the central episode' (D. Miner).

The *Eberhard Prayer-book* (Wuertemberg. Landesbibl., Stuttgart, *Cod. Brev. 4°, No. 1*) may be referred to. It was executed—though not completed—in the years 1492–95 for Count (later Duke) Eberhard V (resp. I) Barbatus (1445–1496), the founder of the Tuebingen University, 1477. The illuminations of the codex may be grouped into (1) copies from the *Vienna Hours* (Nat. Libr., Vienna, *MS. 1855*) of the Bedford Master (*see p. 406*), produced soon after 1420; (2) a work of a North-French illuminator of about 1470; (3) "Kupferstichpassion" by Martin Schongauer; and (4) copper-engravings by the Master ES. (See J. Eschweiler, *Das Eberhardgebetbuch*, Stuttgart, 1951.)

We may end this section with the *Bidpai* (a fictitious Indian poet) or *Pančatantra* (= "five books"), preserved in the Heidelberg Univ. Library (*Cod. pal. germ. 84*). It is the earliest German translation of the cycle of animal stories of Buddhist Indian origin, known in its Arabic form as *Kalīla ve-Dimnah* (see p. 138). The German translation was done by Antonius of Pforr, the court-chaplain of Countess Palatine Mechthild, who commissioned this book for her son Eberhard Barbatus (see above), apparently on the occasion of the foundation of the University of Tuebingen (1477). The illumination of the codex is due to two excellent masters.

Fifteenth Century

In the fifteenth century, German illumination begins to grow gaudy, especially in the revived taste for parti-coloured border-frames, in which green and scarlet are often to be seen. The *Kuttenberg Gradual* (preserved in the National Library at Vienna, *No. 15501*) is of the Bohemian type (see p. 242 ff.). Now and then a MS. will show the influence of Westphalian treatment of foliage and, again, of the school of Cologne, or Nuremberg, or Augsburg. These all differ, whilst still keeping an unmistakable German character. The *Hildesheim Prayer-book*, at Berlin, points to Cologne. The *Frankendorfer Evangeliary*, at Nuremberg, is characteristic of that city. The *Choir-book of SS. Ulrich and Afra*, in their abbey at Augsburg, is also typical of its locality. The *Missal of Sbinco*, Archbishop of Prague, inclines rather to Nuremberg than Prague (preserved in the National Library at Vienna, *No. 1844*); it is eighty years earlier than the Augsburg and Hildesheim manuscripts.

A copy of Durandus, *Rationale*, executed for William the Affable, Duke of

Austria, 1370–1406, is preserved in the National Library at Vienna (*Cod. 2765*). Several hands can be recognized in its miniatures; the most important of its illuminators being Nicholas of Bruenn, the illuminator of the Court at Vienna. An illuminated copy of Aquinas, *Historia de Corpore Christi*, also produced for Duke William, has been attributed to Nicholas. The manuscript is preserved in the H. P. Kraus Collection, New York City.

Another Austrian manuscript, a *Prayer-book* of *c.* 1440, illustrated for an Austrian bishop, is preserved in the Walters Art Gallery (*W. 163*). There are thirty miniatures, three historiated initials, and numerous illuminated borders: Fig. IV-33*d*.

Parts of the eight-volume *Postil* by Nicholas de Lyra, written 1393 by Ruediger Schoepf from Memmingen, and illuminated 1400–06, are preserved in the Univ. Libr., at Bâle (*Codd. A. II. 5* and *13*).

In the fourteenth and fifteenth centuries many manuscripts were produced for popular use, and they provided prototypes for block-books. The majority, of course, were in the vernacular (see p. 234 ff.), but some continued to be in Latin. An example of such manuscripts, an *Apocalypse* of the early fifteenth century, is preserved in the New York Public Library (*MS. 15*). It contains thirty-six miniatures, the figures being drawn 'clearly and vigorously and enlivened . . . with delicate tints of yellow, green, red, etc. Excerpts from the text are scattered over the backgrounds, and red inscriptions in banderolles clarify the significance of the figures' (Miner). Another example, produced in 1414 in the monastery Metten, near Ratisbon, but influenced by Bohemian style of illumination, is a *Biblia Pauperum* (see pp. 236 and 389 f.) with interesting pen-wash drawings (State Library, Munich, *Clm. 8201. d*).

An interesting Canon Table—attributed to the Munich Master of the Augustin altar, and dated to *c.* 1410, is preserved in the Albertina Graphische Sammlung, at Vienna (*Inv. Nr. 4854*)—see *Katalog der Handzeichnungen der Albertina*, Vol. 4, No. 5.

A small *Psalter* (with abbreviated *Hours* and *Canticles*), preserved in the Library of Congress (*MS. 4560: 3: 16*), belongs to the second half of the fifteenth century. It contains twenty-three ornamented initials and a number of figures in borders. It was executed in a Brigittine convent, probably near Cologne, and is a good example of the Rhenish highly decorated provincial style. The first initial, however, is in a more refined style than the rest.

An interesting illuminated manuscript, written in 1434 at Bâle, is preserved in the Civic Museum at Padua (*MS. B.P.954*). It is by Joannes Franciscus Caputlistae, and has the title *De viris illustribus familiae Capitislistae*. There are thirty-one full-page miniatures representing several coats of arms and portraits of personages *de domo de Transelgardis, Forzate et Capite liste*. On fols. 33*r* and 34*r* are represented in half-length, twenty-four *doctores vel licentiati*.

A luxurious copy of the Bible, in seven large volumes, executed in Germany but showing strong Franco-Flemish influences, is preserved in the Casanatense Library, Rome (*MS. 4212*). It contains richly illuminated borders. A *Bible*, written in 1428 by Johannes Freybeck of Koenigsbrueck for Petrus Grillinger, *magister curiae camerae Salisburgensis*, as donation to the Salzburg Cathedral Library, is preserved in the State Library, at Munich (*Clm. 15701*). A *New Testament*, written at Nuremberg in 1422 by the notary Johannes Vorster, is in the Civic Library, at Nuremberg (*Cent. 1. 81*).

A *Missal* from Fritzlar, executed in 1421, is in the Cassel Landesbibl. (*MS. theol. fol. 114*); the last volume of a four-volume *Missal*, written and illuminated in 1481 by Berthold Furtmeyr of Ratisbon, for Archbishop Bernhard of Rohr, is preserved in the Munich State Libr. (*Clm. 15711*); single leaves by the same master, from another *Missal*, are preserved in the Kupferstichkab. at Berlin-Dahlem (*Einzelbl. 14707*); the Adolf von Breithardt *Missal*, produced in 1481 in a Middle-Rhine scriptorium, is at Mainz (Priesterseminar, *Hs. 5*).

Sixteenth Century

Although Germany was a cradle of the printing-press, we find illumination still in vogue there in the sixteenth century. With some exceptions, however, the productions were hardly outstanding. The books became more and more sumptuous, more profusely ornamented than ever.

Emperor Maximilian I Prayer-book. This magnificent volume, printed in 1513 at Augsburg, on parchment, by Hans Schoenperger, contains splendid pen-drawings —executed about 1515—by such artists as Albrecht Duerer, Lucas Cranach, Hans Burgkmair, Hans Baldung Grien, Joerg Breu (State Libr., Munich, *L. imper. 2. fol. m. 64*).

Glockendon. The *Missal cum Prayer-book* of Albert of Brandenburg, Archbishop of Mainz, once at Aschaffenburg, executed about 1524, is among the finest productions in the art of illumination. The painting of this MS. was the work of a famous Nuremberg miniaturist, one of a distinguished family of artists—Nicholas Glockendon. Though design has given way to profusion, and the border flowers and insects—a contemporary characteristic of Netherlandish art also (see p. 451 ff.)— are a sort of portraiture applied to flowers, fruits, and the insect world, the larger miniatures are exquisite paintings, including portraits, differing in nothing but dimensions from the works of the greatest masters of the schools of painting.

A very similar, perhaps even still richer, MS. is the *Prayer-book* of William of Bavaria (preserved in the National Library at Vienna, *No. 1880*), painted by Albert Glockendon. It is one of the most exquisite volumes possible to be met with. A German *Prayer-book*, executed in 1534 for Card. Albert of Brandenburg, is preserved in the Estense Library, Modena (*MS. α. U. 6. 7: Est. 136*). Fol. 2v. depicts the Cardinal's coat of arms under an arch ornamented with jewels and cameos. There are 41 full-page miniatures by Nicholas Glockendon, and numerous coloured initials on gold, and other rich decoration by George Stierlein. (Also *Bona Sforza Horae*—see p. 244—has been attributed to Glockendon.) Another work—though far inferior—by one of the Glockendons is a *Prayer-book* in the British Museum (*Add. MS. 17525*).

Finally, mention may be made of a handsome, large volume (44 by 35·5 cm. or 17¼ by 14 in.), written on paper in Latin and German, which was executed *c.* 1553, in South Germany, and is now preserved in the Hofer Collection, Rockport, Maine (U.S.A.). The text—Cyprian von Leowitz, *Lunar Eclipses*—was composed for Prince Otto Henry, Count Palatine, Duke of Bavaria, and forecasts the sun- and moon-eclipses from 1555 to 1559. There are sixty-one large illuminated astronomical drawings precisely executed and finely coloured, as well as seven miniatures in water-colour, 'showing the activities of men that will be interrupted at the place and time of the prophesied eclipse' (Miner).

PRAGUE, OR BOHEMIAN, SCHOOL OF ILLUMINATION

Bohemian illumination goes back to the eleventh century: Fig. IV-37*a* and *b*.

Prague, the capital of Czechoslovakia, is, of course, a Slavonic city, but in the fourteenth century its art—including illumination—was as German as the art of any German city. With John, the son of Emperor Henry VII, and particularly with the Emperor Charles IV (1316–78)—who in 1348 founded in Prague, his capital, the first of the German universities—apparently the first really important school of illumination was formed in that city.

But long before, several illuminated codices were produced in Bohemia, some going back to the eleventh century. The most famous is the *Coronation Evangeliar of Vratislav*, also known as the *Vyšehrad Gospel-book*, of 1085 (Plate IV-37*a*). In the opinion of a leading Czech art-historian, Jan Kvĕt (see *Czechoslovakian Miniatures*, Milan, 2nd ed., 1964), two illuminated codices preserved in Poland (*Czartoryski Gospels*, in Cracow, and the *Gniezno Cathedral Gospels*) and the *S. Vitus Chapter Library Gospels*, in Prague, are productions of the same school, perhaps the "First School of Bohemian Painting". This school was, apparently, active in the late eleventh and the early twelfth centuries, and was influenced by the Bavarian school.

Mention may also be made of the following illuminated codices of the twelfth and the thirteenth centuries: S. Augustinus, *De Civitate Dei* (*c.* 1140, Prague Castle Archives, *MS. A. 21/1*; *c.* 1200, S. Vitus Chapt. Libr., *MS. A. 7*); *Ostrov Psalter* (S. Vitus Chapt. Libr., *MS. A. 57/1*); *Mater Verborum* (*c.* 1200–1250; Nat. Mus. Libr., *MS. X. A. 11*); *Sedlec Antiphonary* (*c.* 1200–1250; Prague Univ. Libr., *MS. XIII. A. 6*); *Bible*, Second part (late thirteenth cent.; Nat. Mus. Libr., *MS. XII. B. 13*).

Charles IV. A man of brilliant personal accomplishments and cultivated tastes in literature and art, Charles invited painters and scholars from other countries, particularly from Italy and France, to reside in his capital. Also, the new University soon attracted numerous students.

For his 'Collegium Carolinum' he caused many noble volumes to be executed, and among the vast treasures and curiosities of his celebrated Karlstein Castle was a fine collection of illuminated MSS. In the Prague Museum and libraries, in the National Library at Vienna, and in other important collections, are preserved some relics of his great library. They are examples of the great variety of styles of the Bohemian school.

Main Works. Amongst the earliest works of this school is the *Passionale*, composed in 1312–21 for the Princess Cunigunda (daughter of Ottokar II Přemysl, king of Bohemia, 1253–78), Abbess of S. George's, in Prague. The work, composed by the Dominican Kolda and written by monk Benessius, is richly illustrated with interesting miniatures, and is preserved in the University Library at Prague (*xiv. A. 17*). The miniatures, also containing allegories, are painted in tender water-colours, the architectural details being in Gothic style. This work is entirely free from French influence, unlike the *Orationale* of Bishop Arnestus.

Other interesting works—all of the period of Charles IV, and mainly preserved in Prague—are the *Liber Viaticus* of Bishop John von Neumarkt (*c.* 1360; Nat. Mus. Libr., *MS. XIII. A. 12*), the *Pontificale* of Bishop Albert von Sternberg (preserved in the Premonstratensian Monastery at Strahow), the *Missal* of Archbishop Oczko von Wlaschim (in the Library of the Metropolitan Chapter at Prague), *Velislav Historiated Bible* (*c.* 1340; Univ. Libr., *MS. XXIII. C. 124*), *Breviary* of Gr. Master Leo of the Holy Cross Order (1356; Univ. Libr., Prague, *MS. XVIII. F. 6*), Conrad von Haimburg, *Laus Mariae* (*c.* 1364; Nat. Mus. Libr., Prague, *MS. XVI. D. 13*), the *Evangeliary* of Canon John de Oppavia (written and illuminated at Brno, in Moravia, and now in the National Library at Vienna); the last named is most beautifully written, its text is a model of elegant and perfect penmanship, and its ornaments are distinctly Bohemian. We may also refer to the *Evangeliar*, written and illuminated in 1368 by John of Troppau, Can. at Brno, for Duke Albrecht III of Austria, son-in-law of Charles IV (Nat. Libr., Vienna, *Cod. 1182*).

For costumes and curious usages, the *World-chronicle* of Rudolph von Ems, 1350–85 (preserved in the State Library at Stuttgart), the *Legenda Aurea*, of 1362 (preserved in the Public Library at Munich, *Cod. Germ. 6*), and the *Bellifortis* of Conrad Kyeser (preserved in the Public Library at Goettingen, *Philos., No. 63*) are almost encyclopaedias. See also pp. 236, 239, and 389.

Golden Bull. The most important thing associated with Charles IV is the *Golden Bull*, the key to the masterly scheme by which all matters concerning the election to the Empire were in future to be settled. In this book (the name of which derived from the *bulla* or seal of gold appended to it) were written all the Constitutions of the Empire. It was drawn up either at Metz or Nuremberg in 1356, and many copies were distributed throughout the Empire. A splendid copy, executed in 1400 by order of King Venceslaus (Charles' son, 1378–1409), is preserved in the National Library at Vienna (*J. c. 338*); its decoration contains soft curling foliages, variously coloured, and fresh carnations of flesh-tints. This style seems to have influenced the English style of illumination in the reign of Richard II, whose wife, Anne, was the daughter of Venceslaus (see p. 284).

Other Works. A few other works executed for Venceslaus are preserved, the grandest (though incomplete) being the *Venceslaus Bible*, executed by order of Martin Rotloew for presentation to the Emperor. The copy of *Willehalm*, by Wolfram von Eschenbach, of 1387 (now in the collection of Ambras Castle, near Innsbruck, Austria, *No. 7*) affords splendid examples of the fine embroidered and richly coloured backgrounds similar to those of the *Golden Bull* and of early fifteenth-century English MSS. Vol. I of a six-volume *German Bible*, which was produced after 1390 in the Venceslaus scriptorium, is preserved in the Nat. Libr. at Vienna (*Cod. 2759*); Conrad Keyser von Eichstaett, *Bellifortis*, produced in the same scriptorium about 1405 (Nieders. Staats- und Univ. Bibl., at Goettingen, *MS. philos. 63*); *Astrological MS.*, also from the same scriptorium (State Library, at Munich, *Clm. 826*), written after 1398—may also be referred to. A copy of Hugo von Trimberg, *Der Renner* (see p. 236), written by Michael Althaymer at Augsburg, and illuminated in a style influenced by that of the Bohemian school, is preserved in Stockholm (Royal Libr., *Cod. V. u. 14*).

A detached historiated initial U, containing a miniature representing the Holy Trinity, is preserved in the Rosenwald Collection, National Gallery of Art, Washington. Executed *c.* 1430, it is an excellent example of the Bohemian school of the period, showing the extreme delicacy of its style and its colouring. God the Father is represented as a gentle, white-haired giant; with downcast eyes glancing thoughtfully to one side, He places His hands lightly on the shoulders of the small figure of Christ, standing before Him and holding the Cross, on which alights the Holy Spirit in the form of a grey dove.

Arnestus of Pardubitz, Gerhard Groot, and the Brethren of the Pen. The first archbishop of Prague (1344–64)—and previously the twenty-eighth bishop of Prague (1343)—Arnestus or Ernest of Pardubitz, was an industrious collector of MSS. and employed many scribes. Another of the famous patrons of Prague was Gerhard Groot (also known as Gerrit or Geert Groot, or Groote or Groet, Groete, or de Groete)—1340–1384—who employed one of the best artists to copy S. John Chrysostom's *Commentary on S. Matthew*. In 1383 he founded at Deventer the famous House of the Brothers of the Common Life, who made a business of transcribing books; and, indeed, so profitably, that Ian van Enkhuisen of Zwolle received five hundred golden gulden for a Bible. On account of the goose-quill which the Brothers wore in their hats, they were familiarly known as the Brethren of the Pen.

BOHEMIA: BIBLIOGRAPHY

K. Chytl (in Czech), *Monuments of the Czech art of Illumination*: 1, A) *Illuminated MSS. of the fourteenth century—Library of the Museum of the Kingdom of Bohemia*, Prague, 1915.

J. Kvĕt (In Czech), *Italian influences on Bohemian illumination* etc. (with a summary in French), Prague, 1927; (in Czech, with a summary in French) *Queen Rejčka's illuminated manuscripts. Contributions to the history of illumination in Bohemia in the fourteenth century*, Prague, 1931; (in Czech), *Sculpture, painting and the decorative arts*, "Praha románska," Prague, 1948.

J. Krofta (in Czech), *The master of the breviary of John of Středa*, Prague, 1940.

H. Swarzenski and J. Kvĕt, *Czechoslovakia-Romanesque art and Gothic Illuminated manuscripts*, Paris, Unesco, 1959 (Unesco world art series).

POLAND: Illuminated book-production goes back to the twelfth century. Unfortunately, the twelfth-century codex (executed in the monastery of Płock) which until recently was preserved in the Cathedral Library of Płock (Poland) was destroyed in the last World War. It had not been edited, but photographs had been taken, and these have been published by M. Morełowski in the Polish magazine *Biuletyn Historii Sztuki*, Warsaw, XV (1953): see Fig. IV-37c.

All the earlier book-production, both illuminated and non-illuminated, is in Latin. The earliest extant illuminated MS. in the Polish language is the *Puławy Psalter* (preserved in the Czartoryski Museum, Cracow). Interesting is the *Cracow Guild-book*, written in German and Latin by city-scribe Balthasar Behaim, and illuminated in Cracow about 1505. It contains 25 miniatures of the guilds, painted in an apparently German style, influenced by Albrecht Duerer (Cracow, Jagiell. Libr., *Cod. 14, MS. 16*).

In Poland, illumination flourished particularly in the late fifteenth and in the sixteenth centuries, Cracow being its main centre. King Sigismund I (1467–1548) and his wife Bona Sforza (daughter of Gian Galeazzo, Duke of Milan) were great patrons of art. Two Polish illuminators are outstanding: (1) the 'Master of *Behem Codex*', 1505 (preserved in the University Library at Cracow), who also painted the *Liber Pontificalis* of Bishop Erasmus Ciołek, 1500–6 (now in the Czartoryski Museum, Cracow). (2) Stanislas Mogiła (*c*. 1480–*c*. 1540) apparently was a pupil of the 'Master of *Behem Codex*'. The following works are by, or are attributed to, Mogiła: four Books of Hours, *King Sigismund I Horae*, 1524, acquired by the British Museum in 1884; *Queen Bona Sforza Horae*, 1527–28, since 1834 in the Douce collection (Bodleian Library, *MS. Douce 40*, Oxford)—by some scholars attributed to Nicholas Glockendon (see p. 240); *Adalbert Gasztołd Horae*, 1528 (preserved in the National Museum at Munich); and *Christopher Szydłowiecki Horae*, 1528–32 (now in the Ambrosian Library, Milan); as well as Jan Długosz (Longinus), *Lives of the Gniezno Archbishops and of the Cracow Bishops*, 1532–5 (Zamoyski Library, Warsaw, *MS. Cim. 5*) and *Bishop Tomicki Gospel-book*, produced in 1534, which is one of the last representatives of good book-painting in Poland. Fig. IV-37d is from *Adalbert Gasztołd Horae*.

SCANDINAVIA AND ICELAND

Relatively few illuminated books have come down to us from these countries. Dr. Carl Nordenfalk, the greatest living authority in this field, gives the following two reasons for this scarcity: (1) the production of fine books was very modest in this part of the world all through the Middle Ages; (2) the literary legacy of the Middle Ages suffered a severe loss during the time of reformation; the religious policy of the Swedish and Danish governments induced the population to surrender the manuscripts to all kinds of craftsmen (bookbinders, gluemakers, and so on), who could make use of parchment in their daily work; or else, these books were simply thrown away as dangerous remnants of the papistic past.

Dalby-boken or *Dalby Gospels* (Fig. IV-38*a*), of the second half of the eleventh century, now preserved in the Royal Library at Copenhagen (*Gl. Kgl. Saml. 1325, 4°*), is the earliest extant manuscript attributed to ancient Danemark. (Dalby cathedral is in Scania, which was once an independent Danish kingdom, and is now the most southern province of Sweden). But only from the second half of the twelfth century, in Nordenfalk's opinion, there appeared 'something resembling a Northern style of handwriting' and in illumination 'a certain crude power as in the *Scara Missal*', or as in the books illuminated on Iceland in the fourteenth and fifteenth centuries. The earliest preserved Icelandic MS. is a fragmentary copy (consisting of two fragments) of *Physiologus* (see p. 49), preserved in the University Library at Copenhagen (*AM 673a*). It belongs to *c.* 1200 or the first half of the thirteenth century: Fig. IV-38*b*. Slightly later (1250–75) is a copy (also fragmentary) of *Calendarium Latinum*, preserved in the same collection (*AM 249c*). There is also a copy of *Nicholas Saga*, of the first half of the fourteenth century. The following are copies of the *Stjórn*: *AM 227* (*c.* 1350), *AM 350* (1363), *AM 233a* (1350–1400), *AM 673a* (1400–1500), and others. Early Icelandic illuminated manuscripts are also preserved in the Royal Library at Stockholm (*Isl. perg. 5, 16,* etc.).

Kong Magnus Lagaboters Norske Landslov, of 1325–50 (Royal Library at Copenhagen, *Gl. Kgl. Saml. 1154*) is a good representative of early Norwegian illumination. Fig. IV-38*d* is from an early Danish *Necrology*.

A twelfth-century *Gospel-book*, also preserved in the Royal Library at Copenhagen (*Gl. Kgl. Saml. Thott. 20.4*), is either a German production (executed at Helmarshausen: see p. 226) or a Swedish production (executed at Lund): see Fig. IV-38*c*. A copy of *Kong Magnus Erikssons Landslov*, of 1350–75 (Royal Library at Stockholm, *B. 10*) is an excellent representative of fourteenth-century illumination. Another copy of the same work is preserved in the Friherre Rutger von Essen Collection, Skokloster (*MS. 144*).

BIBLIOGRAPHY

J. O. Westwood, *Fac-similes of the Miniatures & Ornaments of Anglo-Saxon and Irish Manuscripts*, London, 1868; *The Bible of the Monastery of St. Paul near Rome, described and compared with other Carolingian Manuscripts*, Oxford, 1876.

L. Delisle, *Mémoire sur d'anciens sacramentaires*, Paris, 1886; *L'Évangéliare de Saint-Vaast d'Arras et la calligraphie franco-saxonne du IXe siècle*, Paris, 1888.

M. MacNair Stokes, *Early Christian Art in Ireland*, London, 1887; Dublin, 1911 and 1928.

K. Menzel, P. Corssen, H. Janitschek, etc., *Die Trierer Ada-Handschrift*, Leipsic, 1889.

W. Voege, 'Eine deutsche Malerschule um die Wende des ersten Jahrtausends,' *Westdeutsche Zeitschr. fuer Gesch. u. Kunst*, Ergaenzungsheft VII, 1891.

A. Goldschmidt, 'Der Utrechtpsalter,' *Repertorium fuer Kunstw.*, 15 (1892), pp. 156–69; 'Die aeltesten Psalterillustrationen,' *ibid.*, 23 (1900), pp. 265–73; *Das Evangeliar im Rathaus zu Goslar*, Berlin, 1910; 'Ueber den Stil d. angelsaechs. Malerei,' *Sitzungsberichte d. Preuss. Akad. d. Wissensch.*, Berlin, 1917, p. 375; *Die deutsche Buchmalerei*: I. *Die karolingische Buchmalerei in Deutschland*, Florence-Munich, 1928; II. *Die ottonische Buchmalerei in Deutschland*, ibid., 1928; 'A German Psalter of the twelfth cent. written in Helmarshausen,' *Journ. of the Walters Art Gallery*, I (1938); 'The decoration of the early Mainz books,' *Magazine of Art*, 1938; 'Die Luzerner illustr. Handschr. d. Schachzabelbuches d. schweizer Dichters Konrad von Ammenhausen: Ein Beitrag z. Gesch. d. Buchmalerei d. 14. und 15. Jahrh.,' *Innerschweizerisches Jahrb. fuer Heimatkunde*, Luzern, 1946.

J. von Schlosser, *Schriftquellen zur Geschichte der karolingischen Kunst*, Vienna, 1892; 'Eine Fuldaer Miniaturhandschrift etc.,' *Jahrbuch d. Kunsthist. Samml. d. Allerh. Kaiserhauses*, 1892.

F. F. Leitschuh, *Geschichte der karolingischen Malerei*, Berlin, 1894; *Die karolingische Malerei, etc.*, Bamberg, 1906.

J. J. Tikkanen, *Abendlaendische Psalter-Illustration des Utrecht-Psalters*, Helsingfors, 1900.

T. K. Abbott, *Catalogue of the Manuscripts in the Library of Trinity College*, Dublin, 1900.

G. Swarzenski, *Die Regensburger Buchmalerei*, Leipsic, 1901; *Karolingische Miniatur und Plastik in Reims*, Berlin, 1902; 'Reichenauer Maleri und Ornamentik im Uebergang v. d. karolingischen zur ottonischen Zeit,' *Repertorium fuer Kunstw.*, 1903; *Die Salzburger Malerei*, Leipsic, 1913; *Vorgotische Miniaturen. Die ersten Jahrh. deutsch. Malerei*, 2nd ed., Koenigstein im Taunus-Leipsic, 1931; *Die lateinischen illuminierten Handschriften des XIII. Jahrh. in den Laendern am Rhein, Main und Donau*, Berlin, 1936; *The Berthold Missal*, New York, 1943; 'The Anhalt Morgan Gospels,' *The Art Bulletin*, 1949.

G. B. Brown, *The Arts in Early England*, 6 vols. London, 1903–57.

J. Romily Allen, *Celtic Art in Pagan and Christian Times*, London, 1904.

J. M. Doran, 'The . . . Origin of the Ornament in the Book of Durrow,' *Burlington Magazine*, 1908.

F. Cabrol, *L'Angleterre chrétienne avant les Normands*, Paris, 1910.

C. Plummer, *Vitae Sanctorum Hiberniae*, Oxford, 1910.

C. W. C. Oman, *England before the Norman Conquest*, London, 1910.

E. H. Zimmermann, 'Die Fuldaer Buchmalerei in karolingischer u. ottonischer Zeit,' *Kunstgeschichtliches Jahrb. d.k.k. Zentralk. f. Kunst- u. Hist. Denkm.*, 1910; *Vorkarolingische Miniaturen*, 5 vols., Berlin, 1916.

L. Gougaud, *Les Chrétientés celtiques*, Paris, 1911; *Christianity in Celtic Lands*, London, 1932.

G. H. Orpen, *Ireland under the Normans*, 4 vols., Oxford, 1911–20.

A. Boinet, *La Miniature carolingienne*, Paris, 1913; *Les manuscrits à peintures de la Bibliothèque Sainte-Geneviève*, Paris, 1921.

L. Weber, *Einbanddecken, . . . Miniaturen, Schriftproben aus Metzer liturgischen Handschriften*, Metz, 1913.

J. Gwynn, *Liber Ardmachanus, The Book of Armagh*, Dublin, 1913.

British Museum, *Schools of Illumination*, Reproductions from Manuscripts, 6th part (Hiberno-Saxon, English and French), London, 1914–30; *Guide to an Exhibition of English Art*, London, 1934.

E. Sullivan, *The Book of Kells*, London, 1914; 5th ed., repr., 1955.

G. Leidinger, *Das sogenannte Evangeliarium Kaiser Otto III* ("Miniaturen aus Hanschriften der Kgl. Hof- und Staatsbibliothek in Muenchen," Heft 1), Munich, s.d.; *Der Codex Aureus* (facsimiles: 253 coloured plates), 4 vols., Munich, 1921–25.

E. G. Millar, *The Lindisfarne Gospels*, London, 1923; *English Illuminated Manuscripts*, 2 vols., Paris and Brussels, 1926–8.

A. Merton, *Buchmalerei in St. Gallen*, Leipsic, 1923.

A. M. Friend, 'Carolingian Art in the Abbey of St. Denis,' *Art Studies*, 1923; 'Two Manuscripts of the School of St. Denis,' *Speculum*, 1926.

K. Porter, 'Spain or Toulouse?,' *The Art Bulletin*, 1924; *The Crosses and Culture of Ireland*, New Haven, 1931.

A. Wilmart, 'Les Livres de l'abbé Odbert,' *Bulletin de la Soc. d. Antiqu. de la Morinie*, 1924.

K. Kuenstle, *Die Kunst des Klosters Reichenau im IX. und X. Jahrb.*, 2nd ed., Freiburg im Breisgau, 1924.

A. Schmidt, *Die Miniaturen des Gerokodex*, Leipsic, 1924.

J. Brøndsted, *Early English Ornament etc.*, London and Copenhagen, 1924.

E. T. de Wald, 'The Art of the Scriptorium of Einsiedeln,' *The Art Bulletin*, 1925.

K. Loeffler, *Der Landgrafenpsalter*, Leipsic, 1925.

N. Åberg, *The Anglo-Saxons in England, etc.*, Uppsala, 1926.

K. Pfister, *Irische Buchmalerei*, Potsdam, 1927.

H. Wegener, *Beschreibende Verzeichnisse der Miniatur-Handschriften der Preussischen Staatsbibliothek zu Berlin*, Leipsic, 1928.

F. M. Carey, 'The Scriptorium of Reims,' *Classical and Medieval Studies in Honor of E. K. Rand*, New York, 1928.

E. K. Rand, *Studies in the Script of Tours, I: A Survey of the Manuscripts of Tours*, Cambridge (Mass.), 1929.

G. Neckel, *Germanen und Kelten, etc.*, Heidelberg, 1929.

L. Coutil, *L'Art mérovingien et carolingien*, Bordeaux, 1930.

A. Boeckler, *Abendlaendische Miniaturen bis zum Ausgang der romanischen Zeit*, Berlin and Leipsic, 1930; *Das Goldene Evangelienbuch Heinrichs III*, Berlin, 1933; 'Die Illustrierung d. deutsch. Profanlit. in Handschr. d. 14. u. 15. Jahrh.,' *Sitzungs-ber. d. Preuss. Akad. d. Wissensch.*, Phil.-hist. Kl., Berlin, 1936; *Codex Wittekindeus*, Leipsic, 1938; *Deutsche Buchmalerei vorgstischer Zeit*, Koenigstein, 1952; *Deutsche Buchmalerei der Gotik*, Koenigstein, 1959; *Das Perikopenbuch Kaiser Heinrichs II*, Stuttgart, 1960.

K. Preisendanz and O. Homburger, *Das Evangelistar des Speyrer Doms*, Leipsic, 1930.

W. Koehler, *Die karolingischen Miniaturen, I: Die Schule von Tours*, Berlin, 1930.

T. D. Kendrick, *A History of the Vikings*, London, 1930; *Anglo-Saxon Art to A.D. 900*, London, 1938.

E. Dewald, *The Stuttgart Psalter*, Princeton, 1930.

J. Ryan, *Irish Monasticism etc.*, Dublin and Cork, 1931.

M. Schott, *Zwei luetticher Sakramentare aus Bamberg u. Paris, u. ihre Verwandten*, Strasbourg, 1931.

G. P. Krapp, *The Paris Psalter and the Meters of Boëthius*, New York, 1932; — and E. van Kirk Dobbie (ed.), *The Anglo-Saxon Poetic Records (The Junius Manu-script, The Vercelli Book, The Exeter Book, etc.)*, New York, 1931–42.

A. Mahr, *Christian Art in Ancient Ireland, etc.*, Dublin, 1932.

E. T. Leeds, *Celtic Ornament in the British Isles down to A.D. 700*, Oxford, 1933.

A. W. Clapham, 'Notes on the Origins of Hiberno-Saxon Art,' *Antiquity*, 1934.

A. Bruckner (ed.), *Scriptoria Medii Aevi Helvetica*, Geneva, 1934.

W. Gernsheim, *Die Buchmalerei der Reichenau etc.*, Munich, 1934.

F. C. Burkitt, 'Kells, Durrow, and Lindisfarne,' *Antiquity*, 1935.

R. P. Hinks, *Carolingian Art*, London, 1935.

B. Salin, *Die altgermanische Tierornamentik etc.*, 2nd ed., Stockholm, 1935.

E. Curtiss, *A History of Medieval Ireland, etc.*, 2nd ed., London, 1938.

G. L. Micheli, *L'Enluminure du haut moyen âge et les influences irlandaises*, Brussels, 1939.

W. Weisbach, *The Pictures of the Evangelists in the so-called Gospels of Otto III etc.*, London, 1939.

R. B. A. Mynors, *Durham Cathedral Manuscripts*, Oxford, 1939.

R. H. Hodgkin, *A History of the Anglo-Saxons, etc.*, 2 vols., 2nd ed., Oxford, 1939.

C. H. Verbist, *Saint Willibrord, etc.*, Louvain, 1939.

F. Henry, *Irish Art, etc.*, London, 1940; *L'Art irlandaise*, 3 vols., Paris, 1963–64.

D. Knowles, *The Monastic Order in England, etc.*, Cambridge, 1940 (repr. 1949).

J. L. Weisberger, *Die keltischen Voelker im Umkreis von England*, Marburg, 1941.

BIBLIOGRAPHY

A. Boutemy, 'Les Enlumineurs de l'abbaye de Saint-Amand and quelques manuscrits à peintures peu connus de l'abbaye de Saint-Amand,' *Revue Belge d'Arch. et d'Hist. de l'Art*, 1942; 'La Miniature (VIIIe-XIIe s.),' *Histoire de l'Église en Belgique*, 1946; 'Un grand enlumineur du Xe siècle: l'abbé Odbert de Saint-Bertin,' *Annales de la Fed. arch. et hist. de la Belg.*, 1947; 'Quel fut le foyer du style franco-saxon?,' *Annales du Congr. arch. et hist. de Tournai*, 1949; 'Odbert de Saint-Bertin et la seconde Bible de Charles le Chauve,' *Scriptorium*, 1950.

O. Homburger, 'Eine unveroeffentl. Evangelienhandschr. aus d. Zeit Karls d. Grossen: *Codex Bernensis 348*,' *Zeitschr. f. schweiz. Kunstgesch. u. Archaeologie*, 1943.

M. L. W. Laistner, *A Hand-list of Bede Manuscripts*, Ithaca, New York, 1943.

P. Salmon, *Le Lectionnaire de Luxeuil*, Rome, 1944–53.

A. M. Mars, 'Polish Miniature Painters in the first half of the Sixteenth Century,' *The Burlington Magazine*, LXXXI (1945).

F. Wormald, 'The Survival of Anglo-Saxon Illumination after the Norman Conquest,' *Proceedings of the British Academy*, 1944; *English Drawings of the Tenth and Eleventh Centuries*, London, 1952; *The Utrecht Psalter*, Utrecht, 1953; *The Benedictional of St. Ethelwold*, London, 1959.

H. Jantzen, *Ottonische Kunst*, Munich, 1947.

F. Masai, *Essai sur les origines de la miniature dite irlandaise*, Brussels and Antwerp, 1947; — and H. Vanderhoven, *Regula Magistri*, Brussels, 1953.

F. Dvornik, *The Making of Central and Eastern Europe*, London, 1949.

M. D. Legge, *Anglo-Norman in the Cloister*, Edinburgh, 1950.

F. M. Stenton, *Anglo-Saxon England*, 2nd ed., repr., Oxford, 1950.

C. Fox and B. Dickins (ed.), 'The Early Cultures of N.-W. Europe,' *H. M. Chadwick Memorial Studies*, Cambridge, 1950.

T. Burckhardt (ed.), *The Book of Kells (Codex Cennanensis)*, 3 vols., Olten and Bern, 1950; *Die irischen Miniaturen der Stiftsbibliothek St. Gallen (The Irish Miniatures in the Abbey Library of St. Gall)*, Olten-Bern-Lausanne, 1953; *Codex Lindisfarnensis—The Lindisfarne Gospels*, Olten and Lausanne, vol. I, 1956; vol. II, 1960; *Codex Durmachensis—The Book of Durrow—*, Olten and Lausanne, 1960; *Von wunderbaren Buechern*, Olten-Lausanne-Freiburg im Breisgau, 1964.

A. M. Cetto, *Miniatures du Moyen Age*, Lausanne, 1950.

E. S. Duckett, *Alcuin, Friend of Charlemagne, his World and his Work*, New York, 1951.

C. M. S. Niver, 'A Study of Certain of the more important Manuscripts of the Franco-Saxon School,' *Harvard University Graduate School of Arts and Sciences*, Thesis, 1951.

D. Talbot Rice, *English Art, 871–1100*, Oxford-London, 1952.

J. Leclercq, 'Les Manuscrits de l'abbaye de Liessies,' *Scriptorium*, 1952.

K. Martin (ed.), *Minnesänger. Achtzehn farbige Wiedergaben a. d. Manesseschen Liederhandschrift*, Baden-Baden, 1953.

A. Gwynn, 'Some Notes on the History of the Book of Kells,' *Irish Historical Studies*, Sept. 1954.

HIBERNO-SAXON, CAROLINGIAN AND OTTONIAN

T. H. White (Editor), *The Book of Beasts* (Translation), London, 1954.

P. H. Feist, *Meisterwerke deutscher Buchmalerei um das Jahr 1000*, Dresden, 1955.

Festschrift zur 900-Jahr-Feier des Klosters Weingarten, Weingarten, 1956.

H. Schnitzler. *Alte Kunst im Schnuetgen-Museum*. Cologne, 1956.

P. Hunter Blair, *An Introduction to Anglo-Saxon England*, Cambridge, 1956.

M. and L. De Paor, *Early Christian Ireland*, London, 1958.

"St. Katharinenthal Gradual": *Neue Zuercher Zeitung*, 10-12-1958; 22-12-1958, and 28-12-1958; D. Schwarz and E. Maurer, *Atlantis*, 1958; A. Knoepfli, *Librarium*, 1959.

D. M. Wilson, *The Anglo-Saxons*, London, 1960.

N. K. Chadwick, *The Age of the Saints in the Early Celtic Church*, London, 1961.

W. Kosch, *Deutsches Literatur-Lexikon*, Bern and Munich, 1963.

J. Beckwith, *Early Medieval Art: Carolingian-Ottonian-Romanesque*, London, 1964.

C. N. L. Brooke, *Europe in the Central Middle Ages, 962–1154*, London, 1964.

W. Braunfels, D. Koetzsche and G. Moersch (ed.), *Karl der Grosse. Werk und Wirkung* (Exhibition), Aachen, 1965.

Der Stuttgarter Bilderpsalter, facsim. ed., 2 vols., Stuttgart, 1965–66.

Chapter V

THE GOLDEN AGE

OF ILLUMINATION

The last three centuries of the Middle Ages were the Golden Age of book-illumination, particularly in Italy, France, and Flanders. Curiously enough, the art of illumination of these countries in the first two centuries of the present millennium was very poor indeed. But during these culturally dark and politically troubled years the real foundations of medieval civilization were laid, and Western civilization was beginning to take shape. In the second half of the tenth century political stability was re-established in the West (Otto the Great was crowned in Rome in 962), the first of the reform movements of monasticism set out from Cluny (see p. 372 f.), and the Romanesque style was created. In certain respects this was the first European style of architecture.

In dealing with the Gothic style of illumination we shall mention the relationship between architecture in general and book-illumination. This relationship is also manifest—though only indirectly and to a much lesser degree—in the Romanesque period.

The Romanesque style—or, rather, styles—of architecture was essentially ecclesiastic. Pevsner has suggested that while actual building operations were the job of the craftsman, the designing of churches and monasteries in the early Middle Ages may often have been due to clerics. And he rightly emphasizes that '. . . during those centuries nearly all the literati, the educated, the sensitive were clerics.' No wonder, therefore, that—as Prof. Pevsner has pointed out—S. Bernward, the bishop who was responsible for the building of S. Michael's at Hildesheim (see p. 224), was 'foremost in writing, experienced in painting, excellent in the science and art of bronze founding and in all architectural work'; that S. Aethelwold (see pp. 192, 194 f., and *passim*) was a 'theoreticus architectus', that Benno, Bishop of Osnabrueck in the eleventh century, was 'an outstanding architect, a skilful planner ("dispositor") of masonry work.'

Also English medieval records mention such versatile clerics, trained in a variety of arts, such as calligraphy, painting, sculpture or metalwork. It will suffice to allude to the twelfth-century monk of St. Albans, Walter of Colchester, who was trained as painter and sculptor, as well as metalworker. Master Hugo, the illuminator of the great Bury Bible (see p. 255), was responsible for the double bronze doors of the church of S. Edmund in Bury St. Edmunds, for the cross in the choir flanked by figures of the Virgin and S. John, and for a great bell cast at Bury—see M. W. Roskill, *Medieval Manuscript Illumination in England as exemplified by the Bury Bible*, Lapsley Essay Prize 1954–5, University of Cambridge.

The effect of Romanesque art throughout Western Europe was to form peculiar styles in each country. The Norman style, which made English medieval architecture, was its 'most consistent variety . . . in the West' (Pevsner). Moreover, by the end of the eleventh century, various changes began to appear, resulting in more complex, more individual, more varied, and more lively forms, and about 1100— with the rebuilding of the monastery of Cluny (see p. 372)—Early Romanesque was transformed into High Romanesque.

ENGLAND

TWELFTH CENTURY—ROMANESQUE OR NORMAN PERIOD

W. Oakeshott considers this period as in some ways the greatest, in all ways the most ambitious period in the history of English illumination. 'The artist is thinking in new terms—severity, dignity, power. . . . It is the exception for any tenderness to be allowed a place.' Thus—concludes Oakeshott—in the books of the twelfth century English art reaches a pinnacle of achievement which outsoared the rest because its aims were loftier.

Indeed, it was a period of experiment and transition. As with most things in this magnificently adaptable island, the first shock of the Norman Conquest and the Normanizing of English civilization were followed by re-adjustment of old traditions and standards to the influx of new thoughts and new influences. The intermingling of Norman and English was progressing fast, and—though only at a later period was the process completed—English was beginning to take pride of place. It was the start of the final phase in the welding of the English nation into one compact body.

At the same time, external influences operated in full. Thanks to the Crusades, influences of Oriental art, particularly Byzantine and Syrian, were felt more than before, and the art of architecture—Romanesque at the height of its development— was not without reflection in the art of illumination. Byzantine influence was, indeed, felt before 1100: striking use of gold paint (for instance, in the *Hereford Gospel-book*, see p. 258), heavy colour, 'mushroom' trees in the background, and other characteristic Byzantine features appeared here and there, but these were not more than isolated instances. It was not until the second or third decade of the twelfth century that a number of clearly Byzantine features became part and parcel of the English style.

Contacts with the art of the Continent were established and maintained; monk-painters and craftsmen were invited from the Continent, or were exchanged. Thus, certain continental influences were accepted, but (again, as with most things in this country) they were completely assimilated and failed to swamp the old traditions. The keynote—writes the leading authority, F. G. Wormald—is the manner in which the English artist took styles from abroad and combined them with the native tradition.

This ability to assimilate each successive innovation, so typical even in modern England, is one of the main characteristics of English twelfth-century illumination. In the most characteristic products of English twelfth-century art, the great illuminated Bibles—writes O. E. Saunders—we find a multitude of elements fused into a distinctive and highly decorative style, which can hold its own with that of any other country.

The main products of this period are fine Bibles, Psalters, Missals, and other liturgical service-books, executed in monumental size, and in a more luxurious manner and with more expensive materials than ever before. These sumptuous codices, which would occupy a worthy place upon the altars of the rich monastic churches, are in a certain way connected with the contemporary monastic liturgical life and the new elaborate and colourful ceremonies introduced during the second great reform of English monasticism.

The eleventh-century initial-illumination was still widely used, but it became enlivened by an interlace of leaves, stems and branches, by the introduction of winged dragons, birds, fighting men, signs of the Zodiac, and so on, as well as by scenes illustrating the text. A characteristic MS. of the period is preserved in Princeton University Library (*Garrett MS. 73*); it contains Haymo of Halberstadt, *Commentary on Isaiah*. It is written in a 'large, handsome script well placed on the suede-like vellum'. There are only three ornamental initials, but they are executed —writes Dorothy Miner—in delicate pen outline in brown ink, showing birds, animals, and grotesques on grounds of light blue, green and lavender. The initial showing Isaiah is in the best English outline style of the period, and resembles the work of Bury St. Edmunds or St. Albans. There is some use of dull gold and of silver.

The full-page miniature, however, became the more characteristic feature of the great books of the twelfth century. The Bible picture-cycle was enlarged, and new *genres* were introduced, such as the Last Judgment, the Jesse Tree, the 'Types and Anti-types' (parallel scenes from the Old and the New Testament), and scenes from the lives of the patron saints of the individual monasteries.

Schools of Illumination

With the beginning of the twelfth century the Winchester school (see p. 256 f.) ceased to be the only important centre of illumination in England, though it continued to be one of the two main centres, the other one being Canterbury. The works executed in the schools at Durham, Westminster, St. Albans, Bury St. Edmunds, Hereford, were, moreover, of much the same high quality as those produced at Winchester. Excellent work was produced in some other *scriptoria*—a very fine *Chartulary*, of *c.* 1146, of Sherborne Abbey, Dorset, acquired in 1947 by the British Museum, and now bearing the mark *Add. MS. 46487*, includes two striking miniatures of SS. Mark and John, showing strong Byzantine influence.

Moreover, not all English twelfth-century productions can be assigned to a definite *scriptorium*. A charming copy of Bede's *Life of S. Cuthbert* (with supplementary chapters from the *Ecclesiastical History* and from the anonymous *Miracles of S. Cuthbert*) is preserved in Oxford (University College, *MS. 165*). It belongs to the second half of the twelfth century and contains interesting drawings: Fig. V-1a.

St. Albans. One of the earliest and best illuminated works of the twelfth century is the splendid *Psalter* executed at St. Albans under Abbot Geoffrey (1119–46). For a time it belonged to S. Godehard's Church, at Hildesheim (see p. 224 f.). In the early nineteenth century it was bought for 2s. 6d. (sic!) by Richard Heber (1773–1833). In February, 1836 it was on sale at Evans, 93 Pall Mall, London, and was bought for £5 18s. by Thomas Thorpe of London; later it was acquired by Sir Thomas Phillips. Several decades later it appeared at Sotheby's; in 1896 it was bought by Quaritch for £34. Afterwards it was bought by William Morris for £56 5s. He gave it the name *The Golden Psalter*. After Morris's death, Richard Bennett acquired the Psalter, but in 1898 it was again on sale at Sotheby's, and was bought by L. W. Hodson of Wolverhampton for £97. In 1909 Hodson sold it to Sir Sidney Cockerell for £150. At the end of 1956 Cockerell gave the codex to B. S. Cron: see, for this exciting history, Cron, *The Recent Owners of the Golden Psalter* ('The Private Library', 1964).

The codex has forty-five full-page miniatures (framed in rectangular patterned borders, which are a characteristic feature of the St. Albans style), representing a cycle of Bible scenes from the Fall of Man to Pentecost, David as musician, three miniatures with scenes from the life of Christ, and one from the lives of S. Martin and S. Alban. It contains also some beautiful initials—there are over 200 initials in this codex—filled with figures (some being fanciful, *e.g.*, boys riding on monsters) or with illustrations of Psalm-passages.

The *St. Albans Psalter* represents 'a complete revolution in English manuscript painting' (F. G. Wormald). It contains various Byzantine elements—the stiff, vertical treatment of the body and the clinging drapery, the rich colour and the elaborate borders—which exercised a great influence on the later English art. At least three different hands can be distinguished, all showing strong European influences.

A copy of Terence, *Comedies*—see p. 40 (preserved in the Bodleian Library, Oxford, *MS. Auct. F. 2. 13*) is another early twelfth-century production of the *scriptorium* of St. Albans.

Bury St. Edmunds. Several early twelfth-century productions of the *scriptorium* of Bury St. Edmunds contain interesting initials: a glossed copy of *Joshua* (preserved in Pembroke College Library, Cambridge, *MS. 54*); a copy of the *Homilies of S. Gregory* (Pembroke College Library, Cambridge, *MS. 16*), containing panelled initials, in four colours, to the Gospels, and historiated and decorative initials, to the remainder of the text; a copy of Bede (preserved in the Bodleian Library,

Oxford, *MS. Bodl. e. Mus. 36*), another Bodleian Library codex (*Leges Langobardorum, MS. Laud. Misc. 742*), and four other manuscripts preserved in Pembroke College Library, Cambridge: *MS. 12*—a copy of *Claudius Clemens*; *MS. 64*—a copy of *Parables*; *MS. 72*—a glossed *Gospel of S. Mark*; and *MS. 78*—*S. Paul's Epistles*. The last MS., and particularly another contemporary codex (a MS. by Florence of Worcester, now in the Bodleian Library, Oxford, *Bodl. MS. 297*), containing an excellent drawing of the Crucifixion, are remarkable for their outline drawings.

The masterpiece of the Bury St. Edmunds *scriptorium* is what is now known as the *Bury Bible*, assigned to the second quarter of the twelfth century. Apparently, the original work consisted of two volumes, but only the first has been preserved; it contains the Old Testament books as far as *Job*. Moreover, a number of illuminations have disappeared; only six large miniatures (the frontispieces to *Numbers, Deuteronomy, Kings, Jeremiah, Ezekiel,* and *Job*), one full-page initial (forming the frontispiece to Jerome's *Prologue*), and forty smaller initials have been preserved (Corpus Christi College Library, Cambridge, *MS. 2*). M. W. Roskill has suggested that three artists worked on the *Bury Bible*: Master Hugo (see also p. 251); a pupil of his; and a third illuminator, 'whose style is somewhat different and probably later in date', and whom Roskill calls the 'Master of the Ezekiel Miniature'. Master Hugo was a particularly skilful painter, who successfully varied 'his palette, subtly blending blue, red, green, purple and orange in alternating combinations and enlivening his designs by highlighting their prominent features with burnished gold': Fig. V-1*b*.

Another good specimen of the school of Bury St. Edmunds is preserved in Pembroke College at Cambridge (*No. 120*). It is a *New Testament*, containing at the beginning twelve pages of Gospel pictures in compartments, giving a particular prominence to scenes involving John the Baptist. They are outline drawings, partly tinted. The codex contains also initials in the main text. The MS. is assigned to *c*. 1130.

Closely related in the facial types, though different in scale and execution, is a *Life, Passion and Miracles of S. Edmund*, executed in the first half of the twelfth century (1130–35 (?)), containing thirty-two full-page miniatures. These—writes Herbert—have plenty of graphic force, but are destitute of charm. Particularly repellent is the prevailing type of face, with long nose, receding chin, and prominent eyes. There is no attempt at realistic figure-drawing; impossibly thin, flat-chested bodies, supported by immensely long, attenuated legs, suggest the human frame well enough for the artist's purpose, which is to tell his story with unmistakable clearness, and which (to do him justice) he never fails to achieve. Gold is used, but sparingly, and is neither raised nor burnished; the colouring generally is somewhat harsh, and the choice of tints quite arbitrary—red, green or violet horses being among the vagaries met with. The decoration of the initials contains scrolls of foliage and various human, animal and monstrous figures. This interesting volume, formerly preserved in Sir G. L. Holford's collection, is now in the Pierpont Morgan Library, New York (*M. 736*): Fig. V-2*a*.

Roskill has pointed out that the Bury style was strongly influenced by the style of St. Albans, and has striking connections with the style of Canterbury, whereas it has little in common with the style of the contemporary illuminators of Winchester and Hereford. Roskill further suggests that Canterbury may have served to some extent as the intermediary between St. Albans and Bury.

Winchester. For the tenth-century Winchester productions, *see* pp. 192 ff. The most outstanding work produced in this period is the *Winchester Bible*, which was written and painted in the Old Minster, or S. Swithin's Priory, at Winchester, in the third quarter of the twelfth century, and is preserved in the Winchester Cathedral Library. In Oakeshott's opinion, one of the artists of the *Winchester Bible* may have worked on the copy of *Terence* (which is probably a mid-twelfth-century work of St. Albans) now preserved in the Bodleian Library, Oxford—see p. 254.

The magnificent *Winchester Bible* (originally in two, but now in three stately volumes) is considered by some scholars the finest of the monumental Bibles which were the fashion in that period. Apparently it is the one which King Henry II borrowed from S. Swithin's Cathedral priory, at Winchester, and in 1173 presented to his Carthusian foundation at Witham; but S. Hugh, Prior of Witham, soon afterwards restored it to St. Swithin's. The beautiful miniatures—two full pages of outline drawings—are distinguished by a fine instinct for composition, the good proportions and modelling of the figures, by the draperies which cling closely to the form, and by the extraordinarily rich and beautiful colouring (dark deep tones predominate, especially a deep blue or green). The splendid historiated initial-ornaments contain human figures, dogs' heads, grotesques, plaits, leaf-moulding or foliated scroll-work, and luxuriant foliage: Fig. V-2c.

According to W. Oakeshott, no fewer than five artists—each with a highly individual style—worked for several decades on the illuminations of the *Winchester Bible*, and even then left the project unfinished. Two of these Masters show strong Byzantine influence (the 'Master of the Genesis Initial' and the 'Amalekite Master'), and they in turn influenced the 'Master of the Morgan Leaf' (of *c.* 1200; it is in the Pierpont Morgan Library, *M. 619*) and the artist of the two miniatures of the *Winchester Psalter*, which will be discussed further on. The leading American authority, Dorothy Miner, describes the artist of *M. 619* as a painter of great power and expressiveness, notable for the versatility of his rendering and the individuality with which he endows the faces and figures of his people, as contrasted with the more standardized types of his contemporary artists. Miss Miner, therefore, considers this folio among the masterpieces of the twelfth century; it may have been prepared for the Winchester Bible, but never used. The leaf ($22\frac{1}{2}$ by $15\frac{1}{4}$ in.), contains illuminations on both sides (one full-page and one three-quarter-page), with illustrations of *Samuel i* and *ii*.

An excellent twelfth-century *Gospel-book*, preserved in the Bodleian Library (*Auct. D. 2.15*), according to Prof. Wormald is related to one of the hands in the *Winchester Bible*. Another *Winchester Gospel-book* is preserved in the Pierpont-Morgan Library, *New York* (*M. 709*): Fig. V-3a.

que pascebat dñs monastiú pete decreuit.
Quoin tế tacien cibos dño peutance pceperit

Cunq: nouú uirtế cómentiom ingressú
sedulo iâ corde meditaret. affuit gra
supna que animú ei arci inpposito firma
ret. ac manifesti edocerec indiciís: qa que
rentíb' regú die iustitia ei. eaque ad uictú
corpori ptinent. beneficio diuine purssionis
adiciunt. Quadá nanq: die dú tế solus
ageret: diuertit hoza ttia inuillá gế mini
posità fozte reppit. intủtủq: domú cuidá

V–1. *a*, Bede, *Life of S. Cuthbert*,
fol. 20 *r*: end of ch. iv. and
beginning of ch. v. *b*, *Bury Bible*:
end of *Foreword* and beginning
of *Book of Ezekiel*. Represented are:
Prophet Ezekiel, Messiah, the four
symbols of the Evangelists; initial E.

interpretes. malint eadem. malint di
uersa transtulerint. Legite igř & hě
iuxta translatione nram quia pcola.
scripus & commata. manifestiorem
sensú legentibus tribuit. Si auř a
mici mei & hunc subsannauerint:

dicemtí ei. qd nemo cos compellat ut
scribant. Sed uereoz ne illud eis eueni
at qd grece significantí dicií ut uocen
tur ΦΑΓΟΛΟΙΔΟΡΟΙ hoc est sagolido
ros. id est manducant senectas.

EXPLIC·PREFATIO:

LE PLIB·R·EZETIEL PRE:
·T·
FACTU
·EST·
IN TRICESIMO
anno·in quarto mense·in quinta men

uisiones dei. In quinta mensis·ipse est
annus quintus transmigrationis regis
ioachin: factú est uerbum dñi ad ezec
hiel filiú buzi sacerdotẽ interra chaldeo
rum secus flumen chobar. Et facta est
sup eum ibi manus dñi. Et uidi. & ecce
uentus turbinis ueniebat ab aquilone·
& nubes magna·& ignis inuoluens·&
splendoz in circuitu ei. & de medio ei
quasi species electri. id est de medio ig
nis. Et e medio eius similitudo quat
uor animaliú. & hic aspectus eoz·hũ
militudo hominis in eis & quatuor facies
uní·& quatuor penne uni·& pedes eoz

V–2. *a, Life, Passion and Miracles of S. Edmund (M. 736)*: Veneration of S. Edmund, whose shrine gave its name to the Benedictine Abbey and town of Bury S. Edmunds. *b, S. Swithin's Psalter*, fol. 7 r: David the Shepherd; David kills the lion; Samuel anoints David. *c, Winchester Bible*, vol. I: beginning of *Book of Jeremiah* and of S. Jerome, *Preface to the Minor Prophets*.

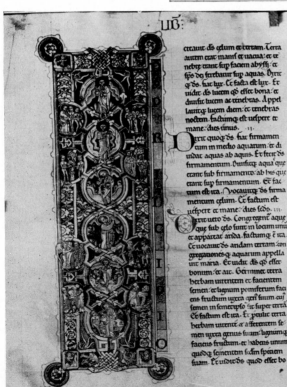

V–3. a, Winchester Gospels,
fol. 48 v : S. Luke.
b, S. Geneviève Bible,
vol. I, fol. 7 v : Genesis, i.

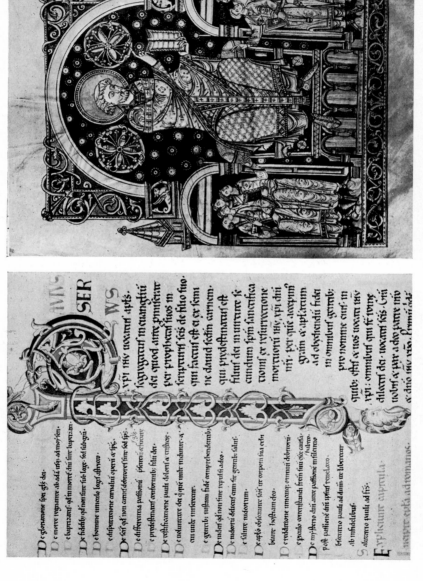

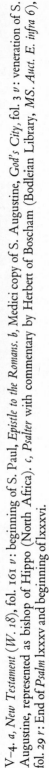

V–4. *a, New Testament (W. 18)*, fol. 161 *v*: beginning of S. Paul, *Epistle to the Romans. b*, Medici copy of S. Augustine, *God's City*, fol. 3 *v*: veneration of S. Augustine, represented as bishop of Hippo (North Africa). *c, Psalter* with commentary by Herbert of Bosham (Bodleian Library, *MS. Auct. E. infra 6*), fol. 29 *r*: End of *Psalm* lxxxv and beginning of lxxxvi.

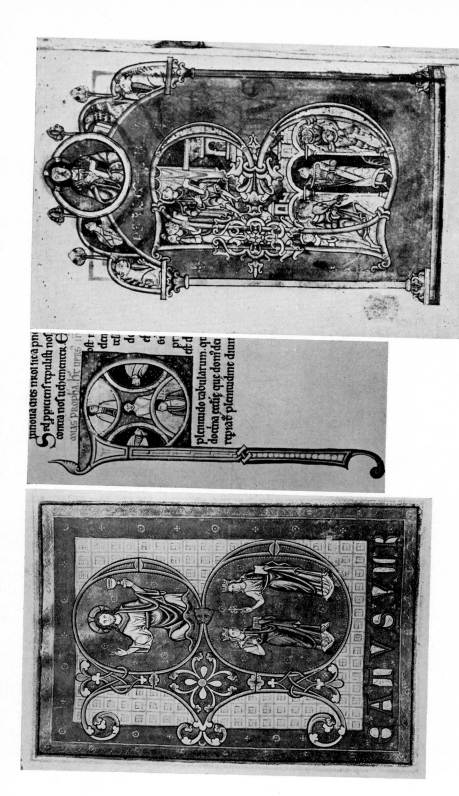

V–5. *a*, *Peterborough Psalter*, fol. 12 *v*: *Beatus* initial. *b*, Initial from *Hugh Puiset Bible*: end of *Lamentations* and *Commentary*. *c*, *Shaftesbury Psalter*, fol. 13 *v*: *Beatus* initial, representing David playing the harp (above, Christ and the symbols of the Evangelists).

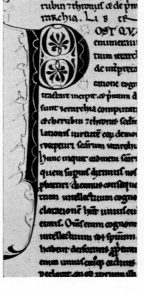

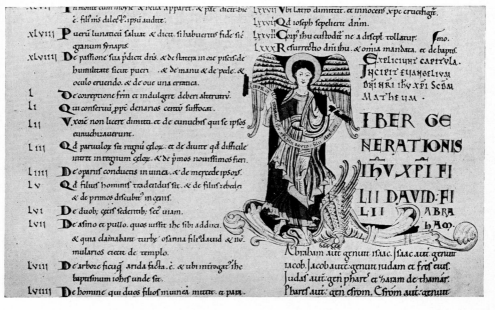

V–6. *a–c*, Initials from codices in Hereford Cathedral Library, *O. 1. viii (a)*, *O. 6. iii (b)*, and *P. 7. iii (c)*.
d, Carilef Bible, fol. 87 *v* : beginning of *S. Matthew.*

V–7. (*a–d*, Initials) *a*, Durham, *Pauline Epistles*, fol. 240 *v* : beginning of *I Thessalonians* ; *b*, Cassiodorus, *De anima*, Durham A. I. 10, fol. 235 *r* : the initial to the Cassiodorus ; *c*, *Works* by Archbishop Anselmus of Canterbury (*MS. Bodley 271*), fol. 43 *v* : initial Q ; *d*, *Bodley Bible MS. Auct. E. infra 1*, fol. 264 *v* : beginning of *Book of Daniel*. *e*, *Guthlac Roll, No. 9* : S. Guthlac.

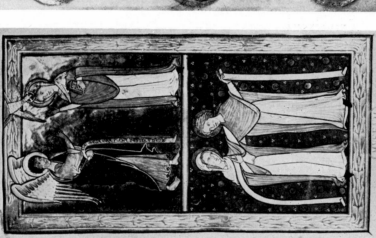

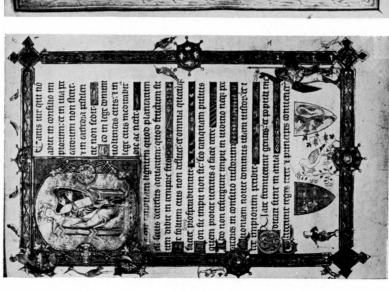

V–8. a, Tenison Psalter, fol. 11 r: Beatus page (initial representing David playing the harp); below, David with the sling and Goliath. b, Psalter MS. Royal. 1. D. X. fol. 1 r: Annunciation and Visitation. c, Lin(de)seye Psalter, fol. 35 v: Crucifixion with S. Mary and S. John; allegories of Church and Synagogue, Sun and Moon, S. Peter and Moses.

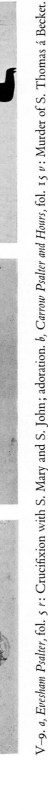

V–9. *a*, *Evesham Psalter*, fol. 5 *r*: Crucifixion with S. Mary and S. John; adoration. *b*, *Carrow Psalter and Hours*, fol. 15 *v*: Murder of S. Thomas á Becket. *c*, *Bible of William of Devon*, fol. 4 *v*: Crowning of the Virgin; Crucifixion with S. Mary, S. John, and two angels; Madonna and Child; SS. Peter and Paul; S. Martin of Tours and the Beggar; William of Devon kneeling in adoration.

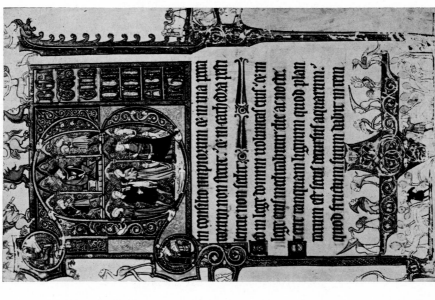

V–10. *a, Cuerden Psalter*, fol. 11 r: *Psalm* i, *Beatus* page with scenes from life of David and Solomon; below, grotesques. *b, Bird Psalter*, fol. 4 r: *Beatus* page; interesting ornamentation.

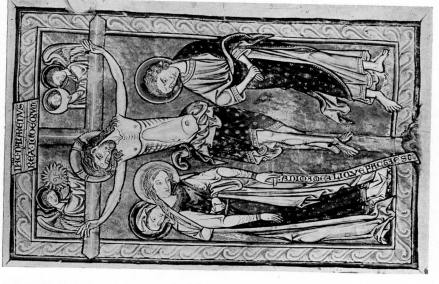

V–II. *a, Bible M. 791*: Trinity, Angels and Saints, the Fall of the Angels, Scenes from *Genesis. b,* Portion of fol. *176 v* from *Bible W. 59*; text: beginning of *Esdra* I; illustration: reconstruction of the Temple. *c, Rylands Sarum Missal (Lat. MS. 24)*, fol. *152 r*: Crucifixion with the two Maries and S. John, and allegories of Sun and Moon.

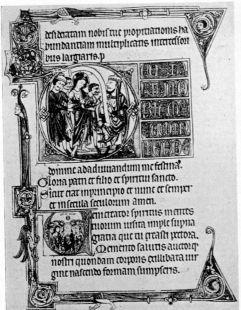

V–12. *a*, *Salvin Horae* (having once belonged to the Salvin family, of Croxdale, Co. Durham), which Sir Chester Beatty presented to the British Museum (now *Add. MS. 48985*); fol. 29 *r*: main initial with Christ before Caiaphas and small initial with Pentecost. *b*, Picture-book of the *Life of Christ* and *Figures of Saints*, fol. 5 *v*: S. Martin of Tours and the Beggar. *c*, *La Estoire de Seint Aedward le Rei Translatee du Latin*, upper part of fol. 32 *v*.

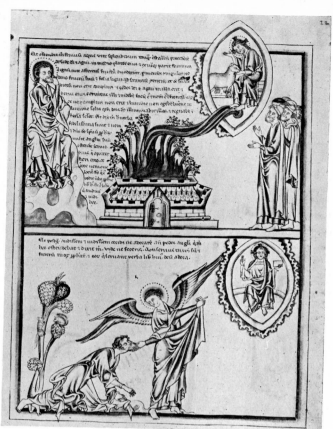

V–13. *a, Apocalypse, MS. Auct.
D. 4. 17*, fol. 22 r. b, *Historia
Anglorum—Chronica Maiora*,
fol. 6 r: Matthew Paris kneeling
before Madonna and Child.

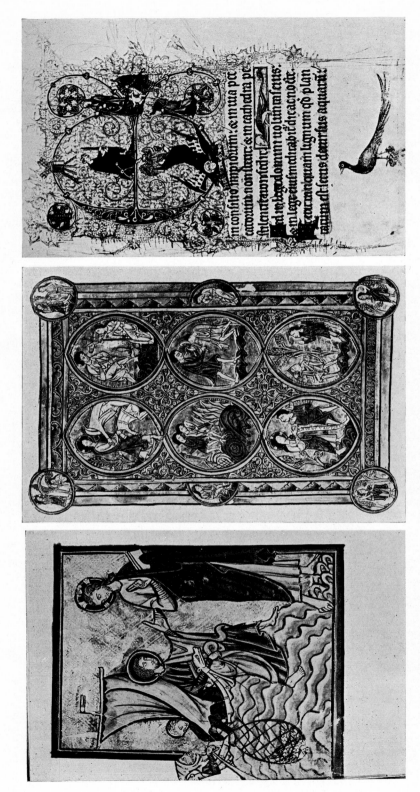

V–14. *a–b*, W. de Brailes: *a*, *W. 106*, fol. *20 r*: scene from the *New Testament* (*S. Matthew*, xiv. 24–33 or *S. Luke*, v. 4–10) ; *b*, *Psalter* Fitzwilliam Museum, *MS. 1016*: six incidents from the stories of Adam and Eve ; Cain and Lamech (according to Isidorus Hispalensis, vii. 6. 14). *c*, *Windmill Psalter*: p. 2 with initial E (from BEATUS), windmill ; judgment of Solomon ; angel ; various ornamentation.

V–15. *a, Grey-Fitzpayn Hours*, fol. 29 *r*: main initial representing adoration of Christ; several smaller initials; grotesques; heraldic bearings, and other ornamentation. *b, British Museum Apocalypse (Royal MS. 15. D. ii)*, fol. 156 *r*: *Apocalypse,* xii. 15 f. *c, Nuneaton Book*, fol. 72 *r*: *Apocalypse,* viii. 10 f.

V–16. *a, Queen Mary's Psalter,*
fol. 71 *v* : Calendar for
January and beginning of
February. *b, Elizabeth
Courtenay Psalter and Hours,*
fol. 243 *r* : Raising of Lazarus.

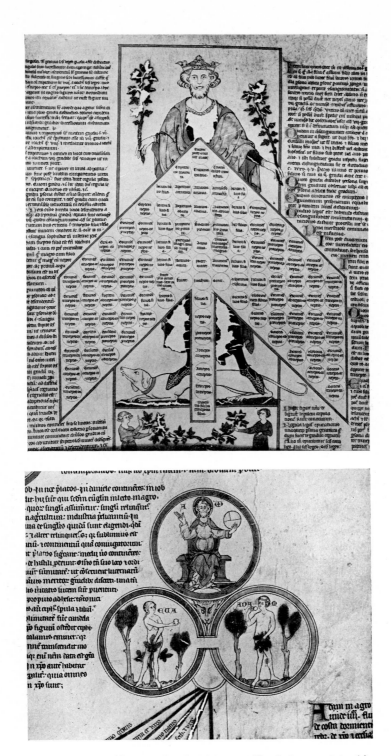

V-17. Portions from Peter of Poitiers, *Table of Consanguinity* (*a*)
and *Genealogy* of Christ (*b*).

V–18. *a, Fitzwilliam Museum Bestiary* (MS. 379), p. 21 : the Swan (*ŏlor*). *b–c,* Details from the borders of the *Romance of Alexander* : a kind of cricket (fol. 22 *r*) and stilts (fol. 65 *r*).

V–19. *a, Du Bois Psalter and
Hours,* fol. 4 *r* : Christ as Judge of
the Universe. *b, Carew-Poyntz
Hours,* fol. 86 *r* : adoration of the
Virgin.

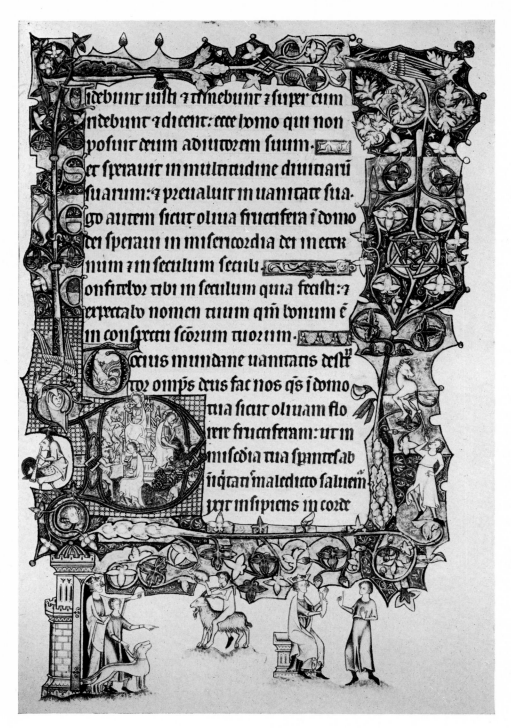

V–20. Ormesby Psalter (Douce MS. 366), fol. 72 r.

custodit dns animaf sanctor suor̃.
de manu peccatoris liberabit eos. Ta.
Lux orta est iusto: i rectis corde leticia
Letamini iusti in dño: et confitemi
ni memorie sanctificationis eius.
Antate domino
canticum nouũ:
er mirabilia fecit.
Saluabit sibi dex
tera eius: et bra
chium sc̃m eius.
Dotum fecit dñs salutare suũ: in cõ
spectu gentium reuelauit iusticiã suã.
Recordatus est misericordie sue: i ve
ritatis sue domui israel.
Viderunt omnes terminos terre:
salutare dei nostri.

V-21. *Bromholm Psalter* (*Ashmole MS. 1523*).

V–22. *a, Arundel MS. 83,* fol.
134 *r*: Crowning of the Virgin.
b, East Anglian Hours W. 105,
fol. 7 *v*: Annunciation.

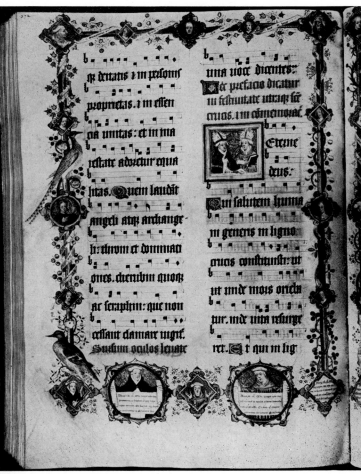

V–23.
a, Thomas Chaundler,
Liber Apologeticus, fol. 7 r:
Death wounding Man
with spear on the right,
Charity holding crown.
b, Sherborne Missal, p. 372:
beginning of text for May
3rd (*inventio S. Crucis*);
historiated initial;
medallion-portraits;
musical notes; beautiful
ornamentation.

tue letificauerunt animam meam.
Numquid adheret tibi sedes iniqui
tatis: qui fingis laborem in precepto.
Captabunt in animam iusti: † san
guinem innocentem condempnabut.

V–24. *a, Luttrell Psalter,* fol. 124 *r*: ploughing. *b, Great Bible of Richard II,* fol. 2 *r*: the scribe presents his book to a Cardinal, probably S. Jerome.

V-25. *a, Hours of Elysabeth ye Queene*: Crucifixion. *b, Bedford Hours and Psalter,* fol. 135 *r*: David playing the harp before Saul; Saul throws his spear at him (1 *Sam.* xvi. 23 and xviii, 10 f.).

V-26. John Lydgate, *Sege of Troy,* copy of *c.* 1420 (*Rylands Engl. MS.* 1): in the background, the city of Troy; in the foreground, combat between Hector and Patroclus; King Menelaus and his army; beautifully decorated border.

V–27. Copy of Chaucer, *M. 817: Troilus and Criseyde*, ii. 1737–iii. 7; floral ornamentation.

V–28. *a*, Fifteenth-century copy of the *Bible* preserved in Dublin, fol. 8 *r*: *Genesis*, xvii. 19–xix. 2. *b*, *Anglo-Flemish Hours*, fol. 6 *v*: Angel holding the image of Death; wide border decorated with birds, leaves, and so on.

It has been suggested that the execution of the *Winchester Bible* was due to the encouragement of Henry of Blois, Bishop of Winchester (1129–71), who was King Stephen's brother, and not only was he a learned prelate, but also a munificent patron of art. In 1151–2 he visited Rome (and went there several times subsequently), whence he is said to have brought works of art. In Sir George Warner's opinion these were used as models for two miniatures (representing the Assumption and the Enthronement of the Virgin), which are part of another superb Winchester product, the *Winchester Psalter* or *S. Swithin's Psalter* (preserved in the British Museum, *Cott. Nero C. iv*), produced in the Winchester St. Swithin's *scriptorium* between 1150 and 1160. It is inferior in quality and slightly later than the *Winchester Bible*, and contains the *Psalter* in Latin and French, preceded by thirty-eight full-page miniatures. Most of their original deep-blue background has been scraped off at some time. With the exception of the two miniatures already referred to—which are in excellent Italo-Byzantine style—the paintings are in English style, allied to that of the *Winchester Bible* miniatures, but their technique is not as good. However, there are some most effective miniatures, such as the Jesse-tree with its white curling tendrils or (the last of the series) the angel locking the door of the Jaws of Death upon the damned: Fig. V-2*b*.

Canterbury (for the earlier productions, see pp. 188 ff.). The great three-volume *S. Geneviève Bible*, of the late twelfth century (preserved in the Library of S. Geneviève at Paris, *MSS. 8–10*), may perhaps be assigned to Canterbury. Its scribe, Manerius, indicates himself as *scriptor Cantuariensis*, but as a matter of fact the work may have been executed anywhere in England, or even in France (as suggested by various scholars, including Dodwell): it is far from easy to ascertain whether twelfth- or thirteenth-century illuminated MSS. are English or French. While its miniatures are inferior in quality to those of the *Winchester Bible*, its initial decoration—it contains seventy-three historiated initials—is freer and more naturalistic: Fig. V-3*b*.

However, the following great works were produced in the two *scriptoria* (St. Augustine's and Christ Church), of Canterbury in the twelfth century: a copy of the *Utrecht Psalter*, executed between 1120 and 1150 (now in the British Museum, *Harl. MS. 603*); the *Eadwine Psalter*, of *c.* 1147–50 (also a copy of the *Utrecht Psalter*), preserved in Cambridge (Trinity College, *MS. R. 17. 1*); the *Lambeth Bible*, 1150–75 (Lambeth Palace Library, London, *MS. 3*); the *Dover Bible* (written for the Dover Priory), of *c.* 1160 (Corpus Christi College, Cambridge, *MSS. 3–4*). Some scholars assign to the Christ Church *scriptorium*, Canterbury, a large Bible, of which two sections survive, an Old Testament section (*Joshua, Judges, Ruth,* and *Kings*) in the British Museum (*Royal 1. C. vii*: it was in the Royal Library as early as 1542), and a New Testament, preserved in Baltimore (Walters Art Gallery, *W. 18*). The text is written in large insular script in two columns. *W. 18*, containing 247 vellum leaves, $14\frac{1}{2}$ by $10\frac{3}{4}$ in., with twenty-six illuminated initials, is—as Dorothy Miner writes—a volume of impressive format, the bold dark brown script being relieved by large initials vigorously wrought of vines and beasts. Red, blue, green, and yellow (instead of gold) are employed. See Fig. IV-14d-e, and V-4a.

Moreover, four detached full-page illuminations, containing scenes from the life of Christ, which probably belonged to a twelfth-century Psalter, are now assigned to Canterbury (M. R. James, who first associated the leaves together, assigned them to Bury St. Edmunds). According to some scholars (Swarzenski and Dodwell), these illuminations may have prefaced the *Eadwine Psalter*. Two of the leaves are in the Pierpont Morgan Library, New York (*M. 521 and 724*), one in the British Museum (*Add. MS. 37472, No. 1*), and one in the Victoria and Albert Museum (*MS. 661*). Roskill suggests that the leaves are connected with the twelfth-century wall-paintings at Canterbury, and that they seem to relate Bury and Canterbury manuscripts together, and bridge the gap which separates the respective styles of the two *scriptoria*.

Amongst other manuscripts assigned to Canterbury there is a beautiful copy of the eleventh or the twelfth century of S. Augustine, *City of God*, which once belonged to Piero di Cosimo dei Medici and is now in the Laurentian Library, Florence (*MS. Plut. 12, 17*). It contains four full-page miniatures, ten historiated or illuminated initials, and a number of smaller decorated initials. Also attributed to Canterbury are two late twelfth-century manuscripts preserved in the Bodleian Library: *MS. Bodley 271* (*Works* by Archbishop Anselmus of Canterbury) and *MS. Auct. E. infra 6* (*Psalter* in Latin, Gallican version, with the *Commentary* by Herbert of Bosham); the first of two volumes, is preserved in Cambridge, Trinity College Library, *B. 5. 4*. Moreover, *B. 5. 6.* and 7, the *Epistles*, also contain Herbert's *Commentary*. See Fig. V-4b, 4c and 7c.

Peterborough. A twelfth-century (or thirteenth-century?) *Psalter*, preserved in the Fitzwilliam Museum, Cambridge (*MS. 12*), is attributed to Peterborough or its neighbourhood. Scholars agree that it is a work of the finest kind and of the best period of Anglo-Norman book-production. According to Prof. Wormald, it was executed *c.* 1220 for Robert de Lin(de)seye, and it is intrinsically related to a MS. belonging to the Society of Antiquaries, London (see p. 265). Fig. V-5a and 8c.

Another *Psalter*—also known as *Peterborough Psalter*—is preserved in the Corpus Christi College (*MS. 53*), at Cambridge. It measures $9\frac{1}{2}$ by $6\frac{1}{2}$ inches and is of the early fourteenth century.

Hereford. The *Hereford Gospels* (now in Pembroke College Library, Cambridge, *MS. 302*) do not belong to this period, the codex being assigned to the middle of the eleventh century. But an excellent representative of the twelfth-century Hereford *scriptorium* is the *Shaftesbury Psalter*, produced 1161–73 (now British Museum, *Lansdowne MS. 383*). The emphasis on angelic messengers in the *Shaftesbury Psalter* —writes M. W. Roskill—suggests a mystical train of thought current in the Hereford foundation: Fig. V-c.

The precious collection of the Hereford Cathedral Library possesses several interesting manuscripts, but it is uncertain whether they, or how many of them, come from the Hereford *scriptorium*. Examples are: *MS. O. 1. viii*, a twelfth-century *Gospel-book*; *MS. O. 6. iii*, a twelfth-century copy of Dionysius, *De celesti Hierarchia*; and *P. 7. iii*, a thirteenth- or fourteenth-century copy of Gratianus, *Decretals* (see p. 314): Fig. V-*6a–c*.

Croyland. A curious and interesting *MS*. is the vellum *Guthlac Roll*, probably executed in Croyland Abbey (and now preserved in the British Museum, *Harl. Roll Y. 6*), containing eighteen charming outline-drawings illustrating the life of S. Guthlac (a hermit, who lived 667–714, in the Crowland or Croyland fens, Lincolnshire). Notwithstanding the still maintained 'tendency to elongate bodies ... the lively quaintness of the characterization, whether of angels, demons, or human beings, gives these drawings an almost unique charm' (Herbert): Fig. V-*7e*.

Durham. Two late eleventh-century illuminated books are interesting as they represent strong Romanesque elements (particularly the second of the two). These are a copy of S. Augustine, *De Psalmis*, of *c.* 1085 (now in Durham Cathedral Library, *B. II. 13*), and the *Carileff Bible*, of 1081–1095 (also in Durham Cathedral Library, *A. II. 4*): Fig. V-*6d*.

Of the Durham twelfth-century productions two deserve special mention: the little book of the *Life of S. Cuthbert* and the great three-volume Bible of Bishop Puiset, the former sometime belonging to the Yates Thompson collection, the latter being still preserved in Durham Cathedral Library. The *Life* contains forty-five full-page miniatures on mostly gold backgrounds (sometimes, however, red, or blue, and once diapered), enclosed in plain banded frames. The pictures—writes Herbert—are on a modest scale, but very charming: the treatment of the face is very careful, and usually judicious; the proportions are good, except for the extended fingers, which are still too long occasionally; and the colours are pleasing, especially the red and blue.

Bishop Hugh Puiset (1153–95). The magnificent Winchester Bible (see p. 256) is perhaps the finest of the preserved monumental Bibles, which were the fashion in the latter half of the twelfth century. The *S. Geneviève Bible* (p. 257) is another; the *Hugh Puiset Bible* is a third. With its finely illuminated initials to each book and prologue; with its very numerous small capitals in red, blue, green (and, very rarely, brown), containing simple scroll-ornament; with the larger capitals having fillings of thin foliage, for which gold is used; with its stately margins; with the original stamped Romanesque bindings, of which the sides have been preserved (vol. i has also its strap-and-pin fastening, the two straps having heavy metal ends, decorated with a delicate foliage-pattern in niello); in its excellent state of preservation (apart from a few leaves, which are lost, and several of the initials which have been cut out)— this Bible is doubtless one of the best specimens of English twelfth-century book-production: Fig. V-*5b*.

If it lacks—writes Prof. Mynors, the greatest authority on the Durham *MSS.*— the skill in rendering movement and expression of the best hands of the *Winchester*

Bible, the originality in colouring and design of the one, of unknown origin, now in the Bodleian Library (*Auct. E. infra 1–2*), and the thundery splendour of the *Bury Bible* now at Cambridge—yet it has a massive grandeur which puts it in the first rank of the productions of the latter twelfth century. (For the Bodleian Bible see Fig. V-7*d*).

This great work, preserved in Durham Cathedral Library (*A. II. 1: No. 146* in Mynors), consists of four large volumes (containing respectively 224, 189, 162, and 148 leaves), all four having on their front fly-leaf the late twelfth-century mark *Hugonis episcopi*. Hugh, Bishop of Durham, is commonly known as Pudsey, but this 'is such a misleading designation for the kinsman of our Norman Royal House, who took his name presumably from the domain of Le Puiset between Orleans and Chartres, that it is better dropped' (Mynors).

The main decoration of the Bible consists in the beautiful initials with figure-subjects, *e.g.* (vol. i, f. 173) David seated on left, mourning; before him lie Saul and Jonathan, blood streaming from their necks; (vol. iii, f. 16) King Solomon throned on left, uttering the word *Vanitas*; corpse lying in tomb before him, over which stands a man holding a scroll inscribed *De utero translatus ad tumulum*; (vol. iii, f. 109) Ahasuerus at the top, then Esther, and below her Haman hanging; (vol. iv, f. 2) two figures, holding scrolls inscribed *Ego Ieronimus mando* and *Damasus papa*. Folios 4–9*v* of vol. iv contain the Canon Tables, 'under arcading, the columns and arches of which are superbly illuminated with different patterns' (Mynors). See Fig. V-5*b*.

Bishop Hugh was a great benefactor of his Cathedral, to which he also donated a library comprising some sixty-two volumes of literature and fourteen service-books. 'Of these, thirteen can be certainly or probably identified with surviving books, and others may be in existence. . . . They vary very much in size and style' (Mynors).

Besides the four-volume Bible, two other works deserve special mention because of their interesting twelfth-century illumination: (*a*) Part of a *Bible*—the second of two volumes (preserved in Durham Cathedral Library, *A. II. 2*, Mynors No. *147*), perhaps a copy of the *Carlieff Bible* (see p. 259); it contains red, blue, green, and, rarely, pale bistre-brown capitals, and initials with either (1) sprays of conventional colour, or (2) a filling of coloured 'petals' and groups of three dots, on a ground left bare. 'The effect is simple, but decorative owing to the brightness of the colours' (Mynors). (*b*) A magnificent copy of the *Pauline Epistles* (preserved in Durham Cathedral Library, *A. II. 19*; Mynors No. *149*) with the gloss of Peter Lombard. Of the finely illuminated large initials, fourteen are preserved; all the initials except two were originally protected with sewn-on linen guards, of which nine are preserved. The majority of the initials are filled with foliage; one has four birds, and four have figure-subjects (S. Paul and Sosthenes; S. Paul; S. Paul and Timothy; S. Paul's martyrdom): Fig. V-7*a*.

Finally, a beautiful initial from an early twelfth-century copy of Cassiodorus, *De anima*, bound with the *Commentary* on *S. Matthew's Gospel*, ascribed to Anselm of Laon (*MS. A. I. 10*, f. 235) is reproduced on Fig. V-7*b*.

PSALTERS

Of all the books of the Bible none has been rendered into English so often (see *The Hand-produced Book*, p. *525*) and none illuminated so frequently as the Psalter. Various copies of the Psalter executed in England in the late twelfth century deserve mention. We may refer to the British Museum *Harley MS. 5102*, the *Hunting field Book* in the Pierpont Morgan Library, New York, the *S. Louis Psalter* in the University Library at Leyden, *Lat. 76A*, the *Psalter* and *Hours* (which in Dr. E. G. Millar's opinion is of English origin) preserved in the National Library at Paris (*MS. Lat. 10433*). But in our sketch we have to limit ourselves to the exquisite *Westminster Psalter*, preserved in the British Museum (*Royal 2. A. xxii*).

At Westminster the traditions of illumination seem to have followed the methods of the earlier Winchester school (see p. 192 ff.). But in the twelfth century its products, as with English work in general, show a greater likeness to the contemporary work of Germany. The *Westminster Psalter* is written in the handsome style of penmanship sometimes called the English Gothic of the latter twelfth century.

It would appear from the frequent copying of the Psalter that it held the place of the later *Book of Hours*, and so we may expect a great similarity among different copies, both in the selection of the illustrations and their mode of treatment. It was usual in all such volumes to prefix to the text a series of subjects from the Old and New Testaments and the Lives of the Saints. In the *Westminster Psalter* are prefixed five full-page miniatures (representing David as Harpist, Annunciation, Visitation, Madonna and Child, Christ in Glory), painted in thick body-colour on burnished gold; the main colours are deep and rich ultramarine blue, red and green. The flesh tones are livid, being of a pale greenish-ochre tint. The rounded, gentle face of the Virgin—writes Herbert—and the stronger, more severe male types, show considerable power of modelling and expression; especially fine is the picture of David, a truly regal, dignified figure.

The Virgin and Child are shown on a seat of the Germano-Byzantine type—formed of tiers of differently coloured steps separated by bands of scarlet, green, etc.—beneath an arch and within a square frame border. The Madonna wears the hood, cape, and robe of the Benedictine nuns, but coloured grey, chocolate, and blue respectively. There is a rich gold brocade border to the robe. An undergarment of pale amber completes her dress. The Infant wears an amber tunic and is wrapped in a scarlet robe. Both have round *nimbi*, the Madonna in plain circular bands of russet and orange, the Child's consisting of bands of pale blue surmounted by a scarlet cross. A very common embroidery of the drapery consists of little stars or triads of white studs (this also being a characteristic of German and early Netherlandish illumination).

The frame-border seems to have been flatly painted in two colours, pale blue and pale red ochre, and on this a foliage scroll of recurring forms in a bold dull red outline finely relieved with white. This is closely repeated as the form of border to the other illuminations. Outside the whole is a characteristic slender frame of bright green in two tints. The arch overhead has two bands of vermilion, with white edge-reliefs and a central band of blue, again in two tints, with pairs of black cross-bars every half-inch or so resting on the capitals of the two pillars which form the sides of the scene. Two lumps of green glass or metal hang from the arch. The pillars have a green abacus at the top of each capital and scarlet beading below. Each pillar is of a dappled-red, marble-like porphyry, with plinths of scarlet and blue. The background is a plate of gold.

David (playing the harp, which is not gilded, but of a drab hue) also wears three garments, white, pale blue, lavender or lilac, and pale chocolate being the main colours. The colours employed for David's throne are: slate-blue, green, orange, white, and buff; the back is of a deep blue and the background of bright flat gold. The outer border is of pale red ochre or pink shade. An outer frame or edging of green completes the page.

For the *Winchester Psalter* see p. 257; for the *St. Albans Psalter* see p. 254; for the *Shaftesbury Psalter* see p. 258.

In the *Hunterian Psalter* (preserved in the Hunterian Museum, Glasgow, *MS. U. 3.2*), which some scholars assign to the York *scriptorium*, we find an exaggerated mannerism in the geometrical treatment of the drapery, a love of movement by the dynamic swirling of the folds across the page. The drapery—writes M. W. Roskill —was made to bear no relation to the figure beneath, but to swing out on either side of the body as though charged with electricity. The main MS (*i.e.*, except the last 13 folios belonging to the fourteenth century) is of the twelfth century. It is beautifully written in one hand; there are fourteen full-page illustrations or illuminations; several gilt, historiated or illuminated initials, and numerous gilt smaller initials. The *Hunterian Psalter* is also known as the *York Psalter*.

GOTHIC PERIOD

In the English styles of the thirteenth and fourteenth centuries may be distinguished two main schools: one, following the Gothic style, resembled the French style of illumination so closely that in many instances it is difficult to distinguish its productions from those of the French schools; the other—the East Anglian school (see p. 278 ff.)—continued the traditional English motifs of the previous century, especially the rich and varied ornamentation.

With regard to the origin of the English Gothic style, Pevsner has suggested that the construction of the choir of Canterbury Cathedral, after the destruction of the old choir in 1174, was a work as revolutionary in England as Saint-Denis was in France (see p. 378). The first architect of the new choir was William of Sens, and Pevsner reminds us that certain features of Canterbury Cathedral are imitations from Sens Cathedral, built about 1140.

For the greater part of the thirteenth century, English illumination in the main— as it has just been pointed out—is so like that of France that it is often difficult to determine its real nationality, but in the late thirteenth century the two branches part company.

Tenison Psalter. Moreover, there is occasionally some feature which we know

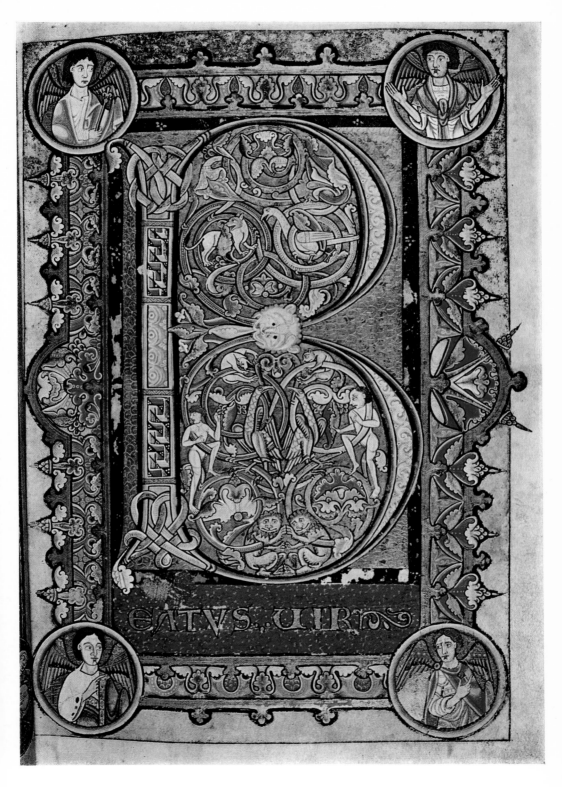

Hunterian (or *York*) *Psalter*. Initial B (of *Beatus*) set in a stylized foliage border,
and containing crouching lions, nude figures, birds, and a cat's mask.

from other sources to be English, or some circumstance in the history of the MS. which fixes its origin; for example, in the *Tenison Psalter* (preserved in the British Museum, *Add. MS. 24686*)—so called because it once belonged to Archbishop Tenison. Although quite in the same style as contemporary French work, it is well known that this was the product of an English school of illumination (perhaps of the Blackfriars, in London). It is also known as the *Alfonso Psalter*; as the arms on the first page show, it was originally intended for presentation to Alfonso, son of King Edward I, on his marriage with Margaret, daughter of the Count of Holland. While the MS. is illuminated throughout, the first gathering is in a slightly earlier style and its miniatures are of finer execution. It has been suggested that the abrupt change in the style of decoration may be due to the death of Alfonso in 1284, and that the successive completion of the MS. was entrusted to somewhat cheaper, inferior artists.

The colouring of the MS. is not confined, as in earlier specimens, to blue and dull pale rose or pale red ochre and gold. It gives us scarlet, crimson-lake, green and brown, besides the blue and pink, and bright gold, which suggest some German influences. The line fillings (see p. 265) are somewhat peculiar in having silver tracery on the blue, side by side with golden tracery on the crimson. The full ivy-leaf appears in the long branch-work of the borders, although some of the initials retain the bird or dragon forms in their construction. The compound bar-frame, gold and traceried colour side by side, is, however, already taking the place of the mere sweeping tail or branch.

But perhaps the best indication of English design is the presence of grotesque animals, with birds and occasional humorous scenes dispersed, not in framed miniatures, but simply among the stems and coils of the foliage. The first page of the MS. is framed in a gold-edged band of tiny lozenges, alternately blue and crimson. On this border, writes Herbert, and in the margins outside, are exquisitely painted birds—gull, bullfinch, etc., drawn and coloured with scientific accuracy, and standing in the most lifelike attitudes—also other figures, lion, leopard, an ape shooting a crane, and at the foot of the page, a dainty little David slinging a stone at Goliath; David also appears as harpist in the initial B, a gracefully posed, well-proportioned figure set on a background of patterned gold: Fig. V-8a.

Characteristics of Gothic Illumination

One of the main features of the thirteenth-century illuminated MSS. was their greatly reduced format. The stately three-volume Bibles referred to on p. 256 were no longer fashionable; their place was taken by single, handy volumes produced in great numbers. In consequence, the large, bold characters had to be supplanted by the small, neat, and clear minuscules, and—for the sense of proportion—illumination had to be adapted to this change. The historiated initial became more and more fashionable, often replacing a miniature, and full-page miniatures were often subdivided into compartments, each containing a picture of the size of the miniatures enclosed in larger initials.

A characteristic feature of the initial decoration was, as Herbert has pointed out, the pendent tail, out of which were gradually evolved the luxuriant borders. At first this tail merely wanders a little way down the margin, to end in a leaf or knob; gradually it lengthens until it reaches the foot of the column of text, whence it proceeds next to turn the corner, becoming eventually a complete border which surrounds the text on all four sides. The main part is at first quite straight and rigid; hence the term 'bar-border' is sometimes given to this type of decoration in the comparatively simple and undeveloped form which is kept throughout the thirteenth century. But the straight edge soon began to be replaced by a series of cusped lines, or other curves; and small figures further relieve the rigidity. Finally, the bars themselves turn into foliage-stems, putting forth leafy branches of ever-increasing lightness, intricacy, and variety, bearing flowers and fruit as well as leaves without regard for species. This last development, argues Herbert, hardly appears before 1300, and does not reach its full luxuriance until the beginning of the fifteenth century; but a tendency had already begun, as early as the middle of the thirteenth century, to transform part of the bar into a thin cylindrical rod, adorned at intervals with rings and other ornaments.

In the late thirteenth century English illumination was fast progressing towards its zenith. Its delicacy of drawing, refinement of taste and advance in freedom, and luxuriance in the decoration of the bar-borders and the margins (containing all kinds of dainty, whimsical animals and birds—often painted with amazing fidelity to nature—and fantastic creatures), are remarkable. The human figure assumed softer, more rounded and gracious contours. All these characteristics may be seen in the *Historia scholastica* of Petrus Comestor (preserved in the British Museum, *Royal 3. D. vi*), which was given to Ashridge College by its founder, Edmund Earl of Cornwall (*d.* 1300), and was executed for him *c.* 1283, perhaps in the Dominican House of the Blackfriars, in London. This MS. is closely related to the *Tenison Psalter* (see p. 262 f.), and, like the same, does not contain large miniatures.

Psalters

In dealing with the finer illuminated MSS. of the thirteenth century, we must in the first place treat of Psalters which were, indeed, the main English productions of the period (see also p. 261 ff.). The Psalters generally contain preliminary Gospel-pictures (miniatures of the life of Christ, in two compartments on a page framed in a narrow band) and Calendar-illustrations—each month having representations of the Zodiacal sign and an appropriate occupation, each being enclosed in a small medallion and being 'so compressed as to be little more than symbols, having mostly only a single figure' (Herbert). The Psalters contained as the first page the words *Beatus vir* (which are the opening words in Latin of *Psalm* i), highly decorated, as well as historiated initials to each Psalm.

One of the best works belonging to this class is preserved in the British Museum (*Royal 1. D. x*); written perhaps at Winchester in the early thirteenth century, it contains miniatures on plain grounds, alternately of highly burnished gold, and of deep blue, powdered with red rings and a small pattern of white dots. The deep, rich blue, so popular in the thirteenth century—emphasizes Herbert—is the dominant note of the colour-scheme; it is balanced by red, light green and lake, and the harmony is completed by passages of warm and cold grey, and of white draperies lightly shaded with buff, grey and pink. In the best pictures, where few figures occur, such as the Annunciation, Visitation, and the Magi scenes, there is a largeness of manner suggestive of fresco-painting rather than miniature, and not often found after this date in English illumination: Fig. V-8b.

This MS. contains also a superb *Beatus Vir* and splendid historiated initials to the individual Psalms, particularly to xxvi, xxxviii, li–ii, lxviii, lxxx, xcvii, ci and cix. The spaces left at the ends of verses are filled with pen-work designs in blue or red, consisting either in flourishes or geometrical patterns or in witty drawings of animals, real or imaginary, fishes, birds, etc.

Other Psalters have similar line-endings, and in later copies there appear heraldic devices or diaper patterns.

It has been suggested that *Royal 1. D. x* and another Psalter of the British Museum (*Arundel MS. 157*), belonging roughly to the same period but probably written at Oxford, derive from a common archetype which may have belonged to the same class, though in a more advanced stage, as the *Westminster Psalter* (see p. 261 f.). Another British Museum Psalter (*Lansdowne MS. 420*), also written in the first quarter of the thirteenth century, perhaps at Chester, contains at the beginning ten pages of Gospel-miniatures which Herbert considers to have been inspired by a series of medallions in stained glass. These interesting illuminations are two on a page and painted on gold, red or blue grounds in roundels which are placed on square fields of a contrasting colour; the gold is burnished and stamped with a star-pattern, and the coloured grounds patterned with white dots and rings. The stiff, elongated, angular figures have all the severity proper to the glass-painter's technique, their heavy black outlines reproduce the leads exactly, and the drapery folds are indicated in the same style by thick lines.

Most exquisite—one may say, in a style well in advance of the period to which it belongs (*c.* 1220–2)—is the *Psalter of Robert de Lin(de)seye*, Abbot of Peterborough, now preserved in the Library of the Society of Antiquaries, in London (No. 59): see also p. 258. It contains a Crucifixion painted on a rich ground of burnished and patterned gold (rather unusual are the shaft and arms of the cross covered with a symmetrical leafy stem), Christ in Glory, a *Beatus vir* equally fine in execution, and historiated initials to five Psalms on backgrounds of highly burnished and elaborately patterned gold: Fig. V-8c.

Two mid-thirteenth-century Psalters also deserve special mention—the magnificent *Evesham Psalter*, executed in, or for, the Benedictine abbey of Evesham (in Worcestershire), and acquired in 1936 by the British Museum (now *Add. MS. 44874*); and the *Carrow Psalter* (so called because in the fifteenth century it belonged to the Carrow nunnery, near Norwich), which was in the Yates Thompson Collection and is now in the Walters Art Gallery, Baltimore (*W. 34*). The numerous miniatures (twenty-nine full-page; eleven historiated and numerous armorial initials) of the *Carrow Psalter* contain some unusual features: there are six scenes from the legend of S. Olaf depicted in the initial ***B***, and full-page miniatures representing the murder of S. Thomas of Canterbury, and an angel giving Adam a spade and Eve a distaff. These miniatures are considered by J. A. Herbert the precursors of the early fourteenth-century East Anglian school (see p. 279 f.): Fig. V-9*a* and *b*.

None of the last-mentioned MSS. come up to the artistic standard of the masterpieces of the latter thirteenth century. The earliest of these splendid works of art is the mid-thirteenth-century *Duke of Rutland Psalter*, containing a nearly unique marginal decoration (exquisite coloured drawings full of life and humour—human figures, animals real and fanciful, grotesques, games and pastimes, such as chessplaying, wrestling and tumbling); large and splendid historiated or foliage-initials to nine Psalms, and smaller initials to the other Psalms; calendar-illustrations; and —its main extraordinary feature—full-page or almost full-page miniatures prefixed to six Psalms. Most charming are the miniatures of Jacob's ladder, Balaam and the Angel, David playing on an organ, and—particularly—Saul aiming a javelin at David.

On the whole, English Psalters of the middle of the thirteenth century are rather rare. It is, therefore, remarkable that—as pointed out by Dr. E. G. Millar— in recent times three such Psalters have come to light, all being of the first rank: a superb Psalter, known as the *Cuerden Psalter*, in the Pierpont Morgan Library, New York (*M. 756*); the *Evesham Psalter*, already referred to, and a *Psalter* executed in the Diocese of York and now in Dr. Millar's possession: Fig. V-10*a*.

The *Cuerden Psalter* is related in style to the *Bible of William of Devon* (see further on) and to a *Book of Hours* preserved in the British Museum (*Egerton MS. 1151*). According to Dr. Millar, the three manuscripts were executed at the same time (*c.* 1250) and place (possibly Canterbury). As to the *York Psalter*, Dr. Millar relates it to the *Psalter of Simon of Meopham*, preserved in Sion College, and a *Bible* in Sir Sydney Cockerell's Collection: if this theory is right, York must have had a flourishing school of illumination in the middle of the thirteenth century: Fig. V-9*c* and 10*a*.

A very fine Psalter, formerly in the Lee of Fareham Collection, and now in the Fitzwilliam Museum, Cambridge (*MS. 2—1954*), is dated between 1280 and 1300. It is known as the *Bird Psalter*. It contains more than fifty naturalistic drawings of birds, amongst which at least twenty different species can be recognised. The grotesques also show much variety and humour, and include a rabbit at the top of one page, sitting with its paws held tightly over both ears, while a fox plays the harp in the margin below: Fig. V-10*b*.

A beautiful Psalter, executed in the second half of the thirteenth century, and known as the *Oscott Psalter*, was preserved in the collection of C. W. Dyson Perrins, and is now in the British Museum (*Add. MS. 50000*). This splendid codex measures $7\frac{3}{4}$ by $4\frac{1}{2}$ ins.

Oscott Psalter: Evangelist or Saint.

Another splendid Psalter—the *Tenison Psalter*—has been discussed on p. 262 f.

Bibles

An important class of thirteenth-century English illuminated MSS. are copies of the Latin Bible, of which a great number have been preserved. The main features of this class are: (1) the small format, the great majority of these MSS. being veritable pocket-books; (2) firm and delicate draughtsmanship, its main importance being calligraphic, neatness and regularity of script; (3) relatively little ornamentation; although book-illustration in outline was still done (either lightly tinted or left uncoloured), and the majority of MSS. were resplendent with burnished gold and warm colouring, the ornamentation was generally restricted to historiated or foliated initials at the beginning of each book; there is hardly any illumination—sometimes a series of Creation-scenes is prefixed to *Genesis*, and a Jesse-tree to *Matthew*; (4) difficulty in ascertaining the country of origin of the single MSS. (especially with regard to France and England), and, in the majority of cases, lack of information concerning their date and provenance.

There are, however, exceptions. The most beautiful mid-thirteenth-century *Bible*, executed—perhaps at Canterbury—by one William of Devon, and preserved in the British Museum (*Royal MS. 1. D. i*) contains extraordinary historiated initials (including, for instance the *In pricipio* of *Genesis*, with miniatures of the Creation, Fall, and Atonement; a Jesse-tree; a miniature of S. Jerome writing), prolonged into bar-borders which often surround the text on three sides. There are two full-page miniatures, divided into compartments. One miniature contains the Coronation of Christ; the Crucifixion; the Madonna and Child with SS. Peter and Paul; S. Martin and the beggar; and a kneeling monk (perhaps the scribe himself); the other contains the Crucifixion, the martyrdom of S. Thomas of Canterbury, the Virgin helping him to mend his shirt, and Christ appearing to him or to another archbishop: Fig. V-9c.

Another remarkable MS. of this class, also preserved in the British Museum (*Burney MS. 3*) is the *Bible of Robert de Bello*, Abbot of S. Augustine's, at Canterbury, 1224–53, probably executed for him in his abbey. This is on a larger scale than the majority of the contemporary Bibles. Apart from the chapter-initials (coloured blue or red, and decorated with delicate pen-flourishes), apart from the smaller historiated initials to nearly all the Biblical books, and the Jesse-tree prefixed to *Matthew*, it contains two large *I*'s, that of *In principio* of *Genesis* with medallion-scenes from the *Creation* on burnished gold grounds, and that of *John*, with stories from his Gospel and representations of the Evangelist with an eagle's head.

An interesting early thirteenth-century *Bible* is preserved in the Pierpont Morgan Library, New York (*M. 791*). Another excellent thirteenth-century *Bible*, now preserved in the Princeton University Library (*Garrett MS. 28*), was one of about a dozen manuscripts owned by Robert Gilmour II of Baltimore, one of the earliest American art collectors. He bought it in 1832. It contains numerous illuminated initials, some being shaped of contorted animals, reminiscent of the *Bestiaries*, well executed on gold or delicately diapered backgrounds. Many initials are in red and blue with foliate *rinceaux*, pen flourishes, drolleries and figures: Fig. V-11*a*.

A thirteenth-century *Bible*, probably executed in England, is preserved in the Walters Art Gallery, Baltimore (*W. 59*). It contains numerous historiated and ornamented initials. The drawing of the scenes—writes Miss Dorothy Miner—is delicate and expressive in outline and has the sureness of works on a far larger scale: Fig. V-11*b*.

Miscellanea. Apart from *Psalters* and copies of the *Bible*, which were the two main classes of illuminated MSS. produced in England in the thirteenth century, numerous other books were executed. They were either liturgical (such as *Missals* and *Breviaries*), or were intended for private devotional use (such as the *Book of Hours*), or else they were of secular nature (such as the illustrated *Bestiaries*, a sort of medieval handbook of natural history: see further on).

An interesting *Missal* for Sarum use is preserved in The John Rylands Library, Manchester (*Lat. MS. 24*). Preceding the canon of the mass are eight full-page illuminations, in one of which a kneeling figure of Canon Henry of Chichester (*c.* 1228–56) is introduced. It is, therefore, suggested that this *Missal* is the earliest known text of Sarum use: Fig. V-11*c*.

The *Book of Hours*, which by the end of the fourteenth century became extremely popular (indeed, by far the most fashionable of illuminated MSS.), already occurs in the thirteenth century. Illuminated *Books of Hours* of earlier date than the latter part of the thirteenth century are extremely rare. An interesting copy, for Sarum use, assigned to *c.* 1240, was preserved in the Library of C. W. Dyson Perrins. For the *Book of Hours* in general see p. 402 ff.

Numerous exquisite *Books of Hours* are preserved in the British Museum, and some of them belong to the second half of the thirteenth century. Two deserve special mention—*Egerton MS. 1151* and *Harley MS. 928*, both being of very small format and both having their bar-borders and margins very richly decorated with animals, birds and grotesques. The former contains, moreover, historiated initials prefixed to several offices, drawn in very fine black outline on a finely diapered background. The latter, unlike the *Egerton MS.*, has in addition a series of full-page miniatures (representing the life of Christ); but on the whole it is of inferior artistic quality.

The *Salvin Horae* (Fig. V-12*a*), Sir Chester Beatty's magnificent gift (in 1955) to the British Museum, as rightly pointed out by T. V. Brown, 'is conspicuous for its early date, for its size ($12\frac{3}{4} \times 8\frac{3}{4}$ in.), and for the dignified splendour of its decoration.' It possibly comes from Lincoln, and may be dated to after 1262—thus being one of the earliest surviving Hours of the use of Salisbury—and it is related to the *Psalter B.M. Add. MS. 38116*.

A beautiful *Book of Hours*, apparently written in England *c.* 1300 but illuminated in the French style, is preserved at Nuremberg (City Library, *Solger in 4°, No. 4*). About 1400 the book was given by King Charles VI of France to a Queen of

England (probably to one of his daughters, Isabella, wife of Richard II, or Catherine, wife of Henry V). At the beginning there is a series of figures of saints standing under canopies, in conventional Gothic style. The full-page miniatures, painted on grounds of stippled gold, are prefixed to the several Hours, and are divided into compartments showing side by side the joyful and dolorous mysteries of the Virgin, the Nativity and Adoration, the Arrest of Christ and His appearance before Pilate, the Crucifixion and Ascension, etc. The faces, left white, are finished with pen-drawing; colour-gradations (particularly vermilion, blue and pink) are used for the draperies.

The illustrated *Bestiaries* (see also p. 49) form a very popular class of English illuminated MSS. of the twelfth and thirteenth centuries, and they are often found in conjunction with illustrated *Herbals*. While the latter go back to the *Dioscorides MSS.* (see p. 44 ff.), the former are partly based on the *Etymologiae* of Isidore, and partly derive from copies of Pliny and the *Physiologus*—see also p. 48 f. Interesting English specimens of the combination of *Bestiary* and *Herbal* are preserved in the British Museum: for instance, the *Harley MS. 4986* of the twelfth century. Superb *Bestiaries* of the second half of the twelfth century are preserved in the British Museum (*Harley MS. 2751*), in the Bodleian Library, Oxford (*Ashmole MS. 1511*), in the University Library at Cambridge (*MS. Ii. 4. 26*), in the State Library at Leningrad (*MS. Qu. V. 1*), and a recently discovered *Bestiary*, in the University Library at Aberdeen. An excellent English specimen, preserved in the Pierpont Morgan Library, New York (*M. 107*) belongs to the late twelfth century; in 1187 it was presented by a Canon of Lincoln to Worksop Priory. Other *Bestiaries* are mentioned on p. 49: see also Fig. I-20.

The most interesting of the pictures, in Herbert's opinion, are those which illustrate the supposed habits of the creatures described: the pelican feeding her young with her blood; the unicorn crouching entranced at a maiden's feet; the watersnake spitefully entering the jaws of a sleeping crocodile in order to devour his entrails; the whale plunging into the depths, to the consternation of the sailors who have lighted a fire on its back; the wonderous white bird *caradrios*, which perches on a king's sickbed and either looks him in the face and cures him, or else turns its back on him, forecasting his speedy death.

A picture-book of the *Life of Christ* and *Figures of Saints*, dated c. 1270 (in the Fitzwilliam Museum, Cambridge, *MS. 370*), and a thirteenth-century copy of *La Estoire de Seint Aedward le Rei Translatee du Latin* (Cambridge University Library, *MS. Ee. 3.59*) may be regarded as examples of other popular book-production: Fig. V-12b–c.

Illustrations of the Apocalypse

The last in the order of the books of the New Testament is known in Christian literature as the *Apocalypse of John*, in the English Bible being called the *Revelation of S. John the Divine*. The term *apocalypse*, derived from the Greek, means 'Revelation', and the expression 'apocalyptic' writings is often used for a special class of religious literature of the Old and the New Testaments containing mystical and symbolical elements. Here we are primarily concerned with the *Apocalypse of John*.

Like other 'apocalyptic' writings, it springs from a time when faith in God is being severely tried by the experience of the world's power and cruelty; indeed, it seems to have been written to comfort the early Church under persecution. Its purpose is to brace the faith of God's people to continued patience, steadfastness, and courage; its keynote is the success of the new religion over every opposition—the triumphant assurance of victory in the end. It is full of prophetic grandeur; awful in its mystic symbols: seven seals opened, seven trumpets sounded, seven vials poured out; mighty antagonists arrayed against Christianity; hostile powers full of malignity against the new religion, and for a season oppressing it, but at length defeated and annihilated; the darkened heaven, tempestuous sea, and convulsed earth fighting against them; while the issue of the long combat is the universal reign of peace and truth and righteousness; the whole scene is relieved at intervals by a choral burst of praise to God the Creator, and Christ the Redeemer and Governor. The future is depicted in such a way as to enhance the conviction that 'the end is at hand'—the end being the vindication of God's rule and the glorious redemption of His people. The form in which these thoughts are expressed is that of a series of visions, the description of the visions being largely conveyed in the language of symbolism. The symbols, however, were borrowed from earlier literature and had already acquired a certain general meaning.

If we take into due consideration on the one hand, what has here been said of the *Apocalypse*, and on the other, what has been said—for instance—in *The Hand-produced Book*, p. 439 and *passim*, on the conditions prevailing in the Middle Ages, we more readily understand why—with the exception of the *Psalms* and *Gospels*—the *Apocalypse* was in the Middle Ages the most popular Biblical book as a subject for pictorial illustration. It should also be emphasized that its contents were most suitable for pictorial representations.

No wonder, therefore, that already in Carolingian times book-illuminators resorted to themes from the *Apocalypse*; no wonder that in Spain, during the struggles between Christianity and Islam, the illustrations of the *Apocalypse* and of its *Commentary* by Beatus de Liébana were extremely popular (see p. 166 f.). In England, the illustrations of the *Apocalypse*—in Gothic style, thus quite different from the Spanish-Mozarabic style (p. 166 f.)—were particularly popular in the thirteenth century. In France and Flanders they were popular from the thirteenth to the late fifteenth century, but artistically much inferior to the English specimens. Of the great number of illuminated MSS. of the *Apocalypse*, which must have existed, about seventy have been preserved.

One of the best specimens, a thirteenth-century English MS. preserved in Trinity College Library, at Cambridge (*R. 16. 2*), was probably executed at St. Albans *c.* 1230. It contains ninety-one miniatures, which, according to Herbert, while lacking the minute delicacy of the smaller designs which adorn the best

French and English Psalters of the time, atone for this deficiency by the richness of their colouring and the dramatic force and vigour of their compositions. It is in the battle scenes, naturally, that the latter quality is displayed most effectively.

Dr. Millar assigns at least three thirteenth-century specimens to a Canterbury group of MSS.: Lambeth Palace Library, *MS. 209*, ex-Yates Thompson Library, *MS. 55*, and British Museum, *Add. MS. 42555*.

Another most beautiful copy of the *Apocalypse*, written and illuminated *c.* 1290, was preserved in the splendid collection of C. W. Dyson Perrins.

The *Apocalypse* MSS. have been classified in various ways: (1) Separating the illustrations in tinted outline from those painted in body-colour; to the former class belong two excellent early thirteenth-century MSS. produced in England. One is preserved in the Bodleian Library, Oxford (*MS. Auct. D. 4. 17*), the other in the National Library at Paris (*Fr. 403*). Very close to the Bodleian copy is an *Apocalypse*, executed *c.* 1260 (at St. Albans?) and preserved in the Pierpont Morgan Library (*M. 524*). It contains forty-two full-page and one half-page illustrations. They are tinted outline drawings, rectangular, two to a page. 'The translucent washes of light green, blue, rose and tan serve only to point up the lyric quality of the outlines' (Miner). The text (confined to excerpts from the *Book of Revelations*) is written in red and blue on the uncoloured backgrounds of the miniatures or on banderolles held by the figures: Fig. V-13a.

(2) According to the subjects illustrated—all the *Apocalypse* MSS. would be distinguished into two classes, and the MSS. mentioned under No. (1) would belong to the first class, as they begin and end with scenes from the life of S. John. A late thirteenth-century English MS. preserved in the British Museum (*Add. MS. 35166*) is placed by Delisle in the second class, but as its illustrations include the two series of scenes from the life of S. John, according to Herbert it would rather form a link between the two classes.

(3) MSS. containing text and illustrations, and MSS. containing no text, only explanatory inscriptions on the backgrounds of the miniatures, which fill the page, being usually divided into two compartments. The Bodleian Library MS. mentioned under (1) would belong to the latter group, while the Paris MS. would belong to the former group—indeed, it contains the full text of the *Apocalypse*, with a commentary, both in French, and both occupying the lower half of the page. Also the British Museum MS. referred to under (2) would belong to the second class—it contains the full text and commentary, both in Latin. Both the Yates Thompson MS. referred to under (4) and the MS. preserved in the Lambeth Palace belong to this group too. The latter, probably executed in the late thirteenth century in S. Augustine's Abbey, at Canterbury, contains seventy-eight half-page miniatures in plain banded frames; slender and elegant figures, outlined in sepia— the drapery folds being indicated with light colours (chiefly grey, brown, and green)— are contrasted against brilliant grounds of blue, purple, or stippled and burnished gold, the blue and purple sometimes diapered. Related to the last-named MS. and, therefore, to the school of Canterbury, is the copy of the *Apocalypse* of the

Abbey of Abingdon (British Museum, *Add. MS. 42555*), executed in the late thirteenth century, the text as well as the commentary being illuminated.

(4) According to the predomination of the grotesque or of the poetical-devotional imagination. The Cambridge MS. would be assigned to the former family. The very beautiful late thirteenth-century MS., already referred to on p. 271, which was formerly preserved in the Yates Thompson Collection (*No. 55*), would belong to the latter family. It is closely related to the Lambeth MS. mentioned under (3), and, like it, contains the Latin text with the commentary of Berengaudus. There are as many as 152 miniatures, illustrating the usual cycle of subjects from the Vision itself as well as their scriptural and historical antitypes according to the commentary.

The best English MSS. come from the thirteenth century, though some excellent specimens belong to the first half of the fourteenth century. In France and Flanders the production of these extremely interesting MSS.—arresting both from the point of view of the poetical imagination of the scribe and of the artistical interpretation of the artist—continued until the end of the fifteenth century, but no attempt can be made here to do more than mention two or three of the masterpieces. However, in the mid-fourteenth century the *Apocalypse* MSS. apparently ceased to be fashionable in the circles of people of better taste, and the artistic quality of the later MSS. is by far inferior to the thirteenth- or early fourteenth-century productions. As an authority in this field, J. A. Herbert, puts it, 'their chief interest, as regards the history of design, lies in the fact that they form a link in the chain which connects the Spanish paintings of the ninth century with Dutch or German woodcuts of the fifteenth.'

Two early fourteenth-century MSS. preserved in the British Museum may be considered representative specimens of the finer (*Add. MS. 17333*) and the average (*Add. MS. 22493*) productions of the Franco-Flemish schools of illumination. *Add. MS. 17333* (which formerly belonged to the Carthusian monastery of Val-Dieu, near Mortagne) contains eighty-three exquisite half-page miniatures, with graceful figures, birds, and monsters, on grounds which are either diapered with a variety of tessellated patterns or are of plain dark colour. *Add. MS. 22493*, a fragment of four leaves, contains in the upper half of each page a miniature on neatly diapered grounds. Herbert emphasizes 'its hard but clean and decided drawing, and its depth of colour, especially its dark blue'.

English Main Centre and Leading Illuminators

St. Albans—Matthew Paris. If we were to assign a leading school of illumination to each period, we would here select the *scriptorium* of the Abbey of St. Albans, which at this period was probably the most noted of all the English centres of book-production; it has left us several fine illuminated MSS. The *scriptorium* was founded about three centuries after the foundation of the abbey. Its library was instituted with eight *Psalters*, two *Gospel-books* bound in gold and silver and set with gems, a book of *Collects*, a book of *Epistles*, the *Evangelia legenda per annum*, and twenty-eight other notable volumes apart from necessary books for ordinary use. But every succeeding abbot considered it his duty to contribute something to the library shelves. The sixteenth abbot, a Norman, Geoffrey, who previously had a school at Dunstable, contributed among other books two *Missals* (one bound in gold, and the other beautifully written and illuminated), a richly illuminated *Psalter*, and a *Benedictional*. His successors, Ralph Gubian and Robert de Gosham, gave many books, and the latter caused 'very many' MSS. to be written and sumptuously bound for presentation to the library.

Abbot Simon, who followed in 1166, created the office of historiographer, repaired and enlarged the *scriptorium*, and kept two or three of the most able scribes and illuminators constantly employed in transcription. He ruled that for the future every abbot should maintain at least one suitable and capable scribe. Moreover, he presented the library with his own precious collection, including a beautiful copy of the Bible specially written with the greatest care and exactness. Another liberal benefactor was John de Cell, a man of vast learning, a grammarian and poet, as well as a physician. His prior, Heymund, caused many valuable books to be transcribed for the library. And so grew in magnitude and importance the great collection which supplied Roger of Wendover and Matthew Paris with materials, for their famous histories.

Matthew Paris, a monk at St. Albans from 1217, scribe-illuminator, painter, and metal-worker, head of the *scriptorium* and historiographer of the Abbey, left important historical writings, *Historia Anglorum* and *Chronica Majora*, which have been preserved in many copies, some having been written by him and illustrated either by him or under his direction. According to E. J. F. Arnould ("Irish Times", 12-7-1958), the unique MS. of Trinity College, Dublin, *Life of St. Albans*, is "not only a valuable specimen of Anglo-Norman literature, but possibly illustrated by the author himself."

Most interesting is a British Museum MS. (*Royal 14. C. vii*) containing the *Historia Anglorum* and the last section of the *Chronica Majora*. A most charming full-page drawing prefixed to the volume, attributed to Matthew Paris, represents him kneeling before the Madonna and Child; it is on a plain vellum ground, framed in bands of pale green and red. Other pages contain lightly tinted outline-drawings—without much attempt at portraiture—of the kings of England from William I to Henry III. At the end of the *Chronica Majora* there is a drawing of Matthew Paris on his deathbed, probably executed by the monk who continued the chronicle: Fig. V-13b.

Another British Museum MS. (*Claudius D. vi*), containing an abridged chronicle of England, has drawings of kings (from the legendary Brutus to Henry III), outlined in brown ink and lightly tinted in water-colour, in a style similar to that of the MS. *Royal 14 C. vii*. Finally, a MS. of the *Lives of the Two Offas*, with historical documents and notes chiefly relating to St. Albans Abbey (British Museum, *Nero D. i.*) contains very fine outline-drawings in the upper half of each page; those of the first six pages, referring to the early life of the first Offa, are exquisite. A charming full-page drawing, almost at the end of the MS., represents the elephant sent by Louis IX to England in 1255 as a present to Henry III; it is usually attributed to Matthew Paris.

Recently, an interesting manuscript in the Bodleian Library (*Ashmole MS. 304*) has also been attributed to Matthew Paris by Dr. E. G. Millar.

W. de Brailes. Thirty-five years ago, Sir Sydney Cockerell discovered another thirteenth-century English artist, also probably a monk, whose name can be associated with at least six books, complete or fragmentary, in Cockerell's possession. There are four instances of Brailes' signed self-portrait. More recently, Dr. H. Swarzenski recognized Brailes' hand in a fragmentary MS. preserved in the Walters Art Gallery, Baltimore (*W. 106*), which contains twenty-seven full-page miniatures of a series of *Bible* illustrations. Swarzenski suggested that *W. 106* may possibly have belonged to a prayer-book, which was partly preserved in the Dyson Perrins Collection, London. E. G. Millar discovered seven more full-page miniatures from the same series in the Georges Wildenstein Collection, Paris. Of particular interest—writes Miss Dorothy Miner—is the great range of scenes, including many episodes rarely depicted, which when considered together with earlier English works, must reflect a tradition going back to a very ancient lost cycle of Bible illustrations. Also, an illuminated *Psalter* in the Fitzwilliam Museum, Cambridge, has been attributed to W. de Brailes: Fig. V-14*a* and *b*. Quite recently W. de Brailes has been identified with William de Brailles, mentioned in five Oxford documents, *c*. 1230–60. At any rate, apparently, W. de Brailes' influence at Oxford 'will have been at its strongest'.

LAST GREAT PERIOD OF ENGLISH ILLUMINATION

The closing years of the thirteenth century and the early years of the fourteenth century may be considered the last great period of English illumination. Some scholars consider it the best period of the English art of illumination. Indeed, the zenith has been reached—a peculiarly satisfying balance was struck between the various conflicting elements of book-decoration: realism, imagination and tradition, illustration and ornament, were blended with unerring nicety of adjustment, by artists possessed of a greater technical dexterity and a more thorough naturalism than their early Gothic predecessors; and a harmonious perfection resulted, which has hardly been surpassed in all the history of the art: Herbert.

Psalters

The Psalters continue to be the main class of superb illuminated MSS. The *Windmill Psalter*, of the closing years of the thirteenth century, was probably executed in Canterbury; it is now in the Pierpont Morgan Library (*M. 102*). It contains not only fine historiated initials and witty line-endings in outline or body-colour, but also two magnificent pages at the beginning of *Psalm* i: the *B* of *Beatus* (filling the first page), in a rectangular frame on a diapered background, with medallions of the Creation on a gold background, a Jesse-tree, etc.; and the *E* (filling half of the next page), which, surrounded with strikingly beautiful lacework design of leaves and flourishes drawn in red and blue outlines and faintly washed with pale green, encloses paintings of an angel, of the Judgment of Solomon, and of a windmill (hence the name of the MS.)—they are, indeed, magnificent specimens of English illumination. This book—writes Miss Dorothy Miner— certainly is one of the most delightful that has come down to us. All the paintings and line-endings appear to be the work of a single artist who is a most expressive and unique personality. His figures are characterized by great freedom of pose and movement, the hands graceful and prehensile, the round-cheeked faces moulded in a kind of pale *grisaille*, the draperies modelled with a most delicate and luscious surface: Miner. Unusual are the colours: a beautiful rose red, a luminous blue, green, golden tan, and others: Fig. V-14c.

Several other Psalters should here be mentioned: the *Arundel Psalter*, in the British Museum (see p. 279 f.), the *Tickhill Psalter*, in the New York Public Library (Spencer Collection, *MS. 26*), the *Ormesby Psalter*, in the Bodleian Library (see p. 282), and others (some of them will be discussed on p. 281 ff.). A specimen of great beauty was acquired by the British Museum (in 1937), and is now marked *Add. MS. 44949*. It is the *M. R. James Psalter*, which was executed in the fourteenth century for use in the diocese of Durham. 'Apart from its own beauty its certain English origin settles that of another Psalter from the same scriptorium and perhaps by the same hand (Egerton MS. 1894)' (A. Esdaile), which hitherto was considered of uncertain origin.

W. Oakeshott has suggested that the English Late Gothic period of book-illumination should be subdivided into two stages. In the first, represented for instance by the *Tickhill Psalter*, the figures still have a childlike air of simplicity about them. More advanced is the second group, its best production being the *Queen Mary's Psalter*.

The *Tickhill Psalter* belongs to an early fourteenth-century group of eight manuscripts, which includes other *Psalters* (Lambeth Palace Library, *MS. 233*, and *Queen Isabella Psalter*, in the Munich State Library, *Cod. Gall. 16*), as well as the *Grey-Fitzpayn Hours* (Fitzwilliam Museum, Cambridge, *MS. 242*), an *Apocalypse* in the British Museum (see p. 280 f.), and other works. These MSS. were painted 'by the same travelling atelier, using the same pattern-books, for prominent inter-related families, nearly all of which were connected with Nottinghamshire' (Miner). The *Tickhill Psalter*, 'one of the richest and most interesting examples of English gothic illumination' was executed for the priory of Worksop (now Radnor), near Nottingham. Its scribe and gilder was John Tickhill, Prior of Worksop (1308–14). It contains 482 miniatures, including seven full-page historiated initials: Fig. V-15a and b.

As some miniatures remain unfinished, the MS. shows every stage of the illuminator's procedure, from the first rough sketch to the finished picture. An unparalleled series, dependent on Petrus Comestor, *Historia Scholastica* (see p. 264), represents episodes in the lives of David and Solomon.

Partly related to the *Tickhill Psalter* is an early fourteenth-century *Psalter* and *Hours*, executed for a foundation of Augustinian monks (St. Julian near St. Albans Abbey?) and preserved in the Walters Art Gallery, Baltimore (*W. 102*). It contains thirty-seven historiated initials and a great number of line-endings and drolleries (thirty-four of them being miniatures), executed by two hands.

Queen Mary's Psalter. The climax in English illumination is reached in the *Queen Mary's Psalter*; it is so named not because it was painted for her—since it was executed more than two centuries before she ever saw it—but in 1553, being about to be sent abroad, it was seized by a London customs officer and presented to Queen Mary I (Mary Tudor, 1553-8); it has been ever since one of the chief treasures of the Royal Library, now at the British Museum (*Royal 2. B. vii*). It is an unusually thick octavo volume—containing 320 leaves—but the great number of miniatures and marginal drawings leave very little space for text on most of the pages. The MS. is bound in what appears to be the binding put on it for the Queen —crimson velvet embroidered on each cover with a large pomegranate, and having gilt corner protections; the golden clasps which it originally had are gone, but the plates remain riveted on the covers, engraved with the Tudor badge.

The first fifty-six leaves of the MS. contain a long series of illustrations from the Old Testament, mostly two miniatures on a page, framed in plain vermilion bands with three leaves growing out of each corner, each picture being accompanied by a sort of caption in French (quaint in phrasing and often of considerable length) taken either from the canonical text or from apocryphal legends from the Creation to the death of Solomon. The drawings are really beautiful—they are so fine, so delicately yet so firmly and cleverly sketched. They are not coloured in full body-colours, but just suggestively drawn in the finest possible outline, and lightly tinted in violet, green and reddish-brown, and are far freer and more truly spontaneous in manner than any previous works of the kind. The draperies are washed over in thin tints, the golds well defined, but lightly shaded. The compositions are spacious and simple; the figures graceful, with just a hint of dainty self-consciousness in their pose; the facial types often of great beauty. We find in the MS. a continuation of the style of drawing, the liveliness of movement, and the delicate, pale colouring of the Winchester school.

After the Old Testament illustrations follows the Psalter with miniatures of New Testament scenes—including a nearly full-page Jesse-tree and a great number of large miniatures of the life of Christ and His kindred—and figures of saints accompanied by most beautiful initials and ornaments. The scenes from the New Testament are painted in body-colour on backgrounds of burnished gold or diapered colours. The high quality of the work abundantly shows that the artist was by no means a novice; it was probably by the same artist who executed the tinted drawings. The MS. also contains the Calendar—its unique feature being the Zodiacal signs and monthly occupations treated in a series of frieze-like drawings, representing scenes of medieval animal-lore, games, sports, and pastimes. Finally there are representations of the miracles of Mary, and of the lives and martyrdoms of saints : Fig. V-16*a*.

One may conclude with the words of W. Oakeshott, 'the workmanship is fine, and the taste impeccable. . . . There is a loveliness about it and an underlying seriousness, which make it more important than most of the comparable books. But it knows nothing of the depths of human emotion, of sorrow, or of pity, or of joy' of the illuminated MSS. of the Renaissance period.

The Psalter and Hours, executed in the second half of the fourteenth century for dame Elizabeth Courtenay, wife of Lord Courtenay (who died in 1375), is a very fine manuscript. It is preserved in the Bodleian Library (*MS. Auct. D. 4.4*) : Fig. V-16*b*.

Apocalypse MSS.

Excellent illuminated copies of the *Apocalypse* were executed in the first half of the fourteenth century, but not many of those preserved are on the same artistic level as those of the thirteenth century described on p. 270 ff. Amongst the best, an *Apocalypse* preserved in the British Museum (*Royal 19. B. xv*) contains seventy-two miniatures of varying size and of varying artistic quality ; a few seem to be related to some miniatures of *Queen Mary's Psalter* (see above). They are effective—writes Herbert—through simplicity rather than strength of colour, relying for effect on the contrast between backgrounds of soft red and blue, and white or faintly tinted figures delicately sketched in pen outline. The faces are rounded in contour and suave in expression, the figures graceful, though tending to an artificial statuesqueness of pose. Simplicity of composition as well as colour marks the happiest efforts of this artist.

A charming copy of the *Apocalypse* is part of a miscellanea codex, called the *Nuneaton Book* (Fitzwilliam Museum, *McClean MS. 123*, folios 66–105), which also includes a *Bestiary*. Nuneaton was a cell to the Abbey of Fontevrault, founded by Robert Bossu, Earl of Leicester. The book is allied in style to *MS. 20* of the same collection (see p. 408). Fig. V-15*c*; see also Fig. V-15*b* as well as p. 272 and p. 280.

An interesting group of about half-a-dozen MSS. of the first half of the fourteenth century, derived from an archetype apparently related to the Paris MS. discussed on p. 271, is represented by the mid-fourteenth-century *Add. MS. 18633* of the British Museum. It contains a paraphrase of the *Apocalypse*. Artistically it does not rank very high, but—as Herbert has pointed out—it is quite expressive as illustration. The backgrounds are mostly blue or pink, diapered, but are sometimes of stippled gold. On the whole the drawing is hard, the technique flat, the composition stiff; the architecture, however, is good and interesting. Silver is used for armour and other accessories.

Miscellanea

Illuminated secular book-production may be represented by an excellent copy of Egidio Colonna or Aegidius Columna, known as Gilles of Rome (1247–1316), *Du Gouvernement des princes*. The original text, in Latin, was composed *c.* 1280 for King Philip the Bold for the instruction of his son, Philip the Fair. The French translation, made by Henri de Gauchy before 1285, became very popular both in France and in England. The present copy, preserved in the Walters Art Gallery (*W. 144*), was executed in England *c.* 1295–1300; it contains ten miniatures, historiated and illuminated initials, and partial borders. 'The illustrations are executed with skill and grace' (Miner).

Another beautiful manuscript of the same collection (*W. 133*) was also executed *c.* 1300, probably in England. It is a copy of the *Decretals of Gratian* with the commentary of Bartholomew of Brescia. It contains thirty-five historiated and four large illuminated initials.

Rather unusual is another Walters Art Gallery manuscript (*W. 80*). It is a fourteenth-century vellum roll (14 ft. $2\frac{1}{2}$ in. × $16\frac{1}{2}$ in.) containing the *Table of Consanguinity and Genealogy of Christ*, illustrated with coloured drawings, 'in a sure and graceful style, many of them in circular medallions' (Miner): Fig. V-17.

An excellent *Bestiary*, preserved in the Fitzwilliam Museum (*MS. 379*) is artistically related to the *Ormesby* and *Bromholm Psalters* (see p. 282). A charming copy of the *Romance of Alexander* (see p. 35), written and illuminated *c.* 1344, is preserved in the Bodleian Library (*MS. Bodley 264*); it is, however, a French or Flemish production: see pp. 35, 380, and 442; see also Fig. V-18*b–c.*

East Anglian School of Illumination

For the first half of the fourteenth century we must mention the richness of ornamentation and the magnificence of the East Anglian school centred at Norwich. This school flourished from 1300 to 1350 and it was then the main artistic centre of England. This period—as W. Oakeshott has rightly remarked—coincided with a period of unparalleled wealth in East Anglia, due to the prosperity of the wool trade at the time, whereas the artistic decline coincided with further economic changes in the region.

The MSS. of this school have very large borders, decorated with ornamental foliage interspersed with cleverly painted human figures, animals and birds, little grotesque pictures, armorial bearings, and so on. J. A. Herbert has summed up the main characteristics of this school as follows: (1) a rich and harmonious colour-scheme, with plentiful use of burnished and patterned gold; (2) luxuriance of ornament, especially in the designing of frame-borders and initial-decoration, where plant forms, animals, and human figures are entwined together in an effective and distinctive manner. Red and green ivy, vine, and oak-leaves—the last combined with acorns—are specially prominent; (3) a passion for the droll and grotesque, not peculiar indeed to this school, but very noticeable and pronounced in it.

The origin of this school is not yet established. While it is doubtful whether Herbert is right in suggesting a connection with late thirteenth-century Flemish art, as exemplified in *Stowe 17* (see p. 439), 'and very likely East Anglian art did owe something to Flemish or North-French influence', his conclusion is more or less generally accepted. 'In the main, however, it was undoubtedly a native growth, and its half-century of duration (1300–50) was the brightest period in English illumination.'

Sydney Cockerell suggested that the East Anglian art of illumination may have derived from the schools which produced the *Duke of Rutland Psalter* (see p. 266) and the *Tenison Psalter* (see p. 263), whereas according to Herbert, the ancestors of East Anglian illumination may have been stylistically connected with a *Peterborough Psalter* (now in the Royal Library at Brussels, *Nos. 9961–2*), a splendid work executed for, and probably at, Peterborough in the late thirteenth century. There is still—writes Herbert—a good deal of archaic angularity about its miniatures; but the borders contain all the elements of ornament noted above as characteristic of the early fourteenth-century East Anglian school, though they lack the rich exuberance of fancy and the fineness of finish which make the best productions of the school so delightful to behold.

East Anglian Masterpieces: Arundel 83. One of the earliest and most interesting productions of the East Anglian school is a miscellaneous book preserved in the British Museum (*Arundel MS. 83*); it contains two fragmentary MSS. of similar style. The first contains a *Calendar*, several pages of allegorical designs, a *Psalter*, *Canticles*, *Litanies*, *Office of the Dead*, and a fragmentary *Hours of the Passion*. Apparently—to judge from the arms on the first page—it was executed either for Sir William Howard (Howard is the family name of the dukes of Norfolk and the earls of Arundel), chief-justice of the Common Pleas (1297–1308), or for his wife, Alice Fitton. The second MS., more fragmentary but of greater artistic merit, contains a *Calendar*, allegorical designs, a series of miniatures (in compartments) illustrating the life of Christ, and a few beautiful full-page miniatures. In the *Calendar*, under November 25, there is a note dated (1339) by Robert de Lyle, or de Lisle (hence the Psalter is also known as the *Psalter of Robert de Lisle*), which records that the book has been presented to his daughters Audrey and 'Alborou' in succession, with remainder to the nuns of Chicksand in Bedfordshire. See Fig. V-22a.

The opening page of the *Psalter* is most elaborate: the *B* encloses a Jesse-tree, and the two columns of text are framed in a border resplendent with gold and colours, filled with intertwining foliage-stems whose curves form panels for figures of Patriarchs and Prophets on both sides, a Crucifixion at the top, and the Evangelistic emblems at the corners. At the foot of the page there is the representation of a woodland scene, with stag and hind, a rabbit, and a fowler crouching under a bush and luring birds with an owl.

In the second MS.,—containing a *Breviary*—we find an interesting painting of the stages of human life in ten medallions (the first an infant on its mother's lap, the last a tomb). Over a very expressive picture of the Three Living and the Three Dead—a subject found in East Anglian wall-paintings of this period (for instance, at Gorleston, to which some scholars assign this MS.)—occur the following lines: *Ich am afert Lo Wet ich se Methinketh hit beth deueles thre.* 'I am afraid. Lo what I see. Me thinketh it be devils three.' *Ich wes welfair Such sheltou be For godes loue be wer by me.* 'I was well fair. Such shalt thou be. For love of God beware by me.' The three living in this illumination are three fashionable ladies—no doubt princesses, for they wear crowns. Generally they are men, as, for instance, in the celebrated fresco *Trionfo della Morte* in the Campo Santo at Pisa.

Miniature-initials on grounds of burnished and stippled gold, borders of cusped bars and foliage-stems, supporting grotesques and decorated with ivy, oak, and vine leaves; daisy-buds, curious emblematic diagrams (including a *seraph* whose wings are inscribed with moral qualities), tables of virtues and vices, a representation of the Cross as the Tree of Life, also occur. The drolleries are very funny. Some of the illustrations are really good pen-drawings—refined, expressive, and graceful, but above all typical of English draughtmanship of the period. In a little scene of the Adoration of the Magi, the kings wear costumes like contemporary English kings as we find them on sculptures, wall-paintings, etc. Two large miniatures show East Anglian painting at its best—one represents the Madonna and Child under a canopy, against a background of gold highly burnished and covered with a finely-stippled pattern of foliage scroll-work; the other is a Crucifixion, on a ground of lozenges filled with fleurs-de-lis and heraldic lions; it also shows two angels with discs (sun and moon), a pelican feeding her young (= Redemption: Christ), Adam, etc.

Related in style to *Arundel MS. 83* is a fragmentary *Book of Hours* of c. 1300, preserved in the Walters Art Gallery (*W. 105*). It contains twelve full-page miniatures and fifteen historiated initials. It is an extremely fine work, but it has been ruined by water: Fig. V-22b.

Apocalypse. In the sections of Spanish (p. 166 f.) and, especially, English (pp. 269 ff. and 277) illumination, several copies of the *Apocalypse* were discussed. It was mentioned that a remarkable series of such MSS., illuminated in the Gothic style, and produced mainly in England, France, or Flanders, is preserved in various collections of Europe and America.

An *Apocalypse* MS. decorated in the style typical of the East Anglian school—one of its main features, occurring on almost every page, being the use of foliage (treated with some attempt at naturalism) for initial and border ornament—is preserved in the British Museum (*Royal 15. D. ii*). Unlike other copies of the *Apocalypse*, it is a book of huge size. It was executed in the early fourteenth century and probably belonged to Greenfield nunnery in Lincolnshire. A characteristic feature of this MS. (and of a contemporary MS. preserved in the Royal Library at Brussels, *MS. B. 282*) is that apart from the *Apocalypse* it contains a copy of the Anglo-Norman poem *Lumière as Lais*. The MS. is decorated with initials containing miniatures or ornamental foliage, on a large diaper-pattern background, with cusped bar and line-and-leaf borders attached. 'The colour-scheme is harmonious and pleasant, but the technique is absolutely flat, without gradation or perspective; the drapery folds are indicated by heavy black lines' (Herbert): Fig. V-15*b*.

Another early fourteenth-century *Apocalypse*, produced in the East Anglian school of illumination, is preserved in the Trinity College at Dublin (*MS. K. 4.31*).

Psalters. There cannot be any doubt that there was an important school of illumination in the neighbourhood of Norwich, perhaps at Gorleston, with which at least two superb Psalters, the *Douai Psalter* and the *Gorleston Psalter*, are associated. Although in that locality there existed houses of the Franciscan and the Austin Friars, apparently 'the best of the artists were laymen, who contracted for given pieces of work, and moved from place to place, at the beck and call of various patrons' (Cockerell).

Douai Psalter. The *Douai Psalter* (*MS. 171* in the Municipal Library at Douai, Dept. Nord, France) was given by Thomas, vicar of Gorleston, to a certain Abbot John; it contains chronological notes, which refer specially to the diocese of Norwich and date the book to 1322–5. It is interesting that the same notes appear in another MS. of the British Museum (*Stowe 12*), a *Breviary* for use in the Diocese of Norwich, containing border decoration and initials, which thus becomes another interesting specimen of East Anglian illumination.

Two superb full-page miniatures prefixed to the *Douai Psalter* represent the Madonna and Child and the Crucifixion on grounds of gold punctured with a scroll-work pattern of foliage. It has a splendid *Beatus vir*, containing a Jesse-tree, with a frame-border filled with figures of kings and New Testament scenes on patterned gold grounds; there is also a picture of David bringing the ark to Jerusalem with an interesting, pompous medieval church procession. Unfortunately, the *Douai Psalter* was completely ruined by damp during the First World War.

Gorleston Psalter. The *Gorleston Psalter*, also known as *Lord Braybrooke Psalter*, was preserved in the collection of C. W. Dyson Perrins. Its association with Gorleston is assured by the inclusion in the Calendar of a festival commemorating the Dedication of Gorleston Church and the prominence given in the illuminations to S. Andrew, the patron saint of Gorleston parish church. Indeed, its style is so closely related to that of the *Douai Psalter*, that both have to be assigned to the same *scriptorium* and period. The *Gorleston Psalter* has no full-page miniatures, but its *Beatus* is as magnificent as that in the *Douai Psalter*, and very similar to it; instead of the picture of David, it has a hunting scene, which takes the place of the woodland scene of the MS. *Arundel 83* (see p. 279 f.).

Herbert rightly says that, in the *Gorleston Psalter*, the small marginal figures and the still smaller ones in the line-endings 'are unrivalled among the productions of this the best period of the school' for variety, humour, and vivacity. Practically the whole range of human activities, as known to the artists—Herbert points out—is represented: ecclesiastics, warriors, hunters, musicians, blacksmiths, etc., practising their respective callings. But it is in whimsical caricature above all that the illustrators delighted, giving free play to an absolutely riotous fancy: foxes masquerading as bishops, rabbits conducting a solemn procession, apes hunting on horseback or driving a team of plough-oxen, and suchlike drolleries. Grotesque and monstrous forms of all kinds abound, of course, and scenes of animal life are often depicted with great spirit.

Ormesby Psalter. The *Ormesby Psalter* (so called because it was presented to Norwich Priory by the monk Robert of Ormesby, a village about six miles north of Gorleston), preserved in the Bodleian Library (*Douce MS. 366*), contains less decoration than the MS. just discussed, but its illuminated pages, particularly the full-page *Beatus vir*, are of such superb artistic quality that authorities like Oakeshott see in it the first promise of the Renaissance, which brings about a complete change in the art of illumination: Fig. V-20.

Saint-Omer Psalter. Notwithstanding this standard of excellence, Herbert considers another East Anglian MS., the *Saint-Omer Psalter*, as representing this style at its greatest height of technical perfection. This masterpiece, begun *c.* 1330 for a member of the Saint-Omer family, of Mulbarton, in Norfolk, was completed at the beginning of the next century. It belonged to Mr. H. Yates Thompson's collection (*MS. No. 58*), but was presented by him to the British Museum (where it is now *Add. MS. 39810*). Its *Beatus vir* page, writes Herbert, is the *non plus ultra* of this particular style of illumination, combining a rich, yet spacious and not overladen, scheme of decoration with minute and exquisite delicacy in the spirited little figure-compositions, and with the utmost fertility in invention; the plant-forms are as varied as in the *Ormesby Psalter*, and bears, unicorns, stags, birds of all kinds, and tiny human figures are perched here and there on the stems, quite irrelevantly and yet with a perfect decorative fitness.

Bromholm Psalter (Bodleian Library, *Ashmole MS. 1523*): in Dr. E. G. Millar's opinion, this charming masterpiece of the early fourteenth century—Fig. V-21—may have been executed by the artist who produced the *Dublin Apocalypse K. 4.31*.

Du Bois Psalter and *Horae*, Sarum use (Pierpont Morgan Library, *M. 700*), executed in East Anglia for Havisia du Bois (who is depicted on fol. 3 *v*), contains four full-page miniatures, twenty-one large historiated and numerous small illuminated initials, as well as brilliant borders enlivened with human and animal figures; the coats-of-arms of the Du Bois and of related families are often introduced into the border decoration: Fig. V-19a.

Luttrell Psalter. A representative specimen of the East Anglian school in its last stage—when its style had already begun to decay—is the celebrated *Luttrell* (or *Louterell*) *Psalter*. Made *c.* 1340 for Sir Geoffrey Louterell or Luttrell, of Irnham, in Lincolnshire, it passed into the possession of the Weld family of Lulworth Castle, Dorsetshire; it was until recently (*i.e.* until 1929, when it was acquired by the British Museum for £31,500) one of the very few English illuminated MSS. remaining in private hands. It is now British Museum *Add. MS. 42130*. Its text, comprising the usual church offices, is embellished with exquisitely drawn illustrations of contemporary life, *e.g.* Geoffrey Louterell on a charger, taking leave of his wife and daughter-in-law, who hand up to him his helmet, shield, and lance; a medieval kitchen, with pots boiling, and game on a spit before an open fire; ladies in a travelling coach; the Castle of Love; Constantinople as a walled city—in short a treasure-house to the antiquary. The beginnings of artistic decadence, on the other hand, may be seen in the bizarre colouring, in the lack of sense of proportion, in the expressionless types of feature, in the partly decadent historiated initials. See Fig. V-24a.

DECADENCE OF THE EAST ANGLIAN SCHOOL AND OF ENGLISH ILLUMINATION

In the middle fourteenth century, the English artistic tradition—which had gone on for four centuries—came to a sudden end: perhaps because of the terrible plague of 1348-9. But even before the middle of the century illuminated books were being produced which were not on the artistic level of the East Anglian productions or *Queen Mary's Psalter*. On the other hand, some of these less artistic productions are very interesting for the insight they give into contemporary life. For instance, a copy of the *Decretals of Gregory IX* (British Museum, *Royal 10. E. iv*), written in Italy, but illuminated in England (probably by the canons of S. Bartholomew's, Smithfield, London), contains in its lower margins drawings which, though not of great artistic value, are very lively and charming, representing scenes from the Bible or from the lives of saints, as well as sketches from everyday life and popular legends and fables. The *Taymouth Horae* (formerly in Yates Thompson's Collection, *No. 57*) contains delightful pictures of the sportswoman's exploits. The *Carew-Poyntz Horae* (Fitzwilliam Museum, Cambridge, *MS. 48*) contains a long series of illustrations of miracles of the Virgin. It is dated *c*. 1350-1360. Fig. V-19b.

In the second half of the fourteenth century English illumination became heavy and dull, though much gold was used. In some MSS.—writes Herbert—the border appears as a framework of narrow rigid bars, sometimes broken midway and replaced by a sort of festoon of close-set foliage, but mostly diversified only by leafy bosses at the corners (a curious reversion to the tenth-century Winchester style: see p. 192 ff.) and by short-stalked leaves or buds, and sprays of foliage thrown at intervals. Good examples of this style are the *Lytlington Missal* (Nicholas Lytlington was Abbot of Westminster, 1362-1386), still preserved in Westminster Abbey, and the huge *Wycliffite Bible* (executed for Thomas of Woodstock, Duke of Gloucester, who died in 1397), now in the British Museum (*Egerton MSS. 617-18*).

There were, however, exceptions: exactly twenty years ago M. R. James published five very fine manuscripts which were executed in England *c*. 1370 and later, for members of the Bohun family. (The Bohun family played a conspicuous part in English history during the thirteenth and fourteenth centuries. Their lands lay on the Welsh borders; from 1199 they were earls of Hereford; later also of Essex and Northampton.) Three of these Bohun MSS. (Exeter College at Oxford, *MS. 47*; Bodleian Library, *MS. Auct. D. 4.4*; National Library at Vienna, *Cod.*

1826) or perhaps four (including also a *Psalter* in T. H. Riches Collection, Kitwells, Shenley, Herts; formerly, H. Y. Thompson, *MS. XCIX*) were executed for Humphrey de Bohun, seventh Earl of Hereford (who lived 1342–1373), while the fifth (Royal Library at Copenhagen, *Thotts Saml. 547*) was produced for his younger daughter Mary de Bohun, whose husband (after her death) became Henry IV. Several other MSS. belong in Dr. Millar's opinion to the Bohun group: a *Psalter and Hours* (National Library of Scotland, at Edinburgh, *MS. 18.6.5*), executed for Eleanor de Bohun, elder daughter of Humphrey, probably after 1382; a *Psalter and Hours* in the British Museum (*Add. MS. 16698*); and also probably a great part of two large scrapbooks, containing illuminated initials and border decorations belonging to a splendid *Missal*, in the British Museum (*Add. MSS. 29704–5*): see M. Rickert, *The Reconstructed Carmelite Missal*, London, 1952.

Another related manuscript was quite recently acquired by the British Museum (it is now *Egerton MS. 3277*); it is a beautiful *Psalter*. In Dr. Millar's opinion, it is one of the most important accessions of the British Museum in recent times.

Also to the fourteenth century belongs a group of excellent manuscripts executed probably at Durham. It includes the *Egerton Genesis* (British Museum, *Egerton MS. 1894*), a British Museum *Psalter* (*Add. MS. 44949*), the *Psalter of Stephen of Derby* in the Bodleian Library (*Rawlinson MS. G. 185*), and the *Fitzwarin Psalter* in the National Library at Paris (*MS. Lat. 765*).

Short Renaissance—German Influence. In the late fourteenth century a new style appeared; it was an imitation of German schools—Rhenish or Bohemian—but decoration of the borders was more or less independent. This decoration of the border with stem and leaves, throwing off thin-twisted tendrils with gold balls at the end—a characteristic shared with Italy—lasted until the middle of the fifteenth century. The main characteristics of the new style were a great softness in the treatment of the face (brush being used instead of pencil or pen), a more harmonious colour-scheme, a more skilful use of architectural ornament, and the introduction of new forms of foliage (conventional, but very decorative) and of a white scroll, with sinuated edges, wrapped round the upright shafts of pillars or initials. The treatment of landscape in miniatures is of interest: while the ground is treated more or less naturalistically, the sky is represented by gilded, tapestried, or checkered backgrounds.

It has been suggested that this new style is mainly due to the influence of German (Rhenish or Bohemian) artists who came to England with Anne of Bohemia, the wife of Richard II (the marriage took place in 1382). Indeed, one of the earliest and most splendid works in this style is the *Great Bible of Richard II* (British Museum, *Royal 1. E. ix*). It contains large miniature-initials and full borders for each book, and, for the prologues, large initials with scrolls of foliage or with pictures of S. Jerome at work among his books. Two large volumes preserved in the British Museum (*Add. MSS. 29704–5*) contain initials and border decorations which some former owner cut out of what must have been a splendid Missal. Some initials are filled with foliage decoration, others contain fine miniatures, representing liturgical ceremonies, lives of saints, and so on; there is also a portrait of Richard II. See Fig. V-24b.

John Siferwas and his School. A superb volume is the huge *Sherborne Missal* (Duke of Northumberland's Collection), containing beautiful initial and border decoration, margins with scenes from the Bible, hagiography, and ecclesiastical history, as well as secular subjects (such as a series of birds inscribed with their English names), highly ornate architectural canopies, and so on. One of the most interesting features of this MS. is that it contains in conjunction portraits of Richard Milford, Bishop of Salisbury (1396–1407)—this, therefore, being the date to which the book has to be assigned—and Robert Bruynyng, Abbot of Sherborne, in Dorsetshire: the two were the joint patrons of the book. Moreover, there are numerous smaller portraits of the scribe, John Whas, a Benedictine monk of Sherborne Abbey, and of the artist John Siferwas, a Dominican friar, who is one of the few English illuminators known to us both by name and by his works. Indeed, he also appears on the frontispiece of a *Lectionary* (British Museum, *Harley 7026*), presenting the book to John Lord Lovel (who died in 1408), who had ordered it as an offering to Salisbury Cathedral. It has been suggested that Siferwas was not the actual painter of the two MSS., but the chief artist, who planned and supervised the work. See Fig. V-23b.

Finally, a charming frontispiece, representing the Annunciation, of a *Book of Hours* (British Museum, *Royal 2 A. viii*), is attributed to an artist trained in the school with which Siferwas was connected. The MS., of the late fourteenth century, contains other miniatures and ornamentation, but these are in decadent style.

FIFTEENTH CENTURY

Last Flicker. The first quarter of the fifteenth century saw the production of a few really fine manuscripts—the first promise of the Renaissance. And 'while books which were purely medieval in ideas and treatment continued to be produced to the end of the fifteenth century, yet in the greatest books the signs of the times are unmistakable'. This is seen particularly in the admirable *Book of Hours* of 'Elysabeth yᵉ quene', the quality of which 'lies in the fusion of medieval and Renaissance minds' (Oakeshott). The MS. was formerly in Mr. Yates Thompson's Collection, and later in the library of C. W. Dyson Perrins. It owes its name to the signature of Elizabeth of York, which it contains; it was probably written for Cecily Neville, wife of Henry Beauchamp, Duke of Warwick. This magnificent manuscript is considered by Dr. Millar to be the finest surviving example of English fifteenth-century Books of Hours: Fig. V-25a.

Henry V's (1413–1422) successful invasion of France introduced a taste for French illumination, which was then at its zenith (see p. 396 ff.). Thus, most of the fifteenth-century Books of Hours and other illuminated books executed in England were the work of French artists or of English artists who imitated foreign models as best they could.

Under Edward IV (1461–83) this fashion gave way to a similar enthusiasm for Flemish painting. Franco-Flemish mixed style in England is represented by a British Museum MS. *Harley 4605* (Christine de Pisan, *Le Livre des fays d'armes* etc.).

Herman and his Atelier

Bedford Hours and Psalter. One of the last Books of Hours, but not the least, a superb work of art, is the *Bedford Hours and Psalter* (not to be confounded with the famous *Bedford Book of Hours*—see p. 405 f.), which A. Esdaile describes as one of the finest examples of the last school of illumination in England. The MS. is 'unique in containing over three hundred exquisite miniature heads, which may be portraits'. This MS.—like the *Bedford Book of Hours*—was executed for John, Duke of Bedford; in 1929 it was bought by the British Museum for £33,000. It bears the mark *Add. MS. 42131*. It was executed before 1422, its chief illuminator being an English (?) artist named Herman. Millar attributes to his atelier the following illuminated books: a *Book of Masses and Private Devotions*, in the British Museum (*Add. MS. 16998*) and a *Book of Hours* of Sarum use, in Millar's possession. The latter contains four miniatures and nine pages with full borders, two miniatures being almost identical in composition with miniatures in the *Bedford Psalter* and in the *Book of Masses*. Also *MS. 69* in the Lambeth Palace Library was apparently executed in Herman's atelier. See Fig. V-25b.

LAST STAGE OF ENGLISH ILLUMINATION

The last important English illuminated manuscripts executed in distinctly English style are not great works of art, but are interesting either as illustrations of local costume or for their genuine depth of mystical devotion. The former may be represented by John Lydgate's—see further on—*Life of S. Edmund* (British Museum, *Harley 2278*), presented to Henry VI in 1433; the latter by the copy of *Desert of Religion* (British Museum, *Cotton. Faust. B. vi, pt. ii*).

Chaundler's Manuscripts. Fig. V-23b reproduces fol. 7 r from Thomas Chaundler, *Liber Apologeticus de omni statu humanae naturae*, which is part of miscellanea works written by Chaundler when he was Chancellor of Oxford (1457–61); the book is preserved in the Trinity College Library at Cambridge (*MS. R. 14.5*). It contains a series of fifteen full-page miniatures of particular delicacy, which were at one time attributed to Chaundler himself. This opinion has been disproved by M. R. James. It is now held that these exquisite drawings were executed in England by an anonymous artist who was strongly influenced by French or, rather, Flemish art. Similar in style, but by a less skilled hand, are the four miniatures in another volume containing Chaundler's works which is now in Oxford (New College, *MS. 288*). On the whole, according to M. Rickert, the miniatures in both these MSS. represent the best miniature style of English drawing of the mid fifteenth century under strong Continental influence (French or Franco-Flemish). M. Rickert also suggests that the miniature on a paper fly-leaf (containing Lydgate, *The Pilgrim*) in a British Museum MS. (*Harley MS. 4826, fol. 1*), which can be dated roughly just before the middle fifteenth century is related in style to the miniatures of the Chaundler MSS. and is probably the work of an artist trained in the same atelier.

The *Missal of Abingdon Abbey*, of 1461 (partly preserved in the Bodleian Library, *Digby MS. 227*, and partly in Trinity College, Oxford, *MS. 75*) is considered by Rickert an excellent example of the late English illumination in painted style.

The following *Miscellanea* manuscripts are also of interest.

A *Book of Hours* in English and Flemish, Sarum use, executed *c.* 1460–1470, may be regarded as an example of the best English production of the period in this field; there are fifty illuminations (Fitzwilliam Museum, Cambridge, *MS. 53*). A Latin *Bible*, preserved in Trinity College Library, Dublin (*MS. No. A. 1.4: No. 36*), contains beautiful initials and ornamentation: Fig. V-28*a* and *b*.

A copy of the English translation of Guillaume de Deguileville, *Pélerinage de la Vie Humaine* (or *The Pilgrimage of the Soul*)—see p. 380—preserved in the Spencer Collection of the New York Public Library, may be regarded as a good example of the fifteenth-century popular book-production in England. Only six manuscripts of this work in English have been preserved. The present copy, probably executed *c.* 1430 for Sir Thomas Cumberworth of Somerby in Lincolnshire, contains twenty-six miniatures.

The prolific Lydgate (*c.* 1370–*c.* 1446), referred to above, a monk of Bury St. Edmunds, follower of Chaucer, wrote *The Hystorye, Sege, and Dystruccyon of Troye*, the *Falls of Princis*, and other poems. A copy of the *Sege of Troye*, of *c.* 1420, is preserved in The John Rylands Library, Manchester (*Engl. MS. 1*). It contains sixty-nine miniatures (some covering half the page) and numerous illuminated initials and ornamental borders. Copies of *The Falls of Princis* are preserved in the British Museum (*Harley MS. 1766*) and in other collections. A copy preserved in the Rosenbach Company Collection, New York City, executed *c.* 1460, 'is among the most elaborately decorated early copies of the work' (Miner). There are seven miniatures and about 260 illuminated initials. See Fig. V-26.

A good example of the English fifteenth-century illumination is John Fordun's *Scotichronicon*, now preserved in Corpus Christi College, Cambridge (*MS. 171*).

Mention must also be made of a few of the finest illuminated fifteenth-century copies of Geoffrey Chaucer, *Canterbury Tales*, preserved in the British Museum (*Harley MS. 1758*), in the Rosenbach Company Collection, the Pierpont Morgan Library (*M. 817*), and in other libraries. The Rosenbach Company manuscript together with two leaves in The John Rylands Library form the *Oxford MS.* (at one time it belonged to the Earls of Oxford). See Fig. V-27 and also *The Hand-produced Book*, p. 533 f.

We add to this short list a handsome copy of the *Magna Charta* with subsequent statues and laws (up to *c.* 1469), preserved in the collection of William K. Richardson, Boston, Mass. There are three historiated initials (showing kings holding court), numerous illuminated initials, and colourful acanthus- and vine-borders.

In the second half of the fifteenth century, the English art of illumination decayed and perished for lack of encouragement. Here reference may be made to two MSS. of the 1470's: the *Ordinances of Chivalry*, preserved in New York (Pierpont Morgan Library, *M. 775*) and the *Warwick Roll* (College of Arms at London).

A later roll—indeed, a very large vellum roll, known as the "Great Tournament Roll of Westminster"—also preserved at the College of Arms, commemorates pictorially a tournament held at Westminster on the occasion of the birth (on New Year's Day, 1511) of a son to Catherine of Aragon and Henry VIII.

BIBLIOGRAPHY

E. M. Thompson, *English Illuminated Manuscripts* (*Bibliographica*, i), London, 1895.

A. Goldschmidt, *Der Albani Psalter in Hildesheim*, Berlin, 1895.

G. B. Brown, *The Arts in Early England*, London, 1903–21.

K. Kuenstle, *Die Legende der drei Lebenden und der drei Toten*, Freiburg, 1908.

G. Warner, *Queen Mary's Psalter*, London, 1912.

S. C. Cockerell, *La Calligraphie et Enluminure modernes en Angleterre*, Paris, 1914; *The Work of W. de Brailes*, Cambridge, 1930.

M. R. James, *The Chaundler Manuscripts*, Oxford, 1916. *The Canterbury Psalter*, London, 1935; *The Bohun Manuscripts* (*Introduction* by E. G. Millar), Oxford, 1936 (see also General Bibliography).

E. G. Millar, *English Illuminated Manuscripts from the Tenth to the Thirteenth Century*, Paris and Brussels, 1926; *The Library of A. Chester Beatty*, Oxford, 1927–, *The Luttrell Psalter*, London, 1932; *The St. Trond Lectionary*, Oxford, 1949; *Fresh Materials for the Study of English Illumination*, in D. Miner (ed.), *Studies in Art and Literature for Belle da Costa Greene*, Princeton, N.J., 1954.

P. Guerrini, 'Il Salterio inglese miniato della Queriniana di Brescia', *Rivista di Archeol. Crist.*, 1926.

T. Borenius and E. W. Tristram, *English Medieval Paintings*, Florence and Paris, 1927.

O. E. Saunders, *English Illumination*, 2 vols., Florence, 1928; *English Art in the Middle Ages*, Oxford, 1932.

A. W. Clapham, *English Romanesque Architecture before the Conquest*, Oxford, 1930.

Victoria and Albert Museum, *Catalogue of an Exhibition of Medieval Art*, London, 1930.

British Museum, *Guide to an Exhibition of English Art*, London, 1934.

R. B. A. Mynors, *The Durham Cathedral Manuscripts*, Oxford, 1939.

BIBLIOGRAPHY

D. D. Egbert (ed.), *Tickhill Psalter and Related MSS.*, New York and London, 1939 and 1940.

D. Knowles, *The Monastic Order in England etc.*, Cambridge, 1940 (repr., 1949).

N. R. Ker, *Medieval Libraries of Great Britain*, Oxford, 1941–.

F. Wormald, 'The Development of English Illumination in the Twelfth Century', *Journal of the Brit. Arch. Assoc.*, 1943; 'The Survival of Anglo-Saxon Illumination after the Norman Conquest', *Proceedings of the British Acad.*, 1944; *English Drawings of the Tenth and Eleventh Cent.*, London, 1952.

O. Paecht, 'A Giottesque Episode in English Mediaeval Art', *Journal of the Warb. and Court. Instit.*, 1943; 'Hugo Pictor', *The Bodleian Libr. Record*, 1950; *The Rise of Pictorial Narrative in 12th Cent. England*, Oxford, 1962.

W. Oakeshott, *The Artists of the Winchester Bible*, London, 1945; *The Sequence of English Medieval Art*, London, 1950.

F. Saxl and R. Wittkower, *British Art and the Mediterranean*, Oxford, 1948.

H. Swarzenski, 'Der Stil der Bibel Carilefs von Durham', *Form und Inhalt*, Festschrift fuer Otto Schmitt, Stuttgart, 1951; *The Berthold Missal*, New York, 1953.

R. G. Chapman (ed.), *Scenes from the Life of Christ in English Manuscripts*, Oxford, 1951.

T. S. R. Boase, *English Romanesque Illumination*, Oxford, 1951; *English Art 1100–1216*, Oxford, 1953; *English Illumination of Thirteenth and Fourteenth Centuries*, Oxford, 1954; *The York Psalter in the Libr. of the Hunterian Museum*, New York, 1962.

M. Rickert, *Painting in Britain: the Middle Ages*, London, 1954.

C. R. Dodwell, *The Canterbury School of Illumination*, Cambridge, 1954.

G. Pollard, 'William de Brailles', *Bodl. Libr. Record*, 1955.

T. J. Brown, 'The Salvin Horae', *The British Mus. Quart.*, 1957.

S. Anglo (ed.), *The Great Tournament Roll of Westminster*, Cambridge, 1965.

Chapter VI

ITALY

Until the end of the twelfth century there was hardly any Italian national style of illumination, and Italy had no great school, perhaps with one or two exceptions, such as that of the Benedictine monastery of Montecassino, which was founded by S. Benedict in the sixth century (see *The Hand-produced Book*, p. 275). Unfortunately during the Lombard and Saracen invasions, and in the disastrous fire at Teano, the main refuge-centre of the monks in the early tenth century, the majority of the early productions of the Montecassino *scriptorium* have been lost, leaving us very little material for the reconstruction of the history of Italian illumination before the tenth century. On the whole, the chief centres of book-production, including illumination, for many centuries were the *scriptoria* of the monasteries (see *The Hand-produced Book*, *passim*).

Byzantine influence predominated until well on in the Middle Ages. Many Greek MSS. were produced in Italy, and they can hardly be distinguished from those produced in Byzantium. It is only to be expected that in the native country of antique Western Roman art, some traces of this art should have lingered on in book-illumination, and that illuminators of Christian Latin books should have been influenced by the frescoes or mosaics of Western Early Christian art. Corroborative evidence for the lingering debased Roman art may be deduced from the few preserved MSS. mentioned on p. 69 f., which are in 'ancient' rather than in medieval style.

Before A.D. 1000 (Fig. VI-1)

The other preserved Italian 'illuminated' MSS. of the last three centuries of the first millennium (A.D.), when compared with the best productions of the Anglo-Saxon or Carolingian *scriptoria* are in a crude style. They are almost exclusively religious in content, having been for the most part produced in the closed Benedictine monasteries. Besides the strong Byzantine influences there were—in the opinion of some modern authorities—Celtic and Anglo-Saxon as well as Frankish influences.

The composition of the miniatures was largely based on Byzantine models, whereas the initial-ornament apparently was partly of Anglo-Celtic and partly of late Carolingian or Ottonian origin. So, for instance, J. A. Herbert writes: In monasteries like Bobbio, founded by Irish missionaries, Celtic influence appears, not only in illuminations directly copied from, or at least founded on, Irish models, but also in the blending of Celtic ornament with Byzantine figure-composition and dress; and this influence is plainly discernible in the South Italian scheme of decoration from the tenth century onwards, where Celtic plait-work and convolutions of interlaced ribbons or foliage-stems are combined with monsters whose weird forms bespeak a Lombardic origin, and sometimes with intertwined branch-and-leaf work in gold on coloured grounds, a motive evidently borrowed from Ottonian illumination. In view of the recent theories on the origin and development of Hiberno-Saxon book-illumination (see pp. 176–8), this theory may partly have to be revised.

As evidence of the mingled styles are adduced the tenth- or eleventh-century *Bobbio Psalter*, a *Psalter* which comes from Lombardy and is preserved in the State Library at Munich (*Cod. Lat. 343*), the *Missale beati Warmundi* (see further on), Paul the Deacon's *Commentary on the Rules of S. Benedict* (see further on), an *Ambrosian Psalter* of the Vatican Library (*Vat. Lat. 83*), and other works. Whereas the *Bobbio Psalter* shows particular Byzantine influence, the *Ambrosian Psalter* shows stronger Insular influences.

Finally, a copy of S. Gregory, *Moralia in Job*, of c. 890, which was presented to the monastery of Bobbio by Abbot Agilulphus (see fol. 295*v*), contains various interesting initials—*R* on fol. 1*r*, *IN* on fol. 4*v*—of Bobbio style, based on the Carolingian style of the school of Rheims (see p. 204 f.). The MS. is preserved in the National Library at Turin (*MS. F. I. 6.*).

The Benedictine monastery of Bobbio (now in the province of Pavia, Lombardy) was founded in 612 by the great Irish saint Columban. For many centuries it was a great centre of book-production, including illumination.

On the whole, with few exceptions, the only decoration of the Italian MSS. of the seventh to ninth centuries was the ornamentation of the initial letters with interlaced ribbon-work, foliage, animals, monsters, and so on; the designs were primitive; the colours crude (mainly yellow, red, and green), the work being probably done not by expert artists but by the calligraphers themselves. It is as yet uncertain whether this art of decoration came from the East, or, as just mentioned, from the North: Fig. VI-1*a–d*.

Noteworthy specimens of this art, apart from the MSS. already referred to, are the following: S. Gregory the Great, *Dialogues*, written c. 747 in Bobbio, and now preserved in the Ambrosian Library at Milan (*Cod. B. 159 sup.*). An eighth- or ninth-century copy of the *N.T.*, Part 2, preserved in the Vallicelliana Library, Rome (*MS. B. 25²*), contains not only various initials and other decorations in Insular style, but also historiated initials (at the beginnings of the *Apocalypse* and of the *Epistles of the Apostles*) and a few full-page miniatures—such as Christ in Glory (fol. 1*v*) and the presentation of the codex by *Iuvenianus humilis subdiaconus* to S. Lawrence (fol. 2*r*), and, on fol. 87*r*, a pen-drawing of S. John the Evangelist.

Secular book-production may be represented by a copy of the Lombardic Laws, *Leges Langobardorum* (S. Gall, *Cod. 730*).

North Italy. The art of illumination of North Italy is mainly represented by interesting MSS. which were produced for S. Warmund (969–1002), Bishop of Ivrea, such as the *Sacramentary* known as *Missale beati Warmundi* (preserved in Ivrea Cathedral, *Cod. LXXXVI*). The style of the *Sacramentary* seems to be particularly composite. The fine miniature of the Maries at the Tomb of Christ is still in the classical tradition (as evidenced by the slender and dignified women, by the flowing draperies of the great angel, by the sleeping soldiers); the figure of Bishop Warmund in the opening page of the Canon is in Byzantine style, though his rectangular nimbus appropriated to living persons betrays the early Italian art, and the gold interlaced lettering of *Te igitur* is in the style of contemporary German MSS.

An interesting book of orations, probably written for Arnolphus, Archbishop of Milan (998–1018), was preserved in the collection of C. W. Dyson Perrins, London.

Generally speaking, in North Italy, overrun as it constantly was from the late Roman times onwards by barbaric invading hordes, Classical and Byzantine influences progressively declined; and the few extant specimens of the book-illumination practised in those troubled ages have a barbaric stamp plainly marked upon them.

There were, however, exceptions: an early ninth-century copy of S. Gregory, *Homilies* (Capitulary Library at Vercelli, *Cod. CXLVIII*) contains an exceptionally rich ornamentation, partly influenced by Frankish and Insular illumination. There are beautiful initials: *L* (fol. 72*r*), representing Christ, *P* (fol. 145*r*), in the shape of a hand, and (on fol. 185*r*) the *Agnus Dei*; numerous initials with interesting zoomorphic elements: *O* (fol. 6*r*), representing two birds; *Q* (fol. 41*r*), a dog holding a round decoration; *S* (fol. 63*v*), several fishes; *D* (76*r*), a bird; *A* (102*v*), two dogs fighting each other, and (200*r*) a peacock holding a long, red snake; and many others (ff. 3*r*, 27*r*, 103*r*, 127*r*, 160*r*, 220*v*, 231*r*). There are also three full-page miniatures, beautifully decorated: fol. 7*v*, depicting the deacon Davidpertus presenting the book to S. Peter; fol. 8*r*, representing Christ *Rex regum* in attitude of blessing; and fol. 9*v*, S. Gregory in attitude of blessing.

A fragmentary Isidore MS. (Isidorus Hispalensis, *Etymologiae*), belonging to the same period and preserved in the same collection (*Cod. CCII*) also contains beautiful initials (in gold and colours) and three full-page miniatures. The initials are insular in style.

Another Vercelli codex (Capitulary Library, *Cod. LXII*), which in fact was produced for the Vercelli church, is an excellent specimen of local North Italian art, based on contemporary painting in Lombardy. It contains a *Psalter* with a Calendar, as well as a *Martyrology*—Necrology and Antiphonary; in the *Psalter* there are, apart from the initials, ten full-page (or nearly full-page) miniatures; nearly all of them represent Christ; the main colours are blue, red, and sometimes also green. Fol. 59*r* contains an interesting composition in pen-drawing, lightly tinted in green.

A tenth-century codex, also produced in North Italy, and now in the Estense Library, Modena (*MS. α. J. I. 23: Lat. 988*), contains Isidore, *Interpretationes nominum hebraeorum* as well as *De Flagellis Dei* and *De Natura rerum*. There are various initials and schematic figures. Main colours: red, blue, yellow, and violet. A great North Italian miniature is contained in a tenth-century copy of Bede, *Expositio in Evangelium S. Lucae*, preserved in the National Library at Turin (*MS. D. III. 16*). Main colours used are red, blue and green. Right, against the background of a church, there is represented S. Luke, writing; on the left, S. Vincent, in profile, holding a book in his left hand; at his feet in a position of humility there is a figure clad in a red tunic, indicated by an inscription as *Walpertus humilis abbas*; another figure, dressed in green, is *Wido humilis monachus*.

Finally, a tenth-century copy of *Leges Salicae* (Capitulary Library, Modena, O. I. 2), containing drawings coarsely tinted with watercolours, may be regarded as a representative of secular book-production.

Central Italy. An interesting manuscript is preserved in the Capitulary Library at Lucca, Tuscany (*MS. 490*). It contains Jerome, *Chronica*; Isidore, *Chronicon*; *Liber Pontificalis*; *Collectio canonum*; Bede, *De Natura rerum*; and the Biblical genealogies. Its interest lies not only in the early age of the codex (late ninth- and early tenth-century) and in the characteristic style of its miniatures and initials, partly influenced by early Christian art, but also in the fact that we know the provenance of the MS. (it was written in the *scriptorium* of Lucca) and the name of the main scribe (in fact, it was written by several copyists), Bishop John, 780–800.

Another Central Italian MS.—which, however, shows northern influences—is preserved in the Capitulary Library at Perugia (*MS. 2*). It is an eighth- or ninth-century *Gospel-book*, and contains, apart from several initials (some coloured, others in pen-drawing), Eusebian Canons, decorated in pen-drawing, and four full-page miniatures (ff. *7v*, *49v*, *70v*, *102r*) at the beginning of each Gospel, representing Christ and an Evangelist (Matthew, Mark, Luke, and John) standing, and each one presenting his book; above each Evangelist there is his symbol. Fig. VI-1e–f.

The most important *scriptorium* was that at Montecassino, and although the majority of its productions have been lost (see p. 290), several interesting codices have been preserved. Moreover, the influence of the Montecassino school spread to the surrounding districts, particularly to Rome, as may be seen in *MS. 29* of the Angelica Library, Rome. It contains ornamented Eusebian Canons (the main colours being red, green, yellow, brown), pen-drawings, two decorated borders, four large initials (in red, green, and yellow) and several small ones, as well as an ornamented arch on two columns, containing in its upper part the figure of Christ, in half-length.

Excellent ninth- or tenth-century Montecassino productions are preserved in the Badia Archives at Montecassino. They are *MS. 3*—a copy of Alcuin's works, *Astronomica*, and *miscellanea*, dated 874–92, with initials, and constellations in pen-drawings; *MS. 175*—Paul the Deacon, *Commentary to the Benedictine Rules*, S. Benedict, *Chronicles*, etc.: it is a Benedictine codex written between 915 and 934 (in the period of Abbot John).

It shows strong Byzantine influence and has an interesting frontispiece, although its execution lacks any great artistic merit; this is noticeable in the rudimentary (though quite original) figure-drawing, with its faulty proportions—the crouching bodies and limbs of the two adoring angels are shrunk almost to nothing, while their heads, hands, and feet are enormous. This frontispiece shows Christ in Glory with the emblems of the Evangelists and two adoring angels, in an ornamental frame of 'Celtic' style: a broad band entwined upon itself so as to form one large central circle and four small ones, and divided into panels filled with interlaced ribbons. It also has a miniature showing Abbot John presenting the book to S. Benedict, who sits in a jewelled chair with an angel standing behind him.

In the Laurentian Library, Florence (*MS. Plut. 73, 41*), there is an early ninth-century Montecassino volume containing Antonius Musa, *De herba betonica*, Pseudo-Apuleius, *Herbarium*, Sextus Placitus Papiriensis, *De bestiis*; Pseudo-Dioscorides, *De herbis* etc., and other miscellanea. See also p. 46 f. and Fig. I-19c.

South Italy. Good specimens of the South Italian schools are the Virgil Codex referred to on p. 38 f.; the *Exultet* rolls referred to on p. 297 ff.; and two liturgical rolls, produced in Campania and attributed to the tenth century, now preserved in the Casanatense Library, Rome—*MS. 724, I: Benedictio fontis*; and *MS. 724, II: Pontifical*.

The *Benedictio fontis*, divided in eight portions, contains fourteen miniatures representing scenes (based on the Old and New Testaments) connected with the blessing of the baptismal font on Holy Saturday. There are also interesting initials. The *Pontifical*, divided into five portions, was apparently produced between 957 and 984 for Landolphus I, bishop of Benevento. There are a number of decorated initials (colours: green, red, and gold) and twelve interesting scenes in pen-drawing, some of the liturgical robes being in colour.

Carolingian Style. Some Italian codices of the second half of the ninth and of the tenth century are illuminated in pure Carolingian style (see p. 198 ff.); *e.g.* the ninth-century *Collectio canonum*, now preserved in the Vallicelliana Library, Rome (*Cod. A. 5*), and a Bobbio missal, preserved in the Ambrosian Library, Milan (*D. 84, inf.*): see also p. 211.

Eleventh and Twelfth Centuries—Romanesque Style (Fig. VI-2–9)

From the eleventh century onwards, the main Italian centres of book-illumination were the *scriptoria* of the Benedictine monasteries, such as that of Montecassino (by far the most important), in Central Italy, and those of Polirone and Nonantola, in North Italy. The most important *scriptorium* of North Italy, however, and perhaps of Italy as a whole, continued to be that of Bobbio.

Instances of the S. Benedetto *scriptorium* of Polirone are the rich eleventh-century *Bible of Countess Matilda* (see p. 302 f.) preserved in the Pierpont Morgan Library (*M. 492*), the late twelfth-century Mantua *Missal* referred to on p. 303, a twelfth-century *Psalter* also in Mantua (*MS. C. III. 20*), and *Vita Mathildis* (see p. 302 f.).

A copy of the *Encyclopaedia* (Books I–XXXII) written by the German theologian Hrabanus Maurus (*c.* 776–856), and copied in, or before, the year 1023, is now preserved in the library of Montecassino (*Cod. 132*); it is illuminated (there are as many as 361 miniatures) in a very primitive style. The same may be said of the copy of S. Gregory's *Moralia*, written for Theobald, Abbot of Montecassino (1022–35), and preserved in the Montecassino collection (*Cod. 73*). It has, however, two full-page miniatures and seven beautiful initials in gold and colours. To the same period belongs the Montecassino *Codex 109*, written by a certain Grimualdus, 'deacon and monk'. It contains *Sermons* and *Homilies*, and is decorated with several initials in gold and colours. These works are in a Montecassino-Byzantine style.

Montecassino School. On the other hand, the MSS. executed in the time of Abbot Desiderius (1058–87)—who later became Pope Victor III—and other codices of the late eleventh and early twelfth centuries, show the excellent style of the flourishing Montecassino school. Instances are (1) the MS. *Vita S. Benedicti*, executed about 1070 for Abbot Desiderius, and now in the Vatican Library (*Cod. Vat. Lat. 1202*); related is a *Lectionary* with charming compositions in pen-drawings and superb initials in gold and colours, executed for Desiderius in 1072 by a certain monk Leo, and paid for by *fr. Johannes Marsicanae dudum*—now at Montecassino (*Cod. 99*); (3) another eleventh-century copy of *Homilies*, also preserved in Montecassino (*MS. 98*), containing three beautiful full-page compositions in pen-drawing, and numerous initials in gold and colour, including four full-page ones (or nearly full-page); (4) artistically allied with Montecassino *Cod. 99* is a slightly later (1094–1105) MS., containing the *Martyrologium Casinense* (and the list of the Montecassino abbots down to 'Seniorictus'), preserved in the National Library at Naples (*MS. VIII. C. 4*). Here are found fourteen large and beautiful initials in Montecassino style. Also interesting are the *Chronicon S. Sophiae* (see p. 297) and the *Chronicle* of S. Vincenzo al Volturno, both now preserved in the Vatican Library (the latter being *Cod. Barb. Lat. 2754*): Fig. VI-2, 3*b* and 4*b*.

Of particular interest is a copy of *Diurnale Benedictinum* executed *c.* 1100 in Montecassino and now also in the Vatican Library (*Urb. Lat. 585*): Fig. VI-3*c*.

Desiderius' activities greatly influenced the art of South Italy (not only book-illumination, but also wall-painting, mosaics, and architecture). He imported artists from Constantinople to decorate the Cassino church with mosaics, and the influence of the Byzantine style is particularly evident in the figure-composition of the MSS. executed for him.

At the same time, however, the initial-decoration, probably imported from Bobbio, is in the style of the Anglo-Celtic MSS. (see p. 178 ff.), combined with Lombardic elements: interlaced ribbons and tendrils, with human figures, grotesques, birds, and greyhounds.

Central Italy (apart from Montecassino). The influence of the Montecassino school spread all over Italy. It is shown, for instance, by an illuminated *Sacramentary* produced in the *scriptorium* of the Benedictine monastery of Subiaco (near Rome).

The codex, commissioned by Abbot John, was written in 1075 by a certain Guittone. It is preserved in the Vallicelliana Library, Rome (*MS. B. 24¹*). Some scholars see in it the influence of Ottonian illumination (see Chapter IV, p. 213 ff.). The same collection possesses a *Gospel-book* of 1104 (*MS. E. 16*) which comes from the Farfa monastery.

Another example of eleventh-century Central Italian art of illumination influenced by Montecassino style is a superb codex, illuminated by various artists and preserved in Perugia since the thirteenth century (now in the Capitulary Library, *MS. 30*). It contains explanations of the Holy Scriptures by S. Augustine, Alcuin, Hrabanus Maurus, Origen, and Bede. There are several initials and miniatures: fol. *1v, 2r, 2v.* (Christ in Glory), *77r* (Alcuin ?), *131r* (Hrabanus Maurus ?), *212v* (Moses receiving the Law), *246r, 300r, 350r* (Bede holding a book), *350v* (Ezra writing with the inspiration of the Dove): Fig. VI-3*a*.

An excellent specimen of the eleventh-century Lucca *scriptorium* is a copy of Hrabanus Maurus (State Library at Lucca, *MS. 370 B*), containing several miniatures and pen-drawings.

North Italy. Not many North Italian illuminated MSS. of the eleventh century have been preserved. An early eleventh-century copy of the *Ambrosian Sacramentary*, executed for a church or monastery of the diocese of Milan and preserved in the Capitulary Library at Vercelli (*MS. CXXXVI*), contains a full-page miniature representing the Crucifixion, and a large initial with a half-length figure of Christ. In this example of illumination from Lombardy there are strong Byzantine and German influences.

Excellent examples of the Nonantola *scriptorium* are the following two codices: a *Gradual*, written in 1039, containing nineteen large miniatures (many filling the whole page) and numerous decorated initials (Angelica Library, Rome, *MS. 123*); and a copy of *Lives of Saints* and *Lectionary*, of the first half of the eleventh century, containing a miniature in pen-drawing and several initials (University Library at Bologna, *MS. 1576*).

A richly illuminated *Psalter* of the eleventh or twelfth century, which belonged to the Benedictine monastery 'de Pado' of Polirone, near Mantua, may represent the important *scriptorium* of Polirone. At any rate, it is a good example of North Italian monastic illumination. There are several miniatures (some full-page) which are influenced by the Byzantine style, though according to Professor Venturi some are dependent on Carolingian models of the Corbie school (see p. 208 f.). There are also several decorated initials. The codex is preserved in Mantua (Communal Library, *MS. C. III. 20*).

South Italy. Interesting codices, produced in Benevento, Troia, Cava dei Tirreni, etc. are characteristic specimens of illumination practised in the monasteries of South Italy, partly influenced by the art of the Montecassino school. The Benevento MS. containing the *Codex Legum Langobardorum* and *Capitularia Regum Francorum*, produced in the early eleventh century and now preserved in Cava dei

Tirreni (Archivio della Badia, *MS. membr. 4*), is ornamented by several initials and by eleven miniatures in rather primitive style.

Fig. VI-4 reproduces characteristic specimens of Beneventan initials and other book-decoration. Byzantine influence combined with South-Italian vigour is at its best in the *Chronicon S. Sophiae* (already referred to), which was executed in Benevento in 1119 and is now preserved in the Vatican Library (*Vat. Lat. 4939*).

To the same period belongs a copy of *Homilies*, probably executed at Troia; it is preserved in the National Library at Naples (*MS. VI. B. 2*). There are thirteen scenes and figures in skilled pen-drawing, painted in red, and several initials, also in pen-drawing, some being painted in red. An eleventh-century MS. of Miscellanea (Bede, *De Temporibus*; *Annales Cavenses*; and *Florilegium*), produced in the *scriptorium* of Cava, is preserved in the Badia Library at Cava dei Tirreni (*MS. membr. 3*). It contains charming pen-drawings.

Exultet (Fig. VI-6 and 7a)

An interesting group of illuminated MSS., mainly written and illuminated in South Italy—for instance, at Benevento, which had close relations with Eastern Christianity—consists of long strips of parchment or vellum rolls, containing liturgical prayers for certain religious ceremonies, such as the strange, mystical, almost rhapsodical canticle for the Resurrection, *Exultet iam angelica turba coelorum, exultent divina mysteria!* which was included in the Missal as early as the seventh century, and was sung on Easter Eve as part of the blessing of the great Paschal Candle, symbolizing not only Christ Himself but also the Pillar of Fire which led the Israelites in the wilderness.

The ceremony—one of the most impressive services in the Catholic Church—was of almost sacramental solemnity.

These manuscripts (known as *Exultet*), produced in the eleventh to thirteenth centuries mainly under Byzantine influence, are rather peculiar in the representation of the figures upside-down in relation to the text (see Fig. VI-6 and 7a). This was done so that they might appear right-side-up to the congregation as the roll was passed over the back of the ambo while the deacon intoned these canticles from the pulpit.

The majority of the copies preserved are written in Beneventan hand, but the few thirteenth-century copies are written in Gothic script.

The compositions and the subjects of the pictures resemble one another very closely, but some rolls contain more illustrations than others. The most complete ones contain the figure of Christ in Glory (or of a prelate enthroned between two priests); an elaborate initial *E* (of *Exultet*); the *angelica turba*; the *Agnus Dei* with six-winged seraphs and the Evangelistic symbols; a rather pagan-Classical representation of the Earth—either a fully draped dignified matron standing between two trees with animals near her feet, or a half-draped or nude figure sitting on the ground or emerging from it, with ox and serpent or two other creatures feeding at her breasts; the censing, blessing, and lighting of the Candle; the Fall of Man; the

Passage of the Red Sea; the Crucifixion; the Mother Church; the Harrowing of Hell; the bees (symbolical of the Virgin Birth) gathering honey and producing the wax for the Paschal Candle; the Annunciation; the Nativity, with bees hovering around the crib; the Madonna and Child with adoring angels. (For the virginity of the bee, see for instance S. Ambrosius, *De Virginitate*, 1, 8.),

Under Abbot Desiderius, Montecassino became one of the main centres (and probably the best one) for the production of the *Exultet* MSS.

A number of copies of *Exultet* have survived: three are in Troia Cathedral (Prov. of Foggia, S. Italy), one belonging to the second half of the eleventh century, another to the early twelfth century, and the third, also of the twelfth century, containing as many as thirty-five miniatures, strongly influenced by Byzantine illumination; of the two produced in Mirabella Eclano, and preserved there in the Archives of the Collegiata, one belongs to the first half of the eleventh century, the other to the second half. A mid-eleventh-century *Exultet*, probably executed in Montecassino, and now preserved in the Curia Vescovile at Avezzano, has no miniatures but contains beautiful initials with zoomorphic elements in colour and gold. Various copies are preserved in Montecassino: one, executed in South-Eastern Italy, belongs to the eleventh century and has very fine miniatures; another one, produced in the early twelfth century in Sorrento (probably for the monastery of S. Salvatore under Pope Pasqual II, Bishop Barbatus and Abbot Peter), contains miniatures painted in red, yellow, violet, green and blue. Three in Gaeta Cathedral belong to the eleventh and the twelfth centuries and are partly of a very primitive style characterized by the misshapen, childish figures. A Beneventan MS. is preserved in the Vatican Library (*Cod. Vat. Lat. 9820*); a twelfth-century roll, probably also produced in Benevento, is preserved in the Casanatense Library, Rome (*MS. 724*); indeed, it is related to *Vat. Lat. 9820*. There are two in Bari Cathedral: one was produced for this Cathedral about the year 1000; it contains exceptionally beautiful miniatures in delicate colours with some traces of gold; the second one, also produced for the Bari church, was executed in the late eleventh century, but was partly re-written in the thirteenth century. The same Cathedral possesses an early eleventh-century *Benedictio ignis et fontis*, also richly illuminated. Four fragments of a beautiful twelfth-century *Exultet* are preserved in Velletri. An excellent copy, produced in South Italy in the thirteenth century, is preserved in the Capitulary Library at Salerno. There is a fragmentary *Exultet* in Capua Cathedral, of the first half of the eleventh century. See Fig. VI-6a–b.

Two interesting copies are preserved in the Civic Museum at Pisa; one belongs to the twelfth century (Fig. VI-6c), the other to the thirteenth (Fig. VI-7a).

One of the finest copies is preserved in the British Museum (*Add. MS. 30377*). It probably comes from Montecassino and may be assigned to the late eleventh or the early twelfth century. Though damaged by the flaking away of the colours—writes J. A. Herbert—it remains one of the finest surviving examples of its class; and its best miniatures already foreshadow that lovely early Italian style which, seen at its best in the Sienese and Umbrian schools, added dramatic expression and a light and brilliant colouring to the grand and spiritual Byzantine types on which it was founded. Its prevailing tints are blue and red; and these, with a plenteous use of gold, give its painting a rich, bright, and yet charmingly soft and harmonious effect. The workmanship is uneven; but in the best pictures, such as the Harrowing of Hell, with its splendid rushing figure of Christ, one sees more the large free manner of the fresco painter than the comparatively cramped technique of the miniaturist. An excellent tenth-century copy, probably executed at Montecassino, is preserved in The John Rylands Library, Manchester; it contains illuminations of great interest, representing the Passion and the Resurrection.

Twelfth Century. The twelfth-century productions of the South Italian schools of illumination (in the Benedictine monasteries) are so improved in their composition, style, and colouring, that we can now speak of a distinctive style of illumination. The richness of colouring in particular (which at a later period became a distinguishing feature of Italian painting) was already such a striking characteristic of Italian twelfth- and thirteenth-century illumination, that it helps to distinguish it from contemporary German and Flemish productions.

This applies especially, writes Herbert, to initial-ornament where the Italian artist seems often to have been content to copy the designs of Northern illuminators, only replacing their light blue and pale green fields by brilliant ultramarine or crimson backgrounds on which orange-yellow or gold letters, panelled with geometrical patterns in red, white, and blue, and filled with intertwining white vine-tendrils, stand in sharp relief.

Herbert regards two British Museum MSS.—the early twelfth-century *Harl. MS. 7183*, a large volume, containing *Homilies* for Sundays and Festivals from Advent to Easter Eve, and the late twelfth-century *Add. MS. 9350*, a smaller book, containing *Psalms* with glosses—as excellent examples of this style, and as examples of the models chosen by Renaissance Italian scribes and illuminators. Both are of uncertain origin, but *Add. MS. 9350* was in the fifteenth century bequeathed to the S. Marco monastery at Florence—celebrated for its association with Savonarola, Fra Angelico, and Fra Bartolommeo. Several initials of *Harl. 7183* contain figures of birds and animals and some are formed of a bird or monster (usually in white on a blue or crimson background); for instance, the *S* may consist of a long-necked bird standing on its own tail and biting its back.

Curiously enough, and somewhat analogously to the Anglo-Celtic MSS. which are earlier by some three centuries or more, while the decorative work is of very fine artistic quality and shows originality in design and composition, the initials which are historiated with half-length portraits of the saints to whose homilies they are prefixed, are of very low standard, the portraits being 'flat, wooden, monotonous' (Herbert). From *c.* 1150 decorated initials predominate in Central Italy.

The *Psalter Add. MS. 9350* is not as fine in design, originality, and colouring, as *Harl. MS. 7183*. Moreover, as Herbert has pointed out, its miniature of David with his four musicians, all red-haired, red-nosed, and ill-proportioned, shows again how much better decorative ornament was understood at this time than figure-painting.

Another twelfth-century MS. of the British Museum (*Add. MS. 18859*) is a *Psalter* produced in Montecassino; it is an excellent example of the Montecassino twelfth-century style. Another Montecassino illuminated codex of the period is the *Register* of S. Angelo in Formis, near Capua (Montecassino, Archivio della Badia, *Regesto 4*); it is dated to 1137–66, and contains nine miniatures.

Strictly allied with the Montecassino school was the Benevento *scriptorium*, as may be shown by two twelfth-century copies of the *Breviary* and *Missal*, preserved in the Capitulary Library at Benevento (*MSS. 19* and *20*). Both have interesting initials. Another Benevento MS. preserved in the same collection (*MS. 28*)—a *Necrology of the Fraternity of the Holy Spirit* of the City of Benevento—was written in 1198 by Abbot Bartholomew. It contains a double-page miniature (fol. 51*v*–52*r*) representing the acceptance of the new members of the fraternity; the miniature of a scribe with a *nimbus* (fol. 53*v*); a full-page Crucifixion (fol. 54*r*); and eighty-four medallions (fol. 55*r*–107*r*) representing the Virgin in half-length and the Patron Saints of the parishes of the dead listed on these pages.

Two characteristic examples of the art of Abruzzi, influenced by the Montecassino style, are a twelfth-century *Martyrology*, with a miniature, pen-drawings, and decorated initials; and an early thirteenth-century *Lectionary*, with several initials. Both codices are preserved in the Capitulary Library at Atri (*MSS. A. 1* and *A. 3*).

An early thirteenth-century copy of *Homilies*, preserved in the Capitulary Library at Spoleto, containing several ornamented initials, may be regarded as a good example of the Umbrian Romanesque style, partly influenced by the Montecassino school of illumination.

A twelfth-century *Epistolarium*, produced and preserved in Palermo (Painiana Library, *S.S.*) shows marked Moslem influence.

Atlantic Bibles. Of particular interest are several Bibles of very large format, thus known as 'Atlantic'. They belong to the period from the late eleventh to the early thirteenth century. The twelfth-century 'Atlantic' Bible which comes from Aquileia—though illuminated in the style of Central Italy—and is preserved in the National Archaeological Museum at Cividale (*Codici Sacri 2*) measures about $24 \times 16\frac{3}{5}$ in. ($61 \times 42 \cdot 5$ cm.). The early thirteenth-century Bible, which comes from Lucca, and is preserved in that Capitulary Library (*MS. 1*), is nearly 24×16 in.; vol. 2 contains forty-two initials with Biblical scenes, several other initials, full-page decorated titles (fol. 1*v* and 231*v*) and other illumination. The illumination is attributed to Marco di Berlinghiero. This seems to be one of the latest 'Atlantic' Bibles.

One of the earliest is a Bible of the second half of the eleventh century, which comes from the monastery of S. Valentino in Piano, near Amelia, and is preserved in the Palatina Library, Parma (*MS. Palat. 386*). It contains a great number of miniatures and initials in the Romanesque style of the Umbria-Rome region.

Several other 'Atlantic' Bibles come from Central Italy. They are mainly of the twelfth century and are preserved in the Vatican Library (*Cod. Vat. Lat. 10405*, which originally belonged to Todi Cathedral; *Cod. Barb. Lat. 587*, from S. Cecilia in Trastevere; *Cod. Vat. Lat. 12958*, formerly belonging to S. Maria ad Martires), in Florence (Laurentian Library, *MS. Mugell. 2*: the miniatures are in Central Italian Romanesque style, with Byzantine influences), in Naples (National Library *MS. VI. AA. 20*: the Bible, in two volumes, belonged to Alfonso II of Aragon), in Perugia (Augusta Library, *MS. L. 59*: richly illuminated), Genoa (Berio Library: several illuminations and numerous decorated initials in Central Italian Romanesque style), Montalcino (Communal Library: two volumes with numerous fine initials and other miniatures in Central Italian Romanesque style with foreign influences; a portion shows Byzantine influences). For the Calci 'Atlantic' Bible, executed in 1169 in the school of Pisa, see further on. See Fig. VI-5, 7*c*, 8*a, c–d*.

Several 'Atlantic' Bibles come from other Italian regions: a codex, which formerly belonged to Florence Cathedral and is now preserved in the Laurentian Library at Florence (*MS. Edili 125*) is attributed by Prof. Toesca to a region influenced by Moslem art (Sicily or South Italy); a superb Bible, in four volumes, executed for S. Mark's, Venice, and now in the Marciana Library (*MS. Lat. I, i: 2108*) is strictly connected with the mosaics of that Basilica; three richly illuminated codices preserved in the National Library at Rome (*MSS. XXV, Sessor. 1. Sessor. 2, Sessor. 3*) are assigned to some *scriptorium* or *scriptoria* in Northern Italy, more particularly in the Po Valley. See Fig. VI-5*d*.

An 'Atlantic' Bible from Farfa (*Cod. Vat. Lat. 5729*) appears to have been illuminated by a Catalan artist: see also p. 211 f.

Byzantine Style. In the famous *scriptorium* of Grottaferrata, near Rome, Greek monks did excellent work in illumination in pure Byzantine style; *Cod. Vat. Lat. 5974* is a good specimen of this production. See also p. 112 f.

Elsewhere, too, Byzantine influence was still very strong. An Italian *Missal*, written and ornamented in the twelfth century and preserved partly in the Casanatense Library, Rome, and partly in the Fitzwilliam Museum, Cambridge, *McClean MS. 49*, is Byzantine in character. Sydney Cockerell rightly compares it with the twelfth-century *Missal of the Holy Sepulchre at Jerusalem* preserved in the National Library at Paris (*Lat. 12056*). See Fig. VI-7*b*.

Central Italy: Rome. The art of illumination of the South Italian schools and—especially as regards ornamentation—of the Montecassino school influenced that of Central Italy, and particularly the *scriptoria* of the monasteries of Rome and of its environs, such as Farfa and Subiaco. Examples are: *Farfa Evangeliarium* of the early twelfth century, now preserved in the Vallicelliana Library, Rome (*Cod. E. 16*); and a MS. which probably comes from S. Cecilia in Trastevere (Rome), and is preserved in the Laurentian Library, Florence (*Plut. 17. 27*). In the former there are decorated Eusebian Canons, several initials, and very fine miniatures representing the Evangelists (fol. 23*r*, 71*r*, 104*r* and 151*v*). Another roughly contemporary codex of the Roman region (preserved in the same collection, *MS. E. 24*) shows very strong Byzantine influence. It contains a *Gallican Psalter* and is illustrated with various illuminations: fol. *25v–26r* (Noah's Ark, with a seven-branch candelabrum and a few musical instruments), *26v* (David playing the harp and two scribes), *27r* (again David playing, and four musicians), *28v* (the Virgin with the Child, and several saints, in pen-drawing), and a few others. There are also numerous decorated initials. See Fig. VI-9*a*.

A twelfth-century *Breviary* (Perugia Capitulary Library, *MS. 12*) is an interesting example of Umbrian book-production: Fig. VI-9*b*.

Tuscany. In Tuscany, apart from the 'Atlantic' Bibles, previously discussed, good work was done in the monasteries of S. Salvatore dell'Amiata, of S. Antimo near Montalcino, and of Pisa. Of particular interest is the beautiful *Pisa Bible* or *Calci 'Atlantic' Bible*. As a matter of fact, it should have been discussed in the section on the 'Atlantic' Bibles, but it is mentioned here as an excellent example of the Pisa school, which in its representational features was strongly influenced by the Byzantine style. The *Pisa Bible*, in four volumes, was executed for the Pisa monastery of S. Vito and is now preserved in the Carthusian monastery of Calci (Certosa di Calci, Pisa). The decorated Eusebian Canons and especially the numerous ornamented and historiated initials were executed by several artists, including a certain *Andreas nepos Gregorii* and an *Adalbertus scriptor de licteris maioris de auro et de colore*. A twelfth-century *Psalter* now in the Laurentian Library (*MS. Acq. e Doni 181*), executed in an allied style for the Vallombrosan monastery of S. Paolo a Ripa d'Arno (Pisa), contains a number of initials, some historiated, others decorated only: Fig. VI-8*a–b*. See also p. 300.

A copy of S. Paul's *Epistles*, of the mid-twelfth-century, preserved in Siena (Communal Library, *MS. F. III. 5*), is a good example of the contemporary art of illumination in Siena, strongly influenced by French art. There are several large initials. A portion (2 folios) of a late-twelfth-century *Antiphonary* and an early thirteenth-century *Liber Census*, both with interesting initials and miniatures, and both preserved in the State Archives at Siena, are other examples of Sienese illumination.

A *Roman Missal*, executed for a Florentine church and still preserved in that city (Laurentian Library, *MS. Gadd. 44*), is an excellent specimen of the Florentine school. There are miniatures and numerous initials: Fig. VI-7*d*.

A monastic *Missal*, which comes from Camaldoli, and is preserved in Florence (Laurentian Library, *MS. Conv. Soppr. 292*), was also produced in Tuscany. It contains interesting initials and a miniature representing Christ in Glory and the symbols of the Evangelists.

North Italy. One of the most famous twelfth-century MSS., known as the *Canossa Codex*, is preserved in the Vatican Library (*Vat. Lat. 4922*). It is Donizo, *Vita Mathildis*. The Vatican MS., written by the author himself, illustrates the life of Matilda, Countess of Tuscany (1046–1115), particularly celebrated for the fact that in 1077 at her castle of Canossa (in the province of Reggio nell'Emilia) the

Emperor Henry IV underwent his humiliating penance before Pope Gregory VII. See also p. 294.

A copy of *Vita Mathildis* produced in 1234 for the Frasinoro monastery (near Modena) is preserved in the Lucca State Library: see p. 304 f.

A few excellent MSS. come from North Italy, particularly from Bobbio; they reflect either Byzantine or German influences. An interesting example of the Nonantola *scriptorium*, of the mid-twelfth-century, is a *Gospel-book* still preserved in that locality (Badia Archives at Nonantola). There are six full-page miniatures and numerous ornamented initials. In the early thirteenth century three miniatures were added, in more artistic style, with strong Byzantine influences.

Other twelfth-century examples of North Italian schools of illumination are preserved in the S. Ambrose Basilica at Milan (*MSS. M. 31, M. 14*, etc.).

A superb codex, containing a Calendar, a Psalter, a Gradual, and an Anti-phonary, which was executed for the church of Piacenza, is now preserved in the Capitulary Library of that city (*MS. 65*). It is an excellent example of twelfth-century illumination of the Emilia region, containing a great number of miniatures and decorated initials.

German influence of the Reichenau school (see p. 219 ff.), or perhaps Flemish influence, is noticeable in a *Gospel-book* produced in 1170 in Padua and preserved in the treasury of that Cathedral. This influence is particularly apparent in the eight full-page miniatures, which are not of great artistic merit—the colouring is pale and hard, and often quite arbitrary (blue hair, green nimbi, and so on); the technique is dry; the figures are angular, the large oval eyes and the clumsy features being indicated by coarse lines, and the stiff and numerous folds of the draperies being outlined with hard bands or hems of colour. There are also thirty-seven rather beautiful initials in red, green, blue or violet, on gold background, containing zoomorphic decoration: Fig. VI-9c. This interesting MS. is known as the *Isidore Evangeliarium*.

Thirteenth Century (Fig. VI-10–12)

The Italian Romanesque style (or styles) of illumination continued well into the thirteenth century. Indeed, as in many parallel instances, for several *scriptoria* it is not easy to ascertain whether a codex belongs to the twelfth or the thirteenth century. Some such transitional MSS. have already been referred to (pp. 299 ff. and *passim.*). Here we may mention a *Missal* executed in the Benedictine monastery 'de Pado', Polirone (see p. 296), now preserved in the Communal Library at Mantua (*MS. D. III. 15*). There are several miniatures and decorated initials in Lombardic monastic style, containing features characteristic not only of Italian Romanesque and Byzantine styles, but also of the early Gothic.

The last features do not appear in contemporary North Italian codices, though they present strong foreign influences, as may be seen in a codex now preserved in Cremona (State Library, *MS. 199*). A superb early thirteenth-century *Gospel-book*, executed for Vercelli, and still in Vercelli (Capitulary Library, *MS. C*), contains fifteen beautiful miniatures on gold or silver backgrounds, and a great number of ornamented initials, some decorated with fantastic or monstrous animals. The illumination is in Northern Italian Romanesque style, influenced by German style.

A *Missal* produced in the early thirteenth century for Modena Cathedral and now in Parma (Palatina Library, MS. 996), is executed in the Romanesque style of the Emilia region. Also executed in Emilian style is a copy—by the monk Guido, who painted it in 1234—of the famous *Canossa Codex* (see p. 302). The copy is preserved in Lucca (State Library, MS. 2508).

We may end this short list with a thirteenth-century parchment roll (of 183 × 61 cm. or 72 × 24 in.) illuminated in the Romanesque style of the region of Piedmont (the roll is preserved in the Capitulary Library at Vercelli). There are eighteen pictures, in pen-drawing in black ink, sometimes also in red and green, reproducing eleventh- or twelfth-century wall-paintings of the old Vercelli Cathedral.

Italian Gothic Style. In the thirteenth century, however, the Gothic style began to appear, but the Italian Gothic is not quite the same as that of the countries to the north of Italy. Moreover, new subjects were introduced and new production-centres arose. Secular subjects (see p. 307), richly illustrated, became popular, as did illustrated law-books, mainly produced in the University of Bologna (see p. 313 f.). Oderisi da Gubbio (see Dante, *Purg. 11. 79* ff.) was the chief illustrator of such books. In the thirteenth and fourteenth centuries, various autonomous schools developed a highly artistic activity; *e.g.* Emilia (particularly Bologna), Genoa, and the schools of Lombardy. The Bolognese school of miniature was soon to attain a position of considerabe importance. Oderisi is mentioned in Bolognese documents of 1269 and 1271. See also further on.

The illumination of these schools sometimes reflects strong influences of the French Gothic style; an interesting instance is a codex, *Decretum Gratiani*, perhaps illuminated in Bologna, now preserved in the Laurentian Library, Florence, *Cod. Ed. 97* (see p. 381). But generally speaking the production of the period shows Byzantine influence. This influence was, indeed, very strong in Italy. An interesting twelfth-century copy of *Job*, probably produced in England, and now preserved in the Laurentian Library, Florence (*MS. S. Croce Plut. 7 dext. 11*), contains on fol. 8*v* (originally left blank) a thirteenth-century South Italian miniature in pure Byzantine style. This style flowed over the whole of the Peninsula, reaching the North Italian schools of Bologna, Parma, Padua, and others. Hence, the Italian productions of the time are quite different from those of England and France, dominated as the last were by the Early Gothic style: Figs. VI-10*c* and VII-9*c*.

In the thirteenth century, Byzantine influences (which in the twelfth century predominated in Italy including Lombardy, as exemplified by the *Atlantic Bible* in the Ambrosiana Library, MS. B. 48. inf.) were particularly strong in the Venetian region and in South Italy. The conquest of Constantinople in 1204 strengthened these influences in the former region. Instances are a *Missal* for the use of a Modena church preserved in Parma (Palatina Library, MS. 996), a *Psalter* formerly in the

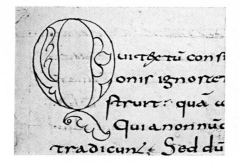

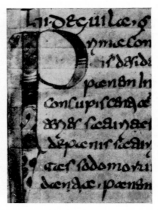

VI-1. Illumination before A.D. 1000. *a–d*, Eighth- and ninth-century initials: *a*, Q in *Vat Pal. 245*, fol. 93 *r*; *b*, Q in British Museum *Royal MS. 15. C. xi*, fol. 15 *v*; *c–d*, O and P in *Cassinensis 753*, fol. 79 *r* and 89 *r*. *e–f*, Eighth-century *Gospels* (Perugia Capitulary Library, *MS. 2*): Christ, Evangelists Luke and John with their symbols.

VI–2. *Lectionary and Vita S. Benedicti* (*Vat. Lat. 1202*), fol. 2 *r*: Abbot Desiderius presents the *Lectionary* to S. Benedict.

VI–3. *a,* Perugia Capitulary Library, *MS. 30*: Explanation of *Genesis*—Christ in Glory, Madonna and Child on the throne. *b, Vita S. Benedicti,* fol. 80 *r*: scenes from the life of S. Benedict. *c, Diurnale Benedictinum,* fol. 257 *v*: Crucifixion with Virgin Mary and St John the Baptist.

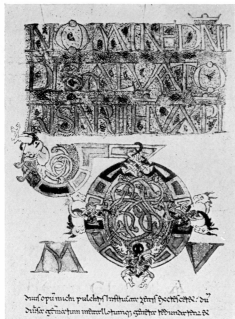
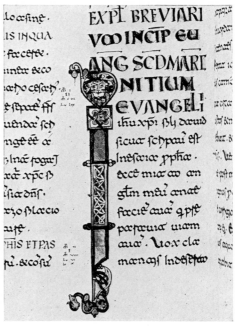

VI–4. Beneventan book-production of the eleventh and early twelfth centuries. a, *Sacramentary-Missal W. 6*, fol. 68 *r*: *Te igitur*. b, *Chronicon S. Sophiae*, fol. 29 *r*: decorated initials and other letters. c, *Vat. Lat. 3741*, fol. 72 *v*: initial I and S. Mark, i. 1–3.

VI–5. *Atlantic Bibles. a, Barb. Lat. 587,* fol. *275 r:* beginning of *Book of Judith. b, Vat. Lat. 10405,* fol. *41 v:* beginning of *Numbers. c, MS. Mugell. 2,* fol. *189 r:* end of *Book of Wisdom. d, MS. Edili 125,* fol. *150 r:* 2 *Kings,* ii. *1–13.*

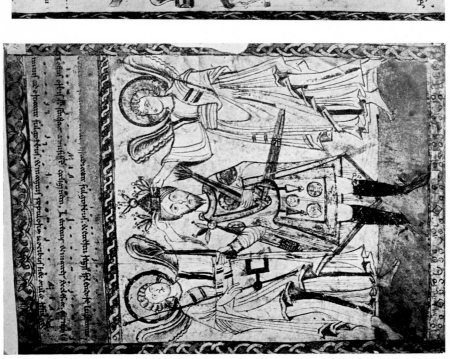

VI–6. *Exultet* rolls. *a*, Benevento, a. 981–7: two angels crown a king (text re-written in the twelfth or thirteenth century), *Vat. Lat. 9820*, section 15. *b*, *Capua Exultet* holding the *Exultet* roll. *c*, Portion of *Pisa Exultet i*: top, vineyard; bottom, deacon with Easter candle and *Exultet* roll.

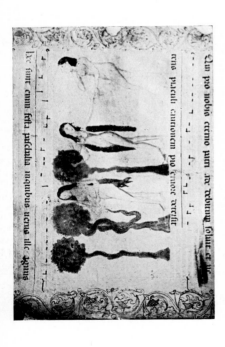

VI-7. *a*, Thirteenth-century *Pisa Exultet ii*: the Fall of Man. *b*, *McClean MS. 49*, fol. 4 *v*: the Lord served by two angels. *c*, *Atlantic Bible Vat. Lat. 12958*, fol. 133 *r*: S. John. *d*, *Roman Missal MS. Gadd. 44*, fol. 114 *v*: Christ in Glory with the symbols of the Evangelists, and Crucifixion.

VI–8. *a, Calci Atlantic Bible*: Moses and beginning of *Deuteronomy*. *b, Vallombrosa Psalter*, fol. 4 *v*: Calendar for August. *c–d, Montalcino Atlantic Bible—c*, Prophet Malachi and beginning of his book; *d, Beatus* page and beginning of *Psalms*, with Christ, David, and other figures.

VI–9. *a, MS. Plut. 17, 27, fol. 77 r*: S. Luke. *b, Perugia Breviary*: Annunciation. *c, Isidore Evangeliarium*: left, Pentecost; right, initial I (text: *S. John*, iv, 23 ff.).

VI–10. (Thirteenth-century illumination: *a–b*, Florence; *c*, South Italy). *a*, *Roman Missal MS. Conv. Soppr. 233*, fol. 127 *r*: Crucifixion with Virgin Mary and S. John. *b*, *Bible MS. Conv. Soppr. 582*, fol. 209 *v*: *Beatus* page (Preface to *Psalms* and *Psalm*, i. 1–3). *c*, *MS. S. Croce Plut. 7. dext. 11*: scenes from *Book of Job*.

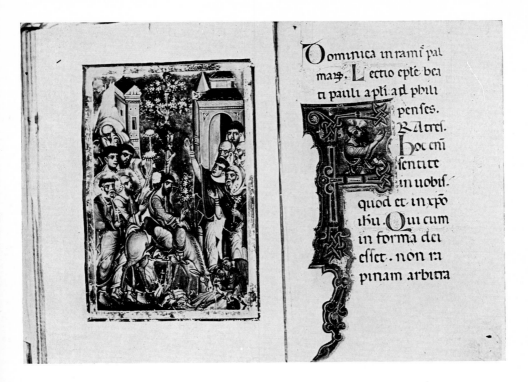

VI–11. Giovanni da Gaibana, *a–b, Padua Epistolarium*: Entry into Jerusalem; initial P; Giovanni's self-portrait. *c, Paduan Psalter* (Fitzwilliam Museum), fol. 22 *v*: *Beatus* page with God the Father between two angels; Christ between S. Mary and S. John the Baptist; King David.

VI-12. Thirteenth-century
North Italian *Bibles. a, W. 122*,
fol. 3 *v* : scenes of the Creation
and beginning of *Genesis*.
b, Conradin Bible, fol. 156 *v* :
Tobias and the Angel, and
beginning of *Book of Tobit*.

VI–13. *a,* Dante, *Divine Comedy* (*Cod. Tempi 1*), p. 1: scenes from *Inferno,* Canto 1, and allegorical figure of Justice. *b, Gradual* attributed to the 'Master of the Dominican Effigies', fol. 42 *r*: initial S with Pentecost.

VI-14. *Augustinian Gradual M. 795,* fol. 202 *r*: S. Bartholomew in an initial G; in the lower margin, two scenes from his martyrdom.

VI-15. *a, Roman Missal* (Cestello Seminary at Florence), pages i and xviii: initials A (Presentation in the Temple) and E (Adoration of the Magi). *b, Ordo Missalis (MS. Edili 107)*, fol. 367 *r*: Miracle of S. Zanobius (in the background, church of S. Reparata = S. Maria del Fiore). *c, De Arte venandi (Pal. Lat. 1071)*, lower portion of fol. 103 *r*.

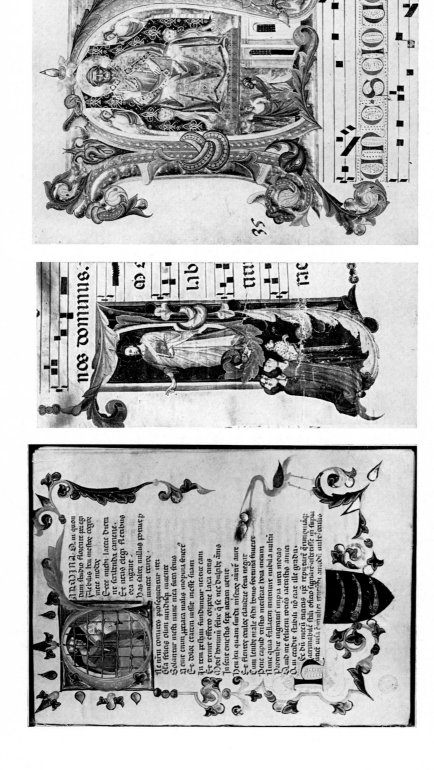

VI–16. *a*, Boëthius, *Philosophiae Consolatio* (*MS. Plut. 78. 15*), fol. 1 *r*: Initial C representing Boëthius in prison writing his work (text: Introduction in verse). *b*, Montepulciano, *Cor. D*, fol. 210 *v*: initial I with Christ appearing to three saints. *c*, *Antiphonary-Sanctorale W. 153*, fol. 35 *v*: initial N (S. Peter on the throne; below, an angel frees him from prison).

VI-17. *a, Il Biadaiolo*: Or S. Michele, Baptistery, and Bargello. *b, Rustici Codex*: the Misericordia and the church of S. Maria del Bigallo.

VI–18. Niccolò di Ser Sozzo Tegliacci: *Caleffo dell'Assunta*.

VI–19. *a,* Thirteenth-century *Chorale* (S. Francis, Zara): decorated initial. *b, Florentine Missal* for the Feasts of the Saints (first half of the thirteenth century), fol. 31 *r:* initial E with two saints. *c,* Impruneta, *A. II.* (first half of the fourteenth century), fol. 51 *r:* initial I with scenes from *Genesis. d,* Fourteenth-century *Chorale* (S. Marco Museum): initial E with the Three Maries at the Tomb.

VI–20. *Chorales. a–b,* Sano di Pietro: *a, Chorale* for Siena Cathedral (now in the Piccolomini Library at Siena): initial representing Presentation in the Temple; *b, Augustinian Missal* (Fitzwilliam Museum), fol. 16 *v*: Crucifixion with S. Mary and S. John. *c,* Impruneta, *A. I.,* fol. 108 *r*: initial N, representing Nativity. *d,* Fifteenth-century *Chorale* in the church of S. Croce: initial N, representing Baptism of Christ.

VI–21. *Chorales* executed in the degli Angeli School. *a, Gradual, a.* 1370, fol. 68 *v* : initial with S. Mark. *b,* Lorenzo Monaco : *Antiphonary* (National Museum at Florence, *Cod. A. 69*), fol. 196 *r* : letter F with S. John the Baptist. *c,* Don Simone Camaldolese : *Cor. 40* (Laurentian Library), fol. 88 *r* : Saint with arrow and sword. *d, Antiphonary, Cor. 5* (Laurentian Library), fol. 105 *r* : S. Michael, dragons and devils.

VI–22. *Chorales. a,* Giuliano degli Amidei: *Chorale* preserved in the S. Marco Museum—page with initial representing S. Andrew. *b,* Giovanni Monte di Miniato del Favilla: *Chorale* in the same collection—in the centre, the Trinity; in the medallions, S. Placitus and Pope Gregory the Great. *c–d,* Sixteenth-century *Chorales* in Florence Cathedral: *c,* page with initial representing Baptism of Christ; the ornamentation includes coats-of-arms of the Commune of Florence; *d,* scenes from Abraham's life.

VI–23. *a,* Niccolò da Bologna:
Lucanus, *De bello Pharsalico*
(*Cod. Triv. 691*), fol. 84 *v.*:
captain (Julius Caesar?) sitting
under a white tent which is
decorated with two coats-of-arms
containing the French *fleur-de-lis*;
armed knights stand around the
captain. *b,* Copy of *Decretum
Gratiani* (Naples, *MS. XII. A. 1*),
fol. 1 *r*: Christ as Judge of the
Universe surrounded by
ecclesiastical dignitaries, and the
beginning of *Corpus Iuris
Canonici.*

c, Perugia Missal (Perugia
Capitulary Library, *Messale
No. 6*), fol. 190 *v*: Crucifixion
with the Virgin and
S. John.

VI–24. *a*, Niccolò da Bologna :
Ordo Missae (M. 800), fol. 39 *v* :
Crucifixion (with the artist's
signature). *b*, Italian copy of
Klimax, *Spiritual Ladder, W*.157,
fol. 10 *v* : initial containing the
'portrait' of the author ; border
decorated with figures and other
ornamentation.

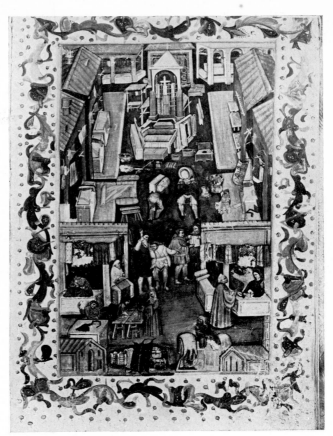

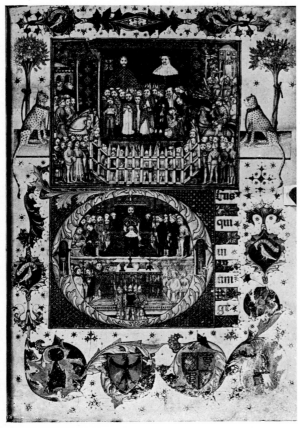

VI–25. *a,* Statutes of the Bologna
Drapers' Guild, of the year
1523 : daily life in a draper's lane.
b, Anovelo da Imbonate : *Gian
Galeazzo Missal*—Emperor
Venceslaus invests Gian
Galeazzo Sforza with the Duchy
of Milan (1395).

VI–26. *a*, Cecco d'Ascoli, *L'Acerba* and *Physionomia* (*MS. Plut. 40. 52*), fol. 24 *v*. *b*, *Apocalypse MS. Ashb. 415*, fol. 3 *r*: *Revelation*, vi. 7–8. *c*, *Speculum humanae salvationis* (Fitzwilliam Museum, *MS. 43–1950*): left, Daniel fed by Habakuk (*Daniel*, xiv. 30–40); right, the ostrich delivers its young.

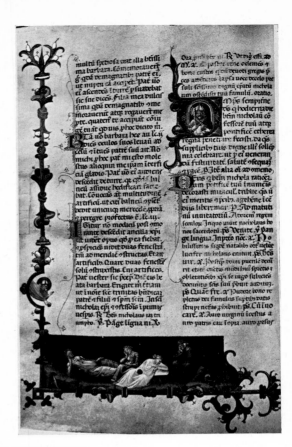

VI–27. *a, Vallombrosan Breviary, MS. Conv. Soppr. 457*, fol. 305 *v*: the story of S. Nicholas of Bari. *b*, S. Augustine, *City of God*, 1433 (National Library at Florence, *MS. II. I. 112*), fol. 33 *v*: veneration of S. Augustine.

VI–28. *a*, Fra Angelico and others: *Diurno Domenicale*, fol. 1 *v*: Resurrection of Christ. *b*, Zanobi Strozzi and Francesco d'Antonio del Cherico: *Gradual MS. Edili 150*, fol. 87 *v*: the Three Magi.

VI-29. *a–b*, Botticelli (?): *Fiore di virtù*, fol. 54 *v* and 62 *v*: representations from *Physiologus* (?). *c*, Filippo di Matteo Torelli: *Gospels*, MS. *Edili* 115, fol. 1 *r*: Last Judgment, Judith with the head of Holofernes, and various ornamentation.

VI-30. *a, Bottega* of Filippo di Matteo Torelli: Josephus Flavius, *De bello iudaico,* fol. 2 *r*: coat-of-arms of Giovanni di Cosimo de'Medici, with various ornamentation. *b,* Francesco d'Antonio del Cherico: *Lorenzo Hours,* fol. 13 *v*–14 *r*: Annunciation and first page of the Office of the Virgin, with Madonna and Child.

VI-31. Francesco d'Antonio del Cherico: copy of Aristotle, *Physics*, fol. 2 *r*—'portrait' of Aristotle, medallions of Cosimo il Vecchio and Piero di Cosimo, putti, cameos, and other ornamentation.

VI-32. Gherardo and Monte di Giovanni del Fora: *a, Bible of Matthias Corvinus*, fol. 3 *v. b, Roman Missal* (National Museum at Florence, *MS. 67*), fol. 150 *v*: Jerusalem (resembling Florence) and Golgotha, Crucifixion, Entombment of Christ, surrounded by Passion scenes.

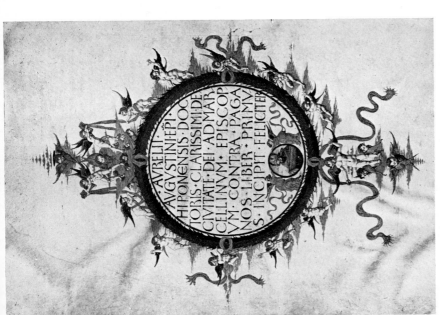

VI-33. *a, Bottega* of Filippo di Matteo Torelli: S. Augustine, *God's City, Plut. 12. 19*, fol. 1 r: title-page with the figure of S. Augustine and two angels in a laurel-garland with little angels. *b*, Attavante: Tommaso Sardi, *Anima peregrina*, fol. 96 r—in the centre, the author arrives at the Golden Gate, which is shut and guarded by S. Paul; above, the Virgin and angels; bottom, the Infernal City (see Dante, *Inferno*, viii. 67–x, 134); decorative border.

S ic martem indomitum / danaosq. ad tecta ruentes

C ernimus obsessumq. acta testudine limen

h erent parietibus scale. postesq. sub ipsos

n ituntur gradibus. clipeosq. ad tela sinistris

P rotecti obiciunt: prensant fastigia dextris

VI–34. *a, Riccardian Virgil,* fol. 84 *r*: storming of Troy (text: *Aeneid,* ii. 437–44). *b,* Boccardino il Vecchio: *Roman Breviary,* fol. 48 *r*: the Three Magi.

VI–35. *a,* Boccardino il
Vecchio: copy of Hippocrates,
Plut. 73. 12—beginning of
Epidemics, book i. *b,* Giovanni
and Francesco Boccardi:
Montecassino Chorale—initial
with SS. Peter and Andrew.

VI–36. *Biccherna* and *Gabella* Tablets—
a, Biccherna a. 1445:
Annunciation by
Giovanni di Paolo or
his school. *b, Gabella
a.* 1479: Duke of
Calabria at Colle Val
d'Elsa, attributed to
Francesco di Giorgio
Martini.

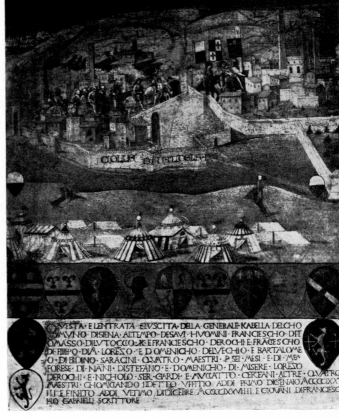

VI–37. Francesco di Giorgio Martini: S. Albertus Magnus, *De Animalibus*—the Unicorn as symbol of Chastity; some of the labours performed by Hercules, and a coat-of-arms.

VI-38. *a*, *Borso Bible*, vol. 2, fol. 233 *v*: richly decorated page containing *2nd Epistle of S. Peter*, iii. 13–*1st Epistle of S. John*, ii. 15. *b*, *Borso Missal*, fol. 7 *r*: beginning of the *Missal* according to Roman use.

VI-39. *a, Ercole Breviary*, fol. 361 *r*: initial representing Visitation; richly decorated border with arms and other ornamentation. *b, Alfonso Officium*: initial with Madonna and Child; border decorated with cameos, flowers, birds, grotesques, and so on.

VI-40. *Visconti Officium*, fol. 46 *v*–47 *r*: Creation of Eve and Heavenly Father; magnificent ornamentation, including angels, animals, the Sforza coat-of-arms, and so on.

VI-41. *a, Milanese Pontifical,* fol. 1 *r*: beautiful border with crowned *Yhs* in gold (at the top) and coat-of-arms (at the bottom); historiated initial representing Confirmation. *b,* Iohannes Franciscus Marlianus, *Epithalamium in nuptiis Blancae M. Sphortiae et ducis Ioannis Corvini,* fol. 5 *r*: portrait of Matthias Corvinus; the Corvinus coat-of-arms; and exquisite ornamentation.

VI–42. *a*, Cornazzano, *Del modo di reggere* (*M. 731*), fol. 4 *v* : dedication page (by Cosimo Tura?). *b*, Marmitta masterpiece : *Missal of Card. Domenico della Rovere*—Crucifixion and scenes of Passion. *c*, *Sforza Book of Hours* : S. Gregory the Great. *d*, *Book of Jesus*, fol. 1 *v* : portrait of Massimiliano Sforza (see p. 344).

VI-41. *a*, *Milanese Pontifical*, fol. 1 r: beautiful border with crowned *Yhs* in gold (at the top) and coat-of-arms (at the bottom); historiated initial representing Confirmation. *b*, Iohannes Franciscus Marlianus, *Epithalamium in nuptiis Blancae M. Sphortiae et ducis Ioannis Corvini*, fol. 5 r: portrait of Matthias Corvinus; the Corvinus coat-of-arms; and exquisite ornamentation.

VI–42. *a*, Cornazzano, *Del modo di reggere* (*M. 731*), fol. 4 *v*: dedication page (by Cosimo Tura?). *b*, Marmitta masterpiece: *Missal of Card. Domenico della Rovere*—Crucifixion and scenes of Passion. *c*, *Sforza Book of Hours*: S. Gregory the Great. *d*, *Book of Jesus*, fol. 1 *v*: portrait of Massimiliano Sforza (see p. 344).

VI–43. *a,* Girolamo da Cremona: initial representing the circumcision of Christ (from a Siena Cathedral *Chorale* preserved in the Piccolomini Library at Siena). *b,* Liberale da Verona: initial representing a sower; in the background, the town of S. Gimignano (from a *Chorale* of the same provenance and in the same collection). *c, Milan Hours (W. 323),* fol. 16 *v*: the disappointed suitors of the Virgin. *d,* Colantonio school (?): Ippolito da Luni, *Sentenze e proverbi Platonici,* fol. 7 *r*—initial P containing the representation of Plato; border ornamented in Neapolitan style.

VI–44. *a*, Neapolitan school influenced by Ferrara style; copyist Peter of Bordeaux: S. Thomas Aquinas, *Super quarto libro Sententiarum,* fol. 11 *r*—top left column, S. Thomas in his study, with a beautiful landscape in the background; lower border, Royal Aragon coat-of-arms painted upon that of Card. John of Aragon. *b*, *Bottega* of Reginaldo Piramo da Monopoli: Virgil, *Aeneid*—beautifully ornamented page; beginning of *Aeneid,* v, with border, initial, and miniature representing women of Carthage seeing departure of Aeneas's fleet. *c*, Neapolitan school with N. Italian influences: *Naples Hours* (*MS. I. B. 26*), fol. 13 *r*—Annunciation, border with arms, putti, medallion, etc. *d*, S. Jerome, *Epistolae* (Naples, *MS. VI. C. 2*): beginning of the *Epistle to Paulinus*; miniature: S. Jerome kneeling before the Crucifix.

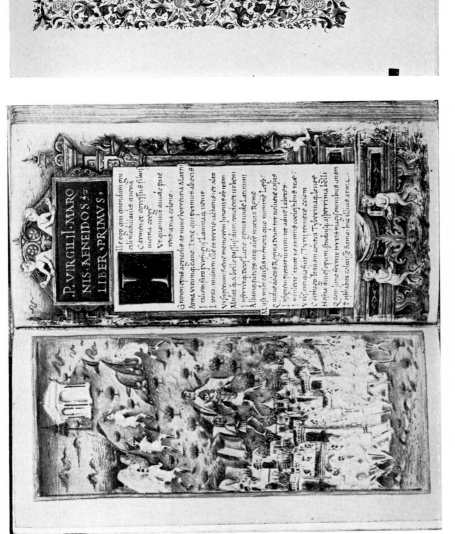

VI-45. *a*, Pocket-size copy of Virgil, *W. 400*, fol. 54 *v*–55 *r*: Conflagration of Troy; Aeneas escapes carrying his father Anchises followed by Ascanius; beginning of *Aeneid*, i, *b*, *Offices of the Virgin*, *W. 328*: S. Catherine of Alexandria,

VI-46. Clovio. *a*, *Grimani Codex*, fol. 8 *r*: Introduction to S. Paul's *Epistle to the Romans*; border elaborately decorated. *b*, *Colonna Missal*, fol. 79 *r*: frontispiece to the *Mass of S. John the Baptist*; initial representing Zacharias (according to *S. Luke*, i. 63); Hercules and Antaeus, and Diana of Ephesus; the extraordinarily rich border contains the arms of the Colonna (a column), various archaeological objects (particularly Egyptian ones), and other ornamentation.

Yates Thompson Collection, and a *Liber de temporibus et aetatibus*, of 1285, executed either in Lombardy or in the Venetian region. In the latter, Byzantine influences occur as late as the fourteenth century; instances are: Burchardus Theutonicus, *Descriptio Terrae Sanctae* (Padua Seminary Library, *MS. 74*), two *Antiphonaries* in the Marciana Library (*Cl. Nos. 98* and *99*), and a *Lives of the Apostles*, written in French with captions in the Venetian dialect (Estense Library, Modena, *MS. α. Y. 4.14*). Strong Byzantine influences in South Italy may be exemplified by a thirteenth-century copy of translated Arabic medical works executed by the Monte-cassino monk John in 1282 for Charles of Anjou (National Library at Paris, *Lat. 6912*).

Italo-Byzantine Style. It would, however, be wrong to assume that the Italian style on the whole was then purely Byzantine. The gentler temper of the Italian religious mind was under the influence of the outlook and spirit of S. Francis of Assisi and of his followers, represented in art by the charming fresco-paintings of the early Italian schools (partly connected with the Franciscan movement) and by the altar-pieces painted in *maniera bizantina* by Duccio di Buoninsegna, Cimabue, and his great disciple, Giotto. In illumination, this Italo-Byzantine art simplified, softened, sweetened, and humanized the Byzantine combination of spiritual mysteries and earthly magnificence.

Thirteenth-century School at Padua? This Italo-Byzantine style of illumination may be exemplified by an *Epistolarium*, executed in Padua, and finished in 1259 (now in the Padua Cathedral). Its scribe and illuminator, Giovanni da Gaibana, is represented in a miniature, sitting at a desk and writing *Ego presbyter Johannes scripsi feliciter*. There are many full-page pictures of the lives of Christ and the saints, painted on highly burnished gold backgrounds in deep, rich colours (blue, which predominates, scarlet, pinkish-blue, and green). The static character of the work (the mannerisms), the fine colouring—the dark complexions of the figures (though with greenish shadows and sharp high-lights on forehead, cheek, and nose), and some other features, and particularly the whole iconography are in Byzantine style, but the vivacity of expression adds dramatic force to the mystic spirituality of this style. Although the figures have faulty proportions—the heads being much too big—they are admirably modelled, mature, noble, profoundly spiritual; they are dignified yet they express emotion. See Fig. VI-11*a–b*.

Also by Giovanni da Gaibana, and signed by him, is a *Psalter* dated 1263 and preserved in the Bodleian Library, Oxford (*MS. Can. Liturg. 370*). On the basis of the Padua *Epistolarium* and the Bodleian *Psalter*, I. Haensel-Hacker has recently reconstructed a thirteenth-century school of illumination in Padua, which is supposed to have produced the following illuminated MSS. in addition to the two codices referred to: the *Admont Missal*, *Cod. 857* in St.-Gall; a *Missal* in the Pierpont Morgan Library, New York (*M. 855*); a copy of the *Pauline Epistles* in S. Paul im Lavanttal (Carinthia); a *Psalter* in the Fitzwilliam Museum, Cambridge (*MS. 36–1950*); and a *Psalter* in the National Library at Vienna (*Cod. 1898*).

These works may have been produced by various artists of the Padua school, partly working in Padua and partly in Austria. See Fig. VI-11c.

On the whole, in the thirteenth and fourteenth centuries excellent work was produced in Padua. Instances are: *Bibles* such as the fourteenth-century *MS. 212* in the Accademia dei Concordi at Rovigo (part of the MS. is in the British Museum) and the *Conradin Bible*, of *c.* 1270 (produced either in Padua or in Venice), which is in the Walters Art Gallery (*W. 152*); a fragmentary *Psalter* in the Estense Library, Modena (*Lat. 1017*); and various secular works preserved in Padua (Seminary, *MS. 67*; Civic Museum, *MS. B.P. 158*), Venice (Marciana Library, *MS. Lat. X. 381*), Florence (Laurentian Library, *Plut. 40.52*), Darmstadt (*Lat. 101*), Paris (National Library, *MS. Lat. 6069. I*, being a copy of Petrarch, of 1379), and in other important collections. Fig. VI-12b.

An interesting codex of the National Library, at Florence (*MS. II. II. 90*)—the *Filostrato* by Giovanni Boccaccio, contains pen designs by a Trecento artist, "probably Paduan".

Conventional Border Ornament. In contrast to Byzantine influence, by the end of the thirteenth century and throughout the fourteenth, there appeared in the Italian illuminated MSS. a conventional border-ornament, probably at least partly derived from the pendent bar-border of the thirteenth-century English and French styles of illumination. Herbert singles out the following four elements of the Italian border-decoration:

(1) The thin wand or rod, normally straight and rigid, but capable of being tied in knots, twisted, or plaited;

(2) the long lobed and pointed leaf, the lobes generally on one side only;

(3) cup-shaped beads threaded on the wands and stems;

(4) comical use of human, animal, and grotesque figures (such as a hare hunting a man, or two men fighting a gigantic snail), exemplified by a small *Bible* in the British Museum (*Add. MS. 37487*).

Bologna Productions. The following liturgical illuminated MSS. produced in Bologna and in allied schools of the Emilian and the Venetian regions may be indicated: a *Bible* in the Bodleian Library, Oxford (*MS. 18949*), written in 1265; a slightly earlier *Bible* formerly preserved in the Dyson Perrins Collection, London; *Bibles* preserved in the National Library at Paris (*Cod. Lat. 18*), the Malatestiana Library, Cesena (*MS. D. XXI. 1*), the Capitulary Library at Verona, the Vatican Library (*Cod. Vat. Lat. 20*), and the Civic Museum at Turin; a *Psalter* with Calendar, executed in Padua in Bolognese style (University Library at Bologna, *MS. 346*); *Chorales* (see p. 313) preserved in the Civic Museum at Bologna (*Nos. 1, 2, 7, 8, 12–14, 16*, and *17*); a codex executed in the monastery of S. Michele in Bosco and preserved in the Estense Library, Modena (*Nos. 1015–6*); *Antiphonaries* in the Capitulary Library at Padua (*Cod. A.5, B.14*, and *B.15*), and in the church of S. Francis at Zara (*Codices A, B, C, G, H*, and *E*); two *Antiphonaries* which come from the S. Dominic Convent of Gubbio and are preserved in the same town (Communal Archives, *Cor. I* and *Cor. II*); and a *Breviary* written in 1291 in Spalato, and preserved in the Correr Museum, Venice: Fig. IV-19*a*.

The productivity of the Bologna school of illumination was not confined to Bibles and liturgical books. Many illuminated codices were produced dealing with other religious matters or with secular subjects. Examples of the former are: Pope Gregory IX, *Decretals* (Marciana Library, Venice, *MS. Lat. IV, 109: 2434*): the miniatures show French influences—some authorities (such as Salmi) assign these miniatures to the group, which in D'Ancona's opinion shows the style of the celebrated Oderisi da Gubbio; a copy of S. Thomas Aquinas, *Summa contra gentiles*, and S. Augustine, *De haeresibus* (Malatestiana Library, Cesena, *MS. D. XVI. 3*); also a copy of the *Statutes* of the Bolognese Congregation *devotorum B. Mariae de Batutis*, of 1260, contains religious miniatures. They are a very fine production of the Bolognese school; here, too, some authorities see the style of Oderisi da Gubbio. According to other experts, the codex shows Byzantine-Romanesque features; it is preserved in the Archiginnasio Library at Bologna (*Fondo Battuti No. 42*).

Examples of secular works are: a copy of the *Statutes* of the Guild of Master Carpenters, of 1248 (State Archives at Bologna), in early Bolognese Gothic with survivals of the Bolognese Romanesque style; a copy of 1270 of similar *Statutes* (the same collection) in Bolognese style with Byzantine influences; a copy of Justinian, *Infortiatum* (middle section of the *Digesta*), preserved in the National Library at Turin (*MS. E. I. 8*), in Bolognese style with French influences—some authorities (such as Salmi) also here assume the style of Oderisi da Gubbio; a copy of Frederick II, *De arte venandi cum avibus* (see p. 309 f.), preserved in Bologna (University Library, *MS. 717*).

For Oderisi da Gubbio and the related French Gothic style see pp. 304, 314, and 381 f.

Tuscan Schools (Thirteenth and Fourteenth Centuries)

The production of the Tuscan schools was not plentiful, and may be regarded as partly dependent on the school of Bologna and of other centres of Emilia.

Florence. Examples of Florentine illumination influenced by the style of Bologna are: a thirteenth-century Bible preserved in the Laurentian Library, Florence (*MS. Conv. Soppr. 582*); a thirteenth- or fourteenth-century Bible in the same collection (*MS. S. Croce, Plut. 5, dext. 1*); part of a copy of *Passio S. Margaritae etc.* (Riccardiana Library, Florence, *MS. 453*), and others: Fig. VI-10*b*.

More independent seems to be the illumination of a thirteenth- or fourteenth-century *Gospel-book* (National Library at Florence, *MS. II. I. 167: Magl. Cl. XXXVI, 92*); two *Antiphonaries* preserved in the Collegiata at Montevarchi (*Cor. A. and B.*); two *Antiphonaries* and three *Graduals*, preserved in the Communal Museum at Montepulciano (*Cor. B., G., A., F.,* and *H.2*); a copy of Dante preserved in the National Library at Naples (*MS. XIII. C.4*); another copy of Dante, preserved in the Laurentian Library (*MS. Tempi 1,*) which is considered one of the best illuminated codices of Dante produced in Florence—it is dated 1398; and other MSS. See Fig. VI-13*a*.

Although there is no evidence that Cimabue (1240–1302), 'the father of modern painting' has done any illumination, his indirect influence may be seen in various codices, such as a late thirteenth-century *Roman Missal* preserved in the Laurentian Library (*MS. Conv. Soppr. 233*), and three thirteenth- or fourteenth-century *Graduals* preserved in Florence (S. Marco Museum, *Cor. F. and G.*) and Bologna (Civic Museum, *Cor. 17–24*): Fig. VI-10*a*.

One of the earliest Florentine artistic *botteghe* (see p. 327 f.) was that of Pacino di Buonaguida; the following illuminated MSS. have been attributed to his *bottega* (or to his followers or imitators): a fourteenth-century *Bible* preserved in the Trivulzio Library, Milan (*MS. 2139*); a copy of *Laudes* in the National Library at Florence (*MS. B. R. 18: II. I. 122*); an *Antiphonary* in the Civic Museum at Montepulciano (*Cor. D.*); a detached leaf in the Fitzwilliam Museum, Cambridge (*MS. 19A*); various miniatures in a copy of Dante, preserved in the National Library at Florence (*MS. Palat. 313*); in *M. 643* of the Pierpont Morgan Library, New York; and in the *Lives of the Holy Fathers*, preserved in the National Library at Rome (*MS. V. E. 1189*), and other codices. An *Augustinian Gradual*, produced in Florence *c.* 1300–30 and now in the Pierpont Morgan Library (*M. 795*), is also in Pacino's style: Fig. VI-14. Closely related are *M. 742* in the same collection, *MS. J. 194* in the Fitzwilliam Museum at Cambridge, and *MS. 303* in the Museum Mayer van den Bergh at Antwerp. An *Antiphonary* in the S. Maria Basilica at Impruneta, near Florence (*Cor. V*) is partly attributed to a follower of Pacino. The anonymous illuminator of *MS. Edili 107* (see further on), according to Prof. Salmi, was more skilful than Pacino.

Another important *bottega* was that of Jacopo del Casentino (a painter from Pratovecchio, who lived from 1297 to *c.* 1358): a *Gradual*, preserved in the S. Marco Museum, Florence; a *Roman Missal*, preserved in the Cestello Seminary, Florence; a copy of *Laudes* and *Sequentiae* (National Library at Florence, *MS. B. R. 19: II. I. 212*); *Cor. I* in the Communal Library at Poppi; and a copy of Bartolomeo da San Concordio (National Library at Florence, *MS. II. II. 319*), partly at least, were produced by, or in the *bottega* of, Jacopo. See Fig. VI-15*a*.

Siena. Thirteenth- and fourteenth-century book-illumination is represented by *Antiphonaries* (S. Maria dei Servi, Siena, *Cor. E.*; Opera del Duomo, Siena, *Cor. C. and D.*; Ospedale di S. Maria della Scala, Siena, *MS. 229*; Communal Library at Siena, *MS. H. I. 7*); *Graduals* (S. Maria dei Servi, *Cor. F. and G.*; Collegiata Museum at Asciano; Communal Library at Siena, *Cor. G. I. 7, MSS. H. I. 1 and 2*); a beautiful copy of *Sequentiae et hymni*, illuminated by at least four artists (Communal Library at Siena, *MS. G. III. 2*); Communal constitutions, Statutes and Rules of trade-guilds, etc. (State Archives at Siena, *Statuti del Comune 16; MS. Arti 61*).

ITALY

The Sienese painter Lippo Vanni was the main illuminator of Siena in the fourteenth century. Various illuminated codices are attributed either to him or to his school or followers: two *Antiphonaries* preserved in Siena (Museo dell'Opera del Duomo, *Cor. 180*, and Seminary Library), *Rules* and *Statutes* (State Archives at Siena, *Patrim. dei Resti Eccles. 682* and *MS. Mercanzia 1*), and a copy of Dante (Augusta Library, Perugia, *MS. L. 70*). An *Antiphonary* preserved in the Fogg Art Museum, Harvard University, contains illuminated borders and forty beautiful historiated initials. It is assigned by Berenson to 1345, and is attributed to Lippo Vanni. Also *Cor. 18* in the Piccolomini Library and *Grad. 4* in the Opera del Duomo Museum, both in Siena, as well as several detached leaves have been attributed to Lippo Vanni, whose artistic activity lasted over thirty years (1344–75).

For Simone Martini see pp. 39 and 311.

An anonymous Sienese artist, influenced by Simone Martini, illuminated in about 1315 a superb MS. known as the *S. Giorgio Codex* (Capitulary Archives, S. Peter, Vatican, *MS. C. 129*); hence this illuminator is known as the 'Master of the S. Giorgio Codex'. A follower of this master, who in Prof. Salmi's opinion came from Viterbo, executed the numerous miniatures of another interesting MS., containing the *Rules of S. Spirito Hospital*, Rome (State Archives at Rome, *MS. Spirito 1*).

Pisa and Lucca. The illuminations of two *Graduals* and two *Antiphonaries*, preserved in the Civic Museum at Pisa (*Cor. O.* and *V., B.* and *E.*) may be considered excellent specimens of the thirteenth- and fourteenth-century Pisan school of illumination. As to the thirteenth century, Siena and Pisa were the only Tuscan cities which had original schools of book-painting from the mid-century onwards: Pisa *Cor. E.* is an example.

A copy of the *Statute of the Comune of Pisa*, of 1302–03, preserved in the State Archives, at Pisa, contains vivid miniatures, still in Gothic style. One miniature represents the election of the Elders; another represents a judge "in cathedra".

Two richly illuminated *Antiphonaries*, executed for Dominican convents and preserved in the State Library at Lucca (*MSS. 2648* and *2654*), are good examples of the thirteenth-century school of illumination of Lucca. One has twenty-six initials with miniatures and several more initials with pure decoration; the other contains eighteen initials with miniatures and a great number of purely ornamented initials.

South Italy

De Arte Venandi. Of great charm is the *Liber de arte venandi cum avibus*, which was written by Emperor Frederick II (1194–1250) and enlarged by his natural son, King Manfred (*c.* 1231–66). A copy beautifully illuminated in Byzantine style by an anonymous artist is now preserved in the Vatican Library (*Cod. Pal. Lat. 1071*). It was probably executed about 1260 in Sicily or South Italy. The bright, lifelike, open-air scenes pleasantly contrasting with the monastic atmosphere of the contemporary books, give to this work a unique character. The drawings are delightful; the marginal paintings, particularly, are of high technical accomplishment; they depict birds and falconers and are remarkable for their naturalism: Fig. VI-15c.

A copy of this book, executed by a French artist (perhaps Simon of Orléans) reflects the French Gothic style; it is preserved in the National Library, at Paris (*MS. Franç. 12400*).

Other instances of the South Italian aulic school—showing not only Byzantine, but also Islamic and North-French influences—are the *Manfred Bible*, of 1258 (*Vat. Lat. 36*)—see, particularly, Adalbert Graf zu Erbach-Fuerstenau, *Die Manfredbibel* ("Kunstgesch. Forsch. herausg. v. koenigl. Preuss. Hist. Inst. in Rom"), Leipsic, 1910—and the earliest extant copy of Petrus de Ebulo, *De balneis puteolanis* (Angelica Library, Rome, *MS. 1474*), which contains eighteen compositions in a highly expressionistic style.

Campania. An interesting, skilfully illuminated document of the second decade of the thirteenth century (a donation to the monastery, confirmed by Pope Honorius III), produced in the monastery of Montevergine, is still preserved in that locality (Archivio della Badia, Montevergine). About ten years later is an illuminated codex, containing (on f. 304*v*) a large miniature depicting the presentation of the book to Abbot Balsamo, and eight ornamented initials on gold background (Badia Library, Cava dei Tirreni, *MS. membr. 18*).

Illuminators

Several artists have already been referred to. Here some more may be added: in the *Gerona Bible* there appears the name of a certain Bernardino of Modena; in a *Chorale* preserved in the Leone Museum, Vercelli, there is the name of a certain Giovanni of Genoa; and a fourteenth-century copy of *Liber Canonum* (*Vat. Lat. 1375*) is signed by Jacopino of Reggio.

Fourteenth Century

The Italian *trecento* saw the first Italian painters of genius, Duccio di Buoninsegna (*c.* 1260–*c.* 1340), the founder of the Sienese school, and the great Florentine Ambrogio di Bondone (*c.* 1266–1337), generally known as Giotto, who re-created Italian painting and who was also sculptor and architect. Both these masters and their fourteenth-century followers were divine painters: they executed strikingly beautiful altar-pieces and glorious frescoes. Apparently the direct influence of Giotto and his school on contemporary Italian book-illumination was not great. Perhaps some traces of his influence may be recognized in the clear-cut profiles, the well-defined types, and the careful treatment of the hair of the figures depicted in a British Museum MS. (*Add. MS. 27488*) containing Simone da Cascia's *L'ordene della Vita Cristiana*, which was composed in 1333. The MS. also contains the lives of saints, in Italian, which are illustrated by very crowded miniatures, set in the column of text and filling its whole width; they are painted on gold backgrounds and have plain rectangular frames.

Of greater importance was the indirect influence of fresco- and panel-painting. Indeed, the best productions of Italian book-illumination of the period—which are far behind the French—are in certain regards fresco- or panel-painting on a small scale.

Good specimens of this art are the frontispieces to all kinds of works, not only literary works but municipal account-books, registers of wills, membership-books of trade-guilds, and so on. Some such frontispieces, which generally are easily dated, are contained in MSS. preserved in the British Museum *Add. MSS. 16532* (executed in Bologna in 1334), *21965* (Perugia, 1368), *22497* (Perugia, soon after 1400), and a few others.

Two frontispieces are outstanding: (1) that of Petrarch's *Virgil* (Ambrosian Library, Milan), which was painted by the great Simone Martini (*c.* 1284–1344), who (or, at least a pupil of his) according to some art-historians also painted the *Codice di S. Giorgio* (referred to on p. 309). The frontispiece to the Virgil which belonged to Petrarch was painted by his friend Simone in Avignon *c.* 1340. Simone combined French with Byzantine influences. (2) Assumption of the Virgin—see Fig. VI-18—prefixed to the *Caleffo* (or Register of Public Documents, the second of the five *Instrumentarii* of the Sienese Republic) of Siena, compiled in 1334–6, and known as the *Caleffo dell'Assunta* (State Archives at Siena). The latter was painted by a great master, Niccolò di Ser Sozzo Tegliacci—the frontispiece is signed *Nicholas ser sozzo de senis me pinxit*—who was influenced by Simone, Lippo Memmi, and Pietro Lorenzetti. Three *Chorales* in the S. Gimignano Museum are attributed to Niccolò. Some scholars assign to a follower of his the copy of Dante preserved in the Augusta Library (others attribute this copy to Lippo Vanni: see p. 309). It has been suggested that the great fifteenth-century altarpiece of Matteo di Giovanni (National Gallery, London) was inspired by the *Caleffo* frontispiece.

Some fourteenth-century illuminated MSS. of the Florentine school show influences of the style of the famous painter Bernardo Daddi. Examples are: a copy of *Ordo missalis* (in the Laurentian Library, *MS. Edili 107*) and a *Gradual* (in the same collection, *Cor. 41*). Two anonymous illuminators, influenced by Bernardo Daddi and somewhat connected with the *bottega* of Jacopo del Casentino, are known to have worked in Florence in the first half of the fourteenth century. They are known as 'the Master of the Corn-chandler' and 'the Master of the Dominican Effigies'. The former is known as the illuminator of a most curious book—Domenico Lenzi, *Specchio umano* (or *Human Mirror*) popularly known as *Il Biadaiolo*, or *The Corn-chandler* (Laurentian Library, *MS. Tempi 3*). The corn-chandler Lenzi gives price-lists of corn and cereals for Or San Michele market for the years 1320–35 and supplements these with various useful notes and moral considerations. The book contains several full-page miniatures, a decorated initial, etc., which depict agricultural and trade-scenes, social historical scenes, and so on, and is one of the best representatives of Florentine popular art. Florentine popular art of the fourteenth century is also represented by a *Life of S. Margaret* (Laurentian Library, *MS. Ashb. 451*) and by several miniatures in Ser Zucchero Bencivenni, *Explanation of the Paternoster* (National Library at Florence, *MS. II. VI. 16: Magl. Cl. XXXV, 179*). A beautiful copy of Dante of 1337 (Trivulzio Library at Milan, *No. 1080*) shows influence of the illuminator of *Il Biadaiolo*. See Fig. VI-15b and 17a. Fig. VI-17b is from the extremely interesting *Rustici Codex* (preserved in the Seminario di S. Frediano in Cestello, Florence).

'The Master of the Dominican Effigies' is known from a post-1336 panel-painting (preserved in the Church of S. Maria Novella, Florence) depicting Dominican Saints and Blessed. The following MSS., at least in part, are attributed to the painter: the *Roman Missal*, already referred to, which is in the Cestello Seminary, Florence; a copy of Boëthius in the Laurentian Library (*MS. Plut. 78, 15*); a copy of Dante in the Palatina Library, Parma (*MS. 3285*); several miniatures in two *Antiphonaries* of the S. Maria Basilica at Impruneta, near Florence (*MS. A. 1* and *Cor. V*); and in a *Gradual* preserved in the Collegiata dei SS. Lorenzo e Ippolito, Castelfiorentino (*Grad. A.*). The copy of Dante preserved in the Trivulzio Library (see above) has been attributed by some scholar to an artist connected with 'the Master of the Dominican Effigies'. Fig. VI-13b and 16a.

Other works painted in the fresco-style are: (1) British Museum, *Royal MS. 6 E. ix*, executed *c.* 1335–40, and containing an address (in verse) by the town of Prato (Prov. of Florence) to Robert of Anjou, King of Naples. The solid and gigantic figures are—as Herbert has pointed out—painted in a thick, rather viscid medium, generally without frames or background. On the best pages the work is very highly finished, face and hair especially being treated with great care. The curious greyish-pink flesh-tints, with a greenish tinge in the shadows, are characteristic of early Italian painting in general, and are found in most of the fourteenth-century miniatures. Gold is used plentifully and the colouring is strong, but with little attempt at gradation or modelling.

(2) Another British Museum work (*Add. MS. 34309*) consists of a series of miniatures attributed to the early fourteenth century. They were made for a large liturgical volume of which, however, there is no trace. These compositions are mainly based, directly or indirectly, on Byzantine models, but it has been suggested that the round table in the miniature of the Last Supper is connected with the paintings of the thirteenth-century German Psalters.

(3) On a much higher artistic level is a similar series of thirty-eight miniatures, formerly in Yates Thompson Collection (*MS. No. 81*; previously *Ashburnham, Appendix 72*). They are painted on a deep blue background, and framed in plain narrow bands of blue and red, the only ornamentation being a little tracery in white on the inner side of the borders. The compositions are in monumental style, solemn and majestic. 'The grouping is well ordered and spacious, the gestures are leisurely and dignified, the faces expressive, with careful preservation of types' (Herbert).

Gigantic Choir-books. The numerous gigantic *Libri Corali*—which are treasured in many chapter-libraries in Italy—form a particular class of the Italian illuminated book-production of the thirteenth to sixteenth centuries. They have no full-page miniatures, but contain the text with full musical setting, being designed each to serve for several choristers; and the principal initials enclose pictures as large as the page of an average modern book. They may be divided into two groups: the *Graduals* (the name derives from the Gradual in the Mass, a short passage from the *Psalms* to be sung after the *Epistle*), which correspond to the *Missals* or Mass-books, and contain the choral parts of the Mass; and the *Antiphonaries* (from the antiphons which make up a large part of the book), which, corresponding to the *Breviaries*, hold the choral parts of the Office.

Unlike the Gothic historiated initials—which at first were characterised by minute compression and later were replaced by purely ornamental initials surmounted by separately framed miniatures—the historiated initials of the Italian choir-books framed pictures 'which in largeness of manner often rivalled the compositions of contemporary panel-painters.' The letters were 'of elaborate design, rich in gold and bright colours and lavishly adorned with pendent decoration' (Herbert).

Several very large *Missals* contain miniatures in the same style as those of the *Choir-books* (see, for instance, Fig. VI-19*b* and 20*b*).

Not many of these enormous volumes are to be found outside Italy. A mid-fourteenth-century *Gradual* of the district of Florence (made perhaps for the monastery of Vallombrosa) is in the British Museum (*Add. MS. 18198*). This has large initials enclosing miniatures—with hardly any border-ornament—painted in soft tints of various colours, including blue and red, the backgrounds being of richly burnished gold. Other initials contain half-length figures of saints, painted on blue or lake grounds, with a little tracery in white, but the majority of the initials contain no figures; they are in blue or in red, and are surrounded by a sort of lace-work design, most elaborate, in red, blue, and white. The last-mentioned decoration was at the time very popular in Italy, and was sometimes extremely fine, as for example in the *Missale Pontificis* of the late fourteenth century, preserved in the British Museum (*Add. MS. 21973*).

Numerous collections in England, including the British Museum and the Victoria and Albert Museum, and in other countries, possess single leaves or historiated initials cut out from Italian *Libri Corali* of the fourteenth-sixteenth centuries; see, for instance, British Museum, *Add. MSS. 18196–97, 21412, 32058,* and *35254.*

Figures VI-16*b*, and 19 to 22 reproduce representative specimens of the thirteenth to the sixteenth centuries.

Law-books and Miscellanea. In the Universities of Bologna and Padua, numerous huge volumes were produced dealing with civil and canon law, many of them still surviving. Although some copies were sent out plain to be illuminated at their place of destination (see, for instance, p. 381), the majority were illuminated where they were written. With few exceptions, these MSS. were very coarsely executed.

A copy of the *Corpus Iuris*, illuminated by a Bolognese master shortly after 1300 is preserved in the Capitular Library, at Padua (*MS. C. 7*). A fourteenth-century *Infortiatum* (or middle part of the *Corpus Iuris*), vividly illuminated by another Bolognese master, is preserved in the Malatestian Library, at Cesena (*MS. S. IV. 2*).

[Gratian or Gratianus, born at Chiusi in Tuscany at the beginning of the twelfth century, spent the greater part of his life in a monastery at Bologna, but was also Professor at the University; he was the founder of the science of Canon Law and the author of *Concordia discordantium canonum* or *Decretum Gratiani*.] A fine illuminated copy of *Decretum Gratiani*, by various artists of the Bologna school, of the early fourteenth century, shows strong French influences (Pïana Library, Cesena, *MS. 3. 207*). A slightly later copy (first half of the fourteenth century), with thirty-seven miniatures and several decorated initials, is preserved in Florence (Laurentian Library, *MS. Edili 97*). The text is written in Bolognese hand, but the miniatures show characteristics of French style, and are considered French by Professor Salmi, whereas according to D'Ancona they are in the style of Oderisi da Gubbio. Similar style is seen in a copy of Gerard of Antwerp, *Abbreviatio figuralis historiae etc.* (Riccardiana Library, Florence, *MS. 1184 bis*). Here, too, Salmi regards the illuminations as French, whereas D'Ancona considers them Italian with strong French influences, and perhaps as the work of Oderisi da Gubbio. See also p. 304.

Fig. VI-23*b* reproduces fol. 1*r* from an early fourteenth-century copy of *Decretum Gratiani* executed in Bologna and now in Naples (National Library, *MS. XII. A. 1.*).

One of the finest works is a two-volume copy of *Decretum Gratiani*, of the second half of the fourteenth century, preserved in the British Museum (*Add. MSS. 15274–75*). The book contains thirty-six chapters, each being preceded by a miniature illustrating its subject-matter, and each beginning with a large initial enclosing a single figure (for instance, the first initial contains a scribe at work). The first half page contains a large picture of the Pope in council; the first page also contains a border beautifully decorated. On the whole, the miniatures are very richly coloured—vermilion and deep blue prevailing—and excellently executed.

We may also refer to an interesting codex of the fourteenth century preserved in the Capitular Library at Padua, the *Consuetudines feudorum*.

In some North Italian schools of illumination, books were produced in the early fourteenth century, allied in style to the coarse production of the law-books, and thus far from attractive. An interesting specimen of this art is a copy of Dante's *Divina Commedia* preserved in the British Museum (*Egerton MS., 943*).

An interesting *Apocalypse*, belonging to the fourteenth century and probably executed in the region of Piedmont, is preserved in the Laurentian Library,

Florence (*MS. Ashb. 415*). A richly illustrated copy, assigned to the same century, of Cecco d'Ascoli, *L'Acerba*, and of *Physionomia*, is preserved in the same collection (*MS. Plut. 40, 52*); it may have been produced in Padua. See Fig. VI-26*a* and *b*. There was no important school in Piedmont or Liguria; the few works extant are in provincial style. Instances are: a copy of *Statutes*, of *c.* 1360, in the Civic Museum at Turin, and the *Malabella Codex*, by various hands, in the Asti Municipal Library.

In Lombardy, under the Viscontis (late thirteenth- to mid-fifteenth century), the Gothic style influenced by French schools lasted longer than in any other Italian region; indeed, it dominated in Lombardy for about 150 years. Instances of the excellent work produced there in the first half of the fourteenth century are *MS. Lat. 4895* in the National Library at Paris and *MS. P. 165. sup.* in the Ambrosiana Library at Milan. A *Missal*, of *c.* 1350, influenced by Giotto, is in the Capitulary Library at Milan.

In the last quarter of the fourteenth century, the Milanese school of illumination reached a high degree of perfection. By then, in Paecht's opinion, the Milanese illuminators had found a solution of the problem of the relationship between miniature and script very similar to that of the 'Master of Mary of Burgundy' (see p. 431 ff.): indeed, the picture space in the miniatures of the Paris *Guizon* (National Library at Paris, *MS. fr. Nouv. Acqu. 5243*) 'is imagined as continuing behind the script, exactly as in the Madrid Hours of the Master of Mary of Burgundy' (Paecht)—see p. 434. A graduale for the Fraternità della Carità (Marciana Library, Venice, *MS. Lat. II–119*), executed in 1365, is already completely free from Byzantine influence.

Verona became in the fourteenth century an outstanding centre of illumination; indeed, already in the late thirteenth century important works were produced in this city (instances: *Cor. N. 742* and *1853* in the Communal Library at Verona). About 1368, seventeen *Chorales* were produced in the *bottega* of Turone (now in Capitulary Library at Verona, *MSS. 1048–65*).

Of particular interest are the curious MSS. *Tacuinum Sanitatis* or *Theatrum Sanitatis*, which are interesting for our study of the late fourteenth-century costumes: one such MS. is in the Kunsthistorisches Museum at Vienna; another in the National Library at Paris (*Nouv. Acq. Lat. 1673*); and a third in the Casanatense Library, Rome (*Cod. 4182*). Cod. 4182 contains, on fol. 1*r*, the portrait of the Arabian physician Elbukhasem in the act of teaching, and 207 nearly full-page miniatures representing scenes of daily life, hunting, fishing, interiors of houses and shops, gardens, castles, fields, etc. The text, of Arabic origin, consists in captions to the miniatures, which describe the plants and their medical characteristics, food and drinks, the influence of the seasons, the spiritual and physical activities of man, hygienic rules to preserve health, and so on. Of similar interest is a small book of drawings made by Giovannino de' Grassi, and preserved in the Civic Library at Bergamo (*Cod. D. VII. 14*). Apart from this *Tacuinum*, Giovannino executed before 1395 a *Book of Hours* for Gian Galeazzo Visconti (now preserved in the collection of the Dukes Visconti di Modrone). Moreover, he and his son worked on the magnificent *Book of Hours* of Filippo Maria Visconti (known as the *Visconti Officium*) preserved in the National Library at Florence (*Fondo Landau Finaly MS. 22*), which was continued by Belbello (see p. 346 f.) : Fig. VI-40. Giovannino, who died in 1398, was the greatest illuminator of Lombardy in the late fourteenth century. With this style, Lombard art became fashionable not only in Italy, but also in France where it was called *ouvrage de Lombardie.*

Various cities and towns of North Italy had their illuminators: Giovanni di Benedetto da Como executed an *Uffiziolo* (State Library at Munich, *Cod. Lat. 23215*); Fra Pietro da Pavia illuminated a copy of Pliny (Ambrosiana Library, *E. 24. inf.*); Anovelo da Imbonate made a *Missal* for Gian Galeazzo Visconti (Basilica di S. Ambrogio, Milan): Fig. VI-25b; he also executed a *Missal*, now in Milan Capitulary Library, a *Book of Hours* (now in the Estense Library, *MS. α. R. 7.3 : Lat. 842*), and a copy of Lancelot du Lac (see p. 381) preserved in the National Library at Paris (*Fr. 343*). Giovannino de' Grassi has already been referred to.

Naturalistic Borders. In the late fourteenth century, some skilled North-Italian illuminators introduced—or perhaps re-introduced—the naturalistic border. The Lombard monk, Pietro da Pavia, used the abstract Gothic scrolls of the French type (see p. 324), but added to them all kinds of naturalistic foliage and other naturalistic elements such as insects: this decoration is adopted in Pietro's copy of Pliny, *Naturalis Historia*, 1389.

Another excellent work in naturalistic style is *Historia Plantorum* (Casanatense Library, Rome, *MS. 459*); it is an encyclopaedia of natural history applied to hygiene; it was executed by various hands, including one extremely refined. Also the *Tacuinum Sanitatis*, referred to above, belongs to this *genre*, but it may be distinguished into two classes, (1) scientific (the Vienna copy), and (2) popular (the copies in Rome and Paris).

Another late fourteenth-century North Italian MS., preserved in British Museum fragments (*Add. MSS. 27695, 28841*, and *Egerton MS. 3127*), will be dealt with under *Cybo the Monk of Hyères*: see p. 320. The naturalistic borders of this MS.—writes Paecht—display a variety of insects or other zoological specimens freely arranged in the margins of the page and in the intervals between the columns of the script. Perhaps the most astonishing of these frames is a border composed exclusively of shells and crustaceans with nothing to link them but the blue colour of the sea with which the margins of the page are tinted. These shells, crabs and lobsters lie and crawl about in no apparent order, casually strewn over the blue foil of the border. It looks—concludes Paecht—as if an artist's sketchbook, full of nature studies, had been emptied on to the pages of a book to fill the space left free by the scribe. See also p. 320.

Byzantine Influence (see p. 304 f.) continued to be felt particularly strongly in book-illumination. Indeed, evidence of this influence may be seen in a *Benedictine*

Italian Naturalistic MS. (*B.M. Add. MS. 28841*), fol. *5r*.

Breviary of the British Museum (*Add. MSS. 15205–06*). The small miniatures enclosed within the initials, according to Herbert, are of course Byzantine in their iconography. But the same influence is apparent here in the subdued colouring, the pose of the figures and the treatment of the faces. The gold nimbi and backgrounds are covered with raised patterns of dots and lines.

Bologna School

Byzantine influence may be seen particularly strong in a few great Bibles, of excellent production, which are assigned to a Bologna school of the early fourteenth century. The main characteristic of this Italo-Byzantine style is the treatment of the figures—the stately pose, the fine modelling of limbs and draperies, the soft, subdued, almost sombre colouring, and the swarthy faces with white highlights and greenish shadows. The Bibles belonging to this group are preserved in the Vatican Library (*Vat. Lat. 20*), in Turin (the *Franciscan Bible*: *MS. D. i. 13*), in the British Museum (*Add. MS. 18720*), in the ex-Yates Thompson Collection (the *Bentivoglio Bible*: *MS. No. 4*), and in the National Library at Paris (*Lat. 18*) where, according to an authority, the figure-compositions and borders are not only effective in themselves, but are controlled by a nice sense of the due proportions between text and illumination—a rare quality in fourteenth-century Italian manuscripts.

In these works other influences have been suggested. For instance, *Add. MS. 18720* in the main outlines of its scheme of decoration seems to follow the pattern of the thirteenth-century French and English Bibles: the series representing the Days of Creation, at the beginning of *Genesis*, the Jesse-tree prefixed to *S. Matthew*, and the historiated initials to the other books, are each set in a tall narrow frame. Human figures are sometimes used as terminals or supports to the stems which form the framework; the first page contains a graceful, exquisitely modelled, nude youth as well as two Dominican friars (at the foot of the page). The borders are less subdued in tint than the miniatures—they brighten up the pages most effectively—and are of the light and pleasing type characteristic of Italian fourteenth-century illumination.

Many other fourteenth-century illuminated codices were executed by artists of the Bologna school; some of them have already been referred to (see p. 313 f.): a few *Antiphonaries* preserved in the Civic Museum at Bologna (*Cor. 13, 15, 24*); two *Graduals* in Modena (Estense Library, *MSS. α. Q. 1. 4: Lat. 1016* and *R. 1. 6: Lat. 1021*); several *Bibles*, illuminated by various artists (Capitulary Library at Albenga; Badia Library, Cava dei Tirreni, *MS. membr. 33*; National Library at Naples, *MS. VI. A. 5*; and others); *Law-books* (see also p. 313 f.), such as Justinian's *Institutions*, and *miscellanea* (Capitulary Library at Padua, *MS. C. 7*, and Malatestiana Library, Cesena, *MS. S. IV. 1*), copies of *Decretum Gratiani* (National Library, at Naples, *MS. XII. A. 1.*, and Marciana Library, Venice, *MS. Lat. Z. 175: 1599*); Papal *Decretals* and *Constitutions*: Gregory IX's *Decretals* (National Library at Naples, *MS. XII. A. 2*), Clement V's *Constitutions* (Marciana Library,

Venice, *MS. Lat. Z. 186: 1603*; Capitulary Library at Padua, *MS. A. 25*), Boniface VIII's *Decretals* (Capitulary Library at Atri, *MS. A. 17*; Capitulary Library at Padua, *MS. A. 24*); *Statutes of Guilds*, and similar documents (Civic Museum at Bologna, *Nos. 85, 86, 93*, etc.; State Archives, Bologna; a copy of *Capitoli della Pia e Devota confraternita e compagnia de tutti gli Manefatori delle Arte de Revedini e Purgatori della cita de Bologna*, of 1 August, 1569, is on sale (L. Gonnelli & Figli, Florence, *Catal. 20-6-1963*)); literary MSS. (Riccardiana Library, Florence, *MS. 1538* and *MS. 237*; Angelica Library, Rome, *MS. 1102*, and other codices). See for instance, Fig. VI-23*b* and 25*a*.

French influences may be seen in various fourteenth-century productions of the Bologna school of illumination. An excellent example is a copy of Pope Gregory IX's *Decretals*, preserved in the Marciana Library, Venice (*MS. Lat. Z. 177: 1478*).

For over 150 years Bologna was the main Italian centre of illuminated book-production. Even as late as the early fifteenth century the Ferrara school of Antonio Alberti and the Gubbio school of Ottaviano Nelli were under the influence of Bologna.

Illuminators

We know the names of a few illuminators who worked in Bologna, but it will suffice to refer to Franco Bolognese—of whom Dante says that he will outshine the glory of Oderisi da Gubbio (*Purg.* 11, 83 f.)—and Niccolò di Giacomo di Nascimbene, known as Niccolò da Bologna (*c.* 1330–1401). Franco Bolognese, a follower of Giotto, was active *c.* 1310; various works (including Estense Library *MS. α. R. 1. 6*) are attributed to him. About 1330–40 the Bologna school of Vitale degli Equi arose, which produced excellent works, such as the copy of Justinianus, *Infortiatum*, preserved in Cesena (Malatestiana Library, *MS. s. IV. 2*).

Niccolò da Bologna. Throughout the second half of the fourteenth century, Niccolò produced in Bologna a great number of illuminated books such as law-books, membership-books of trade-guilds and similar documents (such as the *Book of the Creditors* of the Public Pawn-shop in Bologna, executed in 1394; it is preserved in the State Archives at Bologna), as well as *Antiphonaries* (Estense Library, Modena, *MSS. α. R. 1. 8: Lat. 1013*; and *P. 1. 7: Lat. 1002*; also in the Civic Museum at Bologna), *Missals* (such as *MS. Lat. III. 97: 2115* in the Marciana Library, Venice) and literary works, such as Lucan, *De bello Pharsalico* (Trivulzio Library, Milan, *MS. 691*) and Seneca, *Tragedies* (Marciana Library, Venice, *MS. Lat. XII. 26: 3906*). These books are not first class, but are important because many of them contain the signature of the artist. See Fig. VI-23*a*.

Fig. VI-24*a* represents fol. 39*v* from *Ordo Missae* (Pierpont Morgan Library, New York, *M. 800*): it is a Crucifixion, signed by Niccolò. The MS. also contains eighteen historiated initials. An interesting copy of the Italian translation of Klimax (see p. 106) is preserved in the Walters Art Gallery (*W. 157*). It contains a historiated border and an initial with the 'portrait' of the author: Fig.

VI-24b. It is by a painter 'of unusual ability', who tentatively has been identified with Niccolò. Of the various *Chorales* executed for S. Michele in Bosco (Bologna), now in the Estense Library, Modena, one—marked *MS. Lat. 1008*—is signed and dated 1351.

Two historiated initials cut from an *Antiphonary*, and illuminated by Niccolò, are preserved in the Fitzwilliam Museum, Cambridge (*MS. 278*). They contain the signature *nicholaus de bononia fecit*. Also in the Fitzwilliam Museum there is a leaf from the *Decretals of Gregory IX* attributed to Niccolò (*MS. 331*). An excellent specimen attributed to the same school is preserved in the British Museum (*Add. MS. 23923*): it is a copy of the *Decretals of Boniface VIII*, written between 1370 and 1381—see also p. 318.

Niccolò also executed an excellent copy of Pope Gregory IX's *Decretals* now in the Ambrosian Library, Milan (*Cod. B. 42. inf.*). To an artist of Niccolò di Giacomo's workshop are attributed several miniatures in an interesting *Book of Hours* (or *Officium B. Mariae Virginis*) and *miscellanea*, executed in the fourteenth century by artists of the Emilian school of illumination (Communal Library at Forlì, *MS. 853*).

Niccolò's works were influenced by the Florentine school of Orcagna, by the Rimini school of painting, and by the Bolognese school of Vitale degli Equi (see p. 318). The influence of the last is particularly noticeable in several products of Niccolò's school, exemplified by a copy of *Decretals* of Boniface VIII (Vatican Library, *Palat. Lat. 636*).

Some illuminated codices are attributed to a Pseudo-Niccolò or else to assistants, pupils, or followers of Niccolò: they include a copy of John de Lignano and John Calderinus (University Library at Cagliari, *MS. 2*); a *Roman Missal* (Marciana Library, Venice, *MS. Lat. III, 48: 2291*); a copy of Dante, *Divina Commedia* (Augusta Library, Perugia, *MS. B. 25*); membership-books of trade-guilds (Civic Museum at Bologna, *MSS. 87, 89, 92, 93*); and other works (*MS. 90* in the Civic Museum at Bologna; *MS. 510* in the Angelica Library, Rome). Niccolò's main followers were his son Onofrio, Stefano Azzi, and the Dominican Antonio da Bologna.

Pseudo-Niccolò, whose style was very similar to that of Niccolò, was a skilful artist active from 1340 onwards. Various works are attributed to him; they include the *Decretals Vat. Lat. 1389*; the *Decretum Gratiani Vat. Lat. 1366*; a copy of *Decretals* of Boniface VIII and a copy of *Constitutions* of Clement V. (Capitulary Archives at Padua, *A. 24* and *25*); and a *Missal* of 1346-50 preserved in the Capitulary Archives of S. Peter in Rome (*MS. 63 b*). The last one proves that Bolognese illumination—which spread to Central and Western Europe—also penetrated the Papal *curia*. Part of the *S. Peter Missal* seems to have been executed by Niccolò himself.

Bolognese Unidentified Master. In the late fourteenth and early fifteenth centuries an important Italian artist—not yet identified—worked at Bologna and in France. Dr. Otto Paecht has tried to reconstruct this anonymous artistic personality. Only two of his works can be dated, the historiated initials in the *Brussels Horae* of the Duke of Berry (Royal Library, Brussels, *Cod. 11060–61*), executed before 1401, and a miniature in the book of *Statutes of the Compagnia dello Spedale di Santa Maria della Vita*, dated 1408 (Archiginnasio Library, Bologna, *Deposito Ammin. Osped., Cod. 4*).

British Museum *Add. MS. 34427* was produced by the same artist in Bologna, whereas various works executed in France or for French patrons have been preserved, including four interesting *Books of Hours* (British Museum, *Add. MS. 29433*; Bodleian Library, Oxford, *MS. Douce 62*; Chester Beatty Library, Dublin, *MS. 84*; Palacio Library, Madrid, *MS. 2099*). Paecht refers particularly to the Calendar-pictures of the Chester Beatty *Book of Hours*, which are framed by borders entirely different from the conventional Gothic ivy-leaf scrolls and are freely composed of naturalistic foliage (strawberries, etc.) arranged with a minimum of formal rhythm. They thus—argues Paecht—introduce the proto-naturalistic landscape of the Upper Italian Trecento (*Tacuinum Sanitatis*) into the North, and therefore form a link between Pietro da Pavia (see p. 316) and the columbine border of the Brothers Limbourg (see p. 411 f.).

Other Schools

Neri da Rimini: various works are known to have been illuminated in the early fourteenth century by this artist. A single leaf from a *Chorale* preserved in Venice (Count Cini Collection) is dated 1300. A richly illuminated *Antiphonary*, in three volumes of the early fourteenth century, was executed for the Faenza Cathedral and is still preserved in Faenza (Capitulary Archives, *Cor. II*). Other works of his are: *Chorales* in the Bologna Civic Museum (*No. 20*) and in the Fava Church, Venice, and part of a *Commentary on the Four Gospels* (Vatican Library, *Urb. Lat. 11*).

In the second half of the fourteenth century other schools were active in the Romagna and Emilia regions. A follower of Vitale, Simone dei Crocefissi, probably illuminated a copy of Dante now in the Angelica Library at Rome (*MS. 1102*). Part of an *Officium of the Virgin* (Communal Library at Forlì, *MS. 853*) was executed by an artist influenced by Emilian Romanesque sculpture. Another school produced a charming copy of S. Bonaventura, *Legenda Maior S. Francisci* (National Library at Rome, *MS. Vitt. Eman. 411*).

Cybo the Monk of Hyères. Three interesting MS. fragments in the British Museum (*Add. MSS. 27695* and *28841*, and *Egerton MS. 3127*) are attributed to a certain Cybo, the Monk of Hyères (late fourteenth century), a miniaturist from Genoa. The MSS. contain large miniatures (illustrating the text) not always beautiful, but the margins and line-endings of the pages are covered with drawings of various animals, birds, insects, and plants, painted with such fidelity that, for instance, his spiders, bees, grasshoppers, and stag-beetles seem to be positively starting out of the page. The miniatures show marked Oriental influence. Herbert states that it is hard to find a parallel nearer to Cybo's date than the Flemish miniaturists a hundred years later; 'and even their work seems tame and flat in comparison.' See also p. 315 f.

The fragments belong to the same book, which in R. Flower's opinion (*Brit. Mus. Quart.*, VIII-4; No. 105) contained two Latin texts, analogous in subject, but different in form, one (*MSS. 27695* and *Egert. MS.*) being in prose and the other in "loose rhythmical verse". The prose text is a treatise *On the Vices* by a Cocharelli from Genoa, and the verse treatise, also by a Cocharelli deals with the history of Sicily in the time of Frederick II (1298–1337). Also the decoration scheme of the two parts is different. The prose section contains full-page illustrations of the text; and most of the text pages are framed in borders of decorative work, with roundels containing figures and little scenes, animals, insects, birds, and grotesques; a gold line separates the borders from the text; animals, birds, and insects are represented in the line fillings. The border of the other section is not contained within a formal frame; there are branching sprays with leafage and fruit, breaking out in between the lines of the text at irregular intervals, even extending across the whole breadth of the column. Drawings of insects, shells, and animals (but not birds) are interspersed throughout the borders and in the line-fillings. R. Flowers also emphasizes that the attribution of the illumination to Cybo—"a somewhat shadowy figure"—is far from certain; at any rate, we have here the production of a Ligurian school of miniature, "which does not appear to be elsewhere attested."

Umbria, Rome, and South Italy

Umbria had no important school. A thirteenth-century *Missal* (Perugia Capitulary Library, *No. 6*) written in Palestine, was illuminated in Perugia in Byzantine style: Fig. VI-23c. In the fourteenth century, Perugia production was under Sienese influence. Instances are: *Antiphonary Cor. G. 8* in the Augusta Library, Perugia; *MSS. 1* and *2* in the Collegio della Mercanzia, Perugia; a *Psalter* in Monte Oliveto Maggiore (*Cor. F.*); and a detached leaf of a *Matricola* in the Cini Collection, Venice. Matteo di Ser Cambio, who painted the *Statuta et Matricula Artis Cambii* (Collegio del Cambio, Perugia, *MS. I.*), was the only outstanding illuminator of Perugia.

A much later codex—belonging to the fifteenth century—is still in the early style: it is the *Statuto dell'Arte dei Notari*, of Perugia, preserved in the Augusta Library, at Perugia (*MS. 973*): it contains interesting miniatures of the fourteenth century "Court of Justice" of Perugia, of the procession of notaries, and so on.

Nor did *Rome* have a great school in the late thirteenth and early fourteenth centuries, but several good works were produced there. Instances are an *Exultet* (see p. 297 ff.) in codex form (Capitulary Archives of S. Peter, *MS. B. 78*) and a *Bible* preserved in the Catania Civic Library (*MS. A. 72*).

South Italy. The Court school of Frederick II and Manfred has been referred to on p. 309 f. Under the Anjou dynasty a new style arose, influenced by the Bologna school as well as by Byzantine and French styles. Instances are: *Missal MS. I. B. 22* in the National Library at Naples; a *Pontifical* in Salerno Cathedral; and *Bible MS. 33* in the Badia Archives at Cava dei Tirreni. A Copy of Boëthius (National

Library at Naples, *MS. V. A-14*) is an outstanding product of the Court school. The codex has a fine frontispiece, possibly influenced by Sienese style. Christopher Orimina of Naples illuminated the *Bible of King Robert of Anjou*, 1309–43 (now in the Library of Malines Seminary). *Statut de S. Esprit* (National Library at Paris, *MS. Fr. 4274*) is a later example of the aulic style—the Order of the Holy Ghost was founded in 1356 by Louis of Taranto, husband of Queen Joan.

Naples had also an independent school, which produced excellent secular MSS., such as a copy of Dante (Gerolamini Library, Naples, *MS. C. F. 20*) and of Seneca, *Tragedies* (ibidem, *MS. C. F. 4.5*). The Neapolitan school continued in the fifteenth century (exemplified by a copy of Boniface of Calabria in the Gerolamini Library, Naples, *MS. C. F. 4.10*) and influenced schools in Rome and Abruzzo. Instance of the former: S. Bernard, *Expositio super Cantica Canticorum* (Casanatense Library, Rome, *MS. 970*); instance of the latter: an *Antiphonary* illuminated by Bernardo da Teramo; a detached leaf signed by him is preserved in the Cini Collection, Venice. A *Beneventan Missal* (Benevento Capitulary Library, *MS. 527*) also shows Neapolitan influence.

The *Cava Scriptorium* was particularly active under Abbot Philip de Haya (1316–31); there were then produced excellent MSS., including *Rationale Duranti* (British Museum, *MS. 31032*) and Vincentius Bellovacensis, *Speculum historiale* (Cava Badia Archives, *MS. Membr. 26*). Under Abbot Ranieri (1341–66), the Cava products were in the Anjou Court-style; instances are: Convenevole Pratensis, *Ad Robertum Siciliae Regum* (National Library at Florence, *MS. B. R. 38*). A mid-fourteenth-century *Bible of Abbot Matteo de Planisio*, written by a priest Giorgio da Napoli, is in the Vatican Library (*Vat. Lat. 2550*). Allied in style are: a copy of Dante (British Museum, *Add. MS. 19587*); a *Bible* in Turin (ex-Royal Library, *MSS. vari 175*); and a *Franciscan Breviary* in Madrid (National Library, *N. 6.68*). Of particular interest is the *Hamilton Bible* (Copper Engravings Cabinet, *f. 4*, Berlin).

RENAISSANCE

The intellectual, moral, spiritual, and artistic re-birth of Europe, the revival of ancient classical influences, the rise of a new impulse in culture, in literature and art, the emancipation of the soul of Western humanity from the bondage of scholasticism and, at least in part, of the authority of dictatorial theology: in a word, the 'Renaissance', arose in Italy—to be more precise, in Florence—in the early part of the fifteenth century. About the middle of the century, and in its latter part, the seeds of this new flowering were carried into many countries of Europe, resulting in reforms in religion, literature and art, and the discovery of new lands.

The remark which the great Michelangelo passed upon a medal by Grechetto—that the hour for the death of art had arrived, since it was not possible for a better work of its kind to be done—was true, as has been pointed out, of the whole range of decorative art of that time. It was the age of della Francesca (*c.* 1416–92), Mantegna (1431–1506), Giovanni (*c.* 1428–1516) and Gentile Bellini (*c.* 1426–1507), Botticelli (1444–1510), A. Pollaiuolo (1432–98), Verrocchio (1435–88),

Rosselli (1438–1507), Signorelli (1441–1523), Perugino (*c.* 1450–1523), Ghirlandaio (1449–94), Francia (1450–1517), di Credi (1457–1537), di Cosimo (1462–1521), Giorgione (1477–1510), Titian (1477–1576), del Sarto (1486–1531), Correggio (1489–1534), the three giants, Leonardo da Vinci (1452–1519), Michelangelo (1475–1564), and Raphael (1483–1520), and many other divine artists. It was a moment of history, one of the very rare moments, when formative art found itself endowed with the living gift of perfect utterance and was enabled to flower into that special form which no succeeding age has been able to surpass, or, in its own kind, even to equal. In that great period it was impossible that the making of books, including illumination and bookbinding, should not attain its full artistic development, and at the outset we might naturally have expected to find Italian illumination at its zenith.

As a matter of fact, however, Italy failed to reach in illumination a pre-eminence commensurate with that which she achieved in panel-painting and in other art manifestations. Indeed, in the first half of the fifteenth century, Italian illumination does not reach the sublime height of the French, Burgundian, and Flemish schools. In the latter half it reaches its apogee, producing perfectly superb work, but it still does not surpass Burgundian and Flemish illumination. And finally in the sixteenth century—though some good products still come from Italian ateliers—Italian book-illumination is in gradual but final decadence. Having said all this, we have to make clear that throughout the Italian Renaissance numerous superb works were produced.

Main Characteristics of Renaissance Illumination

The eminent art-historian W. Oakeshott aptly describes the transformation of book-illumination in the Renaissance period. The medieval artists were playing with engaging superficialities: the figures they draw have a childlike air of simplicity about them; there is no hint of mature emotion working below the surface. In the Renaissance period the medieval, pretty, but unreal creatures became men and women of flesh and blood; the modelling of flesh became three-dimensional; the medieval censorship of nakedness was discarded. There was the awareness of the body as something beautiful; the new treatment of flesh makes it seem alive, and there is a new understanding of human feeling, of sorrow, of pity, of joy, of awe, of humility or of pride, these feelings being not those of children but of adults. All this comes from the Renaissance; at the same time, however, the artists of the Renaissance inherited from their medieval predecessors grace, simplicity and faith.

With the Renaissance, illumination of manuscripts became a branch of true art, cultivated especially in the splendid courts of the kings and ruling dukes, who seemed to vie with one another for the enlargement of their libraries with luxurious MSS. A detailed study of the ornamentation of these MSS. really belongs to the history of art, but to complete the treatment of the medieval codex, we must include some account of this special art, which marks the zenith of the hand-produced book. As for Italy, we shall limit our attention to the most famous centres.

One of the most distinctive features of Renaissance book-painting is the decorative framework. This—as Dr. Paecht, a leading authority in this field, points out—has to form a transition from the miniature with its three-dimensional space construction to the flatness of the empty ground of the page. It is a kind of neutral zone which camouflages the antagonism between the part of the page which is imaginary space and the other which is plain surface or flat substratum of script. But, argues Paecht, though the miniaturists of this period, by skilful decorative planning, often succeeded in giving the page a superficial aesthetic unity, they failed to overcome the fundamental divergence and to solve the inner conflict between the conception of the book-page as a primarily planimetric organism and its treatment as an opening into a recession of depth.

In the French and Flemish ateliers, for instance, this decorative framework is mainly 'a foundation of calligraphic spiral work, enlivened by slender acanthus scrolls and some naturalistic foliage and other floreate motifs' (Paecht). In the best work, the earlier productions of the 'Master of Mary of Burgundy' (see p. 431 ff.), the borders, emphasizes Paecht, have the appearance of a rather thinly woven light network with the heavier interludes of flamboyant acanthus ribbons concentrated in the corners. More common in contemporary illumination is another variety of framework, a heavier, densely woven frieze strongly reminiscent in its pattern of tapestry design. Furthermore, in Paecht's opinion, the 'Master of Mary of Burgundy' introduced a radical change in the border-decoration and thus altered the relationship of both miniature and frame to the page—see p. 433 f. Thus, 'book-painting obtained a new lease of life' (Paecht).

In the earliest Renaissance books, which are generally of humanistic contents, only the first leaf is illuminated. This is ornamented with decorated margins similar in style to certain Romanesque initials, which humanists regarded as belonging to Classical antiquity. An interesting instance is *MS. 484* in the Riccardiana Library at Florence. Similar ornamentation was later used in the *incunabula*.

On the whole, the course of development and decay of Renaissance illumination was much the same in any of the great centres of Italian art, though this course cannot as a rule be followed step by step either for lack of material or of precise data with regard to the abundant material which has come down to us. At the same time, there were of course great varieties of style due to the special circumstances of a local school or the individual genius of a great master or the requirements and the artistic tendencies of the patrons (the Medici in Florence, the Este in Ferrara, the Sforza in Pesaro, Pavia and Milan, the Popes (from Eugenius IV to Sixtus IV) in Rome, Federico de Montefeltro in Urbino, the Aragonese kings in Naples) which often differed considerably. This short list of Italian patrons has to be supplemented with several names of foreign personages, such as Matthias Corvinus, King of Hungary, John II, King of Portugal, the English Thomas James, and others.

Finally, it must be borne in mind that the florescence was general, and it is not always easy to distinguish the different local schools. Some leading artists moved about from place to place fulfilling particular commissions. Moreover, while many of their names are preserved in records, there is the usual difficulty in identifying their work in preserved manuscripts; besides, very few illuminators had the habit of signing their productions. And when by fortunate coincidence the records specify individual manuscripts, including such MSS. as are still preserved, they often connect them with the names of several artists without indication of the precise parts executed by any one of them.

Florence

It is a curious fact that the art of illumination practised in Florence, the great home of all the arts, had no great importance before the fourteenth century; an Italian leading scholar, D'Ancona, mentions only five extant codices for the twelfth century and nine for the thirteenth century. In the fourteenth century, however, illuminated codices became more numerous and more varied. In the fifteenth century, when Florence became the cradle of the Renaissance, it also became one of the most important centres of book-illumination; but very little is known of the history of Florentine illumination in the early fifteenth century.

The origins of Renaissance illumination are partly connected with calligraphic developments and with the revival of the style of script and decoration of the eleventh and twelfth centuries. Early examples of this art are a copy of *Valerius Flaccus*, written in Florence in 1429, and a copy of *Justinus*, executed in Verona (North Italy) in 1433, now in the British Museum (*Add. MS. 12012*).

In the course of time, the famous Renaissance border-illumination developed. This was in a rectangular frame consisting of narrow gold bands and containing interlaced scrolls of white vine-tendrils usually painted on grounds of alternating blue, green, and crimson, with *putti*; various animals, such as rabbits, and birds; and medallions enclosed in wreaths of close-set foliage. There were sometimes figure-compositions, heraldic or symbolical designs, or busts copied from antique gems.

The main illuminated productions were Bibles, Missals (such as *Cod. Conv. Soppr. 233* in the Laurentian Library, Florence), Hymnals (such as *Cod. II. I. 122*, in the National Library at Florence), as well as some secular books, such as Dante's *Divine Comedy* (for instance, *Cod. 1080* in the Trivulzio Library, Milan). A charming secular cod., preserved in the Laurentian Library, Florence (*MS. Med. Pal. 87*), the *Squarcialupi Codex* see p. 326, contains beautiful initials and borders. One initial represents the composer Giovanni da Cascia (first half of the fourteenth century), apparently the initiator of the Florentine *ars nova*, the new style of composing. The same page gives the words and the musical notes of Giovanni's song *Agnel son bianco e vo belando*.

An interesting *Missal* (*Messale Borgia*), executed by the Florentine school of the late fifteenth century—for Card. Giovanni Borgia—is preserved in the Capitular Library of the Chieti Cathedral. It contains a miniature representing Pope Alexander VI consecrating a cardinal in the presence of other cardinals.

Earliest Schools. In the second half of the fourteenth century a famous school of religious artists arose in the convent of S. Maria degli Angeli. At its head were famous painters, such as Don Simone Camaldolese (active 1381–c. 1426) and Don Lorenzo Monaco, the famous Sienese painter (1370–c. 1425). Of the two, Don Lorenzo was by far the more gifted. The school was particularly influenced by 'l'Orcagna' and his brothers, and also by Bernardo Daddi.

The superb *Gradual*, completed on the 26 January 1370 and now preserved in the Laurentian Library, Florence (*Cor. 2*), is one of the earliest products of the degli Angeli school. Several works are attributed to Don Simone Camaldolese—particularly *Antiphonaries* (S. Marco Museum, Florence, *Cor. Q.*; Laurentian Library, Florence, *Cor. 37–41*) and *Graduals* (such as *Cor. 33* in the Civic Museum at Bologna). Other productions are attributed to Don Simone Camaldolese's assistants, pupils, or followers: *Antiphonaries* (Laurentian Library, Florence, *Cor. 8*; S. Marco Museum, Florence, *Cor. V*), *Graduals* (such as S. Marco Museum, Florence, *Cor. B.*), the fifteenth-century richly decorated *Squarcialupi Codex* containing old Italian songs (Laurentian Library, Florence, *MS. Med. Pal. 87*), a copy of Francesco da Buti's *Commentary* to the *Divina Commedia* (Riccardiana Library, *MS. 1008*), and a few others. See Fig. VI-21*a* and *c*.

Lorenzo Monaco executed, or collaborated in, the illumination of the following codices: a copy of the *Diurno Domenicale*, preserved in the Laurentian Library (*Cor. 3*), the *Antiphonary*, preserved in the same collection (*Cor. 5*); the *Gradual*, preserved in the National Museum at Florence (*Cor. H.*); an *Antiphonary* (*Cod. A. 69*) and the *Commune Sanctorum* (*Cod. E. 70*), both also preserved in the National Museum: Fig. VI-21*b* and *d*, and 28*a* (see also below). See also p. 328.

A *Gradual* preserved in the Civic Museum at Bologna (*Cor. 30*) is attributed to a Florentine school connected with Agnolo Gaddi. An *Antiphonary* in the S. Marco Museum (*Cor. s. s.*), containing five large initials decorated with various scenes, animals, foliage etc. was executed by a certain Bartolomeo di Fruosino, a pupil of Agnolo Gaddi.

Other excellent productions in fifteenth-century Florentine late Gothic style are found in the following collections: an *Antiphonary* in the S. Marco Museum (*Cor. L. E.*); a *Breviary* in the Laurentian Library (*MS. Conv. Soppr. 457*); a copy of *Vaticinia Pontificum* in a miscellanea volume in the Riccardiana Library (*MS. 1192*); a copy of S. Francis of Assisi in the Laurentian Library (*MS. Gadd. 112*); a copy of S. Augustine, *City of God* in the National Library at Florence (*MS. II. I. 112*); a copy of Dante in the same collection (*MS. B.R. 215: Palat. 320*); a codex of Dante and miscellanea in the Riccardiana Library, Florence (*MS. 1040*). See Fig. VI-27*a* and *b*.

About the mid-fifteenth century Renaissance illumination entered on its most brilliant period, but a *Roman Missal*, executed in 1457 in or near Florence for the abbess of Rosano (Diocese of Fiesole), Sandra, the daughter of Giovanni Cianchini of Gavignano, still presents a transitional character, and in certain respects it marks the chronological limits of the pre-Renaissance tradition. Its only full-page miniature (a Crucifixion prefixed to the Canon) is crude, 'but the initial and border decorations are simple and effective, especially on the opening page of the Temporale (f. 7), where they form a pleasing harmony in pale blue, pale green, and burnished gold' (Herbert).

Medici. If the origins of the Renaissance could be connected with any family-name, that of the Medici—the wealthy and liberal merchants and bankers, and later the splendid rulers, of Florence—would have to be chosen for this great honour. Cosimo de' Medici (1389–1464), the 'uncrowned king of Florence', the friend and patron of the Italian humanists, may almost be styled the foster-father of the revival of learning. His grandson Lorenzo 'the Magnificent' (1448–92) was a distinguished scholar and poet, and one of the greatest patrons of art of all times and lands. His collection of MSS. and books—which became the famous Laurentian Library—of pictures and *objets d'art* was one of the finest in Europe.

Two British Museum MSS. (*Add. MS. 25697* and *Harley MS. 5761*) containing the Medici arms were perhaps made for Lorenzo, but they are not first-class productions. They are small books and contain characteristically Florentine border-ornament, rich in rayed discs, painted on the plain vellum. *Add. MS. 25697* is a *Breviary*; *Harley 5761* is a *Petrarch*. The latter has also tiny vignette miniatures at the foot of the pages representing the Triumphs in 'a sketchy, but skilful and effective manner' (Herbert). Much more beautiful is the *Lorenzo Book of Hours* (see below).

Contemporary productions, executed for other private individuals and for churches, are often of great artistic value. The *Smeralda Horae* was made in Florence after 1472 for a lady named Smeralda: the half-length portrait of a fair-haired girl, which appears on almost all the illuminated pages, evidently represents this lady. The book has a beautiful border-decoration in brilliant colouring, consisting mainly of arabesques in dead gold on blue, green, or crimson grounds, enclosed in a rectangular frame.

A good example of excellent Renaissance work made for a monastery is the late-fifteenth century *Breviary* of the S. Croce Franciscan monastery in Florence, now preserved in the British Museum (*Add. MS. 29735*). In its decoration two styles may be recognized: (*a*) the lighter and more graceful one of the borders and figure-initials, which appear throughout the book (including the interesting miniature of fol. 127*v* showing the miracle of the Invention of the Cross); and (*b*) a more sumptuous type which appears on fol. 7*r*, the most elaborate page in the book; it is the opening page of the Temporale—the grounds are crimson, blue and green; the side borders consist of arabesques interrupted by half-length figures of saints set in richly jewelled medallions; the lower border is filled by a miniature of the Annunciation, which is very carefully painted and has a stylistic resemblance to panels by Lorenzo di Credi. An excellent example of the late Quattrocento Florentine school is a *Borgia Missal* (Capitul. Library of the Chieti Cathedral), produced for Cardinal Giovanni Borgia. An interesting miniature shows the famous pope Alexander VI Borgia creating a cardinal.

'*Botteghe*'. The famous *botteghe* (or 'shops') of the great stationers—a characteristic institution of Renaissance Florence—became important meeting places for humanists and *dilettanti* in books. The most famous of these *botteghe* was that of Vespasiano da Bisticci (1421–98), amongst whose customers were the dukes of Urbino (see p. 353 ff.), the kings of Aragon and Naples (see p. 356 ff.), Corvinus (1443–90), king of Hungary—see also pp. 330 f. and 363—and especially the Medici. Vespasiano mentions that, on the order of Cosimo de' Medici, he prepared 200 codices for the Badia Fiesolana (near Florence); these codices were written in twenty-two months by forty-five copyists. From the elegant writing and tasteful illumination one would not guess the speed with which these manuscripts were written and illuminated.

Whilst Bolognese book-production was mainly concerned with law-books, in Florence books dealing with the history of thought, classics and science predominated.

Great Masters of Illumination. One of the earliest of the great Florentine painters who is said to have practised book-illumination is Fra Giovanni Angelico (1387–1455), or Beato Angelico, from Fiesole, the Dominican painter whose works include the remarkable series of frescoes of S. Marco in Florence. He has actually been credited with the illumination of some choir-books now preserved in the S. Marco Museum, and he exercised great influence on Florentine art.

Indeed, the influence of Fra Angelico upon contemporary Florentine illuminators is evident, for instance, in a miniature representing the Virgin surrounded by Angels, on a detached leaf from an *Antiphonary* (Cleveland Museum of Art, *No. 28652*). This influence is revealed, as Miss Dorothy Miner points out, by the conservative composition, the fresh but delicate colouring with almost imperceptible modelling and the gentle charm of the figures.

Moreover, according to several authorities Fra Angelico collaborated with Lorenzo Monaco (see also p. 326) and other artists of the degli Angeli school of Florence (see p. 326) in the illumination of the *Gradual* executed in 1409 for the monastery of S. Maria degli Angeli and now preserved in the Laurentian Library, Florence (*Cor. 3*). This magnificent codex, known as the *Diurno Domenicale*, is reproduced on Fig. VI-28a.

In his earliest works Fra Giovanni was still late Gothic. Allied in style was Battista di Biagio Sanguigni (*Chorales* for the S. Gaggio monastery, now in the Corsini Collection at Florence).

A pupil of Beato Angelico, Zanobi di Benedetto Strozzi (1412–c. 1470), worked in the S. Marco monastery; in the years 1446–53 he painted nineteen codices for his monastery. Outstanding are the following *Graduals* and *Antiphonaries* now preserved in the S. Marco Museum: *Cor. A., B., F., G., S., s.s.* These magnificent codices were executed on Cosimo il Vecchio's commission. It has been suggested that some of the finest parts of the compositions were executed by Fra Angelico and others by Fra Benedetto Toschi. Some of the ornamentation may have been done by Filippo di Matteo Torelli (see further on). Zanobi Strozzi also illuminated a *Missal* now in the S. Marco Museum, and collaborated with Francesco d'Antonio del Cherico (see below) in the illumination of *Graduals* for

Florence Cathedral, which were executed *c.* 1463–71 and are preserved in the Laurentian Library, Florence (*MSS. Edili 149–51*). Zanobi worked in pure Renaissance style: see Fig. VI-28*b*.

The divine painter Sandro (or Alessandro) Botticelli, 1444–1510, illustrated for Lorenzo the Magnificent the famous copy of Dante Alighieri's *Divine Comedy.* (See, particularly, J. B. Supino, *Sandro Botticelli. I disegni per la Divina Commedia di Dante Alighieri*, Bologna, 1921.) The master worked on the MS. between the years *c.* 1480 and 1490, but the illuminations have not been completed; as a matter of fact, the work of the painter had only been begun. The majority of the drawings were preserved in the Hamilton Collection, whence they passed in 1882 to the Kupferstich Cabinet of the Berlin Museum. Eight leaves, formerly in the collection of Christina of Sweden, passed in 1690 to the Pontifical Library (only in 1887 they were rediscovered and identified by Strzygowski) and are preserved in the Vatican Library (*Reg. Lat. 1896 A.*). In another MS., executed between the years 1475 and 1482, and also preserved in the Vatican Library (*S. Cyprian: Urb. Lat. 63*), there is a full-page miniature, representing S. Cyprian writing in his cell. It was executed by a master close to Botticelli. A beautiful fifteenth-century copy of *Fiore di virtù*, preserved in the Riccardiana Library, Florence (*MS. 1711*) contains on fol. *2v* an illuminated title-page by an artist related in style to Botticelli. The MS. also contains thirty-five interesting miniatures painted in the bottom margin; some scholars attribute them to Botticelli himself: Fig. VI-29*a* and *b*.

Amongst the numerous partly contemporary illuminators the following may be singled out: Francesco d'Antonio del Cherico (who worked from about 1455 to 1485); Gherardo (1444?–97) and Monte di Giovanni detto Fora, 1448–1529 (who worked in the late fifteenth and the early sixteenth century); Francesco Pesellino, 1422–57 (C. Silius Italicus, *De bello Punico*: copy preserved in the Marciana Library, Venice, *MS. Lat. XII. 68: 4519*); Bartolomeo and Giovanni d'Antonio (*Lectionary*, executed in 1448, now in the Laurentian Library, *MS. Edili, 147*); Antonio Sinibaldi; the brothers Boccardi; and particularly Attavante degli Attavanti, also known as Attavante Fiorentino.

Francesco d'Antonio del Cherico was one of the greatest masters in the art of illumination. His *Lorenzo Hours*, produced in 1458 for Lorenzo the Magnificent (preserved in the Laurentian Library, *MS. Ashb. 1874*), is a masterpiece of Florentine illumination. Its little miniatures—writes Herbert—are surrounded with very lovely borders, in which tiny but wonderfully lifelike *amorini* uphold festoons and vases of fruit and flowers, amidst a well-ordered medley of medallions, cherubs, birds, sphinxes, etc., and the characteristic scrolls of foliage, flowers, and rayed gilt discs. All this sounds crowded, especially when one considers that the whole page measures only six inches by four; and yet, painted on the plain white vellum, it produces a light and charming effect: Fig. VI-30*b*. See also p. 328.

Another *Book of Hours* by Francesco d'Antonio is preserved in the Vatican Library (*Barb. Lat. 382*). Francesco also illuminated (partly in collaboration with other artists) the superb *Gradual* for the Florence Cathedral already referred to on p. 328 (*MS. Edili, 150*) and another *Gradual* (SS. Annunziata Basilica, Florence,

Cor. C.), a *Pontifical* (Laurentian Library, *MS. Plut. 23, 1*), a *Hebrew Bible* (Laurentian Library, *MS. Plut. 1, 31*), a *Roman Breviary* (the same collection, *MS. Plut. 17, 28*), a copy of Cristoforo Landino, an eminent humanist (Vatican Library, *Urb. Lat. 508*), a copy of S. Augustine's *Works* (Vatican Library, *Urb. Lat. 79*), of S. Jerome and Didymus (the same collection, *Urb. Lat. 52*), of S. John Chrysostom (the same collection, *Urb. Lat. 33*), of Aristotle (Laurentian Library, *MS. Plut. 84, 1*), of Petrarch (Trivulzio Library, Milan, *MS. 905*), of Homer (Laurentian Library, *MS. Plut. 32, 4*), of Pliny (National Library at Naples, *MS. V. A. 3*), and other works. Francesco was at his best in his humanistic and small liturgical books. See Fig. VI-28*b* and 31.

The masterpiece of Gherardo and Monte di Giovanni is the superb *Bible* in three volumes which in the second half of the fifteenth century was executed for the Hungarian king Matthias Corvinus (1458–90)—see also p. 328; the Bible is now preserved in the Laurentian Library (*MS. Plut. 15, 15–17*). Other magnificent works produced by the two artistic brothers, or attributed to them, are: a *Roman Missal*, produced in the late fifteenth century for the S. Maria Nuova Hospital in Florence and now in the National Museum at Florence (*MS. 67*); a miniature in a copy of Homer, executed for Cardinal Alessandro Farnese (1468–1549), who became Pope Paul III—the superb work is preserved in the National Library at Naples (*MS. S.Q. LV. G. 2*); a copy of S. Augustine's *Epistles* (Laurentian Library, *MS. Plut. 12. 1*); a copy of *Sonate* by various authors (National Library at Florence, *MS. B.R. 229—Magl. Cl. XIX. 59*). Moreover, Monte di Giovanni executed, or is credited with the execution of, the following illuminations: a *Roman Missal*—a masterpiece—produced in 1509–10 for the Florentine church of S. John and preserved in the Vatican Library (*Barb. Lat. 610*), an *Antiphonary* and a *Gradual* produced for Florence Cathedral (Museo dell'Opera del Duomo, *MSS. C.* and *F²*); also *Chorales R. F. 88, D*, and others. He executed a *Missal* for the S. Orso Church at Aosta. Gherardo, Monte and their elder brother Bartolomeo also executed the *Missal MS. Edili 109* in the Laurentian Library, the *Breviary Add. MS. 29735* in the British Museum, and musical works such as *MS. B. R. 229* in the National Library at Florence. See Fig. VI-32.

Antonio Sinibaldi, who was a calligrapher rather than an illuminator, in 1485 wrote two beautiful books. One is the *Liber Precatorius*, preserved in the State Library at Munich (*Cimel. 22*). The other is the superb little *Lorenzo Book of Hours*, already referred to; this was formerly in the Ashburnham Library (*MS. 1874*), but has now been restored to the Laurentian Library (see p. 329).

A great artist now known as the 'Master of the Riccardian Virgil' illuminated a copy of Virgil (Riccardiana Library, Florence, *MS. 492*), a copy of Petrarch, *I Trionfi* (the same collection, *MS. 1129*), and a copy of Aesop (the same collection, *MS. 1185¹*). The *Riccardian Virgil* (Fig. VI-34*a*) was formerly attributed to Benozzo Gozzoli or Francesco Pesellini (p. 329).

Filippo di Matteo Torelli illuminated a *Gospel-book* (executed in 1466; now preserved in the Laurentian Library, *MS. Edili, 115*), a *Breviary* (1470, Riccardiana Library, *MS. 284*), and a copy of Petrarch and Dante, *Rime* (the same collection,

MS. 1108). Various works are attributed to Filippo Torelli's workshop or to artists influenced by him (*De bello iudaico*, Laurentian Library, *Plut. 66.9*: Fig. VI-30a, and S. Augustine, *City of God, Plut. 12.19*: Fig. VI-33a, are instances). Filippo, whose work is documented for the years 1440–68, was particularly skilful in ornamentation; he decorated a beautiful *Roman Breviary* for the Florentine Church of S. Egidio (now in the National Museum at Florence, *MS. 68*); the compositions of the codex are by Girolamo da Cremona (see p. 348 f.). For Filippo's work see also, *e.g.*, Fig. VI-29c. His son, Fra Giacomo Torelli, in 1466 illuminated *Chorales* for Siena Cathedral.

Attavante. Attavante Fiorentino (1452–1517) is the most famous of the Florentine illuminators. Many manuscripts illuminated by him have been preserved—Bradley, *Dictionary of Miniaturists*, enumerates thirty-one such codices—and we are fortunate in that he had the helpful habit of signing most of his work. He was only thirty-one when he received a commission from Thomas James, Bishop of Dol, to illuminate a Missal (now preserved in the treasury of Lyons Cathedral). Soon after this he illuminated several books for Matthias Corvinus (see p. 328) including a *Missal*, executed in 1485–7 and now in the Royal Library at Brussels (*No. 9008*). It is one of the works most representative of Attavante's best production and it is typical of Renaissance illumination at its zenith, characterized by artistic taste and dexterous technique. It may also be said to exemplify the characteristic qualities of a great book-illuminator as distinct from a great panel-painter. The MS. is splendidly decorated throughout; his large miniatures are excellent, particularly the great double-page paintings prefixed to the Temporale (fol. 8b–9) and to the Canon (fol. 193b–4), including a fine Crucifixion with a Tuscan landscape. If his large figure-compositions are excellent, the border-decorations and other accessories are superb: he delights—writes Herbert—in gorgeous colouring and rich and varied ornament; his pages glow with crimson, blue, and gold, his borders are filled with a bewildering wealth of 'humanistic' decoration—copies or imitations of classical friezes, cameos, and coins; arabesques, *putti*, pearls, and rubies; all painted with great skill, against grounds of brilliant hues. Attavante's works show influence of Ghirlandaio, Pollaiuolo, and Cosimo Roselli.

In collaboration with Gherardo and Monte he executed the *dos Jeronimos Bible* in seven volumes commissioned by King John II of Portugal (1495–7), now preserved in the National Archives at Lisbon. He worked on all sorts of books, secular as well as religious, such as *Chorales* and Tommaso Sardi, *Anima peregrina* (Corsiniana Library, Rome, *MS. 612: 55. K. 1*): Fig. VI-33b.

In 1475–8 Attavante collaborated in the illumination of the *Urbino Bible* (now Vatican Library, *Urb. Lat. 1–2*). This masterpiece was one of the books which Vespasiano da Bisticci (see p. 328 f.) had prepared to the commission of Federico di Montefeltro, Duke of Urbino, who wanted to have a copy of the *Book of Books* which would surpass everything in magnificence. Vespasiano, looking over the completed work, is supposed to have said: 'This is the book, none like it has been made in our time.' 'The duke'—writes Vespasiano—'has had the Bible, the most excellent of books, written in two volumes ornamented with historical figures, decorated in an inexpressibly rich and worthy manner, and covered with gold brocade richly plated with silver.' Indeed, in the opinion of one authority (Dr. Luigi Michelini Tocci of the Vatican Library), in the *Urbino Bible* there is a splendour and elegance of decoration beyond expression; its richness and artistic accomplishment have no match in this type of work. There is a profusion of precious borders, conceived with bold phantasy and executed with wonderful delicacy; a glorious variety of colours: acanthus-like designs in gold and in colours, filigree pen-work, flowers and fruit, gold chandeliers, jewels and gems, *putti*, animals and many-coloured birds; titles in gold majuscules on grounds stippled with gold. There are a large number of medallions with historical scenes representing—with the effectiveness and power of pictorial art—crowds or movements or dramatic scenes.

The *Corvinus Breviary* (Vatican Library, *Urb. Lat. 112*) is another great masterpiece of the Italian Renaissance. Attavante and his pupils worked on it from about 1487 to after 1492. Other outstanding works illuminated by Attavante or his school are: a *Gradual* preserved in the Laurentian Library (*Cor. 4*), a copy of Plotinus (in the same collection, *MS. Plut. 82. 10*), a *Book of Hours* (*Vat. Lat. 5493*), a copy of Maximus of Tyre (*Vat. Lat. 2196*), a copy of Apollonius Rhodius (National Library at Florence, *MS. B. R. 110¹: B. R. 4. 1. 6*), a copy of Florentius (Trivulzio Library, *MS. 2146*), a copy of the *Hebrew Bible* (Palatina Library, Parma, *MS. 2162*), and various others. Littifredi Corbizi, a follower of Attavante, illuminated a *Book of Hours* and *miscellanea*, preserved in the Communal Library at Siena (*MS. X. V. 3*). Attavante had many other followers, including Boccardino il Vecchio, Stefano di Tommaso, Frate Eustachio, and Antonio di Girolamo.

Giovanni di Boccardi (1460–1529) was a direct follower of Attavante, but he was also influenced by Filippino Lippi (see, for instance, a *Book of Hours* now in the Aquila Museum). He added to his pages drawings of cameos and coins (similar method is adopted in works by other artists; for instance, *MS. Vitt. Eman. 1004* in the National Library at Rome, by an anonymous illuminator).

Of the two brothers Boccardi, Giovanni, commonly known as Boccardino il Vecchio, is the more famous. He collaborated with Attavante (fol. 88*v* of the *Gradual* illuminated by Attavante—see above—is Boccardino's work) and illuminated a number of MSS. including a *Roman Breviary* (Laurentian Library, *MS. Plut. 17, 1*)—Fig. VI-34*b*—part of a *Missal* now in Chieti (Capitulary Library) and the *Book of Hours* in the Guarneriana Library, S. Daniele del Friuli (*MS. 198*). The younger Boccardi, known as Boccardino il Giovane, in 1536 illuminated the *Book of Hours* preserved in the Corsiniana Library, Rome (*MS. 1232: 55 K. 16*). Boccardino il Vecchio executed the majority of the books illuminated for the Badia Fiorentina, and with his son Francesco as well as with Matteo da Terranova and Luigi di Napoli he worked for Montecassino. In the years 1509–23 he worked on commission in Florence (for the Cathedral, 1511–18), Perugia, Siena, and in other cities. He illuminated secular codices, such as a copy of Hippocrates (Laurentian Library, *MS. Plut. 73.12*): Fig. VI-35*a*. He worked for Matthias Corvinus, Leo X, the Commune of Florence (1526 onwards: *Pandects* in the National Library at Florence, *MS. Magl. Cl. XXIX. N. 16*). In his works and those of Francesco, illumination became heavier and heavier. Indeed, with Francesco Boccardi (who died in 1547) Florentine Renaissance illumination decayed. Francesco worked for Montecassino and Perugia (*Chorales*), and executed several aulic works, including a *Book of Hours* for Duke Alessandro de' Medici or his wife Margaret of Austria (Corsiniana Library, Rome, *MS. 1232: 35.K.16*). Fig. VI-35*b* reproduces an initial from a *Chorale* executed by Giovanni and Francesco Boccardi for the Montecassino Abbey, and preserved there in the Badia Archives.

Johannes Franciscus Martius of San Gimignano wrote for Matthias Corvinus three manuscripts containing parts of Livy's *Roman History*. One of these manuscripts, of *c.* 1475, is preserved in the New York Public Library (Spencer Collection). Don Bartolomeo della Gatta's work may be exemplified by the *Antiphonary* in Urbino, Capitolo della Metropolitana (*Cor. 6*); 'Don Bartolomeo della Gatta' is the name given by Vasari to Pietro di Antonio Dei (1448–1502), a Camaldoli monk, born in Florence, who lived and worked in Arezzo. Matteo de' Contugi of Volterra decorated an elegant copy of Libanius (Vatican Library, *Urb. Lat. 336*) and other volumes. In the first half of the sixteenth century, excellent work was produced by a certain Frate Eustachio (*Antiphonary*, Museo dell'Opera del Duomo, Florence, *Cor. O*); by Antonio di Girolamo (*Antiphonary*, the same collection, *Cor. H*); and particularly by Jacopo Giallo (*Psalter*, executed in 1538, now in S. Giorgio Maggiore, Venice, *Cor. 12 A; Missal*, executed in 1538–9, now in the Casanatense Library, Rome, *MS. 458*).

Text-books. MSS. 2580 and *2669* in the Riccardiana Library at Florence are excellent representatives of popular text-books.

Other Centres

Siena. Not many first-class productions in the Sienese Late Gothic style of illumination have come down to us from the early fifteenth century. Moreover, only a few MSS. of certain date and provenance have been preserved complete. Examples are a *Roman Missal* (Communal Library at Siena, *MS. X. II. 2*), and a *Gradual* (the same collection, *MS. H. I. 2*). Of other contemporary illuminated productions only single leaves or miniatures—such as British Museum *Add. MSS. 37955, A* and *35254, C*—are preserved. For this period we can hardly speak of a Renaissance in illumination. The fourteenth-century style continues and achieves some very pleasant results. Indeed, in Siena the Gothic style continued in the late fifteenth century. Earliest Renaissance illumination was introduced by the Florentine Giacomo Torelli, who worked in Siena in 1466 and executed an interesting *Roman Missal* (Siena Communal Library, *MS. G. III. 11*).

In the first half of the fifteenth century a Sienese school of illumination came into prominence. One of its best productions, a Sienese *Austin Hymnal*, dated 1415, is preserved in the British Museum (*Add. MS. 30014*). It is full of exquisite lace-work initials in red and blue, and is particularly remarkable for its borders which are a modification of the old rod-and-acanthus design—the rods, usually curved, becoming less prominent, the leaves growing more freely and luxuriantly; there are introduced human figures (a monk praying, a woman with a basket on her head), grotesques, animals and birds (a bird flying with food to its nestlings), flowers, etc. The most elaborate is fol. 51, relating to Christmas; it contains the Nativity in an initial miniature, the Annunciation to the Shepherds in the lower margin, half-length figures of David and John the Baptist, and medallions of angel-musicians in the borders.

An excellent *Roman Missal*, illuminated in 1427–8 for Cardinal Antonio Casini, Bishop of Siena (1426–39), is preserved in the Communal Library at Siena (*MS. X. II. 2*). The same collection possesses an illuminated *Gradual* of the second half of the fifteenth century (*MS. H. I. 2*).

The Sienese school produced a number of choir-books (see p. 313 f.)—the British Museum cuttings referred to, have evidently been taken from such MSS.— which form a link between the productions of Niccolò di Ser Sozzo (see p. 311) and those of Sano di Pietro. A number of such choir-books are still preserved in Siena Capitulary Library. Sano di Pietro (1401–81), a pupil of Sassetta (see p. 337), was one of the greatest masters in book-painting.

Many of his works are extant: the illuminations in *Statuto dell'Arte di Mercanzia*, executed in 1474 (now in the State Archives at Siena), in *Antiphonaries U* and *V* (Chiusi Cathedral), in five *Antiphonaries* of the Piccolomini Library, Siena; a miniature in *Cod. Vat. Lat. 1742, Cart. 2* (Vatican Library); an illuminated *Franciscan Breviary* (Communal Library at Siena, *MS. X. IV. 2*); a number of illuminations in *Graduals Nos. 1, 2, 3, 6, 10*, and *11* (Siena Capitulary Library); two miniatures in Pienza (Baptism and Prophet receiving Vision of Christ); and *Cor. 52* in the Bologna Civic Museum. See Fig. VI-20a.

A *Missal* for Roman use, executed *c.* 1450 for the Augustinian Friars Hermits at Siena and preserved in the Fitzwilliam Museum, Cambridge (*MS. 6–1954*), has been attributed to Sano di Pietro. It contains a half-page miniature of the Cruci-fixion and eighteen historiated initials with partial borders. Some of the initials may be the work of other artists. Sano di Pietro also painted some *Biccherna* and *Gabella* tablets (see further on). Fig. VI-20b.

Pellegrino di Mariano (who died in 1492), a follower of Sassetta, painted several *Chorales* which are preserved in the Pienza Museum and in the Piccolomini Library at Siena.

Some of the choir-books, executed in perfect Renaissance style, are very fine productions of two famous illuminators, Girolamo da Cremona (see p. 348) and Liberale da Verona (see p. 348 f.). The former worked in Siena from 1468 to 1473, the latter from 1470 to 1476. Their miniatures, enclosed in the large initials, are exquisite (for instance, the parable of the Labourers in the Vineyard, in Liberale's

Gradual, of *c*. 1475, now in the Piccolomini Library, Siena), whereas the pure decoration, done perhaps by their assistants, is conventional and of little artistic merit. See Fig. VI-43*a* and *b*.

Francesco Rosselli (1445–1513), brother of Cosimo, collaborated with Girolamo and Liberale. Their follower Benvenuto di Giovanni (1436–1518?) *c*. 1480 illuminated part of a *Psalter* preserved in the Cava Badia Library.

Other Sienese illuminators produced excellent work. Francesco di Giorgio Martini (who lived 1439–1502) was a pupil of il Vecchietta and was also influenced by Pollaiuolo, Girolamo da Cremona, and possibly by Botticelli. Of his illuminated works the following have been preserved: S. Albertus Magnus, *Commentary on Aristotle's De Animalibus*, executed in 1463 and preserved in the Osservanza Convent near Siena (*Cod. 3*); Fr. Alfon. Ord. S. Augustini, *Super Primum Sententiarum Commentum*, 1466 (the same collection); fol. 3 in *Antiphonary B*, Chiusi Cathedral: Fig. VI-37. See also p. 338.

A copy of Virgil (Vatican Library, *Urb. Lat. 350*), magnificently ornamented, shows the influence of Francesco. The inner side of the first cover of Cristoforo Landino's *Disputationes Camaldulenses* (Vatican Library, *Urb. Lat. 508*), of *c*. 1475, contains a beautiful painting *a tempera* attributed to Francesco di Giorgio. In this miniature, Federico di Montefeltro, Duke of Urbino, is depicted holding a book in his hand, and standing together with a person who according to some scholars is the painter himself (according to others it is Landino).

A fine illuminated *Gradual* of the Osservanza Convent, Siena (*Cor. F*) is the production of a skilled artist, who according to Salmi was connected with Neroccio di Lando. Another excellent example of Sienese art is a *Roman Missal* in the Siena Communal Library (*MS. G. III. 11*); it shows influences of the famous Benozzo Gozzoli. Four *Antiphonaries* in the Piccolomini Library (*23F., 18G., 19M., 4Q.*) were illuminated in the second half of the fifteenth century by two Sienese masters Bernardino Cignoni and Guidoccio Cozzarelli (1450–1516): see also p. 338.

Bartolomeo Neroni, better known as il Riccio, in 1532 illuminated a *Gradual*, now preserved in the Berio Library, Genoa. Il Riccio (who worked between 1520 and 1571 or 1573) was a good painter. He was a pupil of Sodoma, and also a follower of Beccafumi and Bronzino.

Biccherna Tablets. The course of development and decay of Renaissance illumination in any of the great centres of Italian illumination—we said above—cannot, as a rule, be followed step by step for lack of material or of precise data with regard to the abundant material which exists. There are two main exceptions, but in neither of them are the main objects in question illuminated books. In the Sienese school the successive stages are shown by the *Biccherna Tablets*; in the Venetian school by the *Ducali* (see p. 351 f.). The *Biccherna Tablets* are book-covers of a sort—as such they will be dealt with in the volume on *Bindings*—but they contain miniatures which could hardly have differed from contemporary book-miniatures; they are painted by artists who are known to have also been book-illuminators; and they are exactly dated so that they are of great importance for the dating of Sienese illuminated books.

These unique documents, known as the *Tavolette dipinte della Biccherna e della Gabella*, i.e. the 'painted tablets of the Biccherna and the Gabella', are of great interest from various angles. The name *Biccherna* is thought by some scholars to be connected with *Buecher*, the German term for 'books', but this theory is out of the question. The more probable explanation is that which connects *Biccherna* with the name of a public building in the Parish of S. Pellegrino, at Siena—the *Bacherna senensium Consulum*, mentioned from 1193 onwards—the first headquarters of the Treasury of the Siena Republic. The *Biccherna*, at any rate, was the office in which were received and disbursed the revenues of the Republic. The *Gabella* was the office charged with the collection of taxes.

The books of these important magistracies were at first bound in plain boards of wood, and fastened with leather thongs. The plain surfaces of these boards— curiously enough, on books dealing with taxes, fines, contracts, salaries and wages, etc., on which nobody would today expect illumination or decoration—about the middle of the thirteenth century gave place to a series of painted decorations.

The earliest contained merely a portrait of the chief officer of either the *Biccherna* or the *Gabella* and the relative inscription or the coats-of-arms of these officers. Succeeding centuries added scenes of allegorical significance or those connected with the history of the city.

From 1457-9 onwards the tablets became objects of art without any practical purpose: the books of the *Biccherna* and *Gabella* were bound with covers of leather and the tablets became true pictures to hang up on the wall. From 1460 onwards, they were framed. Later their size gradually increased, and the last two *Biccherna* tablets (dated 1619 and 1677-82) are large panel-paintings on canvas.

It goes without saying that these *Biccherna* tablets are of artistic and historical importance. The majority of the tablets are in the State Archives at Siena, but some are preserved in other collections (in Berlin, Budapest, in the Victoria and Albert Museum, London, the National Library at Paris, the Vatican Gallery, etc.). The merit of the tablets varies, some being masterpieces, others being average good work, and others having no artistic value at all. Enzo Carli published 124 such tablets in 1950, and has given a list of another 49 tablets which are either lost or whose present whereabouts is unknown.

The tablet of 1258 painted by Gilio di Pietro (an artist mentioned in documents from 1249 onwards, who died in 1261) is the earliest in date. It presents Frate Ugo, monk of S. Galgano, seated at his desk as *Camarlingo* (chamberlain or chairman) of the *Biccherna*. This and some of the later tablets by predecessors and contemporaries of Duccio (see p. 310), rank among the earliest attempts at individual portraiture in the history of Italian art.

Tablets of 1264, 1267, 1270, 1278, 1282, and probably some others, were painted by Dietisalvi di Speme, an artist mentioned in documents from 1256 to 1291. The tablet of 1291 was painted by Massaruccio, who has been identified with Massarello di Gilio (died in 1339), the son of Gilio di Pietro. The tablet of

1320—representing S. Galgano plunging his sword into the rock—shows the influence of the famous Simone Martini (see p. 311).

The *Gabella* tablet of 1344 is of particular interest: it represents Good Government, symbolized by an old king dressed in white and black (the colours of Siena), seated on a throne. This tablet is generally attributed to Ambrogio Lorenzetti (1319–48), and is a good example of the miniature-style of this great Sienese artist. Also the *Biccherna* tablet of 1340, representing a receiving officer and a citizen paying his taxes, is attributed to this master. The *Gabella* tablet of 1357, formerly attributed to Ambrogio Lorenzetti's school, is now assigned to Lippo Vanni (see p. 309), as its resemblance to Vanni's miniatures would indicate: for instance, those of a Choir-book of 1345 in Siena Cathedral, and those in the Van Regteren Altena Collection.

The *Biccherna* tablet for 1367 is attributed to another master, Niccolò di Buonaccorso; those for 1388 and 1393 to Taddeo di Bartolo, another great master of the Sienese school. Taddeo di Bartolo (*c.* 1362–1422) was an excellent painter (his panel-paintings are preserved in Siena, Pisa, Genoa, Perugia, and Sicily) and illuminator. In 1407 he illuminated a parchment folio which covers the *Deliberations of the Siena Commune*, and is preserved in the State Archives at Siena (*MS. Concist. 250*). A *Roman Missal* in the Communal Library at Siena (*MS. G. III. 7*) is illuminated in Taddeo's style. A follower of Taddeo illuminated another *Missal* (*MS. X. II. 2* in the same Library).

The *Biccherna* tablets for 1433 (Pope Eugenius IV crowning Emperor Sigismund of Luxembourg), for 1436 (S. Jerome in the desert—a realistically delightful composition), with the *Gabella* tablet of 1440 (S. Peter of Alexandria enthroned between two Angels) and those of 1444 (S. Michael fighting the Dragon) and 1445 (Annunciation) are attributed either to Giovanni di Paolo or to his school. This master also painted the tablet of the *Libro Vitale* (executed in 1458) of the Spedale di S. Maria della Scala (State Archives at Siena). See Fig. VI-36a.

Giovanni di Paolo (*c.* 1403–82), a close follower of Sassetta (Stefano di Giovanni Sassetta, 1392–1450) and of Gentile da Fabriano, is sometimes called 'the Greco of the Quattrocento'—he must have been in touch with the contemporary Byzantine paintings. He was also a master in illumination, as may be seen from his *Antiphonary*, preserved in the Communal Library at Siena (*MS. G. I. 8*).

Biccherna a. 1451 (*Camarlingo* Bellanti washing his hands and the Virgin protecting the city of Siena) and *a.* 1457 (two monks with a dove), *Gabella a.* 1471 (the Eternal sending forth the Angel of Wisdom) and *a.* 1473 (marriage of Count Sanseverino and Lucrezia Malavolti, 16 February 1473) are attributed to Sano di Pietro (see p. 334). So also is the tablet of the manuscript *Concistoro* or *Liber andatarum* (State Archives at Siena).

Another pupil of Sassetta, Lorenzo di Pietro (*c.* 1412–80), known as il Vecchietta, painted various tablets, including *Biccherna a.* 1460 (Pope Pius II being crowned, 3 September 1458, with the Virgin above; here we have probably an authentic portrait of Pius II) and *Gabella a.* 1460 (Pius II making his nephew Francesco Piccolomini Todeschini a Cardinal, 5 March 1460; some authorities attribute this tablet to il Vecchietta's school); also the tablets of *Libro della cera* (*No. 464*), of *Libro delle donazioni ed oblazioni* (*No. 176*), 1347–1437, and of *Libro 466* (all three of the Spedale di S. Maria della Scala and now in the State Archives at Siena), and of *Opera Metropolitana*, executed in 1458, are by this master. Lorenzo il Vechietta is the illuminator of fol. 29 (Christ in the midst of Disciples) of *Antiphonary No. 26* in the Piccolomini Library, Siena.

An interesting *Biccherna* tablet, *a.* 1467, representing Siena under the protection of the Virgin during the earthquakes of August 1466, is by Francesco di Giorgio Martini (see p. 335). *Gabella a.* 1484 is by Guidoccio Cozzarelli (see p. 335).

Two tablets, *Gabella a.* 1468 (allegory of Peace and War) and *a.* 1474 (allegory of Good Government), are by Benvenuto di Giovanni (1436–c. 1518), who also illuminated an Epiphany in Letter *O* in a Choir-book of the Osservanza Museum. Another *Gabella* tablet, *a.* 1479 (triumphal Entrance of Alfonso Duke of Calabria into Colle Val d'Elsa, 15 November 1479), is by some scholars attributed to Benvenuto, by others to Giovanni di Cristofano and Francesco d'Andrea, or to Francesco di Giorgio Martini: Fig. VI-36b.

Two other small masterpieces may be referred to: *Gabella a.* 1480 (the Virgin invokes Jesus Christ's protection of Siena; the inscription reads *Hec est Civitas Mea*), attributed to Neroccio di Bartolomeo (1447–1500), a pupil of il Vecchietta, and *Biccherna a.* 1548 (the Mystical Nuptials of S. Catherine of Alexandria and S. Catherine of Siena), attributed to Domenico Beccafumi (see p. 335), by whom also other tablets were painted.

Ferrara

The Ferrara school became important with the *signoria* of the Estensi—the enlightened rulers of the House of Este, from a branch of which House, established in Germany, are descended (through Henry 'the Lion', Duke of Bavaria and Saxony) the Brunswick and Hanoverian sovereigns of Britain. The importance of the Estensi mounted from the fifteenth century onwards, and was especially marked under Niccolò III (d. 1441), and under his three sons, who ruled until 1505. In 1452 the Emperor made Borso d'Este duke of Modena, and in 1471 the Pope made him duke of Ferrara. The Estensi were great patrons of art and literature and their splendid and cultivated court at Ferrara became a great centre of art and culture. They also founded the Universities of Ferrara and Padua; the latter became one of the greatest in Europe. Belbello da Pavia (see p. 346 f.) illuminated for Niccolò III a *Bible* 'in lingua gallica' (Vatican Library, *Barb. Lat. 613*).

Masters of Illumination. Notable artists in the Ferrarese school of book-illumination were Guglielmo and Alessandro Giraldi, Franco de' Russi, Giorgio d' Alemagna and his son Martino da Modena, and Marco dell' Avogaro, but the illuminator in chief was Taddeo Crivelli. These and a few other illuminators were patronised by those liberal patrons of art, the Este dukes Leonello (1441–50), Borso (1450–71), and Ercole I (1472–1505).

Crivelli accomplished many works but, except for his masterpiece the *Borso Bible* (see below), the documentary evidence concerning the individual books is rather scanty. At any rate, it is known that from 1452 to 1476 he illuminated choir-books for the Certosa di Pavia and the Bolognese monasteries of S. Procolo and S. Petronio. He died *c.* 1479. In his work for S. Petronio he was assisted and succeeded by Martino da Modena, who worked for this monastery from 1477 to 1480, and from 1480 to 1485 illuminated choir-books for Modena and Ferrara cathedrals : see also further on.

Borso Bible. The gem of the Ferrara school—and indeed one of the most magnificent masterpieces of Italian illumination—is the great two-volume *Bible of Borso* (now in the Estense Library, Modena, *MSS. V. G. 12: Lat. 422–3*), which contains about a thousand miniatures. We are fortunate that certain data with regard to its execution have been preserved in Borso's accounts. Its illumination began in 1455 and was completed in 1462; its main illuminator was Taddeo Crivelli, who was assisted by Franco de' Russi, Giorgio Tedesco or d' Alemagna, Marco dell' Avogaro, Giovanni da Lira, Giovanni Todesco da Mantova, Giovanni da Gaibana, Sebastiano del Portello, Rodrigo Bonaccorsi, Cristoforo Mainardi, Jacopo Filippo d'Argenta, Pietro Maiante, G. M. Spari, Niccolò d'Achille, and Malatesta di Pietro (a Roman painter). The calligrapher P. P. Maroni wrote the text. See Fig. VI-38*a*.

This magnificent work, formerly owned by the Dukes of Modena, was brought to Austria in 1859. Archduke Franz Ferdinand sold it to the Emp. Franz Joseph I, from whom it passed on to the Emp. Karl. Soon after World War I, Karl sold it to a Parisian dealer in antiquities. Several American dealers tried to buy it and to export it to America, but the Italian industrialist Giovanni Treccani (the famous founder of the Italian *Encyclopaedia Treccani*) succeeded to outbid them; he paid for it five million It. lire, and presented the codex to the Italian State who deposited it in the Modena Estense Library.

The double-page illumination at the beginning of *Genesis*—painted by Crivelli himself—is superb. The wide border which surrounds the three columns of text— writes Herbert—is filled with a great variety of decorative elements, but these are so well adjusted as to result in an admirable design, rich and yet harmonious and not overloaded. The two inner margins are in the same style as many Ferrarese MSS. of the time. But decoration—Herbert continues—is freely lavished on the two broad outer bands, which, with the upper and lower margins, contain a series of Creation-scenes, placed in a gorgeous setting of Renaissance architectural and other ornament, *putti*, vases, doves, and conventional foliage. The Creation-scenes show much originality in composition, especially that in which the Almighty is putting the finishing touches to a lion under the interested surveillance of a horse. The animals and nude human figures are treated in a naturalistic and graceful manner, the *putti* are particularly charming; in the purely decorative work a fertile fancy is combined with excellent taste; the drawing is firm and delicate, the whole execution finely finished. The decoration is mainly influenced by the works of Belbello da Pavia (see p. 346 f.), whereas in the miniatures there are influences of the great masters Pisanello, Andrea Mantegna, Piero della Francesca, Cosmè (or Cosimo) Tura, and others.

Other Ferrarese Masterpieces and their Illuminators. The *Roman Missal* known as the *Borso Missal*, also preserved in the Estense Library, Modena (*MS. α. W. 5. 2.: Lat. 239*) is another famous codex executed for Borso d'Este. This Ferrara masterpiece was illuminated by Taddeo Crivelli, assisted by Giovanni da Lira and other artists. Taddeo Crivelli also illuminated a *Gradual* (now preserved in the S. Petronio Museum, Bologna, *Cor. 111*) and a copy of S. Augustine's *Sermons* (Malatestiana Library, Cesena, *MS. D. III. 3*). A copy of S. Augustine's *City of God*, executed in 1450 for Malatesta, Lord of Cesena (the same collection, *MS. D. IX. I*), is illuminated in Taddeo Crivelli's style. See Fig. VI-38*b*.

A magnificent copy of *The Divine Comedy* (Vatican Library, *Urb. Lat. 365*) contains one hundred and ten large miniatures painted between the years 1474 and 1482, by various artists, including Franco de' Russi, and Guglielmo and Alessandro Giraldi. A superb *Gospel-book* of the same period, containing full-page miniatures, decorated initials in gold and colours, finely figured medallions, and magnificent ornamental work, is another Ferrara masterpiece executed by various artists, including Franco de' Russi and Guglielmo Giraldi (Vatican Library, *Urb. Lat. 10*). A beautiful copy of Francesco della Rovere, *De Sanguine Christi etc.* (Vatican Library, *Urb. Lat. 151*) has been attributed to Franco de' Russi. A magnificent full-page miniature added after 1474 to a copy of Peter Lombard's *Commentaries* (Vatican Library, *Urb. Lat. 18*), has also been attributed to Franco de' Russi. He, too, executed a book of *Ducali* (see p. 351 f.) now in the British Museum.

Giorgio Tedesco (or d'Alemagna) painted in 1453 a long poem describing Charlemagne's enterprises (Ariosto Library, Ferrara, *MS. Cl. II. 132*); according to Salmi he may have illuminated a copy of Joannes Blanchinus, *Tabulae astrologiae* (the same collection, *MS. Cl. I. 147*).

Guglielmo Giraldi di Giovanni del Magro, known as 'il Magri', is documented for the years 1445–76. He was perhaps a pupil of Giorgio d'Alemagna with whom he worked on a copy of Aulo Gellio (*Cod. Scotti*) now in the Ambrosian Library at Milan. In the late 'sixties he worked on the *Borso and Ercole Bible* (see below) and and on the *Certosa Chorales* (now partly in the Schifanoia Museum at Ferrara). In the latter and in the *Estense Psalter* (see further on) he was assisted by his nephew Alessandro Leoni. Perhaps with de' Russi he executed for Federico di Montefeltro a copy of Dante, *c.* 1480 (Vatican Library, *Urb. Lat. 365*). He also illuminated a *Treatise of Good Government* (Trivulzio Library at Milan, *Cod. 86*).

The *Borso and Ercole Bible*, a superb work in four volumes, executed for the Carthusian monastery of S. Christopher (near Ferrara) on commission by Dukes

Borso and Ercole d'Este, may be considered Guglielmo Giraldi's masterpiece (Schifanoia Museum, Ferrara). Other outstanding works by Guglielmo Giraldi are: a copy of Candido Bentempi, *Libro del Salvatore* (Estense Library, Modena, *MS. α. T. 5. 27: Ital. 353*), two *Graduals* (Schifanoia Museum, Ferrara, *Cor. 3 and 9*), a *Pontifical* (University Library at Bologna, *MS. 661*), and a *Psalter* (Estense Library, Modena, *MS. α. Q. 4. 9: Lat. 990*). Other excellent works were produced by Guglielmo Giraldi's pupils; they include a copy of Eusebius, *Ecclesiastical History* (National Library at Florence, *MS. B. R. 40: II. I. 214; C. XXXVII, 51*).

Followers of Giraldi illuminated a copy of Plutarch (Bologna University Library, *MS. 2325*) and a *Liber iurium* (Bologna Civic Museum, *MS. 95*). An excellent copy of Pliny was executed by another anonymous illuminator of the Ferrara school (Turin National Library, *MS. I. I. 22–23*; it was badly damaged in the fire of 1904). D'Argenta (or l'Argenta) continued Giraldi's style in the *Chorales* for Ferrara Cathedral executed in the years 1477–1501 (see also further on).

Jacopo Filippo Medici d'Argenta was another illuminator of the Ferrara school. To him or to his *bottega* are assigned various codices, including the following: an *Antiphonary* (Queriniana Library, Brescia, *MS. G. I. 5*), a *Gradual* (Duomo Museum, Ferrara, *Cor. XVII*), and a copy of Xenophon, *Cyropaedia* (Estense Library, Modena, *MS. α. G. 5. 1.: Ital. 416*). He painted a copy of Pliny (printed by Ienson, Venice, 1472), now in the Turin National Library (*XV, I, 39*). He also worked in Bologna (in 1465) and in Brescia, where with several assistants he executed seventeen MSS. for the church of S. Francis.

A famous *bottega* of Ferrara was that of Andrea delle Viezze (exemplified by a copy of Procopius, preserved in the Estense Library, *MS. α. H. 4. 2: Ital. 463*).

A *Ferrara Breviary* (British Museum, *Add. MS. 17294*), of *c.* 1472, probably executed for Ercole I (it contains his arms, together with the *diamante impresa*), is beautifully written, though its decoration is not of particular interest. The decoration of the margins—similar to that of many Ferrarese MSS. and to that of the inner margins of the *Borso Bible*, already referred to—consists of flowers and golden discs, connected by a sort of network of filigree lines, representing the stems, and enclosing plaques painted with the Este arms and *imprese*.

A splendid *Missal* (Trivulzio Library, *Cod. 2165*) has been assigned to Martino da Modena. Professor Salmi assigns to the same illuminator a beautiful miniature (fol. 1 r) in an *Avicenna* codex of the Laurentian Library, Florence (*MS. Gadd. 24*). Other outstanding works by Martino da Modena are: two *Graduals* (preserved in the S. Petronio Museum, Bologna (*Cor. 119* and *120*), a *Roman Missal* (Palatina Library, Parma, *MS. 851*), and a *Roman Breviary* (National Library at Palermo, *MS. I. B. 21*). Martino was a very able and original painter of landscapes, and his treatment of the human face is much ahead of his contemporaries.

Late fifteenth-century illumination of the Ferrara school is well represented by Matteo da Milano, Tommaso da Modena, and by a few other masters (*Ercole Breviary* preserved in Modena, Estense Library, *MS. V. G. II: Lat. 424*; a richly illuminated codex containing *Orations* executed for Duke Ercole, Marciana Library, Venice, *MS. Lat. II, 60: 2075*; and other works).

The *Ercole Breviary* (executed by Matteo, Cesare delle Viezze, and Tommaso di Cesare) was completed *c.* 1502; it is a very fine book. It contains some gorgeous pages with elaborately painted landscape-backgrounds. On the other hand—as Herbert has emphasized—it already shows signs of decadent taste. The details of ornament, exquisitely painted though they be, are ill-distributed, now crowding up the borders with reckless profusion, now arranged in stiff and monotonous symmetry. The miniatures, too, are often hampered with incongruous details, and lacking in spaciousness of composition. See Fig. VI-39*a*.

A translation of Avicenna's *Canon Medicinae* (*see* p. 149), with a magnificent miniature of the Ferrarese school, is preserved in the Laurentian Library, Florence (*MS. Gaddiano 24*).

A beautiful MS. preserved in the Pierpont Morgan Library (*M. 731*) contains Antonio Cornazzano, *Del modo di reggere e di regnare*. It was written (in silver) and illuminated for presentation to Leonora of Aragon (1450–93), sister in law of Matthias Corvinus, probably on the occasion of her second marriage (in 1473, to Ercole I d'Este). Fol. 4*v* contains a profile painted against a lapis-lazuli background, surrounded by a lavender frame; a golden wand is given to the lady by a celestial hand in the upper right corner: Fig. VI-42*a*. Bernard Berenson, a foremost authority on Italian painting, attributed this miniature to Cosimo Tura. In this connection, the reader may be referred to an excellent article by P. Wescher, *Buchminiaturen im Stil Cosimo Turas*, Berliner Museen, LI/4, 1930, pp. 78–81.

In the early sixteenth century the Ferrarese art of illumination was in full decadence, though some excellent works were still produced. Amongst the better productions the following two deserve special mention: the *Officium of Alfonso I* (Academy of Fine Arts at Zagreb) of *c.* 1505–10, and the *Missal of Cardinal Ippolito I* (University Library at Innsbruck, *MS. 43*) of 1503–20. See Fig. VI-39*b*.

Marmitta

Other Schools of Emilia Region. The Ferrara school of illumination strongly influenced other schools of Emilia, as well as those of the Venetian region (see further on). This influence can be seen in various excellent works, produced in Emilian style, such as a copy of Gualterius Burlaeus (Marciana Library, Venice, *MS. Lat. Z. 255: 1486*), a copy of *Decretum Gratiani* preserved in the National Library at Florence (*MS. B.R. 108*), a superb small *Book of Hours* assigned to Marmitta (Berio Library, Genoa), a miniature detached from a *Missal* painted in the style of Angelo and Bartolomeo degli Erri. The *Hours* assigned to Marmitta is known as *Uffiziolo Durazzo*: it is a magnificent very small MS. written in gold on purple vellum with numerous extremely fine miniatures.

Marmitta, a sixteenth-century artist—who by some scholars has been identified with Gian Marco Cinico, a court-painter to the Aragon kings of Naples—worked in Parma as painter, engraver and illuminator; the illumination of the *Book of Hours*, referred to above, is allied in style to the miniatures of the magnificent *Missal of Cardinal Domenico della Rovere* (preserved in the Civic Museum at Turin), which Professor Venturi had ascribed to Gian Francesco de' Maineri of Parma. A detached miniature of the Crucifixion preserved in the Fitzwilliam Museum, Cambridge (*Marley Leaves, I. 28*) has been attributed by Professor Wormald to Marmitta. Finally, an elegant small copy of Petrarch's *Trionfi* (State Library at Cassel, *MS. poet. 4°. 6*) is also in Marmitta's style. See Fig. VI-42b.

Examples of the Bologna school of illumination influenced by the Ferrara school are: a *Psalter* preserved in the Civic Museum at Bologna (*Cor. 53*), and another codex in the same collection (*MS. 95*).

Giovanni Battista Cavalletto was one of the best illuminators of Bologna. An illuminated membership-book of the Bologna Guild of Drapers, signed by Cavalletto and dated to 1523, is preserved in the Civic Museum at Bologna (*MS. 97*). Other works illuminated in Cavalletto's style or in a similar style are an *Antiphonary* and a *Psalter* in the same collection (*Cor. 78* and *75*) and a *Gradual* in the Taroni Library, Bagnocavallo. See also p. 317 f. and Fig. VI-25a.

A Nativity by Amico Aspertini in the *Albani Hours* (see p. 354) shows influences of Filippino Lippi, Pinturicchio, and Boccardino.

Romagna: best instances of the illumination of this region are seven *Graduals* executed for Cesena Cathedral; they are influenced by panel-painting (particularly by Melozzo and Palmezzano). Henry of Amsterdam began to write them in 1486. (They are preserved in the Malatestiana Library at Cesena.)

Milan and Lombardy

Gothic illumination continued during the Renaissance period and strongly influenced the works executed in Renaissance style. An excellent instance is a copy of Antonius Averulinus 'il Filarete', *Architecturae Libri XXV* (Marciana Library, *MS. Lat. VIII. 2*); this codex was executed in Buda for Matthias Corvinus by a skilful artist dependent on Belbello da Pavia (see p. 346 f.). Otherwise, Lombard illumination of the period was mainly of the Sforza Court-style, the main Court-illuminator being Cristoforo de' Predis.

Storia degli Umiliati (Ambrosian Library, Milan, *MS. 301 inf.*) is an excellent Milanese product of 1421. It deals with members of the Order of the Umiliati, an order which flourished in thirteenth-century Milan.

Not many Milanese masterpieces are extant and very little is known of their illuminators. One name of the earlier phase of Milanese illumination is well known —that of Cristoforo de' Predis (the brother of Ambrogio, see below). Not only have Cristoforo's works been preserved, but some are signed and (with one exception) dated. They are the *Lives of SS. Joachim and Anna* (ex-Royal Library, Turin, MS. *Var. 124*), of 1476; a *Missal* (in the church of Madonna del Monte, near Varese, of the same year; a detached leaf is in the Wallace Collection, London), c. 1475–? (the last number being illegible); and the *Borromeo Hours*, undated (Ambrosian Library, Milan). The Calendar-pictures in the last-named book are of some interest. As in the later French Books of Hours, they fill the lower margins and part of the sides of each page, and contain some curious illustrations of contemporary life.

Other illuminated, or partly illuminated, works assigned to Cristoforo, or to a master of similar style, are: a *Gradual* preserved in Modena (Estense Library, MS. α. P. 1. 6: Lat. 453), a *Roman Breviary* (Pïana Library, Cesena, MS. 3. 226), a copy of Virgil (National Library at Naples, MS. IV. E. 7), and of Plutarch and *miscellanea* (Communal Library, Siena, MS. I. VII. 23), a copy of *De Sphaera*, produced for the Sforza family (Modena, Estense Library, MS. α. X. 2. 14: Lat. 209). He also executed a *Choir-book* for the chapel of Ercole I, Duke of Ferrara (Estense Library, MS. α. P. I. 6: Lat. 453) and the *Leggendario*, 1474 (ex-Royal Library at Turin, MSS. Varî 124).

Cristoforo adopts—writes Herbert—the full Renaissance style of ornament, filling his frame-borders with festoons, arabesques, vases, pearls and precious stones, cameos and medallions, as well as birds and innumerable *putti*; but his figure-drawing and perspective are poor, and his colouring, though deep and brilliant, is ill-harmonized and unpleasing in effect.

The following excellent works show the influence of Cristoforo de' Predis: Gaspare Visconti, *Paolo e Daria Amanti*, 1492 (Copper-Engravings Cabinet, Berlin); *Antiphonaries* in the Lodi Civic Museum; a copy of Virgil in the National Library at Naples (MS. IV. E. 7); a copy of *Donatus* in the Trivulzian Library, Milan (MS. 2167).

One of the greatest treasures of the Fitzwilliam Museum, Cambridge, is the *Milanese Pontifical* (MS. 28). Indeed, the extraordinarily fine quality of its work, 'the touch most delicate, the colouring beyond praise' induced M. R. James in 1895 to regard it as 'probably the most beautiful MS. in the collection.' It contains 115 illuminated pages. The arms, which occur in the MS., formerly identified with those of Franciscus de Regatiis, Bishop of Bergamo, 1403–37, have recently been identified by Mlle. E. Pellegrin with those of Francesco Piccolpasso, Archbishop of Milan, who died in 1443. Toesca attributes the illumination of this MS. to the 'Master of the *Vitae imperatorum*' (see p. 347). Fig. VI-41a.

The most superb production of the Milanese school is preserved in the British Museum (*Add. MS. 34294*). It is the *Sforza Book of Hours*, executed c. 1490 for Bona of Savoy, widow of Galeazzo Maria Sforza, Duke of Milan (d. 1476). The MS. contains forty-eight Milanese miniatures and various ornamentations and frame-borders also executed at Milan, as well as sixteen Flemish miniatures (see p. 456)—including a portrait of Charles V, dated 1520—which were added in 1519–20 to replace some leaves formerly taken away. See Fig. VI-42c.

Bona Sforza gave this MS. to her daughter Bianca Maria; it has been suggested that it was originally intended as a wedding-gift on her proposed marriage to John Corvinus, natural son of King Matthias (see p. 346), but the marriage-project fell through, and in 1493 Bianca Maria married the Emperor Maximilian I. Apparently the pages which contained allusions to the previous marriage project were then removed, and when in 1519 Charles V, who succeeded Maximilian, inherited the MS., he caused the insertion of the new pages to make good the imperfections of the book.

The great majority of the earlier pages, in Herbert's opinion, represent Milanese illumination at its highest pitch of excellence. They are painted in the sharp, vivid manner of the Lombard school; as crisp as medals, as brilliant as enamel, they yet avoid hardness, and their saints and angels have all the tense, ardent spirituality of expression which the great North Italian masters knew so well how to convey.

The miniatures include three portraits of Evangelists, ten scenes from the Passion, the Death and Assumption of the Virgin, and a long and interesting series of saints, including many of the most beautiful compositions of the book (for instance, the two Catherines, the SS. Clare, Bernardino, Albert of Trapani, and Gregory). The borders are painted with the same brilliancy as the miniatures, and are designed with equal freedom and originality with regard to details of conventional ornament—which, though of the conventional Renaissance type, is varied with an amazing fertility of invention—as well as figure-compositions, including an extremely interesting and charming series of angel-musicians, saints whimsically depicted as *putti*, and a *putto* teaching a dog to beg.

Illuminators. The illuminations vary in style and in their artistic merit and are evidently the work of several artists, but none is signed and there is no sufficient evidence to identify the masters. A letter from a *presbiter Johannes Petrus Biragus miniator* refers to an *officiol imperfecto* in preparation for Bona Sforza. It is uncertain whether this *officiol* is the *Sforza Book of Hours*; even assuming that the priest Giovanni Pietro da Birago (see below) was this *presbiter*, in no case could he have painted the whole book.

In more recent times, two other names have been suggested: Ambrogio de' Predis and Antonio da Monza. The latter, a Franciscan friar, was an excellent illuminator. He painted a *Missal* for Pope Alexander VI (1492–1503); a miniature of the Descent of the Holy Spirit (in the Albertina Museum, Vienna), the only one preserved from this book, is allied to some of the *Sforza Book* miniatures, but is not sufficient to substantiate the theory that Antonio was one of the illuminators of this book.

Ambrogio de' Predis, active in Milan 1472–1506 and probably later, was a great panel-painter (it will suffice here to mention his association with Leonardo da Vinci), but very little is known of him as an illuminator of books. However, Ambrogio has been credited (by Dr. Mueller-Walde) with the illumination of Elio Donato, *Grammatica* (now in the Trivulzio Library, *MS. 2167*, Milan): see below. If this attribution is correct, he must at least have executed the Passion-series of the *Sforza Hours*, and would have been a leading illuminator as well as panel-painter. The copy of *Grammatica*, just referred to, is allied in style to the beautiful *Codex Leggendario*; it was executed *c.* 1496 for Massimiliano Sforza, son of Ludovico il Moro and Beatrice d'Este. Cristoforo de' Predis (who died *c.* 1486) could not have executed the book. It is thus attributed to Ambrogio de' Predis, who was the most able pupil and collaborator of Leonardo da Vinci. Another MS., a Lombard masterpiece, attributed to Ambrogio is I. F. Marlianus, *Epithalamium in nuptiis Blancae M. Sphortiae et ducis Johannis Corvini*, dedication copy to Matthias Corvinus (father of Duke John), executed in 1487 and now in the Communal Library Guarnacci at Volterra (*MS. 49.3.7*). Certain details of the miniatures are in Leonardo's style: Fig. VI-41*b*.

The Milanese style of illumination is also represented in two British Museum specimens, the printed *Sforziade* (Milan, 1490) with fine examples of Milanese border-decoration, and a grant of lands from Ludovico Sforza to his wife Beatrice d'Este, dated 1494 (*Add. MS. 21413*). These—argues Herbert—are in the same style as the *Sforza Book* borders, though on a larger scale, and are specially interesting for the splendid medal-like portraits of Ludovico and Beatrice, and of Ludovico's father Francesco Sforza-Visconti.

A few other fifteenth-century Lombard illuminators may be mentioned: Giovanni Pietro da Birago, who executed a *Gradual* (now in the Estense Library, MS. α. R. 1. 7: *Lat. 1022*); miniatures preserved in the Uffizi Gallery, Florence (*Nos. 843, 4423–30*); perhaps also a copy of the *Legend of S. Josaphat*, which is preserved in the Braidense Library, Milan (*MS. AC. XI. 37: AN. XIV. 21*). Giovanni Pietro, assisted by five artists, executed in the years 1471–4 eighteen *Chorales* for the Brescia Cathedral. Recently he has been identified with Pseudo-Antonio da Monza (see p. 349). See also p. 346.

Andrea Solari probably executed the folios 6*r* and 9*v* of the *Libro del Jesus*, preserved in the Trivulzio Library, Milan (*MS. 2163*); Michelino Molinari da Besozzo worked *c.* 1388–1442; he executed the *Orazione funebre* (National Library, Paris, *Lat. 5888*) and a copy of Boëthius (Malatestiana Library, Cesena, *MS. D. XIV. 2*); his son Leonardo (active *c.* 1421–35) executed a copy of *Imagines pictae virorum illustrium* (Vittorio Crespi Collection, Milan); Giovanni di maestro Ugolino da Milano illuminated a *Roman Missal* (Fermo Capitulary Library), 1436. A follower of Leonardo illuminated one of the most beautiful Hebrew codices (Avicenna, *Canon Maior*) preserved in the Bologna University Library (*MS. 2197*); see also p. 149. Fig. VI-42*d*.

Fig. VI-43*c* reproduces fol. 16*v* from a *Milan Hours* of *c.* 1440 preserved in the Walters Art Gallery (*W. 323*). It is a fine small MS. ($4\frac{1}{8} \times 3\frac{1}{4}$ in.) in the style of the so-called Zattavari school.

Belbello da Pavia (active *c.* 1430–62) was one of the foremost Italian illuminators of the first half of the fifteenth century. The following works have been attributed

Initial C in *Catho's Life*, from the sumptuous fifteenth-century B.M. *Add. MS. 22318*
(attributed by Charles Mitchell to a Lombard Renaissance *bottega*,
which had affinities with Belbello da Pavia and the 'Master of *Vitae Imperatorum*').

to him or to his school: a *Lives of Saints* of *c.* 1431 (Braidense National Library, Milan, *MS. AE. XIV. 20*); a *Gradual* preserved in the Malatestiana Library, Cesena (*Cor. I.*); (in collaboration with Girolamo da Cremona) a *Missal* preserved in Mantua Cathedral; (in collaboration with Jacopino d'Arezzo, who painted the initials) a *Bible*, preserved in the Vatican Library (*Barb. Lat. 613*); a Greek copy of Ptolemy, *Geography* (Marciana Library, Venice, *MS. Gr. Z. 388: 333*); an *Antiphonary*, of which detached leaves are preserved in Count Cini Collection, Venice; an *Antiphonary* of which a leaf is preserved in the Rosenwald Collection, National Gallery of Art, Washington; ten cuttings now preserved in the Wildenstein Collection, New York City; and one cutting in the Fitzwilliam Museum, Cambridge (*Marlay Leaves, I, 18*). An elegant copy of Homer, *Iliad* and *Batrachomyomachia*, preserved in the Laurentian Library (*MS. Plut. 32, 1*) is in a Lombard style influenced by Belbello; the magnificent frontispiece is decorated with elegant friezes, *putti*, emblems, human figures (including Homer), and the initials of the famous humanist Francesco Filelfo (1398–1481) for whom the codex was executed.

Belbello continued to work on the magnificent *Visconti Officium* (see p. 316): Fig. VI-40.

'Master of Vitæ Imperatorum'

A great contemporary master illuminated the codex *Vitae imperatorum*, translated by Pier Candido Decembrio, which was written in 1431 for Filippo Maria Visconti (National Library at Paris, *It. 131*); this illuminator is known as the 'Master of *Vitae imperatorum*'. He also illuminated a copy of Dante (partly in the National Library at Paris, *It. 2017*, and partly in the Imola Communal Library, *MS. 32*). See also below and p. 350.

Milanus Burrus. In recent years, Dorothy Miner, H. Baron, S. Morison, and Élisabeth Pellegrin have drawn attention to the activity of Milanus Burrus, a fifteenth-century Milanese copyist. All his books are dated and signed. They are illuminated, but it is not known who the artists were. The illumination of some MSS. is attributed to the 'Master of *Vitae imperatorum*'. The latest list, by Mlle. Pellegrin, contains seven works copied by Milanus Burrus: (1) Suetonius, *De vita Caesarum*, copied in 1443, and preserved in the Fitzwilliam Museum, Cambridge (*McClean, 162*). Each biography of the Emperors was preceded by a full-page miniature, but only those of Otto, Vespasian, and Domitian have survived; (2) Leonardo Bruni, *Commentary* to the *First Punic War*, copied in 1444, is preserved in the Philadelphia Free Library (*Lewis MS. 54*): it contains decorated borders, initials, coat of arms, and other ornamentation: (3) Suetonius, *De vita Caesarum* (Princeton University Library, *Kane MS. 44*), copied in 1433; it contains twelve miniatures (probably by the 'Master of *Vitae imperatorum*'), a coat of arms, the *nodo* emblem, and other decoration; (4) Aulus Gellius, *Noctes Atticae* (Newberry Library, Chicago, *MS. 90. 5*), copied in 1445; there are decorated initials; (5–6) two illuminated copies of Aristotle, *Ethica* (Communal Library, Mantua, *MS. 46: A. II. 15*, copied in late 1449; and Museum of the Zeeland Archaeological Society, Middelburg, *MS. 103*, written six years earlier: this MS. perished in 1940); and (7) a *Bible*, dated 1442, preserved in the Toulon Municipal Library (*MS. 1*).

Cremona, Verona, and Miscellanea from North Italy. The city of Cremona had an important school of illumination: Giovanni Gadio in 1482 illuminated an *Antiphonary* for Cremona Cathedral (Duomo Capitulary at Cremona, *Cor. 6: F. 2*); Antonio Cicognara in 1483 illuminated another *Antiphonary* for the same Cathedral (in the same collection, *Cor. 4: D. 1*). There are other codices illuminated in a style similar to that of Cicognara, including a *Breviary* now in Naples (National Library, *MS. I. B. 52*). Fra Andrea da Cremona in 1467 executed a *Breviary*, now in the Casanatense Library at Rome. A charming codex of the *Società dei Falegnami* ("Society of Carpenters"), of Cremona, executed in that city in 1478 (in the time of the Visconti, whose arms are depicted on one of the leaves), is preserved in the Civic Museum, at Cremona.

Girolamo da Cremona (1467–83) and Liberale da Verona (c. 1445–1529) have been referred to on p. 334 f. Girolamo da Cremona is credited with the illumination of various MSS. including a work attributed to Raymond Lully or Raimundus Lullus (National Library at Florence, *MS. B.R. 52: II. III. 27; Cl. XVI, 41*); the compositions of the *Breviary* now in the National Museum at Florence, *MS. 68* (see p. 331); and part of a *Gradual*, preserved in the Piccolomini Library, Siena (*Cor. 12*). Another *Gradual* of the same collection (*Cor. 4*) is illuminated in the same style, and so is also a miniature in a *Roman Missal* preserved in the National Library at Naples (*MS. I. B. 29*). Girolamo also worked in Mantua, where he continued Belbello's decoration of the exquisite *Missal of Barbara of Brandenburg* (now in Brandenburg Cathedral Library). See Fig. 43*a* and *b*.

A detached leaf from a choir-book signed *Ieronimus F*, is preserved in the Victoria and Albert Museum, London (*MS. 1184*); five initials probably from the same choir-book, are now in the Fitzwilliam Museum, Cambridge (*Marlay Bequest, 1912*). For Girolamo da Cremona see also p. 351.

Bonifacio Bembo da Cremona, who worked c. 1440–78, collaborated on *Cod. Palat. 556* (in the National Library at Florence, c. 1446). He also illuminated *MSS. α. L. 5. 16* and *M. 5. 27* in the Estense Library at Modena; *MS. V. E. 293* in the National Library at Rome; and a copy of Tarocchi in the Carrara Academy at Bergamo.

Liberale da Verona illuminated a *Roman Missal* for the Siena Cathedral (now in the Communal Library, Siena, *MS. X. II. 3*) and two *Graduals* preserved in Chiusi Cathedral (*Cor. Q. and R.*). A detached initial *D*, of monumental size, from an *Antiphonary*, contains the miniature depicting the *Entry into Jerusalem*; the fragment, now preserved in the Robert Lehman Collection, New York City is attributed to Girolamo da Cremona or Liberale da Verona. It may, however, be part of the same manuscript as the cuttings in the Victoria and Albert Museum and in the Fitzwilliam Museum, previously referred to. See also p. 334. Some other works, at least in part, are in the style of the Verona school of illumination, such as a miniature detached from a *Choral* (Count Cini Collection, Venice) or a copy of the *Tractate* by Pope Sixtus IV, Rome, 1472 (National Library at Turin, *XV, XII, 106*). A superb copy of a *Roman Missal*, now in the National Braidense Library, Milan (*MS. AE. X. 30: AN. XV. 14*) is in the style of a Verona artist, Girolamo dai Libri, who is quoted by Vasari as a fine illuminator. Girolamo's father, Francesco (1452–c. 1514), according to Vasari, illuminated a great number of works; a *Pontifical* executed for Card. Domenico della Rovere (Pierpont Morgan Library, *M. 306*) is attributed to Francesco. It contains drawings only.

Giacomo de Balsamo, of Milan, in 1470–89 executed four *Graduals* and eight *Antiphonaries* for the basilica S. Maria Maggiore at Bergamo.

An unidentified artist, commonly known as the Pseudo-Antonio da Monza, illuminated a superb minute *Book of Hours* on commission by Ludovico il Moro to be presented to Emperor Charles V (Count Cini Collection, Venice); an *Uffiziolo* for Bona of Savoy (British Museum, *Add. MS. 34294*); a *Pontifical* (Vatican Library, *Ottob. Lat. 501*); a few miniatures in *MS. 2167* in the Trivulzio Library, Milan, and other works. Some scholars have identified Pseudo-Antonio with Zuan Andrea from Mantua, but the identification with Giovanni Pietro da Birago (see p. 346) suggested by Prof. M. Salmi, appears to be the most probable.

Privilegi delle famiglie bresciane (Queriniana Library, Brescia) is a charming example of illumination of the school of Brescia.

A fine choir-book, apparently illuminated for a North Italian church dedicated to SS. Cosmas and Damian—the patron saints of physicians—is now preserved in the Library of the Society of Antiquaries of London. It contains at the beginning a half-page miniature representing the miracle of the Ethiopian's leg (a popular episode in the legend of SS. Cosmas and Damian); there are also several large historiated initials and beautiful borders, allied in style to book-productions of Ferrara of *c.* 1460–70. The MS. may come from Mantua, but the sixteenth-century inscription signed *Frater Iacobus de Mantua* attributing the illuminations to Andrea Mantegna (1431–1506) and to his son Francesco, court-painters to the Gonzagas at Mantua, can hardly be correct.

An interesting product of North Italy, executed about 1470, is preserved in the Victoria and Albert Museum, London (*L. 101–1947*). It is a copy of Petrarch's *Sonnets and Triumphs*.

Lombard Humanists and their Libraries. In an article (*Bibliothèques d'Humanistes lombards de la Cour des Visconti Sforza*, 'Bibliothèque d'Humanisme et Renaissance', 1955), Mlle. E. Pellegrin has reconstructed a fifteenth-century group of eminent humanists connected with the Court of the Visconti and the Sforza, the Dukes of Milan. These personages were also book-collectors; many illuminated manuscripts were executed for them, and some are still preserved in European or American collections.

Francesco Pizzolpasso or Pic(c)olpasso, already referred to, Bishop of Dax and Pavia and Archbishop of Milan (until his death in 1443), had a very important library of theological, liturgical, and classical books. He presented at least eighty-two manuscripts to the Chapter of Milan Cathedral which in the seventeenth century passed to the Ambrosian Library. Some of his MSS., however, are in the Vatican Library (for instance, a copy of Lactantius, *Vat. Lat. 215*) or in the National Library at Paris (a copy of Josephus Flavius, translated by Pseudo-Hegesippus, *Lat. 5068*), or in other collections. Two important works are in England: the superb *Pontifical* in the Fitzwilliam Museum (see p. 344) and a Biblical *Glossary* in the British Museum (Add. MS. 17397).

Bartolomeo Visconte, bishop of Novara (1402–57), commissioned many books and about half-a-dozen of them were decorated by the 'Master of *Vitae imperatorum*'. Two illuminated copies of Suetonius were executed for him, one in 1434 (now in the National Library at Madrid, *Vit. 16–2*), the other in 1444 (now in the Trivulzio Library, Milan, *MS. 696: D. 132*). Also a copy of *Vitae imperatorum* (Vatican Library, *Urb. Lat. 437*); a copy of *Historia Augusta* (*Vat. Lat. 1903*); a copy of Lactantius (National Library at Paris, *Lat. 1677*); a copy of Cicero, *Philippicae* (Bodleian Library, *D'Orville MS. 76*); a copy of Papias (British Museum, *Add. MS. 14806*), and other works were executed for Bartolomeo Visconte.

Several illuminated MSS. were executed on the commission of Gian-Matteo Bottigella. Two of them were copied by Milanus Burrus (see p. 347 f.); they are dated 1443 and 1444. Some MSS. may have been illuminated by the 'Master of *Vitae imperatorum*' or by his atelier. The following MSS. may be referred to: Fitzwilliam Museum, *McClean MS. 162* (see p. 347); Bodleian Library, *Can. Class. Lat. 295*; Philadelphia Free Library, *Lewis MS. 54* (see p. 347); Royal Library at Brussels, *MS. 14638*; National Museum at Budapest, *MS. 761*. Fig. VI-41*a*.

Baldo Martorelli (who died in 1475) was preceptor to the children of Duke Francesco Sforza. He wrote some books (now in the Trivulzio Library, Milan, *MS. 786*; Wolfenbuettel, Ducal Library, *MS. 22*) or had them written (Ambrosian Library, Milan, *T. 16. sup.*), and had a good collection of Classical and theological books. Mlle. Pellegrin lists the following MSS., which were in Martorelli's possession: Ambrosian Library, *L. 87. sup.*; Trivulzio Library, *MS. 727*; University Library at Valencia, *MS. 766*; National Library at Vienna, *MS. 3187*; *Vat. Lat. 1854*; National Library at Paris, *Lat. 6088* and *7576*; British Museum, *Add. MS. 21984*; Royal Library at Brussels, *MS. 15560*; Holkham Hall, Leicester, *MS. 510**.

Finally, we may refer to a copy of Paolo Veneto's *Commentary* to Aristotle's *De anima*, preserved in the Pavia University Library.

Venetian Region

Padua. Giovanni Vendramin da Padova is credited with the illumination of various works, including an *Antiphonary* executed for Ferrara Cathedral and now in the Duomo Museum, Ferrara (*Cor. II*), and a copy of *Offici della Beata Vergine* etc. (Badia Archives, Montecassino, *MS. 620*). In 1482 Giovanni worked on the Ferrara *Chorales*.

Girolamo da Cremona (see pp. 334 and 348 f.) was of Lombard origin, but he was connected with Paduan art and has been identified with Girolamo Padovano referred to by Vasari.

Excellent examples of the Padua school of illumination, strongly influenced by the school of Ferrara, are: an *incunabulum* of Pliny (Classense Library, Ravenna, *Inc. 670*), a copy of Robertus Valturius (Capitulary Library at Padua, *MS. D. 11*) and of Macrobius (the same collection, *MS. W. 2*), a copy of *Decretum Gratiani* (Schifanoia Museum, Ferrara), etc. Other examples of Padua illumination are a very fine copy of Domitius Calderinus, of 1474, preserved in the Laurentian Library, Florence (*MS. Plut. 53, 2*); a copy of Petrarch in the National Library at Florence (*B. R. 103: B. 2. 3*); another copy in the Guarneriana Library, S. Daniele del Friuli (*MS. 139*); a copy of Pliny in the Marciana Library, Venice (*MS. Lat. VI, 245: 2976*); an *Epistolarium*, dated to 1509, with beautiful miniatures and fine decoration, preserved in the Seminary Library at Padua; perhaps also a mid-fifteenth-century *Pontifical Missal*, illuminated with strong German influences (Vatican Library, *Vat. Lat. 8700*), and other fine works. A *Flemish*(!) *Lectionary*, written and illuminated in Padua in 1436, is preserved in the Pierpont Morgan Library, at New York (*MS. 150*).

Belluno. Two excellent examples of the Belluno school of illumination may be referred to: (1) *Statutes of the City* (Library of the Gregorian Seminary), of the early fifteenth century; of particular charm is a miniature showing the magistrate "in cathedra"—in the presence of lawyers—administering justice. (2) *Statutes of the Monte di Pietà of Belluno* (Civic Library, Belluno) of the sixteenth century; it contains the Coat of Arms of Girolamo Zeno, "podestà" of Belluno, with a beautiful landscape background.

Venice—the Ducali

The productions of the Venetian school of illumination cannot be compared in excellence with the masterpieces of Florence, Ferrara, and Milan. The unique importance of this school lies in the fact that, thanks to the *Ducali*, the development of its art can—with a few gaps—be followed fairly closely from the fourteenth to the eighteenth centuries. The *Ducale* was a kind of covenant, which the Doge made with the Venetian people on his election, but in its wider sense the term also applies to other ducal documents such as ducal commissions, congratulatory addresses offered to a Doge, etc.

The earlier *Ducali* were of no great artistic merit; they usually contained a figure-initial with pendent border-ornament. From the mid-fifteenth-century onwards, the *Ducali* may be regarded as representative of Venetian illumination. Many of these *Ducali* are preserved in the British Museum: *Add. MSS. 21463* (dated 1486),

18000 (*1521*), *21414* (*c. 1530*), *17373* (*1554*), *King's MS. 156* (*1568*), and several others. A volume (*Add. MS. 20916*) contains a number of detached frontispieces from the late fifteenth century to 1620. The later *Ducali* are usually decorated by a full-page frontispiece; this is gorgeous in its colouring and florid design, but it is rather a poor imitation of panel-painting on a reduced scale than a refined miniature. The art of true illumination is better represented by the early Renaissance *Ducali*, which preserve a due balance between text, ornament, and figure-composition.

An excellent specimen of such a *Ducale* is British Museum *Add. MS. 15816*, the covenant of Cristoforo Mauro (1462). The first page contains a full border of flowers, rayed discs, and filigree-stems with numerous small figures of birds, foxes, etc. painted on the plain vellum, and enclosing medallions of apes, lions, and other animals, with the Mauro arms within a wreath supported by *putti* in the lower margin. There are three illuminated initials, the principal one being replaced, so to speak, by a fine miniature in subdued colours of the Doge adoring the enthroned Madonna and Child between S. Mark and S. Bernardino; the deep crimson of the Doge's robe lights up the whole miniature.

Of similar nature are the fourteenth- and fifteenth-century *Mariegole* of Venetian confraternities (such as those of S. Teodoro, S. Caterina da Siena, S. Marco, as well as of the 'calderari', the last being of 1446), which are preserved in the Civic Museum Correr at Venice (*MSS. IV. 21; 118*, etc.) and in the Marciana Library (*MS. Ital. VII, 2098*).

It is interesting to note that even in the fourteenth century several non-Venetian book-illuminators worked in Venice. It will suffice to refer to names such as Giovanni da Bologna, Niccolò di Giacomo (Crucifixion in *Missal MS. Lat. III. 97* in the Marciana Library) and Belbello da Pavia (see p. 346 f.). Giustino di maestro Gherardino da Forlì in 1365 executed a *Gradual* (Marciana Library, *MS. Lat. II. 119*). Moreover, Giovanni da Bologna influenced the Venetian Cristoforo Cortese (a leaf from a work of his is in the Wildenstein Collection at New York), whereas the degli Angeli school of Florence (see p. 326 f.) influenced the illuminators of *MS. Busta 956, 17, f. 21* in the Seminary Library at Venice. Instances of other MSS. showing external influences are: the fourteenth-century *Entrée de Spagne* (Marciana Library, *MS. Fr. 21*) and a copy of Dante (*MS. Ital. IX, 276 : 6902*, also in the Marciana Library).

Other Illumination. Few names of Venetian illuminators have come down to us. Benedetto Bordone (sixteenth century) is one of them. He painted a *Psalter*, in two volumes, which is now preserved in the Civic Museum at Padua (*MS. C. M. 811–12*). Also the illumination of *MS. 906* in the Correr Museum, Venice, is in Benedetto Bordone's style.

An otherwise unknown master Franciscus of S. Paul (a note says: *magister Franciscus miniator de S. Paulo Verone miniavit*) executed a copy of Giovanni Giacomo da Padova, *Libro della perfezione della vita* (Seminary Library at Padua, *MS. 432*).

Venetian illuminated works include the following codices: a *Bible* of 1454, in the Vatican Library (*Vat. Lat. 1*); *MSS. Lat. II, 39: 2999; and X, 190: 3555*; and *MS. It. XI, 196: 7577*, in the Marciana Library, Venice; the illuminations of a *Bible*, Venice, 1476, preserved in the Estense Library, Modena (*α. B. 1. 15*); a miniature in a printed copy of Dante (Marciana Library, *Inc. 157*), and other works. An interesting copy of *Antiquitates*, codex compiled by Giovanni Marcanova is preserved in the Estense Library, at Modena (*MS. α. L. 5. 15*); it was written in 1465 for Malatesta Novello, Lord of Cesena. A miniature in a printed copy of Petrarca's *Trionfi* of 1478 is in Florence, Bibl. Naz., B.R. 103.

Piedmont and Liguria. Excellent examples of Renaissance illumination produced in Piedmont partly influenced by Lombard, Ferrara and Flemish illumination, are: a fifteenth-century *Antiphonary* preserved in the Cathedral Archives at Casale Monferrato (*Cor. XI*); a late fifteenth-century *Book of Hours* preserved in the ex-Royal Library, Turin (*MS. Var. 78*); an early sixteenth-century *Book of Hours* preserved in the Riccardiana Library, Florence (*MS. 456*); a sixteenth-century copy of Antonius Pennetus, *Officium S. Sidonis*, preserved in the National Library at Turin (*MS. E. IV. 13*), and many other works.

A *Roman Breviary* produced for Leonardo Marchesi, Bishop of Albenga (1476–1513), and preserved in the Capitulary Library at Albenga, is a good example of Ligurian illumination of the period.

We may conclude this section with a beautiful *Gospel-book* which until 1932 was part of the Chester Beatty collection and is now in the Marciana Library (*Lat. I, 103: 11925*). The codex was written in 1528 by a certain presbyter Sebastian Cavazonus on commission by Cardinal Marino Grimani, Patriarch of Aquileia.

There are twelve fine compositions (containing the figures of the Evangelists, scenes from the life of Christ, etc.) decorated initials and borders. The illumination is attributed to two artists, an earlier and a later; the latter was by some scholars wrongly identified with Giulio Clovio—see p. 361 f.

The Marches and Umbria. Urbino, the birthplace of Raphael, was a famous centre of art and literature during the fifteenth and sixteenth centuries. Federico di Montefeltro and the other Dukes of Urbino were enlightened patrons of arts and their famous library—which in 1658 was acquired by Pope Alexander VII and is now part of the Vatican Library—contained the best examples of the art of illumination of the Renaissance.

It is therefore to be assumed that Urbino was also a great centre for the production of illuminated manuscripts, but it never reached the importance of other outstanding Italian centres such as Florence, Ferrara, and Milan. Although no great school of illumination arose in Urbino, and no names of outstanding illuminators of this city are known, in the Urbino collection of the Vatican Library and in some of the main libraries are preserved beautifully illuminated books produced there. Moreover, the Dukes of Urbino commissioned a great number of books in other centres of illumination (see, for instance, p. 331 f.).

Federico Veterani, the custodian of the library of the Dukes of Urbino, was a famous copyist and calligrapher. He copied a number of codices for the Urbino library, and apparently illuminated some of them. He also worked in Gubbio (now in the province of Perugia), which then belonged to the Duke of Urbino. Veterani has been credited with the execution in Urbino of a beautiful copy of Livy, in three volumes, now in the Vatican Library (*Urb. Lat. 423, 424, 425*). An illuminated copy of Appian (*Urb. Lat. 419*) may be considered an example of Veterani's book-production in Gubbio. The illumination of all these volumes shows strong influence of the Ferrara school.

Some volumes written by Veterani were illuminated by other artists, the majority being in the style of the Ferrara school (*Urb. Lat. 353, 325, 326*): see p. 337 ff.

Matteo de' Contugi of Volterra (see p. 333) was another famous copyist and calligrapher who worked for the Dukes of Urbino. He executed the Vatican Library codices *Urb. Lat. 336, 324, 427, 548, 10*, and other MSS., but nearly all of them were illuminated by Ferrara artists.

Pesaro was another centre of book-illumination which produced codices for the Dukes of Urbino. Examples (preserved in the Vatican Library) are *Urb. Lat. 1765, 1764, 899*.

The great Perugino—properly Pietro Vannucci (1446–1523)—head of the Umbrian school of painting, a pupil of Piero della Francesca and master of Raphael, was also an illuminator. Perugino executed a full-page Martyrdom of S. Sebastian, collaborating with Amico Aspertini and others in the illumination of the superb *Albani Hours* (ex-Yates-Thompson Collection at London). Another great master, Bernardino Pinturicchio (1454–1513), is credited with the painting of a full-page miniature of the Crucifixion in a *Roman Missal* preserved in the Vatican Library (*Barb. Lat. 614*); the illumination of the rest of the codex was executed by Florentine artists.

The brothers Giacomo (or Giapeco) and Bartolomeo Caporali who worked in the second half of the fifteenth century and in the early sixteenth are the best representatives of the Perugia school of illumination. Bartolomeo (1420–c. 1505) was rather a painter than an illuminator; he was a pupil of Gozzoli and was also influenced by Boccati, Piero della Francesca, Baldovinetti, and Perugino. Only in recent times scholars such as Gnoli and Salmi have recognized that Bartolomeo collaborated with Giacomo in the illumination of several books. Bartolomeo executed a series of miniatures depicting the Gates of Perugia with their Patron-saints and citizens. One such leaf, depicting Porta S. Angelo, is dated 1486 and is preserved in the Academy Gallery at Vienna. A *Missal*, written in 1496 and preserved in the Count Paolo Gerli di Villagaeta Collection at Milan, contains a large Crucifixion by Caporali in a style allied to that of Benozzo Gozzoli.

Examples of the works executed by Giacomo Caporali are: a *Roman Missal* preserved in the Capitulary Library at Perugia (*MS. 10*); an *Antiphonary*, executed in 1473, and preserved in S. Peter Basilica at Perugia (*Cor. M.*); and a *Liber publicorum negotiorum etc.*, preserved in the State Archives at Perugia (*MS. 108*). A

Missale Fratrum Minorum, executed in 1469 for the S. Francis convent in Montone (Perugia), and preserved in the Library of Count Paolo Gerli di Villagaeta, is a good example of the collaboration of the two brothers.

An *Antiphonary* of 1472, preserved in the S. Peter Basilica (*Cor. I*), was illuminated by Pierantonio di Giacomo da Pozzuolo. A contemporary codex, containing the rules of the public pawn-shop of Perugia (State Archives at Perugia, *MS. 33*) was illuminated by a Perugia artist, Lorenzo Spirito.

Interesting codices illuminated in Umbrian style are: Giacomo degli Oddi, *Specchio de l'Ordene*, known as *Franceschina* (fifteenth century; Augusta Library, Perugia, *MS. 1238*); an *Antiphonary* (fifteenth or sixteenth century; Badia, Monteoliveto Maggiore, *Cor. H.*); a *Psalter* (early sixteenth century; the same collection *Cor. T.*); a *Gradual* (sixteenth century, the same collection, *Cor. A*); and numerous other works. A fifteenth-century (*a.* 1464) *Roman Missal*, preserved in the Capitulary Archives at Urbino, is in a mixed Marches-Umbrian style of illumination.

Rome. There is no evidence of important original schools of illumination in Rome, though it is obvious that the Court of Rome must have attracted some of the best illuminators from various Italian centres. It is also certain that the Popes and various Roman noble families from time to time hired the services of famous artists, or commissioned illuminated books. On p. 345 f. reference has been made to Antonio da Monza, who illuminated a *Missal* for Pope Alexander VI.

Most of the works of the Roman school of illumination show influences of other schools. For instance, an exquisite copy of Riccobaldus Ferrariensis, *Pomerium Ecclesiae Ravennatis*, executed in 1462 for Pope Pius II and preserved in the Vallicelliana Library (*MS. D. 22*), is a product of the Roman school influenced by Ferrara illumination. A Greek copy of Pausanias illuminated in Rome in 1485 and preserved in the Laurentian Library, Florence (*MS. Plut. 56, 11*) shows Emilian influences.

Giacomo da Fabriano, documented for the years 1470-4, had a flourishing *bottega*, which worked for Federico d'Urbino, Pius II and Sixtus IV; interesting instance is a copy of Diodorus Siculus, *MS. Vat. Lat. 1816*.

A group of interesting codices is preserved in the Angelica Library, Rome (*MSS. 537, 551, 560,* and *577*). They were executed about 1470 for Niccolò di Cattaro, Bishop of Modrus. The illumination of this Roman school is in a transitional style from late Gothic to Renaissance.

A group of illuminated manuscripts in exquisite style, though influenced by North Italian styles of illumination, has recently (in 1950) been identified as a Roman school of illumination of the second half of the fifteenth century, allied with Humanists (such as Platina, Guazzelli, Persona, and others) connected with the Vatican Library and the Roman Academy. At least nine codices seem to belong to this group. They are: a copy of Caesar, in the Casanatense Library, Rome (*MS. 453*), a copy of *Scriptores historiae Augustae* (National Library at Rome, *MS. V. E. 1004*), and seven codices preserved in the Vatican Library: *Vat. Gr. 1626* (a copy of Homer, written and illuminated in 1477 for Cardinal Francesco

Gonzaga), *Reg. Lat. 1931* (a copy written before 1487, of Ludovico Guasti and Plutarch), *Vat. Lat. 2094* (a Latin copy of Aristotle, written for Sixtus IV), *Vat. Lat. 2058* (the presentation copy to Sixtus IV of George Trapezuntius, *Commentary on Ptolemy's Almagest*), *Vat. Lat. 3595* (a copy of Statius, *Sylvae*, and Ovid, *Letter from Sappho to Phaon*), *Vat. Lat. 2044* (presentation copy to Sixtus IV of Bartolomeo Platina, *Lives of the Roman Pontiffs*), and *Vat. Lat. 263* (Cristoforo Persona's Latin translation of Theophylactus, *Commentary on the Epistles of S. Paul*).

Naples

It is not certain the Naples had a proper and important school of illumination. The Aragonese kings of Naples were, however, great patrons of art and their court became a centre of art and culture, but the works produced for the court were neither outstanding nor characterized by a definite style. Indeed, it would be difficult to point out any definite feature which stamps these works as Neapolitan as distinct from contemporary works produced in other parts of Italy.

For instance, the *Psalter Add. MS. 28962* in the British Museum, which was executed in 1442 for Alfonso of Aragon, King of Naples (1442–58), is in a great mixture of styles; the artists were probably Spanish, and part of the MS. seems to be an imitation of French work.

Of exceptional interest is the *S. Martha Codex*, preserved in the State Archives at Naples. It consists of seventy-two parchment folios, containing the arms (and sometimes also decorated initials with personalities depicted in them) of sovereigns and high dignitaries who became members of the S. Martha Confraternity, Naples, from its foundation in 1400 until 1600. The miniatures, executed in various periods and styles, have a similar significance to the Sienese *Bicchernae* (see p. 335 ff.) and the Venetian *Ducali* (see p. 351 f.). The greater part of the artists probably belonged to the Neapolitan school of illumination, influenced by other schools (fols. 17r, 55r, 56r, 57r, and 58r, are attributed to Cola Rapicano), but some miniatures are attributed to artists of other Italian schools (fol. 2r, for instance, is attributed to a Lombard illuminator stylistically near to Leonardo da Besozzo) or even to foreign schools: fol. 9r is in a Franco-Flemish style, and some scholars even have suggested the name of Jean Foucquet (see p. 412 ff.). Because of its contents (see above) the *S. Martha Codex* is also known as *Catalogus illustriorum sodalium*.

King Ferdinand. Under Alfonso of Aragon, King of Naples, and particularly under Ferrante or Ferdinand I (Alfonso's natural son and successor), 1458–94, excellent Renaissance illumination was produced by the calligrapher Hippolytus Lunensis. Many books were illuminated either by him or under his direction. A sumptuous copy of *Joannis Scoti super libros Sententiarum quaestiones*, in several large volumes, is partly preserved in the British Museum (*Add. MSS. 15270–3*) and partly in the National Library at Paris (*Lat. 3063*). The borders of the pages, in the usual decorative scheme of Italian illumination, contain the scroll-work design with *putti*, rabbits and other animals, medallions enclosed in wreaths, and busts copied from antique gems, all painted on grounds of alternating blue, green, and crimson, set in a rectangular frame composed of narrow gold bands. The opening page of vol. V (*Add. MS. 15273*) is of special interest. Besides a full border as just described, it contains, attached to an initial, a neatly executed miniature of a scribe at work. Johannes Scotus is better known as Duns Scotus.

An excellent copy of Onosander, *De optimo imperatore*, signed *P. Hippolyti Lunensis manu*, and produced for Alfonso, is preserved in the Hofer Collection, Rockport, Maine. The codex contains four illuminated pages, finely drawn borders, and several ornamented initials.

Hippolytus worked chiefly for the King, but he also illuminated books for private personages; for instance, about 1480 he produced for Antonello Petrucci an Ovid (formerly in C. W. Dyson Perrins' Collection), in which the border-frames are in two styles, the usual Renaissance interlaced scroll-design of white vine-tendrils, and—as Herbert has pointed out—a scroll of thread-like stems with tiny leaves and large flowers on a plain vellum ground. This 'tendency to spoil the decorative effect of a page by overloading it with ill-assorted ornaments, was a besetting sin of the Renaissance illuminators' (Herbert). See further on and Fig. VI-43*d*.

Hippolytus was not the only illuminator who worked for King Ferdinand. We know of at least one other distinguished calligrapher who was a court-illuminator, Rudolfo Brancalupo. In 1480 he executed for Ferdinand a copy, in four bulky volumes, of S. Augustine's *Commentary on the Psalms* (British Museum, *Add. MSS. 14779–82*). The decoration, typical of the period, consists mainly of gold initials with pendent borders of interlaced white vine-tendrils on coloured grounds. Moreover, the first page of text of the third volume contains an elaborate Renaissance border-frame, and is preceded by a well-designed title-page: Herbert emphasizes that these late Italian title-pages are amongst the most pleasing features of Renaissance illumination, being usually characterized by a good taste checking that delight in ornament which so often ran riot elsewhere. See also further on.

Matteo Felice was another court illuminator of the Aragonese kings: an excellent copy of Virgil, preserved in Turin (ex-Royal Library, *MS. Var. 190*), has been attributed to him.

A luxurious manuscript (containing Valerius Maximus, *Factorum et dictorum memorabilium*), executed for King Ferdinand, is preserved in the New York Public Library, Spencer Collection. Apart from the ornamented borders, there are 133 illuminated initials. The borders—writes Miss Dorothy Miner—are ornamented in the humanist taste with representations of candelabra, coins, engraved gems, garlands, *putti*, and other classical motives, often executed in *camaieu d'or* and relieved against grounds of shredded blue, lavender, rose, etc. Miss Miner also points out that the work is notable for the integration of all these favourite humanistic motifs into the page design, and for the luminosity of colour and exquisite finish of the painting.

Other Neapolitan Bibliophiles and Patrons of Art. Cardinal John of Aragon, King Ferdinand's son, was also a book-collector. Peter of Bordeaux copied for him various MSS., such as a copy of Aquinas (National Library at Naples, *MS. VII. B. 4*), and a copy of Albertus Magnus (University Library of Valencia, *Cod. 838*). See Fig. VI-44*a*.

The scholar and bibliophile Andrea Matteo Acquaviva, Duke of Atri, was another famous book-collector. There are many luxurious codices which were executed for him. A copy of Apuleius (see further on), a luxurious copy of Livy, a copy of Themistius, a copy of Cicero (see below), and a copy of Pliny (preserved in the Gerolamini Library, Naples, *MS. C.F. 5.5.*), are a few of the MSS. which were produced for Duke Acquaviva.

A charming *Book of Hours*, dated 1478, executed in Naples for Lorenzo Strozzi by 'Alexander Antonii Simonis' of Florence, is preserved in the Fitzwilliam Museum, Cambridge (*MS. 153*). It contains twenty-six full-page illuminations and numerous initials.

Title-pages. An interesting title-page is contained in another MS. produced for a member of the Court of Naples, Don Iñigo Davalos, Count of Monte Odorisio and Grand Chamberlain to King Ferdinand. It is a copy of S. Augustine's *City of God* and is preserved in the British Museum (*Add. MS. 15246*). Its decoration is excellent, particularly the first page of text (containing a beautiful miniature-initial and a charming highly ornate border-frame). Of interest is its delightful, symmetrical and tasteful title, written in plain Roman capitals. It 'is encircled by a garland, which again is surrounded by a scroll-work design of foliage, flowers, and rayed gilt discs, with the patron's arms and with numerous putti disporting themselves among the branches' (Herbert). The decoration is in Florentine style.

Other Neapolitan Productions. A charming Neapolitan product is a *Book of Hours* executed in Naples for George Castriota Scanderberg (*c.* 1403–67), King of Albania. Some illuminated MSS. are attributed to the Neapolitan Colantonio school of illumination; for instance a copy of Hippolytus Lunensis, *Sentenze e proverbi* (National Library at Naples, *MS. XII. E. 32*): Fig. VI-43*d* (see also p. 357).

Some fine illuminated codices are assigned to the Neapolitan *bottega* of Reginaldo Piramo da Monopoli: a copy of Virgil, *Aeneid*, preserved in the National Library at Naples (*MS. IV. E.25*); a copy of Apuleius (Gerolamini Library, Naples, *MS. C.F. 5.7.*); a copy of Cicero (the same collection, *MS. C.F. 5.4*); a copy of Themistius (the same collection, *MS. C.F. 5.6*), and others. Other works are attributed to the *bottega* of Nicola Rapicano or to his followers. Examples are: a copy of Caesar, preserved in the Riccardiana Library, Florence (*MS. 1569*); a copy of the Spanish-Portuguese *Cancionero* in the Casanatense Library, Rome (*MS. 1098*); and a copy of Cyprian in the National Library at Naples (*MS. VI. C. 4*). See Fig. VI-44*b*.

Reginaldo Piramo and Nicola (or Cola) Rapicano, who worked from 1451 onwards, were under Flemish influence; this is particularly noticeable in the naturalistic features of Cola's works. Cola was also influenced by Francesco d'Antonio (see p. 329 f.): hence, his medallions and *putti*. Cola's sons Filippo and Nardo continued to produce illuminated books, mainly in Paduan style on Classical background; example: a charming copy of Pliny now in the Gerolamini Library at Naples (*MS. C. F. 5.5*). Paduan style (with Flemish and Lombard influences) also appears in works executed by Cristoforo Maiorana, who worked in the years 1480–92; an instance: an elegant copy of Aesop, now in Valencia. Gaspare da Padova, also called Gaspare Romano, worked in Paduan style, whilst Giovanni Todeschino, documented for the years 1488–95, who was born in Lombardy, naturally enough was mainly influenced by Lombard illumination.

A copy of Caesar, written by a certain Jacobus Laurentianus and preserved in the National Library at Naples (*MS. XI. AA. 51*), is illuminated in the style of Gioacchino de Gigantibus, influenced by the Ferrara and Padua schools. He also executed a copy of Bessarion, now in the National Library at Paris (*MS. Lat. 12946*).

Under Alfonso's and Ferdinand's reigns, excellent illumination was done in Naples. A beautiful copy of Arrianus, *De rebus gestis Alexandri Magni*, produced for Alfonso of Aragon, is preserved in the Vatican Library (*Urb. Lat. 415*). A copy of Bonifacio Calabro, *Libro di maniscalcia*—in a popular form—produced in the fifteenth century, is preserved in the Gerolamini Library, at Naples (*MS. C.F. 4. 10*). Slightly later works are: a *Life of S. John the Baptist* (Tuscan influences; National Library at Naples, MS. XIII. F.24); a *Roman Breviary* (Umbrian and Ferrara influences; the same collection, MS. I.B. 23); a copy of S. Jerome, *Epistolae* (the same collection, *MS. VI. C. 2*); a *Book of Hours*, illuminated by two artists of the Neapolitan school (the same collection, *MS. I. B. 26*); a copy of Petrarch's *I Trionfi*, preserved in Florence (National Library, *MS. Palat., 197*). A copy of Bessarion, *Opuscula*, illuminated in Naples, is preserved in Venice (Marciana Library, *MS. Lat. Z. 135: 1694*); a copy of Sext. Propertius, *Carmina* is in the Casanatense Library (*MS. 915*); a copy of Diodorus Siculus is preserved in the University Library at Bologna (*MS. 618*); a beautifully illuminated *Psalter* is in the Badia Archives, Montevergine (*MS. 12*). Two *Antiphonaries*, of the late fifteenth and the early sixteenth century, are preserved in the National Library at Naples (*MSS. XV. AA. 6* and *18*); a richly illuminated copy, dated to 1465, of *Vaticinia* is in the Angelica Library, Rome (*MS. 1146*). See, for instance, Fig. VI-44c and *d*.

A beautiful, pocket-size copy of Virgil, now preserved in the Walters Art Gallery, Baltimore (*W. 400*), was produced in Naples about the year 1500. It contains two full-page miniatures, painted in *camaieu d'or* on lavender-stained leaves, with some use of green, blue, and red for the landscape, and silver (now oxidized) as highlights on flesh. There are two 'architectural frames with *putti* that surround the initial text pages of the separate works' (D. Miner) and one historiated frame (introducing the *Georgics*) consists of a craggy landscape, with men plowing, woodcutters, olive trees, and beehives: Fig. VI-45a. Fig. VI-45b reproduces a miniature from a slightly earlier (of *c.* 1480) *Horae*, also in the Walters Art Gallery (*W. 328*). It contains seven miniatures, six historiated initials and complex gold vine borders with birds and animals. Its ornamentation incorporates a heraldic motto *Spera in Dio*, also appearing in *W. 329* of the same collection.

Sicily. A *Benedictine Breviary*, of the late fifteenth or the early sixteenth century, executed for the monastery of S. Martino delle Scale, near Palermo, is preserved in the National Library at Palermo (*MS. XV. H.1*). The first page contains a wide frame with foliage and coloured flowers (golden on sky-blue background, and sky-blue on golden backgrounds in the lower border), with *putti*, birds, etc., and four historiated medallions in the margins. Fol. *54v* also contains a richly illuminated border. There are eight large, decorated initials. The illumination of this codex is attributed to various Sicilian artists.

The difficulty of assigning certain MSS. with Renaissance illumination, and particularly the mediocre ones, to a definite region can be exemplified by two codices which have been assigned to Sicily for one reason or another, though the MSS. give no direct evidence for such an attribution:

A small *Book of Hours* (British Museum, *Add. MS. 28271*) of Roman use, was made for a patron whose name began with C (fol. 159) and whose arms—per bend, azure and or, over all a leopard rampant argent—are on the first page. There is a certain coarseness in the miniatures, especially in the facial types, but this would not suffice to identify the origin of the MS. The only indication is the Litany, which points distinctly to Sicily or the extreme south of Italy.

Another British Museum MS. (*Add. MS. 21120*) contains a copy of Prince Charles of Viana's Spanish translation of Aristotle's *Ethics*; it was evidently executed for the translator himself. There are no miniatures, but there are beautiful initials and border-frames. It has been suggested that the MS. was decorated in Sicily during the Prince's residence there (1458–9). This is possible, but Herbert suggests a Spanish origin which may be indicated by the language and what little is known of the history of the book, as well as by the resemblance in style between its decoration and that of a fragmentary *Toledo Missal* in the British Museum (*Add. MS. 38037*)—see also p. 169.

Sixteenth Century—End of Italian Illumination

In the early sixteenth century the illumination of manuscripts decayed as a feature of book-production. This was largely the result of the development and spread of printing and of the wood-cut book-illustration; moreover, the progress in the manufacture of paper and the consequent cheapness of books rendered almost impossible the competition of copies written one by one, and illuminated on parchment.

Be it as it may, the days of book-painting were numbered. Although for a short time here and there it still continued to flourish as a branch of art, its quality became decadent, its vitality was ebbing rapidly, and very soon it lost any real significance in the history of painting. In short, at a time when panel-painting was nearing perfection, the art of illumination was nearing its end. Book-illumination lost its originality and became little more than a distant echo of the divine productions of the Renaissance panel-painters.

Not that there was a sudden falling off in the output of illuminated MSS. Their quantity was still considerable, both in the great choir-books (see p. 313) which were required for use in monastic and other churches, and in smaller but even more sumptuous volumes of devotional or secular character, produced for prelates, princes, and other nobility. Certain types of illuminated books—for instance, the *Book of Hours*—continued to be popular, and there was also an abundance of highly skilled craftsmen who devoted their talents to the illumination of books, taking their inspiration from panel-paintings, from cartoons, from tapestries, or even from woodcuts. There was little originality, however, and with one or two exceptions, such as Perugino (see p. 354), who painted one of the miniatures in the *Albani Book of Hours*, hardly any great master took further interest in this art.

Clovio and Apollonio. Two famous illuminators are outstanding: Giorgio Giulio Clovio and Apollonio de' Bonfratelli. Their productions are the last Italian flashes of a dying art. Clovio was a Croatian by birth (he was born at Grizane in 1498): his original name was Jurai (or George) Glovichsich. At eighteen he migrated to Italy, where (in Perugia, Rome, and Florence) he worked as book-illuminator until his death in Rome in 1578. His work was influenced by his friend Giulio Romano (Raphael's pupil), by Michelangelo and Bronzino, and by Flemish artists. Clovio's work, though often technically good, never rises above an 'insipid elegance'. He was fond—writes Herbert—of weak suave forms, cheap sentiment, and soft broken colours. His usual weaknesses peep out continually, especially in the larger compositions: his mawkish sentiment, want of dignity, and florid taste.

He actually executed many illuminations, but a great number of works attributed to him are now regarded as the productions of his pupils or imitators. Two of his best works are in London, both having been made for his patron, Cardinal Marino Grimani, Patriarch of Aquileia (*see also* p. 455). These works are a copy of the *Commentary on S. Paul's Epistle to the Romans* (now in the Soane Museum, London, *MS. 11*), and a *Book of Hours* (British Museum, *Add. MS. 20927*). The former contains a large, beautifully finished frontispiece of the Conversion of S. Paul. The other book is much smaller, but it has several full-page illuminations containing, as Herbert points out, frame-borders of the amazingly miscellaneous character so loved by the late Renaissance illuminators: satyrs, pieces of armour, birds, nude athletes, scriptural scenes, all jostling one another on the gilded and coloured grounds. Many of the miniatures are exquisitely painted, soft and delicate, and occasionally vigorous, too, as in the vignette of David beheading Goliath, which forms part of the admirable frontispiece to the Penitential Psalms (fol. 91*v*). Fig. VI-46*a*.

A superb *Missal*, in six volumes, executed *c.* 1517 for Cardinal Pompeo Colonna, is preserved in The John Rylands Library, Manchester (*Lat. MS. 32*).

The tradition handed down by the family was that the large full-page illustrations were executed by Raphael about 1517 on the elevation of Colonna to the cardinalate; but modern investigations have shown that there is a close similarity in style to that of the *Farnese Hours*, which is attributed to Clovio. Indeed, this *Book of Hours*, executed in 1546 for Card. Alessandro Farnese and now preserved in New York (Pierpont Morgan Library, *M. 69*) is Clovio's masterpiece. Fig. VI-46*b*.

One of the best of the great number of works formerly attributed to Clovio and nowadays regarded as the production of his pupils or imitators is that of the *Victories of Charles V* (British Museum, *Add. MS. 33733*).

Apollonio de' Bonfratelli, Clovio's pupil, has in Herbert's opinion many of his master's affectations; but he composes in a larger, freer manner, and adopts a deeper and more brilliant colour-scheme. His conception of the human form, too, is essentially different; instead of Giulio's slender and often absurdly elongated figures, he prefers a more robust type, and gives us thickset, clumsy, yet vital and actual men and women. He cannot be called a great artist, argues Herbert, but his work is not without merit, and he may fitly be taken as the last representative of the great Italian illuminators.

(This particularly concerns secular books which then were mainly decorated with woodcuts, whereas religious books, particularly *Chorales*, continued to be illuminated. It has, thus, rightly been remarked that the art of illumination ended as it had begun, as an art for the nearly exclusive use of the Church: see, for instance, Fig. VI-19–22.)

His output does credit to his industry; some of his miniatures are signed, including those executed in 1564 for Pope Pius IV; the MS. is lost, but the miniatures cut out from it are preserved in the *Rogers Album* (British Museum, *Add. MS. 21412*, fol. 36–44). Amongst these miniatures there are a Crucifixion and Pietà (fol. 42 and 43) which led us to assign to Apollonio a large miniature of the Crucifixion preserved in the Condé Museum, at Chantilly (N. France), formerly attributed to Clovio.

Some other names may be referred to. Benedetto Bordone, illuminator and woodcutter, worked in Padua in the late fifteenth and early sixteenth century; he died in 1539. He illuminated a *Missal*, now in the British Museum (*Add. MS. 15813*); a *Gospel-book*, signed, preserved in the Holford Collection; and a *Psalter* in two volumes produced for the church of S. Giustina at Padua, and now in the Padua Civic Museum.

Agostino Decio flourished in the Duchy of Milan under Francesco II Sforza (1492–1535). He illuminated religious books at the courts of Rodolfo II and the Duke of Savoy. His son Ferrante worked also for the Pope. Their works were influenced by Renaissance panel-painting. Instances are *Chorales* in the Certosa di Pavia; a *Missal*, a *Gospel-book*, and an *Epistolarium* in Vigevano.

In the early sixteenth century Florentine illumination was cultivated at the court of Pope Leo X (1513–21), who was a Medici.

Jacopo Grillo of Florence illuminated a *Psalter*, signed and dated 1538, for the church of S. Giorgio Maggiore at Venice (now *Cor. 12A*).

In Perugia, Giovan-Battista Caporali (1476–1560), son of Bartolomeo (see p. 354 f.), in 1553 illuminated a copy of *Annali Decemvirali*, preserved in the Augusta Library at Perugia; he also executed a *Missal* for Perugia Cathedral (now in the Beco Collection at Buenos Aires).

A fine Greek MS. written by Giovanni Onorio de Maglie of Lecce, a copyist and calligrapher of the Vatican from 1535 to 1550, is preserved in the Hofer Collection, Rockport, Maine. The codex, commissioned by Pope Paul III (1534–49), a great patron of art, contains the *Life and Reign of Octavius Caesar* (an excerpt from Dio Cassius, *History of Rome*). There are two illuminated pages, and the 'tiny volume shows delicate penmanship and wide, finely balanced margins' (D. Miner).

Also in Rome, a French artist Raymond Vincent in 1549 was appointed by Paul III as illuminator of the Pope. Influenced by Raphael and Michelangelo, he executed a famous *Psalter* now in Paris (National Library, *MS. Lat. 8880*).

The last important event in the history of Italian illumination was the commission by Pius V for the church in Bosco, near Alessandria, of thirty-seven *Chorales* and four *Collettari*. They were executed *c.* 1585 and are preserved in the Alessandria Communal Library.

Bernardo Buontalenti (1536–1608), a famous Florentine architect, sculptor and painter, may be considered the last important artist of Italy who was also an illuminator.

HUNGARY

Mainly for political reasons, Hungary has made hardly any contribution in the field of book-illumination. The only luminous exception, Matthias Corvinus, was a great patron of art and a great bibliophile. The artists who worked for him were, however, Italians; hence, he was dealt with in the chapter on Italy (pp. 328, 330 f., 333, 342 f.).

One of the great treasures of the Vatican Library, *Ottobonianus Lat. 51*, is also a product of a central Italian school. The codex is known as the *Ottobonian Pontifical*. It measures 355 × 252 mm. and contains 208 leaves with 24 miniatures (11 large and 13 small ones, some of the latter not completed), all enclosed in shrines, and very richly decorated with borders, animals, *putti* and the raven (the emblem of Matthias Corvinus).

The volume was probably produced, between 1489 and 1490, in Hungary for Vitéz János junior, bishop of Veszprém. Indeed, Vitéz himself, portrayed with great effect, appears in several miniatures, at various functions of his office, surrounded by his clergy.

The codex is written in "Gothic" minuscule-hand; the superb illuminations are by a great master, and show Florentine influences, especially of Ghirlandaio (who worked for Matthias Corvinus).

BIBLIOGRAPHY

A. Caravita, *I codici e le arti a Monte Cassino*, 3 vols., Montecassino, 1869–70.

E. Cheney, *Remarks on the Illuminated Official Manuscripts of the Venetian Republic*, London, 1869.

G. Campori, 'Notizie dei miniatori dei principi estensi', *Atti e memorie delle RR. Deput. di Storia Patria per le Prov. Modenesi e Parmensi*, 1872.

Bibliotheca Casinensis seu codicum manuscriptorum qui in Tabulario casinensi asservantur, 5 vols., Montecassino, 1873–94.

I codici petrarcheschi delle Biblioteche Governative del Regno, Rome, 1874.

O. Piscicelli Taeggi, *Paleografia artistica di Monte Cassino*, Montecassino, 1876.

A. Bartoli, *I manoscritti italiani della Biblioteca Nazionale di Firenze*, 3 vols., Firenze, 1879–83.

G. Porro, *Catalogo dei codici manoscritti della Trivulziana*, Torino, 1884.

A. Venturi, 'L'arte a Ferrara nel periodo di Borso d'Este,' *Rivista Storica Italiana*, 1885; 'La mostra d'arte antica a Bologna', *Rassegna Emiliana di Storia etc.*, 1888; 'La miniatura ferrarese nel sec. XV e il "Decretum Gratiani",' *Le Gallerie Naz. Ital.*, 1899; *Storia dell'arte italiana*, 10 vols., Milan, 1901–1937; 'Antifonario miniato di Giovanni di Paolo,' *L'Arte*, 1923; 'Un grande miniatore quattrocentesco (Francesco di Giorgio Martini),' *L'Arte*, 1925.

G. Mongeri, 'L'arte del minio nel ducato di Milano dal sec. XIII al XVI etc.', *Archivio Storico Lombardo*, 1885.

M. Caffi, 'Miniature cremonesi', *Il Bibliofilo*, 1885.

G. B. Cavalcaselle and J. A. Crowe, *Storia della pittura in Italia etc.*, Florence, 1886–1908; Engl. transl. (J. A. Crowe and G. B. Cavalcaselle), *History of painting in Italy*, 6 vols., London, 1903–14.

R. Zazzeri, *Sui codici e libri a stampa della Biblioteca Malatestiana di Cesena*, Cesena, 1887.

A. M. Latil, *Le miniature nei rotoli dell'Exultet etc.*, Montecassino, 1889.

G. Ottino, *I codici bobbiesi nella Biblioteca Nazionale di Torino*, Torino and Palermo, 1890.

G. W. Bradley, *The Life and Works of Giorgio Giulio Clovio*, London, 1891.

F. Carta, *Codici, corali e libri a stampa miniati della Biblioteca Nazionale di Milano*, Rome, 1891.

F. Malaguzzi Valeri, 'I codici miniati di Niccolò di Giacomo e della sua scuola in Bologna,' *Atti e Memorie della R. Deput. di Storia Patria p. le prov. di Romagna*, 1892–3; 'La collezione d. miniature nell'Archivio di Stato di Bologna,' *Archivio Stor. d. Arte*, 1894; 'La miniatura in Bologna dal XIII al XVIII sec.', *Archivio Stor. Ital.*, 1896; 'Le pergamene, i codici miniati e i disegni del R. Archivio di Stato di Bologna,' *Atti e Memorie d. R. Dep. di Storia Patria p. le prov. di Romagna*, 1897–8; *La corte di Ludovico il Moro*, 4 vols., Milan, 1913–23.

R. Galli, *I manoscritti e gli incunaboli della Biblioteca Comunale d'Imola*, Imola, 1894.

L. Frati, *I corali della Basilica di S. Petronio in Bologna*, Bologna, 1896.

A. Bassermann, *Dantes Spuren in Italien*, Heidelberg, 1897.

BIBLIOGRAPHY

G. Gruyer, *L'Art ferrarais à l'époque des Princes d'Este*, 2 vols., Paris, 1897.

G. Mazzatinti, *Invent. d. manoscr. ital. d. bibliot. di Francia*, 3 vols., Rome, 1886–8; *Invent. d. manoscr. d. bibliot. d. Convento di S. Francesco d'Assisi*, Forlì, 1894; *La bibliot. dei Re d'Aragona in Napoli*, Rocca S. Casciano, 1897.

S. Borghesi and L. Banchi, *Nuovi documenti per la storia dell'arte senese*, Siena, 1898.

H. J. Hermann, 'Miniaturhandschriften aus d. Bibl. d. Herzogs Andrea Matteo III Acquaviva', *Jahrb. der kunsthist. Samml. d. allerh. Kaiserhauses*, 1898.

L. Volkmann, *Iconografia dantesca etc.*, Firenze and Venezia, 1898.

A. Zorzi, *Notizie, guida e bibliografia dei RR. Museo Arch., Archivio e Bibliot. già Capitolari ed antico Archivio Comun. di Cividale del Friuli*, Cividale, 1899.

S. Morpurgo, *I manoscritti d. R. Bibliot. Riccardiana di Firenze: Manoscritti italiani*, I, Rome, 1900.

P. Toesca, 'Il "Liber Canonum" d. Bibl. Vallicelliana (cod. A.5),' *L'Arte*, 1902; 'Michelino da Besozzo e Giovannino de'Grassi, Ricerche sull'antica pittura lombarda,' *L'Arte*, 1905; 'A proposito di Giovannino dei Grassi,' *L'Arte*, 1906; 'Di alcuni miniatori lombardi della fine del Trecento,' *L'Arte*, 1907; *La pittura e la miniatura nella Lombardia dai più antichi documenti alla metà del Quattrocento*, Milan, 1912; 'Ancora della pittura e della miniatura in Lombardia nei secoli XIV e XV,' *L'Arte*, 1913; *Storia dell'arte italiana*, I, 1–2: *Il Medioevo*, Turin, 1927; II: *Il Trecento*, Turin, 1951; 'Miniature romane dei sec. XI e XII. Bibbie miniate,' *Rivista del R. Ist. d'Archeol. e Storia d. Arte*, 1929; *Monumenti e studi per la storia della miniatura italiana, I: la Collezione di Ulrico Hoepli*, Milan, 1930; 'Francesco Pesellino miniatore,' *Dedalo*, 1932; 'Quelques Miniatures vénitiennes du XIVᵉ siècle,' *Scriptorium*, 1946–7; *L'Uffiziolo visconteo Landau-Finaly donato alla città di Firenze*, Florence, 1951.

Masséna Prince d'Essling and E. Muentz, *Pétrarque: ses études d'art, son influence sur les artistes etc.*, Paris, 1902.

P. Lugano, *Memorie dei più antichi miniatori e calligrafi olivetani*, Florence, 1903.

Biblioteca Vaticana, *Le miniature del Pontificale Ottoboniano (cod. Vat. Ottob. 501) etc.*, Rome, 1903.

E. Bertaux, *L'Art dans l'Italie méridionale*, Paris, 1904; 'Le Missel de Jean Borgia,' *Revue de l'art anc. et mod.*, 1905.

P. d'Ancona, 'La miniatura alla mostra senese d'arte antica,' *L'Arte*, 1904; 'Un ignoto collaboratore del Beato Angelico (Zanobi Strozzi),' *L'Arte*, 1908; 'Un'opera ignorata di Attavante degli Attavanti nella Bibliot. Corsiniana di Roma,' *Rivista d'Arte*, 1910; 'I bagni di Pozzuoli raffigurati in un codice napoletano de' primi del secolo XIV,' *L'Arte*, 1913; *La miniatura fiorentina*, 2 vols., Florence, 1914; 'Due preziosi cimelii miniati nel Duomo di Casale Monferrato,' *L'Arte*, 1916; 'L'arte di Oderisio da Gubbio,' *Dedalo*, 1921; *L'uomo e le sue opere nelle figurazioni italiane del Medioevo (miti, allegorie, leggende)*, Florence, 1923; *La miniature italienne du Xᵉ au XVIᵉ siècle*, Paris, 1925; 'Virgilio e le arti rappresentative,' *Emporium*, 1927; 'L'arte e la cultura italiana in Ungheria sotto il regno di Mattia Corvino,' *Emporium*, 1927; *La Divina Commedia. Tavole illustrative*, Bergamo, 1934.

F. Menčik, 'Die neapolitaner Handschriften der Hofbibliothek,' *Mitteilungen des oesterreichischen Vereins fuer Bibliotheksw.*, 1904 and 1905.

A. Graf zu Erbach Fuerstenau, 'Pittura e miniatura a Napoli nel sec. XIV,' *L'Arte*, 1905; 'La miniatura bolognese nel Trecento (Studi su Nicolò di Giacomo),' *L'Arte*, 1911.

O. Sirén, *Don Lorenzo Monaco*, Strasbourg, 1905.

R. Bratti, 'Arte retrospettiva : miniature veneziane,' *Emporium*, 1907.

C. Cipolla, *Codici bobbiesi della Biblioteca Nazionale Universitaria di Torino*, 2 vols., Turin, 1907.

T. Gnoli, *L'arte umbra alla Mostra di Perugia*, Bergamo, 1908.

A Muñoz, 'Un Theatrum Sanitatis con miniature veronesi del sec. XIV d. Biblioteca Casanatense,' *Madonna Verona*, 1908.

T. Gerevitch, 'Le relazioni tra la miniatura el la pittura bolognese nel Trecento,' *Rassegna d'Arte*, 1909.

R. Baldani, 'La pittura a Bologna nel sec. XIV,' *Documenti e Studi d. R. Dep. di Storia Patria p. le prov. di Romagna*, 1909.

L. Testi, *Storia della pittura veneziana, I: Le origini*, Bergamo, 1909.

V. Balzano, *L'arte abruzzese*, Bergamo, 1910; *Guglielmo di maestro Berardo di Gessopalena, miniatore del sec. XIV*, Lanciano, 1920; 'Berardo di Teramo, antico miniatore abruzzese ignorato,' *Rassegna di Storia e d'Arte d'Abruzzo e Molise*, 1927.

C. Frati and A. Segarizzi, *Catalogo dei codici marciani italiani*, 2 vols., Modena, 1909-11.

C. Ricci, *L'arte in Italia*, Bergamo, 1910.

A. de Hevesy, 'Les miniaturistes de Matthias Corvin,' *Revue de l'art chr.*, 1911; *La Biblioth. du roi Matthias Corvin*, Paris, 1923.

W. Bombe, *Geschichte der peruginer Malerei bis zu Perugino und Pinturicchio*, Berlin, 1912.

T. Borenius, ed., *History of Painting in North Italy*, London, 1912.

A. Serafini, 'Ricerche sulla miniatura umbra (sec. XIV–XVI),' *L'Arte*, 1912.

G. Biagi, *Cinquanta tavole . . . da codici d. Bibliot. Mediceo-Laurenziana*, Florence, 1914.

L. Dami, *Siena e le sue opere d'arte*, Firenze, 1915; 'La miniatura fiorentina dall'XI al XVI sec.,' *Rassegna d'arte*, 1915; 'Giovanni di Paolo miniatore e i paesisti senesi,' *Dedalo*, 1923.

Codicum Casinensium manuscriptorum catalogus, 3 vols., Montecassino, 1915-41.

A. M. Bessone Aureli (ed.), G. Vasari, *Vita di Giulio Clovio*, Florence, 1915.

G. Pacchioni, 'Belbello da Pavia e Gerolamo da Cremona miniatori. Un prezioso Messale gonzaghesco del sec. XV,' *L'Arte*, 1915.

G. Carbonelli and R. Ravasini, *Commenti sopra alcune miniature e pitture italiane a soggetto medico, specialmente dell'arte d'illustrare il Tacuinum Sanitatis nei secc. XIV e XV etc.*, Rome, 1918.

R. van Marle, *Simone Martini et les peintres de son école*, Strasbourg, 1920; *The Development of the Italian Schools of Painting*, 19 vols., The Hague, 1923-38.

BIBLIOGRAPHY

A. Bellucci, 'Il codice Filippino della Divina Commedia è anteriore al 1323?' *Bollettino del Bibliofilo*, 1921.

M. Salmi, 'Gerolamo da Cremona miniatore e pittore,' *Bollettino d'Arte d. Min. d. Pubbl. Instruz.*, 1922-3; 'Intorno al miniatore Neri da Rimini,' *Bibliofilia*, 1931; 'La scuola di Rimini,' *Rivista d. Instit. d'Archeol. e Storia d. Arte*, 1931-2; 'La miniatura,' *Tesori d. Biblioteche d'Italia: Emilia e Romagna*, 1932; 'Bartolomeo Caporali a Firenze,' *Rivista d'Arte*, 1933; 'Un Evangelario miniato fiorentino,' *Rivista d'Arte*, 1937; 'La Bibbia di Borso d'Este e Piero della Francesca,' *La Rinascita*, 1943; 'Problemi dell'Angelico,' *Commentari*, 1950; 'Contributo a Belbello da Pavia,' *Miscellanea Giovanni Galbiati*, Milan, 1951; 'Due miniatori urbinati,' *Commentari*, 1952; 'La miniatura fiorentina medioevale,' *Accademie e Bibliot. d'Italia*, 1952; 'Nota su Bonifacio Bembo,' *Commentari*, 1952; *La miniatura fiorentina gotica*, Rome, 1954; *La miniatura italiana*, Milan, 1955 (Engl. translation, 1957).

C. H. Weigelt, 'Lombardische Miniaturen im Kupferstichkabinett,' *Jahrbuch d. preuss. Kunstsamml.*, 1923; *La pittura senese del Trecento*, 1930.

U. Gnoli, *Pittori e miniatori nell' Umbria*, Spoleto, 1923.

G. Biagi, *La Divina Commedia nella figurazione artistica etc.*, 3 vols., Turin, 1924-39.

B. Berenson, 'Un Antiphonaire avec miniatures par Lippo Vanni,' *Gazette di beaux-arts*, 1924; *Pitture italiane del Rinascimento*, Milan, 1936.

A. Moschetti, 'Il tesoro della Cattedrale di Padova,' *Dedalo*, 1925-6; *Il Museo Civico di Padova etc.*, 2nd. ed., Padua, 1938.

G. Bertoni, *Il maggior miniatore della Bibbia di Borso d'Este: Taddeo Crivelli*, Modena, 1925.

D. Fava, *La Biblioteca Estense etc.*, Modena, 1925; *I tesori delle biblioteche italiane: Emilia e Romagna*, Milan, 1932; 'Il Breviario di Ercole I d'Este,' *Accademie e Bibliot. d'Italia*, 1939; *La Biblioteca Nazionale Centrale di Firenze etc.*, Milan, 1939; 'I corali degli Olivetani di Bologna,' *Miscellanea di bibliogr. ed erud. in memoria di L. Ferrari*, Florence, 1952; 'Documenti artistici della educazione dei principi nella corte sforzesca di Milano,' *Accademie e Bibliot. d'Italia*, 1952; 'La miniatura ferrarese etc.,' *Studi Riminesi etc. in onore di C. Lucchesi*, Faenza, 1952; — — and M. Salmi, *I manoscritti miniati della Biblioteca Estense*, I, Florence, 1950; *Mostra di manoscritti e incunabuli del Decretum Gratiani*, Bologna, 1952.

E. Martini, 'Sui codici napoletani restituiti dall'Austria,' *Atti d. Reale Accad. di Archeol., Lettere e Belle Arti*, 1926.

Bibliotheca Corvina, *La Biblioteca di Matteo Corvino, re d'Ungheria*, Budapest, 1927.

J. P. Gilson, *An Exultet Roll etc. (B.M. Add. MS. 30377)*, London, 1929.

G. Castelfranco, 'I corali miniati di S. Domenico di Gubbio,' *Bollettino d'Arte del Min. d. Pubbl. Istr.*, 1929; 'Contributi alla storia della miniatura bolognese del '200,' *Bologna*, 1935.

L. Serra, *L'arte nelle Marche*, I: *Dalle origini cristiane alla fine del Gotico*, Pesaro, 1929; II: *Il periodo del Rinascimento*, Roma, 1934.

E. Berkovits, 'Un codice dantesco nella Biblioteca della R. Università di Buda-pest,' *Corvina*, 1930; 'Un antifonario sconosciuto miniato da Giovanni di Paolo,' *Corvina*, 1943.

R. Brenzoni, *Liberale da Verona (1445–1526)*, Milan, 1930.

R. Offner, *A Critical and Historical Corpus of Florentine Painting*, New York, 1930 ff.

G. Salvoni Savorini, 'Monumenti della miniatura negli Abruzzi,' *Atti d. Conv. Storico Abruzz.-Molisano*, Casalbordino, 1931.

P. Schubring, *Illustrationen zu Dantes Goettlicher Komoedie, Italien 14. bis 16. Jahrh.*, Zurich-Leipsic-Vienna, 1931.

N. Gabrielli, 'La Bibbia atlantica della Biblioteca Beriana di Genova ed i suoi rapporti con l'arte dell'Italia Centrale,' *Accademie e Bibliot. d'Italia*, 1932–3.

C. Brandi, 'Niccolò di Ser Sozzo Tegliacci', *L'Arte*, 1932; *La R. Pinacoteca di Siena*, Rome, 1933; *Giovanni di Paolo*, Florence, 1947; *Quattrocentisti senesi*, Milan, 1949.

A. M. Ciaranfi, 'Lorenzo Monaco miniatore,' *L'Arte*, 1932; (A. M. Francini Ciaranfi) 'Mostra di manoscritti medicei in occasione del V. centenario di Lorenzo il Magnifico alla Bibliot. Laurenz. di Firenze,' *Bollettino d'Arte del Min. d. Pubbl. Istr.*, 1949.

G. H. Edgell, *A History of Sienese Painting*, New York, 1932.

V. Golzio, *Lorenzo Monaco*, Rome, 1932.

J. Sala, 'Un miniatore d. sec. XVº: Cristoforo De Predis,' *Archivio d. Soc. Stor. Varesina*, 1932–3.

F. Filippini, 'Oderisi da Gubbio,' *Il Comune di Bologna*, 1933.

M. R. Gabrielli, 'Un Exultet cassinese dell'XI sec.,' *Bollettino d'Arte d. Min. d. Pubbl. Istr.*, 1933.

R. Longhi, *Officina ferrarese*, Rome, 1934.

F. Wittgens, 'Cristoforo De Predis,' *Bibliofilia*, 1934.

M. Avery, *The Exultet Rolls of South Italy*, 2 vols., Princeton and Oxford, 1936–7.

G. Jezzi, *Le miniature in Guardiagrele*, Guardiagrele, 1937.

M. C. Ferrari, 'Contributo allo studio della miniatura riminese,' *Bollettino d'Arte d. Min. d. Pubbl. Istr.*, 1938.

A. van Schendel, *Le Dessin en Lombardie jusqu'à la fin du XVᵉ siècle*, Brussels, 1938.

A. Daneu Lattanzi, 'Un breviario della Bibl. Naz. di Palermo miniato da Martino da Modena,' *Accademie e Bibliot. d'Italia*, 1939; 'I "Vaticinia pontificum" ed un codice monrealese del sec. XIII-XIV,' *Atti d. R. Accad. di Scienze, Lett. ed Arti di Palermo*, 1943.

S. Ameisenowa, 'Opere inedite del Maestro del codice di San Giorgio,' *Rivista d'Arte*, 1939.

E. Berti Toesca, 'Un romanzo illustrato del '400,' *L'Arte*, 1939.

V. Dainotti, 'I corali della Cattedrale di Cremona,' *Accademie e Bibliot. d'Italia*, 1939.

V. Viale, *2ᵃ Mostra d'Arte a Palazzo Carignano. Gotico e Rinascimento in Piemonte. Catalogo*, Turin, 1939.

BIBLIOGRAPHY

W. F. Volbach, 'Le miniature del codice Vat. Pal. lat. 1071 "de arte uenandi cum avibus",' *Rendiconti d. Pont. Accad. Rom. di Archeol.*, 1939.

M. F. Turrini, 'Il Genesi e Ruth istoriati della Concordiana di Rovigo,' *Atti d. Accad. dei Concordi di Rovigo*, 1939.

P. Ginori Conti, *Un antifonario miniato della scuola bolognese*, Florence, 1940.

O. Lehmann Brockhaus, 'Tierdarstellungen der Fiore di Virtù,' *Mitteilungen d. kunsthist. Inst. in Florenz*, 1940.

G. De Francovich, 'Arte carolingia ed ottoniana in Lombardia,' *Roemisch. Jahrb. f. Kunstgeschichte*, 1942–4.

E. Carli, *Capolavori dell'arte senese*, Florence, 1945; *Le tavolette di Biccherna*, Florence, 1950; *Miniature di Liberale da Verona dai corali per il Duomo di Siena*, Milan, 1953.

R. Pallucchini, *Cinque secoli di pittura veneta. Catalogo della Mostra*, Venice, 1945; *Exposition 'Trésors de l'art vénitien' etc. Catalogue des oeuvres*, Lausanne, 1947.

F. Filippini and G. Zucchini, *Miniatori e pittori a Bologna*, Florence, 1947.

T. De Marinis, *La Biblioteca Napoletana dei Re d'Aragona*, 4 vols., Milan, 1947–52.

Kunsthaus Zuerich, *Kunstschaetze der Lombardei, November 1948–Maerz 1949*, Zurich, 1948.

Bodleian Library, *Italian Illuminated Manuscripts*, Oxford, 1948 (G. Paecht).

G. Bazin, *Fra' Angelico*, London-Paris-New York, 1949.

P. Bargellini, *La pittura ascetica del Beato Angelico*, Florence, 1949.

T. Lodi and S. Vagaggini, *Mostra della Biblioteca Medicea Laurenziana etc.*, Florence, 1949.

A. Barzon, *Codici miniati della Biblioteca Capitolare della città di Padova*, 2 vols., Padua, 1950.

R. Filangieri di Candida, *Il codice miniato della Confr. di Sta. Maria in Napoli*, Florence, 1950.

P. Sambin, 'Tra miniatori e "scriptores" forestieri a Padova nella prima metà del sec. XIV,' *Archivio d. Istit. Veneto di Scienze, Lett. ed Arti*, 1950.

F. Zeri, 'The Beginnings of Liberale da Verona,' *The Burlington Magazine*, 1951.

S. Vagaggini, *La miniatura fiorentina*, Florence, 1952.

P. Baldass, 'Disegni d. scuola cassinese d. tempo di Desiderio, *Bollettino d'arte del Ministero d. Pubbl. Istr.*, 1952.

C. Baroni and G. A. Dell'Acqua, *Tesori d'arte in Lombardia*, Milan, 1952; —— and S. Samek Ludovici, *La pittura lombarda del Quattrocento*, Messina and Florence, 1952.

C. Santoro, *Biblioteca Trivulziana. Codici miniati del Rinascimento italiano*, Milan, 1952 (incl. MSS. of the fourteenth to the sixteenth century).

S. Morison, *Byzantine Elements in Humanistic Script*, Chicago, 1952.

M. Harrsen and G. K. Boyce, *Italian Manuscripts in the Pierpont Morgan Library*, New York, 1953.

E. B. Garrison, *Studies in the History of Mediaeval Italian Painting*, I/1 Florence, 1954.

Ministero della Pubblica Istruzione, 2nd ed., *Mostra Storica Nazionale della Miniatura. Catalogo* (G. Muzzioli, ed.), Florence, 1954.

I. Haensel-Hacker, 'Eine italo-byzantinische Malerschule . . . in Padua', *Jahrbuch der oesterreichischen byzantinischen Gesellsch.*, 1954.

E. Pellegrin, *La Bibliothèque des Visconti et des Sforza*, Paris, 1955; 'Bibliothèques d'Humanists lombards', *Bibliothèque d'Humanisme et Renaissance*, 1955.

F. Redenbacher, 'Zur Buchmalerei des Mittelalters,' *Zeitschr. f. Bibliothekwesen*, etc., 1955.

E. Pirani, 'Aspetti della miniatura emiliana,' *Accademie e Biblioteche d'Italia*, 1955.

G. S. Martini, *La bottega di un cartolaio fiorentino etc.*, Florence, 1956.

U. Procacci, in A. Sapori, *Merchants and Companies in Ancient Florence*, Florence, 1955.

G. S. Martini, *La bottega di un cartolaio fiorentino*, etc., Florence, 1956 (La Bibliofilia, 1956—supplemento).

Chapter VII

FRANCE – BURGUNDY,
THE NETHERLANDS – FLANDERS

FRANCE

Book-illumination in France in the Carolingian period was followed by a decadence (see p. 213). The art was almost paralysed by the constant strife and disorder which preceded, accompanied, and followed the decline and extinction of the Carolingian dynasty. Indeed, the century and a half from 843 to 987 is a period of great obscurity and confusion, partly caused by the attacks of the Norsemen, who made themselves masters of important cities such as Rouen, Bordeaux, and Aix-la-Chapelle, and who in 912 became the masters of Normandy. With the increased feudal power of the great nobles, the authority of the French monarchy became merely nominal. In 987, with Hugh Capet, the third French dynasty began, but for another century the fortunes of France were still very obscure.

c. 1000–1150—NORMAN OR ROMANESQUE STYLE (Fig. VII-1-2)

In the eleventh century, however, there was a partial revival of art. According to J. A. Herbert, the recovery of art was doubtless retarded, and its progress checked, by the puritanic tendencies of the Cistercian Order. One of the greatest preachers of all times, S. Bernard of Clairvaux (who died in 1153), called it his aim as a preacher to move hearts, not to expound Scripture. Associated with these puritanic tendencies are certain characteristics of the Norman style: the confinement of the design within its surrounding panel, the employment of a heavy gouache paint upon a colour ground, and particularly the stiffness of the style of the initials. At the same time it was the age of differentiation and of individual expression. A British authority in the field of illumination, Professor Francis Wormald, has pointed out that the eleventh-century revival of art was fostered by the important revival of monasticism which was taking place in the latter part of the tenth and throughout the eleventh century, and which produced new monastic *scriptoria* (Fig. VII-1a).

Moreover, the economic development of Western Europe, the increase of trade between the various countries, the growth of new towns and the increasing wealth of some of the old cities, combined with a renewed interest in classical studies in centres like Paris and Chartres, were also responsible for the revival of art in the eleventh and early twelfth centuries.

Here and there Carolingian reminiscences lingered on and in the South there was a certain Catalonian influence. Both these features may be seen in two MSS. of South France, one preserved in the Méjanes Library, Aix-en-Provence (*MS. 7*), and the other, a *Gospel-Book*, preserved in the Walters Art Gallery, Baltimore (*W. 17*). The latter, containing one miniature and three decorated initials, preserves 'in its large, simple forms a reminiscence of Carolingian proto-types, and in its thick, flatly applied areas of bright red, blue and yellow a suggestion of Catalonian taste. The introductory pages of the Gospels are written in alternating lines of red and blue capitals, with numerous monogrammized contractions' (D. Miner), whereas the rest of the MS. is written in minuscule. See Fig. VII-1*b*.

On the whole, while the beginning of the eleventh century witnesses the rise of the first South-French schools of illumination, in the North the contacts with the Anglo-Saxon schools became more frequent and the influence of the latter became very strong: this is particularly notable in the Saint-Omer MSS. (see further on).

Actual illustration of books was, however, rare; their main decoration consisted in the initial letters. Indeed, late eleventh-century MSS.—such as the *Lives of Saints* from Cluny (National Library at Paris, *Lat. 3779*) or a MS. containing the *Lives* of S. John, of the Fathers, and of the Eastern monks (National Library at Paris, *Nouv. Acq. Lat. 1491*)—are decorated with ornamented initials, but have no illustrations.

Romanesque Initial—Odbert

Thus appeared the true Romanesque initial. It was ornamented with interlaced ribbon-work, human figures, clawing, clambering, and biting monsters, etc.; and it recalls S. Bernard's condemnatory remarks on the carvings—which, as is known, were inspired by the initial decorations of the MSS.—at the monastery of Cluny in Burgundy. (This was the famous Benedictine monastery and abbey which, founded in 910, under the abbots Berno, Odo, Mayeul, Odilo, and Hugh of Semur became the centre of monastic revival, and spread with such amazing rapidity in the next century that it possessed more than 1200 dependent houses, including some great abbeys.) See Fig. VII-1*a*.

One of the earliest illuminated MSS. of the period in question is the richly illustrated *Odbert's Psalter*, written about the year 1000 by Odbert, Abbot of S. Bertin in Saint-Omer (986–1007) and preserved in the Municipal Library at Boulogne (*MS. 20*). It contains drawings in outline, tinted work, and red outlines on a pale blue ground. Like the *Gallican Missal*, written about half a century later in another North-French school of illumination, and formerly preserved in the Yates Thompson Library (*Cod. No. 69*), the *Odbert Psalter* shows a very close affinity to contemporary MSS. executed in Southern England. Moreover—as

Herbert has emphasized—it is additionally interesting because it shows the progressive and informal art of outline-drawing at work upon compositions of the strictly conservative Byzantine type, and combined with decorative ornaments of Carolingian design.

Odbert knew and utilised the English MSS. illuminated in the Winchester style, but he was able to create a style of his own which influenced all the eleventh-century artists of S. Bertin. In comparing the Saint-Omer MSS. executed before the production of the *Odbert Psalter—Life of S. Wandrille*, tenth century, Saint-Omer Municipal Library (*MS. 764); Lives of SS. Valery, Philibert,* and others, late tenth century, Municipal Library at Boulogne (*MS. 106*); and *Gospels*, late tenth century, Boulogne (*MS. 11*)—with the MSS. illuminated by Odbert and his associates, we realize the great importance of Odbert's artistic activity. Examples of Odbert's work produced about the year 1000 (apart from *Odbert's Psalter*, already referred to) are the following: *Gospels* and *miscellanea*, Saint-Omer, *MS. 342 bis; Lives of SS. Bertin, Folquin, Silvin* and *Winnoc*, Boulogne, *MS. 107*; a copy of Aratus, referred to on p. 54, Boulogne, *MS. 188*. Two *Gospel-books*, preserved in Saint-Omer (*MS. 56*) and in the Pierpont Morgan Library, New York (*M. 333*) belong to the early eleventh century, and are examples of Odbert's later work.

Abbey-scriptoria and their Productions

During the eleventh and twelfth centuries excellent work was produced in the *scriptoria* of various abbeys in Northern France. The following are examples of this production:

S. Bertin Abbey and region of Saint-Omer: Betrothal of Joseph and Mary, eleventh century, Saint-Omer, *MS. 154; Life of S. Omer,* Saint-Omer, *MS. 698; Gospel-book,* early twelfth century, Boulogne, *MS. 14; The Soul of Lambert* (Abbot of S. Bertin, 1095–1125), c. 1125, Boulogne, *MS. 46;* a copy of Isidore of Seville, *Collectio canonum,* mid-twelfth century, Boulogne, *MS. 115;* Zachariah of Besançon, *Concordances of the Gospels,* twelfth century, Saint-Omer, *MS. 30;* a copy of S. Augustin and Boëthius, twelfth century, Saint-Omer, *MS. 73;* a late-twelfth-century *Bible* and a copy of S. Gregory, *Moralia in Job,* Saint-Omer, *MSS. 1* and *12.*

Corbie Abbey: Gospels, second half of the eleventh century, Municipal Library at Amiens, *MS. 24;* Amalaire, *De ecclesiastico officio,* the same period, National Library at Paris, *Lat. 12033; Gospel-book,* late eleventh century, National Library at Paris, *Lat. 13170;* twelfth-century MSS. preserved in the National Library at Paris: *Corbie Recueil, Lat. 17767;* S. Gregory, *Homilies, Lat. 13392;* S. Jerome, *In Ecclesiasten, Lat. 13350;* a copy of Amalaire, *Lat. 11580;* Gilbert de la Porrée, *Commentary on the Psalms, Lat. 12004;* Julian of Toledo, *Prognosticorum . . . de futuro saeculo* etc., *Lat. 12270;* a copy of S. Augustine, *Exposition of S. Paul's Epistles,* 2 vols., *Lat. 11575–6;* Raoul de Flay, *Exposition of Leviticus, Lat. 11564;* and other works.

S. Vaast Abbey: the three following works belonging to the first half of the eleventh century may be referred to—a copy of S. Augustine, *Confessions,* Arras

Municipal Library, *MS. 748*; a copy of S. Jerome, *Assumption of the Virgin*, Arras, *MS. 684*; and a *Gospel-book*, Boulogne, *MS. 9*.

Marchiennes Abbey: Life of S. Rictrude, first half of the eleventh century, Douai Municipal Library, *MS. 849*; a copy of S. Gregory, *Moralia in Job*, first half of the twelfth century, Douai, *MS. 301*; a copy of S. Augustine, *Enarrationes in Psalmos*, 3 vols., mid-twelfth century, Douai, *MS. 250*. A contemporary copy of S. Gregory's *Epistles*, executed in the Abbey of S. Martin de Tournai (National Library at Paris, *Lat. 2288*) contains a full-page portrait of S. Gregory, which appears to be a copy of S. Augustine in Douai *MS. 250*.

Anchin Abbey: various MSS. produced in the twelfth century are preserved in Douai—*MSS. 2, 42, 253, 309, 315, 339, 340, 372.*

S. Amand Abbey: eleventh-century MSS. are preserved in the Valenciennes Municipal Library (*MSS. 169, 502, 39*); some twelfth-century MSS. are in Valenciennes (*MSS. 75, 512, 186, 197, 500, 501, 80, 108*) and some in the National Library at Paris (*Lat. 1699, 2287, 1808*, and others).

Various eleventh- and twelfth-century MSS. produced in North-French abbeys are preserved in Cambrai Municipal Library (*MSS. 215, 528, 234, 559, 330*); in Bergues Municipal Library (*MS. 19*); in Boulogne (*MS. 2*); in Saint-Omer (*MS. 193*); in the S. Geneviève Library, Paris (*MS. 1042*); in Lille Municipal Library (*MS. 33*), in the libraries of the Avesnes Archeological Society and of the S. Quentin Basilica, and in other collections.

In Normandy, too, several abbey-*scriptoria* were active. The Avranches Municipal Library possesses some good work produced in the eleventh and the first half of the twelfth century in the *Abbey of Mont-Saint-Michel* (*MSS. 50, 72, 75, 76, 90, 103, 210*); other Mont-Saint-Michel MSS. are preserved in the Pierpont Morgan Library, New York (*M. 641*) and in the National Library at Paris (*Lat. 2639, 2079*, etc.). Productions from other abbeys are preserved in Bayeux Cathedral (*MSS. 57* and *58*), in the Municipal Libraries of Évreux (*MS. 131*), Alençon (*MSS. 14* and *11*), Le Havre (*MS. 332*), Rouen (*MSS. 456, 498, 1409*); in the National Library at Paris (*Lat. 2058, 2342, 1684, 668*). About the year 1000 two magnificent works were produced in Rouen with strong English influences: the *Winchester Pontifical* (Rouen, *MS. 369*) and *Robert's Sacramentary* (Rouen, *MS. 274*). Robert was Archbishop of Canterbury.

In the late tenth and the early eleventh century good work was produced in the *Fleury Abbey* (Orléans Municipal Library, *MSS. 45-6, 175*; National Library at Paris, *Lat. 1126*). From other abbeys of the Loire Region there are tenth-, eleventh- and twelfth-century MSS. in the Municipal Libraries of Angers (*MS. 24, 3-4, 102, 150, 154, 25*), Le Mans (*MSS. 214, 228, 263*), Amiens (*MS. Lescalopier 2*), Poitiers (*MS. 250*), Bordeaux (*MS. 1*), Tours (*MSS. 1018, 291, 924*), Vendôme (*MSS. 28, 193, 117, 23*), Troyes (*MS. 894*), in the National Library at Paris (*Lat. 10, 1126, 9865; Nouv. acq. Lat. 1390*). In the Arsenal Library, Paris (*MS. 1169*) there is a fine illuminated collection of liturgical chants dated to 977-1024.

...ed leaf from a large *Gospel-book* (now lost) from Liessies. C. R. Dodwell ascribes the *Liessies Gospels* (of which two ...ed leaves are preserved, in the possession of the Société Archéol. of Avesnes) to the artist of the Lambeth Bible (see p. 257), but suggests that the Liessies MS. was produced at the Abbey of Liessies about 1146.

In the Paris region, three abbey-*scriptoria* were particularly active mainly in the eleventh century: S. Denis (MSS. preserved in the National Library at Paris, *Lat. 103* and *9436*, and Mazarine Library, *MS. 384*), S. Maur-des-Fossés (National Library, *Lat. 12054, 3778*, and *1654*; and Troyes, *MS. 2273*), and S. Germain-des-Prés (National Library, *Lat. 11751, 11550, 12610, 11685, 12117, 11615*). National Library *Lat. 18303* and *17970* also come from the Paris region.

Examples of eleventh- and twelfth-century *Rheims* productions are mainly preserved in the Rheims Municipal Library (*MSS. 194, 18, 21, 460*). In the region of Lorraine and Alsace there were the *scriptoria* of the abbeys of Senones (National Library, *Lat. 9392*), of S. Vanne (Verdun Municipal Library, *MSS. 52, 95, 1, 119, 43, 62, 66*), of S. Martin in Metz (Épinal Municipal Library, *MS. 73*). Other tenth- to twelfth-century MSS. are in the 'Grand Seminary' at Metz, at Strasbourg (*MS. 78*), in the Laon Municipal Library (*MS. 550*), and in the National Library at Paris (*Lat. 9392, 15392, 9453, 15307*).

S. Martial Abbey, Limoges: the *Sacramentary of S. Étienne Cathedral*, at Limoges (now in the National Library, Paris: *MS. Lat. 9438*) was probably produced, about 1100, at Limoges, in the S. Martial Abbey. Jean Porcher (*Le Sacramentaire de Sainte Étienne de Limoges*, Paris) regards this codex—thanks to the richness and originality of the illuminations and the "impetuous talent" of the painter—as one of the most precious monuments of French Romanesque art. In his opinion, the illuminator seems to be a "Limousin" with a southern temperament; at the same time, he finds in the codex traces of a long local tradition. The codex measures 270 × 165 mm. and contains 14 full-page illuminations and nine beautifully decorated letter-initials.

Very interesting examples of South French illuminated productions are preserved in the Calvet Museum, Avignon (*MS. 22*), in Rheims (*MS. 13*), in the Municipal Libraries of Arles (*MS. 4*), Méjanes, Aix (*MS. 7*), Perpignan (*MS. 1*), Albi (*MSS. 45, 6, 5*), in the Pierpont Morgan Library (*M. 44*), and in the National Library at Paris (*Lat. 889, 1084, 8878, 1118, 94, 776, 2077, Nouv. acq. Lat. 1871, Lat. 5058, 254, 2819, 2293, 1720, 1120, 1121, 5927, 5296 A., 9438*).

Ornamented Letters. In the eleventh and twelfth centuries, the elaborately ornamented letters assumed such importance that in some instances the pages of MSS. hold only single words. Moreover, some initials, such as *A, B, V*, often fill a whole page; often the *T* makes a cross which fills the page. In the Psalters, the initial *B* (of *Beatus vir*, the first words of the first Psalm) often fills the whole page, and sometimes provides sufficient scope for a beautiful miniature. The Gospel-books usually have a superb initial at the beginning of each Gospel, i.e., *L* (for the words *Liber generationis*, with which the *Book of S. Matthew* begins), *I* (for *Initium evangelii* in *S. Mark*), *Q* (for *Quoniam quidem* in *S. Luke*), and once more, *I* (for *In initio* in *S. John*): Fig. VII-1a.

Bibles and Miscellanea. As to illuminated Bibles, it would suffice to refer to the *First Bible of S. Martial*, in 2 vols., of the second half of the tenth century (National

Library at Paris, *Lat. 5*), and particularly to the *Second Bible of S. Martial*, the latter consisting of two great volumes which contain as many as seventy-seven initials magnificently ornamented in Limoges in the second half of the eleventh century (National Library at Paris, *Lat. 8*). The eleventh-century *Bible of Anjou Cathedral*, in two volumes (British Museum, *Harley MSS. 2833–4*), is also of particular interest.

Bibles, of course, were produced all the time. Examples of eleventh-century illuminated Bibles are the *S. Vaast Bible* (3 vols., first half of the eleventh century, Arras, *MS. 435*), the *Bible of S. Aubin d'Angers* (2 vols., illumination of the late eleventh century; Angers, *MSS. 3–4*), the *Rheims Bible* (third part of a Bible, of about 1100; Rheims, *MS. 21*), the *Albigeois Old Testament* (about the year 1000; National Library at Paris, *Lat. 94*), another *Bible* of the National Library (*Lat. 52*), and the *S. Yrieix Bible* of the late eleventh century. However, with the second half of the twelfth century there appeared great *Bibles*, produced in various *scriptoria* all over France. We may refer to the following: Valenciennes, *MSS. 1–5*, Boulogne, *MS. 2*, National Library, *Lat. 10, 11535, 8823, 16743–6* (4 vols.), Bordeaux, *MS. 1*, Clermont-Ferrand, *MS. 1*, Lyons, *MSS. 410–11*, Moulins, *MSS. 1 and 14*, Bourges, *MS. 3*, Troyes, *MS. 2391, Bible of Saint-Omer*, Saint-Omer, *MS. 698*, Sens, *MS. 1*, Grenoble, *MSS. 17, 12, 28*, and others. See also Fig. VII-2a.

A copy of the *New Testament*, written in Gothic script and produced in North France, *c.* 1200, contains ten pages of decorated Canon Tables, eight historiated initials, and thirty-three ornamented initials. 'The illuminations are by several hands, the finest being responsible for a representation of St. James of impressive proto-Gothic style. The Canon Tables, on the other hand, preserve archaic features reminiscent of early romanesque art' (D. Miner). The MS. is preserved in the Walters Art Gallery, Baltimore (*W. 67*).

Numerous decorated initials are contained, too, in the *Lectionary of the Abbey of Montmajour* from Arles (National Library at Paris, *Lat. 889*), the *Lives of Saints* from S. Martial de Limoges (National Library at Paris, *Lat. 5301*), and a few other codices.

A twelfth-century fragmentary *Sacramentary* written for the use of Rheims Cathedral, but probably produced in the region of Arras or Marchiennes (now preserved in the Walters Art Gallery, Baltimore, *W. 28*), presents various unusual features. It contains, for instance, an abridged coronation formula according to the Gallican rite. The two full-page miniatures and the two large ornamental initials are rather archaic in style; as Miss Dorothy Miner points out, they are extremely delicate of outline and light of colour. Moreover, contrasting colours, shot through the draperies to indicate folds and highlights, produce an iridescent effect.

Thus, as in the Carolingian period, these illuminated MSS. were almost all of a religious nature—Bibles, Psalters, Gospels, Sacramentaries, Lectionaries, Homilies, Lives of Saints and Commentaries on Holy Books were the main productions— and, as mentioned, the pure ornament by far outweighed the illustrations or miniatures.

There were, however, exceptions. It will suffice to refer to an unidentified text on *Cosmography*, written in the twelfth century, and illustrated with twenty coloured diagrams of interesting decorative character. The MS. is preserved in the Walters Art Gallery, Baltimore (*W. 73*). It contains various medieval astronomical drawings, such as representations of the Zodiacal signs, movements of the planets, eclipses, the winds, and the elements: see also p. 51 and Fig. I-24*b*.

Tonaria. Finally, mention should be made of three interesting eleventh-century *tonaria*, adorned by figures of musicians and dancers, which accompany but do not illustrate the text and notes of hymns. These MSS. have been described by Dr. Joan Evans; one of them comes from S. Martial de Limoges, and is illustrated with nine figures of musicians (National Library at Paris, *Lat. 1118*); the second apparently belonged to the monastery of S. Étienne de Toulouse; it represents four musicians and a dancing woman (part of *Harl. MS. 4951*, in the British Museum; the third MS. is in the National Library at Paris (*Lat. 7964*).

Cistercian Illumination. The Cistercian illuminators, or rather calligraphers, while they constantly repudiate the golden splendour and monstrous follies of their rivals, absolutely excel in this same ornamental draughtsmanship. The ornament is mostly in a red ink, with flat-coloured blue, green, or yellow backgrounds, but has not been surpassed. The interlacements and coils, foliages and panels, of the twelfth century are without any doubt among the finest examples of ornamental lettering ever conceived. See Fig. VII-2*b* (Dijon Municipal Library, *MSS. 168–70*).

Illuminating seemed at this epoch to be more and more closely following the details of contemporary architecture, and so paving the way to the next great variety of the art which is looked upon by some writers as the real beginning of medieval illumination. The excellence, however, limits itself to the ornament. The human figure is wretchedly incorrect—even barbarous. This is partly explained by the fact that monastic education did not permit the study of the nude, hence the monkish ignorance of figure drawing. But the monstrous hands and feet, and the exaggerated facial expression of the figures depicted have no explanation.

Decline of the Scriptoria. The middle of the twelfth century witnessed the decline of the great monasteries, of their *scriptoria*, and of their artistic production. Furthermore, the *Consuetudines* (1134) of the Cistercian Order forbade illuminated initials in manuscripts, and the newly-built Cistercian monasteries did not include *scriptoria*. Artistic book-production was passing into the hands of the secular clergy, and later on it passed to the ateliers of professional secular scribes.

THIRTEENTH AND FOURTEENTH CENTURIES

About the middle of the twelfth century a wonderful change came over the architecture of Europe. In various European countries we have the simultaneous appearance of the pointed arch.

Gothic Style

The new style, laying aside both the Classical cornice and the Romanesque arch, makes use of a new vertical principle of construction, called in French the *ogive* (or pointed) arch, composed of two sections only, instead of the whole semi-circle. At first it was a simple lancet arch, but by degrees—through adding clustered pillars, the buttress, the flying buttress, the rib-vault, and mullions of manifold form and tracery—a degree of perfection and refinement never before dreamt of was obtained. The new architectural style, which supplanted the Romanesque, is known as Gothic, though no satisfactory explanation can be given of the reasons why this term was adopted (interesting is the explanation given by Giorgio Vasari, the famous Italian historian of art, 1511–74).

In 1140—writes N. Pevsner—the foundation stone was laid for the new choir of S. Denis Abbey near Paris. It was consecrated in 1144. Abbot Suger, the mighty counsellor of two Kings of France, was the soul of the enterprise. There are few buildings in Europe—argues Pevsner—so revolutionary in their conception and so rapid and unhesitating in their execution. Whoever designed the choir of S. Denis, one can safely say, invented the Gothic style, although Gothic features had existed before, scattered here and there; in the centre of France, the provinces around S. Denis, they even developed with a certain consistency. In the succeeding sixty years —concludes Pevsner—the following new cathedrals were begun: Sens, Noyon, Senlis, Paris, Laon, Chartres, Rheims, Amiens, and others. Not all scholars agree with this theory—indeed, according to Frankl the Gothic style begins with S. Trinité at Caen—but on the whole Pevsner's thesis appears to be the most likely.

Generally speaking, according to eminent scholars, whatever appears in illumination has appeared first in architecture and its auxiliary arts; it is certain, however, that the new fashion gave an impetus to the development of the Gothic style of illumination incomparably greater than any architectural type before or after. Indeed, the decorative and illustrative ideas characteristic of Gothic architecture, and the Gothic period in general were specially suited to the limitations under which the illuminator worked, and this fact began to change almost entirely the character of the ornamentation of books.

The relationship between the Gothic style of architecture and the Gothic style of illumination can best be studied in an album of sketches, a sort of textbook on architecture, written *c.* 1235 by Villard de Honnecourt (from the region of Cambrai, Northern France). The book (National Library at Paris, *MS. Fr. 19093*) is one of the most instructive relics of this period: it contains drawings with descriptions of architectural details—such as plans of church choirs, choir stalls, windows, cathedral towers, as well as geometrical motifs and figures of men and animals (some realistic, some fantastic). There are also personifications of Pride, Humility, the Church Triumphant, and the Wheel of Fortune, New Testament scenes (the Crucifixion, the sleeping disciples in the episode on the Mount of Olives), and even worldly scenes (such as wrestlers, a king with his retinue), and geometrical schemes for drawing human heads and animals.

An interesting fragment (six vellum leaves) from a lost *Missal* of a luxurious nature, is preserved in the Hofer Collection, Rockport, Maine (U.S.A.). There are seven historiated and six ornamented initials. The 'delicately rotating foliate initials populated by springing beasts are the very essence of French thirteenth-century painting in its "purest" and most refined phase'. The particular interest of the miniatures lies in the fact that their style is very close to Villard de Honnecourt's style, though outright 'attribution of these paintings to Villard is no longer agreed to by scholars' (D. Miner).

In Oakeshott's opinion the main characteristics of the Early Gothic style (*c.* 1200–*c.* 1340) are a tenderness and a softness which were alien to Romanesque art. In the main, writes Herbert, Gothic illumination is minute, refined, delicate, contrasting sharply with the broad manner of the preceding age.

Moreover, apart from the gracious illustration of the main story, we find in Gothic codices a great number of whimsical diversions unconnected with the text such as humorous figures playing in the margins, women at their work, playing children, nobles at their pleasures, monsters and grotesques, fantastic line-edgings, and so on.

Re-emergence of France. It is generally agreed that there are few facts more striking in the history of illumination than the sudden re-emergence of France about the beginning of the thirteenth century, from comparative obscurity, and her rapid advance to the leading position which she occupied from the time of S. Louis (1226–70) until the middle of the fifteenth century. Of the various factors which may have contributed to this new revival, the following two, suggested by J. A. Herbert, seem to be the most important: (1) the rule of Philip Augustus (Philip II, 1180–1223), who strengthened and thoroughly reorganized the administration of the country, and firmly re-established the royal power; (2) the growing importance of Paris and its University as one of the main European centres of art, culture, and learning, drawing students and artists thither from all parts of Europe, and creating there a great demand for book-production.

Secular Illuminators and Secular Manuscripts

Much more than in Italy, the French school of illumination of the thirteenth century freed itself from the traditional motifs of the previous centuries, and new elements were introduced by non-religious literature (such as *chansons de gestes*).

The earliest extant signature of a secular illuminator dates to 1285 (National Library at Paris, *Fr. 412*), but there is hardly any doubt that lay manuscript-painters were active much earlier. In *The Hand-produced Book* (p. 208) it has been pointed out that in the Middle Ages, in addition to the monks who were regular scribes and illuminators, there were special classes of secular scribes (such as *illuminatores* and *rubricatores*) who were brought to the monasteries when there were no competent men there to do the required work. There were also men who, though generally living within the monastic precincts and often adopting the outward dress of monks, were in fact only lay brethren, skilled in various handi-crafts or trades.

Moreover, it is known that important university towns had scribes and illumin-ators who worked on a fixed tariff of charges. Here particular mention should be made of the guild of binders, scribes and illuminators of the University of Paris. It has also been suggested that there were numerous groups of travelling artists and urban bookshops, and that among the various systems of book-production, including illumination, there was a considerable degree of overlapping.

From the thirteenth century onwards, other personages besides abbots (kings, dukes and other feudal lords, rich merchants, etc.) began to collect books.

Literature of Chivalry. Gradually, pictures drawn from other themes found their way into books, and secular writings—such as histories, chronicles, romances, *chansons de gestes* and other poems—were produced in a decorated form. Dr. Joan Evans has rightly emphasized that in the late twelfth and early thirteenth centuries it was the knights and ladies, the troubadours and minstrels, who were represented in art, rather than the subject of their lays, while the chief inspiration of thirteenth-century secular decoration was heraldic; this period saw the beginning of feudal art. Curious architectural backgrounds, such as pierced balustrades or pinnacles, were added; sometimes the characteristic circular medallion is to be seen. Later on, beautiful landscape backgrounds with a new richness of colour, naturalistic grotesques, and other elements marked the skill and originality of the artists. Influence of this secular art on religious books may be seen in many works: for instance, in a beautiful Italian *Psalter* now preserved in the Library of the Padua Seminary.

A few outstanding illuminated secular MSS. may here be mentioned: *Didactic works*, of *c.* 1278 (Arras Municipal Library, *MS. 139*); *Historical texts*, *c.* 1280 (National Library at Paris, *Fr. 17177*); *French poetry*, *c.* 1280–90 (Arsenal Library at Paris, *MS. 3142*); *Chansonnier de Paris*, *c.* 1280–1315 (Faculty of Medicine at Montpellier, *MS. 196*); the poems of Robert de Blois, of the late thirteenth century (Paris, Arsenal Library, *MS. 5201*).

Fourteenth century: the MS. of the *Chronicles of France*—or *Grandes Chroniques de France* (*see* also pp. 398 f., 411)—copied in 1318 by Thomas de Maubeuge, and now preserved in the National Library at Paris (*Fr. 10132*); a MS. written by Gillis li Muisis, formerly in the Dyson Perrins Collection (*No. 36*); a copy of *La Dame à la Licorne*, written *c.* 1350 (National Library at Paris, *Fr. 12562*); the MS. Guillaume de Deguileville, *Le Pèlerinage de la vie humaine*, a very much favoured medieval allegory, copied in 1393 in the atelier of Oudin de Carvanay, and illuminated by Pierre Remiet (ibidem, *Fr. 823*). The copy of the *Romance of Alexander*, now in the Bodleian Library, Oxford (*Bodl. MS. 264*), illuminated by Jehan de Grise, in 1344, has been referred to on p. 35; see also pp. 278 and 442.

An interesting example of secular book-production is a copy of Vegetius, *De re militari,* executed *c.* 1270 and preserved in the Fitzwilliam Museum, Cambridge (*Marley Add. MS. 1*). The text is written in Anglo-Norman French (it is the earliest known French translation of the work, and the only MS. extant), followed by the Latin text. There are two miniatures and two pen-work-initials: Fig. VII-5*a*.

These works are written in the vulgar tongue. Amongst the various tales of chivalry, there is the story of *Lancelot of the Lake;* a beautiful copy is *MS. Fr. 95* in the National Library at Paris: the grounds are of applied gold-leaf, which 'imparts to the figures the luminosity of stained glass' (van Moé). Perhaps the finest illuminated example of the *Roman de Lancelot du Lac* is a copy in two volumes (originally in one), preserved in the Pierpont Morgan Library, New York (*M. 805–6*). It was produced *c.* 1300 in North-East France, and contains thirty-nine miniatures. The long, rectangular miniatures—writes Miss Dorothy Miner—extending across the page, are each divided into halves, the background at the left being of burnished gold, while the right is diapered in blue or pink. They are executed with exceptional charm, the graphic elegance and vivacious colours, as well as the over-refined figures with their rhythmic and delicate movements appearing to modern eyes as the very epitome of the age of chivalry. An earlier copy, of *c.* 1274, is preserved in Paris (National Library, *Fr. 342*); another copy is *Rylands French MS. 1*: Fig. VII-4.

There is the story of *Tristan and Isolde;* the songs of *troubadours* and *trouvères.* There are also curious satirical stories, such as the *Roman de Renart* or the charming *Roman de Fauvel*—the name FAUVEL being formed by the initials of the allegorical personages (Flattery, Avarice, Villainy, Variability, Envy, and Lâcheté (= Lily-livered Cowardice)), whose views are expressed in this interesting medley of prose and music centred round a fabulous horse. A charming copy, of *c.* 1325, is in the Paris National Library (*Fr. 146*). Instances of other Romances are: *Chevalier au cygne, c.* 1270 (National Library, *Fr. 12569*); *Roman de la Poire, c.* 1275 (*Fr. 2186*); Robert de Borron, *L'Histoire du Graal, c.* 1280 (*Fr. 95*).

Other instances of illuminated literature of chivalry are: a copy of the French translation of William of Tyre, *History of Jerusalem,* of *c.* 1250 (Paris National Library, *Fr. 9081*); Girardin d'Amiens, *Le Conte de Héliacin, c.* 1260 (*Fr. 1633*); *Roman de Troie,* of 1264 (*Fr. 1610*); *Roman de Godefroi de Bouillon, c.* 1331 (*Fr. 22495*); *Roman d'Artus, c.* 1325 (*Fr. 761*); *Roman de l'Atre périlleux,* of *c.* 1330 (*Fr. 1433*).

A copy of *Decretum Gratiani,* executed *c.* 1300, is an excellent example of the secular book-production, especially of law-books, in Latin. The copy is preserved in the Walters Art Gallery, Baltimore (*W. 133*); it may have been executed in N. France or England: Fig. VII-5*b*. Fig. VII-9*c* reproduces a beautiful copy of the first half of the fourteenth century preserved in the Laurentian Library at Florence. Other excellent copies of *Decretum Gratiani,* with gloss by Bartholomew of Brescia, are preserved in the Tours Municipal Library (*MS. 558;* of *c.* 1288) and in Paris (National Library, *Lat. 3893;* of 1314). Instances of Roman literature are: a copy of Caton, *Distichs,* and other texts (National Library, *Lat. 15158;* of 1289); a copy of Livy, *Roman History* (Sainte-Geneviève Library at Paris, *MS. 777;* of *c.* 1370); a copy of Boëthius (Faculty of Medicine at Montpellier, *MS. 43;* of *c.* 1325).

Religious Works produced by Lay Artists. Book-production dealing with such literature continued for a few centuries and was very popular in Burgundy (see p. 423), and in various other regions. The bulk of French illuminated MSS., however, continued to be religious works, such as Bibles, Psalters, or Missals.

As a matter of fact, lay artists—who worked for kings and queens, dukes and high prelates of the Church, and other rich or noble patrons of art, particularly ladies—produced not only secular manuscripts, but also devotional books, such as Psalters, Breviaries, and Books of Hours, usually superbly illuminated; these books were commissioned either for private chapels, such as the Sainte Chapelle (or royal oratory), or for domestic use.

Psalters

It will suffice to mention a few masterpieces of the thirteenth century: the *Ingeburg Psalter*, or the Psalter of Queen Ingeborg of Denmark, the second wife of Philip II Augustus (1180–1223). This codex executed perhaps in Paris *c.* 1213, is preserved in the Musée Condé, Chantilly; it contains twenty-seven pages of preliminary miniatures, painted on burnished gold backgrounds. Related in style are: *Blanche (of Castile) Psalter*, executed *c.* 1200–23, for Blanche of Castile, wife of King Louis VIII (1223–6); it was formerly in the Sainte Chapelle, and is now preserved in the Arsenal Library, Paris (*MS. 1186*); the Psalters given by S. Louis (1226–70) to the Sainte Chapelle, and now preserved in the National Library at Paris (*Lat. 10525*)—see p. 386—and in the British Museum (formerly in the Yates Thompson Collection); a MS. apparently written *c.* 1260 by the same hand as the last two codices, now known as the *Psalter of Joan of Navarre* (because at one time it belonged to this queen, wife of Philip the Fair); it is preserved in The John Rylands Library, Manchester: Fig. VII-5c. See also p. 330.

Other excellent *Psalters* are: *Lat. 10434* and *Nouv. acq. Lat. 1392* in the National Library at Paris, of the first half of the thirteenth century; copies of the *Psalter cum Hours* in Rouen (*MS. 3016*); in the National Library (*Lat. 1073A*) of the same period; in the Arsenal Library (*MS. 280*), of the second half of the thirteenth century; and *Lat. 1328* in the National Library, of *c.* 1300; *Psalters* in the Sainte-Geneviève Library (*MS. 2689*; of *c.* 1260), in the National Library (*Smith-Lesouëf 20*, of *c.* 1280; and *Lat. 10435*, of *c.* 1290).

Hours and Breviaries

A few interesting thirteenth-century MSS. preserved in the Walters Art Gallery, Baltimore, may here be referred to: *W. 39*, a *Book of Hours*, produced in Northern France, and containing nine historiated initials, twelve Calendar-illustrations, and numerous drolleries; *W. 98*, also a North-French *Book of Hours*, with five large and seven small historiated initials; *W. 109*, a *Breviary*, for Dijon use, containing thirty-three historiated initials, eight ornamental initials, and as many as forty-one partial borders and drolleries. Several *Hours* and *Breviaries* are, of course, preserved in the major French collections. Instances are, of the late thirteenth century: National Library at Paris, *Lat. 1023*, and Cambrai Municipal Library, *MSS. 102 and 103*; of the early, or the first half of the fourteenth century: Cambrai, *MS. 87*; Arras Municipal Library, *MSS. 639 and 717*; Marseilles Municipal Library, *MS. 111*; Arsenal Library, at Paris, *MS. 570*, and National Library, *Nouv. acq. 560*; of the second half of the fourteenth century: National Library, *Lat. 1394* and *Lat. 1403*.

Pontificals, Gospels, Missals. The richly decorated *Chartres Pontifical* of the early thirteenth century (Orléans Municipal Library, *MS. 144*) and the *Châlons Pontifical* of the second half of the thirteenth century (Châlons Municipal Library, *MS. 45*) are outstanding. As to the *Gospels*, we may refer to *Cambrai Cathedral Gospels*, of *c.* 1260 (Cambrai Municipal Library, *MS. 189*), and *Sainte-Chapelle Gospels*, of *c.* 1260–70, 2 vols. (National Library, *Lat. 8892* and *17326*). Instances of fine *Missals* are: *Anchin Missal*, of *c.* 1200, 2 vols. (Douai Municipal Library, *MS. 90*); *Saint-Denis Missal* of *c.* 1270–80 preserved in Paris (National Library, *Lat. 1107*); *Missal of the S. Augustine Hermits*, of *c.* 1362 (Toulouse Municipal Library, *MS. 91*); *Missal of Mont-Saint-Éloi*, of the second half of the thirteenth century (Arras Municipal Library, *MS. 38*); *Missal of Saint-Corneille de Compiègne* (National Library, *Lat. 17322*) and *Corbie Missal* (Amiens Municipal Library, *MS. 157*) of the early fourteenth century; *Saint-Vaast Missal* of the mid-fourteenth century; and four *Cambrai Missals* preserved in the Cambrai Municipal Library (*MS. 233* of the late thirteenth century; *MS. 156* of the mid-fourteenth century; *MSS. 185* and *232* of the late fourteenth).

Bibles

Copies of the Latin Bible were produced in great numbers, but these volumes—writes Herbert—are for the most part interesting as curiosities, from the exquisite minuteness of script and figure-initials, rather than strictly beautiful or important in relation to the development of art. Herbert cites as an excellent specimen of the most compressed type, a *Bible* written *c.* 1250 in a French Dominican house (perhaps at Clermont in Auvergne), and preserved in the British Museum (*Add. MS. 35085*): its pages measure 5 × 3 inches, and 'its Jesse-tree and its tiny miniature-initials, with architectural backgrounds and partial bar-borders usually ending in a single leaf, are marvellous in their combination of accuracy and softness'.

Instances of thirteenth-century *Bibles* are: *Corbie Bible* of the first half of the century (Amiens Municipal Library, *MS. 23*); *Bible of Mont-Saint-Éloi* of *c.* 1250 (Arras Municipal Library, *MS. 1*); and *S. Louis Bible* of *c.* 1270 (National Library, *Lat. 10426*). Early fourteenth-century *Bibles* are: *Celestine Bible* (Arsenal Library, *MS. 590*); *Rheims Cathedral Bible*, 4 vols. (Rheims Municipal Library, *MSS. 39–42*); and *Bible of Philip the Fair*, 2 vols. (National Library, *Lat. 248*).

Miscellanea

More popular productions are the *Bible moralisée* and the *Bible historiale*. Of the former, of *c.* 1250, one copy is partly in the Pierpont Morgan Library and partly in the Toledo Capitulary Library; one copy is in the National Library at Vienna; and a third copy is partly in Oxford (*Auct. B. IV. 6*), partly in the British Museum (*Harl. MSS. 1526–7*), and partly in the National Library at Paris (*Lat. 11560*). Four early fourteenth-century copies of *Bible historiale* by Guiart Des Moulins (French translation of Pierre Le Mangeur, *Historia scholastica*) are preserved in the Sainte-Geneviève Library at Paris (2 vols., *MSS. 20–1*), the Arsenal Library (*MS, 5059*), the Troyes Municipal Library (*MS. 59*), and the National Library (*Fr. 8*).

Various other works belong to this category, but they are of inferior quality. Even the *Vie de S. Denys*, produced as late as 1250 in the great abbey of S. Denis near Paris—and now preserved in the National Library at Paris, *Nouv. acq. Fr. 1098*—is still in a very crude style. So, too, is a much earlier work, a *Missal* in the British Museum (*Add. MS. 17742*), which was written in 1218 by a certain Geroldus, clerk of Amiens. The MS. contains one full-page miniature (a Crucifixion) prefixed to the Canon, a few historiated initials and various decorative initials. See also p. 387.

Illuminated copies of the *Apocalypse* have already been dealt with in other parts of the present book (pp. 269 ff., 277, and *passim*). Here we may refer to more French products. A beautiful copy of the *Apocalypse* in Latin, with the *Commentary* by Berengandus, preceded by a portion of the commentary in French, is preserved in the Bodleian Library (*MS. Douce 180*). This exquisite MS., according to Herbert shows "English" painting of the late thirteenth century at its best; it has advanced—writes Herbert—beyond the formalism and severity of early Gothic, and has not yet begun to grapple with the problems and subtleties of modern art. The white vellum backgrounds, soft pale colours, and careful space-filling, together with the sweet and gracious forms of the personages represented, give these miniatures a dainty, poetical, and altogether irresistible charm. Some of them are merely drawn in outline, in others the colouring and gilding have been left at various stages of incompleteness. The angels are of monastic type, massive and dignified, with tonsured heads, grave and gentle expressions. Another copy of the *Apocalypse* is in the Valenciennes Municipal Library (MS. 99). Fig. VII-2*c* and 3. A copy of the Apocalypse (in French), with numerous beautiful illuminations, is preserved in the Nat. Libr., at Paris (*MS. franç. 13096*).

MSS. dealing with Natural History. Many MSS. do not lend themselves readily to precise chronological or topographical arrangement. These are the illustrated *Bestiaries*, the Medieval handbooks of natural history. Based on Isidore's *Etymologiae*, and more remotely on Pliny and the *Physiologus* (see p. 49), they were often profusely illustrated, especially during the twelfth and thirteenth centuries, with coloured drawings of beasts, birds, and fishes, actual or legendary, and more rarely with fully illuminated miniatures in gold and colours. They are often found in

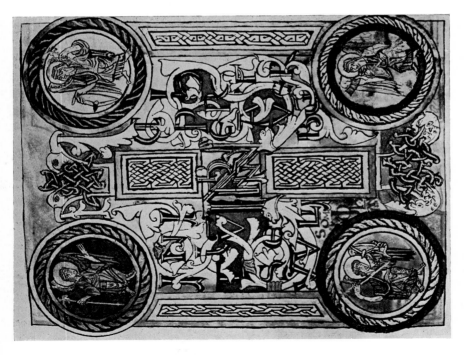

VII–1. Eleventh-century Gospels. *a*, North France, *McClean MS. 19*, fol. *91 v*: beginning of *S. John* (letters curiously connected and orna-mented); in the corners, four strange angels with cross-staffs and other objects. *b*, South France, *W. 17*, fol. *8 v*: S. Matthew.

VII–2. *a*, North-West France, *Bible of Saint-Omer*, fol. 395 *r*. *b*, Early twelfth-century Cistercian MS.: S. Gregory, *Moralia in Job*; initial O. *c, Apocalypse Valenciennes MS. 99*, fol. 21 *r*: John taking a book from the Angel.

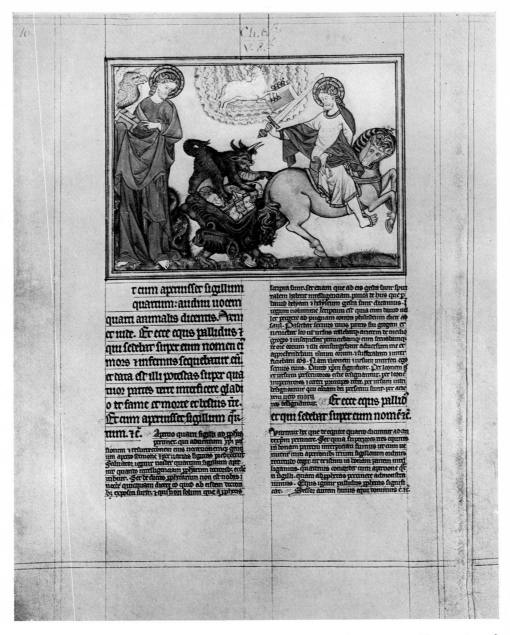

VII–3. *Apocalypse MS. Douce 180*, p. 16: *Apocalypse*, vi. 7–9 and *Commentary* (the opening of the fourth seal).

VII–4. Copies of Lancelot du Lac of c. 1300. a, Rylands French MS. 1. b, M. 805. fol. 67 r.

VII–5. *a*, Copy of Vegetius, *Marley. Add. MS. 1*, fol. 86 *r*: sea-battle. *b*, W. *133*: copy of *Decretum Gratiani* of *c.* 1300, fol. 179 *r*: Pars II, causa I. *c, Psalter of Queen Joan of Navarre*. fol. 12 *r*: New Testament scenes.

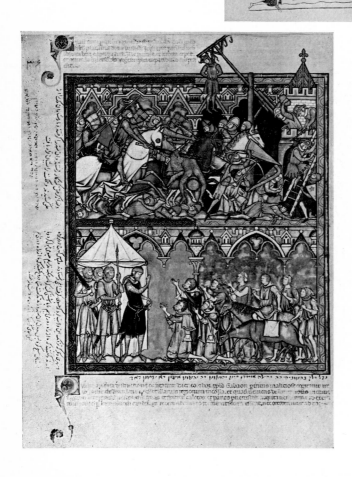

VII–6. *a, Psalter and Hours of Isabelle of France,* fol. 174 *r*: decorated initials; beautiful line-endings and grotesques; liturgical text. *b, M. 638,* fol. 10 *v*: *Josh.* viii. 1–29, ix. 3–15.

VII–7. *a*, *Bible W. 56*, fol. 101 *v* :
1 *Sam.* xxx, 21—2 *Sam.* i. 10;
the initial represents the beginning
of 2 *Sam.* (Saul's death). *b*, *M. 751*,
fol. 109 *r* : episode from the life of
S. Anselm of Canterbury.

VII–8. *a, Missal of S. Louis* (Lower church of S. Francis, Assisi): Crucifixion and Christ in Majesty with the Evangelists and their symbols. *b, Psalter of the Counts of Arras,* fol. 153 *r: Psalm* cx. 1–3; the initial represents the Holy Trinity. *c, Bible Historiée (Rylands French MS. 5),* fol. 27 *r:* Christ as 12-year old boy in the Temple (according to *Luke,* ii. 41–51).

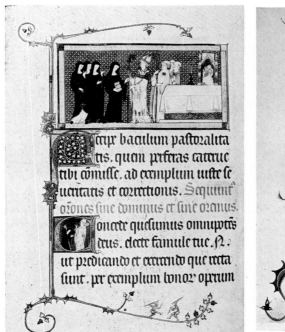

VII–9. *a,* Two leaves from a copy of *Somme le Roi* (Fitzwilliam Museum, *MS. 368*); upper zone: the allegorical figures of Chastity, Luxuria, Equity and Felony; lower zone: Judith and Holofernes, Joseph and Potiphar's wife, Noah's ark, and Moses (*Exod.* ii. 13). *b, Metz Pontifical:* consecration of an abbess. *c,* French masterpiece or French-influenced Oderisi da Gubbio (?), *Decretum Gratiani Edili 97,* fol. 104 *r*: Pars II, causa I.

VII–10. *Bible Historiée MS. Fr. 9561. a*, Crucifixion; *b*, Joseph of Arimathaea requests from Pilate the body of Christ (according to *Matthew*, xxvii. 57 f.).

VII-11. *a*, Pucelle: *Breviary of Belleville*, fol. 258 *v*: the Three Magi and liturgical text. *b*, *Psalter W. 119*, fol. 55 *v*: *Psalm* lii. 7–11 and *Psalm* xiv. 1; initial representing the Fool. *c*, *Hours and Psalter* written for Philip the Bold, fol. 62 *v*: the Baptism of Christ and liturgical text.

VII–12. a, *Missal of Saint-Denis* : initial representing the Annunciation ; various ornamentation ; musical notes ; and liturgical text. b, 'Maître aux Bouquetaux' : *Hours and Psalter*, Fitzwilliam Museum, *MS. 3–1954*, p. 203 : the Three Magi.

VII–13. *a*, André Beauneveu : *Psalter of the Duke of Berry*, fol. 23 *v*—a Prophet. *b, The Most Rich Hours* : The Fall of Man ; Adam and Eve driven out of Paradise.

VII–14. *a, Horae W. 96,* fol. *60 r*: Nativity; ornamented initial; ornamented border. *b, Horae W. 265,* fol. *90 r*: Flight into Egypt; ornamented initials; decorated border. *c, Horae W. 90,* fol. *151 r*: beautifully decorated page with historiated initial, animals, grotesques, etc. *d, Horae MS. Douce 144,* fol. *5 v*: S. Mark; rich border.

VII–15. *a*, Boucicaut Master (Victoria and Albert Museum, *MS. 1646–1902*): Christ as Judge of the Universe with Cross and Column carried by angels. *b, W. 232*, fol. 73 *r*: Flight into Egypt. *c, W. 260, fol. 92 r: Dormitio Virginis*; Christ receives Her soul; the Apostles mourning. *d, W. 287*, fol. 46 *r*: Visitation.

VII–16. *a, Grandes Heures de Rohan*: Annunciation and *Conceptio per aurem*; Prophet. *b, Hours of Isabel Stuart,* fol. 136 *v*: Madonna and Child with SS. Peter and Paul; above, the Holy Trinity carried by *Seraphim*.

VII–17. *a, Horae W. 449, fol. 9 v*:
Calendar for August. *b, Hours,*
Fitzwilliam Museum, *MS. 60,* fol. 96 *r*:
Christ enthroned; Moses with the
Tables of the Law; Angel with the
hostia; Psalm, vi. 2.

VII–18. *a, Bedford Hours*, fol. 256 *v*: the Duke kneeling before his patron-saint; richly decorated border with coat-of-arms, martyr-doms of saints (crucifixion of S. Andrew, S. John the Evangelist in boiling oil, Apostle Simon Zelotes, etc.), and other orna-mentation. *b*, Bedford atelier: *Hours of Jeanne de Lannoy (Walters Art Gallery, W. 281)*, fol. 234 *r*: S. Christopher.

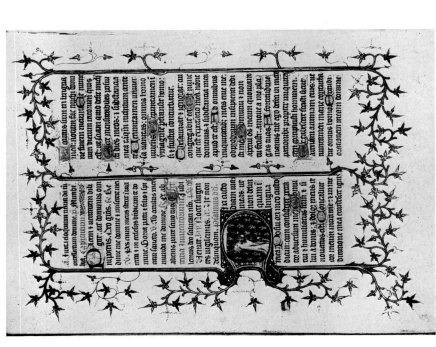

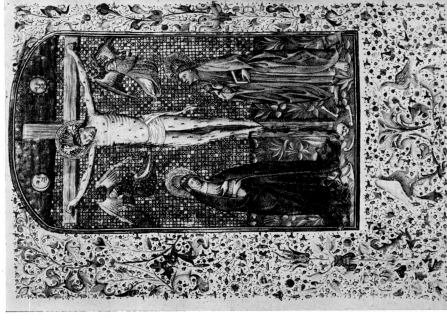

VII–19. a, *Roman Breviary Rylands Lat. 136*: initial with King David and liturgical text. b, *Missal of Pope Felix V*, fol. 111 v: Crucifixion with the Virgin and S. John.

VII–20. *a*, Indulgence to a Bevagna church (*M. 697*): Madonna and Child; symbols of the Evangelists; S. Vincent (martyr, d. 303), first bishop and patron of Bevagna. *b*, Copy of *Life of the Virgin*, Fitzwilliam Museum, *MS. 20*, fol. 9 *r*: Annunciation; historiated initial; decorated border with grotesques. *c*, Copy of *Description des douze Césars* fol. 34 *v*: Hadrian.

VII–21. *a*, Guillaume de Nangis, *Chronicle of the Kings of France* (up to
1300), *W. 306,* fol. 14 *v*: the King prays before the beginning of the battle;
on the left, the Christian army; on the right, the army of the infidels. *b*, Copy
of *Great Chronicles of France* (up to 1340–50), *W. 139,* fol. 20 *r*: four scenes
representing travel; writing of the *Chronicles*; battle; and crowning; the text
is the beginning of the *Prologus.*

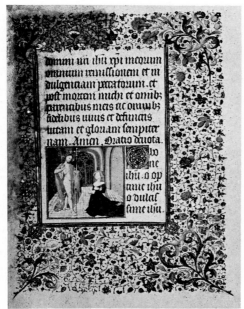

VII–22. *a, Horae W. 219,* fol. *16 r*: Creation of Eve and beginning of *S. John. b, Chevalier Hours*: Annunciation. *c,* Early work of Maître François: *Horae W. 285,* fol. *107 r*: adoration of the Resurrected Christ. *d,* Maître François: *Horae W. 252,* fol. *130 r*: burial.

VII–23. *a, Hours for Adelaide of Savoy*: Assumption of the Virgin at the side of the Moon, and adoration by six Sybils. *b*, Fitzwilliam Museum, *MS. 3–1954*, fol. *253 v* (Burgundian addition): Christ appears on the altar as S. Gregory the Great celebrates Mass. *c*, Lyoset Liédet: National Library at Paris, *MS. 22547*: Alexander the Great receives mother and wives of King Darius (note the costumes and armour of late fifteenth-century Burgundy).

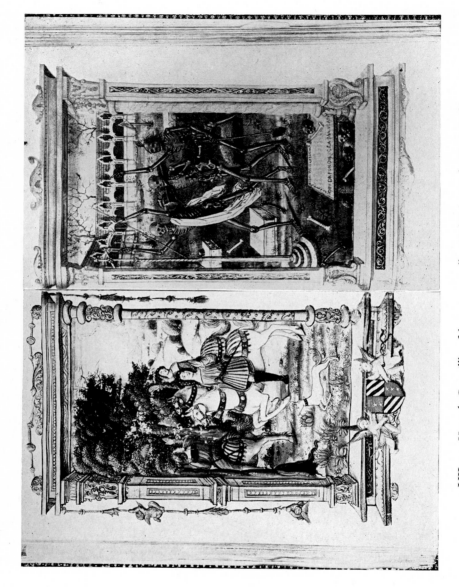

VII–24. *Horae de Genouilhac*, fol. 94 *v*–95 *r*: 'les Trois Morts et les Trois Vifs'.

VII-25. *a*, Jacques de Besançon: *Psalter and Abbreviated Hours, W. 286*, fol. 11 *r*: adoration of Madonna and Child by donor commended by Mary Magdalen; liturgical text. *b*, *Hours of Anne of Brittany*: Anne commended by three saints (including S. Anne, to the right).

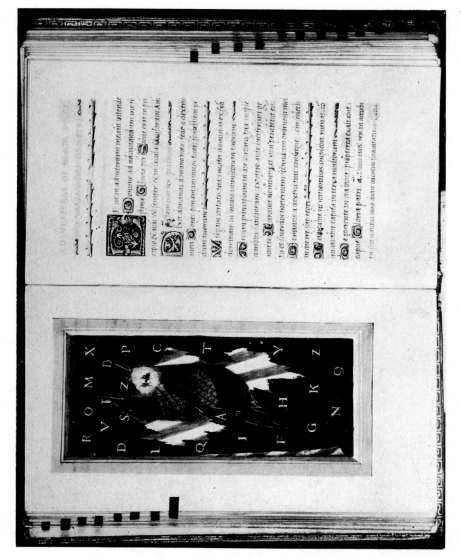

VII–26. *Hours for Jehan Lallemant the Younger*, fol. 37 v–38 r: Flight into Egypt (?).

VII–27. a, B. M. Harl. MS. 2897, fol. 188 v: *Acta Apostolorum* i. 1–2. b, B. M. Add. MS. 35311, fol. 8 r: *Beatus* page and beginning of *Psalms*. c, *Stavelot Bible*, British Museum, *Add. MS. 28107*: initial A (beginning of *Book of Judith*). d, *Floreffe Bible*, British Museum, *Add. MS. 17738*.

VII–28. *a*, *W. 85*, fol. 31 *v*–32 *r*: historiated initial representing Crucifixion; ornamented initials; marginal drolleries and grotesques. *b, Bodley MS. 264*, fol. 220 *r*: the 'Great Cham' receives Niccolò, Maffio (Matteo) and Marco Polo. *c, M. 785*, fol. 50 *r*: (Astrological Treatise) *Luna, Exaltatio: Taurus*.

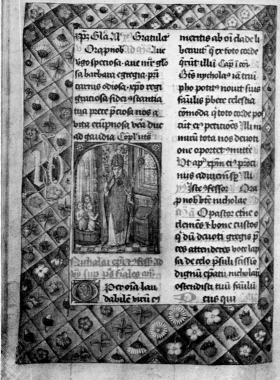

VII–29. *a, W. 166,* fol. 161 : Madonna and Child adored by angels. *b, Rylands Lat. 39,* fol. 151 *v* : S. Nicholas and the three children in the tub ; ornamented initial and decorated border.

VII–30. *a, W. 171* (Dirc van Delft, *Tafel van den Kersten Ghelove*), fol. 4 *r*: Christ as Judge of the Universe. *b, Rylands Dutch MS. 15,* fol. 37 *r*: ornamented initial; beautifully decorated border. *c, Horae W. 185,* fol. 14 *v*: Christ arrested; kiss of Judas. *d, Missal W. 174,* fol. 98 *v*: Resurrection of Christ; the Three Maries at the Tomb.

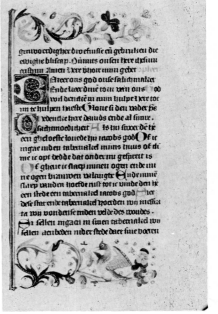

VII–31. *a, Horae W. 168*, fol. 81 *v*: Flagellation of Christ. *b, Utrecht Horae W. 188*, fol. 122 *r*: Christ in the Limbo, Adam and Eve. *c, Utrecht Bible* (Fitzwilliam Museum, *MS. 289*), vol. I, fol. 2 *r*: S. Jerome writing; historiated initial; decorated border; text: S. Jerome's *Epistle* to presbyter Paulinus. *d, Utrecht Horae, C.U.L. Add. MS. 4097*, fol. 39 *r*: ornamented initials; decorated upper and lower borders.

VII–32. *a, Flemish Horae W. 428,* fol. 132 *v*–133 *r*: Bathsheba (2 *Sam.* xi. 2); text: *Psalm,* vi. 2–5. *b, Flemish Horae W. 427* fol. 89 *v*–90 *r*: Annunciation to the Shepherds; liturgical text.

VII–33. *a, Flemish Horae, C.U.L. Add. MS. 6689, fol. 13 r: Beatus* page (*Psalm* i. *1–5*). *b, Flemish Horae W. 430*: Flight into Egypt; the motto of the original owner (Ie Lay de Vev) is worked into the border of the miniature. *c, Ghent-Bruges Horae, W. 425, fol. 1 v–2 r*: Calendar for January and February.

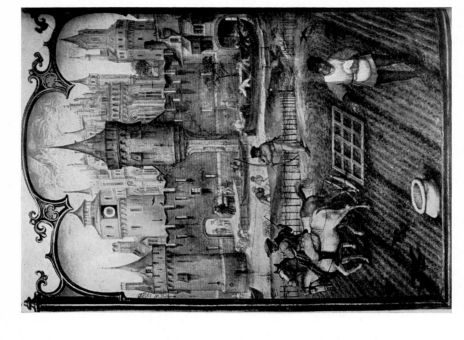

VII–34. *Grimani Breviary*: *a*, The Virgins (in the foreground from left to right, S. Catherine of Alexandria, S. Cecilia, and S. Barbara). *b*, Agricultural occupation for October.

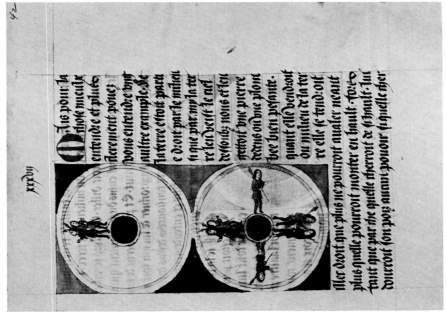

VII-35. *a*, Jehan de Wavrin, *Chroniques d'Angleterre* (*W. 201*), fol. 261 *r*: coronation in Westminster Abbey of Henry IV (1399) and murder of Richard II at Pontefract (1400). *b*, Gautier de Metz, *Image du monde* (*W. 199*), fol. 42 *r*: cosmologic speculation.

VII–36. *W. 442*: Quadriptych (cf. p. 452) attributed to Simon Bening (third wing); scenes from the passion of Christ.

conjunction with illustrated *Herbals* which, tracing their descent from the *Dios-corides MS.* (see also p. 44 ff.), have the same carefully outlined and delicately tinted drawings of plants, the monotony of their solid instructiveness always broken by a picture of the ill-fated dog chained to the mandrake's monstrous roots.

Interesting specimens of this class have been mentioned on p. 269. A charming copy of Guillaume le Clerc, *Bestiary*, of *c.* 1285, is in the National Library at Paris (*Fr. 14970*). A late thirteenth-century copy of the French translation of Frederick II, *De Arte venandi* (see p. 309 f.) is in the same collection (Fr. *12400*).

There are various works which deal with similar subjects, but their titles are often deceiving. The great majority of these books are written in Latin—an excellent specimen is Lambert d'Ardres, *Liber Floridus* (National Library at Paris, *Lat. 8865*). There are, however, a few MSS. written in vulgar tongues, particularly in Provençal; for instance, Maître Ermengau's sort of encyclopaedia *Breviari d'amor* (National Library at Paris, *Fr. 857*). 'The text is illustrated by miniatures often of considerable interest, setting forth the seasonal and daily occupations, the classification of temperaments and other topics' (Van Moé).

Another class of scientific picture-book, more strictly scientific and therefore far less popular and numerous, is also of great interest. The majority of medieval text-books of medicine and surgery have no illustrations at all, but some contain diagrams carefully drawn in outline, and a few have fully illuminated pages in gold and colours. J. A. Herbert mentions an admirable example of this class, a French translation of the *Treatise on Surgery* by Roger of Parma (British Museum, *Sloane MS. 1977*). The French copy, written *c.* 1250, contains at the beginning sixteen full-page miniatures, each divided into nine compartments, and—writes Herbert—planned so as to combine professional instruction with a reminder of the homage due to religion: the three topmost compartments contain scenes from the life of Christ, etc., painted on gold or diapered grounds under trefoil-arched canopies, and forming a complete series from the Annunciation to the Last Judgment, while the remaining compartments are filled with illustrations of surgical treatment, on plain blue or lake grounds. Further on in the volume are four pages, each in twelve compartments, entirely devoted to surgery, preceded by a full-page representation of the master and his pupil in the dispensary. The delicate and expressive draughtsmanship of these little pictures, concludes Herbert, is a delight to the layman, while members of the faculty find an added joy, not unmixed with surprise, in recognizing their scientific soundness and accuracy.

Finally, reference may here be made to a pseudo-scientific text-book on hygiene, compiled mainly on the basis of Arabic sources by Aldobrandino da Siena (+ Troyes, 1287), physician and writer at the court of Countess Beatrix of Savoy. The work, known as *Régime du Corps*, contains several illuminated initials. A thirteenth-century MS. is preserved in the British Museum (*Sloane*, 2435); a fourteenth-century MS. in the National Library, at Paris (*Franç.*, 12323); and a fifteenth-century MS. (containing the arms of Henry VII and his queen Elizabeth of York) in the University Library, Cambridge (I. i. 5. 11).

Paris School of Illumination

Paris, with its great University at the Sorbonne, was then the main artistic and cultural centre of France, and its thirteenth- and fourteenth-century school of illumination produced excellent work. As a result of the impetus given to Biblical studies by the scholars of the University, great numbers of small, handy *Bibles* were produced for personal use. They were finely written in minute Gothic script on tissue-thin vellum. An excellent specimen is preserved in the Walters Art Gallery, Baltimore (*W. 51*). It contains two full-page miniatures, thirty-eight historiated, and thirty-seven ornamented initials. 'The initials . . . avoid the use of gold, but the scenes are virorously designed and finely drawn' (D. Miner).

Amongst the best productions of the Paris school of illumination, there are two little *Psalters*, which were executed for S. Louis and his sister, and 'represent the highest achievement of thirteenth-century illumination in France' (Herbert). The *S. Louis Psalter* (National Library at Paris, *Lat. 10525*), which has no fewer than seventy-eight full-page miniatures of Old-Testament subjects at the beginning, was produced between the years 1253 and 1270.

The other, *Psalter and Hours*, probably executed for Isabelle of France, sister of S. Louis (and foundress of Longchamp Abbey, where she lived out her last ten years, 1260–70), was almost a replica of the above, but only very few of the miniatures have been preserved; the *Psalter* was in the Yates Thompson Collection, and is now in the Fitzwilliam Museum, Cambridge (*MS. 300*). Both books— writes Herbert—are remarkable, among other things, for their exquisite architectural backgrounds, consisting in every instance of two or four bays of a Gothic interior, with gables, wheel or quatrefoil windows, and fretted arcadings and pinnacles above, forming as it were a scenic setting before which the personages of Bible-history play their parts like actors in the miracle-plays, which were actually performed in churches. These personages indeed, full of that gentle and ingenuous gaiety of which Gothic painters held the secret, seem less historical characters than the delighted actors of a pious play: Fig. VII-6*a*. Reference may here be made to the *Missal of S. Louis*, preserved in Assisi: Fig. VII-8*a*.

A little *Psalter* (measuring $5\frac{3}{4} \times 4$ in.), containing eight historiated initials which show exceptional excellence of workmanship, is preserved in the Walters Art Gallery (*W. 115*). Each large initial, 'its form lightened by areas of interlace, sends forth a fine ivy border to surround the page'. The elegantly drawn figures are shown against diapered grounds of colour and gold, or, in some cases, carefully tooled and burnished gold leaf' (Miner). The MS. was executed in Paris for the Counts of Arras: Fig. VII-8*b*.

In contrast to these small-sized Psalters, very large Psalters were also produced. The Pierpont Morgan Library, New York (*M. 638*), possesses forty-three vellum leaves, measuring $15\frac{3}{8} \times 11\frac{3}{4}$ in., which apparently were originally prefixed to a Psalter. There are eighty-six full-page miniatures containing 283 scenes, painted *c.* 1250 by several excellent artists. Two other leaves from this MS. are preserved in the National Library at Paris, and one in London, formerly in Cockerell's collection. In the sixteenth century, the codex belonged to the Polish Cardinal Bernard Maciejowski, who in 1604 presented it as a gift to Abbas the Great Shah of Persia. The latter ordered to be added on the margins (already containing explanatory inscriptions in fourteenth-century Italian hand) explanations in Persian and in Hebrew: Fig. VII-6*b*.

The illustrations—writes Dorothy Miner—commence with the Creation and terminate with *II. Samuel xx.* Many rarely represented episodes are included, all presented with great richness of narrative detail. As customary at the time, the events are depicted as if of contemporary occurrence, so that the miniatures present us with a detailed picture-book of thirteenth-century life. Particularly notable is the facile rendering of unusual and foreshortened poses, and the dignity and serenity with which the figures move through the complex narratives represented.

Less advanced in technique is a mid-thirteenth-century *Gospel-lectionary*, which was given by S. Louis to the Sainte-Chapelle, and is now preserved in the National Library at Paris (*Lat. 17326*). An excellent copy of this work, a product of the Paris school, is preserved in the British Museum (*Add. MS. 17341*). These books do not contain full-page miniatures, but there are miniature-initials with partial borders attached. 'The foliate scroll-work inside the initial-frames is finely finished, and already foreshadows the rich designs which fill the margins of fifteenth-century Horae' (Herbert).

Another interesting book is the Latin-French *Life of S. Denis*, written in 1317 by the monk Yves of the Paris abbey of S. Denis, and presented by the abbot to King Philip V; the MS. is now preserved in the National Library at Paris (*Fr. 2090–2*). There are 77 finely-executed miniatures (74 being full-page), on diapered or tapestried grounds, representing the lives and martyrdoms of S. Denis and his companions. It is assumed that the artist was a Parisian lay illuminator. Particularly charming are the foreground-pictures of everyday street and riverside life in Paris: people walking or riding in the streets, men bathing from boats or fishing with rod or net, and the towing or unloading of boats. The pictures are, for the fourteenth century, unusually realistic and full of animation. See also p. 384.

Other Schools of Illumination

The mid-thirteenth-century productions of other schools—though excellent— are inferior in quality to those executed in Paris. Amongst the preserved specimens there are a number of fine Psalters. One of them, assigned to a North-French school (probably Rheims), is preserved in the British Museum (*Add. MS. 17868*). It contains historiated initials and, on almost every page, bar-borders, supporting little figures, such as manikins, rabbits, etc. In its preliminary series of eighteen full-page miniatures of the life of Christ, on grounds of raised and brilliantly burnished gold—argues Herbert—we have a collection of true Gothic types: slender, pale-faced, sweet though formal personages, now far removed from the crudely outlined figures of earlier time. The architectural ornament, too, is typical of Gothic art, and particularly of that branch of it which flourished in France at this period: trefoil-arched gables supported by very slender columns.

Another thirteenth-century North-French *Psalter*, perhaps produced in the region of Sens, is preserved in the Philadelphia Free Library (*Lewis MS. 185*). It contains twenty-four full-page miniatures, twenty-four small Calendar-illustrations, one large and a great number of smaller historiated initials, and numerous fantastic line-endings. On the whole, in D. Miner's words, it is a MS. 'of exceptional richness and beauty, which is a noteworthy example of the luxury books of the thirteenth century'. The scenes are composed with clarity and grace, the abundant drapery folds being modelled by succeeding washes of grey and even black over the basic colour, which is always soft: rose, blue, grey, grey-blue, light green, and dull lavender. The general effect, concludes Miss Miner, is luminous, but not brilliant.

Another *Psalter* (it is combined with a *Book of Hours*), preserved in the same Library (*Widener MS. 9*), comes from North-Eastern France and belongs to the late thirteenth century. It contains twelve full-page miniatures (mainly illustrating scenes from the life of Christ), twenty-four Calendar-illustrations, twenty historiated initials, and a great number of drolleries.

Similar in style is a *Bible*, containing as many as 64 historiated initials, which is preserved in the Walters Art Gallery, Baltimore (*W. 56*): Fig. VII-7a.

A *Psalter* and *Canticles*, from Northern France, belonging to the thirteenth century, is also preserved in the Walters Art Gallery (*W. 44*). It contains ten full-page miniatures and ten historiated initials.

Slightly less advanced in technique is a *Psalter* in the British Museum (*Royal 2. B. ii*) which was written for a nun of a monastery apparently situated near Nantes. There are no full-page miniatures, but there are exquisite medallions and Calendar-squares, and large initials enclosed in diapered rectangles with miniatures on grounds of burnished gold.

A *Psalter* of Franciscan use, produced *c.* 1250 for the family Fieschi, Counts of Lavagna (near Genoa), and now preserved in the Walters Art Gallery (*W. 45*), contains eight beautiful historiated initials and a great number of marginal drolleries.

An excellent late thirteenth-century *Psalter* is preserved in The John Rylands Library, Manchester (*Lat. MS. 117*).

Popular Picture-books for Religious Instruction

An interesting codex, executed *c.* 1300 in Northern France, and preserved in the Spencer Collection of the New York Public Library, may exemplify the production in France of popular picture-books. 154 leaves, containing 846 miniatures, have survived, but according to the table of contents of the MS., originally there were 1034 figures, illustrating the histories of the Old and the New Testaments, the lives and miracles of the Apostles, saints and martyrs, and 'explained in writing'. Indeed, the most frequent arrangement of this *Historiated Bible*

FRANCE

and Lives of Saints is a column of text paralleled by a column of illustrations on various patterned backgrounds. The miniatures are by several hands, 'the finest distinguished for the graceful and expressive character of the drawing' (D. Miner).

In the lower social classes, amongst the nearly illiterate laymen, three richly illustrated books became fashionable in the late thirteenth and the early fourteenth centuries. They were the *Biblia Pauperum,* the *Legenda aurea,* and the *Speculum Humanae Salvationis* (*see* also pp. 233 and 236); the last, which was the Dominican manual of devotion, first appeared *c.* 1324. See, particularly, J. Lutz and P. Pedrizet, *Speculum humanae salvationis,* 2 vols. (text and plates), XX. 351 pp., folio, 1907.

The *Biblia Pauperum,* as it is commonly called, or as it should be called, the 'Bible of the Illiterates' (see pp. 234 and 236), contains the old allegories rendered into later forms. The use of the *Legenda* and the *Speculum* was so widespread, and their influence so great, that, in Dr. Joan Evan's opinion, while the *Summa* of the Dominican S. Thomas Aquinas was the foundation of learned thought, the *Legenda* and *Speculum,* also Dominican productions, were the bases of popular iconography.

The preserved copies of the *Speculum,* generally speaking, are unpretentious, didactic manuscripts for popular use, abundantly illustrated with rough drawings. There are, however, exceptions: two luxurious French copies, one produced *c.* 1440, and the other somewhat later, are similar in style and elegance. They are preserved in the National Library at Paris (*Fr. 6275*) and in the Rosenbach Company Collection, New York City. See also p. 441 f.

The *Bible Historiale,* a French paraphrase of the Sacred Scriptures, a translation (made in 1295 by Guiart des Moulins, Canon of Aire in Artois) of Petrus Comestor's *Historia Scholastica,* was one of the most popular works of the fourteenth century. A copy written in Paris in 1317 by Jean de Papeleu (and preserved in the Arsenal Library, Paris, *No. 5059*), contains a frontispiece, representing Christ surrounded by angels, and 176 illustrative miniatures on gold or diapered grounds. Of great interest are the preliminary sketches still visible in the margins; such sketches also appear in other manuscripts, as, for instance, in an early fourteenth-century French Bible of the British Museum (*Royal MS. 18. D. viii*). See also pp. 394, 399 f., and 450.

An excellent copy of the *Bible Historiée*—a series of 48 full-page paintings representing scenes from the books of *Genesis* and *Exodus*—is preserved in The John Rylands Library, Manchester (*French MS. 5*). The miniatures, executed *c.* 1250, are on a background of burnished gold. The descriptions, in French, are above and below the miniatures: Fig. VII-8c. Particularly charming is the Paris copy, National Library, *MS. Fr. 9561*: Fig. VII-10.

Of great interest, though not of great artistic merit, is a four-volume *Moralized Bible* (British Museum, *Harl. MS. 1526–7*; National Library at Paris, *Lat. 1150*; Bodleian Library, *Bodl. 270b*). There are on every page two narrow text-columns (each containing two short passages from the Bible, followed by moralization or allegorical interpretation) and two wide miniature-columns (in oblong frames covered with diaper patterns) containing four medallion-scenes painted on gold ground.

Of much better quality is a British Museum copy (*Add. MS. 18719*) of the same work, also containing eight illustrations to the page, but these are square, and, as Herbert has pointed out, are freely and crisply drawn in brown ink without any use of colour. Simple, expressive, dramatic, they tell their stories apparently without effort, yet always with effect. The illustrations 'give a mixed but altogether pleasing impression of brisk narrative, popular theology, and sure and easy draughtsmanship' (Herbert).

Perhaps the best specimen of this class of illuminated MSS. is a book containing religious treatises, executed in France *c.* 1300, and later divided into two volumes, of which one is in the British Museum (*Add. MS. 28162*) and the other was in the Yates Thompson Collection. The former contains the *La Somme le Roy*—a French popular compendium of Catholic doctrine, composed (in 1279) for Philip III the Bold by his confessor, Fr. Laurent—and has at the beginning full-page miniatures by Honoré (see p. 391 f.), painted in brilliant colours (particularly scarlet) on backgrounds of burnished and patterned gold, within Gothic arcades. They represent the Decalogue, the Creed, the cardinal virtues, and the seven deadly sins with their corresponding virtues. There are also exquisite initials enclosing foliage-scrolls or figures and bar-borders. Three of the four full-page miniatures of the second volume have 'a beauty of conception, a delicacy and refinement of colouring, and a perfection of technique, which mark them out as among the most exquisite productions of the illuminator's art' (Herbert). A slightly earlier copy of this work (of *c.* 1295) is in the Mazarine Library at Paris (*MS. 870*), and a copy of *c.* 1311 is in the Arsenal Library (*MS. 6329*).

A fragmentary copy of *La Somme le Roy* was in the possession of Dr. Eric Millar, London, but two leaves are preserved in the Fitzwilliam Museum, Cambridge (*MSS. 192* and *368*): Fig. VII-9a. Millar ascribes them to Honoré (see p. 391 and facing plate).

A fine British Museum volume of the fourteenth century (*Arundel MS. 83*) is a good representative of a curious class of manuscripts, containing the *Danse macabre*.

LATE THIRTEENTH- AND FOURTEENTH-CENTURY MASTERS IN ILLUMINATION

Names of several French illuminators (including that of a lady) of the thirteenth-fourteenth centuries are known, but very little is known of their work. The work of Honoré—last decades of the thirteenth century—and of his son-in-law Richard de Verdun (associated with him in 1292; apparently by 1318 he had inherited Honoré's atelier) was of special account. The motifs introduced by Honoré dominated the field during the whole of the fourteenth century. Amongst the most famous artists of the century may be mentioned Jean Purcelle (who worked *c.* 1320 to *c.* 1370); the artist known as the *Maître aux Boquetaux* (of the late fourteenth century); André Beauneveu (of the closing years of the fourteenth century), and Jacquemart de Hesdin (of the early years of the following century). Each of these great artists has been associated with a well-marked distinctive style.

An interesting Latin-French *Book of Hours* and *Missal* (formerly in the collection

Honoré(?), *La Somme le Roy*, fol. 107. Above, personifications of the Virtue of Friendship and the Vice of Hatred; below, David and Jonathan (= friendship) and Saul threatening David's life (= hatred).

of the Viscountess Lee of Fareham, and now in the Fitzwilliam Museum, *MS. 3–1954*) was executed in Paris *c.* 1370 for Philip the Bold of Burgundy for the use of the Sainte-Chapelle (see also p. 426). It was illuminated by the 'Maître aux Boquetaux' and his assistants. In the fifteenth century a number of Flemish miniatures were added, some of them being by Jehan Dreux, *c.* 1470 (see p. 429). The MS. now contains 14 large and 115 small miniatures apart from Calendar-illustrations and borders. Fig. VII-11*c* and 12*b*.

Honoré and Richard de Verdun. The *Breviary of Philip the Fair* (National Library at Paris, *Lat. 1023*), of 1296, is attributed to Honoré.

A *Psalter and Hours of the Virgin*, produced perhaps in Amiens *c.* 1275, and preserved in the Pierpont Morgan Library, New York (*M. 729*), contains 40 full-page miniatures, 66 historiated initials, and a great number of borders with armorial decoration, and many drolleries .This richly illustrated MS., executed for Yolande, Vicomtesse de Soissons, wife of Bernard V, sire de Moreuil, is by several hands, 'the most skilful employing a style resembling that ascribed to "Maître Honoré" ' (D. Miner). See also p. 390.

Two most beautiful works, obviously executed by the same artist, are attributed to Richard de Verdun: they are the *Verdun Breviary* and the *Metz Pontifical*, and both contain a great number of beautiful historiated initials and charming borders, consisting of slender cusped bars ending in foliage-stems or in little human heads or grotesque forms, with a great variety of single humorous figures or groups, executed in fine taste and with good sense of proportion.

The former work, in two volumes (Vol. I, formerly Yates Thompson Collection *No. 31*; Vol. II, in the Public Library at Verdun, *No. 107*), was executed for Margaret de Bar, Abbess of S. Maur at Verdun, 1291–1304. The *Metz Pontifical*, executed for her brother, Raynaud or Reinhold, Bishop of Metz, 1302–16, contains also a splendid series of half-page miniatures illustrating many rites and ceremonies which are mentioned in the text. The first nineteen depict the dedication of a church, including a picture showing the bishop tracing with his crosier the Greek and Latin alphabets on the floor of the church. The delicately drawn figures, argues Herbert, stand out well against the diapered backgrounds; they still have the almost ascetic slenderness of early Gothic art, but its austere rigidity has now given place to a curious and distinctive sway of the body, not ungraceful, though somewhat artificial and suggestive of sentimentality. The faces, placid, smooth, and rounded, are of refined types, and are drawn with extraordinary delicacy. This beautiful codex, formerly in the Yates Thompson Collection, is now preserved in the Fitzwilliam Museum, Cambridge (*MS. 298*): Fig. VII-9*b*.

Jean Pucelle and his School. The illumination of the following three books is credited to Jean Pucelle: a *Book of Hours* completed between 1325 and 1328 (see p. 392); a *Bible*, completed in 1327 (now preserved in the National Library at Paris, *Lat. 11935*); and the *Belleville Breviary*, completed before 1343 (now in the National Library at Paris, *Lat. 10483–4*). The Bible, very neatly written by one Robert de Billyng, has beautiful pen-tracery in blue and red, and excellent, though scanty, illumination; there is also a dated colophon, stating that Jehan Pucelle, Anciau de Cens, and Jaquet Maci *hont enluminé ce livre ci*. See Fig. VII-11*a*.

Some memoranda in the *Belleville Breviary* indicate that Pucelle was the *chef d'atelier* commissioned to execute the book, and that he was assisted by Mahiet, Ancelet, and J. Chevrier (copyists or illuminators), the first two being perhaps identical with the aforementioned Maci and Anciau. The *Breviary* contains 76 small but exquisite miniatures: an interesting new feature consists in these miniatures being not enclosed in the initials but set in the column immediately above them. Also the border-frame tends to become an independent ornament. It consists of narrow bars (cusped and knotted at the angles) surrounding the text on all sides but the upper one, where the bars branch out into the foliage-stems (consisting mainly of the conventional three-lobed ivy-leaf) which nearly meet and complete the frame: among the foliage, or used as terminals, are human figures, birds, insects, dragons, and grotesques. Unlike the earlier book-production and that of contemporary England, there is little striving after naturalism or variety, the main purpose of the border being to present a graceful and symmetrical arrangement of purely conventional foliage. Some pages contain in their lower margins, between the text and the bar, charming little scenes from the Bible and allegorical representations of virtues and of the mysteries of the Church.

On the whole, to quote Miss Dorothy Miner, Pucelle was distinguished for a most elegant and graceful style, free and fluid of action and expressive of narrative, which was enhanced by light and delicate modelling. His incidental drolleries show a direct and tender observation of the natural characteristics of birds, beasts, insects and flowers.

An interesting problem is presented by the *Pucelle Hours*, mentioned in the inventories of Duke of Berry's Library. It has been identified with a small *Hours* (known as the *Hours of Jeanne d'Évreux*), which formerly belonged to the collection of Baroness Adolphe de Rothschild, and it has been suggested that it may be the same as the *bien petit livret d'oroisons . . . que Pucelle enlumina* between 1325 and 1328 for Charles IV to be presented to his third wife, Jeanne d'Evreux, who bequeathed it in 1370 to Charles V, from whom it passed to his brother, Jean de France, Duke of Berry. Though rather small ($2\frac{3}{8} \times 3\frac{1}{2}$ inches), it is one of the most splendid examples of the perfection of French fourteenth-century illumination. Offered for sale by Baron Maurice de Rothschild, in 1954 it was purchased by the Metropolitan Museum of Art, New York, and is now preserved in the Cloisters.

An attractive copy of Guilielmus Durandus, *In sententias Petri Lombardi*, written in Paris in 1336 by the English scribe William of Kirkby (in Lincolnshire), is preserved in Princeton University Library (*Garrett MS. 83*). There are two historiated initials and several illuminated borders. The ornament in general, the patterns used in the drolleries, and the aristocratic decorative charms are strikingly close to the Pucelle MSS., 'yet the peculiar lightness, vitality and subtle modelling of veritable Pucelle works are missing' (D. Miner). In consequence, the Durandus MS. is attributed to an atelier using some of the Pucelle models.

A rather charming feature of the *Belleville Breviary* is the Calendar-illustrations (unfortunately only the two pages for November and December have been preserved), which are explained in the *exposition des ymages* at the beginning of the book. Two other Parisian masterpieces, probably belonging to the 'Pucelle School', contain a complete series of Calendar-illustrations. Both were in the collection of Mr. Yates Thompson (*MSS. 75* and *LXXXVI*) and in 1941 were donated to the British Museum. They are the *Hours of Joan II*, Queen of Navarre (daughter of Louis X of France), a book completed between 1336 and 1348, and the *Hours of Yolande of Flanders* (Joan's daughter-in-law), completed about 1353. The former contains, apart from the Calendar-illustrations, 68 half-page miniatures and 37 historiated initials, with minor initial and border decoration on nearly all pages. The series of miniatures of the *Hours of Joan II* is most interesting. The pictures depict scenes from the life of S. Louis, who was a direct ancestor of Joan. A most charming historiated initial represents Joan kneeling, with a prayer-book before her, below a large miniature of the Trinity. The miniatures of the *Hours of Yolande of Flanders* have been badly damaged through a Thames flood, but their design is exquisite.

The Calendar-illustrations of these books are of great interest, both because of their artistic value and their theological symbolism. The whole year symbolizes the gradual destruction of the Synagogue of the Old Testament: at the foot of each page is the Synagogue building, from which a prophet removes a stone, symbolizing a prophecy, and gives it to an Apostle, in whose hands it turns into a scroll inscribed with an article of the Catholic Creed; thus the Synagogue, complete in January, crumbles away as the year advances, till in December it falls to the ground in ruins. Each month is identified with one of the twelve apostles, with one of the twelve articles of the Creed, and with S. Paul's conversion or one of his Epistles. At the top of each page is a battlemented gate, one of *les xij portes de Jérusalem de Paradis*; from the battlements the Virgin, *par quoi nous fu la porte ouverte*, waves a banner containing a device illustrating one of the articles of the Creed, corresponding with the inscription on the scroll held by the apostle. Below the Virgin, S. Paul crouches beneath the Hand of God or preaches to the Romans, Corinthians, and others. From the right-hand side of the gateway springs an arch, bearing the sun in a position which marks its meridian altitude for the month; below is the appropriate zodiacal sign, with a landscape sketch suggestive of the season (bare trunks and frozen earth in January, rain in February, etc.).

A reflection of the style introduced by Jean Pucelle may be seen even in MSS. belonging to the last quarter of the fourteenth century; examples are two codices illuminated in Paris *c.* 1380, and preserved in the Walters Art Gallery, Baltimore: *W. 119*, a *Psalter*, containing eight historiated initials and several illuminated borders; *W. 124*, a *Missal* for the use of Paris, with seventeen historiated initials and illuminated borders: Fig. VII-11*b*.

Painting in Grisaille. Pucelle's influence may be seen in various exquisite MSS. of the second half of the fourteenth century. Some of these present a new feature: the figures are no longer painted in full body-colour like the rest of the miniature, but are in pale, semi-lucent monochrome. This monochrome technique—writes Dr. Paecht—was one of the means by which miniaturists attempted to give book-painting a more restrained note to distinguish it from the richer effects of the panel picture and to place illumination in a category of its own, halfway between paint-ing and the graphic arts. The colour abstraction of *grisaille* miniatures, argues Paecht, makes for a distinct decorative harmony between picture and script which could never exist between black lettering and miniatures painted in full colour.

The figures are usually on a patterned or coloured ground; they are very faintly shaded and modelled in a cold grey, and, like cameos, appear as though moulded or carved in relief, enhanced by the splendid brocaded and tessellated gold grounds and the bright colours of the rest of the miniature.

A good example of *grisaille* art is a two-volume copy of the *Bible Historiale*, of 1357 (now in the British Museum, *Royal MS. 17. E. vii*), containing two half-page miniatures—one at the beginning of each volume—with full borders, and 87 smaller ones.

The *grisaille*-method is also employed in the mid-fourteenth-century *Breviary of Jeanne d'Evreux*: see also p. 392 (now in the Condé Museum, Chantilly, N. France). Jeanne (1328–70) was the widow of King Charles IV. This MS. contains 114 miniatures: although the draperies are sometimes fully coloured, the figures are delicately painted in *grisaille* on diapered, trellised, or damasked backgrounds.

Fine examples of *grisaille*-painting, with improved technique, are (1) two great volumes of S. Augustine's *City of God* (British Museum, *Add. MSS. 15244-5*). Apart from the finely modelled figures in *grisaille*, the miniatures here are also characterised by improved technique in the painting of landscape, the foreground being executed with great care and naturalism; (2) the *Missal of S. Denis Abbey* (Victoria and Albert Museum, London), containing charming small figures in the lower margins in the numerous historiated initials. The birds, butterflies, and grotesques of the borders are well-drawn and in faintly tinted outline; (3) *Harley MS. 2952*, of the British Museum, 'a dainty specimen' (Esdaile) of the fifteenth century. See Fig. VII-12a.

Reference may also be made to MSS., which are not in *grisaille* proper, though they may appear as such: for instance, a fourteenth-century richly-illustrated copy (it contains as many as 81 miniatures) of Jacques de Longuyon, *Les Voeux du paon* ('Vows of the Peacock'), preserved in the Spencer Collection of the New York Public Library. In it—as Miss D. Miner has pointed out—the figures, simply drawn in outline upon the plain parchment, give the effect of *grisaille*, while colour is achieved mainly by means of the patterned backgrounds of rose or lavender.

André Beauneveu and Jacquemart de Hesdin (or Houdain). André Beauneveu, from Hainault, worked as a sculptor and painter from 1361 for over forty years; in 1364 he was commissioned by Charles V for the royal tombs of the basilica of S. Denis; later he worked for the Count of Flanders; in 1386 he worked in Bourges as *ymagier* to the Duke of Berry, and slightly later he was *maistre de ses oeuvres de taille et de peintures*.

In the famous Latin-French *Psalter of the Duke of Berry* (National Library at Paris, *MS. Fr. 13091*) we have 24 miniatures, prefixed to the text, which are the only ones painted by Beauneveu that have come down to us with documentary evidence. They represent twelve prophets and (on the opposite pages) twelve apostles, all in *grisaille*, seated on faintly coloured thrones, against backgrounds which are either diapered or tessellated, or coloured reddish-brown or very dark blue, with patterns of oak-leaves or other foliage outlined in black. The faces of the figures appear to be portraits from life; the draperies are soft and beautifully modelled. As in Michelangelo's paintings, the figures have the stamp of a great sculptor—as Beauneveu was—more than of a great painter: Fig. VII-13*a*.

Other masterpieces may have been the work of this great artist. A superb *Book of Hours* (Royal Library at Brussels, *Nos. 11060–1*) contains at the beginning two full-page miniatures, on opposite pages, forming a single composition and representing the Duke of Berry (between SS. Andrew and John the Baptist) kneeling before the Virgin and Child. These miniatures seem to have been executed by Beauneveu, but some critics have assigned them to Jacquemart de Hesdin (or Houdain). Other critics have assigned to Jacquemart seventeen of the twenty miniatures which the *Brussels Book of Hours* contains; they have the characteristics (in their colour-scheme and landscape-backgrounds) of the early fifteenth century. See also p. 399.

Jacquemart de Hesdin is believed to have been a pupil of Jean de Bruges, a court painter to Charles V. He worked for the Duke of Berry in 1384 and 1399, and after the latter year he was active for nearly fifteen years. With Beauneveu and others he worked on the *Brussels Hours*, the *Great Hours*, the *Small Hours*, and on the Latin-French *Psalter* (see below). These show him, writes Herbert, to have been a painter of consummate skill. His work is neater and crisper and more conventionally perfect than Beauneveu's, but it lacks the sculptor's large conception of form. Distinct signs of primitive Italian influence are visible in his miniatures (as in those of most French painters of his time), notably in the landscape, now claiming more and more of the space hitherto given up to conventional patterns. On the whole—concludes Herbert—Jacquemart seems to have been an eclectic copyist of great expertness, rather than an original artist.

The following masterpieces are, in part at least, ascribed to Jacquemart: John de Berry's *Great Book of Hours* (National Library at Paris, *Lat. 919*), which was finished in 1409; the best miniatures of John de Berry's *Small Book of Hours*, finished in or before 1402 (National Library at Paris, *Lat. 18014*); and the miniatures of the *Latin-French Psalter* (National Library, *Fr. 13091*), except the twenty-four already referred to.

Various Books of Hours have been attributed, at least in part, to the atelier or the followers of Jacquemart de Hesdin. Some MSS. of this group are preserved in Walters Art Gallery, Baltimore. They are *W. 94*, produced in Paris *c.* 1390, containing eleven miniatures and several illuminated borders; *W. 231*, produced between 1400 and 1410, with twenty miniatures and illuminated borders throughout; *W. 232,* of *c.* 1415, with sixteen miniatures and illuminated borders through-out; *W. 219,* of *c.* 1415–20, with twenty-six miniatures and a great number of illuminated borders. A detached leaf of *c.* 1400, representing the bearded giant S. Christopher, contains a beautiful grey-green landscape with distant towers and fantastically spiralling crags, which reflect the backgrounds in miniatures attributed to Jacquemart de Hesdin. (The leaf is preserved in the Rosenwald Collection, National Gallery of Art, Washington.) Fig. VII-22*a*.

A *Book of Hours* for use of Rome, preserved in the Bodleian Library (*MS. Lat. Lit. f. 3*), and containing seventeen miniatures, several borders and marginal illuminations, was executed by two artists, one of whom (who painted the miniature with the portrait of Anne of Bohemia) worked in a style related to that of Jacquemart de Hesdin. The book was executed in Brussels, for Anne of Bohemia, Queen of Richard II, before her arrival in England, in 1382.

The 'Maître aux Boquetaux' has been referred to on p. 391.

FRANCE, THE LEADING CENTRE IN ILLUMINATION
(FIFTEENTH CENTURY)

The transition from the thirteenth to the fourteenth century marks in England and in France the zenith of the early Gothic illumination. The English and the French styles, which in the thirteenth century resembled one another so closely as to be practically indistinguishable—see p. 262—took, curiously enough, absolutely divergent paths in their development during the fourteenth century. English illumination continued its glorious tradition for a few decades, but about the middle of the century it suddenly decayed (see p. 283 f.); whereas in France, although the art of illumination proceeded more or less continuously, the first half of the fourteenth century marked a somewhat characterless period.

The great and saintly Louis IX (see p. 379) was succeeded by Philip III the Bold (1270–85) and Philip IV the Fair (1285–1314). The latter's reign marked the zenith of the royal power, but was the prelude to a very rapid decline. His three sons (Louis X, Philip V, and Charles IV) reigned in quick succession. The period of their rule and of that of the first two kings of the House of Valois (Philip VI, 1328–50, and John II, 1350–64) is marked by a deep depression of French power owing to the initial disasters of the Hundred Years' War (1337–1453), and to the violent 'revolutionary' movement that seemed for a time to destroy the power of the monarchy. No wonder, therefore, that the condition of the country at large was deplorable and for a time there was a standstill in the development of both arts and letters.

With Charles V 'the Wise' (1364–80), victorious against the English and against his feudal nobility, reformer of the administration of justice and of taxation, the situation greatly improved. By collecting a great number of manuscripts, he laid the foundations of a French National Library at Paris. Indeed, his famous collection, housed in the Louvre, became the nucleus of the Royal Library, *i.e.,* of what is now the *Bibliothèque Nationale.* Charles V caused many manuscripts to be copied and others to be translated from Latin into French. The brothers of Charles V, and particularly John Duke of Berry, were also great collectors of books and patrons of brilliant illuminators, such as the brothers Limbourg, Jacquemart de Hesdin, Jacques Coene, and André Beauneveu (see *passim*).

Moreover, the superb books produced for the kings and princes were only a part of the output of fourteenth- and fifteenth-century illuminated MSS. The love of beautiful books was extended to all educated classes of society; not only the great personages of the day, but the middle-class bourgeois were also keen to possess finely executed *Books of Hours*, and other illuminated books. It was an age of great activity, good, bad, or indifferent in the production of illuminated manuscripts. The French painters, as Herbert has rightly emphasised, went on from strength to strength, preserving the excellent tradition they had inherited, yet continually vitalizing and developing it by the rejection of worn-out conventions and the introduction of new ideas, and progressing steadily towards a more perfect mastery of technique.

By the end of the fourteenth century, French illumination had reached a very high level, and the beginning of the fifteenth century saw the production of a great number of first-class manuscripts, though these are eclipsed by the supreme beauty of a few outstanding masterpieces—just as, in an allied field, one finds very great masters in the Uffizi Galleries in Florence who would be superlative in any other art-gallery, but who are there outshone by a Botticelli, a Leonardo da Vinci or a Michelangelo.

However, the first half of the fifteenth century was the flowering-time of French illumination in the proper sense of the term. An immense quantity of work was produced in this century and in the early sixteenth century, and some of the illuminated codices have considerable artistic merit. The special beauty of the period lies in real paintings—executed on vellum instead of canvas or wood—rather than in ornamented manuscript pages.

New styles arose, represented primarily by Jean Foucquet (see p. 412 ff.) and Jean Bourdichon (p. 418 f.), and new foreign influences are noticeable, particularly the influence of the Flemish school in the North, and of the Italian school in the South-East.

Amongst the main features of this period was the border, which developed from a sort of pendant or excrescence which encroached on the margin. This excrescence developed into a leafy branch, running completely around the text, and could have the form of a natural branch, with leaves and animals or grotesques intertwined among the boughs, or else the form of a narrow formal stem or fanciful foliage, or other device.

The most famous Books of Hours—the jewels of French book-production—belong to this period.

Charles V and John Duke of Berry

This period may well be considered the Golden Age of French illumination.

We may start with a MS. which has no great artistic merit, but is of considerable historical importance: this is a Latin-French copy of Charles V's coronation service (now in the British Museum, *Tib. B. viii*, fol. 35–80), containing the King's autograph note, and made on his order in 1365. It contains thirty-eight miniatures, some with the portrait of Charles V, painted in various colours and gold, on diapered, tessellated, or damasked backgrounds.

Of greater artistic value is another British Museum MS. (*Landsdowne MS. 1175*), the first volume of a French Bible, translated by Raoul de Presles for Charles V; it was probably the actual copy given to the King; and is the only preserved codex containing de Presles's dedicatory preface. This is prefixed by a miniature showing Raoul presenting the book to Charles. The work contains the name of the scribe (Henri du Trevou) and has charming little miniatures at the beginning of several Biblical books. The figures, with extremely small heads, are in *grisaille*, on checkered, tessellated or damasked backgrounds; the landscapes are of Italo-Byzantine style, containing flat-topped hillocks with smooth, steep, terraced slopes.

Another book (also in the British Museum, *Royal MS. 19. C. iv*) produced for Charles, the *Songe du Vergier*, written in 1378 by Philippe de Maizières, has a very curious frontispiece: the author is shown asleep in an orchard, and is dreaming of Spiritual and Temporal Power, represented by two charming queens, who are on the left and the right of the King sitting in state; the disputed merits of these powers are argued upon by a clerk and a knight. The manuscript contains an autograph note by Charles V.

Although belonging to a slightly later period, mention may here be made of another curious frontispiece, painted in brilliant colours and prefixed to the *Epistle to Richard II*, written by the same author in 1395–6, to promote friendship between France and England (British Museum, *Royal MS. 20 B. vi*). The crowns of the two countries, on blue and red grounds, and, in between, the Crown of Thorns on a black field, are represented under Gothic canopies in the upper half of the frontispiece with the inscription *Charles roy de France, Jesus roy de paix, Richart roy d'Angleterre*, while in the lower half there are the arms of the two countries and the Sacred Monogram written in gold. A large miniature, painted on the opposite page, contains a beautiful initial and border decoration, and represents the writer offering his work to King Richard.

Of the important works translated into French for Charles V, at least two should here be added: Augustine's *City of God*, translated into French by Raoul de Presles (already referred to), in 1378; and the *Treatise on the Properties of Things*, by the English Franciscan friar Bartholomaeus Anglicus, translated into French by Jean Corbechon in 1371: an excellent copy, in two volumes, executed about 1380 for Charles V, is preserved in the Nat. Libr., at Paris, *Fr. 20090* (see also p. 403). Finally, mention should be made of a beautiful copy of the *Grandes Chroniques de France* (see also pp. 380, 410, 418), preserved in the National Library at Paris (*MS. Fr. 2813*). The *Chronicles* are a sort of official version of history, tracing the story of France from mythical origins down to 1380; in fact, it is a typical medieval history consisting of a compilation of romance, legend, and fact. The MS. was produced by the monks of the Abbey of S. Denis. An interesting late fourteenth-century copy of the *Grandes Chroniques de France* (containing one large and 36 small miniatures, and 40 illuminated initials) with drawings in *grisaille*, is preserved in the Walters Art Gallery, Baltimore (*W. 139*) see p. 410.

More important for our purpose was the interest in book-illumination shown by Charles' brother, John Duke of Berry, 'the prince of medieval bibliophiles'.

Indeed, as Herbert puts it, the history of French illumination in the fourteenth century is largely a catalogue of John's library, though the majority of its best works belong to the opening years of the next century. The Duke of Berry, as already mentioned, was not only a great collector but also a great patron. In or before 1386, he appointed André Beauneveu (see p. 394) as his salaried *ymagier*, and—according to the chronicler Jean Froissart, under the year 1390—as *maistre de ses ouvres de taille et de peintures*. See Fig. VII-13a.

Jacquemart de Hesdin was another miniaturist who worked for the Duke of Berry (see p. 395 f.).

The Walters Art Gallery, Baltimore, possesses a very fine *Book of Hours* (*W. 96*), produced in Paris *c.* 1400. It contains fourteen miniatures and illuminated borders throughout. According to Miss Dorothy Miner, its illustrations are by two hands, both very delicate in delineation and modelling, and reminiscent of the artists who worked for the Duke of Berry on such MSS. as his *Grandes Heures*: Fig. VII-14a (see also p. 395).

A fine copy of Raoul de Presles's French translation of S. Augustine's *City of God*, produced *c.* 1380 for the Duke of Berry, is now partly preserved in the Hofer Collection, Rockport, Maine (U.S.A.) and partly in the Municipal Library at Angers (*MS. Fr. 162*). The Hofer MS. contains twelve miniatures and a great number of illuminated initials and borders. The illustrations, by at least three different hands—writes Miss Miner—are delicately drawn in *grisaille*, partly tinted in colour, against grounds ornamented with diapering or *rinceaux*. The finest of the hands has much of the grace and freshness associated with the artist known as the 'Maître aux Boquetaux' (see p. 391).

Two other copies of the *City of God* have been attributed to the same atelier: British Museum, *Add. MSS. 15244-5* (see p. 394), and National Library at Paris, *Fr. 22912-3*. A slightly later copy (of *c.* 1410) of the work, containing only books I–V, is preserved in the Philadelphia Museum of Art. It is a *de luxe* MS. executed by several artists of the Paris school. Each 'book' is preceded by a large miniature with full ivy border, while 59 small miniatures are dispersed throughout the text.

A good example of late fourteenth-century illumination is the *Berry Bible*, containing the *Bible Historiale* in two large volumes (British Museum, *Harley MSS. 4381-2*). The magnificent opening page of the first volume, referring to *Genesis*, represents the Trinity, with the Virgin, SS. Peter and Paul, the four Doctors of the Church, some pagan philosophers (including Plato, Aristotle, and Seneca), and personifications of Dialectics and Arithmetic. The first page of the second volume, much coarser in execution than that of the first volume, refers to the book of

Proverbs, and contains a large square with four scenes from the life of Solomon. The opening pages of other books of the Bible or their chapters contain smaller miniatures, with ivy-leaf borders and initials on burnished gold. Some miniatures, such as the Nativity, in *S. Matthew*, are very good, but others do not reach the same standard. The miniatures on burnished gold or minute diaper are very effective; others on red grounds, patterned with gold, are less so. Other copies of the *Bible Historiale* have been referred to on pp. 389 and 394.

A very fine production appears in the inventories of Robinet d'Estampes, keeper of the jewels to the Duke of Berry, as *une très belles heures de Nostre Dame*. It was begun about 1390 for the Duke, but was left unfinished. This *Most Beautiful Book of Hours*, is now known as the *Turin Hours*. Apparently, a portion, detached at an early period, belonged to William IV of Bavaria, Count of Hainault and Holland (who died in 1417); a new Calendar, of Netherlandish origin, was added at the beginning, and several uncompleted pages were filled up with miniatures executed by Flemish artists (see p. 444). The history of this beautiful work reads like a detective story: before 1413 it belonged to Robinet d'Estampes; later it was separated into three portions. (I) The portion, which had belonged to William IV, at a later stage, was again separated into two fragments. One was given in 1720 by Victor Amaedeus II to the National University Library of Turin (which he then founded); the other one passed to the Trivulzio Library (Prince Trivulzio, Milan), and just before the last World War was sold to the Museo Civico in Turin. The first fragment, however, was destroyed in the disastrous fire of the Turin National University Library, in 1904; fortunately, however, it was previously published (though with "indistinct and sometimes blotchy collotype illustrations") by Paul Durrieu (*Les heures de Turin*, 1902). (II) A portion of the book belonged until the last war to Baron Maurice de Rothschild, but (according to Prof. E. J. F. Arnould, *Irish Times*, 12-7-1958) "it somewhat mysteriously disappeared during the German occupation and was found by an officer of the French Second Armoured Division, Captain Francis Rogé, on May 6th, 1945, among litter left the day before in Goering's house at Berchtesgaden by G.I. souvenir hunters. Identified some time later and returned to its owner, it was ultimately presented to the Bibliothèque Nationale, Paris, by Baron de Rothschild, shortly before he died."

In a private letter, written on April 8th, 1965, Prof. Arnould (cousin of Capt., now Lt. Col., Ret., Rogé, of the French Army) adds some interesting data, partly based on information received from Rogé himself. ". . . the codex was found in the 'sous-sols' of the Berchtesgaden station. . . . We have 'stolen the march' on the Americans. . . ." Prof. Arnould and Rogé got in touch with M. Porcher of the French National Library. "Ultimately the ownership was traced to Maurice de Rothschild, who agreed to leave the manuscript at the National Library, and it was finally deposited there and exhibited formally from 10th January to 9th February 1957, a different page being shown every day. The number is *Nouv. acq. lat., 3093*."

(III) The smallest portion, consisting of only four folios, were given by Jules Maciet in 1896 to the Louvre Museum (now preserved in the Cabinet des dessins).

Apparently, several leading artists collaborated in the illumination of this book, including Jacquemart de Hesdin (see p. 395 ff.) and the brothers Limbourg (p. 411 f.). Several miniatures of the portion supplemented in Flanders (see p. 444) are attributed to one master, the "chief master" of the *Turin Hours*. This has been identified by some modern art-historians (such as Friedlaender, Winkler and Beenken) with either Hubert or Jan van Eyck, but this attribution is highly controversial (see, for instance, L. Balduss, *Jan van Eyck*, London, 1952).

For the small Book of Hours, known as the *Hours of Jeanne d'Évreux* or *Pucelle Hours*, see p. 392; for the much larger, known as the *Belles Hours*, see p. 411 f.

All these superb works of art almost pale into insignificance beside *Les très riches heures* or *Most Rich Book of Hours* (now preserved in the Condé Museum, at Chantilly, *MS. 1284*). Pol de Limbourg and his brothers Jehannequin and Hermann were engaged by the Duke to paint this masterpiece for him (see pp. 411.) when in 1416 Berry died. The zenith of the whole art of illumination was here reached, and though subsequently various superb, luxurious, and brilliant masterpieces were executed by great painters, a definite gradual decadence in point of taste may be noted: Fig. VII-13*b*. See also p. 405.

The influence of the Flemish artists working for the Duke of Berry is reflected in various French illuminated MSS., exemplified by a richly illustrated *Book of Hours*, of 1420–5, now preserved in the Walters Art Gallery, Baltimore (*W. 265*): Fig. VII-14*b*.

To illustrate the Duke of Berry's splendid collection of books, quite apart from those specifically executed for him, it will suffice to mention two British Museum manuscripts of the mid-fourteenth century, *Burney MS. 275* and *Harley MS. 2891*; the former was a gift of Anti-Pope Clement VII (1378–94), having previously belonged to Pope Gregory XI (1370–8); and the latter was probably given by Itier de Martreuil (Bishop of Poitiers, 1395–1405) to the Duke of Berry, and by him to the Sainte-Chapelle at Bourges. *Burney MS. 275*, a secular book (comprising works of Priscian, Euclid, and Ptolemy), contains fine and charming personifications of the arts and sciences, and borders with numerous animals and grotesques. *Harley MS. 2891*, a *Missal* of Paris use, contains two full-page miniatures prefixed to the Canon (a Crucifixion, in beautiful composition, and a Christ in Glory), and a number of delicate historiated initials, with exquisite borders. The opening page of the *Temporale—Ad te levavi animam meam*—contains a charming little miniature of the celebrant lifting up his soul to God.

Finally, mention may be made of a copy of the *Moralized Bible* (National Library at Paris, *Fr. 166*), a beautiful picture-book for religious instruction (see p. 389); it was not completed until after the Duke's decease.

In addition to the devotional books, the Duke's library also contained beautifully illuminated secular books. A copy of the *Book of Marvels* (National Library at Paris, *Fr. 2810*) was given to the Duke in 1413 by John the Fearless, the son of Philip the Bold, Duke of Burgundy (who died in 1404), for whom the MS. was apparently executed. It is a narrative of Eastern travel, or rather a collection of Oriental tales compiled from the narratives of Marco Polo, Sir John Mandeville, and others. It contains 265 charming and amusing illustrations. In the Arsenal Library, Paris (*MS. 664*), is to be found the Duke of Berry's magnificent copy of the plays of Terence (see p. 40). It is known as *Térence des ducs*, having been in the possession of two dukes, Louis, Duke of Guyenne and Dauphin (d. 1415) and the Duke of Berry. The codex is abundantly illustrated and—as Herbert writes—its miniatures have a special value from the complete absence of any marvellous or symbolical element to interfere with the simpler aim of depicting actual life as the artists saw it. The faces are well and clearly drawn, the posing and grouping of the figures full of dramatic expressiveness, the costumes carefully painted. The provenance of this copy (which was produced between 1405 and 1410) is uncertain. Another copy of Terence, *Comedies*, which belonged to the Duke of Berry, is now in the National Library at Paris (*Lat. 7907A*). It was executed *c.* 1407. Although derived from the same model, this copy is much simpler than the *Térence des ducs*. Under the illumination of fol. 39r there appears the name *Hainbert*, who has been identified with Imbert Steiner, a painter at the Court of Philip the Bold (see p. 423 f.).

The Duke of Berry also possessed a beautiful copy of the works of the great musician Guillaume de Marchaut (it is now preserved in the National Library at Paris, *Fr. 9221*). The codex, of *c.* 1390, contains 38 very fine miniatures executed by two hands. Finally, astrology was well represented by the extremely interesting illuminated MS. now preserved in the Pierpont Morgan Library (*M.785*): see p. 442.

Books of Hours (also known as Hours or Horae)

When the illuminated book productions of the best period are grouped according to subject, the *Books of Hours* head the list, immensely out-numbering the contents of any other class. The name derives from the main section of these books, containing the 'Hours' (or Office) of the Virgin, *i.e.*, services to be said or sung by the clergy at the canonical hours of Matins, Lauds, Prime, Tierce, Sext, None, Vespers, and Compline. The opening words of Matins (or Matin Hours) are *Domine labia mea aperies*; the other Hours, except Compline, begin *Deus in adjutorium meum intende*. The Hours of the Virgin are usually followed by the Hours (in a very condensed form) of the Cross and of the Holy Ghost, and are generally preceded by the following three sections: Calendar; four lessons—one from each Gospel: the opening verses of S. John, the Annunciation from S. Luke, the Adoration of the Magi from S. Matthew, and the conclusion of S. Mark; and two prayers to the Virgin (beginning *Obsecro te* and *O intemerata*). Other sections follow the Hours. Usually they are the following: the Seven Penitential Psalms, followed by Litany and prayers, Memorials of Saints, and Vigils (or Office) of the Dead, consisting of Vespers and Matins. French Hours contain also Hours of S. Catherine, the Mass of the Trinity, and other additions; English Hours have other additions, such as the Commendation of Souls. On the whole, the contents of the Hours vary greatly both in matter and arrangement.

The decoration also varies, but the Hours almost always include the following full- or half-page miniatures: the *Hours of the Virgin* contain the illumination of the Annunciation, the Visitation, Nativity, Angel and Shepherds, Adoration of the Magi, Presentation in the Temple, Flight into Egypt, Coronation of the Virgin; the *Hours of the Cross* and *of the Holy Ghost* contain the Crucifixion and Pentecost; there are Calendar-illustrations; the *Gospel-lessons* contain the portraits of the four Evangelists; the *Penitential Psalms* contain the miniature of David kneeling; the *Memorials of Saints* contain miniatures of saints; the *Vigils of the Dead* contain the Raising of Lazarus, and so on.

A great number of illuminated Books of Hours have been referred to in various sections, dealing with English, Italian, or French books of the thirteenth and fourteenth centuries, but by the end of the latter they had become extremely popular especially in France, and the most famous Hours belong to this period or to the following decades.

Here a few more fourteenth- and fifteenth-century *Horae* may be mentioned.

An interesting *Book of Hours*, written *c.* 1325 for a lady of the region of Thérouanne in French Flanders, is preserved in the Walters Art Gallery (*W. 90*). It contains seven full-page miniatures and twenty-four historiated initials. Moreover, ornamental borders with marginal grotesques decorate nearly every page: Fig. VII-14*c*.

A beautiful *Horae*, in Latin, with a Calendar in French, written in 1407 for the use of a church in the Diocese of Paris, is preserved in the Bodleian Library, Oxford (*MS. Douce 144*): Fig. VII-14*d*.

The *Boucicaut Hours* (Jacquemart-André Museum, Paris, *MS. 2*), made between 1410 and 1415 for the Maréchal de Boucicaut and his wife, is particularly interesting because of the realism which begins to show itself in the representation of landscape and the improved perspective; indeed, a few of the miniatures, for instance, have instead of the checkered and brocaded backgrounds, a deep blue sky spangled with stars. Some scholars have suggested the identification of the 'Master of the Boucicaut Hours' with the painter Jacques Coene (see p. 457). The MS. contains 45 large miniatures.

Various Books of Hours, partly at least, have been attributed to the atelier or to followers of the 'Boucicaut Master'. Examples are: *MS. Lat. 10538* in the National Library at Paris; three MSS. in the Walters Art Gallery, Baltimore (*W. 232, W. 260, W. 287*; the last containing as many as thirty-nine large miniatures and twenty-four in the Calendar, and illuminated borders on every page); and a *Book of Hours* for Paris use, of *c.* 1425, preserved in the Library of Congress, Washington (*Acc. 4560: 7*). A very fine early fifteenth-century copy of Corbechon's translation of Bartholomaeus Anglicus (see p. 398) is preserved in the Fitzwilliam Museum, Cambridge (*MS. 251*). It contains nineteen miniatures (three are missing) in the style of the 'Boucicaut Master'. There are also initials in gold and colour, and elaborate borders with grotesques. Other copies of the same work are in the British Museum (*Royal MSS. 15. E. ii, iii*). Also *MS. 1646-1902* in the Victoria and Albert Museum at London is attributed to the 'Boucicaut Master': Fig. VII-

15. A *Missal* of the first half of the fifteenth century, containing sixteen large miniatures, numerous initials, and illuminated borders (State Library at Lucca, *MS. 3122*) is in a style allied to that of the 'Boucicaut Master'.

Related in style to the *Boucicaut Hours*, though on a much smaller scale, is an *Hours* in the National Library at Paris (*Lat. 1161*), containing charming borders with, among other details, the long sinuous leaf entwined about a slender stem, popular in late fourteenth-century English MSS. One of the best of the miniatures—characterized by their brilliant and finely harmonized colours—is the Madonna and Child adored by a lady with her guardian angel; of interest is the composition of the burial-scene in a monastic cemetery, prefixed to the Vigils of the Dead.

Closely allied to the latter MS., but with an admixture of Italian elements—such as *putti* among the leaves, or growing Clytie-wise out of flowers—in the borders (which are filled with various forms of natural or conventional foliage, birds, butterflies, rayed gilt discs, and so on), are two British Museum *Books of Hours, Add. MSS. 29433* and *32454*. They show a brilliancy of colouring; and some pages, very finely executed, glow with burnished gold. The latter MS. contains a splendid Coronation of the Virgin, while the former contains a fine Annunciation, though this miniature and that prefixed to the Penitential Psalms are full of light-hearted, Italian humour.

Admixture of Italian influence, especially in the border-ornament, may be seen in the Books of Hours produced in South-Eastern France.

An excellent example is *W. 237* in the Walters Art Gallery, Baltimore. It belongs to *c.* 1400 and contains eighteen miniatures and a great number of illuminated borders. Its Calendar celebrates a number of Cluniac saints and points to South-East France between the High Alps and Provence. There are hints of Italian influence in the *Anjou Hours*, made for King René of Anjou (1409–80), and preserved in the British Museum (*Egerton MS. 1070*) and in the National Library at Paris (*Lat. 1156*). This influence is particularly strong in some later Books of Hours such as the *Saluces Hours* (British Museum, *Add. MS. 27697*), made *c.* 1450–60, probably for Amadeus de Saluces.

The *Louis de Savoy Hours* (Nat. Library, Paris, *Lat. 9473*) is a magnificent example of the school of Savoy. The Hours, of Roman use, produced between 1440 and 1465 for the Duke Louis de Savoy, was the work of a Savoyard artist. Its composition is French, but the painting is strongly influenced by North-Italian art, particularly by that of Cristoforo de Predis (see p. 343 f.).

Among the finest French book-products of the period are another two *Hours* of the National Library at Paris, known as the *Rohan Hours* (*Lat. 9471*) and the *Laval Hours* (*Lat. 920*). The former contains eleven very fine full-page miniatures—*e.g.*, one represents in a particularly vivid scene Christ as an old man, leaning over a dying Christian, while the archangel Michael and the devil are fighting for the possession of his soul. Fig. VII-16a.

The *Laval Hours* contains 54 half-page miniatures, and the medallion-scenes of the borders number no fewer than 1155. This beautiful book is attributed to Jean Colombe, who c. 1485 completed the *Most Rich Hours* (see p. 401) for Charles, Duke of Savoy, and his Duchess, Blanche de Montferrat. Although these latter pages are hardly to be compared with those painted by the Limbourg brothers (see p. 401), they are excellent examples of the best work produced at the period.

The *Rohan Hours*, as Miss Miner has pointed out, is one of the most remarkable and enigmatic of all fifteenth-century Books of Hours. It is also notable for the monumental scale of its illuminations. The works of the 'Rohan atelier' are also distinguished for highly original presentation of both narrative and symbolic scenes. 'Not only the iconography, but the rendering of figures in unusual poses of great expressiveness, the emphasis on intense emotion and avoidance of prettiness, set these works apart from the whole body of illumination produced by other Paris ateliers of the period' (Miner). Of the various MSS. attributed to the 'Rohan atelier', the following, executed c. 1425, may be referred to: a *Book of Hours* preserved in the Harvard College Library, containing 19 large and 58 smaller miniatures; two *Books of Hours* for the use of Troyes (one is in the Eisemann Collection, London; the other partly in the Princeton University Library, *Garrett MS. 48*); the British Museum *Harley MS. 2934*; and *MS. 1278* in the S. Geneviève Library, Paris. Finally, mention must be made of the beautiful *Hours of Isabel Stuart*, preserved in the Fitzwilliam Museum, Cambridge (*MS. 62*): some scholars regard it as one of the best productions of the 'Rohan atelier', second only to the *Rohan Hours*: Fig. VII-16b.

Another excellent *Book of Hours*, preserved in the Fitzwilliam Museum (*MS. 60*), was executed in 1420 for a lady in Brittany. It is characterised by a great variety in the borders: Fig. VII-17b.

One of the most celebrated Hours—though not as fine or beautiful as the *Most Rich Hours*—is the gorgeous, indeed excessively sumptuous, *Bedford Hours*. It was written and illuminated in 1423–30 for John of Lancaster, Duke of Bedford (1389–1435), the brother of Henry V and Regent of France from 1422 until his death in 1435; the *Hours* was probably executed on the occasion of John's marriage (in 1423) to Anne, daughter of John the Fearless, Duke of Burgundy (see p. 424 f.). The book contains her portrait, arms, and motto as well as his, and she gave it (with his consent) to King Henry VI on Christmas Eve, 1430. The British Museum bought it in 1852 for £3,000 (it is *Add. MS. 18850*), and Esdaile regards it as one of the very finest illuminated books in the Library. Every page of the text has a luxuriant full border with brilliant little medallion-miniatures, columbines, violets, and other lavish flowers, ivy-leaf and acanthus. There are four beautiful full-page miniatures depicting scenes from *Genesis*. The four Gospel-lessons have large pictures of the Evangelists writing, with vignettes representing scenes from their lives, and the Annunciation is framed by twelve scenes from the Virgin's life. The last miniature (fol. 288b) illustrates the legend of the divine origin of the royal arms of France, and two superb portrait-pages (fols. 256v and 257v) represent in pure profile the Duke and Duchess, magnificently dressed, kneeling before their respective patron-saints: Fig. VII-18a. *See*, also, p. 407 for the *Sarum Breviary*.

Various MSS. have been attributed to the 'Bedford atelier', including two preserved in the Walters Art Gallery, Baltimore: a *Missal* for the use of Paris (*W. 302*), executed in 1429, and containing seventeen historiated initials (with tiny miniatures) and several illuminated borders; and a *Book of Hours* (*W. 281*), executed between 1430 and 1435, containing twenty-seven miniatures and illuminated borders: Fig. VII-18b.

More important is *MS. 1855* of the Nat. Library, Vienna. It was executed soon after 1420 by the "Bedford Master" and was later presented to King Charles VII (1422–61) and his queen Marie d'Anjou.

Another splendid *Book of Hours*, contemporary with, and artistically related to the *Bedford Hours*—in part probably decorated by the same artist—is the *Sobieski Hours*, having once belonged to John Sobieski, King of Poland (1624–96). The MS., bequeathed by Cardinal Henry Stuart to George IV, is now in the Royal Library at Windsor. Apparently it was made for Margaret (sister of Anne, Duchess of Bedford) on the occasion of her marriage, in 1423, to Arthur, Count of Richemont. Some pages of the MS. are superior to those of the *Bedford Hours*; they are more restrained, delicate, and harmonious in colouring, and are in certain aspects a link between the refined art of the *Most Rich Hours* and the gorgeous art of the *Bedford Hours*. The admirable large miniatures are composite pictures either divided into compartments (such as the scenes from the life of the Virgin, prefixed to the Hours of the Virgin) or representing several incidents continuously (for instance, the picture of Mont Saint-Michel at the *Memoria* of S. Michael). The Calendar-illustrations, with their symbolic figures of prophets and apostles and with the figures of saints in the margins opposite their respective days, are very interesting.

The *Dunois Hours* (Yates Thompson Collection, *No. 11*), a beautiful small book by a brilliant Parisian artist of the period of the regency of the Duke of Bedford, was made for the great soldier Dunois, Bastard of Orléans, after his capture of Paris in 1436. In three miniatures there is the portrait of Dunois. The representation of the seven deadly sins, illustrating the Penitential Psalms, is outstanding ('Idleness' is a copy of 'Vierge au donateur' by Jan van Eyck, in the Louvre). On the whole, it is in brilliant colours.

An interesting *Horae* of the Bodleian Library, at Oxford (*MS. Auct. D. inf. 2. 11*), was executed in France about 1430–40. A French Dominican *Horae* of the British Museum (*Add. MS. 35312*) was executed between 1425 and 1450.

A *Book of Hours* for the use of Sarum, now in the Fitzwilliam Museum, Cambridge (*MS. 375*), was executed *c.* 1450 by a North-French (Rouen?) artist, working for the English market: there are sixteen miniatures, eighteen historiated initials, and one historiated border.

Some other fifteenth-century *Horae* preserved in the Fitzwilliam Museum are particularly interesting: the *Beauchamp Hours*, Sarum use, executed in 1424 for Margaret Beauchamp, second wife of John Talbot, first Earl of Shrewsbury; with prayers in English (*MS. 41—1950*: it is a companion volume to *MS. 40—1950*, made for John Talbot); a *Liturgical Psalter and Hours*, of Roman use, executed *c.* 1450 in North France or South Flanders (*MS. 4—1954*); fifteenth-century *Horae* (*MSS. McClean 80 and 81*, and *MS. 63*); and a *Horae*, of Paris use, executed in 1480 (*MS. 74*).

Also the Trinity College Library, Cambridge, possesses some excellent French *Horae* of the fifteenth century (*MS. B. 11. 19*; *MSS. B. 11. 31 and 32*; *MS. o. 8. 18*).

The *Coëtivy Hours* (Yates Thompson Collection, *No. 85*) contains more miniatures, but is not on the highest artistic level though of some brilliancy; most of the miniatures are painted in a method which is a modification of *grisaille* (see p. 343 f.): while the backgrounds are in light colours, the draperies are left white.

The beautiful *Hours of Marguerite d'Orléans* (Nat. Libr., Paris, *Lat. 1156 B*), probably of the early sixteenth century, contains on f. 135 a number of emblems and alphabetic letters spread over the page, which may be a mystic game of words or names.

Finally, *Harley MS. 2877*, in the British Museum, executed about 1500, is a fine volume 'by an artist of (or imitating) the later Tours school' (Esdaile); and a charming *Horae* for Toulouse use, of 1524 (Walters Art Gallery, *W. 449*) may be regarded as one of the last fine specimens of this 'genre': Fig. VII-17a.

Other Devotional Books. The *Breviarium* or Breviary was in certain respects closely related to the Book of Hours. It is a book which contains the office for the eight canonical hours in the Catholic Church. It is a compendium of the various books —such as the Psalter, the Book of Prayers, etc.—needed in any one service of the canonical Hours. It thus contains psalms, antiphons, verses, responses, hymns, prayers, lessons from Scripture, patristic homilies, and lives of saints. Its normal arrangements are in part similar to that of the Book of Hours: (1) Calendar; (2) Psalter; (3) Temporale; (4) Sanctorale; (5) Common of Saints; (6) Hours of the Virgin; (7) Office of the Dead; and other special services.

Being similar in contents to the Book of Hours, the Breviary also provides ample opportunities for illustration, but preserved copies of finely illuminated Breviaries are much rarer, because the books were in daily use. Still, some preserved illuminated Breviaries are outstanding. The *Sarum Breviary* (National Library at Paris, *Lat. 17294*), made for the Duke of Bedford, was probably executed by the same artists as those who worked on the *Bedford Hours*, but must be of slightly later date, because it contains the arms of his second wife, Jacqueline of Luxembourg, whom he married in 1433. Canon Victor Leroquais counted in the *Sarum Breviary* no fewer than four thousand three hundred vignettes.

Examples of very fine earlier Breviaries are: the *Breviary of Philip IV the Fair* (1268–1314)—see p. 396, now in the National Library at Paris (*Lat. 1023*); the *Belleville Breviary*, produced *c.* 1340; the *Breviary of Charles V* (1337–80), preserved in the National Library at Paris (*Lat. 1052*)—see p. 396 f.

There is in the Walters Art Gallery, Baltimore (*W. 300*), a Breviary with Franciscan Calendar and saints, executed in 1422 in Rouen (Normandy). It contains one half-page miniature, 67 historiated initials, and numerous illuminated borders with drolleries. According to Miss Miner, the abundant and unusual miniatures are by several hands, including one much influenced by Italian painting. This artist painted the Last Judgment (in the large miniature), and a similar scene, 'also strongly Italianate in style', is to be found in *Add. MS. 29433* of the British Museum.

An exquisite *Roman Breviary* for the use of Notre-Dame (Paris), of the early fifteenth century, is preserved in The John Rylands Library, Manchester (*Lat. MS. 136*). The miniatures and historiated initials have grounds of plain gold, blue or red, with gold flourishing; some are tessellated. Dragons occur frequently on the terminations of the ornaments. The ivy-leaf borders are in blue, red, or gold. Another excellent *Breviary* of the fifteenth century, for Sarum use, is preserved in the University Library at Cambridge (*MS. Dd. 5.5*). See Fig. VII-19*a*.

For the *Burgundian Breviary* see p. 424; for the *Isabella Book* and *Grimani Breviary* see pp. 453 and 455 f.

A very fine *Missal*, of the mid-fourteenth century (now preserved in the British Museum) was presented by John, Duke of Berry, to the Sainte-Chapelle at Bourges.

Elsewhere (see pp. 398 ff., 416 ff., and *passim*) other illuminated devotional works have been dealt with. Psalters are no longer as popular as before, the less so as Psalms are included in Books of Hours and Breviaries. There are, however, some splendid productions in this genre, too. It will suffice to refer to the *Psalter of Henry VI* (British Museum, *Cotton MS., Domitian A. xvii*). It is generally assumed that this was a gift from his mother, Queen Catharine, on the occasion of his coronation in 1430. It contains fifteen fine miniatures and in six of them the young king is shown (kneeling before the Image of Pity, or the Virgin and Child, or looking on at the combat between David and Goliath, etc.). The borders, as Herbert has pointed out, show the gilt ivy-leaf style at its best, and the church scenes, with nuns and friars singing the office, are admirable both for the display or architectural detail and for the soft and delicate treatment of the faces.

Fig. VII-19*b* reproduces the magnificent *Missal* executed for Amadeus VIII, Duke of Savoy, who as Felix V was set up as anti-Pope by the Council of Basel (1439) in opposition to Eugene IV, but resigned his dignity in 1449.

An interesting product of South-East France is preserved in the Pierpont Morgan Library at New York, *M. 697*: it is an 'indulgence' granted by Pope Clement VI at Avignon, on 18 July 1343, to the church of S. Maria by the Stone Bridge at Bevagna in the diocese of Spoleto. It contains the initial U enclosing the representation of the Virgin and Child flanked by an angel holding a scroll and a saint in the regalia of bishop (probably S. Vincent who died in 303, who was the first bishop and patron of Bevagna). On the left, there are the symbols of SS. John and Mark: Fig. VII-20*a*.

A copy of a *Life of the Virgin*, in French, executed in 1323 (Fitzwilliam Museum, *MS. 20*), and a fifteenth-century copy of *Le Livre de la Vigne nostre Seigneur* (Bodleian Library, *MS. Douce 134*) are excellent representatives of other classes of devotional books: Fig. VII-20*b*.

Secular Manuscripts. The production of beautiful secular MSS. (see p. 380 f.) continued in the fourteenth and fifteenth centuries—see also further on. An admirable sample of the first-rate class is a strikingly beautiful copy of Gaston Phébus, Comte de Foix, *Le Livre de la chasse* (National Library at Paris, *Fr. 616, ancien 7097*), produced in the years 1387–91. It contains numerous extremely interesting illuminations, depicting in a most clear manner and in fullest detail the various operations of the chase and of game-hunting, such as questing for trails, setting snares, traps and nets. Indeed, nothing is forgotten, not even the hunter's meal in a glade of the forest.

The various species of game, the appropriate breeds of dogs, etc., are all recognizable at a glance. But the realism which shows itself in the increasing attention to landscape and the improved perspective of these pictures—the whole of the foreground, vegetable as well as animal, shows a genuine and careful study of nature—matches ill with the comparatively flat, conventional treatment of the background: behind the treetops, instead of skies, we find the usual, stereotyped, lozengy, tessellated or brocaded patterns, which are thus quaintly combined with a spirited and by no means unsuccessful attempt at naturalistic treatment of woodland hunting scenes. *See* W. A. Baillie—Grohman, *The Finest Hunting Manuscript Extant*, "BURLINGTON MAGAZINE", II–4 (June, 1903), pp. 8 ff.

Another excellent copy (also in the National Library, *Fr. 1291*) is of *c.* 1450; it contains 28 charming drawings.

An early fifteenth-century copy of Henri de Ferrières, *Le Livre du roy Modus et de la reyne Ratio*—the earliest French prose work on sports, which was composed in the first half of the fourteenth century, is preserved in the Rosenbach Company Collection, New York City. There are 34 miniatures, which are in *grisaille* against coloured grounds; they 'illustrate the various aspects and phases of the chase as performed in the early fifteenth century, thus providing a vivid and gay picture of contemporary life and costumes' (D. Miner).

A *MS.* preserved in the National Library at Paris (*Fr. 12399*) is dated 1379 and is signed by a monogram which some scholars have deciphered as giving the names of the author and the copyist (Denis d'Hormes). It shows marked Italian influence. A MS. of the same work, also in the National Library (*Fr. 1302*), was executed between 1405 and 1410 by two great artists: one of them has been identified as the future Master of the 'Rohan atelier' (see p. 404 f.); the same artist also decorated another copy of this work, preserved in the National Library at Vienna (*MS. 2573*); the other artist later collaborated with the 'Boucicault Master' and the 'Bedford Master' (see p. 405 f.).

B. M. *Harley MS. 1319* is the most beautiful copy (there are several other copies) of a famous poetical work dealing with the *Deposition and Death of Richard II* (b. 1367; king 1377–1399; + 1400); there are 16 miniatures, of an unknown painter of the first quarter of the fifteenth century. The authorship of the poem is controversial; Sir E. Maunde Thompson ("BURLINGTON MAGAZINE", 1904) attributed it to Jehan Créton, Chamberlain to Charles VI, whereas Evan J. Jones ("SPECULUM", 1940) ascribes it to Bishop Trevor of St. Asaph, Chamberlain of Chester,

Flint, and North Wales castles (+1410). The first owner of *Harley MS. 1319* was Charles d'Anjou, Count of Main and Mortain (1414–1472), brother of King René d'Anjou.

A copy, executed in 1437, of *Le Pèlerinage de la vie humaine* (see p. 380), containing 284 miniatures (originally there were more than 300), is preserved in the Rosenbach Company Collection, New York City. A copy, executed *c.* 1440, of Jacques Bruyant, *Le Chastel de labour* (also known as *La Voie de povreté et de richesse*), an allegorical poem composed in 1342, is preserved in the Philadelphia Free Library (*Widener MS. 1*). A mid-fifteenth-century copy of *Le Livre du Petit Artus*—'Little Arthur' being the son of the 'good' Duke John of Brittany—is preserved in the Spencer Collection, New York Public Library.

Of the more famous secular works, René of Anjou's *Livre du Cueur d'amour épris* (National Library at Vienna, *No. 2597*), produced about 1470–80; Boccaccio's *Theseid* (the same collection, *No. 2617*), executed by the same master; and *Traité de la forme et devis d'un tournoi*, belonging to the same period (National Library at Paris, *Fr. 2695*), are of particular importance.

Already in 1890, the French art-historian Henri Bouchot suggested that Foucquet (*see* p. 412 ff.), in his young age, before he left for Italy, executed a copy of *Bible Moralisée* (Nat. Library, at Paris, *MS. Fr. 166*), but it has been pointed out by Count Durrien and particularly by Sir Trenchard Cox, that this codex is artistically connected with Boccaccio's *Theseid*, already referred to, and with three other MSS. (Frontin's *Stratagèmes*, Royal Libr., at Brussels, *MS. 10474*; the *Mer des Histoires*, Nat. Library, at Paris, *MS. Lat. 4915*; and *Des Cas des nobles hommes et femmes malheureux*, Bibl. de Genève, *MS. Fr. 191*). Apparently all these MSS. were executed for René of Anjou, and it is thus possible that Foucquet as a young artist was also patronised by René.

A very fine copy (of *c.* 1425–30) of Livy, *Decades*, in two volumes (being Pierre Berceure's French translation of Livy's *Roman History*), made for John II the Good, is preserved in the Richardson Collection, Boston, Mass. (U.S.A.).

A copy of Jean Cuvelier, *Rommant de Bertrand de Gleaquin* (Illustrations from the Life of Bertrand Duguesclin) was formerly in the Library of Henry Yates Thompson (MS. No. 100). Cuvelier, the "last of the troubadours", composed this long poem (of 23,000 verses) between 1380 and 1387.

An excellent early fifteenth-century copy of Guillaume de Lorris and Jehan de Meung, *Roman de la Rose*, containing three large and 106 smaller miniatures, is preserved in the Carleton Richmond Collection, Milton, Mass. (U.S.A.). As Miss Dorothy Miner has pointed out, the figures, delicately drawn and painted with thinly laid colours, appear not against the patterned backgrounds usual at this time, but upon the uncoloured vellum.

A fine copy of the *Great Chronicles of France* (see pp. 380, 398, 415, and 446) of *c.* 1400 is preserved in the Walters Art Gallery (*W. 139*): Fig. VII-21*b*. Another copy is in the Royal Library, Brussels (*MS. 3*); it is of the early fourteenth century, and was produced in Paris.

A copy of Guillaume de Nangis, *Chronicle of the Kings of France*, executed *c.*

1470, is preserved in the same collection (*W. 306*). It contains fine pen-drawings, lightly tinted with colour. See Fig. VII-21*a*. A copy of the *Letters and Poems* by Jehan Robertet (Secretary to the Duke of Bourbon), executed *c.* 1480, is preserved in the Cambridge University Library (*MS. Nn. 3.2*). Another secular codex, also containing poems, is preserved in the British Museum (*Harley MS. 4431*): it belongs to the early fifteenth century.

Some other excellent secular MSS. are dealt with further on. Here we may mention a less sumptuous codex, but one still belonging to the superior class. The volume in question is a copy of Statius preserved in the British Museum (*Burney MS., 257*). Its figures are mostly *en grisaille*, and are very softly and delicately executed, with much grace and charm.

We end this section with an extremely fine early sixteenth-century manuscript also preserved in the British Museum (*Harley MS. 6205*). It is a copy of Albert Pigghe's *Commentaires de la Guerre Gallique*, made for, and given by Pigghe, to Francis I in 1520. The MS. is one 'of the finest illuminated volumes in the Harley Library'; 'in the pictures in grisaille, touched with gold and colour, we see the Renaissance arriving' (Esdaile). See also Fig. VII-20*c*, reproducing fol. 34*v* from a copy of *Description des Douze Césars* (see also p. 419).

The Great Masters of the Fifteenth Century

The *Limbourg brothers* were salaried artists to the Duke of Berry (they worked for him in the last years of his life), but otherwise we know very little of them. Pol de Limbourg and his brothers Jehannequin and Hermann painted the most superb pages of that great masterpiece which is known as the *Most Rich Hours* (see p. 401). Most of the miniatures of this manuscript—as Dr. Paecht has pointed out—have been left without decorative framework, as the Duke who ordered them died before the illuminators' work had been completed. But in the one page they completed, the brothers Limbourg show themselves masters of decorative invention. There the conventional picture-enclosure formed by a band of ivy, or acanthus scrolls, is replaced by a free grouping of sprigs of columbine, each sprig with a snail at its base which looks as though it were fastening the spray to the frame. The clusters of flowers—continues Paecht—are spread over the margins not entirely casually, but at rhythmical intervals; this concession to a metrical form of decoration is, however, more than offset by the freely naturalistic treatment of the single plants. Indeed, the whole layout of the page gives the impression of a quasi-temporary arrangement such as the adornment of a picture trimmed with flowers for some festive occasion. In this and in other respects—concludes Paecht—the Limbourgs fully anticipate the illusionistic effects of the Flemish borders of the end of the century. Indeed, according to Paecht, compared with the columbine border of the *Très riches heures* the great majority of Flemish and French borders for the next sixty years look conventional, unimaginative and lifeless.

Various other miniatures have been attributed to the Limbourgs, including those of the *Beautiful Hours*—not to be confused with the *Most Beautiful Hours* (p.

400 f.)—of the Duke of Berry (formerly Collection of Baron Edmond de Rothschild) and two miniatures—a Crucifixion and a Majestas Domini—in a Missal presented in 1412 to the church of S. Magloire, Paris (now in the Arsenal Library, *No. 623*). The *Belles Heures*, also known as the *Heures d'Ailly* (because they once belonged to the Ailly family), until the last war in the possession of Baron Maurice de Rothschild, were kept during the Nazi occupation of France in the National Library, Paris. In 1954, they were purchased from Baron Maurice de Rothschild, by the Metropolitan Museum, New York, through the munificence of John D. Rockefeller, Jr., and were deposited in the Cloisters. There are 224 folios with 94 full-page and 54 column illustrations, 24 calendar-medallions, and marginal vignettes decorating all the folios. The illuminations are of the same workmanship and even in the same style as the *Très Riches Heures* of Chantilly (see p. 401), and like these are generally attributed to the Limbourg brothers.

The *Limbourg Horae* (preserved in the Count Seilern Collection) is also a product of the Limbourg atelier. Its margins contain naturalistic flower borders, backed by a broad frieze of calligraphic scroll-work, but in Dr. Paecht's opinion, this trellis-like structure of delicate tendrils and wiry scrolls on which the naturalistic foliage rests is definitely not the work of the Limbourgs themselves, though whether it is a contemporary or later addition is a question not easy to decide. As this MS. was already in the Low Countries in the first half of the fifteenth century, Paecht considers it of particular interest regarding the development of Flemish border-decoration.

Masterly artists in every way, to quote Herbert, it is as colourists above all that the Limbourg brothers show their consummate powers. At once brilliant and delicate, clean without hardness, and infinitely varied without loss of unity, the colouring could hardly be surpassed in beauty; on vellum, at any rate, it assuredly never has been. Most of the pages glow with bright and joyous sunlight; but night-effects are attempted with great success in a few pictures, as in the dusky blue of the Gethsemane scene, where the soldiers fall prostrate before the divine majesty of Christ; or in the lurid darkness of Hell, with the devils, and the lost souls whom they torture with every circumstance of medieval ingenuity, seen dimly in the smoky room.

Jean Foucquet, Maître François, and their Schools. About the middle of the fifteenth century there arose in Tours a great school of miniaturists. Jean Foucquet or Fouquet was its master. Little is known of his artistic activity before 1461, when he was commissioned to paint the portrait of the dead King Charles VII. Born at Tours between 1410 and 1420, in his twenties and thirties he was in Rome (probably between 1443 and 1447), where he painted Pope Eugenius IV's portrait for the church of S. Maria sopra Minerva. See, however, p. 410. Foucquet died about 1480, and in the last twenty years of his life he resided in Tours. He worked for Louis XI: he was commissioned to paint certain 'tables' for the Order of S. Michael, instituted on 1st August 1469; he painted the frontispiece to the copy of the *Statutes* of this Order (now in the National Library at Paris, *Fr. 19819*) —representing Louis XI in the centre, attended by the Knights of the Order, including Charles Duke de Guienne (brother of Louis XI), Duke Louis II of Bourbon, and others; in the back, there is the portrait of Jehan Robertet.

Foucquet also painted the King's portrait for the royal tomb prepared in advance. In 1472 he was commissioned to paint a *Book of Hours* for the Duchess of Orléans, and, a couple of years later, another for Philippe de Commines, but it is not known whether these books exist. In 1475 he was given the title *Painctre du Roy*. Several portraits painted or drawn by him are preserved in the Louvre, in the Kupferstich Cabinet, Berlin, and in private collections in Vienna, New York, and London. Foucquet's masterpiece in panel-painting is the famous "Melun diptych": this name is due to the fact that the diptych was in the Nôtre Dame church of Melun (on the Seine, south of Paris). The diptych was executed for Étienne Chevalier (*see* further on), who is painted with his patron S. Étienne (S. Stephen) on the left-hand panel; the right-hand panel represents the Madonna and Child. The left-hand panel was preserved in the Deutsches Museum, Berlin; the other is in the Musée Royal des Beaux-Arts, Antwerp.

Philippe de Commines (also Comines or Commynes), 1444/7–1509/11, was one of the greatest historians of the period. He was also an important diplomat, firstly in the services of the Burgundian dukes Philippe le Bon (see p. 424 f.) and Charles le Témeraire (p. 425 f.), and from 1468 in the services of the king of France, Louis XI. A beautiful vellum MS.—containing the 4th book of Froissart, *Chroniques* (see pp. 430 and 458)—was written for Philippe: his arms appear on many of the illuminated pages. It is preserved in the British Museum, and is now divided into two volumes (*Harley MSS. 4379–4380*), consisting respectively of 184 leaves with 29 illuminated folios, and 200 leaves with 51 illuminated folios. The illuminations, in gay colours with a great number of coats of arms and flags, represent the courtly life at its best. The MS. seems to have been produced in Paris —f. 3 of *MS. 4379*, contains the entry of Queen Isabel of Bavaria (the wife of Charles VI) and the remarkably exact representation of Nôtre-Dame and the Sainte-Chappelle. Was the painter connected with Foucquet or with his school?

Foucquet's great masterpiece is the *Chevalier Hours*: as a matter of fact, there is no documented evidence that it is by Foucquet, but all authorities agree in this attribution. Only 47 leaves, in the eighteenth century brutally torn from their context, remain of this beautiful book. Forty are in the Condé Museum, at Chantilly; two in the Louvre (*Nos. 50* and *50a*); one in the National Library at Paris (*Nouv. Acq., Lat. 1416*); one in the British Museum (*Add. MS. 37421*); one more in a London private collection (Lord Bearsted); one in the Georges Wildenstein Collection in Paris; and one in the Robert Lehman Collection, New York City—the last two having been 'discovered' in 1946. Fig. VII-22b.

The book was painted for Étienne Chevalier, an important personage who was connected for over thirty years with the court of Charles VII and Louis XI, and who died in 1474. Chevalier's portrait occurs in a superb double-page miniature at the beginning (he kneels with his patron S. Stephen before the Madonna and Child) and again in the Entombment scene, where he is shown kneeling at the foot of the Sepulchre; his name or initials (E C) occur in many miniatures or ornamental initials. Also Charles VII's portrait appears (as one of the Magi).

Some of the miniatures are very beautiful indeed. In truth, according to Herbert, there is a touch of monotony in the battles, ceremonial processions, and murders with which the Jewish and French chronicles and the *Cas des nobles hommes et femmes* are illustrated; but here, well worn as the themes are, Foucquet has found ample scope in their presentation for his imagination and originality of design. Of special interest are the majestic composition of some of the miniatures (*e.g.* the Enthronement or the Coronation of the Virgin), the addition of legendary scenes (*e.g.*, the woman forging nails for the Crucifixion) or of realistic scenes (*e.g.*, a man drawing water from a well, in the Visitation), and the originality of a few other pictures (such as the Mission of the Apostles or the charming picture of the Angel's visit to the Virgin announcing her approaching death).

Several other *Books of Hours* have been rightly or wrongly attributed to Foucquet: (1) the *Book of Hours*, executed between 1466 and 1469 for Charles Duke of Normandy (younger brother of Louis XI); 217 leaves, measuring 180 × 132 mm. It contains only one finished miniature, probably by Foucquet, representing "the kiss of Judas"; it is preserved in the Mazarine Library, Paris (*MS. No. 473*). (2) *Book of Hours of Anne de Beaujeu*, formerly in the Durrieu Collection, Paris: executed about 1470; contains 209 leaves, measuring 165 × 115 mm., and seven miniatures, attributed to Foucquet. (3) The *Hague Book of Hours* (*A.A. 266*) with a beautiful miniature of the Crucifixion. (4) The *Charles de Bourbon Hours*, now preserved in the Royal Library at Copenhagen (*G.K.S. 1610. 4°*). (5) Even more likely is the attribution to Foucquet of the *Chester Beatty Hours*, which was formerly preserved in the Holford Collection. At least two (Annunciation and Visitation), or perhaps three, of the miniatures are most probably the work of Foucquet.

A copy of Giovanni Boccaccio's *Decameron*, in the French translation by Laurent de Premierfait, apparently executed for Chevalier, is preserved in the Richardson Collection, Boston, Mass. (U.S.A.). Even more famous and much more complicated is the problem of the codex, generally (but not quite correctly) known as the *Munich Boccaccio* (State Library, Munich, *Cod. gall. Mon. 369*). The volume *Des Cas des nobles hommes et femmes malheureux*, by Laurent de Premierfait —under the auspices of the Duke of Berry (*see* p. 410)—is a translation from Latin of Boccaccio's *De casibus virorum et mulierum illustrium*, but it is much more than a pure translation. As the greatest authority on Foucquet, Sir Trenchard Cox, has pointed out, "The translator, being a man of scholarship and with knowledge of the world, amplified and embellished Boccaccio's original by the fruits of his own experience and transformed the book from reiteration of moral problems into a nutshell history of social developments from Adam and Eve until the fourteenth century."

Premierfait's version became very fashionable, and many illustrious people— such as Jehan Sans Peur, Charles the Bold and many members of Louis XI's family, perhaps also Henry VII of England—possessed the book. One copy— which may have been in the Duke of Berry's library—is now in Geneva; it is profusely illustrated and contains 144 miniatures.

The Munich codex was written (it was completed on 24-11-1458) at Aubervilliers, a Paris suburb, by the priest Pierre Faure or Favre, for Laurens Gyrard, financial administrator of the King (the successor of Étienne Chevalier). It is divided into nine sections, at the head of each there is a large miniature; there is a large frontispiece, and eighty small miniatures head each new chapter. Even the small miniatures are of great historical and social interest. But the large and celebrated frontispiece, the *Lit de Vendôme*, peculiar to the Munich codex, represents a great historical incident, the *Lit de Justice*, or "Solemn Assembly of Justice", of Vendôme under the French king Charles VII, in 1458, in which John, Duke of Alençon, was condemned to death for high treason. In Sir Trenchard Cox's opinion, Foucquet painted the frontispiece, while the smaller miniatures were partly painted by him and partly by his pupils.

Another masterpiece—indeed, the only definitely documented work—painted by Foucquet is a French translation of Josephus's *Jewish Antiquities* and *Jewish War*. This beautiful work, now reunited in the National Library at Paris (*Fr. 247* and *Nouv. Acq. Fr. 21013*) through the generosity of King Edward VII and the late Mr. Yates Thompson, is the only one for which we have documented evidence that it was painted by Foucquet. The evidence consists in a note by François Robertet inserted between 1488 and 1503 in the first volume of Josephus, which then belonged to Pierre de Bourbon, Sire de Beaujeu and Duc de Bourbon. The volume was written for Duke of Berry between 1403 and 1413. According to the note, the first three *ystoires* of the volume are by *l'enlumineur du duc Jehan de Berry*, and the remaining nine—actually there are eleven—by *un bon peintre et enlumineur du roi Loys XI[e], Jehan Foucquet, natif de Tours*. The second volume, long considered lost, was bought in 1903 at Sotheby's, London, but it contained only one of its thirteen miniatures. Fortunately, another ten were identified two years later in an album of detached miniatures in the Royal Library at Windsor. The miniature at the beginning of the volume is without any doubt the work of Foucquet; the others very possibly so, or, at least, by the hand of a very able disciple of his.

An interesting codex—the *Estrif de vertu et fortune*—of the Leningrad State Library has a beautiful frontispiece, representing the allegorical figures of Virtue and Fortune; it is artistically related to *Jewish Antiquities* and may have been, at least in part, executed by Foucquet.

Various other works have been attributed to Foucquet—including, for instance, the *Book of Hours*, British Museum, *Add. MS. 28785*, and two leaves from a *Book of Hours*, made for Charles of France, Duke of Normandy (1465), preserved since 1958 in the Cloisters Collection, Metropolitan Museum of Art, New York—but, apart from those already referred to, the following is unmistakably by his hand: a copy of the *Chronicles of S. Denis* or, rather, *Grandes Chroniques de France* (National Library at Paris, *Fr. 6465*). This luxurious codex, executed about 1460, contains 470 leaves (measuring 460 × 350 mm.) and fifty-one miniatures (one large and the others rather small). "The marvellous talent for the values of composition; the excellent manipulation of the groups; the refined and poignant characterization; the dignity of bearing and natural gesture; . . . views of cities and rivers;

stretches of green pasture land and measureless expanses of azure sky," and some other dominant characteristics, indicate—in Sir Trenchard Cox's opinion—"that Foucquet played a large part in the decoration of the manuscript, although glimpses of a feebler hand can at times be seen."

Only four full-page miniatures have been preserved of another historical MS., the *Histoire ancienne jusqu'à Jules César et des faits de Romains*. Two of the miniatures have been preserved in the Yates Thompson Collection, at London, and two are in the Louvre. According to Sir Trenchard Cox, these miniatures may be either by Foucquet himself or should be regarded as the finest products of his school.

Herbert, referring to the splendid paintings of the Josephus, rightly emphasizes that they show plainly the hand of a great master in the plenitude of his powers, though their large manner bespeaks the painter rather than the illuminator. In his faculty for handling landscape, writes Herbert, and his understanding of open-air effects, Foucquet rivals the great Flemish painters of his time; he resembles them too in the homely directness of his portraiture. From Italy he seems to have borrowed little directly beyond architectural details, in particular the twisted columns of S. Peter's; but there are suggestions of Italian influence in some of his figure-compositions. His pictures are admirably planned, with an unerring sense of balance and due proportion between the several parts. In battle-scenes and processions, especially, he excels in combining the total effect of serried crowds with life and individuality in the single figures.

Foucquet had two sons, Louis and François, and both were good painters, but we know very little about them except that François has been identified by some scholars with *Maître François* or *egregius pictor Franciscus* (as he is called in a letter written in 1473 by the scholar Robert Gaguin to his friend, Charles de Gaucourt, the Governor of Paris). He was the skilful and versatile illustrator of a huge and beautiful copy of S. Augustine's *City of God*, executed for Charles de Gaucourt *c*. 1473 and now in the National Library at Paris (*Fr. 18–19*); two other copies of the *City of God* (Nantes, *MS. 8*, and Mâcon, *MSS. 1–2*); a copy of *Les Cérémonies et ordonnances qui se appartiennent à gage de batailles* (Nat. Libr., at Paris, *Fr. 2258*); a copy of the *Golden Legend*, made for Antoine de Chourses; a two-volume copy of Valerius Maximus, made for Philippe de Commines *c*. 1475, and now in the British Museum (*Harley MSS. 4374–5*), and various other works. These include some very small *Books of Hours*, such as the one executed for René II, Duke of Lorraine, 1473–1508 (Yates Thompson Collection), and a British Museum MS. (*Egerton MS. 2045*), perhaps executed for Louis of Luxembourg, Count of Saint-Pol (who died in 1475). A *Lectionary* attributed to Maître François was preserved in the Dyson Perrins Library—it was on sale at Sotheby's in December, 1959.

Some *Books of Hours* attributed to Maître François are preserved in the Walters Art Gallery, Baltimore (*W. 214, 251, 252*, and *285*). A detached miniature, apparently from a copy of Valerius Maximus, *Memorabilia*, executed *c*. 1460–70 and preserved in the Cleveland Museum of Art (*No. 24. 1015*) has been regarded either as an early production of Maître François or as the work of one of his associates. Whether Maître François was or was not François Foucquet, he certainly belonged to Jean Foucquet's school, and was active from 1463 to 1481. See Fig. VII-22c-d.

The *Adelaide of Savoy Hours* (Condé Museum, Chantilly, *MS. 1362*), a product of the school of Foucquet, has interesting Calendar-illustrations. The layout of the page is similar to that of the *Madrid Hours*, one of the latest works of the Master of Mary of Burgundy (see p. 432 ff.) : the artist, to quote Paecht, 'instead of surrounding the script with a decorative border has framed it with a narrative picture'. But the problem, continues Paecht, of how to unify the space-illusion for the whole page, margin and centre alike, was never taken too seriously by the French and many of their illuminated pages introduce a central picture within the opening of the marginal scenery which is seen from a different view-point and rendered on a different scale. Fig. VII-23a.

Several other *Horae* are to be attributed to the school of Foucquet: National Library, at Paris, *Lat. 1417*; contains 231 leaves, measuring 130 × 105 mm.; use of Paris; Tours calendar; executed about 1470; *Durrieu Horae* (formerly Durrieu Collection), executed about 1465; contains 169 leaves, measuring 95 × 75 mm.; use of Paris; two *Horae* of the use of Rome, of which one was executed about 1460 (Smith-Lesouëf Collection *MS. No. 30*), and the other about 1465 (National Library, at Paris, *Lat. 13305*); and one *Horae* of Tours use, executed about 1475 (National Library, at Paris, *Lat. 1179*). Of greater significance is the *Diane de Croy Horae*, preserved in the John Ruskin Museum, at Sheffield. The codex contains 178 leaves and 20 full-page miniatures. Notwithstanding the great similarities with the *Chevalier Hours* (see p. 413 f.), in Trenchard Cox's opinion, "the work cannot be considered that of the master himself but the product of a member of his *atelier* at Tours".

Other works have been attributed to the school of Foucquet, including excellent MSS., such as a large copy of Boccaccio preserved in the British Museum (*Add. MS. 35321*). The attribution of these works is based upon composition, the pose of individual figures and the treatment of the draperies, the frequent touches of gold to heighten effects, etc. Also a copy of Jehan de Breuil's *Jouvencel*—preserved in the Wolfenbuettel Library, *Cod. 137*—is probably the work of Foucquet's school rather than by the master himself.

Various works have been attributed to followers of Foucquet. A skilful artist produced (between 1458 and 1473) the *Hours of Olivier de Coétivy and Marie de Valois*, now preserved in the National Library at Vienna, *MS. 1929*, as well as a *Breviary* (executed between *c.* 1460 and 1470), which is preserved in the Walters Art Gallery, Baltimore (*W. 297*). Other followers of Foucquet produced a *Book of Hours*, also preserved in the Walters Art Gallery (*W. 274*) and a *Book of Hours* for the use of Tours, preserved in the Library of Congress (*MS. acc. 4560, 8*).

Also the illumination of the *Horae* made for Jacques Galliot de Genouilhac (1465–1546), Seigneur d'Acier, has been attributed to an artist of the school of Foucquet. The book was executed in the South of France. The borders are of classical architecture in fluid gold, the pictures carefully painted, the landscapes excellent. The MS. is preserved in the John Rylands Library, Manchester (*MS. 38*): Fig. VII-24.

Whether rightly or wrongly, next to Foucquet Maître François has been regarded as the greatest French miniature painter. He developed a school of his own 'notable for an excellent technique of crosshatching and broken strokes, wherewith he develops his effects of form and atmosphere' (D. Miner).

He had various pupils. Jacques de Besançon was the closest in style of those associated with him. Jacques was a skilful miniaturist and collaborated with his master on some important commissions. In the late fifteenth century, he turned to illuminating the woodcuts of printed books (such as some of the *de luxe* copies printed by Antoine Verard and presented to Charles VIII). An excellent example of Jacques de Besançon's manuscript-illumination is preserved in the Walters Art Gallery, Baltimore (*W. 286*). It is a *Psalter* with abbreviated *Hours* for Carthusian use, executed in 1489; it contains two miniatures and several illuminated borders: Fig. VII-25*a*.

Bourdichon. Jean Bourdichon was born in 1457, and was a fellow-citizen and perhaps also a pupil of Foucquet; he died about 1521. Commissioned in 1478 to decorate the Royal Chapel at Plessis-lez-Tours, in 1484 he was given the title *painctre du roy*. He was a portrait-painter, but also painted banners and views of towns, and designed coins, reliquaries, and lamps. He may be considered the last good French illuminator. Apparently he had several pupils—illustrators of numerous works, including British Museum, *Add. MSS. 18854*, made in 1525 for the Bishop of Auxerre, François de Dintville; *18855*, of the early sixteenth century; *35254, T-V*; a *Book of Hours*, of *c.* 1515, and a copy of *Description des douze Césars* etc., of *c.* 1520, in the Walters Art Gallery, Baltimore (*W. 452* and *W. 463*); and many others—but none of them was outstanding. Émile Mâle has attributed to Bourdichon at least six manuscripts preserved in French libraries, and H. J. Hermann has attributed to him a *Prayer-book* in Innsbruck University Library, a MS. apparently painted soon after 1490 for Jean Bourgeois.

A magnificent *Book of Hours* preserved in the Vatican Library (*Vat. Lat. 3781*) has also been attributed to Bourdichon and to his school. It contains many very fine miniatures and borders of most variegated designs, with flowers and foliage in colours upon a gold ground or in gold upon a coloured or black ground, with birds, animals, and grotesque figures. Another very fine *Book of Hours*, by some scholars attributed to Bourdichon (by others, to Foucquet, or else to 'a competent painter of the Tours school'), is preserved in Princeton University Library (*Garrett MS. 55*). It was executed *c.* 1480 for Margaret de Rohan, wife of John d'Orléans, Count d'Angoulême, and contains fifteen miniatures and several illuminated borders.

Bourdichon's chief title to fame, however, is the *Book of Hours* (National Library at Paris, *Lat. 9474*) executed for Anne of Brittany, Queen Consort of Charles VIII (1491–8) and of Louis XII (1499–1514). This MS., perhaps the last masterpiece of French illumination, was previously attributed to Jean Poyet, but is now generally attributed to Bourdichon; the main evidence being a warrant (dated 14 March 1507) for the payment of 600 crowns to Jean Bourdichon for having *richement et somptueusement historié et enlumyné une grans heures* for Queen Anne's use. In this MS. the groups are well planned, the landscapes and architectural ornaments are finely painted, but the faces, though not without a certain individuality, are sentimental, sleek, lacking in animation: Mâle describes Bourdichon as 'a lyric poet who gives tireless expression to the vision of beauty which haunts his soul'. And in van Moé's opinion, the splendour of his colouring is unsurpassed for decorative effect, though his style lacks the vigour of the old Romanesque illuminators. The 'golden shadows that play round his figures and still life' (van Moé) are the main characteristics of Bourdichon's works. See Fig. VII-25*b*. A replica of Queen Anne's *Hours*—known as the *Holford Hours*, after an early owner, is preserved in the Pierpont Morgan Library, New York.

An excellent copy of the *Description des douze Césars* (an abridged version of Suetonius, *Twelve Caesars*, but extended to the times of Antoninus Pius) is preserved in the Walters Art Gallery (*W. 467*). It contains sixteen large miniatures painted in the style of the school of Bourdichon, though the portraits seem to go back to ancient coins or gems. Each Emperor is depicted in profile against a blue background within a round frame: see p. 411.

Various works have been attributed to the school of Tours, or regarded as influenced by this school. A *Book of Hours* (for use of Tours), preserved in Trinity College, Hartford, U.S.A. (*MS. 096, 3*), containing nine miniatures, was executed *c.* 1470 'by several artists of the school of Tours with a predilection for the use of black in garments, which is exceptional in French manuscripts of this period' (D. Miner). Another *Book of Hours*, of the same period, is partly preserved in the Walters Art Gallery (*W. 210*). As Miss Miner has remarked, each of its pages is surrounded by a border of foliage enlivened with courtly figures, peasants, grotesques and animals, all executed in *grisaille* and dull gold. The work is by several hands of the Tours school, the best of them being artists of considerable skill. *W. 207* of the Walters Art Gallery, of *c.* 1470–80, contains six large and thirty-four small miniatures, painted in a semi-*grisaille* method (the figures are in white garments, the rest being painted in full colour), which for a period of time was in fashion with the school of Tours.

End of French Illumination

It has been said (on p. 411 and *passim*) that excellent illuminated codices continued to be produced in France in the early sixteenth century, long after the introduction of printing, and much skill and labour were expended on them. But, without grave inaccuracy, it may be said that book-painting generally had lost its originality by the end of the fifteenth century. With one or two exceptions, indeed, it was no longer infused with life and capable of natural development. As Giulio Clovio in the history of the Italian art of illumination, so Jean Bourdichon (see p.

418 f.) may be regarded as the last representative of the dying efforts of French illumination.

One of the exceptions was Geoffrey Tory, the great calligrapher, type-designer, and book-binder. It was in large part his influence that swung France from Gothic hand to Roman type. A few MSS.—because of their elegance and beautiful script —are attributed to Geoffrey Tory: A small *Book of Hours* for the use of Bourges, executed in Bourges in 1506 for Jehan Lallemant the Younger, Seigneur de Marmagnac; it contains one large and forty small miniatures, 'all painted with great finish of detail', and all 'both heraldic and enigmatic in subject' (D. Miner). It is preserved in the Rosenwald Collection of the Library of Congress, Washington. Another MS. of the same Collection, executed in 1524, is a very fine copy of *Offices of the Virgin* for the use of Bourges; it contains sixteen large and twenty-four small miniatures, as well as sixteen illuminated borders. Because of its fine Roman type, it too has been ascribed to Geoffrey Tory. Two *Books of Hours*, preserved in the Walters Art Gallery (*W. 446* and *W. 449*), one for the use of Bourges and the other for the use of Toulouse, are connected with the two Rosenwald MSS. *W. 446*, like the *Hours* of 1506, was executed for Jehan Lallemant the Younger, and presents the same elegant and enigmatic features. *W. 449*, executed for an Abbot Bertrand, was produced in the same atelier and in the same year (1524) as the other Rosenwald MS. Also *W. 451* of the Walters Art Gallery was executed (c. 1540) for Jehan Lallemant, and its miniatures, again, are enigmatic. (See Fig. VII-26.)

BURGUNDIAN GOLDEN AGE OF ART AND CULTURE

Burgundy (in French, Bourgogne), now forming all or part of the French departments of Ain, Aube, Côte-d'Or, Haute Marne, Nièvre, Saône-et-Loire, and Yonne, was an independent state in the fifth and sixth and from the ninth to the fifteenth centuries. In 1477, on the death of its last duke, Charles the Bold, Burgundy was attached to the crown of France. At various periods the art practised in this region reached the highest level—it will suffice to mention Cluny (see p. 372 f. and *passim*)—but here we shall refer mainly to that period of struggle for supremacy in France between the powerful Burgundians (under their dukes who were also great patrons of the arts), the French, and the English, which fills an important chapter of medieval history.

Before the fifteenth century there existed important centres of illumination in Burgundy, though their productions are hardly distinguishable from those of other French regions.

Romanesque Period

In the Romanesque period, the *scriptoria* of three Burgundian abbeys were particularly active. Very few illuminated books have been preserved belonging to the tenth or the eleventh century. A late tenth-century copy of Haimon d'Auxerre, *Commentary on Ezekiel*, executed in the abbey of S. Germain d'Auxerre, and preserved in the National Library at Paris (*Lat. 12302*) contains three miniatures: two (on fol. 1*r* and *v*) depict scenes from the book of *Ezekiel*, and one (fol. 2*r*) represents the scribe Heldric, Abbot of S. Germain d'Auxerre (d. 1009) praying before S. Germain. Two Burgundian illuminated MSS. are preserved in the Library of the Faculty of Medicine at Montpellier: *MS. 76* is a late tenth-century copy of the works by S. Ambrose; *MS. 48* is an eleventh-century copy of *Lives of Saints*.

Cluny Abbey was founded in 910 by William, Duke of Aquitaine, and about the end of the eleventh century it rivalled Rome as one of the largest and richest seats of learning in Christendom. The Cluny Cathedral was only surpassed by S. Peter's in Rome.

The late eleventh-century *Cluny Lectionary* (National Library at Paris, *Nouv. Acq. Lat. 2246*) is an outstanding production of this abbey. Only six miniatures have been preserved: they show strong Byzantine and also Ottonian influences. The initials are in gold and silver—and not in green or blue, like the Cistercian MSS.—on purple background. The style of the *Cluny Lectionary* influenced later work produced in Cluny and its dependencies, as may be seen from an excellent MS. executed a century later (about 1190) in S. Martin-des-Champs, a priory of Cluny: *Recueil historique et liturgique concernant Cluny* (National Library at Paris, *Lat. 17716*).

Cîteaux Abbey was founded in 1098, as the first Cistercian house. Its illuminated book-productions (see under *Cistercian Illumination*, p. 377) include the *S. Stephen Harding Bible*, in 4 vols., executed in the twelfth century (Dijon Municipal Library, *MSS. 12–15*); a copy of S. Gregory, *Moralia in Job*, 4 vols., early twelfth century (Dijon, *MS. 168–70* and *173*); a contemporary copy of S. Jerome, *On the Prophets* and the *Ecclesiastes* (Dijon, *MS. 132*) and *On Isaiah* (Dijon, *MS. 129*); the *Cîteaux Lectionary*, vol. IV and V of the early twelfth century; vol. I–III were re-written in the thirteenth century (Djion, *MSS. 641–2*); *S. Benigne Bible*, of the early twelfth century (Dijon, *MS. 2*); S. Jerome's *Epistles*, of the first half of the twelfth century (Djion, *MS. 135*). A copy of S. Gregory, *Moralia in Job*, executed in 1134 by the scribe Pierre of Toul, at the Cistercian abbey La Ferté-sur-Grosne, and preserved in the Municipal Library at Châlon-sur-Saône (*MSS. 7–9*), is in the same style as the precedent works.

Clairvaux Abbey was founded in 1115 by S. Bernard. It is only too obvious that the teaching of S. Bernard (see, for instance, p. 372) and the Cistercian reforms (see p. 377) should be reflected in the MSS. executed in this abbey. Excellent examples of Clairvaux production are the following: mid-twelfth-century productions: the *Clairvaux Bible*, 5 vols. (Troyes Municipal Library, *MS. 27*); a *New Testament* (Arsenal Library, Paris, *MS. 579*); a copy of S. Augustine (Troyes, *MS. 40*). A copy of the *New Testament and Psalter*, produced in the second half of the twelfth century (Bourg-en-Bresse Municipal Library, *MS. 1*) and an early thirteenth-century copy of Pierre Lombard, *Exposition sur les Psaumes*, 2 vols. (Troyes, *MS. 92*) also present the characteristic features of the Cistercian illuminated MSS. (see p. 377).

However, a few centuries were to pass before Burgundian illumination becomes really outstanding.

Burgundian Illumination

The court of Burgundy was a great centre of cultural and artistic activity particularly in the fifteenth century. The large majority of the works written for the Dukes of Burgundy or those assembled in their splendid collections are preserved in the Royal Library in Brussels, though many excellent specimens are in Paris (in the National Library, in the Arsenal Library, or in other collections), and elsewhere. Of the various codices now in Paris, we may mention the National Library MSS. *Fr. 5594* (Sebastian Mamerot on the *Crusades*) and *Fr. 9087* (Bertrandon de la Brocquière, *Voyage d'Outremer*), and the Arsenal Library *MS. 5087* (Jean Mansel's *Roman Stories*).

As a matter of fact, Burgundian Renaissance book-painting was part and parcel of Flemish illumination; moreover, the artists who worked for the Burgundian court were mainly Flemish, employing the same style as in Flanders. However, for various other reasons it seems more fitting to deal with Burgundy as an autonomous entity, the more so as Burgundy was not part of Flanders, but vice-versa. (Hence, in certain respects Flemish illumination may be said to be part of Burgundian illumination.)

Amongst the various general characteristics of the Burgundian works are the beautiful backgrounds, formed by landscapes or interiors replete with realistic details. Curiously enough, these backgrounds are highly anachronistic. Events are visualized as if they happened in the artist's own time and among the people of his own surroundings. Even in historical works, which do their best to give a text as accurate as possible, there is no attempt to introduce a touch of chronological and local colour; thus, classical or Oriental figures are attired in Western fifteenth-century costume, the setting shows characteristics of Burgundian town and country scenery, and in illustrations representing ancient battles we may find medieval cannon. See, for instance, Quintus Curtius, *History of Alexander*, translated by Vasco de Lucena: Fig. VII-23c (National Library at Paris, *MS. 22547*; see also p. 428).

Yet it would be wrong—writes Dr. Paecht—to dismiss this kind of narrative art as naïve realism. The artists lived in a world which, at least in the higher strata of society, ardently endeavoured to conform to certain ideal standards. The courtly life portrayed by the Flemish miniaturists was in itself a reality already cast into firm shape. Here fiction and reality had become one. The extravagant fashions of the time, continues Paecht, are only the most conspicuous and tangible effect of a very complex and systematic transformation affecting every side of human life. All the typical features of Burgundian fashion are designed to recast the human figure in accordance with an ideal of Gothic linear elegance and one-sided refinement. The formalized life of Burgundian society—argues Paecht—had in a certain sense prefigured the 'style of the long line', a style at first seemingly highly subjective and mannered, yet containing all the ingredients of descriptive naturalism which characterize the great tradition of Flemish painting. On the other hand, in the work of minor painters this artistic movement easily deteriorated into mannered routine-work.

The curious entertainments at the Burgundian Court—such as the performances in which monkeys and other animals imitated knightly combats—found their artistic reflection in marginal grotesques of manuscripts. According to Olivier de la Marche, among the 'entremets' of the wedding-feast of Charles the Bold and Margaret of York, there were scenes enacted by persons dressed up as monkeys (*singeries*).

The luxurious Burgundian books often contain large miniatures occupying half, and sometimes a whole, page.

Philip the Bold. Philip the Bold (Philippe le Hardi), 1342–1404, the founder of the second and last ducal house of Burgundy, was the fourth son of John II (the Good), King of France, and the brother of Charles V and of John Duke of Berry (see pp. 397 ff. and 399 ff.). No less than his brothers, Philip was a great patron of art, a Maecenas of artists, and an animator of contemporary culture. He was a great book-collector, and his library contained numerous historiated works, in Latin or French or Flemish, of religious or secular character, the latter being predominant. His library naturally included Bibles, Psalters, Missals, Prayer-books, Books of Hours, Breviaries, Patristics (such as Gregory the Great's *Dialogues*), and suchlike. Classical literature was represented by a superbly illuminated Livy, written on gold (it was a present from Dino Rapondo, a financier from Lucca), and *Hector of Troy*, a Latin paraphrase of the *Iliad*.

There were, of course, the popular medieval books, the Bestiaries, the Atlases, the Fables, and the treatise *On the Properties of Things* by Bartholomaeus Anglicus (see p. 403); but particularly rich was the section treating of chivalry and knightly deeds, the *Chansons de gestes*, the *Roman de la Rose*, the *Roman de Renart*, the French *Chronicles* and the *Chronicles of the Counts of Flanders*, the romances of *Ogier le Danois*, *Baldwin of Jerusalem*, the *Sultan Saladin, Fleur des Ystoires d'Orient*, the *Conquest of Constantinople*, and the *Ballades et Virelais* and *Miroir de Mariage* by Eustache Deschamp (or Eustache Morel), *c.* 1338–1415, the author of numerous ballades, satires, and farces, who styled himself *roi de Laidure*.

We end this list with the works of Christine de Pisan (*c.* 1363–1430), one of the most interesting literary figures of the French Middle Ages. Of Italian parentage, the daughter of Charles V's astrologer, and the wife of this king's secretary, after her husband's death she dedicated herself to writing, and enjoyed the patronage of Charles VI and the dukes of Berry and Burgundy. Her books are of great interest for their portraits of contemporary personages, and for their descriptions of the domestic and social life of the times. Her works include *Cent Ballades, Mutacion de Fortune, Épitre au dieu d'amour* (1399), and *Dit de la rose* (1402). She was commissioned by the Duke to write a book on Charles and his court, which she completed after Philip's death—*Le Livre des faits et bonnes moeurs du Sayge Roi Charles le Quint* (1405). It was soon followed by her autobiography, *La Vision* (1405), and *La Cité des Dames* (1407).

An interesting MS., a copy of the *Book of Marvels*, which was apparently made for Philip the Bold, has been mentioned on p. 401. A *Book of Hours* and *Missal* executed for him has been referred to on p. 391 : Fig. VII-11*c* and 12*b*.

John the Fearless and Philip the Good. Philip's son, John the Fearless (1371–1419), lived mainly in Flanders, had a Flemish tutor, and spoke Flemish; his reign was too turbulent to allow him to dedicate much time to cultural and artistic interests. He was occupied in constant warfare, playing a leading part in the Civil War of 1410–35 between the Burgundians and the Armagnac (or Orléans) Party. Philip the Good (1396–1467), though also occupied in warfare, either in alliance with the English or against them, took more interest in patronising the arts than did his father. Indeed, Philip was a great collector of books and other treasures.

It is interesting to note that one of the best masterpieces of Burgundian art was executed for John the Fearless and his wife, Margaret of Bavaria. The evidence that this splendid work was done for these personages is on fol. 188*v* of *Harley MS. 2897* (British Museum), the page illustrating the Ascension Day; its border contains the graceful picture of a lady who sits on a daisy-studded lawn and holds the shields of arms of the Duke and Duchess. The book is known as the *Burgundian Breviary*: Fig. VII-27*a*.

Soon after its completion it was divided into two parts, and, in order that these should appear as entire Breviaries, the second part was supplemented by a Calendar and Psalter, the miniatures of which were copied either from the first part or from the same models. The two volumes, somewhat mutilated, are preserved in the British Museum, the first one having been acquired through the Rothschild Bequest in 1899 (now *Add. MS. 35311*), whereas the second volume is the *Harley MS. 2897*. Only three large miniatures are preserved—two in *Add. MS. 35311* and one in *Harley MS. 2897*—but there are numerous smaller ones, all being of striking beauty and finish. The larger ones—as Herbert has emphasized—are especially remarkable for their luxuriant and yet harmonious colour-scheme. Particularly lovely is the blue, so characteristic of French illumination of this time; at once cold and brilliant, exquisitely transparent yet capable of forming a solid mass upon the page, its effect is always beautiful and satisfying, whether it be used in a pure or modified form, for skies, draperies, or ornament.

The border-ornament of gilt ivy-leaves, which surrounds the pages, is varied and sumptuous; particularly beautiful are the borders of the three principal pages, the most splendid being fol. 8*r* of *Add. MS. 35311* (at the beginning of the Psalter), with plaques of burnished and delicately patterned gold, containing charming pictures of birds and flowers, and enclosing half-length figures of David, Goliath, and angel-musicians. On the same page there is an initial *B* containing 'a wonderfully tender Madonna holding the Child closely to her and sheltering Him with her cloak'. The most charming of the smaller miniatures is that of S. Anne teaching the Virgin to read; 'the soft treatment of the face, the delicate gradations of colour, the fine modelling of the draperies, are here seen at their best' (Herbert): Fig. VII-27b.

A *Book of Hours*, executed in a Flemish atelier (in Ghent or Malines)—see p. 444 —on commission by John the Fearless, is preserved in the National Library at Paris (*Nouv. acq. Lat. 3055*).

Under Philip the Good, Flanders became the main political, cultural and artistic centre of the Duchy of Burgundy, and about the middle of the fifteenth century the following Flemish illuminators worked for the Burgundian Court: Jean de Pestivien, Willem Vrelandt, Jehan Dreux, Jean Tavernier, Lyoset Lyédet (Liédet), Jean Hennecart, and the celebrated Simon Marmion. Several of these artists will be discussed further on.

Charles the Bold. With Charles the Bold (le Téméraire), 1433–77, Philip the Good's only son, the fourth and last of the great dukes of Burgundy, this duchy reached the zenith of its power, culture, and art.

He was a great soldier and a very ambitious ruler. He desired the restoration of the middle kingdom of France and aspired to the kingship himself. He had added to his territory and power, but in doing so he had raised many enemies, including the Emperor. Having become a widower for the second time, in 1468 he married Margaret of York, the sister of King Edward IV.

Philip de Mazerolles, Sanders Bening, and several other artists worked for Charles the Bold.

Charles the Bold's *Ordinance*, illuminated for him and his Duchess between 1473 and 1476, by the 'Master of Margaret of York', is preserved in the British Museum (*Add. MS. 36619*).

An excellent *Book of Hours*, executed c. 1470 by the 'Master of Margaret of York', is preserved in the Fitzwilliam Museum, Cambridge (*MS. 268*); it contains Calendar illustrations, fifteen full-page miniatures, and several historiated borders.

Charles's third marriage consolidated his friendship and alliance with his brother-in-law Edward IV, and promoted the cultural and artistic relationship between the two courts. Burgundian-Flemish illumination began to supplant French in the esteem of the English nobility. The king himself added to his library a large collection of huge books written and illuminated in the then Burgundian duchy, especially at Bruges and Ghent. Amongst the books which have been preserved, there is an interesting copy of Josephus (now in the Soane Museum, London), but the majority are copies of the *Bible Historiale*, and of histories and romances; there are even some philosophical works in French.

The miniatures of these works—not of a very high artistic level—resemble scene-painting in their technique; they are very large (filling half the page or more), and are pleasant only when viewed from a distance. The great majority of these MSS. are now in the British Museum, *Royal MSS.*, having been transferred there from the old Royal Library. Amongst the better executed works, the following may be mentioned: a copy of Valerius Maximus, dated 1479 (*18. E. iii* and *iv*); a copy of the *Livre des propriétéz des choses* (see pp. 398 and 403), executed in 1482 at Bruges (*15. E. ii* and *iii*); a copy of Boccaccio (*14. E.v.*); a compilation of Roman history, known as *Romuleon* (*19. E. v*); and especially a copy of D. Aubert's *Vita Christi*, written at Ghent in 1479 (*16. G. iii*), which contains much smaller miniatures, executed, however, in a more individual and artistic style (see also p. 444).

Of the numerous books of Charles the Bold's rich library, the Latin-French *Book of Hours* and *Missal* discussed on pp. 390 f. and 429 deserves special mention. Formerly in the collection of the Viscountess Lee of Fareham, it is now preserved in the Fitzwilliam Museum, Cambridge (*Lee of Fareham Bequest, 1954*): Fig. VII-23*b*.

It goes without saying that numerous other works were produced in Burgundy. Here it will suffice to refer to the famous *King René's Horae* (British Museum, *Egerton MS. 1070*), executed in Dijon in 1437. Amongst the general characteristics for the figure-style, as Paecht has remarked, are the elongated proportions and the strictly parallel alignment of towering verticals which give the composition a somewhat arid and often monotonous rhythm.

The illuminators, particularly of profane books (writes Paecht), found in the style of the 'sixties and 'seventies—the style of the long line as it has been called—a most congenial vehicle of expression. In it formalism and realism—which generally exclude each other—could be blended.

An interesting example of book-illumination executed in a popular style—frequently found in Germany at the period, but rather unusual in Burgundy—is preserved by H. P. Kraus, New York City. It is a copy, of *c.* 1460, of a MS. by Jean Germain (prelate and counsellor of Philip the Good) on *Le Chemin de Paradis*. The book deals with the allegorical subject matter of two tapestries, which Germain had ordered for Châlon-sur-Saône Cathedral. The MS. contains five double-page water-colour drawings, which in Miss Miner's opinion suggest the composition of the tapestries.

Charles's death extinguished the male line of the dukes of Burgundy, and with it the grandeur and importance of the duchy. His only daughter succeeded to the Burgundian possessions outside France; she married Archduke Maximilian of Austria, and thus the Flemish possessions descended to the Spanish branch of the house of Austria.

Burgundian Masters of Illumination

Willem Vrelandt. Among the many illuminators who are known to have worked for—or at least during the reign of—Philip the Good and Charles the Bold, the name of Willem Vrelandt can be evidenced by the accounts of the illuminators' guild at Bruges; it occurs there from 1454 until 1480–1 (when he died). In 1467–8 he was paid for the miniatures in vol. ii of the *Chroniques du Haynaut* (Royal Library at Brussels, *Nos. 9242–4*). It is assumed that not all these miniatures were actually painted by him, but they were certainly executed under his direction.

An interesting copy of Virgil, written by 'Florius Infortunatus' in Paris, *c.* 1460, possibly for James III, contains two miniatures by a French artist, and two by Vrelandt. The book contains the Royal Arms of Scotland. It belonged to John Colville, who presented it to Edinburgh University Library in 1564. It is still preserved in this collection (*MS. D. b. VI. 8*).

Master of the Chronique de Jherusalem. This great illuminator seems to have been the earliest master to have worked almost exclusively for the Burgundian court in the years 1446–1468 (or even later). His first work was vol. I of the *Chroniques du Haynaut* (Brussels, Royal Libr., *9242–4*), at the second volume of which Willem Vrelandt worked in the years 1467–68. Before 1447, the Master of the *Chronique* illuminated the old *chanson de geste* of Girard de Rousillon (Nat. Libr., at Vienna, *Cod. 2549*) in a still somewhat crude style. His masterwork is the *Chronique de Jherusalem* (Vienna Nat. Libr., *2533*). Our Master may have been influenced by the great painter Rogier de la Pasture (von der Weyden), but he surpasses him in the delicacy by which he groups his figures and cities in the given frame, by his scintillating colours, by the charming illustrations depicting war-operation, by his dramatic tension and the quiet sheet of water mirroring heroic actions. Possibly, he may have also illuminated the *Livre des œuvres de misericorde* (Royal Libr., Brussels, *Cod. 9296*) for Margaret of York, Edward IV's sister who in 1468 married Charles the Bold and survived him for 26 years. It is most likely that Simon Marmion (*see* p. 446) and Philippe de Mazerolles were deeply influenced by our Master.

Winkler attributes to this Master several other works, including *Compos. of the Sacred Scripture*, of *c.* 1462 (Brussels, *Cod. 9017*); *Miroir de l'humilité*, of 1462 (in Madrid); the beginning of the *Prayerbook of Charles the Bold*, before 1466 (Vienna, *Cod. 1857*), *Crucifixion* (Kunstbiblioth., Berlin).

A Flemish illuminator whose style, according to Dr. Paecht, is similar to that of the young Vrelandt, executed a MS. for William, Count of Montfort (National Library at Vienna, formerly in the Fideicommiss Library). This MS. contains the Annunciation to the Shepherds copied from the *Limbourg Horae* (see p. 412). Paecht also suggests that the same illuminator painted four miniatures which were later added to the *Limbourg Horae*.

A *Book of Hours*, now preserved in the University Library at Glasgow (*MS. BE. 9–c. 16*), was illuminated *c.* 1460 by two artists, one of whom worked in a style related to that of Willem Vrelandt; there are eighteen miniatures and a number of borders. A *Book of Hours* for the use of Rome, formerly in C. W. Dyson Perrins Collection, London (*MS. 100*), was executed in Ghent by a follower of Willem Vrelandt: it contains 24 miniatures in *grisaille*, 30 historiated initials, and several borders.

At any rate, it is generally held that Vrelandt headed an important school of illumination which executed very fine books, including the *Histoire de bon roi Alexandre* (Dutuit Collection, Paris).

The *Breviary of Philip the Good* (Royal Library at Brussels, *Nos. 9511* and *9026*) has also been assigned by Durrieu to the school of Vrelandt, but according to van den Gheyn it may have been executed in the same atelier before Vrelandt belonged to it. Curiously enough, H. Karlinger (*Die Kunst der Gotik*, Berlin, 1927, p. 649) refers to *Philip the Good Breviary*, as a Dutch production of the first half of the fifteenth century preserved in the Royal Library, at Brussels, *MS. 9062*.

Tavernier. Jean le Tavernier, of Oudenaarde, probably belonged to the same school. A copy of Jehan Mielot, *Les Miracles de Nostre Dame*, 2nd series, made soon after 1456 for Philip the Good, is attributed to Tavernier; there are 73 miniatures in *grisaille*, being painted in bluish-grey shaded from white to nearly black. Some are expressive and humorous. The copy preserved in the Bodleian Library (*MS. Douce 374*) will be referred to on p. 429.

In 1458 Tavernier illuminated for Philip the Good a copy of *Conquêtes de Charlemagne* (now in the Royal Library at Brussels, *Nos. 9066–8*). The Royal Library at The Hague possesses an interesting *Book of Hours* (*MS. 76*) executed for Philip the Good (it is therefore not later than 1468); the majority of its miniatures were painted by Tavernier, but a second artist, as yet unidentified, painted 39 miniatures of the book.

In Guillaume Adam, *Advis pour faire le passage d'outremer* (Royal Libr., Brussels, *Cod. 9095*; written in or after 1455, perhaps in Lille) there are three beautiful illuminations which remind of the art of Jean le Tavernier. One of them shows the city of Jerusalem, glittering from gilded cupolas of mosques and minarets looking like European church towers in a fine green landscape; the margin is enlivened by flowers.

Lyoset Liédet (or *Lyédet*) may also have belonged to the same school as Tavernier. From 1460 to 1478 he worked at Hesdin and at Bruges, becoming a member of the guild of illuminators of the latter place in 1469. He was 'if not a great or original artist, at least a highly accomplished craftsman' (Herbert). In 1463–5 Loyset Liédet illuminated for Philip the Good a copy of the *Histoire de Charles Martel* (now in the Royal Library at Brussels, *Nos. 6–9*), and several other works of his are extant.

A superb copy of the *Histoire Universelle*, containing many miniatures, initials, and illuminated borders, has been attributed to Lyoset Liédet; in the opinion of some authorities he may have executed this codex for the Burgundian court. A copy of the French translation of Quintus Curtius Rufus, by Vasco de Lucena, *Faictz et gestes d'Alexandre le Grand* executed after 1469, and preserved in the British Museum (*Burney MS. 169*), was illuminated by pupils of the school of Lyoset Liédet, including the 'Master of the *Chronicle of England*', so called from the MS. preserved in the National Library at Vienna (*Cod. 2534*). See also Fig. VII-23c, from another copy of Vasco de Lucena, now at Paris, which has been attributed to Liédet. (See also p. 422.)

In Paecht's opinion, neither Vrelandt nor Lyoset Liédet were great or original masters. Artists like Vrelandt or Liédet, he writes, made the fatal mistake of conventionalizing form in order to portray a conventionalized world. Their figures become lifeless marionettes, their compositional arrangements empty formulas of court ceremonial or of knightly combats.

Unidentified Masters and Jehan Dreux. Another great illuminator who worked for the dukes of Burgundy is known as the 'Master of the Girard de Rousillon' (Jehan Dreux?—see also further on). Amongst the various works attributed to him, there is *Add. MS. 7970*, in the British Museum, which was executed for Margaret of York. Dr. Paecht, however, regards this as a typical example of the conventional, unimaginative, and lifeless border-decoration and mannerisms of the Flemish style of illumination before 1470, reflecting the affectations of Burgundian court manners and fashions.

Another book-painter who has not been identified is known as the 'Master of the *Dresden Hours*'. Winkler has assigned to him the Calendar-pictures of the *Madrid Hours* (see p. 434), which Paecht in part ascribes to the 'Master of Mary of Burgundy'. Paecht, indeed, regards the 'Dresden Master' as a very conservative landscape painter whose imagination cannot possibly be credited with the invention of the most advanced landscape compositions which the fifteenth century produced.

The 'Dresden Master' collaborated with various anonymous masters, such as the 'Master of the Prayerbooks' (*Book of Hours* in C. W. Dyson Perrins Library, *MS. 105*), as well as with great masters such as Gérard David and Gerard Horenbout (British Museum, *Add. MS. 18851*). See also pp. 449 and 454 f. Other illuminators have not been identified: the 'Master of the Prayerbooks' (he worked in Bruges *c.* 1500), who executed, or collaborated in the execution of, *MS. 105* in Dyson Perrins Library; *Add. MS. 4100* in the University Library of Cambridge; *MS. 311* in the Earl of Leicester's Library, and so on; the 'Master of Edward IV': *MS. 6* in Lambeth Palace Library and *MS. Douce 383* in the Bodleian Library, Oxford, and others.

The Latin-French *Book of Hours* and *Missal* (Fitzwilliam Museum, *MS. 3–1954*), mentioned on pp. 390 f. and 426, was enriched in the fifteenth century with a number of Flemish miniatures (one containing the portrait of Charles the Bold), some of them being by Jehan Dreux, *c.* 1470.

We have just seen that only very few of the names of the galaxy of artists who worked for the Burgundian dukes can be identified. Many names will perhaps never be known. A strikingly beautiful two-volume copy of Mielot's *Miracles de Nostre Dame* (see p. 428) is preserved in the National Library at Paris (*Fr. 9198–9*). The illustrations are amongst the finest examples of painting *en grisaille* (see p. 393 f.). The first volume was executed in 1456 at The Hague; the second is attributed to a slightly later period, its representations of landscape, architecture, figure-composition, etc., being on a more advanced level. The Bodleian Library is in possession of a MS. (*Douce 374*)—see p. 428—which is a copy, or rather replica, of vol. II, attributed to the early period of Charles the Bold's reign.

Alexander Bening. Another uncertain attribution is that of the miniatures of the *Vita Christi* MS., referred to on p. 426. Durrieu has assigned them to Alexander Bening or Bennik, and if this suggestion is correct, Bening must have been an illuminator of distinction and individuality. More recently, another modern critic,

Hulin de Loo, tried to identify Alexander Bening with the 'Master of Mary of Burgundy' (see below). These 'identifications' have now been dismissed. We have more data regarding Alexander Bening's life than his artistic activity. In 1469 he became a member of the Ghent guild of painters, two great artists of the town being his sponsors: Hugo van der Goes and Joes van Wassenhove (known as Justus van Ghent). His wife was Catherina van der Goes (a near relative of Hugo), and they had two sons, Paul—who is comparatively unknown—and Simon (the most famous Flemish miniaturist of the sixteenth century), who settled in Bruges—see p. 456 f. Alexander died in Ghent in 1519.

Philippe de Mazerolles. Philippe de Mazerolles, who died in 1479, was the court painter of Charles the Bold. He completed the *Book of Hours* which the Bruges town-council bought from Marc de Bougeteur of Bruges, and presented to Charles the Bold, then Count de Charolais (National Library at Vienna, *Cod. 1857*) and a small *Prayerbook* of Charles's, now in the Count Durrieu Collection. In these books— remarks Paecht—the script of the top and bottom lines is elaborated by means of calligraphic flourishes and strapwork (called 'cadeaux') which prolong some of the letters into the space of the margins. Often the pen-scrolls turn into caricature-like faces or masks. In the margins of the Prayer-book 'are further added small grotesque figures, monkeys and fabulous creatures, painted in colours' (Paecht). It is interesting to note that *Cod. 1857* is a black vellum MS. (see also *Cod. 1856*: the *Black Prayerbook*—p. 431), written in gold and silver.

An interesting *Book of Hours* illuminated by Mazerolles and his assistants was preserved in the C. W. Dyson Perrins Library (*MS. 102*). The book, containing nineteen miniatures, borders, and historiated initials, was written for a couple bearing the arms of Sachsenheim and Breitenstein (?). Another MS. illuminated (*c.* 1460) by Mazerolles is a free copy of *MS. Douce 374* (Bodleian Library)—see above. The MS., probably written by David Aubert, was executed for Philip the Good. It contains 67 large miniatures in *grisaille* (see p. 393 f.), touched with pink and gold. The MS. is preserved in the National Library at Paris (*MS. 9199*).

There is little doubt—writes Dr. Paecht—that we have in Mazerolles' practice of framing columns of plain text with a light sprinkling of playful little figures the prelude to the 'Master of Mary of Burgundy's' little marginal scenes set against an empty ground. The *Alphabet of Mary of Burgundy* (Coll. Rothschild, Louvre Museum, Paris) has similar calligraphic embellishment.

Perhaps the most important work of Philippe de Mazerolles is the Froissart in the civic library of Breslau (nowadays, Wrocław, Poland), written by David Aubert (see p. 432) for Antoine, Bâtard de Bourgogne. The vividness of the scenes described by Froissart and illuminated by Philippe is very great, and the floral and figurative borders are highly imaginative. Perhaps the most beautiful page is that showing the "bal au château de St. Pol" in Paris in the year 1392, at which the king Charles VI was nearly burnt to death (Froissart, *Chron.*, 4°, ch. XXXII); it is painted in *grisaille*, heightened by white lights; only the musicians are on a red tribune. (For Froissart, *see* also pp. 413 and 458.)

Dr. Paecht assigns the border of the British Museum *Add. MS. 36619*, some pages in a *Book of Hours* of the Salting Collection in the Victoria and Albert Museum, and some in the *Virgil MS.* in the Holkham Hall Library (*MS. 311*) to a rather mediocre illuminator who was a follower of Mazerolles.

The "Black Prayerbook" and the "Master of Anthony of Burgundy" (?). The National Library at Vienna possesses (*Cod. 1856*) a magnificent black-vellum MS., which is one of the most notable products of the fifteenth-century Flemish art of illumination. Strangely enough, also *Cod. 1857* (see p. 430) is a black-vellum MS. written in silver and gold. It contains a folio of the Arms of Galeazzo Maria Sforza, Duke of Milan (+1476), and 154 illuminated leaves, measuring 252 × 180 mm., written in silver (and partly in gold), in "Gothic" minuscule style. The codex was thus illuminated (probably in the years 1470–76) for Galeazzo Maria, but was the product of a great Flemish master.

It has been suggested that this master worked for the famous patron of art Anthony of Burgundy (1421–1504), illegitimate son of Philip the Good and Jeanette des Presles, who collected in the castle de la Rochelle, in the Ardennes, a magnificent library of illuminated MSS. The illuminator is, thus, generally referred to as the "Master of Anthony of Burgundy", but very little is known about him.

The following illuminated MSS. (apart from the *Black Prayerbook*) have been attributed to the "Master of Anthony": Valerius Maximus, *Factorum ac dictorum memorabilium libri IX* (Civic Library, Wrocław, *R. 48/49*), produced for Anthony of Burgundy; Bartholomeus Anglicus, *Livre des propriétés des Choses* (Nat. Libr., at Paris, *MS. Fr. 134*); Aegidius de Roya, *Chronique* (Mus. Meerm.—Westreen., The Hague, *MS. 10 A 21*); Valerius Maximus, as above, produced for Wolfart de Borselle (Bibl. de l'Arsenal, Paris, *Cod. 5196*); *Pembroke Hours*, perhaps produced for William Herbert, Earl of Pembroke (preserved in New York); Raoul Lefèvre, *Recueil des histoires de Troye*, produced for the Library of the Burgundian Dukes (Royal Library, Brussels, *MSS. 9262* and *9263*); Jean Froissart, *Les Chroniques*, Tome 4, produced for Louis de Bruges (Nat. Libr., Paris, *MS. Fr. 2646*); Jean Robertet, *Les 12 dames de Rhétorique* produced for Louis de Bruges (Nat. Libr., Paris, *MS. Fr. 1174*). Also a copy of Jaques le Grant, *Le Livre de bonnes mœurs* (in a private Parisian collection), and some other illuminated MSS. have been attributed to the "Master of Anthony of Burgundy".

The 'Master of Mary of Burgundy'. Various illuminated manuscripts are extant which in recent times have been assigned to another anonymous illuminator of outstanding artistic importance (see pp. 347, 403 f., 429, and *passim*). The difficulty in the identification of this artist is the more curious and disturbing as we know (1) that he was patronized by the Burgundian dukes—the cultural activities of the artists who worked for the Burgundian Court being among the best documented of any historic milieu; (2) that he worked for Margaret of York, Mary of Burgundy, and her husband, the Archduke Maximilian, and their son, Philip the Fair; and

(3) a number of preserved masterpieces can be assigned to this artist. One would therefore expect to find in the Burgundian archives documents or references to payments related to the production of this master. But all the researches in this connection have been unsuccessful.

Dr. Paecht holds that the Master may have belonged to the personal household of Margaret of York, but the accounts of this household have not been found either in the archives of Brussels or those of Lille.

F. Winkler was the first to recognize this personality and to compile a list of his works. Paecht, more recently, has reconstructed the whole artistic personality of this illuminator of genius, considering him and Jean Foucquet (see p. 412 f.) as the last really great and original book-illuminators.

At the time when panel-painting was at the zenith of its glory, 'the aesthetic equilibrium of Gothic book decoration began to break down and from this moment the days of book-painting were numbered.' Even in France and Flanders —argues Paecht—book-painting had lost its originality and was in fact, judged from a wider historical angle, little more than a distant echo of the brilliant achievements of the great school of panel-painters from Eyck to Gérard David. The only exceptions were Jean Foucquet and the 'Master of Mary of Burgundy', who 'succeeded in inventing new systems of book-decoration which enabled them to produce once more . . . genuine book-painting'.

Dr. Paecht recognizes two main stages in the artistic career of the 'Master of Mary of Burgundy'. His earliest productions are miniatures in *grisaille* (see p. 393 f.) —mostly using, however, not a simple grey, but a grey shaded with coloured (violet or salmon-pink) tints, and having the highlights often picked out in gold— thus following the best artistic conventions of the Burgundian court-painters. Paecht regards these productions as being of 'the highest perfection of an old style and its most poetical expression'.

This early work is represented by a group of sumptuous manuscripts, such as chronicles, religious tracts, and moral treatises, executed about 1475–7 for Margaret of York. These works include the following illuminated MSS.: *Apocalypse and Commentary*, in French, written *c.* 1475 in the *scriptorium* of David Aubert in Ghent, and containing seventy-eight miniatures; *MS. Douce 365* in the Bodleian Library, Oxford, written in 1475 in Ghent by David Aubert, with four miniatures; Boëthius, *De consolatione philosophiae*, in French, written in 1476 by David Aubert, with one miniature, University Library at Jena (*MS. Gall. f. 85*); *Chronique des Comtes de Flandre*, also written in the *scriptorium* of David Aubert, and completed in 1477, with twenty miniatures (Holkham Hall Library of Lord Leicester, *MS. 659*); *Breviary*, use of Sarum, before 1477 (?), only partly preserved: seven miniatures, now in Cambridge (St. John's College, *MS. H. 13: 215*).

In Paecht's opinion, a number of illuminated MSS. of the Royal Library at Brussels (*Nos. 9030–7, 9106, 9272–6*), also made for Margaret of York, though of much weaker execution, are stylistically related to the books just referred to, and were presumably executed in the same atelier.

Within a very few years the Master had not only completely changed his style, but his work 'marks at the same time the opening of an entirely new chapter in the history of Flemish illumination.' To this group belong two *Books of Hours* (*Cod. 1857* in the National Library at Vienna—see also p. 430—and *78 B 12* in the Print Room, Berlin, containing 41 miniatures) illuminated between 1477 and 1482 for Mary of Burgundy and her husband, the Archduke Maximilian. The later of the two—argues Paecht—the Berlin MS., shows already fully developed that new system of book-decoration which was to become common law for Flemish illuminators until book-painting died out, and which was imitated by French (Bourdichon), German (Glockendon), Spanish and even Italian miniaturists.

With this new method, according to Dr. Paecht, the Master undertook a complete reorganisation of the illuminated page, changing radically the relationship of both miniature and border to the page. The border—previously an incongruous flat decoration—was set within the same frame of perspective as the miniature which it surrounded. Flowers, insects or jewels, or, when appropriate, skulls, were sprinkled over a lightly coloured foil, in a quite accidental arrangement in the border with shadows behind them so that they seemed to stand out in front of the page. The *trompe-l'œil* strew-pattern still-life ornament 'looks as if an artist's sketchbook, full of nature studies, had been emptied on to the pages of a book to fill the space left free by the scribe' (Paecht).

Even the script could be regarded as in the same plane as the page itself. It looks, suggests Dr. Paecht, as if a fragment of the page (covered with script) were floating in the air and had, therefore, somehow to be tied with strings to the edges of the book. The scenes in the border appear to lie at a remote distance, the only thing near to us is the piece of writing in the middle: it is so near that we can read it. Previously—concludes Paecht—the written page contained the picture; now the picture contains the written page. See also *Douce MS. 223* of the Bodleian Library, Oxford: it is a *Book of Hours* illuminated by the 'Master of Mary of Burgundy' *c.* 1480.

A new type of marginal decoration—used, however, only in exceptional cases— is found in *MS. Douce 219-20* of the Bodleian Library (a *Book of Hours*, which will be discussed further on). It consists of small figures or groups of figures performing little scenes (little grotesques or satirical scenes, episodes of hunting and jousting, and other pastimes of Burgundian court-life), similar to those of the marginal paintings or drawings of Byzantine or Anglo-Saxon Psalters, or else to the Gothic drolleries. Hulin and Paecht have proved that this lavishly illuminated manuscript was originally made for Engelbert of Nassau, Lieutenant of the Realm at the time of the minority of Philip the Fair. It may be assumed that Engelbert gave 'the precious little book as a present to Philip, the young Sovereign of the Burgundian State, and that at this moment the playful marginal scenes with Philip's arms were added' (Paecht).

Another innovation is the window-aspect given to the main scene of the illuminated page. The centre—writes Paecht—seems to have become transparent like a pane of glass and through it we see familiar Biblical subjects as distant visions. Thus, the miniature is a window opening in the page to disclose a distant vista beyond. The need to contrast the distant view of the miniatures with the minute detail of the decorative borders led the Master to replace the earlier technique by a more summary treatment in which tone values play an ever increasing part. It was this concern with tone values that made possible the most remarkable innovations: the monochrome technique of the *grisaille* was abandoned and the Master 'started to paint *histoires en toutes couleurs*'. Moreover, argues Paecht, an attempt is made to characterize an object by painting its colour-impression on our eye, without giving the linear and plastic data of its material shape.

In later phases of the development, the miniature becomes a kind of vignette: freeing himself from the medieval conception of the landscape as pure accessory to figure, the Master 'began to treat landscape as an independent genre', thus becoming a pioneer in this field. The human figures, at the same time, became mere accessories to their landscape settings. The Master has shown himself a pioneer in other directions of artistic evolution. One miniature of his is 'the first example of plein-air painting in Northern art'.

The following are the main illuminated MSS. attributed by Dr. Paecht to the 'Master of Mary of Burgundy': *Book of Hours* (Bodleian Library, Oxford, *MS. Douce 219–20*) of *c.* 1485–90, use of a Flemish Diocese: the MS. originally made for Engelbert of Nassau and completed for Philip the Fair, contains 62 miniatures; *Book of Hours* (National Library at Madrid, *MS. E. XIV. Tesoro*), of *c.* 1490, formerly in Toledo Cathedral: it contains numerous decorative and five historiated borders, and 29 miniatures; *Book of Hours* (Lazaro Collection, Madrid), use of Sarum, 24 miniatures, *c.* 1490 (?); *Book of Hours* (Czartoryski Museum, Cracow, *Cod. 3025*), written for a Benedictine monk, four miniatures; fragmentary *Book of Hours* (Print Room, Berlin, *MS. 78 B. 13*), *c.* 1490 (?): contains at least eight miniatures by the Master, the rest being the work of Simon Marmion (see p. 446) and Philippe de Mazerolles (?)—see p. 430; and a few other works.

Two other MSS. have been attributed to the 'Master of Mary of Burgundy' or to his school: a very fine codex which was bequeathed to the British Museum by Alfred H. Huth (now *Add. MS. 38126*) and a fragmentary *Book of Hours*, of *c.* 1490, belonging to Mrs. William Emerson, Cambridge, Mass. (U.S.A.). The latter, containing seven large and twenty-four small miniatures, nineteen historiated initials, seven historiated borders, and a great number of illuminated borders, was apparently executed for Joanna the Mad, of Castile, mother of Emperor Charles V. In Miss D. Miner's opinion, its miniatures are of a refinement and beauty unsurpassed by any Flemish MS. now in America. 'The illustrations are in a style of great clarity and refinement of finish, the landscapes fresh and rolling, the drapery handled without any touch of banality.' The colour 'is clear, but restrained in brilliance, with a liberal use of pearly grey and pale lavender'. Each of the historiated borders contains 'a series of little scenes, amplifying the legend of the saint whose full-page picture adjoins. These are painted softly around the text ...'. (Miner). According to Miss Miner, figure and facial types, colouring, refinement of finish, all correspond to the works assigned to the 'Master of Mary of Burgundy'.

There is no unanimity amongst the critics with regard to all the works ascribed

MS. Douce 219 (Bodleian Library, Oxford), fol. 36v–37r: S. Anthony in the Desert.

to the Master. So, for instance, Winkler assigned to him the border and miniature —representing Margaret of York and Mary of Burgundy kneeling in prayer before an altar with the statue of S. Anne—of a MS. containing the Register of the Guild of S. Anne in Ghent, executed in 1477 (now preserved in the Royal Library at Windsor); whereas in Dr. Paecht's opinion, the composition of the picture resembles in its main features one of our Master's compositions (frontispiece of the *Legend of S. Adrian*, in the National Library at Vienna), the Windsor miniature 'lacks all the personal characteristics of our artist's style'.

All the evidence seems to point to Ghent as the Master's headquarters during the period of his earlier productions; there he illuminated numerous books written in the *scriptorium* of David Aubert. In later times he apparently worked mainly at Bruges.

The School of the 'Master of Mary of Burgundy'. In Dr. Paecht's opinion, not only had the Master many followers and imitators, but practically the whole Ghent-Bruges school stands on his shoulders. Dr. Paecht suggests that although the Master's followers sought to modernize book-painting by consolidating the substance of the figures and by clarifying the space construction, thereby gaining in correctness of design, they irretrievably destroyed the visionary qualities of their Master's creations.

Amongst the manuscripts which contain copies of compositions by the 'Master of Mary of Burgundy', reference may be made to British Museum *Add. MS. 35313*, by an artist who has not yet been identified. On the other hand, the master of the *Grimani Breviary* (see p. 455 f.), though strongly influenced by the 'Master of Mary of Burgundy', is to be considered a great artist and not an imitator.

According to Dr. Paecht, the 'Master of Mary of Burgundy's' immediate pupil was the 'Master of the Prayerbook of Maximilian', formerly erroneously called the 'Master of the *Hortulus Animae*', an illuminator who, on the one hand, copied his Master's 'compositions so faithfully that master and pupil have sometimes been confused' and, on the other hand, introduced 'the new compositional formulas of the Bruges school (Memling, Gérard David) into illumination'. This master painted, amongst other manuscripts, the *Books of Hours* in the ex-C. W. Dyson Perrins Library (*MS. 104*) and the Stonyhurst College Library (*MS. LX*); the *Quarré Horae* (Bodleian Library, Oxford, *Douce MS. 311*), executed in 1488 for Louis Quarré; a *Roman Breviary* in the University Library at Glasgow (*Hunterian MS., S.2.15*); as well as a *Prayerbook*, now preserved in the State Library at Munich (*Cod. 3506*). Simon Bening (see p. 456 f.)—the reputed illuminator of the *Hortulus Animae MS.*—was a pupil of this master.

THE NETHERLANDS—FLEMISH ILLUMINATION

We must not overlook the fact that the Netherlands once belonged partly to Germany and partly to France or were part of Burgundy. Also Netherlandish art till the thirteenth century at least, and even in some respects until the fifteenth century, was a variety either of North-German art (Holland, Limbourg, Luxemburg) or of North-French art (the earlier schools of Flanders and Hainaut, and perhaps of Brabant). With regard to illumination it is hardly possible to fix exact frontiers, particularly between France and Flanders. We find the same style in works produced at Soissons, Laon, Cambrai, and in Flanders, and even as far south-eastwards as Trèves (as shown by the border-decoration of a *Kopialbuch*, written for Archbishop Baldwin, and now in the Archives at Coblenz). For the sake of convenience we may regard the productions of Soissons and Laon as French, those of Cambrai as Flemish, and those of Trèves as German.

However, where there is no other distinguishing feature, the later Netherlandish miniatures may be detected by (1) their preference for plain burnished gold backgrounds to diapered ones; (2) a plain, deep blue colouring paled towards the horizon; (3) the replacement of the background by a natural, or what was intended to be a natural, landscape. As a general test between French or German influence, the use of green shows the latter, that of blue the former. Not that this was any aesthetic point of difference in taste, but somehow the Germans had the green paint (while the French had not), and so they used it.

Its Beginnings

The most ancient writings known in this region were charters and other documents, apart from the pious effusions of the occupants of monasteries, such as those of S. Amand, Lobbes, Stavelot, and others. It was the revival of art and literature under Charlemagne that was the beginning of artistic calligraphy; then followed the production of books outside the monasteries: classical authors, chronicles, and 'mirrors' of various sciences.

The earliest notice of illumination in the Netherlands is in a ninth-century Benedictine chronicle, where mention is made of Harlinda and Renilda, or Relinda, daughters of the Lord of Denain, who were educated in the convent of Valenciennes. 'In 714'—we are told—'they left their native province to found a monastery on the banks of the Maas—among the meadows of Alden and Maas-Eyck. They there consecrated their lives to the praise of God and the transcription of books, adorning them with precious pictures'.

About the year 1730 an *Evangeliary*—small folio—of great age was discovered in the sacristy of the church by the Benedictine savant Edmond Martène, which was attributed to the two sisters. Notwithstanding the acceptance of this attribution by some experts, it is rather uncertain. The MS., still in existence (in 1880 it was exhibited in Brussels), contains a great number of miniatures in the Franco-Saxon style (see p. 208). There are portraits of the Evangelists, figures of saints, demons, and monsters, scrolls of foliage and birds. Draperies and other details are heavy, dull, and ill-drawn, but the blue, red, green, and gold of the borders have all kept their brilliancy.

Eleventh and Twelfth Centuries

In the eleventh century we find monastic books and others, such as Psalters, Evangeliaries, Bibles, and Missals, of which the ornamentation is sometimes splendid, glowing with gold and colours. Already the abbeys of Stavelot and Liége were superior centres of production. S. Martin of Tournay also had a famous *scriptorium* which was noted for the beauty of its writing and its grand initial letters. Immediately following S. Martin, the abbeys of Gembloux, S. Bavon at Ghent, and others, produced or acquired MSS. of the most sumptuous kind, and before the thirteenth century the Netherlands had established quite a distinguished reputation.

But, on the whole, the style of illumination of the Dutch *scriptoria* was much the same as in other German districts, though Gospels and Psalters exhibit features somewhat akin to English works. There is a style of calligraphic ornament deriving its origin from the Northern Dutch foundations such as Zwolle, which is confined almost entirely to the painting of the initial letters and the decorating of the borders with flourished scrolls of pen-work very neatly drawn and terminating in equally neat but extremely fanciful flowers finely painted. It seems to have been brought at some time from the North of Italy, where a similar kind of initial and exceedingly neat penmanship is found in the choir books.

Many South-German choir books are similarly ornamented, so that it is not always easy to say at once where the work was done. The Dutch illuminators, however, may usually be recognised by the characteristic miniatures combined with neat and sometimes rigidly careful penmanship in the scrolls and tendrils and a hardness in the outline of the flowers. Sometimes the large initials are produced entirely by the pen, the labyrinthine patterns in blue or vermilion being filled in with circlets, loops, and other designs, with infinite patience and excellent effect.

Some of the border scrolls are exceedingly pretty, and these borders differ from the Flemish in mixing natural flowers painted in thin water-colours with the more conventional flowers painted in a different medium, and not, as in the later Flemish manner, with flowers which are direct imitations of nature and painted in the same medium as the rest of the illumination.

Stavelot

An important *scriptorium* existed from early times in the Benedictine abbey of Stavelot. A tenth-century *Missal*, preserved in the British Museum (*Add. MS. 16605*), is decorated in a style which has been considered a continuance, rather than a development, of the Franco-Saxon style (see p. 208). There are no figure-compositions, only a few initials in gold and colours, and four pages of the Canon written in silver uncials on a purple ground, with large interlaced initials in gold, green, and white. They are partly in the style of the school of Saint-Denis, near Paris.

Another product of Stavelot, a tenth-century *Psalter* also preserved in the

British Museum (*Add. MS. 18043*), shows a different style. Indeed, in Herbert's opinion, it is more nearly allied to the *Boulogne Psalter*, so far as one may judge by the brightly yet softly coloured pages, with gold and red plait-work initials enclosing quaint little figures, prefixed to *Psalms li* and *ci*; the initial-page of *Psalm i*, doubtless the most elaborate of the three, has unluckily been cut out.

The most important production of the Stavelot school of illumination, now preserved in the British Museum (*Add. MSS. 28106-7*), is the great two-volume *Stavelot Bible*, executed by the monks Goderannus and Ernestus in 1093-7. It is rightly considered the precursor of the series of the huge Bibles of Worms, Arnstein, etc. (see p. 218). It contains one full-page miniature, in Carolingian style, representing Christ in Glory—the figure of Christ being of immense size—uninteresting Canon-arcades, and large illuminated initials to several books, particularly to *Genesis* (an *In principio* series of medallion-scenes from *Genesis* and the life of Christ), *Exodus, Judges, I* and *II Kings*. In many of these illustrations, the figures are drawn in outline and left wholly or partially uncoloured; and these are for the most part drawn with much delicacy, expressiveness, and even charm: Fig. VII-27*c*.

S. Marie de Parco. This Premonstratensian abbey, situated near Louvain, was another important *scriptorium*. One of its main products—a three-volume great *Bible*, written in 1148, and preserved in the British Museum (*Add. MSS. 14788-90*) —contains initials which are either purely ornamental (plaited gold ribbons on a coloured field and entwined with white vine-branches, or else coloured foliations on a gold ground) or contains figures. Some initials contain pen-drawn red and green patterns, and dragons used for the tails of letters. The only full-page illumination (prefixed to *Genesis*) contains the first verse of the Bible, Christ in glory, medallion-scenes from *Genesis*, and foliate scroll-work with birds, animals, etc.

Floreffe. Another great *Bible* (in two volumes, written *c.* 1160) preserved in the British Museum (*Add. MSS. 17737-8*) was executed at the abbey of Floreffe, near Namur. Herbert has pointed out that this book with its neat execution and its slender, almost Gothic figures, shows that Flemish painting had by this time reached at least as high a level as that of contemporary German schools. The miniatures (in the second volume), however, although brilliant in colour, are rather hard in technique. The subjects are mystical and allegorical. The initials, of the usual scroll and dragon type, are very finely drawn in red and black outline, with great elaboration of detail, but without any illumination properly so called: Fig. VII-27*d*.

Thirteenth-Century Transition to Artistic Excellence

Flemish illumination of the first half of the thirteenth century follows—though at a certain distance—in the steps of English and French illumination. The early thirteenth-century *Missal of S. Bavon's*, at Ghent (British Museum, *Add. MS.*

16949), contains one full-page miniature (a Crucifixion) and initials decorated with white foliage-scrolls on pale blue fields powdered with white spots; it has all the characteristics of a twelfth-century MS.

Even the much later Flemish Psalters—exemplified by excellent copies in the British Museum (*Royal MS. 2. B. iii; Add. MSS. 19899* and *24683*), written about the middle of the thirteenth century—can at their best be considered as transitional to the glorious Flemish illumination. The best of them, *Royal 2. B. iii*, contains full-page miniatures of the life of Christ with no attempt at effective composition. In the colouring, on raised and highly burnished gold grounds, the very dark blue of thirteenth-century Flemish painting predominates.

Characteristic features of these Flemish Psalters are as follows: With some exceptions, the cycle of Calendar-pictures does not contain the signs of the Zodiac; the occupation-pictures are rather large and are executed on blue or pink backgrounds framed in gold; peculiar subjects representing some months (February: a woman holding a great Candlemas taper; June: a man carrying a load of wood; October: grape-picking, etc.).

Maestricht School of Illumination. The transition to Flemish artistic excellence may be studied in the products of Maestricht, as, for instance, in a thirteenth-century *Psalter*, preserved in the British Museum (*Harl. MS. 2930*), containing miniatures, historiated initials, and bar-borders, decorated with birds and grotesques, of rich and brilliant colouring, partly spoilt by a vivid crimson. In another Brit. Mus. MS. (*Royal MS. 2. A. iii*), as pointed out by Herbert, the tiny figures are on gold grounds in medallions and the treatment shows something already of the refinement and delicacy typical of the best thirteenth-century art.

The British Museum *Maestricht Hours* (*Stowe MS. 17*), of the closing years of the thirteenth century, is considered the masterpiece of this school. It measures only $3\frac{3}{4} \times 2\frac{3}{4}$ in., or $9 \cdot 5 \times 7$ cm. (small books seem to have been fashionable there), and contains exquisite miniatures such as the Childhood and Passion, and wonderful marginal ornament, including delightful scenes, such as the fox shamming death; the three living and three dead kings; wrestlers, tilting knights, tumblers, musicians. Bible-history, legends of the saints, folk-lore, scenes in daily life—all these, says Herbert—are illustrated with an exuberance of fancy and a delightful inconsequence thoroughly typical of this fascinating phase in the history of art.

Other Flemish Productions. In the thirteenth century, with works like the last referred to, Flemish illumination reached the first height of its glory. To this superb class also belongs a small, very richly illustrated, volume of miscellaneous contents (a sort of *Hortus Deliciarum*: see p. 217), including passages from the Bible and the Fathers, hortatory and other tracts, legends, etc. The volume, known as *Sneyd Cantica Canticorum* (having formerly belonged to the Sneyd Collection) was sold *c.* 1907 by Bernard Quaritch to a French collector. Apart from the rich borders and grotesques, the book contains full-page tinted drawings of scenes from the lives of the hermits, illuminated illustrations—on elaborately diapered and stippled backgrounds—of Christian dogmas and of the arts and sciences, allegories of monastic discipline, mystical or symbolical representations from the *Song of Songs*, and the attributes of the Trinity, etc. Even apart from the brilliant colouring, with its almost exclusive use of white, gold, rose, deep blue, and scarlet, this volume is extremely interesting for the study of medieval symbolism.

A fine *Psalter*, containing nine historiated initials and twelve Calendar pictures, belongs to *c.* 1270. It is preserved in the Walters Art Gallery, Baltimore (*W. 112*). A *Psalter* and *Book of Hours*, executed for a lady at Liége, *c.* 1280–90, is preserved in the Fitzwilliam Museum, Cambridge (*MS. 288*): it contains Calendar-illustrations, one full-page miniature, twenty-six historiated initials, and decorated borders. A late thirteenth-century Flemish *Book of Hours*, containing fourteen full-page miniatures, eleven large and numerous small historiated initials, twenty-four Calendar-pictures, and a great number of marginal drolleries, is preserved in the Walters Art Gallery (*W. 37*). Two Walters Art Gallery manuscripts—*W. 85*, a *Psalter*, and *W. 127*, a *Missal*—belong to the year *c.* 1300. *W. 85* contains numerous historiated initials and marginal grotesques; *W. 127*, thirteen very fine and unusual historiated initials. Another *Missal* of 1300, was preserved in C. W. Dyson Perrins' Library, London (*MS. 98*): it was made for the use in the Benedictine Abbey of S. Peter at Blandigny (near Ghent), and it contains one miniature, three historiated initials, and decorated borders. See Fig. VII-28*a*.

A three-volume large *Antiphonary*, of 1290, assigned by its previous owner, Yates Thompson, to the Cistercian nunnery of Beaupré, near Grammont, contains exquisite historiated initials, marginal figures, and cusped and leafy borders. Especially charming in their demure grace are the kneeling patronesses, 'Domicella de Viana' and 'Domicella Clementia'.

During the second half of the thirteenth century, a small though interesting group of illuminated MSS., executed in Franco-Flemish style, was produced in the region of Saint-Omer (for Saint-Omer see also p. 373). An excellent example belonging to this group is preserved in the Pierpont Morgan Library, New York (*M. 72*). It is a *Psalter* containing sixteen full-page miniatures and twelve Calendar-illustrations. The miniatures—writes Miss Dorothy Miner—are characterized by particular refinement of style, the figures appearing against the heavy burnished gold backgrounds with a charming elegance of pose and movement. Draperies fall with a Gothic grace that has not yet become mannered. Accessories, reduced to the minimum essential for the narrative, are incorporated into the compositions as a subtle emphasis to the rhythm of the figures.

Fourteenth Century

In the early fourteenth century there is close affinity between the Flemish, the East Anglian, and the French schools. This affinity is noticeable in the late thirteenth-century *Maestricht Hours* (see p. 439), as well as in the *Sneyd MS.* (see p. 439), which was more French in style. Similar strong French influence may be seen in the *Val-Duchesse Breviary* in the British Museum (*Harley MS. 2449*), which belonged to the Dominican convent of Val-Duchesse, at Auderghem (near Brussels). In this little book—writes Herbert—the miniatures, with their daintily swaying, white-faced figures painted against diapered or burnished gold grounds, and their use of black pen-lines to indicate all details of drapery and features, have little to distinguish them from French illuminations of the time except the characteristic Flemish dark blue.

A copy of Albertus Magnus, *De laudibus Virginis*, of *c.* 1300, executed in French Flanders (it is preserved in the Wellesley College Library, *MS. 19*), and a *Psalter* of Dominican use, in a closely allied style, of *c.* 1310, also produced in French Flanders (Arras), and now preserved in the Walters Art Gallery, Baltimore (*W. 115*) are excellent representatives of Franco-Flemish illumination of the early fourteenth century. Both MSS. are exceptionally fine. *MS. 19* contains twelve historiated initials with interesting allegorical miniatures. *W. 115* has eight historiated initials, with elegantly drawn figures shown—as D. Miner has pointed out—against diapered grounds of colour and gold, or, in some cases, carefully tooled and burnished gold leaf. Each large initial, its form lightened by areas of interlace—concludes Miss Miner—sends forth a fine ivy-border to surround the page.

An early fourteenth-century *Psalter*, executed in Ghent, and preserved in the Bodleian Library, Oxford (*MS. Douce 38*), contains eighteen miniatures, six historiated initials, and borders.

A richly illustrated *Psalter* in two volumes, probably executed at Ghent *c.* 1320–30, contains Calendar-illustrations, twenty-six miniatures, numerous historiated initials and marginal illustrations. It is also preserved in the Bodleian Library (*MSS. Douce 5–6*).

Great affinity with East-Anglian MSS.—in the predilection for grotesques, and sometimes in the whole decorative scheme, or even in the larger compositions—may be noticed not only in the *Maestricht Hours*, already referred to, but also in two MSS. from Blandigny Abbey (see p. 440), now in the British Museum (*Add. MSS. 29253 and 30029*), the *Saint-Omer Horae*, of *c.* 1320 (also in the British Museum, *Add. MS. 36684*), a Cambrai *Missal* (Municipal Library, *MS. 87*), a two-volume *Bible* (in the same collection, *No. 327*), and other works.

In the latter half of the fourteenth century the affinity with French illumination is even greater, the more so as many of the best Flemish illuminators, such as André Beauneveu and Jacquemart de Hesdin, worked for French patrons of art (see p. 394 f.). Works produced in Flanders—such as the *Kuerbouc d'Ypres*, of 1363, rich in marginal figures, mainly grotesques—did not attain the same level of excellence.

An interesting *Missal*—of Laurentius of Antwerp—a Dutch production of 1365, is preserved in the Meermanno—Westreenianum Museum, at The Hague.

There was a copious production of illustrated popular books, such as the *Biblia Pauperum* and *Speculum Humanae Salvationis* which present a very interesting iconography. These works are mainly of German origin and not of great artistic value, and many are on paper. Amongst the best Flemish productions there is a British-Museum (*King's MS. 5*) illuminated copy on vellum of the *Biblia Pauperum*, executed *c.* 1400. See also p. 389 and *passim*.

The MS. is one of the best and most excellently finished examples of the popular works produced in Flanders. It now contains thirty-one long narrow pages, each one having in the centre a scene from the life of Christ, with four half-length figures of prophets bearing scrolls, and on each side an Old Testament scene which is supposed to have foreshadowed the New Testament episode of the centre. Herbert refers to the scenes of the widow from Zarephath gathering sticks (*1 Kings, 17.10*) and Christ carrying the Cross, to show how curiously far-fetched are the parallelisms given in this and other MSS. Some compositions are absurd, for instance that of Michal letting down David from a window in full view of Saul. Other negative sides of the MS. are: the still undeveloped representation of the landscape; the backgrounds which are either gilded or diapered in the old style; and the restricted range of colours. On the other hand—according to Herbert—in the faces of the figures there is a distinct striving after individual types, especially in the grave, intensely pathetic Christ; the colours are generally used with felicity, a favourite tint being a particularly soft and pleasing violet; and the flat treatment of the figure has now given way to careful modelling by means of skilful and delicate gradations of colour.

A superb example of Flemish fourteenth-century secular illumination is preserved in the Bodleian Library, Oxford (*MS. Bodley 264*): it is a copy of *Li Romans d'Alixandre* and other poems. The copy was written probably at Bruges; its excellent illumination, by Jehan de Grise, was completed in 1344. It contains as many as 166 miniatures and a great number of historiated initials and marginal illustrations: Fig. VII-28*b*. See also pp. 35, 278 and 380.

Fifteenth Century

In a wider sense, Burgundian book-illumination was Flemish, but fifteenth-century productions of Flanders, the mother-country of the Burgundian artists, did not reach the level of those executed for the Burgundian Court.

Although the best Flemish illuminators worked for this court and for French dukes and high religious and secular nobility, particularly for the Duke of Berry (see p. 399 f.), it would be wrong to assume that in Flanders itself the productions were not first-rate. On p. 402 reference has been made to an illuminated astrological MS., which belonged to the library of the Duke of Berry and is now preserved in New York (Pierpont Morgan Library, *M. 785*). This charming volume, containing astrological treatises by the Arabic astrologist Albumazar or Abū Ma'shar (*c.* 805–85), was illuminated in Bruges *c.* 1400. According to F. Saxl and H. Meier, this work belongs to a group of three astrological manuscripts (National Library at Paris, *MS. Lat. 7330*; British Museum, *Sloane MS. 3983*; and *M. 785*), based on an original apparently produced in the twelfth century in South Italy. The earliest of the three extant MSS. is the one preserved in Paris, which belongs to the early thirteenth century. Fig. VII-28*c*.

Already in the early fifteenth-century Flemish illumination—as Herbert has remarked—had been brought to a high state of perfection; and for the next hundred years Flemish illuminators not only held their ground against their French and Italian fellow-craftsmen, but ultimately eclipsed them completely, maintaining great excellence and even continuing to improve, especially in the delicacy of their handling of landscape and portraiture, long after their rivals had sunk into tasteless decadence. This remarkable fact is largely due—as has rightly been suggested—to the propensity of Flemish art in general throughout this period for methods peculiarly appropriate to miniature.

Specialization in Flemish book-painting. By then, book-painting had become a highly specialized craft 'and the illumination of a manuscript was more often than not the collective work of two or even three specialists' (Paecht). Paecht doubts whether the borders were executed by the artist who painted the miniatures. In his opinion, the *enlumineur* was responsible for the purely decorative part; the *historieur* (*l'ystorieur*) painted the miniatures (*histoires*), and the craftsman who did the borders was sometimes called *vigneteur*—the word *vignette* (from *vigne*, 'vine-scroll') being the proper term for 'border'. So, for instance—in Paecht's opinion—the impersonal borders in the early manuscripts containing miniatures by the 'Master of Mary of Burgundy' (see p. 431 ff.) may have been the work of such a professional *enlumineur* or *vigneteur*. Here we may refer to an interesting Flemish *Book of Hours* of the fifteenth century, preserved in the Lambeth Palace Library, *MS. 496*.

If this specialization was a rule, there certainly were numerous exceptions, and each individual master-illuminator must have had a permanent *vigneteur*. Indeed, Paecht himself points out, referring to the same master, that every one of the early miniatures by this master is framed by the same kind of border, designed in the same way and executed in the same colours, whereas in the later period of the Master, border and miniature became 'interdependent parts of one single painterly vision, too closely interconnected to be separately executed by different artists'.

Masterpieces. One of the earliest-known examples of excellent Flemish illumination—a veritable masterpiece, characterized by freedom from conventionality and firm but delicate draughtsmanship—was executed at the beginning of the fifteenth century in or near Liége. It is a series of twenty-eight full-page monochrome miniatures (without text) illustrating the travels of Sir John de Mandeville (d. 1372 (?)); it is preserved in the British Museum (*Add. MS. 24189*). We have here one of the first attempts to dispense with the conventional background and to paint the figures in their natural setting. Buildings or landscapes of quite an elaborate description fill the whole picture, within frame lines, and 'despite the rudimentary perspective, resembling that of a bird's-eye view, the artist goes far towards achieving his aim of making us see the actual scene which he has in mind.' The architecture 'is drawn with characteristically Flemish attention to detail.' The outlines are drawn in ink on a ground tinted in pale milky green, and delicately shaded with washes of pale grey, with occasional touches of opaque white. The figures are often faulty (they are out of proportion to the tiny buildings which surround them), but 'are spirited and expressive'. The main colouring is in the foliage (usually a sombre green), as well as in the sea and sky (tinted in blue, but sometimes patterned in white); very little gold is used (for accessories, such as crowns and nimbi); faces and hands are faintly tinted.

The *Turin Book of Hours*, referred to on p. 400 f., was apparently supplemented by its first additions in Flanders, in the second decade of the fifteenth century. The new *Calendar* is Netherlandish, as is shown by the preponderance of local saints, and the added miniatures are of the Flemish style of the period. Some of these—to quote Herbert—are superb, displaying a remarkable advance in perspective and in all the problems of landscape-painting, especially the picture which contains Count William's portrait; a sea-shore piece, with a long line of breakers along the coast; and that of SS. Martha and Julian in a small sailing-boat, guiding the sailors into harbour, with its masterly treatment of the choppy sea; the boat and its occupants; and the distant wooded hills.

Concerning the controversial attribution of some miniatures of the supplementary portion of the *Turin Hours* to the famous van Eyck brothers—Hubert (d. 1426?) and Jan (fl. 1422–1436, d. 1441)—see p. 401.

Flemish Ateliers Working for Export. An *Apocalypse*, in Flemish, executed *c.* 1400, is preserved in the National Library at Paris (*MS. Néerl. 3*): it contains several illuminated borders and twenty-three miniatures, the first six being the work of a Flemish master, the rest by his workshop. A richly-illustrated copy of Jacobus de Varagine, *Legenda Aurea*, executed *c.* 1400–10, in the region of French Flanders, is preserved in the University Library at Glasgow (*BE. 8–x.6*): there are 102 miniatures, six borders, and several initials. A skilful Flemish master, who worked at Tournai *c.* 1440–50, is known as the 'Master of the *Privileges of Flanders*', from a manuscript illuminated by him and now preserved in the National Library at Vienna (*Cod. 2583*). He also executed a *Book of Hours* for the use of Tournai, now preserved in the Bodleian Library, Oxford (*MS. Rawl. Lit. e. 14*), which contains twenty-six miniatures and several illuminated borders.

In the first quarter of the fifteenth century an important atelier was active in Ghent or Malines. Although the majority of its productions were for export, some were executed on commission by famous patrons of art (see for instance pp. 446, 449 f., 455). Several of the MSS. of this atelier are preserved in important American collections: two are in the Pierpont Morgan Library, New York (*M. 46* and *439*), two in the Walters Art Gallery, Baltimore (*W. 166* and *170*), one in the John Carter Brown Library, Providence (*MS. 3*), and so on. See Fig. VII-29a.

W. 166 of the Walters Art Gallery contains thirteen full-page miniatures, several historiated initials and illuminated borders, and a great number of grotesques. *W. 170* has as many as twenty-seven large miniatures and eight historiated initials. On the whole, the products of this atelier 'are characterized by abundant and vigorous foliate ornament, amusing drolleries, and a competent decorative painting style, still essentially gothic' (D. Miner).

A *Book of Hours* of the Ghent-Bruges school, produced *c.* 1500, is preserved in the Fitzwilliam Museum, Cambridge (*MS. McClean 93*).

It is of course true that this was not the only Flemish atelier which produced illuminated devotional books for export. Near the Franco-Flemish border an important atelier was active which produced interesting books. Miss Miner points out that, as in other ateliers producing for export, the technique is somewhat routine in character, the iconography is rather unusual, 'being very eclectic, and revealing the process by which elements of representation were transferred from one region to another through the pattern-books of the most productive guilds'. Indeed, according to Miss Miner, a *Missal*, produced in this atelier about 1435 (and now in the Gutman Collection, Baltimore), 'retains elements of the "Bedford atelier" as well as of the so-called "gold-scroll" group'. An interesting feature of this *Missal*, which contains twenty-five miniatures, five historiated initials, and several illuminated borders, is the introduction of the main illustration into the margins. Another product of this atelier, a *Book of Hours* (Walters Art Gallery, *W. 211*), contains twenty-one miniatures and several illuminated borders. Its illumination is characterized by unusual features 'drawn from French, Italian, Flemish and Lower Rhenish art' (Miner).

Other Franco-Flemish Schools. The production of the Franco-Flemish schools was abundant. Here and there, some of these manuscripts have been referred to.

But many other MSS. may be added; the following are examples: a fifteenth-century *Book of Hours* preserved in the National Library at Naples (*MS. I.B. 27*); four detached miniatures, preserved in the Royal Library at Turin (*MS. Var. 74 a–d*); a *Book of Hours* of the second half of the fifteenth century in the National Library at Florence (*MS. B.R. 320*); a *Book of Hours* preserved in the Trivulzio Library, Milan (*MS. 446*). Later productions of these schools include: A *Horae*, of 1482, with nineteen full-page miniatures and decorated borders (Badia Library, Cava dei Tirreni, *MS. membr. 45*); other fifteenth-century *Books of Hours* executed in Franco-Flemish schools are preserved in the National Library at Palermo (*MS. I.A. 14*, containing fourteen full-page miniatures, fifteen polychrome naturalistic borders, decorated initials, etc.), in the Royal Library at Turin (*MS. Var. 88: 46* miniatures and decorated borders throughout), in the Trivulzio Library, Milan (*MS. 481*: fourteen pages with miniatures and borders, initials, etc.), in the National Library at Naples (*MS. I.B. 53*: six full-page and 36 smaller miniatures, illuminated borders throughout, Calendar-pictures), and many others in the main European and American collections.

We may also mention that Flemish influence on the North-French illumination was very strong. In many instances, Flemish productions can hardly be distinguished from the French. Here reference may be made to two magnificent *Books of Hours* preserved in the Vatican Library, which are North-French productions with strong Flemish influences: *Barb. Lat. 381* contains many fine bordered miniatures with initials in gold and colours, and illuminated borders with gold berries, coloured foliage, flowers lightened up with gold, angels and figures; *Ottob. Lat. 2919* contains a great number of miniatures by different hands, initials in gold and colours, illuminated and decorated borders, with foliage, flowers, animals, mythical creatures, angels, and so on.

Simon Marmion. Simon Marmion, born between 1425 and 1440, probably in Amiens; died in 1489 in Valenciennes. He was a leading illuminator of his time, if the appellative given to him—*prince d'enlumineure*—by a contemporary poet was proper, and if Reinach's attribution to him and to his school of the copy of the *Grandes Chroniques*, now in Leningrad, which was painted in 1456 for Philip the Good, is correct. The miniatures of this work are superb, and the best of them, as Herbert has pointed out, are unquestionably by a great master, who rivalled Jean Foucquet (see p. 412 ff.) in his power of giving individuality and character to the personages of a group.

In Dr. Paecht's opinion, the practice of packing massive half-figures into the picture-space seems to have been introduced by Simon Marmion (*cf.* British Museum, *Add. MS. 38126*). Various cuttings from an illuminated MS. by this artist are extant: a Crucifixion in Sprincels Collection, Portinscale; a miniature of the Pentecost, of *c.* 1480, in the Fitzwilliam Museum, Cambridge (*MS. 304*); and some which were sold with Lord Northwick's Collection at Sotheby's, London, on 21.5.1928.

Amongst the works, partly at least, attributed to Simon Marmion, there is a superb *Book of Hours*, known as *La Flora*, which was executed for Charles VIII, King of France (*1483–98*). It contains twenty-four Calendar-pictures (two for each month) with architectural frames, occupational scenes and Zodiac signs, as well as about one hundred miniatures, including thirty-six full-page, and others arranged around the text. There are illuminated or decorated borders throughout the book. Some miniatures are attributed to the 'Master of the *Hortulus Animae*', by Winkler identified with Gerard Horenbout (see p. 454 f.); other scholars see a stylistic connection with the 'Master of the *Dresden Hours*'. The manuscript is preserved in the Vatican Library. See also p. 456.

A beautiful Crucifixion in a *Missale Fratrum Minorum* (executed between 1450 and 1460, and now preserved in the Royal Library at Turin, *MS. Var. 186*) is also attributed to Simon Marmion. An Italian copy of Livy, containing eleven historiated initials (including one with a miniature depicting the author) is preserved in the Estense Library, Modena (*MS. α. D. 3.9: Ital. 1015*). The illumination, in Flemish-Burgundian style, appears to be related to Simon Marmion's style, though it seems to be slightly earlier.

North-Flemish Schools. A luxurious fifteenth-century *Book of Hours*, probably executed for the French Royal family (whose arms in gold on blue background appear in the border decoration of fols. 54*r* and *v*, 126*r*, 162*r* and *v*), is preserved in the Riccardiana Library, Florence (*MS. 429*). The codex is attributed to the North-Flemish school. There are twenty-two large miniatures, all with wide decorated borders. Moreover, several pages contain illuminated borders with scenes or figures related to the text, and throughout the MS. there are decorated borders with multi-coloured flowers and gold leaves, with figures, animals, birds and grotesques.

Another fifteenth-century *Book of Hours*, executed in a North-Flemish school is preserved in the Pïana Library, Cesena (*MS. 3. 176*). It is fragmentary, and contains seven very fine illuminated borders.

A fine Psalter with several full-page and other miniatures, with decorated initials and ornamented borders, is preserved in the National Library at Palermo (*MS. II. C. 7*).

Fifteenth-century Dutch Illumination

In 1404, Dirk van Delft, chaplain to Duke Albrecht of Bavaria, Count of Holland, wrote a 'Table of the Christian Faith', known as *De Tafel van den Kersten Ghelove*. Several fragmentary copies of this work have been preserved. An early copy of the first part, known as the *Somerstuc* is in the Pierpont Morgan Library, New York (*M. 691*). In similar style and format (but not belonging to this MS.) is a fragmentary copy of the part known as the *Winterstuc*, preserved in the Walters Art Gallery, Baltimore (*W. 171*). Another copy of the MS., much larger in format, is preserved in the British Museum (*Add. MS. 22288*). Particularly interesting is *W. 171*, which contains thirty-four historiated initials with miniatures painted by two hands, one being related to those of the other two MSS., the other being more accomplished and 'extraordinarily skilful in constructing form and expression entirely by means of soft modelling in light and shade, a completely "painterly" technique' (D. Miner): Fig. VII-30a.

Maria of Geldern Prayerbook, executed in 1415 in Marienhorn near Arnhem, in a fine court-style, is preserved in the Univ. Libr., at Tuebingen (was formerly in the State Libr., at Berlin, *Cod. germ. 4°. 42*).

Fig. VII-30b reproduces fol. 37r from a beautiful Dutch *Horae* of the fifteenth century preserved in The John Rylands Library, Manchester (*Dutch MS. 15*).

School of Utrecht. In the early fifteenth century an important school developed in Utrecht. A fine *Book of Hours*, executed c. 1410 and preserved in the Walters Art Gallery (*W. 185*), contains twelve large miniatures, one historiated initial, several illuminated initials and an illuminated border. The miniatures—writes Miss Dorothy Miner—are painted in a fluent, rapid style, lightly modelled. 'The border springs of trefoils and daisies are sparse and simple.' A contemporary manuscript preserved in the Bodleian Library (*MS. 18392*) is in allied style. See Fig. VII-30c.

The two best artists of the Utrecht school are known as the 'Master of Zweder van Culemborg', and the 'Arenberg Master' or 'Master of Catherine van Cleef'. The 'Master of Zweder van Culemborg' is so called from a manuscript which he illuminated for Zweder, Bishop of Utrecht from 1425. He also painted various other MSS. A *Missal* for Carthusian use, executed in Utrecht c. 1430 and preserved in the Walters Art Gallery (*W. 174*), contains as many as 56 miniatures and 59 historiated initials. Of the miniatures, a great full-page Crucifixion and many small pictures are by the 'Master of Zweder van Culemborg': Fig. VII-30d.

A fine *Missal* preserved in the University Library at Muenster (*MS. 41*) is also attributed to the 'Master of Zweder van Culemborg'. A *Book of Hours*, executed in Utrecht *c.* 1430 and preserved in the Walters Art Gallery (*W. 168*), contains eleven full-page miniatures, twenty historiated initials, and several illuminated borders. Several styles may be distinguished, one of them being very close to that of the 'Zweder Master'. Another *Book of Hours* of the Walters Art Gallery (*W. 188*) contains eighteen historiated initials and several illuminated borders painted in similar style. See Fig. VII-31a–b.

Various miniatures of *W. 174*, previously referred to, are by the 'Aremberg Master', who in Miss D. Miner's opinion shows careful study of the works of the van Eycks. Similar style of illumination appears in the *Egmont Breviary*, preserved in the Pierpont Morgan Library (*M. 87*); in the *Table of the Christian Faith* (British Museum, *Add. MS. 22288*); in a three-volume Latin Bible preserved in the Fitzwilliam Museum, Cambridge (*MS. 289*); and in other works. See Fig. VII-31c. *Add. MS. 22288* has been referred to on p. 447.

The greatly significant problem of the influence of the van Eyck brothers on the Utrecht school of illumination, has been thoroughly re-examined by Dr. Ulrich Finke (*Anmerkungen zu einem van Eyck-Problem*, "BERLINER MUSEEN", N.S., XV, 1965/2; with copious bibliography).

MS. 289 of the Fitzwilliam Museum, written *c.* 1420, contains miniatures, historiated initials, borders, and grotesques. It belongs to an important group of Utrecht MSS. 'with pronounced characteristics recalling the style of the Lower Rhine region' (Byvanck). According to Byvanck, it was executed by five masters, including the 'Master of Zweder van Culemborg' and the 'Master of the *Treatise of Tierry of Delft*'. An interesting Dutch Bible, with charming rather unusual illustrations in frames, is preserved in the State Library at Munich (*Cod. Germ. 1102*). It was produced in Utrecht, in 1439.

The later production of the Utrecht school are skilful, but more or less routine work. On the whole the developments in the Utrecht school—as well as in Dutch illumination in general—were rather conservative, as may be seen in a fine manuscript executed in Utrecht *c.* 1480, and preserved in the British Museum (*Add. MS. 29887*). A *Book of Hours* in closely allied style is preserved in the Collection Dimitri Tselos, New York City. The MS. contains four full-page miniatures, six historiated initials, and several illuminated borders. See also Fig. VII-31d, which reproduces fol. 39r from a very fine *Horae* of the Utrecht school, of *c.* 1470 (now Cambridge University Library, *Add. MS. 4097*).

School of Delft. Another important school was active in Delft. A group of illuminated books attributed to Delft—as Miss Dorothy Miner remarks—is in striking and expressive *grisaille* technique, lightly relieved by colour. 'The angularity of the poses and drapery folds and the sharp contrasts of the modelling recall Netherlands wood-carvings of this same period.' An excellent example of this group is preserved in the Walters Art Gallery (*W. 165*). It is a *Book of Hours* for the use of Utrecht, and contains eighteen full-page miniatures.

Influence of the Great Flemish Masters. In contrast to the greatest Italian masters of the Renaissance, who, as far as we can tell from evidence, with few exceptions were hardly interested in book-painting, there is no doubt that several of the greatest Flemish masters practised illumination. This has been supposed of Hans Memling (active *c.* 1435–94) who was born at Seligenstadt-on-Main but settled in Bruges before 1479. The theory is quite probable, as the style of Memling's panel-painting was in so many ways aptly suited for book-painting. On the whole, leading authorities have pointed out that the influence of the panel-paintings of the great Flemish masters upon the current productions of book-illumination was notable. An excellent example of such a production is preserved in the Walters Art Gallery, Baltimore (*W. 208*). It is a small *Book of Hours*, containing eleven miniatures. Some of these, in Miss Dorothy Miner's opinion, are based upon the compositions of Petrus Christus and other Flemish masters. However, the various attributions to Memling of preserved miniatures are not supported by available evidence. Modern critics, therefore, prefer to assign to direct imitation the re-semblance to his work often noticed in the late fifteenth- and early sixteenth-century illuminations executed at Bruges, Memling's centre of activity.

Quite different is the case of another great Flemish master, Gérard David (*c.* 1450–1523), who was born at Oudewater (in Holland), but was active in Bruges, and became in 1501 dean of the flourishing Bruges Painters' Guild. After the death of Memling he became the leading painter in Flanders. He is known to have practised book-painting. Indeed, amongst his various book-illuminations, there are three (Nativity, Epiphany, S. Barbara) in British Museum *Add. MS. 18851*; a Nativity in *Add. MS. 4100* in the University Library at Cambridge, and so on.

Last and Most Attractive Phase of the Flemish Illumination
   (*Second Half of the Fifteenth Century*)

Fine work was executed in this period, but it is hardly possible to give a detailed description of the books produced or even of all the ateliers which produced them. The majority of the illuminated books—mainly Books of Hours—were produced in excellent ateliers which worked particularly for export.

One of the best examples of this export-production is the very fine *Prayerbook* executed *c.* 1470 for Galeazzo Maria Sforza, Duke of Milan, and preserved in the National Library at Vienna (*MS. 1856*). It contains large miniatures, marginal medallions, and historiated initials executed in *grisaille*, silver, and gold on vellum painted black. It has been dealt with on p. 431.

Other work produced in the same atelier was routine work. Very few artists who worked in this or similar ateliers are known by other than the name given to them from their productions. In this atelier the 'Girart Master' was active. Similar in style is a *Book of Hours* of *c.* 1465 preserved in the Walters Art Gallery (*W. 190*).

There are nine large miniatures executed in *grisaille* on dark colours, and eight historiated initials containing small scenes executed in *grisaille* and gold on black grounds.

W. 439 of the Walters Art Gallery is a *Book of Hours* of c. 1485, and is an example of the routine-work of another Flemish atelier. It contains fourteen large miniatures, thirty-two historiated initials, and a number of historiated borders.

A very interesting musical MS., containing Masses, hymns and sacred chants is preserved in the Vatican Library (*Chig. C. VIII. 234*). The main decoration, of a Flemish school of the second half of the fifteenth century, consists in illuminated borders, with drawings of figures, fantastic animals, and grotesques; there are also naturalistic borders with flowers on a ground of opaque gold, with birds and butterflies, musical notes, etc.

A late fifteenth-century *Book of Hours*, also preserved in the Vatican Library (*Ottob. Lat. 548*) contains numerous miniatures, gold and coloured initials, and decorated borders with bands of dark gold or delicate colours, sprinkled with flowers, butterflies, and animals. A contemporary *Book of Hours* in the Vatican Library (*Ross. 94*) has a more superb illumination: it contains a great number of beautiful miniatures with decorative borders in dark gold sprinkled with flowers, fruits, animals, rosaries of jewels, etc. All the initials are either historiated or decorated, the larger containing borders in gold. Illuminated or decorated borders are on all pages. Very fine *Books of Hours* of the late fifteenth century are also preserved in the National Museum at Syracuse (Sicily), in the National Library at Naples (*MS. I.B. 28; I.B. 41*; and many others). A richly illuminated *Psalter and Offices* is in the Trivulzio Library, Milan (*MS. 448*).

In the latter half of the fifteenth century in Flanders, and particularly at Bruges and Ghent, huge illuminated volumes came into fashion. They were mainly copies of the *Bible Historiale*, of histories and romances, and even of philosophical works—see p. 388 f. But towards the end of the century these volumes became much less popular; as the most characteristic Renaissance class of book, the devotional books intended for private use, mainly Breviaries and Books of Hours, became more fashionable. It was the zenith of Flemish book-painting. Indeed, in technical skill the best Flemish book-painters—writes Herbert—had now reached the utmost heights attainable in the art, and their rendering of landscape leaves little to be desired by the most exacting critics; while their close relations with the great painters saved them from the decadence into which their French and Italian fellow-craftsmen fell, and gave their compositions something of that sincerity and homely simplicity, combined with dignity and intense spirituality, which give such character to the masterpieces of Memling and his contemporaries.

Some of these MSS. were shown in the 'Exhibition of Flemish Art 1300–1700' at the Royal Academy of Arts, London 1953–4 (*Catalogue Nos. 565, 569, 571*, and so on). A Latin *Psalter and Book of Hours*, with the Calendar of Mons, now in Cambridge University Library (*Add. MS. 6689*), was illuminated in the third quarter of the fifteenth century. It contains thirteen beautiful floral borders. The

University Library at Glasgow (*MS. BD. 19–h. 12*) possesses a beautiful *Book of Hours* with a Calendar pointing to Saint-Omer of *c.* 1460–70. There are twelve miniatures in addition to the floral borders. See Fig. VII-33a.

Jehan Mielot, whose works were fashionable *c.* 1460, wrote *Le Miroir de l'humaine salvacion* and *Les Miracles de Nostre Dame* (see pp. 428 and 429). A copy of the former, written at Bruges in 1455, and probably illuminated by the author himself, is preserved in the University Library at Glasgow (*Hunterian MS. T.2.8*): it contains one large and forty-two fourfold miniatures, partly in *grisaille*.

The majority of books illuminated after 1480 are Prayer-books of very small size; the lettering, on the other hand, is comparatively large, producing extremely short and narrow columns of script. 'These short columns, thrown up by the coloured border, detach themselves like little posters picturesquely mounted on the page' (Paecht). A charming *Horae* of 1487 is preserved in The John Rylands Library, Manchester (*Lat. MS. 39*): Fig. VII-29b.

Renaissance devotional books—particularly Books of Hours and Breviaries—have been discussed in other sections (see pp. 382 f., 402 ff., and *passim*); here something may be said about the style of border-decoration introduced by the Flemish masters. This decoration consists of broad rectangular bands mainly of dead gold (sometimes, however, of a monochrome, such as pale grey or purple), covered with beautifully and accurately painted flowers, such as cornflowers, carnations, columbines, and pansies, fruits (particularly wild strawberries), butterflies, bees, snails, birds, etc.; it is interesting to note that the depicted objects appear as though slightly raised above the ground, this illusion being caused by a shadow given to each object. Indeed, as Miss Giles points out, sometimes the spray of flowers is actually secured to the page by a painted pin. Although each of the objects painted is delightful in itself, and is an admirable illustration from natural history, the decorative scheme is not on the whole successful. Some modern critics have compared it with the illustrated catalogue of a seedsman.

Devotional Books with Naturalistic Borders. Herbert refers to an excellent example of a manuscript (British Museum, *Add. MS. 25698*) containing such naturalistic borders; it is a fragmentary *Prayer-book* (only eleven leaves being preserved) of unknown origin, probably executed *c.* 1492–3 in connection with the military Order of S. George (founded in 1490 by Emperor Frederick III, but given more scope by Maximilian), which was supposed to organize a crusade against the Turks: fol. 2 represents the Elevation of the Host in a church which is probably intended to represent the Church of Jerusalem; on fol. 3 Frederick and Maximilian together with the Kings of England, France, and Spain, and the Archduke of Austria, are kneeling before the altar of S. George; on fol. 4 the Pope and prelates invoke S. Peter; fol. 5 represents a great lady on her deathbed (her name apparently began with *M*—is it Mary of Burgundy, who died in 1482?) as Michael and the devil fight for her soul, but she is cheered by a vision of the Virgin and Child; on fol. 8 various secular personages invoke Christ; on fol. 10 monks and friars invoke the Holy Ghost, all probably with the aim of insuring victory against the Turks.

An extremely interesting picture—not at all related to the subjects of the book—is fol. 1 which represents a landscape for its own sake. It is a charming Flemish scene—a village by a river, animals grazing in the fields, with trees and low hills in the background.

A *Book of Hours*, for the use of Rome, produced *c.* 1490 in Flanders, with nine large and thirty-seven small miniatures, and illuminated borders throughout, is preserved in the Walters Art Gallery, Baltimore (*W. 176*). It is—as Miss Dorothy Miner points out—a tiny book of silky vellum, whose chief charm is in the naturalistic and carefully studied flowers, birds and insects that are strewn through the borders. Like other main collections of America and Europe, the Walters Art Gallery possesses a number of such MSS. with naturalistic borders. Two *Books of Hours* belong to *c.* 1500: *W. 423* (with nine full-page miniatures and several illuminated borders) is a tiny book on extremely thin, silky vellum. 'The dull gold borders are strewn with large flowers, carefully studied after nature' (Miner); *W. 428* contains seventeen large and twenty-nine small miniatures, as well as several illuminated borders, 'with the characteristic designs of naturalistic flowers, birds, jewelry and similar motives' (Miner). Even more interesting are two other *Books of Hours*, *W. 209*, of *c.* 1510, and *W. 210*, of *c.* 1530. *W. 209* contains fifteen large and five small miniatures, and illuminated borders. Here—as Miss Miner points out—the carefully observed renderings of flowers are more finely executed than in the average examples, but the chief charm lies in the refreshing treatment of all the intervening pages, on which the uncoloured margins are strewn with a few tenderly observed flowers, birds, jewels, or other objects. The style of this book is closely connected with that of the *Croy Prayer-book* preserved in the National Library at Vienna (*MS. 1858*). *W. 425* contains forty-five miniatures and several illuminated borders. The latter 'feature not only the usual carefully studied flowers, insects and birds, but jewels and renaissance architectural motives. The handling of lighting and of distant landscape in the miniatures is good, despite the tiny scale of the paintings' (Miner). Another excellent representative of this class, also preserved in the Walters Art Gallery (*W. 427*), belongs to *c.* 1510. It is 'more finely executed' than other average examples. Fig. VII-32*a–b*, and 33*c*.

Dr. Paecht has pointed out that this newly awakened interest in nature studies from plant-life did not remain confined to artists practising book-painting. Shortly after the first *trompe-l'œil* borders had been designed—writes Paecht—two herbals were printed in Mainz, the *Herbarius Latinus* in 1484, and the *Gart der Gesundheit* in 1485, both containing large sets of woodcuts which mark an important event in the history of herbal illustration. For the latter edition—Paecht suggests—the Mainz printer had secured the collaboration of a craftsman from the Netherlands. The systematic portrayal of plant-life in the herbals, and the playful assortment of nature studies in the manuscript borders are undoubtedly complementary historical phenomena. Taken together they demonstrate that there was no essential difference of approach to the treatment of artistic representation, or to the treatment of scientific illustration, by the painters of the Low Countries and their German pupils.

In Winkler's opinion, the style of the *Croy Prayer-book* (referred to above) is related to that of the artist whom he calls "Jakobsmeister", and to whom he attributes the following works: the title miniature of *James IVth* (of Scotland) *Prayerbook* (Nat. Libr. at Vienna, *MS. 1897*), executed about 1503–13; Brussels, *Cod. 9126*, executed about 1500–10; four title-miniatures of the *Great Missal* of Philip I (el Hermoso) of Spain (Nat. Libr. at Vienna, about 1500); *Cod. 1858* of the Vienna National Library; British Museum *Add. MS. 35313*, and a few other works, preserved in Jena, Venice, and the Vatican Library.

Isabella Book. Another excellent example of a devotional book produced in the late fifteenth century is a *Breviary* of Spanish Dominican use written in Spain, but illuminated by Flemish artists probably working in Spain. About 1497 the book was given by Francisco de Roias to Queen Isabella, hence its name the *Isabella Book*. It is preserved in the British Museum (*Add. MS. 18851*). It contains over one hundred small miniatures and forty-five half-page ones, many of the compositions being very beautiful; the influence of Memling and his pupils is very strong. Outstanding are the Nativity (fol. 29), the Adoration of the Magi (fol. 41), S. Barbara (fol. 297), and the Apocalyptic vision of S. John (fol. 309). The Calendar-illustrations, typical of the period, do not constitute separate miniatures, but the whole text for each month is inlaid, as it were, in a picture of an appropriate occupation. A new characteristic feature of this and of a few other Calendar-illustrations of the late fifteenth and early sixteenth centuries is the representation of May as a boating pleasure-party on a river. There are numerous borders and their decoration is of three styles: (*a*) the old scroll-work; (*b*) the naturalistic type (see above); and (*c*) striped repeat-patterns, which in Herbert's opinion may have been copied from brocaded work.

Two exquisite little *Books of Hours* were probably made for Isabella's daughter Joan, perhaps also for Philip the Fair, Joan's husband: they are British Museum, *Add. MS. 17280*, which contains portraits of Joan and Philip, and British Museum, *Add. MS. 18852*, which contains many charming miniatures—Joan's portrait is on fols. 26 and 288.

Sixteenth Century

Apart from the great masterpieces, which will be discussed below, the early sixteenth century saw no new styles or trends in book-painting. Some of the books contained simple copies or imitations of miniatures in other works. The *Egmont Horae* (British Museum, *Add. MS. 35319*)—a book executed for Floris van Egmont, Count of Buren and Knight of the Golden Fleece (1505–39) and his wife, Margaret van Bergen—contains on fol. 33*b* a bad but faithful copy, down to the minutest detail (including the kneeling figures in the nave), of the Elevation of the Host as shown on fol. 2 of *Add. MS. 25698* (see p. 451).

Some of the routine-works show greatly improved technique; this is the case, for instance, with a fine *Book of Hours*, of *c.* 1500, preserved in the Walters Art Gallery, Baltimore (*W. 430*). It contains twelve miniatures which are executed in a dark *grisaille* relieved with slight colour. Also to *c.* 1500 belong a charming little *Book of Hours*, with thirty-two miniatures, which passed from the Felix M. Warburg Collection to the Library of Congress, Washington, and a series of twelve miniatures, which belong to the Boston Public Library. See Fig. VII-33*b*.

A remarkable book of the period is a British Museum *Book of Hours* (*Add. MS. 35313*). This is not of great originality but it contains an interesting Annunciation, Nativity, and Augustus with Sybil. In the design prefixed to the *Vigils of the Dead* —three skeletons with darts attacking a lady in the hunting-field—some scholars have seen an allusion to the death of Mary of Burgundy. The following interesting devotional books are, moreover, outstanding: *Prayer book of Maximilian* (see also pp. 433 and 435) in the National Library at Vienna; three manuscripts in the State Library at Munich; and the *Albert of Brandenburg Horae*. To a slightly later period belong the British Museum *Egerton MS. 1147*, and a fragment—perhaps the finest of all Flemish fragmentary manuscripts—of four leaves, of which two are in the British Museum (*Add. MS. 18855*) and two in the Salting Collection, Victoria and Albert Museum, London.

We may end this list with a *Book of Hours*, for which, thanks to its colophon, we have full information. The codex (now in the Philadelphia Free Library, *Lewis MS. 109*) was executed in 1537 at the Abbey of S. Amand for François Duquesne, Duke of Orléans. Miss Dorothy Miner draws attention to the interesting development in this book of the use of architectural borders of complex silhouette, rendered with scrollwork and occasional figures, similar to the borders in the *Book of Hours of Henry II* (National Library at Paris, *Lat. 1429*).

Production of superior illuminated religious books, apart from Books of Hours, was not plentiful. Examples are: a *New Testament* in two volumes—vol. I, in the University Library at Cambridge (*MS. Dd. VII. 3*), vol. II, in the British Museum (*Royal MS. I.E.v.*); a *Missal*, of 1521, in Wadham College, Oxford (*MS. A.7.8*). Interesting is a copy of *Motets*, executed for Henry VIII and Catherine of Aragon, *c.* 1519–33 (British Museum, *Royal MS. 8. D. vii*).

Gerard Hore(n)bout. About 1500 a great Flemish illuminator, Gerard Hore(n)-bout, executed very fine MSS. A set of three richly illuminated books is preserved in the Vatican Library: *Vat. Lat. 3768–70*. They contain the *Office of the Dead* and other prayers, the *Office of the Holy Trinity* and other prayers, a *Psalter* and the *Office of the Virgin*. Throughout there are illuminated or decorated borders with bands of opaque gold, black or light colours, with scattered flowers, and leaves, butterflies and dragon-flies etc. 'Many excellent miniatures of figures and historical scenes are executed with extremely fine workmanship and often with vivid expression' (Michelini Tocci). Hore(n)bout also executed a few miniatures in British Museum *Add. MS. 18851*. An *Obituary Roll* on John Islip, Abbot of Westminster (*d.* 1532), which is preserved in the Library of Westminster Abbey, contains interesting drawings attributed to Gerard Hore(n)bout, at that time court painter to Henry VIII. An *Epistolary* (Christ Church Library, Oxford, *MS. 101*) and a *Gospel-book* (Magdalen College, Oxford, *MS. 223*) are attributed to a member of the Hore(n)bout family. *See* also p. 446.

Grimani Breviary. This Roman *Breviary*, a masterpiece, preserved in the Marciana Library, Venice (s.s.), is not only of uncertain authorship and provenance, but also of uncertain date. It is, however, mentioned in the first will (dated 5 October 1520) of Cardinal Domenico Grimani (see p. 361), who had bought it from Antonio Siciliano for 500 ducats. The contents of the Calendar suggest that it was made for the Italian market, but we do not know whether it was written in Italy or not. The styles of the miniatures—there is no doubt that many masters collaborated in their execution—suggest a date between 1490 and 1510, probably nearer the latter. The main interest of this work lies in its unique bulk: there are 832 leaves of large size (28 × 22 cm.), the last one being blank. They contain 110 miniatures, including 49 full-page, and twelve superb full-page Calendar-pictures, as well as several smaller miniatures and numerous minor decorations; throughout the whole book are illuminated borders with naturalistic or architectural elements, with figures and scenes from daily life. The 49 full-page miniatures depict scenes connected with the main holy-days and the feasts of the saints. Other nineteen large and eighteen smaller miniatures depict scenes from the Old and New Testaments. The miniatures are by different hands—Flemish and, perhaps, French. See Fig. VII-34.

The Calendar-pictures (one for each month, depicting the seasonal occupations, particularly those relating to agriculture), are without doubt an imitation or a copy of the corresponding series of the *Most Rich Hours* (see p. 401); they are, however, a homogeneous unity and are attributed to the Benings, particularly to Simon (see p. 456 f.). Some of the miniatures are directly or indirectly influenced by David's pictures (see p. 449). The Adoration of the Magi—which closely resembles a miniature in the *Isabella Book*—was either derived from a lost panel by David (in which case it may have been a model to the artist of the *Isabella Book*), or was itself copied from the latter book.

Some miniatures are attributed to Jean Gossaert, others to Gerard of Ghent.

The Master of the David scenes in the *Grimani Breviary* is credited with the illumination of various *Books of Hours* such as *MS. Douce 112* in the Bodleian Library (containing fifty-three pages with miniatures and floral borders throughout) and *Douce MS. 256* of the same collection (containing 38 miniatures and several floral borders).

The *Grimani Breviary* had a very great influence on Flemish illumination; indeed, in the opinion of some authorities it overwhelmed the more serene and subtle trends in Flemish painting. Its influence was particularly strong in the Bruges atelier, which produced a number of fine *Books of Hours*, such as that executed in 1531, and now preserved in the Pierpont Morgan Library (*M. 451*), and that in the Walters Art Gallery (*W. 426*).

The Ghent atelier, also, was under the spell of the *Grimani Breviary* tradition. In Miss Dorothy Miner's opinion, the influence of this tradition can be seen in the famous *Hortulus Animae* (see below); in the *Breviary of Eleanor of Portugal* preserved in the Pierpont Morgan Library (*M. 52*); and particularly in eleven detached miniatures (now scattered in various collections) from a MS. executed in Ghent *c. 1515*. Two of these miniatures, preserved in the Robert Lehman Collection, New York City (*Nos. 102–3*) represent the *Pietà* with the Virgin and S. Brigitt writing her *Revelations*. In the *Grimani Breviary* as well as in all these MSS., the historiated borders 'have been treated as whole paintings upon which the main illustration has been imposed in the form of an additional and independent painting, a development of Flemish fascination with the representation of spacious landscape vistas' (D. Miner).

Flemish Miniatures of Sforza Horae. The Flemish additions to the *Sforza Book of Hours* have been referred to on p. 344. It is generally assumed that they were executed in 1519–21 by various artists working for the Emperor Charles V. These additions consist of the first page of the *Penitential Psalms*, containing—apart from the border-decoration, imitating the work of the Milanese artists of the original part —Charles' portrait, dated 1520, painted in gold within a medallion; and of sixteen full-page miniatures, which in conception, design, and colouring, are perhaps the finest production of the Flemish school. It will suffice to refer to the Adoration of the Magi and the Presentation—to quote Herbert—with their masterly portraiture, simple yet effective grouping, and skilful, characteristically minute and careful treatment of architecture and costume; the *O intemerata*, with its placid, dreamy Madonna and the delightful group of angel-musicians; and loveliest of all, perhaps, the *Salve Regina*, with its beautiful soft colouring and large, gracious manner.

Hennessy Horae, the 'Golf' Book, Dixmude Missal, and Simon Bening. The *Hennessy Hours* (Royal Library at Brussels) and the *Golf Book* (British Museum, *Add. MS. 24098*) are the last masterpieces of Flemish illumination. The former contains 27 full-page miniatures (including a complete Calendar-series, portraits of the Evangelists, and scenes of the Passion) and numerous pages with interesting marginal decoration. The *Golf Book* is fragmentary; it consists of 30 leaves, containing 21 full-page miniatures (the Calendar-pictures, eight Passion scenes, and S. Boniface). The two MSS. agree in the Passion pictures and in some Calendar-illustrations, and it is evident that they were the product of the same school. This has been identified by some scholars as the school which produced in 1530 the *Dixmude Missal*, as well as the *Hortulus Animae* MS., already referred to (preserved in the National Library at Vienna, *MS. 2706*). It was the school of Simon Bennik or Bening—also known as Binnik, Binnink, Bynnynch—(1483–1561), the last great master of Flemish book-painting. He was the son of Alexander (see p. 429 f.), and was born in Ghent, but in 1508 he went to Bruges where he settled permanently in 1517. He worked for the Emperor Charles V.

Two self-portraits of Simon Bening have been preserved, one in the Victoria and Albert Museum, London (*P. 159–1910*), the other in the Robert Lehman Collection, New York City (*No. 191*). The latter measures $3\frac{1}{8} \times 2$ in., and shows the artist at half-length; near him there is an easel with colours and a painting. Beneath, there is the inscription *SIMON BENNIK. ALEXANDRI. F. SE. IPSU. PIGEBAT. ANO. AETATIS. 75. 1558.* This painting was apparently conceived as a separate picture and not as a book-painting. Roughly in the same format ($3\frac{1}{8} \times 2\frac{3}{8}$ in.) there is in the Walters Art Gallery (*W. 442*) a remarkable series of 64 miniatures on vellum, mounted in the form of a quadriptych. It has been suggested that this arrangement was the original one, and thus these miniatures were not intended to be part of a book. 'The subjects commence with the meeting of Joachim and Anna at the Golden Gate and continue through the story of Christ and of the Virgin to a final scene showing the Day of Judgment. Many scenes seldom represented in painting are included and many unusual conceptions of familiar subjects, the whole forming a kind of repertory of all the inventions of the school' (D. Miner). These miniatures are usually attributed to Simon Bening. See Fig. VII-36.

Five single miniatures, preserved in the Fitzwilliam Museum, Cambridge (*MS. 294*), are by Simon Bening. According to Professor Wormald they are related to 'the Master of the *Hortulus Animae*'. A *Benedictional*, executed *c.* 1520, and preserved in the University Library at Cambridge (*MS. Nn. IV.1*) was illuminated by Simon Bening and his school at Bruges. A *Book of Hours*, illuminated at Bruges and dated to 1524, contains eight miniatures by Simon Bening and nineteen miniatures, Calendar-illustrations and floral borders by another artist. An unfinished *Genealogy of the Portuguese Kings*, in Portuguese, commissioned *c.* 1530, was beautifully illuminated after designs (some of which are in the style of Duerer's school), by Simon Bening and other Flemish artists. It is preserved in the British Museum (*Add. MS. 12531*).

Bruges. This city, which was the headquarters of Simon Bening and of nearly all the leading Flemish illuminators, was from the twelfth to the sixteenth century one of the largest commercial cities in Europe, an *emporium* of English, Scandinavian, Hanseatic, Venetian and other Italian merchants. Its school of illumination was the most important in Flanders.

A great number of Franco-Flemish illuminated books are attributed to one or another artist of the Bruges school. A fine codex of the late fourteenth or early fifteenth century, containing the *Office of the Virgin, Penitential Psalms* and the *Office of the Dead*, preserved in the Royal Library at Turin (*MS. Var. 77*), is illuminated in the Franco-Flemish style: it has been attributed to Jacques Coene of Bruges (see also p. 403). Some authorities have identified this artist with the 'Boucicaut Master' (see p. 403 f.). A copy of Vitruvius, Cato, and Varro (Laurentian Library, Florence, *Plut. 30, 10*) is in a style similar to that of Jacques Coene.

Secular Manuscripts. To end this section, a few excellent examples of secular manuscripts will be briefly dealt with. The British Museum *Royal MS. 16. F. ii,* containing a copy of poems by Charles, Duke of Orléans, was apparently executed for King Henry VII or his son Arthur, Prince of Wales. There are six large miniatures, of different artistic value, none being outstanding. The work was apparently done in England by Flemish artists, who were perhaps court-painters to Henry. The miniatures are allied in style to those of the British Museum *Royal MS. 19. C. viii*, which was written for Henry, at Sheen in 1496. One of the most interesting miniatures of *Royal 16. F. ii* is a picture of the Tower of London (where the Duke of Orléans spent most of his captivity, from 1415 to 1440); we see the Thames, Traitor's Gate, London Bridge, and the City. The miniature is in the old 'continuous' method (see pp. 30 and 43): we see the Duke (*a*) writing at a table, (*b*) in his prison-chamber in the White Tower, (*c*) looking out of a window, and (*d*) giving a letter to a messenger—all shown in the same picture!

A beautiful fifteenth-century copy of *Hystoire du Roi Arthus*, preserved in the National Library at Turin (*MS. L. III. 31*), was partly destroyed in the fire of 1904. The second portion of the book (fols. 233–343) contains 25 very fine monochrome miniatures (with little gold) representing various scenes illustrating the text.

A copy *de luxe* of Jehan de Wavrin, *Chronicle of England*, executed *c.* 1490 by a fine Flemish painter, is an example of the best production in illuminated historical works. Vols. II, III, and V are preserved in Holland in the Royal Library at The Hague, whereas Vol. IV, containing six large miniatures, apart from several illuminated borders, is preserved in the Walters Art Gallery, Baltimore (*W. 201*). A copy of *Histoires de Thèbes et de la destruction de Troye*, written on paper by Jacquotin de Lespluc in 1469, probably in Lille, and illuminated by the 'Wavrin Master', was preserved in C. W. Dyson Perrins Library (*MS. 99*): it contains 128 pen-and-ink drawings. Another MS. of the same collection (*MS. 101*) is a copy of Jean de Vignay, *Mireoir Historial*, executed *c.* 1470 for a member of the family of Lannoy d'Amerancourt, of Picardy: there are 56 miniatures and several historiated borders. See Fig. VII-35*a*.

A copy of Gautier de Metz, *Image du monde*, executed in Bourges in 1489, and preserved in the Walter Art Gallery (*W. 199*), is of particular importance. It is 'a "scientific" synopsis of the elements of astronomy, natural history, the seven arts ... illustrated by astronomical diagrams as well as by *grisaille* illustrations' (Miner). It contains 37 miniatures: Fig. VII-35*b*.

Copies of Jean Duchesne's French translation made in 1474 of Caesar, *De Bello gallico*, are preserved in the Bodleian Library (*Douce MS. 208*) and in the British Museum (*Egerton MS. 1065*). The Oxford MS. contains eleven miniatures and historiated borders; the British Museum copy has ten illuminations, four being by the artist of the Oxford copy, and six in a style related to that of Philip de Mazerolles (see p. 430 f.). The artist of the Oxford MS. also illuminated the frontispiece of the copy of Jean Corbechon, *Des Propriétéz des choses* (translation of Bartholomaeus Anglicus—see p. 398), referred to on p. 403.

A copy of Froissart, *Chroniques*, with miniatures by various masters, such as the 'Master of Anthony of Burgundy' and the 'Master of the *Dresden Hours*' (see p. 429, 431 f.), is preserved in the Nation. Libr. at Paris (*MS. Fr. 2643–6*). Copies of Jean Robertet, *Les Douze dames de Rhétorique*, illuminated between 1473–5 by the 'Master of Anthony of Burgundy', are preserved in the University Library at

Cambridge (*MS. Nn. III.2*) and in the National Library at Paris (*MS. Fr. 1174*). Other outstanding secular MSS. are: a copy of Ovid, written and illuminated in 1497 at Ghent (Earl of Leicester's Library, *MS. 324*); a copy of Virgil, *c.* 1473–1500 (the same collection, *MS. 311*); a copy of Guillaume de Lorris and Jean de Meun, *Roman de la Rose*, of *c.* 1500 (British Museum, *Harley MS. 4425*); a copy of Hélie de Borron, *Gyron le Courtois*, of *c.* 1500 (Bodleian Library, *Douce MS. 383*); three MSS. produced *c.* 1500 by the same artist: Jacques de Guise, *Chroniques de Hainaut* (Bodleian Library, *Douce MS. 205*; Earl of Leicester's Library, *MS. 658*), and *Le Livre des échecs amoureux* (National Library at Paris, *MS. Fr. 9197*). Jehan Franco, *Généalogie de l'Empereur Charles V*—dedication copy executed in 1527 for Margaret of Austria (National Library at Paris, *MS. Fr. 5616*).

In a mid-sixteenth-century MS. of the National Library at Paris (*Fr. 1872*), the various episodes of the *Chasse au faucon* have been reassembled within one landscape setting to form a calendar-picture.

The remarkable British Museum manuscript previously referred to is a sumptuous copy of the *Roman de la Rose* (*Harley MS. 4425*): it seems to have been made for Englebert of Nassau, Lieutenant of the Realm at the time of Philip the Fair's minority. Curiously enough, the text seems to have been transcribed from one of the early printed editions of the work. The MS. has four large and 88 small miniatures. There is—as Herbert writes—a quaint artificial elegance (French rather than Flemish in spirit) about the large garden-scenes; but the great merit of the book consists in the admirable figure-drawing and characterization shown in many of the smaller pictures.

Two other fine manuscripts executed for Englebert of Nassau are preserved in the Bodleian Library. They are a copy of Vasco de Lucena's translation of Quintus Curtius (*Laud. Misc. 751*) and a Guizon (*Douce MS. 383*). Both bear the arms of Engelbert, decorated with peacocks' eyes.

BIBLIOGRAPHY

L. Delisle, *Le Cabinet des Manuscrits de la Bibliothèque Impériale (Nationale)*, Paris, 1868–81; *Inventaire des Manuscrits de la B.N.: fonds de Cluni*, Paris, 1884; *Les Manuscrits de Saint-Martial de Limoges*, Limoges, 1895; *Notice de douze livres royaux du XIIIᵉ et du XIVᵉ siècle*, Paris, 1902.

S. Berger, *La Bible française au moyen âge*, Paris, 1884.

Can. Dehaisnes, *Histoire de l'art dans la Flandre etc. avant le XVᵉ siècle*, Lille, 1886.

E. Baes, 'Notes sur le Bréviaire Grimani et les manuscr. a miniat. du commenc. du XVIᵉ siècle,' *Bulletin d. Comm. Roy. d'Art et d'Archéol.*, 1889.

P. Durrieu, *Un Grand Enlumineur parisien au XVᵉ siècle: Jacques de Besançon, etc.*, Paris, 1892; *Jacques Coene, peintre de Bruges établi à Paris sous le règne de Charles VI: 1398–1404*, Brussels, 1906; *Les Antiquités judaïques et le peintre Jean Foucquet*, Paris, 1908; 'Un Siècle de l'histoire de la miniature parisien, etc.,' *Journal des Savants*, 1909; *La Miniature flamande*, Brussels, 1921.

A. de Champeaux and P. Gauchery, *Les Travaux d'art exècutès pour Jeàn de France, duc de Berry*, Paris, 1894.

D. Ciàmpoli, *I codici francesi d. R. Bibl. Naz. di San Marco in Venezia*, Venice, 1897.

O. Sohring, 'Werke bildender Kunst in altfranzœsischen Epen,' *Romanische Forschungen*, 1900.

H. Pirenne, *Histoire de Belgique*, 1902–1932.

E. Mâle, *L'Art religieux du XIIIe siècle en France*, 2nd ed., Paris, 1902; *L'Art religieux en France de la fin du moyen âge*, Paris, 1908; *L'Art religieux du XIIe siècle en France*, Paris, 1928.

Rohault de Fleury, *Gallia Dominicana, etc.*, 2 vols., Paris, 1903.

S. de Vries and S. Morpurgo, *Breviarium Grimani* (Germ. transl.), 15 parts, Leipsic, 1903–08.

H. Martin, *Les Miniaturistes français*, Paris, 1906; *Les Peintres de MSS. et la miniature en France*, Paris, 1909; *La Miniature française du XIIIe au XIVe siècle*, Paris and Brussels, 1923.

G. Vitzthum, *Die pariser Miniaturmalerei*, Leipsic, 1907.

P. Aubry, *Le Roman de Fauvel . . .* , Paris, 1907.

A. Vidier, 'Le Trésor de la Sainte-Chapelle,' *Mem. de la Soc. de l'Hist. de Paris etc.*, 1907–10.

G. Coggiola, *Le Bréviaire Grimani*, Leyden, 1908–10.

K. Voll, *Memling*, Stuttgart, 1909.

G. Doutrepont, *La Littèrature française à la cour des ducs de Bourgogne etc.*, Paris, 1909.

F. de Mely, 'Le Bréviaire Grimani et les inscript. de ses miniat.,' *Revue de l'Art Anc. et Mod.*, 1909.

L. Bréhier, 'La Bible de Souvigny et la Bible de Clermont,' *Bull. de la Soc. d'Émulation du Bourbonnais*, 1910; *L'Art en France etc.*, Paris, 1930; —— and R. Aigrain, *Grégoire le Grand etc.*, Paris, 1938.

Académie de Mâcon, *Millénaire de Cluny*, 2 vols., Mâcon, 1910.

P. Toesca, 'Le miniature dell' "Entrée de Spagne" d. Bibl. Marciana (cod. fr. XXI),' *Scritti vari d'erudiz. e di crit. in onore di R. Renier*, Turin, 1912.

J. Vogelstein, *Von franzœsischer Buchmalerei*, Munich, 1914.

A. Wilmart, 'Cluny (Manuscrits liturgiques de),' *Dictionnaire d'Archéol. Chrétienne*, III, Paris, 1914.

W. M. Conway, 'The Abbey of Saint-Denis and its Ancient Treasures', *Archaeologia*, 1915.

F. Winkler, 'Studien zur Geschichte der niederl. Buchmalerei', *Jahrbuch d. kunsthist. Samml. d. allerh. Kaiserhauses*, Vienna, 1915; *Die Flaemische Buchmalerei des XV. und XVI. Jahrhundert*, Leipsic, 1925; *Neuentdeckte Niederlaender, I*: 'Sanders Benning,' *Pantheon*, 1942; *II*: 'Gerard Horenbouts,' *Pantheon*, 1943.

J. Huizinga, *Herfsttij der Middeleeuwen*, Haarlem, 1919 (2nd ed., 1921); German transl., 1924 (2nd ed., 1928); also French transl.

A. Weese, *Skulptur u. Malerei in Frankreich im XV. u. XVI. Jahrh.*, Wildpark in Potsdam, 1922.

BIBLIOGRAPHY

A. W. Byvanck and G. J. Hougewerff, *La Miniature hollandaise*, The Hague, 1922-5; G. J. Hougewerff, *De Nord-Nederlandsche Schilderkunst*, The Hague, 1936; A. Byvanck, *La Miniature dans les Pays-Bas Septentrionaux*, Paris, 1937 (also in Dutch and English).

C. Oursel, *Les Manuscrits à peintures de la biblioth. de Dijon*, Paris, 1923; *La Miniature du XIIe siècle à l'abbaye de Cîteaux*, Dijon, 1926; *L'Art roman de Bourgogne*, Dijon and Boston, 1928.

J. Evans, *Life in Mediaeval France*, London, 1924; *Monastic Life at Cluny, 910-1157*, Oxford, 1931; *Pattern etc.*, 2 vols., Oxford, 1931; *Nature in Design etc.*, Oxford, 1933; *Art in Mediaeval France, 987-1498*, Oxford, 1948; *Cluniac Art of the Romanesque Period*, Cambridge, 1950.

V. Leroquais, *Les Sacramentaires et les Missels manuscrits*, Paris, 1924; *Le Bréviaire de Philippe le Bon*, Brussels, 1929; *Un Livre d'Heures de Jean sans Peur*, Paris, 1939.

A. Kleinclausz, *Histoire de Bourgogne*, Paris (2nd ed.), 1924.

J. Destrée, *Les Heures de Notre Dame, Dites de Hennessy*, Paris, 1925.

C. Lorenzetti, 'Di due codici miniati inediti di Jean Bourdichon in Italia,' *Bollettino d'Arte d. Minist. d. Pubbl. Istruz.*, 1925-6.

O. Cartellieri, *Am Hofe der Herzœge von Burgund*, Basel, 1926; *The Court of Burgundy*, Paris, 1929.

S. C. Cockerell and M. R. James, *A Book of O.T. Illustrations etc.*, Cambridge, for the Roxburghe Club, 1927.

British Museum, *Guide to an Exhibition of Flemish Miniatures etc.*, London, 1927; *Miniatures from a French Horae (B.M. Add. MS. 16997) etc.*, London, 1927.

J. Calmette and H. Drouot, *Histoire de Bourgogne*, Paris, 1928.

J. Lafond, *Un Livre d'Heures rouennais enluminé d'après le 'Speculum humanae salvationis,'* Rouen, 1929.

A. de Laborde, *Les Miracles de Notre Dame*, Paris, 1929.

T. A. Cook and W. H. Ward, *Twenty-five Great Houses of France*, Paris, 1930.

O. Smital, *Das schwarze Gebetbuch*, Vienna, 1930.

A. Blum and P. Lauer, *La Miniature française au XVe et XVIe siècles*, Paris and Brussels, 1930.

Fr. Lyna, *De Vlaamsche miniatur van 1200 tot 1530*, Brussels—Amsterdam, 1930; see also under 1944.

L. Mercier, *Les Primitifs français La peinture clunysienne en Bourgogne à l'époque romane*, Paris, 1931.

T. Cox, *Jehan Foucquet*, London, 1931; *Jean Foucquet etc.*, Paris, 1931.

P. A. Lemoisne, *Gothic Painting in France. Fourteenth and Fifteenth Centuries*, Florence and Paris, 1931.

A. Bruel, *Romans français du moyen âge*, Paris, 1934.

H. R. Hahnloser, *Villard de Honnecourt*, Vienna, 1935.

L. Morel-Payen, *Les plus beaux manuscrits etc. de Troyes*, Troyes, 1935.

N. Gabrielli, 'Opere di maestri fiamminghi a Chieri nel Quattrocento,' *Bollettino Stor. Bibliogr. Subalpino*, 1936.

G. Bazin, *La peinture française* etc., Paris, 1937; *L'École franco-flamande*, Paris, 1941; *L'École parisienne*, Paris, 1942.

Bibliothèque Nationale, Paris, *Bibliothèque Nationale. Les plus beaux manuscrits français du VIIIe au XVIe siècle*, Paris, 1937; *Les Manuscrits à peintures en France du VIIe au XIIe siècle*, 2nd ed. (Catalogue of the Exhibition), Paris, 1954; *Les Manuscrits à peintures en France du XIIIe au XVIe siècle* (Catalogue), Paris, 1955.

H. David, *Philippe le Hardi, duc de Bourgogne, protecteur des arts*, Dijon, 1937; *Philippe le Hardi, duc de Bourgogne et co-régent de France de 1392 à 1404*, Dijon, 1947.

R. L. Kilgour, *The Decline of Chivalry as shown in French Literature*, Cambridge, Mass., 1937.

G. Mourey, *Tableau de l'art français*, Paris, 1938.

J. Adhémar, *Influences antiques dans l'art du moyen âge français*, London, 1939.

J. Courcelle Ladmirant, 'Le Bréviaire Flamand dit "La Flora" de la Bibl. Nat. de Naples,' *Bulletin de l'Inst. Hist. Belge de Rome*, 1939.

L. Réau, *La Peinture française du XIVe au XVIe siècle*, Paris, 1939; *L'Art religieux au moyen âge*, Paris, 1946; *Hist. de la peinture au M. -â. La miniature*, Melun, 1946.

P. Colin, *Les Ducs de Bourgogne*, Brussels, 1941.

F. Ingham, *Philippe le Bon*, Brussels, 1941.

J. de Jongh, *Margaretha van Oostenrijk*, Amsterdam, 1941.

Uisages de la Bourgogne, Paris, 1942.

É. A. van Moé and R. Brun, in *Le Livre*, Paris, 1942. (See also under 1950).

R. Schilling, 'A Book of Hours from the Limbourg Atelier,' *Burlington Magazine*, 1942; 'Two Unknown Flemish Miniatures of the XIth century,' *Burlington Magazine*, 1948.

P. Bonenfant, *Philippe le Bon*, Brussels, 1943.

J. Bartier, *Charles le Téméraire*, Brussels, 1944.

H. van Ussel, *Maria van Bourgondië*, Bruges, 1944.

L. Hommel, *Marie de Bourgogne ou le Grand Héritage*, Brussels, 1945.

C. Gaspar and Fr. Lyna, *Philippe le Bon et ses Beaux Livres*, Brussels, 1944.

E. Faral, *La Vie quotidienne au temps de Saint Louis*, Paris, 1944.

E. Panofsky, *Abbot Suger of the Abbey Church of St. Denis and its Art Treasures*, Princeton and London, 1946; *Early Netherlandish Painting*, 2 vols., Cambridge (Mass.), 1953.

A. Lejard (Edit.), *The Art of the French Book*. From early manuscripts to the present time. Introd. by Philip James, London, 1947.

P. Wescher, *Jean Fouquet and his Time*, Bâle, 1947.

R. Brun, *Le Livre français*, Paris, 1948.

O. Paecht, *The Master of Mary of Burgundy*, London, 1948.

S. Gevaert, *Étude sur les miniatures mosanes prégothiques*, Brussels, 1948.

E. Trenkler, *Das schwarze Gebetbuch*, Vienna, 1948; *Meisterwerke d. franz. Buch-malerei in d. œsterr. Nationalbibliothek* (*Nationalmusei Arsbok*), 1947-8.

G. Ring, *A Century of French Painting, 1400-1500*, London, 1949.

J. Calmette, *Le grands ducs de Bourgogne*, Paris, 1949.

BIBLIOGRAPHY

É. A. van Moé, *Illuminated Initials in Mediaeval Manuscripts* (transl. by J. Evans), London and Paris, 1950.

Y. Deslandres, *La Décoration des manuscrits dans la région parisienne du IXe au début du XIIIe siècle* (École Nationale des Chartes: Position des thèses), 1950.

J. Chailley, *L'École musicale de Saint-Martial de Limoges jusqu'à la fin du XIe siècle,* Paris, 1951.

F. Wormald and P. M. Giles, 'A Handlist of the Additional Manuscripts in the Fitzwilliam Museum,' Pts. 1–4, *Transactions of the Cambridge Bibliographical Soc.,* 1951–4.

J. Porcher, *Les Belles heures de Jean de France, duc de Berry,* Paris, 1953; *Chefs-d'œuvre de l'Enluminure française du 15e siècle,* Paris; *Medieval French Miniatures,* London, 1960.

E. G. Millar, *An Illuminated Manuscript of La Somme le Roy* . . . attributed to . . . Honoré (Roxburghe Club), Oxford, 1953.

Royal Academy of Arts, *Flemish Art, 1300–1700* (Catalogue of the Exhibition), London, 1953–4.

B. Woledge, *Bibliographie des romans et nouvelles en prose* etc., Geneva, 1954.

R. Limousin, *Jean Bourdichon,* Lyons, 1954.

T. Gasparrini Leporace, *Il Calendario del Breviario Grimani,* Milan, 1957 (2nd ed.).

Metropolitan Museum of Art, *The Hours of Jeanne d'Évreux, Queen of France,* New York, 1957.

The Metropolitan Museum of Art, "BULLETIN", June, 1958.

R. Hassal, *The Douce Apocalypse,* London, 1961.

U. Finke, *Utrecht—Zentrum nordniederlændischer Buchmalerei. Seine Bedeutung in der erst. Hælfte d. 15. Jhrdts.,* "OUD HOLLAND", LXXVIII. 1/2, 1963, pp. 27–66; *Nordniederlændische Buchmalerei des Spætmittelalters,* Dissert., 1964.

L. N. Valentine, *Ornament in Medieval Manuscripts. A Glossary,* London, 1965.
See also Chapter IV and General Bibiography.

GENERAL BIBLIOGRAPHY

F. G. Delamotte, *A Primer of the Art of Illumination*, London, 1860; 2nd ed., 1925; new ed., New York, 1950.

J. W. Bradley, *A Manual of Illumination*, 7th ed., London 1861; *A Dictionary of Miniaturists, Illuminators, Calligraphers, and Copyists*, 3 vols., London, 1887–9; repr., New York, 1958.

J. Labarte, *Histoire des arts industrielles, etc.*, Paris, 1864–6.

W. R. Tymms, *The Art of Illuminating*, London, 1866.

H. Shaw, *A Handbook of the Art of Illumination*, London, 1866.

L. Delisle, Paris, 1868–81: see Chapter VII.

G. Valentinelli, *Bibliotheca manuscripta ad S. Marci Venetiarum*, 6 vols., Venice, 1868–73.

Grimouard de Saint-Laurent, *Guide de l'art chrétien*, Paris, 1872–4.

B. Bucher, *Geschichte der technischen Kuenste*, 3 vols., Stuttgart, 1875–93.

W. de Gray Birch and H. Jenner, *Early Drawings and Illuminations*, London, 1879.

Bibliothèque Nationale, Paris, *Bibliothèque Nationale. Imprimés, manuscrits, estampes. Notice d'objets exposés*, Paris, 1881; *Catalogue Général d. manuscrits latins*, 3 vols., Paris, 1939.

C. Lamprecht, *Initiale Ornamentik etc.*, Leipsic, 1882.

H. L. Bordier, *Description des peintures et autres ornements contenus dans les manuscrits grecs de la Bibl. Nat.*, Paris, 1883–5.

J. L. Propert, *History of Miniature Art*, London, 1887.

C. Paoli, E. Rostagno, T. Lodi, *I codici Ashburnhamiani d. R. Biblioteca Mediceo-Laurenziana di Firenze*, Rome, 1887–.

C. Duraud, 'Monuments figurés du moyen âge exécutés d'après les textes liturgiques,' *Bull. mon. liv.*, 1888.

L. Gentile, 'Il codice Poggiali della Divina Commedia, *Rivista d. Biblioteche*, 1888; *I codici Palatini d. R. Bibl. Naz. Centrale di Firenze*, 2 vols., Rome, 1889–90.

L. von Kobell, *Kunstvolle Miniaturen etc.*, 4th ed., Munich, 1890.

J. H. Middleton, *Illuminated Manuscripts in Class. and Mediaev. Times*, Cambridge, 1892.

S. Beissel, *Vaticanische Miniaturen*, Fribourg, 1893; *Geschichte der Evangelienbuecher*, Fribourg, 1896; *Bilder aus der Geschichte d. altchristlichen Kunst und Liturgie*, Fribourg, 1899.

S. Berger, *Histoire de la Vulgate pendant les premiers siècles du moyen âge*, Paris, 1893.

J. J. Tikkanen, *Die Psalter-Illustrationen im Mittelalter*, Helsingfors, 1895 and 1903; *Abendlændische Psalter-Illustrationen des Utrecht-Psalters*, Helsingfors, 1900; *Die Beinstellung in der Kunstgeschichte*, Leipsic, 1912.

GENERAL BIBLIOGRAPHY

R. W. Hunt and others, *A Summary Catalogue of Western Manuscripts in the Bodleian Library at Oxford*, 7 vols. (in 9), London, 1895–1953.

M. R. James, *Descriptive Catalogues of MSS. (Eton College; Fitzwilliam Museum; Jesus College, Trinity, King's, Peterhouse, Queens', Gonville and Caius, Clare, Corpus Christi, Christ's, Emmanuel, Pembroke, etc.,* of Cambridge; *Lambeth Palace; Westminster Abbey; The John Rylands Library,* and so on), Cambridge, 1895 onwards; *The Apocalypse in Art* (The British Academy, Schweich Lectures, 1927), London, 1931; *The Romance of Alexander*, Oxford, 1933.

F. X. Kraus, *Geschichte der christlichen Kunst*, Fribourg, 1896–1900.

E. Molinier, *Histoire générale des Arts appl. à l'industrie*, 3 vols., Paris, 1896–7.

A. Ebner, *Quellen und Forschungen z. Geschichte u. Kunstgesch. des Missale Romanum im Mittelalter. Iter italicum*, Freiburg i. Br., 1896.

J. von Schlosser, *Quellen zur Kunstgeschichte d. abendlaendischen Mittelalters*, Vienna, 1897.

E. Mandarini, *I codici manoscritti della Biblioteca Oratoriana di Napoli*, Naples and Rome, 1897.

F. Carta, C. Cipolla, and C. Frati, *Monumenta palæographica sacra. Atlante paleografico artistico compilato sui mss. esposti in Torino alla Mostra d'arte sacra nel mdcccxcviii*, Turin, 1899.

E. von Dobschuetz, *Christusbilder*, Leipsic, 1899.

G. F. Warner, *Illuminated Manuscripts in the British Museum*, London, 1899–1903; *Descriptive Catalogue of the Library of C. W. Dyson Perrins*, Oxford, 1920; — and J. P. Gilson, *Catalogue of Western Manuscripts in the Old Royal and King's Collections* (in the B.M.), London, 1921.

H. Omont, *Reproductions de manuscrits et miniatures de la Bibl. Nat.*, 32 vols., Paris, 1901–11; 'Peintures de L'Ancien Test.,' in *Monuments Piot*, 1909.

J. E. Weis-Liebersdorf, *Christus- und Apostelbilder*, Fribourg, 1902.

W. L. Schreiber, *Biblia pauperum*, Strasbourg, 1903.

E. Berger, *Die Maltechnik des Altertums*, Munich, 1904.

F. Wickoff (ed.), *Beschreibendes Verzeichnis d. Illum. Handschr. in Oesterreich*: H. J. Hermann, *Die illum. Handschr. in Tirol*, Leipsic, 1905; H. Tietze, *Die illum. Handschr. in Salzburg*, Leipsic, 1905; R. Eisler, *Die illum. Handschr. in Kærnten*, Leipsic, 1907; P. Buberl, *Die illum. Handschr. in Steiermark*, Leipsic, 1911; H. Tietze, *Die illum. Handschr. der Rossiana in Wien-Lainz*, Leipsic. . . .

S. C. Cockerell, *The Book of Hours of Yolande of Flanders. A Manuscript of the 14th Century in the Library of Henry Yates Thompson*, London, 1905.

A. Michel, ed., *Histoire de l'art*, vols. I-III, Paris, 1905–23 (vol. 2, p. 1: A. Haseloff, *Les miniatures, les vitraux, la peinture murale*).

J. Lutz and P. Perdrizet, *Speculum Humanae Salvationis*, 2 vols., Mulhouse, 1907.

British Museum, *Reproductions from Illuminated Manuscripts*, Series I-III, London, 1907–8; 3rd ed., 1923–5; 4th ser., London, 1907–28; *Guide to the Exhibited Manuscripts.* Part III (*Illuminated Manuscripts etc.*), London, 1923; *Schools of illumination*, 6 pts., London, 1914–30.

H. Y. Thompson, *Illustrations of 100 MSS.*, 7 vols., London, 1907–18.

W. Singer, *Allgemeines Kuenstler-Lexicon*, Frankfort, 1907.

U. Thieme and F. Becker, *Allgemeines Lexikon der bildenden Kuenste*, 37 vols., Leipsic, 1907–50.

S. C. Cockerell and E. F. Strange, *Catalogue of Illuminated Manuscripts*, London, 1908.

F. Young and P. Henderson Aitken, *A Catalogue of the MSS. of the Hunterian Museum in the Univ. of Glasgow*, Glasgow, 1908.

Burlington Fine Arts Club, *Exhibition of Illuminated Manuscripts* [catalogued, with introduction by S. C. Cockerell], London, 1908.

L. Dorez, *Les Manuscrits à Peintures de la Bibl. de Lord Leicester*, Paris, 1908.

M. Couderc, *Bibliothèque Nationale, Album de portraits*, Paris, 1908.

H. Kehrer, *Die Heiligen Drei Koenige in Literatur und Kunst*, Leipsic, 1909.

H. Martin, *Les Peintres de manuscrits etc.*, Paris, 1909.

A. Gastone, *L'Art Grégorien*, Paris, 1911.

Bull. de la Société Française de Reproductions des Mss. à Peintures, Paris, 1911 onwards.

J. A. Herbert, *Illuminated Manuscripts*, 2nd ed., London and New York, 1911; repr., New York, 1958.

H. Hieber, *Die Miniaturen des fruehen Mittelalters*, Munich, 1912.

H. M. Bannister, *Monumenti vaticani di paleografia musicale latina*, 2 vols., Leipsic (Rome and Turin), 1913.

G. Biagi, *Cinquanta tavole in fototipia da codici d. R. Biblioteca Medicea-Laurenziana*, Florence, 1914.

E. A. Lowe, *The Beneventan Script etc.*, Oxford, 1914; *Scriptura Beneventana*, 2 vols., Oxford, 1929; *Codices lat. antiqu. etc.*, 6 vols., Oxford, 1934–53.

E. G. Millar, *Les Manuscrits à peintures des Bibliothèques de Londres*, Paris, 1914–25; *The Library of A. C. Beatty, etc.*, Oxford, 1927–.

A. Pellizzari, *Trattati attorno le arti figurative*, Naples, 1915.

E. H. Zimmermann, *Vorkarolingische Miniaturen*, 4 vols., Berlin, 1916–18.

E. Bishop, *Liturgica historica etc.*, Oxford, 1918.

G. Leidinger, *Meisterwerke der Buchmalerei aus Handschriften der bayerischen Staatsbibliothek*, Munich, 1920; *Der Codex Aureus der Bayerischen Staatsbiblioth. in Muenchen*, Munich, 1921–5.

R. van Marle, *La Peinture romane au Moyen-âge*, Strasbourg, 1921.

H. J. Hermann, *Die fruehmittelalterlichen Handschriften des Abendlandes*, etc., 8 vols., Leipsic, 1923–31.

G. G. Coulton, *Five Centuries of Religion*, 3 vols., Cambridge, 1923–6; *The Chronicler of European Chivalry*, London, 1930.

A. Merton, *Buchmalerei in St. Gallen*, Leipsic, 1923.

E. Benezit, *Dictionnaire d. peintres, sculpteurs, etc.*, 3 vols., Paris, 1924.

V. Leroquais, *Les Sacramentaires et les Missels etc.*, Paris, 1924; *Les Livres d'heures manuscrits de la Bibliothèque Nationale*, 3 vols. (Supplément), Paris, 1927–43; *Les Pontificaux manuscrits etc.*, 4 vols., Paris, 1937; *Les Psautiers manuscrits etc.*, 2 vols., Paris, 1940–1; *Le Sacramentaire de Gellone* (in MS. at the National Library, Paris).

GENERAL BIBLIOGRAPHY

J. Huizinga, the *Waning of the Middle Ages*, London, 1924; later ed., 1937.

A. W. Byvanck, *Les Principaux MSS. à peintures de la Bibl. Roy. d. Pays-Bas*, Paris, 1924.

H. Cornell, *Biblia pauperum*, Stockholm, 1925.

A. von Le Coq, *Bilderatlas zur Kunst- und Kulturgeschichte Mittel-Asiens*, Berlin, 1925.

J. Strzygowski, *Der Norden in der bildenden Kunst etc.*, Vienna, 1926. (See also Chapter I.)

C. G. Crump and E. F. Jacob (ed.), *The Legacy of the Middle Ages*, Oxford, 1926.

E. Mâle, *Art et Artists du moyen âge*, Paris, 1927. (See also Chapter VII.)

C. H. Haskins, *The Renaissance of the Twelfth Century*, Cambridge, Mass., 1927.

P. Lauer, *Les Enluminures romanes des manuscrits de la Bibliothèque Nationale*, Paris, 1927.

K. Lœffler, *Romanische Zierbuchstaben und ihre Vorlæufer*, Stuttgart, 1927.

M. Hautmann, *Die Kunst des fruehen Mittelalters*, 2nd ed., Berlin, 1929.

T. Gnoli, *Biblioteca Nazionale di Brera, Milano. Catalogo descrittivo della mostra bibliografica: manoscritti e libri miniati*, Milan, 1929.

A. Bœckler, *Abendlændische Miniaturen bis zum Ausgang der romanischen Zeit*, Berlin and Leipsic, 1930.

R. Byron and D. T. Rice, *The Birth of Western Painting*, London, 1930.

F. Wormald, *The Book of Psalms etc.*, Westminster (London), 1930. (See also Chapters V and VII.)

H. Dupin, *La Courtoisie au moyen âge*, Paris, 1930.

P. Wescher, *Beschreibendes Verzeichnis d. Miniatur-Handschr. etc. d. Kupferstichkab. d. staatl. Museen in Berlin*, Leipsic, 1931.

J. Evans, *Pattern etc.*, Oxford, 1931; *Nature in Design etc.*, Oxford, 1933.

J. J. Tikkanen, *Studien ueber die Farbgebung in der mittelalterlichen Buchmalerei etc.* (ed. by T. Borenius), Helsinki, 1933.

Pierpont Morgan Library, New York (Belle da Costa Greene and Meta P. Harrsen), *Exhibition of Illuminated Manuscripts etc.*, New York 1933-4; *Illustrated Catalogue of an Exhibition etc.*, New York 1940; *The Pierpont Morgan Library, 1936-1940*, New York, 1941; *The Bible*, New York, 1947.

L. Réau, *L'Art primitif. L'Art médiéval*, Paris, 1934; *L'Art religieux au moyen âge*, Paris, 1946.

D. T. Rice, *The Scope of Art History etc.*, Edinburgh, 1934; see also R. Byron and D. T. Rice, 1930.

National Museum, Copenhagen, *Greek and Latin Illuminated Manuscripts etc.*, Copenhagen, 1934.

Wallace Collection, London, *Miniatures and Illuminations*, London, 1935.

S. de Ricci and W. J. Wilson, *Census of Medieval and Renaissance MSS. in the U.S. and Canada*, 3 vols., New York, 1935-40.

T. Klauser, *Das Rœmische Capitulare Evangeliorum*, Muenster i. W., 1935.

Walters Art Gallery, *Handbook of the Collection*, Baltimore, 1936; *Illuminated Books of the Middle Ages and Renaissance*, Baltimore, 1949.

E. Lavagnino, *Il Medioevo*, Turin, 1936.

D. V. Thompson, *The Materials of Medieval Painting*, London, 1936.

F. Harrison, *Treasures of Illumination*, London, 1937.

C. Gaspar and Fr. Lyna, *Les princ. manuscrits à peintures de la Bibl. Roy. de Belgique*, 2 vols., Paris, 1937–1945.

E. Wolf, *A Descriptive Catalogue of the J. F. Lewis Collection etc., in the Free Library of Philadelphia*, Philadelphia, 1937.

A. Melter, *Catalogue of Illuminated Manuscripts*, Worcester, Mass., 1937.

Worcester Art Museum, *The Dark Ages*, Worcester, 1937.

J. C. Webster, *The Labors of the Month in Antique and Medieval Art*, Princeton, 1938.

H. Focillon, *Art d'Occident: le moyen âge et gothique*, Paris, 1938.

C. Nordenfalk, *Die spætantiken Kanontafeln*, Gœteborg, 1938; *Die Buchmalerei*, in A Grabar and C. Nordenfalk, *Das fruehe Mittelalter* (*Die grosse Jahrhunderte der Malerei*), Geneva, 1957.

H. Haseloff, *Die Psalterillustration im 13. Jahrh.*, Kiel, 1938.

R. S. and L. H. Loomis, *Arthurian Legends in Medieval Art*, London and New York, 1938.

D. Fava, *La Biblioteca Nazionale Centrale di Firenze e le sue insigni raccolte*, Milan, 1939;— — and M. Salmi, *I manoscritti miniati della Biblioteca Estense*, I, Florence, 1950.

L. Gillet, *Histoire artistique des Ordres Mendiants*, 2nd ed., Paris, 1939.

G. Hulin de Loo, 'La Vignette chez les enlum. gantois,' *Acad. Roy. de Belg.— Bull. de la Cl. d. B.-A.*, 1939.

A. Katzenellenbogen, *Allegories of the Virtues and Vices in Medieval Art*, London, 1939.

E. Panofsky, *Studies in Iconology*, New York, 1939.

E. Kitzinger, *Early Medieval Art in the British Museum*, London, 1940.

Boston Museum of Fine Arts, *Arts of the Middle Ages*, Boston, 1940.

N. R. Ker, *Medieval Libraries of Great Britain*, London, 1941.

M. Dœrner, *Malmaterial u. s. Verwendung i. Bilde*, 8th ed., Stuttgart, 1944.

R. Rey, *L'Art roman et ses origines*, Toulouse, 1945.

W. Weisbach, *Religiœse Reform und mittelalterliche Kunst*, Einsiedeln and Zurich, 1945.

M. R. Rogers and O. Gœtz, *Handbook to the Lucy Maud Buckingham Collection*, Art Institute of Chicago, 1945.

C. Jacques, *Les Peintres du moyen âge*, Paris, 1946.

R. J. Gettens and G. L. Stout, *Painting Materials*, etc., 4th ed., New York, 1947.

Bodleian Library, *Exhibition of Renaissance MSS.*, Oxford, 1948; *Illuminated Manuscripts in the Bodleian Library*; I: *German, Dutch, Flemish, French, and Spanish Schools* (ed. by O. Paecht and J. J. G. Alexander), Oxford, 1965. (See also further on.)

O. Demus, *The Mosaics of Norman Sicily*, London, 1949.

P. d'Ancona and E. Æschlimann, *Dictionnaire d. miniaturistes du Moyen âge et de la Renaissance*, 2nd ed., Milan, 1949.

GENERAL BIBLIOGRAPHY

National Book League, *Exhibition of Flower Books*, London, 1950.

E. van Moé, *Illuminated Initials in Medieval Manuscripts* (transl. by J. Evans), London and Paris, 1950. (See also Chapter VII.)

Trésors des bibliothèques d'Italie, IVᵉ–XVIᵉ siècle, Expos. à la Bibl. Nat., Paris, 1950.

L. Michelini Tocci, *Miniature del Rinascimento. Catal. d. Mostra (nel quinto centenario d. Bibl. Vatic.)*, Vatican City, 1950.

H. Swarzenski, *(Introduction to) Early Medieval Illumination*, 'IRIS COLOUR BOOKS,' London, 1951; *Monuments of Romanesque Art*, London, 1954.

Bodleian Library, *Bodleian Picture Books*, Oxford, 1951 onwards (see also Chapter II—under Paecht—and Chapter V—under Boase and Chapman; as well as under 1948).

Goldsmiths' Exhibition of Oxford Treasures, London, 1953.

F. Saxl and H. Meier, *Verzeichnis astrologischer und mythologischer illustrieter Hand-schriften des lateinischen Mittelalters*, III (English Manuscripts), London, 1953.

A. Grabar and C. Nordenfalk, *Early Medieval Painting*, New York, 1957.

The Faber Library of Illuminated Manuscripts:

F. Wormald, *The Benedictional of St. Ethelwold*, London, 1959.

J. Porcher, *The Rohan Book of Hours*, London, 1959.

C. R. Dodwell, *The Great Lambeth Bible*, London, 1959.

E. G. Millar, *The Parisian Miniaturist, Honoré*, London, 1959.

E. Wellesz, *The Vienna Genesis*, London, 1960.

Ch. Mitchell, *A Fifteenth Century Italian Plutarch*, London, 1961.

A. G. and W. O. Hassall, *The Douce Apocalypse*, London, 1961.

T. S. R. Boase, *The York Psalter*, London, 1962.

R. S. Bruce Mitford, *The Book of Durrow*; F. Henry, *The Book of Kells*, and others in preparation. See also The Faber Gallery of Oriental Art, including D. Barrett, *Persian Painting of the Fourteenth Century* and R. H. Pinder-Wilson, *Persian Painting of the Fifteenth Century*.

A. Nesbitt (ed.), *Decorative Alphabet and Initials*, New York, 1959.

L. C. MacKinney, *Bilder aus. der Geburtshilfe im Mittelalter*, CIBA-SYMPOSIUM, 8/5–6, 1960.

C. R. Dodwell, *Theophilus: The Various Arts*, London–Edinburgh, 1961.

R. Lister, *The Miniature defined*, Cambridge, 1963.

Adolph Goldschmidt zum Gedæchtniss, 1863–1944, Hamburg, 1963.

T. Burckhardt, *Von wunderbaren Buechern*, Lausanne and Freiburg i.B., 1964.

D. Talbot Rice (ed.), *The Dark Ages*, London, 1965.

INDEX

N.B. Arabic names preceded by the article al- are to be found under the commencing letter of the name; e.g. for al-Ḥallaj see under H. Names of Saints are also to be found under the commencing letter of the name. The number following the letters f. p. (facing page . . .) refers to the colour plates. Roman numbers refer to the monochrome plates.

INDEX

INDEX

INDEX

INDEX

INDEX

Horae of Anne de Bretagne, 418 f.; VII-25

Isidorus Hispalensis (Lat. 5543), 209

Jacob Monachus (Jakobus Monachos) of Kokkinobaphos, 104; II-23

S. Jerome, Tractatus in librum Psalmorum, 70; II-3

John Cantacuzen (Johannes III Kantakuzenos), Theological Works, 110 f.; II-26

S. John Chrysostom (S. Johannes Chrysostomos), Homiliae, 104; II-22

Kalīlah wa Dimnah (MS. Arabe 3465), 138; III-4

(General) Kandurān (Prints OD. 44), III-15

Lothar Gospels (Lat. 266), 207

Martianus Capella (Lat. 7900 A), 209

Marvels of Creation (Suppl. Pers. 332), 143

MS. 22547, see Curtius Rufus

MS. Lat. 10514, 220

MS. Suppl. Gr. 75, 79

MSS. Coptes-Arabes 13–48, 125; II-40

Monastic Psalter (Cod. Gr. 20), 98; II-14

Paris Psalter (Cod. Gr. 139), 96 f.; II-11 f.

Psalter of Charles the Bald, 209

Psalter of the Duke of Berry, 395 f.; VII-13

Psalter of S. Louis, 382; 386

Pucelle Bible, 391

Rāz Bahādur and Rupmati (Prints OD. 43), III-15

Sacra Parallela (Gr. 923), 65; 104; II-21

Sacramentarium Gellonense, 200; IV-15

Sacramentary of Limoges, 375

Second Bible of Charles the Bald, 208; IV-22

Suppl. Turc. 190, III-16

Tacuinum Sanitatis, 315 f.

Terence (Terentius) (Lat. 7899; 7900; 7907A), 40; 205; 209; 402

Theocritus (Gr. 2832), 34

Villard de Honnecourt, 379

Vivian Bible: Lat. 1, 72; 207

M. H. Vever Collection:

Firdousī, Shāh nāmeh (or nāma), 142 f.; III-5 f.

Paris: Matthew Paris, 52; 272 ff.; V-13

Historia Anglorum et Chronica Majora, 273; V-13

Parma: Palatina Library:

Abraham ben Juda ibn Ḥayyim (Cod. 945), 140

Atlantic Bible from S. Valentino in Piano (near Amelia), 300

Marmitta, 343; VI-42

Parma, Roger of, Treatise on Surgery, 385

Patrons, see the following entries:

'Abbās Shāh; 'Abd-al-Raḥmān III; Adelaide de Savoye; Adelheid of Burgundy; S. Aethelwold; Agnes de Poitou; Agrippa; Akbar; Albert or Albrecht of Brandenburg; Archbishop of Mainz; Alcuin(us); Alexios; Alfonso d'Aragon; Alfonso VI; Alfonso X el Sabio; Alfonso, son of King Edward I; Amadeus VIII, Duke of Savoy, later Pope Felix V; Anne de Bretagne; (Duke Alexios) Apokaukos; Aragons of Naples; Arnestus of Pardubitz, Archbishop of Prague; (Count of) Arras; Athelstan; Babur; Badī az-Zāmān Mīrzā; Basilios II; (John Duke of) Bedford; Bernward of Hildesheim; (Duke of) Berry; Berthold; Blanche de Castile; Boucicau(l)t; (Robert) Bruynyng, Abbot of Sherborne; Carilef(f); Casini; Cassiodorus Senator; Ceolfrid; Charlemagne; Charles IV; Charles V; Charles VII; Charles VIII; Charles d'Anjou; Charles le Téméraire (the Bold); Charles of Viana; Charles the Bald; (Étienne) Chevalier; Conradin von Hohenstaufen; Constantine VII Porphyrogennetos; (Dame Elizabeth) Courtenay; Cunigund, Empress of S. Henry II; Cunigund, Princess and Abbess; Davalos; Desiderius; (Havisia) Du Bois; S. Dunstan; Eadyth or Edith, first wife of Emperor Otto I; Egbert; Egmond; Este of Ferrara: Lionello, Borso, Ercole I, Alfonso; Eugenius IV; Farnese; Ferdinand I d'Aragon; Fredericus II; Gasztołd; Geoffrey, Abbot of St. Albans; Gertrud, daughter of Henry the Lion; Grimani; al-Ḥakam II; Hazecha; Hedwig, sister of Emperor Otto I; S. Henry II; Henry III; Henry VI; Henry de Blois; Henry, Canon of Chichester; Hitda von Meschede; Ḥusayn Mīrzā Bāyqarā; (the) Ilkhāns; Ingeborg; Isabelle de France; Isabelle, Queen of Castile; Ismā'il Shāh; Jacques Galliot de Genouilhac; Jahān; Jahāngīr; (Thomas) James, Bishop of Dol; Jean sans Peur; Jeanne de Navarre; João II, King of Portugal; Johannes Komnenos; Johannes III Kantakuzenos; (Fr.) Johannes Marsicanae dudum; Johannes Protospatharios; John of Aragon; John de Cell; Judith; Justinianus; (Queen) Keran; Kunigunde; Lallemant; Leo X; Leo Patricius; Leonhard Layming; Leonora d'Aragon; Lin(de)seye; S. Louis; (Sir Geoffrey) Louterell or Luttrell; Maciejowski; Manfred; Mani; Martorelli; Mary of Burgundy; Mat(h)ilda, Countess of Tuscany; Mat(h)ilda, mother of Emperor Otto I; Ma-

INDEX

212

INDEX

Thebes (in Egypt):
  Ani and his wife, 28; I-1
  Leyden papyrus, 29; I-6
  Ramesseum ceremonial papyrus, 27; I-1
Theobald, Abbot of Montecassino, 295
Theocritus: Paris, National Library, 34
Theodore Psalter, 98 f.
Theodoulos (scribe), 111; II-27
Theodulphus, Bishop of Orléans, Abbot of
  Fleury, 209
Theophano, wife of Emperor Otto II, 214
Theophilus (*qui et Rugerus*), 226
Theseus, 30; I-7
Thessalonike (Salonica), 94
S. Thomas Aquinas, 358; VI-44
S. Thomas a Londinio (or à Becket), V-9
Thot (Egyptian god), 28; I-1
Tickhill Psalter, 275 f.
Tīmūr lenk, 143
Tīmūrid princes, 143 f.
Tobias, VI-12
Toledo, 161 ff.; 169
Tōrah shrine, 148; I-29; III-17, and passim
Torelli: Filippo di Matteo Torelli, 328;
  330 f.; VI-29 f.; VI-33
Torelli: Giacomo Torelli, 333
T'oros Roslin, 122; II-37 f.
T'oros (of) Taron, 124
Torriti: Jacopo Torriti, 112
Toschi: Frà Benedetto Toschi, 328
Tours scriptorium, 206 f.; 412 ff.; IV-19
Transfiguration of Christ, 111; II-26 f.; II-37
Translators: Gospels of the Translators, 121;
  II-36
Trapezuntion: Trebizond Gospels, 121;
  II-35
Tree of Houris (Sūra 56), III-11
Trèves (or Trier):
  Cathedral:
    Ada Gospels, 203; IV-15
    Codex Egberti, 219 f.; IV-26
    Gospels (Treasury No. 61), 186; IV-11
  Scriptorium, 202 f.; 223; 227
    Gospel-Lectionary, British Museum (Eg-
      erton 809), 227
Tristan und Isolde, 381
  Gottfried von Strassburg, Tristan und
    Isolde, 235
Troia Cathedral:
  Three Exultet Rolls, 298
Troilus (and Cryseida), 30; I-7; V-27
Troy, VI-34
Tura: Cosimo Tura (?), 342; VI-42
Turin:
  Civic Museum:
    Missal of Cardinal Domenico della
      Rovere, 343; VI-42

Egyptian Museum:
  Kha' papyrus, I-1
National Library:
  Gregorius Magnus, Moralia in Job (from
    Bobbio), 291
  Bede, Expositio in Evangelium S. Lucae,
    293
  Hrabanus Maurus, De Laudibus S.
    Crucis, 210
  Van Eyck (?), 400; 444
Turkish book illumination, 147; III-16
  Ottoman Genealogy, 147
Turone, 315
Tuota (or Uta) Codex, 214; 222
Typikon: Oxford, Lincoln College, 110

Ulfila, Codex argenteus, 82; II-4
Ultramarine, 83
Umbria, 354 f.
Unicorn as symbol of chastity, VI-37
Uppsala: Codex argenteus, 82; II-4
Urbino, 353 f.
  Federigo di Montefeltro, Duke of Urbino,
    39; *331 f.*; 353 f.
al-Ushmūnayn, 131 ff.
Uta, 214; see also Tuota
Utrecht:
  Scriptorium, 447 f.; VII-30 f.
Utrecht Bible, 448; VII-31
Utrecht Horae, 448 f.; VII-31
Utrecht University Library: Cod. No. 32
  (Utrecht Psalter), 197 f.; 205 f.; 257 f.;
  IV-18

S. Vaast scriptorium, 373 f.
Valenciennes, Municipal Library:
  Prudentius, 209
  Apocalypse, 384; VII-2
S. Valentino in Piano (near Amelia), scrip-
  torium, 300
Vallombrosa Breviarium, 326; VI-27
Vallombrosa Psalter, VI-8
Van, 120
Van Eyck, 400; 444; 448
S. Vanne scriptorium, 375
Vanni: Lippo Vanni, 309; 337
Varagine: Jacobus de Varagine, Legenda
  aurea, 242 f.; 444
Varro, Imagines illustrium aliquot modo
  hominum, 35 f.
Vasco de Lucena, translator of Curtius Rufus,
  422; 428; VII-23
Vaticana (Vatican Library):
  Agrimensores, 53 f.; I-26
  Apicius, De re coquinaria, 206; IV-19

503

INDEX

INDEX HISTORICUS

(Chronological Index)

This is an attempt to give a chronological survey of the history of the illuminated manuscript, mainly as far as it is dealt with in this book. It goes without saying that the majority of the dates are only approximate. In some rare cases we may know the date when a manuscript was finished; seldom we are so fortunate to know both the dates of the beginning and the end of the work, as in the case of the Vet. Testam. from L'Abbaye de Bonne Espérance (Hainaut)—now in the Burgundian Library of the Royal Library at Brussels—in which the scribe, frater Henricus, states that he started on 26th August 1132 and finished in July 1135.

B.C.

c. 1971: Ramesseum ceremonial papyrus, 27; I-1
c. 1900–c. 1250: various recensions of the Book of the Dead, 27 f.; I-1–3
c. 1420/1413–c. 1385/1377: a copy of the Book of the Dead, preserved in Cairo, 28; I-3
c. 600–c. 500: Etruscan fresco in the Tomba dei Tori, at Tarquinia, 30; I-7
c. 560/550: Ergotimos and Klitias, François vase, 30; I-8
c. 460: Attic crater preserved in Florence, 30; I-7
c. 306–c. 30: Nesikhonsu papyrus, 28
c. 300–c. 200: Etruscan alabaster-urn, preserved in Florence, 30; I-7
c. 200–c. 0: Ayer papyrus, 32
165: Papyrus Letronne, 32; I-8
47: Destruction of the Library of Alexandria
39: Varro, Imagines illustrium aliquot hominum, 35 f.

A.D.

c. 30 B.C.–c. 325 A.D.: Rhind papyrus, 28; I-3
c. 100–c. 200: Holy Eucharist: Mosaic in the catacomb of S. Priscilla at Rome, II-1
c. 100–c. 200: Apuleius, Amor et Psyche, I-9
c. 100–c. 200: Greek romance, 32
c. 200–c. 300: the chaste Susanna: Catacombs of SS. Pietro and Marcellino at Rome, II-1
before 256: Jewish frescoes in the Synagogue at Dura-Europos, 61 ff.; I-30
c. 300–c. 350: Virgil (Cod. Vat. Lat. 3225), 37 ff.; I-11 f.
c. 300–c. 400: Leyden papyrus, 29; 33; I-6
c. 300–c. 400: Oslo papyrus, 29; I-5
c. 300–c. 400: Quedlinburg Itala fragment, 69 f.; II-3
c. 300–c. 400: Rome, S. Pudenziana, Mosaic in the Apse, 68 f.; II-1
c. 400: Symbols of the four Evangelists in the Battistero di S. Giovanni in Fonte, in Naples—perhaps the oldest representation of Evangelist symbols, 101 f.
c. 400: Papyrus No. 13296 (Berlin, State Museum), 29
c. 400: Chronicles of the World (Alexandrian), 29; I-4
c. 432–440: Mosaics in Rome (S. Maria Maggiore) based on biblical MSS., 69; II-2
c. 450: Ravenna, Mosaics in the Mausoleum of Galla Placidia, 69; II-2
c. 450: Ravenna, Mosaics in the Battistero degli Ortodossi, 69
c. 400–c. 500 (?): Virgil (Cod. Vat. Lat. 3867), 37 ff.; I-12
c. 400–c. 500: Coptic MS. (Naples, Nat. Libr.), 125; II-40
c. 400–c. 500: Cotton Genesis, 84 f.; II-4
c. 490: Virgil, Codex Mediceus, 37

Date Due